Enterprise Information Systems III

Enterprise Information Systems III

edited by

Joaquim Filipe

School of Technology,
Polytechnical Institute, Setúbal, Portugal

Bernadette Sharp

School of Computing,
Staffordshire University,
Stafford, England, U.K.

and

Paula Miranda

School of Technology,
Polytechnical Institute, Setúbal, Portugal

KLUWER ACADEMIC PUBLISHERS
DORDRECHT / BOSTON / LONDON

A C.I.P. Catalogue record for this book is available from the Library of Congress.

ISBN 1-4020-0563-6

Published by Kluwer Academic Publishers,
P.O. Box 17, 3300 AA Dordrecht, The Netherlands.

Sold and distributed in North, Central and South America
by Kluwer Academic Publishers,
101 Philip Drive, Norwell, MA 02061, U.S.A.

In all other countries, sold and distributed
by Kluwer Academic Publishers,
P.O. Box 322, 3300 AH Dordrecht, The Netherlands.

Printed on acid-free paper

Printed in the Netherlands.

TABLE OF CONTENTS

PART 4 – INTERNET COMPUTING AND ELECTRONIC COMMERCE

PREFACE

This book includes a set of selected papers from the third "International Conference on Enterprise Information Systems" (ICEIS 2001), held in Setúbal, Portugal, 7 to 10 July 2001.

Since its beginning, in 1999, ICEIS focuses on real world applications and aims at becoming a major point of contact between research scientists, engineers and practitioners in the area of business applications of information systems. In 2000 the conference was held in Stafford, United Kingdom, and in 2001 it returned to its origins in Setúbal, Portugal.

The conference included four simultaneous tracks, as usual, covering different aspects related to enterprise computing, including: *Databases and Information Systems Integration*, *Artificial Intelligence and Decision Support Systems*, *Information Systems Analysis and Specification* and *Internet Computing and Electronic Commerce.* Although ICEIS 2001 received more than 200 submissions, only 64 papers were accepted as full papers and presented in regular 30-minute oral presentations. There were also short papers and poster presentations. From the set of 64 full papers only 33 were selected for inclusion in this book. These numbers demonstrate stringent quality criteria and the intention of maintaining a high quality forum for future editions of this conference.

A number of additional keynote lectures, case studies and technical tutorials were also held. These presentations, by specialists in different knowledge areas were an important contribution to increase the overall quality of the Conference, and are partially expressed in the first 5 papers of the book. We would like to thank in particular the collaboration of the following invited speakers: Anatol Holt (University of Milan), Frank Dignum (University of Utrecht), Gio Wiederhold (Stanford University), Jean Bézivin (Université de Nantes) and Nuno Martins (MIT).

All the regular papers were selected based on detailed classifications provided by the members of the program committee and additional reviewers, whom I would like to thank for their diligence and expert reviewing. The complete list of all reviewers is provided below. Each paper had at least two reviewers drawn from 19 countries in all continents.

Many people contributed to the success of ICEIS 2001, but we owe special thanks to the organizing team, composed by the subscribers of this preface and Aníbal Ponte, José Braz, José Cordeiro, Hugo Gamboa, Nuno Pina, Nuno Ribeiro and Sara Silva (all from the School of Technology of Setúbal).

We have received strong encouragement, both during the conference and afterwards, from many friends who urged us to continue the ICEIS series. There is a general feeling of confidence that leads us to believe that the ICEIS conference has now established itself and will continue growing during the next few years. People in various countries have expressed their interest in organizing future editions of ICEIS but it was finally decided that the ICEIS 2002 edition would be hosted by our Spanish friends from the University of Castilla-La Mancha, at Ciudad Real. The ICEIS 2003 will be held by ESEO (École Superieure d'Electronique de l'Ouest) at the beautiful city of Angers, France.

Joaquim Filipe
Bernadette Sharp
Paula Miranda

CONFERENCE COMMITTEE

Conference Chair:

Joaquim Filipe, Escola Superior de Tecnologia of Setúbal, Portugal

Programme Chairs:

Bernadette Sharp, Staffordshire University, School of Computing, Beaconside, Stafford, UK
Algirdas Pakstas , University of North London, UK

Organising Committee:

José Braz, José Cordeiro, Hugo Gamboa, Paula Miranda, Nuno Pina, Aníbal Ponte, Sara Silva and Nuno Ribeiro, Escola Superior de Tecnologia of the Instituto Politécnico de Setúbal, Portugal.

Programme Committee:

Alderson, A. (UK)
Amaral, L. (PORTUGAL)
Aparicio, J. (PORTUGAL)
Belo, C. (PORTUGAL)
Bernus, P. (AUSTRALIA)
Bittel, O. (GERMANY)
Boavida, F. (PORTUGAL)
Bonsón, E. (SPAIN)
Cavalho, J. (PORTUGAL)
Cernuzzi, L. (PARAGUAY)
Cheng, A. (USA)
Chu, W. (TAIWAN)
Clarke, R. (AUSTRALIA)
Claude, C. (FRANCE)
Coelho, H. (PORTUGAL)
Costa, E., (PORTUGAL)
Coulette, B. (FRANCE)
Dietz, J.(NETHERLANDS)
Dignum, F. (NETHERLANDS)
Dingley, S. (UK)
Dorffner, G. (AUSTRIA)
Eardley, A. (UK)
Emery, D. (UK)
Ferreira, P. (PORTUGAL)
Figueiredo, A. (PORTUGAL)
Fred, A. (PORTUGAL)
Gough, T. (UK)
Grönlund, Å. (SWEDEN)
Guarino, N. (ITALY)
Guimarães, N. (PORTUGAL)
Gupta, J. (USA)
Gustavsson, R. (SWEDEN)
Hammoudi, S. (FRANCE)
Heng, M. (AUSTRALIA)
Huang, K. (NETHERLANDS)
Kim, H. (CANADA)
Kouloumdjian, J. (FRANCE)
Lazzarini, H., (ARGENTINA)
León de Mora, C. (SPAIN)
Libourel, T., (FRANCE)
Linna, M., (FINLAND)
Liu, K. (UK)
Loogen, R. (GERMANY)
Lopes, G. (PORTUGAL)
Lopes, J., (PORTUGAL)
Luker, P. (UK)
Lyytinen, K. (FINLAND)
Machado, A. (PORTUGAL)
Madeira, E. (BRASIL)
Madeira, H. (PORTUGAL)
Malekovic, M. (CROATIA)
Mamede, N. (PORTUGAL)
Martins, J. (PORTUGAL)
Martins, M. (PORTUGAL)
Moghadampour, G. (FINLAND)
Monteiro, E. (PORTUGAL)
Odell, J. (USA)
Paiva, A. (PORTUGAL)
Penzel, T. (GERMANY)
Piattini, M. (SPAIN)
Pires, F. (PORTUGAL)
Pirotte, A. (BELGIUM)
Ramos, P. (PORTUGAL)
Rees, S. (UK)

Revenu, M. (FRANCE)
Rodriguez, P. (SPAIN)
Rosa, A. (PORTUGAL)
Schoop, M. (GERMANY)
Shah, H., (UK)
Shankararaman, V. (UK)
Shao, J. (UK)
Shi, Z. (CHINA)
Silva, A. (PORTUGAL)
Silva, A. (PORTUGAL)
Silva, J. (PORTUGAL)
Silva, M. (PORTUGAL)
Smirnov, A. (RUSSIA)
Soule-Dupuy, C., (FRANCE)
Stader, J. (UK)
Stamper, R. (NETHERLANDS)
Sun, L. (UK)
Taniar, D. (AUSTRALIA)
Tari, Z. (AUSTRALIA)
Tribolet, J. (PORTUGAL)
Ultsch, A. (GERMANY)
Verdier, C. (FRANCE)
Vernadat, F. (FRANCE)
Walley, W. (UK)
Wang, H. (HONG KONG)
Warkentin, M. (USA)
Weigand, H. (NETHERLANDS)
Welty, C. (USA)
Wijnhoven, F. (NETHERLANDS)
Wilson, D. (UK)
Wood-Harper, T. (UK)
Yang, H. (UK)
ZongKai, L. (CHINA)

Invited Speakers:

Jean Bézivin, University of Nantes, France

Satya Chattopadhyay, University of Scranton, USA

Frank Dignum, University of Utrecht, Holland

Thomas Greene, MIT Lab for Computer Science and NSF, USA

Anatol Holt, University of Milano, Italy

Qusay Mahmoud, University of Carleton, Canada

Nuno Martins, MIT, USA

Giorgio De Michelis, University of Milano, Italy

Ulrich Reimer, Swiss Life, Information Systems Research Group, Switzerland

Gio Wiederhold, University of Stanford, USA

OBTAINING PRECISION WHEN INTEGRATING INFORMATION

Gio Wiederhold
Computer Science Department, Stanford University,
Stanford California, 94305, USA
email: gio@cs.stanford.edu

Abstract: Precision is important when information is to be supplied for commerce and decision-making. However, a major problem in the web-enabled world is the flood and diversity of information. Through the web we can be faced with more alternatives than can be investigated in depth. The value system itself is changing, whereas traditionally information had value, it is now the attention of the purchaser that has value.

New methods and tools are needed to search through the mass of potential information. Traditional information retrieval tools have focused on returning as much possible relevant information, in the process lowering the precision, since much irrelevant material is returned as well. However, for business e-commerce to be effective, one cannot present an excess of unlikely alternatives (type 2 errors). The two types of errors encountered, false positives and false negatives now differ in importance. In most business situations, a modest fraction of missed opportunities (type 1 errors) are acceptable. We will discuss the tradeoffs and present current and future tools to enhance precision in electronic information gathering.

1. INTRODUCTION

While much progress in Information Science is triggered by progress in technology, when assessing the future we must focus on the consumers. The consumers have to provide the financial resources over the long haul, and repay the investments made by governments, venture funders, and dedicated individuals. The current (Spring 2001) malaise is certainly in part due to technological capabilities outrunning the capabilities of the customers. The expectations of the consumer are fueled by the popular and professional press, namely that any need, specifically in the domain of information, can be satisfied by going to the computer appliance and in few seconds, satisfy that need. What are some of those needs?

Customers can be partitioned into a wide range, from a professional, who is focused on work, to a teenager who, after school, focuses on entertainment. In practice the groups overlap quite a bit. Many professionals use their laptops on airplanes to play games; and teenagers perform research or even start Internet enterprises at home [Morris:99]. In this paper we consider business needs, consumer and professional needs were also addressed in the source report [W:99]. Business needs are characterized by including a large volume of repetitive tasks. These tasks must be done expeditiously, with a very low rate of error and modest human supervision.

1.1 Business-to-business needs

Business-to-business covers the early parts of the supply chain from raw materials and labor to consumer.. In manufacturing, the traditional needs are obtaining information about material and personnel, the best processes to produce merchandise, and the markets that will use those goods. In distribution industries, the information needed encompasses the producers, the destinations, and the capabilities of internal and external transportation services. In these and other situations data from local and remote sources must be reliably integrated so they can be used for recurring business decisions.

The needs and issues that a business enterprise deals with include the same needs that an individual customer encounters, but also involve precision. In business-to-business interaction automation is desired, so that repetitive tasks don't have to be manually repeated and controlled (JelassiL:96). Stock has to be reordered daily, fashion trends analyzed weekly, and displays changed monthly. However, here is where the rapid and uncontrolled growth of Internet capabilities shows the greatest lacunae, since changes occur continuously at the sites one may wish to access.

J. Filipe et al. (eds.), Enterprise Information Systems III, 1–14.

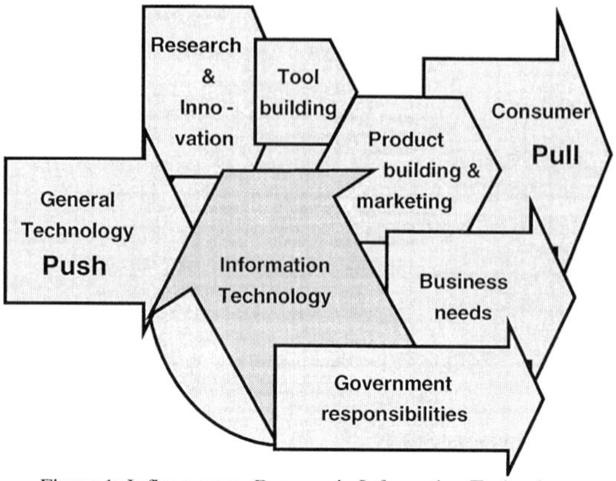

Figure 1: Influences on Progress in Information Technology

1.2 Infrastructure

Supply chain management has been the topic of automation for a long time (Hoffer:98). Initiatives as Electronic Interchange (EDI) and Object Management Group (OMG) CORBA have developed mechanism for well-defined interchanges. Java Enterprise Beans (JEB) provide an attractive, more lightweight mechanism. Recently Microsoft and IBM have teamed up in the Universal Data Interchange (UDDI) initiative to support a broad range of business services on the we.. The ongoing move to XML provides a more consistent representation. However, none of these efforts directly address the semantic issues that must be solved for the next generation of on-line services.

2. SELECTION OF HIGH-VALUE INFORMATION

The major problem facing individual consumers is the ubiquity and diversity of information. Even more than the advertising section of a daily newspaper the World-Wide Web contains more alternatives than can be investigated in depth. When leafing through advertisements the selection is based on the prominence of the advertisement, the convenience of getting to the advertised merchandise in one's neighborhood, the reputation of quality, personal or created by marketing, of the vendor, and features -- suitability for a specific need, and price. The dominating factor differs based on the merchandise. Similar factors apply to online purchasing of merchandise and services. Lacking the convenience of leafing through the newspaper, greater dependence for selection is based on selection tools.

2.1 Getting the right information

Getting complete information is a question of breadth. In traditional measures completeness of coverage is termed *recall*. To achieve a high recall rapidly all possibly relevant sources have to be accessed. Since complete access for every information request is not feasible, information systems depend on having indexes. Having an index means that an actual information request can start from a manageable list, with points to locations and pages containing the actual information.

The effort to index all publicly available information is immense. Comprehensive indexing is limited due to the size of the web itself, and the rate of change of updates to the information on the web. Some of these problems can be, and are being addressed by brute force, using heavyweight indexing engines and smart indexing engines. For instance, sites that have been determined to change frequently will be visited by the *worms* that collect data from the sources more often, so that the average information is as little out-of-date as feasible (Lynch:97). Of course, sites change very frequently, say more than once a day, cannot be effectively indexed by a broad-based search engine. We have summarized the approaches currently being used in (W:00).

The problems due to the variety of media used for representing information is being addressed (PonceleonSAPD:98). Although automatic indexing systems focus on the ASCII text presented on web pages, documents stored in alternative formats, as

Microsoft Word or Portable Document Format (PDF) (Adobe:99) are covered by some search engines. Valuable information is often presented in tabular form, where relationships are represented by relative position. Such representations are hard to parse by search engines. Image data and Powerpoint slides may be indexed via ancillary text.

Information that is stored in databases that are only accessed via scripts remains hidden as well. Such information, as vendor catalogs contents are not indexed at all, and the top-level descriptive web-pages are rarely adequate substitutes. There are also valuable terms for information selection in speech, both standalone and as part of video representations.

Getting complete information typically reduces the fraction of actual relevant material in the retrieved collection. It is here where it is crucial to make improvements, since we expect that the recall volume of possibly relevant retrieved information will grow as the web and retrieval capabilities grow. Selecting a workable quantity that is of greatest benefit to a customer requires additional work. This work can be aided by the sources, through better descriptive information or by intermediate services, that provide filtering. If it is not performed, the customer has a heavy burden in processing the overload, and is likely to give up.

High quality indexes can help immensely. Input for indexes can be produced by the information supplier, but those are likely to be limited. Schemes requiring cooperation of the sources have been proposed (GravanoGT:94). Since producing an index is a valued-added service, it is best handled by independent companies, who can distinguish themselves, by comprehensiveness versus specialization, currency, convenience of use, and cost. Those companies can also use tools that break through access barriers in order to better serve their population.

2.2 The Need for Precision

Our information environment has changed in recent years. In the past, Say ten years ago, most decision makers operated in settings where information was scarce, and there was a inducement to obtain more information. Having more information was seen as being able to make better decisions, and reduce risks, save resources, and reduces losses.

Today we have access to an excess of information. The search engines will typically retrieve more than a requestor can afford to read. The metrics for information systems have been traditionally recall and precision. Recall is defined as the ratio of relevant records retrieved to all relevant records in the database. Its complement, the count of relevant records not retrieved is termed a type 1 error in statistics. Precision is defined similarly as the ratio to relevant records to irrelevant records. The number of irrelevant records retrieved are type 2 errors. In practical systems these are related, as shown in Figure 2. While recall can be improved by retrieving more records, the precision becomes disproportionally worse.

There are a number of problems with these metrics: measuring relevance and precision, the relative cost of the associated errors, and the scale effect of very large collections.

Relevance. Well recognized is that the decision on relevance of documents is fluid. When the resources, as on the web, are immense, the

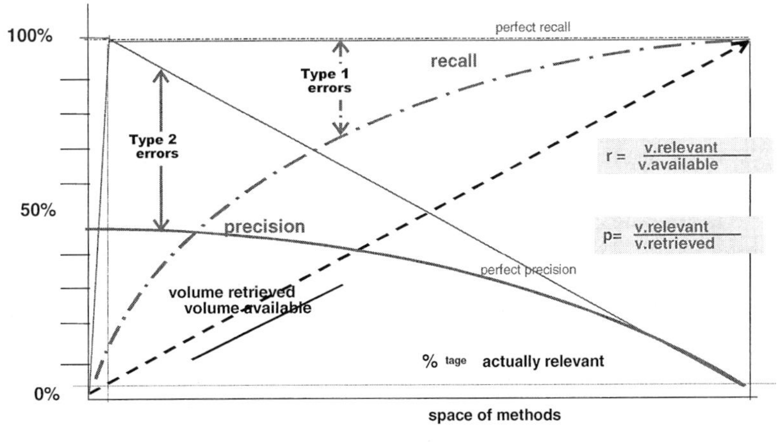

Figure 2: Trading of Relevance versus Precision

designation of relevance itself can become irrelevant. Some documents add so little information that an actual decision-making process will not be materially affected. A duplicate document might be rated relevant, although it provides no new information. Most experiments are evaluated by using expert panels to rate the relevance of modest document collections, since assessing all documents in the collection is a tedious task.

Precision. The measurement of precision suffers from the same problem, although it does not require that all documents in the collection be assessed, only the ones that have actually be retrieved. Search engines, in order to assist the user, typically try to rank retrieved items in order of relevance. Most users will only look at the 10 top-ranked items. The ranking computation differs by search engine, and account for much of the differences among them. Two common techniques are aggregations of relative word frequencies in documents for the search terms and popularity of webpages, as indicated by access counts or references from peer pages (Google ref). For e-commerce, where the catalog entries are short and references harder to collect these rankings do not apply directly. Other services, as MySimon, and Epinion (Epinion:00) try to fill that void by letting users vote.

Cost. Not considered in most assessments of retrieval performance are relative costs to an actual user of the types of errors encountered. For instance, in a purchasing situation, the cost of not retrieving all the possible suppliers of an item may cause paying more than necessary. However, once the number of suppliers is such that a reasonable choice exists, the chance that other suppliers will offer significantly lower prices is small. The cost of type 1 errors is then low, as shown in Figure 3.

The cost of an individual type 2 error is borne by the decision-maker, who has to decide that an erroneous, irrelevant supplier was selected, perhaps a maker of toy trucks when real trucks were needed. The cost of an individual rejection may be small, but when we deal with large collections, the costs can become substantial. We will argue that more automation is needed here, since manual rejection inhibits automation.

Scale. Perfection in retrieval is hard to achieve. In selected areas we find now precision ratios of 94% (Mitchell:99). While we don't want to belittle such achievements, having 6% type 2 errors can still lead to very many irrelevant instances, when such techniques are applied to large collections, for instance, a 6% error rate on a million potential items will generate 60 000 errors, way too many to check manually. It is hard to be sure that no useful items have been missed if one restricts oneself to the10 top-ranked items.

2.3 Errors

The reasons for having errors are manifold. There are misspellings, there is intentional manipulation of webpages to make them rank high, there is useful information that has not been accessed recently by search engines, and there are suppliers that intentionally do not display their wares on the web, because they want to be judged by other metrics, say quality, than the dominant metric when purchasing, namely price. All these sources of errors warrant

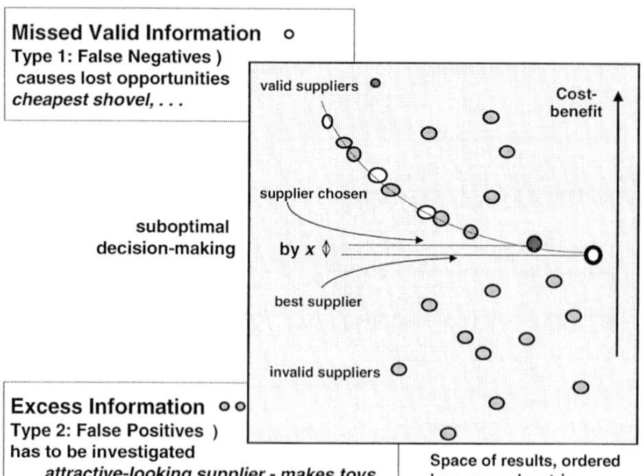

Figure 3: Costs of type 1 versus type 2 Errors

investigation, but we will focus here on a specific problem, namely semantic inconsistency.

The importance of errors is also domain-dependent. A database which is perfectly adequate for one application may have an excessive error rate when used for another purpose. For instance, a payroll might have too many errors in the employee's address field to be useful for mailout. It's primary purpose is not affected by such errors, since most deposits are directly transferred to banks, and the address is mainly used to determine tax deduction requirements for local and state governments. To assure adequate precision of results when using data collected for another objective some content quality analysis is needed prior to making commitments.

3. SEMANTIC INCONSISTENCY

The semantic problem faced by systems using broad-based collections of information is the impossibility of having wide agreements on the meaning of terms among organizations that are independent of each other. We denote the set of terms and their relationships, following current usage in Artificial Intelligence, as an *ontology*. In our work we define ontologies in a grounded fashion, namely:

Ontology: a set of terms and their relationships Term: a reference to real-world and abstract objects
Relationship: a named and typed set of links between objects
Reference: a label that names objects
Abstract object: a concept which refers to other objects
Real-world object: an entity instance with a physical manifestation

Grounding the definitions so that they can refer to actual collections, as represented in databases, allows validation of the research we are undertaking [WG:97]. Many precursors of ontologies have existed for a long time. Schemas, as used in databases, are simple, consistent, intermediate-level ontologies. Foreign keys relating table headings in database schemas imply structural relationships. Included in more comprehensive ontologies are the values that variables can assume; of particular significance are codes for enumerated values used in data-processing. Names of states, counties, etc. are routinely encoded. When such terms are used in a database the values in a schema column are constrained, providing another example of a structural relationship. There are thousands of such lists, often maintained by domain specialists. Other ontologies are being created now within DTD definitions for the eXtended Markup Language (XML) (Connolly:97).

3.1 Sources of Ontologies

Although the term ontology is just now getting widespread acceptance, all of us have encountered ontologies in various forms. Often terms used in paper systems have been reused in computer-based systems:

- Lexicon: collection of terms used in information systems
- Taxonomy: categorization or a classification of terms
- Database schemas: attributes, ranges, constraints
- Data dictionaries: guide to systems with multiple files, owners
- Object libraries: grouped attributes, inherit., methods
- Symbol tables: terms bound to implemented programs
- Domain models: interchange terms in XML DTDs, schemas.

The ordering in this list implies an ongoing formalization of knowledge about the data being referenced. Database schemas are the primary means used in automation to formalize ontological information, but they rarely record relationship information, nor define the permissible range for data attributes. Such information is often obtained during design, but rarely kept and even less frequently maintained. Discovering the knowledge that is implicit in the web itself is a challenging task (HeflinHL:98).

3.2 Large versus small ontologies

Of concern is the breadth of ontologies. While having a consistent, world-wide ontology over all the terms we use would cause the problem of semantic inconsistency to go away, we will argue that such a goal is not achievable, and, in fact, not even desirable.

3.2.1 Small ontologies

We have seen successes with small, focused ontologies. Here we consider groups of individuals, that cooperate with some shared objective, on a regular basis. Databases within companies or interest groups have been effective means of sharing information. Since they are finite, it is also possible for participants to inspect their contents and validate that the individual expectations and the information resources match. Once this semantic match is achieved, effective automatic processing of the information can take place. Many of the ongoing developments in defining XML DTD's and schemas follow the same paradigm, while interchanging information to widely distributed participants. Examples are found in diverse applications, as petroleum trading and the analysis of Shakespeare's plays. The participants in those enterprises have shared knowledge for a long time, and a formal and processable encoding is of great benefit.

There is still a need in many of these domains to maintain the ontologies. In healthcare, for instance, the terms needed for reporting patient's diseases to receive financial reimbursement change periodically, as therapies evolve and split for alternate manifestations. At a finer granularity, disease descriptors used in research areas evolve even faster, as we learn about distinctions in genotypes that affect susceptibility to diseases.

The maintenance of these domain ontologies often evolves onto professional associations. Such associations have a membership that has an interest in in sharing and cooperating. Ontology creation and maintenance is a natural outgrowth of their function in dissemination of information, and merges well with the role they have in publication and organizing meetings. An example of such a close relationship in Computer Science is the classification of computer literature (ACM:99), published by the ACM and revised approximately every 5 years. This document provides an effective high-level view to the literature in the scientific aspects of the domain, although it does not provide a granularity suitable for, say, trading and purchasing of software.

3.2.2 Large ontologies

A major effort, sponsored by the National Library Medicine (NLM), has integrated diverse ontologies used in healthcare into the Unified Medical Language System (UMLS) (HumphreysL:93). In large ontologies collected from diverse sources or constructed by multiple individuals over a long time some inconsistencies are bound to remain. Maintenance of such ontologies is required when sources change (Oliver:00). It took several years for UMLS to adapt to an update in one of its sources, the disease registry mentioned earlier. Still. UMLS fulfills is mission in broadening searches and increasing recall, the main objective of bibliographic systems.

Large ontologies have also been collected with the objective to assist in common-sense reasoning (CyC) (LenatG:90). CyC provides the concept of *microtheories* to circumscribe contexts within its ontology. CyC has been used to *articulate* relevant information from distinct sources without constraints imposed by microtheories (ColletHS:91). That approach provides valuable matches, and improves recall, but does not improve precision.

The inconsistency of semantics among sources is due to their autonomy. Each source develops its terminology in its own context, and uses terms and classifications that are natural to its creators and owners. The problem with articulation by matching terms from diverse sources is not just that of synonyms -- two words for the same object, or one word for completely different objects, as *miter* in carpentry and in religion. The inconsistencies are much more complex, and include overlapping classes, subsets, partial supersets, and the like. Examples of problems abound. The term *vehicle* is used differently in the transportation code, in police agencies, and in the building code, although over 90% of the instances are the same.

The problems of maintaining consistency in large ontologies is recursive. Terms do not only refer to real-world objects, but also to abstract groupings. The term `vehicle' is different for architects, when designing garage space, versus its use in traffic regulation, dealing with right-of-way rules at intersections. At the next higher level, talking about transportation will have very different coverage for the relevant government department versus a global company shipping its goods.

There are also differences in granularity with domains. A vendor site oriented towards carpenters will use very specific terms, say *sinkers* and *brads*, to denote certain types of nails, that will not be familiar to the general population. A site oriented to homeowners will just use the general categorical term *nails*, and may then describe the diameter, length, type of head, and material. For the homeowner to share the ontologies of all the professions involved in construction would be impossible. For the carpenter to give up specialized terms and abbreviations, as 3D for a three-penny sized nail, would be inefficient -- language in any domain is enhanced to provide effective communication within that domain. The homeowner cannot afford to learn the thousands of specialized terms needed to maintain one's house, and the carpenter cannot afford wasting time by circumscribing each nail, screw, and tool with precise attributes.

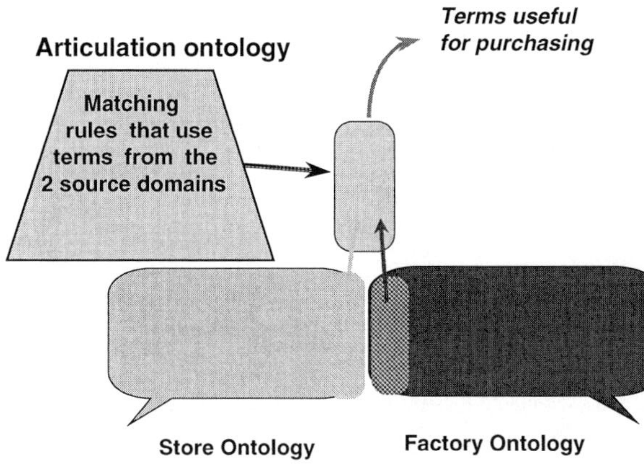

Figure 4: Articulation of Two Domains

The net effect of these problems, when extended over all the topics we wish to communicate about is that **it is impossible to achieve a globally consistent ontology**. Even if such a goal could be achieved, it could not be maintained, since definitions within the subdomains will, and must continue to evolve. It would also be inefficient, since the subdomains would be restricted in their use of terms. The benefits to the common good, that we all could communicate consistently will be outweighed by the costs incurred locally and the cost of the requirements that we all acquire consistent global knowledge.

3.2.3 Composition of small ontologies

If we have proven here, albeit informally, that large global ontologies cannot be achieved, even though they are desirable to solve broader problems than can be solved with small ontologies, we are faced with one conclusion. It will be necessary to address larger problems we interoperating with small ontologies. Since a simple integration of small ontologies will lead us directly into the problems faced by large ontologies, we must learn to combine the small ontologies as needed, specifically as needed for the applications that require the combined knowledge.

However, inconsistent use of terms makes sharing of information from multiple sources incomplete and imprecise. As shown above, forcing every category of customers to use matching terms is inefficient. Mismatches are rife when dealing with geographic information, although localities are a prime criterion for articulation (MarkMM:99).

Most ontologies have associated textual definitions, but those are rarely sufficiently precise to allow a formal understanding without human interpretation. Although these definitions will help readers knowledgeable about the domain, they cannot guarantee precise automatic matching in a broader context, because the terms used in the definitions also come from their own source domains. The result is that inconsistencies will occur when terms for independent, but relatable domains are matched.

These inconsistencies are a major source for errors and imprecision. We have all experienced web searches that retrieved entries that had identically spelled keywords, but were not all related to the domain we are addressing - type 2 errors. When we augment the queries with possible synonyms, because we sense a high rate of missing information, type 1 errors, the fraction of junk, type 2 errors, typically increases disproportionably. The problems due to inconsistency are more of a hindrance to business than to individuals, who deal more often with single instances.

4. ARTICULATION

Since we cannot hope to achieve global consistency, but still must serve applications that span multiple domains, we must settle composition. The theme, that only focused, application oriented approaches will be maintainable, directs us to limit us to the concepts needed for interoperation, for which we will reuse the term articulation.

Once we have clear domain ontologies that are to be related within an application we must recognize their intersections, where concepts belong to multiple domains. For clarity, we restrict ourselves to intersections of two domains. More complex cases are certainly feasible, but we will address them using the algebraic capabilities presented in Section 5. We will deal in this section with the binary case.

4.1 Semantic rules

An application requiring information from two domains must be able to join them semantically, so that there will be a semantic intersection between them. Such a match may not be found by lexical word matching. For instance, checking for a relationship of automobile purchasing and accidents requires looking for the car *owners* in dealer records that list the *buyers*.

We define then the articulation to be the semantically meaningful intersection of concepts that relate domains with respect to an application. The instances should match according to our definition of an ontology, given in the introduction to this section.

An articulation point hence defines a relevant semantic match, even if the actual terms and their representation do not match. For instance, for vacation travel planning a *trip segment* matches the term *flight* from the airline domain, and term *journey* from the railroad domain. Terms at a lower level of abstraction, defining instances also have to made to match. For instance, to take a train to San Francisco Airport one must get off at the San Bruno Caltrain station. Here the terms are at the same granularity, and once matched, the articulation is easy. Understanding such articulation points is a service implicitly provided now by experts, here travel agents. In any application where subtasks cross the boundaries of domain some experts exist that help bridge the semantic gaps.

Often the matching rules become complex. In listings of the California Department of Motor Vehicles (DMV) houseboats are included. To match vehicles correctly for, say, an analysis of fuel consumption, the articulation rule has to exclude those houseboats. The attributes that define the classes now become part of the input needed for the execution of the articulation. Such differences in scope are common, and yet often surprising, because the application designer has no reason to suspect that such differences exist. A good way to check correctness of matches is to process the underlying databases.

The concept is not to force alignment of entire base ontologies, but only present to the application consistent terms in the limited overlapping area. Typical applications that rely on intersections are in purchasing goods and services from another domain, the example above cited *journeys* and *lights*. Terms only used in one domain need not be aligned, as *sleeping compartment* and *in-flight movie*.

4.2 Creating Articulations

There are already people in all kinds of business settings who perform such work. Any travel agent has to be able to deal with the diversity of resources. However, when interacting the phone or directly with diverse webpages on the Internet, the problems are not widely recognized. For automation they will need to be solved formally.

Keeping the rules that define an articulation specific to narrow application contexts simplifies their creation and maintenance. Even within an application area multiple rule sets can exist, for instance one might specific to logistics in drug distribution. The logical organization to be responsible for the rules which define such a specific *articulation ontology* for, say, pharmaceutical drugs would be the National Drug Distributors Association (NDDA) in the USA. There will be a need for tools to manage those rules, and these tools can serve diverse applications, both in creation and maintenance (Jannink:01).

When two sources come from the same organization, we would expect an easy match. i.e., a consistent ontology. However, we found that even in one company the payroll department defined the term *employee* differently from the definition used in *personnel*, so that the intersection of their two databases is smaller than either source. Such aberrations can easily be demonstrated, by computing the differences of the membership from the respective databases, following an ontological grounding as we use here.. In large multi-national corporations and in enterprises that have grown through mergers, differences are bound to exist. These can be dealt with if the problems are formally recognized and articulated, but often they are handled in an isolated fashion, and solved over and over in an ad-hoc fashion.

Such analyses are not feasible when source information sources are world-wide, and contexts become unclear. Here no comprehensive matching can be expected, so that certain operation cannot be executed reliably on-line, although many tasks can be carried out. These difficulties are related to the applicability of the closed-world-assumption (CWA) (Reiter:78).

It requires an effort to define articulations precisely. The investment pays off as it reduces the wasted effort in taking care of the effects of errors that are now avoided. The initial effort becomes essential to support repetitive business transactions, where one cannot afford to spend human efforts to correct semantic mismatches every time.

To summarize, articulations that are needed among domains are made implicitly by *smart* people. Converting human expertise in dealing with domain intersections to permit automation will require a formalization of the domain ontologies and their semantic intersections. Such research will be an important component of moving to the semantic web (BernersLeeHL:01).

5. AN ALGEBRA FOR ONTOLOGIES

There will be many applications that require more than a pair of ontologies. For example, logistics, which must deal with shipping merchandise via a variety of carriers: truck, rail, ship, and air, requires interoperation among many diverse domains, as well as multiple companies located in different countries. To resolve these issues we are developing an ontology algebra, which further exploits the capabilities of rule-based articulation (MitraWK:00).

Once we define an intersection of ontologies through articulation, we should also define union and difference operations over ontologies (W:94). We apply the same semantic matching rules we used for articulation to transform the traditional set operations to operations that are cognizant of inter-domain semantics. Assuring that soundness and consistency, mirroring what we expect from traditional set operations, is a challenge.

Having an algebra not only achieves disciplined scalability to an unlimited set of sources, but it also provides a means to enumerate alternate composition strategies, assess their performance, and, if warranted, perform optimizations (JanninkEa:99). We expect that the semantic union operation will mainly be employed to combine the results of prior intersections, in order to increase the breadth of ontological coverage of an application.

The semantic difference operation will allow the owners of a domain ontology to distinguish the terms that the owners can change as their needs change. The excluded terms, by definition, participate in some articulation, and changes made to them will affect interoperation with related domains, and hence make some application less precise, or even disable it. Informally, difference allows ontology owners to assess the scope of their local autonomy.

6. FILTERING

The amount of information that becomes available after articulation may still be excessive. Filtering the results may be required, or a ranking may be computed to bring the most relevant results to the attention of the information users (Resnick:97).

6.1 Suitability

The suitability of the information for use once it is obtained also needs assessment. Medical findings of interest to a pathologist will be confusing to patients, and advice for patients about a disease should be redundant to the medical specialist. Some partitioning for roles exists now; for instance Medline has multiple access points (Cimino:96). But smart selection schemes might well locate information via all paths, and most information that is publicly available is not labeled with respect to consumer roles, and it may even be presumptuous to do so.

There is hence a role for mediating modules to interpret meta-information associated with a site and use that information to filter or rank the data obtained from that site (Langer:98). Doing so requires understanding the background and typical intent of the customer. Note that the same individual can have multiple customer roles, as a private person or as a professional.

6.2 Quality-based ranking

Assessing the quality of information and the underlying merchandise and services is an important service to consumers, and should be integrated into mediating services. There is currently an excessive emphasis on ranking of products solely by price, but price is only one factor in deciding on a purchase. Without tools that can assess quality there is a disincentive for high-quality suppliers to participate in electronic commerce, since they will be ranked as being non-competitive on price. To assess quality three parties are involved in the mediation:

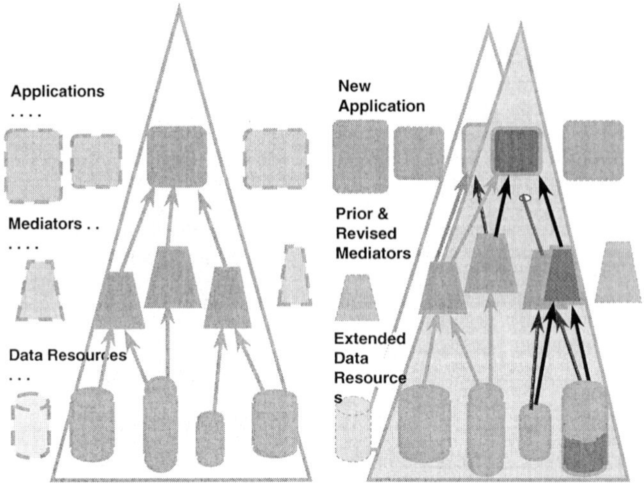

Figure 5: Mediator Architecture

1. sources of the data, which should be up-to-date and highly available;
2. customers, to whom information is to be delivered;
3. assessors, who apply criteria and specific annotations to the data, adding value to the information.

The assessors must understand the sources as well as the expectations for various categories of customers, and also be able to respond to feedback from the customers. Several current systems rely wholly on informal consumer input, others attempt some validation of feedback and membership (Epinions:00). Today use of these services requires more complexity in on-line interactions, but a better integration of tools that help rank the quality of data into electronic commerce should be feasible (NaumannLF:99).

When quality information is gathered by surveying customers, it represents the actual outcome, rather than a model based on relevant parameters. However, such evaluations tend to lag and are easily biased. Bias occurs because of poor selection of customers and unbalanced response rates. Stable customers are reached more easily. Unhappy customers are more likely to respond. Questionnaires include leading entries, say, by starting with questions about safety of a car, subsequent questions about reliability will be viewed differently by the customer. It is difficult to eliminate bias from statistical reports (Huff:54).

6.3 Personalization

Tools that take the customer into account should be able to determine specific features important for the purchaser. Personalization has become a popular topic in web-oriented research, and a major task when developing community portals (JinDW:01). Unfortunately, much input is needed before we have enough information to model the customer's needs. Today, most personalization is quite primitive. There is a great deal of reluctance for an individual to specify their interests to any degree of detail (Maes:94), so that other means of acquiring profiles are preferred;

Learning from on-line interactions and behavior avoids placing a burden on the customer (Mitchell:01). Typically the computer used for an interaction is taken to be a surrogate for an individual. Interactions performed are categorized, and become the model for a user, ignoring that an individual can assume multiple, distinct roles and that the computer may serve multiple individuals. Specific objectives of an interaction span a wide range, and are hard to identify within the collected information. Examples of detailed objective in a series of related interactions maybe a search for the shade of a color wanted to match a piece of apparel, the location of the theater performance one wants to attend, a check of one's bank account before ordering tickets, and the search for a book describing the locale of the play. Recognizing a cluster here is beyond current technology. In practice, a consumer may during that period also seek secondary measurements of a piece of furniture wanted for a specific odd location, further confusing learning process..

There is an obvious tension in providing more specifications. Organizing the information to make it suitable for the consumer requires insight and care. Many of the parameters are hard to specify, especially factors describing quality. If much detail, irrelevant to many, is given, then the consumer who is not interested will be overloaded, and may give up on the purchase altogether. At the same time, information of interest is often lacking from catalogs, forcing the consumer to search many sources. For instance, the noise made by a projector is rarely reported, and information as battery life in laptop computers is notoriously inaccurate.

Modeling the customer's requirements effectively requires more than tracking recent web requests. First of all a customer in a given role has to be disassociated from all the other activities that an individual may participate in. We should distinguish here customers, performing a specific role, and individuals, who will play several different roles at differing times. In a given role, complex tasks can be modeled using a hierarchical decomposition, with a structure that supports the divide-and-conquer paradigm that is basic to all problem-solving tasks (W:97). Natural partitions at an intermediate level will typically correspond to the domains

7. ARCHITECTURE

We use the term architecture to refer to the composition of modules of information systems. Traditional information systems have depended on human experts. Their elimination through the capability of providing direct linkages on the web has led to disintermediation (W:92) .

We see these services being replaced by automated engines, positioned between the information clients and the information resources. Within the mediators will be the intelligent functions that encode the required expertise for semantic matching and filtering. Composition of synergistic functions creates a mediator performing substantial service. Such a service is best envisaged as a module within the networks that link customers and resources, as sketched in Figure 5.

Domain-type mediators can integrate domains as financial information, personnel management, travel, logistics, technology etc. (WC:94). Within these domains will be further specialization, as in finance to provide information about investing in precious metals, bonds, blue-chip stocks, utilities, and high tech. There will be meta-services as well, helping to locate those services and reporting on their quality. Mediators encompass both experts and software to perform these functions, and sustain the services as functional requirements and underlying ontologies evolve.

Domain-type mediators can integrate domains as financial information, personnel management, travel, logistics, technology etc. (WC:94). Within these domains will be further specialization, as in finance to provide information about investing in precious metals, bonds, blue-chip stocks, utilities, and high tech. There will be meta-services as well, helping to locate those services and reporting on their quality. Mediators encompass both experts and software to perform these functions, and sustain the services as functional requirements and underlying ontologies evolve.

7.1 Middleware and Mediation

The need for middleware to connect clients to servers has been well established. although it has only attracted a modest amount of academic interest (Gartner:95). However, middleware products only enable communication, and deal with issues as establishing connectivity, reliability, transmission security, and resolution of differences in representation and timing. A mediator can exploit those technologies and avoid dealing with the problems that arise from having an excess of standards. However, middleware never deals with true semantic differences and only rarely with integration of information, leaving these tasks to a superior layer of software.

There is today a small number of companies building mediators with transformation and integration capability (W:98). However, the available technology is not yet suitable to be shrink-wrapped and requires substantial adaptation to individual settings. Many products focus on specific increments. When the added value is modest, then the benefit gained is likely outweighed by the cost in performance incurred when adding a layer into an information system architecture. In those cases, making incremental improvements to the sources, as providing object transforms, or in applications, as providing multiple interfaces, seems to be preferable.

However, if the services placed into an intermediate layer are comprehensive, sufficient added value can be produced for the applications that access the mediators and the cost of transit through the additional layer will be offset.

7.2 Scalability and Maintenance

It is important that the architecture in which mediators are inserted is scalable and maintainable (WC:94). These concepts are directly related, since a failure to provide for growth means that orderly maintenance is inhibited, while a failure to provide for maintenance inhibits growth.

Many initial demonstrations of mediator technology used a single mediator and provided impressive results by combining, say three sources and supporting two applications. Such a design creates a central bottleneck, both in terms of performance as more customers find the services attractive, and in terms of maintenance, as more resources have to be dealt with. All resources change over time, some perhaps every couple of years, others much more frequently. Any mediator must be of a size that its operation can be maintained without excessive hassles, and that means that systems will have multiple, specialized mediators.

Some mediators may provide information to higher level mediators as well as to customers. Having consistent interfaces will be valuable, although no single standard dominates today. For the delivery of services XML is today the prime candidate, and allows for the specification of basic ontologies (Connolly:97).

The interfaces to the sources are likely to remain more varied, so that in order to achieve a large scale through broad access a variety of interface types will have to be supported (ChangGP:96). The diversity means also that maintenance, as sources change will be hard to automate. Feedback to trigger mediator maintenance may have to come from polling of the sources, triggers placed within the mediators, and reports of errors from customers or customer applications.

7.3 Incremental Maintenance

To deliver valuable services, mediators will have to be updated as well. Some changes are bound to affect the customers, as new interfaces or changes in the underlying ontologies. Unwanted updates, scheduled by a service, often hurt a customer, even though in the long run the improvement is desired. To allow customers to schedule their adaptation to new capabilities when it is suitable for them, mediator owners can keep prior versions available. Since mediators are of modest size and do not hold voluminous data internally, keeping an earlier copy has a modest cost.

The benefits of not forcing all customers to change interfaces at the same time are significant. First of all customers can update at a time when they can do it best. A second benefit is that first only a few customers, namely those that need the new capabilities will be served. Any errors or problems in the new version can be repaired then, in cooperation with those customers, and broader and more serious problem will be avoided (W:95).

Since maintenance of long-lived artifacts, including software, is such a large fraction of the lifetime cost it is crucial to plan for maintenance, so that maintenance can be carried out expeditiously and economically. being able to be responsive to maintenance needs increases consumer value and reduces both consumer and provider cost. Where maintenance today often amounts to 80% of lifetime cost, a 25% reduction in those costs can double the funds available for systems improvements, while a 25% increase can inhibit all development and lead to stasis.

8. SUMMARY

Information presented to customers or applications must have a value that is greater than the of obtaining and managing it. A large fraction of the cost is dealing with erroneous and irrelevant data, since such processing requires human insight and knowledge. More information is hence not better, and less may well be, if relevance per unit of information produced is increased

The need for assistance in obtaining relevant information from the world-wide-web was recognized early in the web's existence (BowmanEa:94). This field has seen rapid advances, and yet the users remain dissatisfied with the results. Complaints about *information overload*' abound. Web searches retrieve an excess of references, and getting an actually relevant result, requires much subsequent effort.

In this paper we focused on one aspect, namely precision, the elimination of excess information.. The main method we presented is constrained and precise articulation among domains, to avoid the errors that occur when searches and integration of retrieved data is based on simply lexical matches.

We refer to the services that replace traditional human functions in information generation as mediators, and place them architecturally between the end-users, the human professionals and their local client software, and the resources, often legacy databases and inconsistently structured web sources. Such novel software will require more powerful hardware, but we are confident that hardware-oriented research and development is progressing, and will be able to supply the needed infrastructure. The major reason for slow acceptance of innovations is not the technology itself, but the massiveness of the organizational and human infrastructure.

ACKNOWLEDGEMENT

Background material for this paper came from a study prepared for JETRO / MITI (W:99) , and in turn was based on many published resources as well as on discussions with wonderful people that I have encountered in my work and studies. Work on mediation in general was supported by DARPA for many years. The research focusing on articulation is being supported by AFOSR under the New World Visions initiative and by DARPA's DAML project.

REFERENCES

ACM:99 Neal Coulter, et al: ACM Computing Classification System; http://www.acm.org/class, 1999.

Adobe:99 Adobe Corporation: PDF and Printing; http://www.adobe.com/prodindex/postscript/pdf.html, 1999

BernersLeeHL:01 Tim Berners-Lee, Jim Hendler, and Ora Lassila: "The Semantic Web"; *Scientific American*, May 2001.

BowmanEa:91 C. Mic Bowman, Peter B. Danzig, Darren R. Hardy, Udi Manber and Michael F. Schwartz: "The HARVEST Information Discovery and Access System"; *Proceedings of the Second International World Wide Web Conference*, Chicago, Illinois, October 1994, pp 763--771.

BrinP:98 Sergey Brin and Larry Page: "The Anatomy of a Large-Scale Hypertextual Web Search Engine"; *WWW7 / Computer Network,s* vol.30 no.1-7, 1998, pp.107-117.

ChangGP:96 Chen-Chuan K. Chang, Hector Garcia-Molina, Andreas Paepcke : Boolean Query Mapping Across Heterogeneous Information Sources ; *IEEE Transactions on Knowledge and Data Engineering*; Vol.8 no., pp.515-521, Aug., 1996.

Cimino:96 J.J. Cimino: "Review paper: Coding Systems in Health Care"; *Methods of Information in Medicine*, Schattauer Verlag, Stuttgart Germany, Vol.35 Nos.4-5, Dec.1996, pp.273-284.

ColletHS:91 C. Collet, M. Huhns, and W-M. Shen: "Resource Integration Using a Large Knowledge Base in CARNOT"; *IEEE Computer*, Vol.24 No.12, Dec.1991.

Connolly:97 Dan Connolly (ed.): *XML: Principles, Tools, and Techniques*; O'Reilly, 1997.

Epinions:00 R.V. Guha: *Check Before you Buy*; Epinions.com, 2000.

Gartner:95 The Garther Group: *Middleware*; Gartner group report, 1995.

GravanoGT:94 L. Gravano , H. Garcia-Molina ,and A. Tomasic: "Precision and Recall of GlOSS Estimators for Database Discovery"; *Parallel and Distributed Information Systems*, 1994.

HeflinHL:98 J. Heflin, J. Hendler, and S. Luke: "Reading Between the Lines: Using SHOE to Discover Implicit Knowledge from the Web"; in *AAAI-98 Workshop on AI and Information Integration,* 1998.

Hoffer:98 Stephen Hoffer: TBBS: Interactive electronic trade network and user interface; United States Patent 5,799,151, August 25, 1998

Huff:54 Darrel Huff: *How to Lie with Statistics*; Norton, 1954.

HumphreysL:93 Betsy Humphreys and Don Lindberg: "The UMLS project : Making the conceptual connection between users and the information they need"; *Bulletin of the Medical Library Association*, 1993, see also http://www.lexical.com.

JanninkEa:99 Jan Jannink, Prasenjit Mitra, Erich Neuhold, Srinivasan Pichai, Rudi Studer, Gio Wiederhold: "An Algebra for Semantic Interoperation of Semistructured Data"; in *1999 IEEE Knowledge and Data Engineering Exchange Workshop (KDEX'99),* Chicago, Nov. 1999.

Jannink:01 Jan Jannink: *Towards Semantic Interoperation of Semistructured Data*; Stanford University, Computer Science Department PhD thesis, March 2001; http://www-db.stanford.edu/~jan/http://www-db.stanford.edu/~jan/..

JelassiL:96 Th. Jelassi, H.-S. Lai: CitiusNet: The Emergence of a Global Electronic Market; INSEAD, The European Institute of Business Administration, Fontainebleau, France; Society for Information Management, 1996; http://www.simnet.org/public/programs/capital/96paper/paper3/3.html.

JinDW:01 YuHui Jin, Stefan Decker, and Gio Wiederhold: OntoWebber: Model-Driven Ontology-Based Web Site Management; in preparation, Stanford University CSD, Ontoweb project, May 2001.

Langer:98 Thomas Langer: "MeBro - A Framework for Metadata-Based Information Mediation"; *First International Workshop on Practical Information Mediation and Brokering, and the Commerce of Information on the Internet*, Tokyo Japan, September 1998, http://context.mit.edu/imediat98/paper2/.

LenatG:90 D. Lenat and R.V. Guha: *Building Large Knowledge-Based Systems*; Addison-Wesley (Reading MA), 372 pages.

Lynch:97 Clifford Lynch: "Searching the Internet"; The Internet: Fulfilling the Promis, *Scientific American;* March 1997.

Maes:94 Pattie Maes: "Agents that Reduce Work and Information Overload"; *Comm.ACM*, Vol 37 No.7 July 1994, pp.31-40.

MarkMM:99 David Mark et al.: Geographic Information Science: Critical Issues in an Emerging Cross-Disciplinary Research Domain; NCGIA, Feb.

1999, http://www.geog.buffalo.edu/ncgia/workshop report.html.

Mitchell:99 Tom Mitchell: "Machine Learning and Data Mining"; *Comm. ACM*, Vol. 42, No. 11, November 1999.

MitraWK:00 Prasenjit Mitra, Gio Wiederhold, and Martin Kerstens "A Graph-Oriented Model for Articulation of Ontology Interdependencies"; Proc. *Extending DataBase Technologies, EDBT 2000*, Konstanz, Germany, Springer Verlag LNCS, March 2000;

Morris:99 Bonnie Rothman Morris: You Want Fries With That Web Site?; *The New York Times*, 25 Feb.1999, p. D1.

NaumannLF:99 F.Naumann, U. Leser, J-C. Freytag: "Quality-driven Integration of Heterogeneous Information Sources"; VLDB 99, Morgan-Kaufman, 1999.

OliverS:99 Diane E. Oliver and Yuval Shahar: "Change Management of Shared and Local Health-Care Terminologies"; *IMIA Working Group 6 Meeting on Health Concept Representation and Natural Language Processing,* Phoenix, AZ, . 1999.

PonceleonSAPD:98 D. Ponceleon, S. Srinivashan, A. Amir, D. Petkovic, D. Diklic: "Key to Effective Video Retrieval: Effective Cataloguing and Browsing"; *Proc.of ACM Multimedia '98 Conference*, September 1998.

Reiter:78 Ray Reiter: "On Closed World Data Bases"; in *Logic and Data Bases*, Gallaire and Minker(eds) Plenum Press NY., 1978,

Resnick:97 Paul Resnick: Filtering Information on the Internet"; The Internet: Fulfilling the Promise; *Scientific American,* March 1997.

W:92 Gio Wiederhold, Gio: "Mediators in the Architecture of Future Information Systems"; *IEEE Computer*, March 1992, pages 38-49; reprinted in Huhns and Singh: *Readings in Agents*; Morgan Kaufmann, October, 1997, pp.185-196.

W:94 Wiederhold, Gio: "An Algebra for Ontology Composition"; *Proceedings of 1994 Monterey Workshop on Formal Methods*, Sept 1994, U.S. Naval Postgraduate School, Monterey CA, pages 56-61.

W:95 Gio Wiederhold: "Modeling and System Maintenance"; in Papazoglou: *OOER'95: Object-Oriented and Entity Relationship Modelling*; Springer Lecture Notes in Computer Science, Vol. 1021, 1995, pp. 1-20.

W:97 Gio Wiederhold: "Customer Models for Effective Presentation of Information"; Position Paper, Flanagan, Huang, Jones, Kerf (eds): *Human-Centered Systems: Information, Interactivity, and Intelligence*, National Science Foundation, July 1997, pp.218-221.

WG:97 Gio Wiederhold and Michael Genesereth: "The Conceptual Basis for Mediation Services"; *IEEE Expert, Intelligent Systems and their Applications*, Vol.12 No.5, Sep-Oct.1997.

W:98 Gio Wiederhold: "Weaving Data into Information"; *Database Programming and Design*; Freeman pubs, Sept. 1998.

W:99 Gio Wiederhold: Trends in Information Technology; report to JETRO.MITI, available in English as http://www-db.stanford.edu/pub/gio/1999/miti.htm.

W:00 Wiederhold, Gio: "Precision in Processing Data from Heterogeneous Resources"; in B.Lings and K.Jeffreys (eds.): *Advances in Databases*. Proc. 17th British National Conf. on Databases, Exeter, UK, July 2000, pages 1-18.

BIOGRAPHICAL NOTES

Gio Wiederhold is a professor of Computer Science at Stanford University, with courtesy appointments in Medicine and Electrical Engineering. Since 1976 he has supervised 30 PhD theses in these departments. Current research includes privacy protection in collaborative settings, large-scale software composition, access to simulations to augment decision-making capabilities for information systems, and developing an algebra over ontologies.

Wiederhold has authored and coauthored more than 350 publications and reports on computing and medicine, including an early popular Database Design textbook. He initiated knowledgebase research through a white paper to DARPA in 1977, combining databases and Artificial intelligence technology. The results led eventually to the concept of mediator architectures.

Wiederhold was born in Italy, received a degree in Aeronautical Engineering in Holland in 1957 and a PhD in Medical Information Science from the University of California at San Francisco in 1976. Prior to his academic career he spent 16 years in the software industry. His career followed computer technologies, starting with numerical analysis applied to rocket fuel, FORTRAN and PL/1 compilers, real-time data acquisition, a time-oriented database system, eventually becoming a corporate software architect.

He has been elected fellow of the ACMI, the IEEE, and the ACM. He spent 1991-1994 as the program manager for Knowledge-based Systems at DARPA in Washington DC. He has been an editor and editor-in-chief of several IEEE and ACM publications.

FROM OBJECT-ORIENTED PROGRAMMING TO ONTOLOGY-DRIVEN MODELING

Some considerations on the MDA organization

Jean Bézivin
CRGNA, University of Nantes, Nantes, France
Email: Jean.Bezivin@sciences.univ-nantes.fr

Keywords: MDA; MOF; UML; Meta-Modeling; Ontology engineering

Abstract: This paper discusses the recent paradigm shift - from objects to models - that is currently spreading in the software development area. The transition will be illustrated by the move of the Object Management Group from its previous Object Management Architecture (OMA) to the newest Model-Driven Architecture (MDA). We review some achievements of object technology but also discuss some promises that have not been fully realized. We suggest instead that these challenges may be met in the future by advances in the field of model engineering. This will not happen instantaneously and a long period of maturing is still necessary before we can automatically generate code from models for a variety of execution platforms. What we need is a clear understanding and a regular organization of large libraries of models and meta-models that will help capturing the various specific aspects of software systems. Starting from there, a number of operations, based on widely available tools, will progressively become available and change the nature of the software engineer work: model transformation, merging, specialization, verification, browsing, reutilization, code generation, reverse engineering, etc. These new possibilities may greatly improve the global productivity of the software production and maintenance chain. Alternatively they may also be easily misused and occasionally become counter-productive.

1. INTRODUCTION

The paradigm shift that is presently taking place in the information systems and software engineering areas may have a very high impact on the computer science industry. The move from objects and components to models is probably as important as the move from procedures to objects that occurred twenty years ago. The Object Management Group (OMG) has changed its previous Object Management Architecture (OMA) to the newest vision of the Model Driven Architecture (MDA). However the MDA framework has still some way to go in order to reach the level of maturity of the previous OMA framework centered on CORBA, IDL, IIOP, and related standards. The MDA will have the best chances of being industrially adopted when the general organization of models becomes completely regular. We are witnessing today a number of tools being proposed to populate the MDA scene. Each of them implements some operations on models and meta-models.

This paper is organized as follows. We first show how object and component technology presently seems to be reaching its applicability limits. We then sketch some of the characteristics of model engineering as implemented in contexts like the OMG MDA. Finally we conclude by discussing some of the possibilities offered by the new model-centered approaches as well as some dangers and potential pitfalls.

2. HOPES AND LIMITS OF OBJECT TECHNOLOGY

There is now more than thirty years that the Simula language has been defined and more than twenty years that the Smalltalk language has found its way to industrial usage. The object-oriented programming scene seems to have recently stabilized with the apparent convergent solutions of Java and C#. The time seems thus right to question which benefits were brought during this period by object technology.

J. Filipe et al. (eds.), Enterprise Information Systems III, 15–21.

The fact that object-oriented programming is now considered as mainstream practice in software production is a sufficient proof of the basic value of the technology. Nobody today would seriously advocate a return to procedural technology. Even if some criticisms may be occasionally heard, reusability has been dramatically improved, with the corresponding impact on productivity of software production and increased robustness of the systems. Object-oriented systems seems to be much more stable and resistant to specification changes than their corresponding procedure-based systems. There are plenty of operational systems of significant size written in C++ for example that may testify of the solidity of the technology. Since the systems we are building today are more complex, more evolutive, more open on their environment than the systems we were building in the eighties, the passage from procedures to objects may be globally qualified of an important technological progress. These advantages have been discussed at length in the computer science literature.

However a fair evaluation should also present the darker side of object orientation. Some potential qualities may have been over-emphasized in the initial stages of the transitions from procedures to objects. One of them was conceptual simplicity. The argument was that object would dramatically reduce the average number of concepts used by the software engineer. Since everything would be an object, the handling of these features should be easy. We know today that this is not true and that the average number of different concepts used by the information system engineer is probably much higher now than it was in the procedural era. Classes, interfaces, objects, methods, use cases, components, beans, patterns - to name only a few - populate a development environment that is rather complex.

The problem of portability and interoperability was also probably underestimated. Due to the increase in abstraction level from procedures to objects, it was recognized more difficult to make a Smalltalk and a C++ program communicate than a Pascal and a C program communicate. In a distributed context this was even worse since simple RPC protocols were far from being sufficient. This problem was fortunately identified very early and efforts by the OMG to provide a general object broker started immediately. Nevertheless it took more than ten years to reach the technology level of IDL, IIOP and CORBA3. Even with this high quality long-term work, inter-language inheritance (as in Microsoft DotNet) was not provided by the OMG middleware platform.

Then there was this naïve idea of a "natural" correspondence between the objects in a computer system and the entities in the environment of this system. We know today that the situation is much more complex. If we can identify so called "business objects" in a given system, there are many different kinds of objects as well and the seamless correspondence between the business model and the final design model is far from being straightforward. Each object in the final system originates from a particular design decision, but only a few of them from the mere observation of the business domain. The idea of an analysis object progressively transformed into a design object and then into a code object in a completely seamless way ("object refinement") never did really work, but no completely satisfactory methodological solution was proposed instead.

The procedural technology had the advantage of providing natural functional entry points for applications. The parallel decomposition of procedures into sub-procedures and problems into sub-problems was called functional refinement. Since this was found to produce non–stable architectures, it was advantageously replaced by object composition. Unfortunately, in this process, we lost track of the functional entry points. It was like putting objects together and just hoping that the resulting system would perform the exact service we wished it to perform, without specifying it in any way. On practical grounds this could not work and the concept of a "use case" was introduced to compensate for this conceptual hole. Today the lack of this central notion of service is more and more often expressed, especially in the context of Web application deployment. Moreover, non-functional properties (QoS attributes like performance, reliability, security, etc.) are much more naturally associated to application services than to objects or components.

At another stage of object technology development it was found that the complexity of a system did not lay within the objects composing this system, but outside these objects, in the way these objects were supposed to work together in order to solve a particular problem. The new concept of a design pattern had to be invented to express this knowledge. Unfortunately, no more than for the use case, the design pattern may be considered as a true object.

Some time later, an even more serious problem arose: how to manage separately the different aspects of a system, functional and non-functional? The demonstration that this was not possible within plain object-oriented programming was followed by several proposals of aspect-oriented programming (Kikzales, G. & al.). Here again the tentative to solve this real problem within the context of code-centered approaches does not seem completely satisfactory. Neither object technology nor component technology provides the necessary mechanisms for aspect separation and combination.

Finally another initial hope of object technology was that it would be possible to find a unique canonical and minimal object scheme (I refrain voluntarily to use the word "model" here). From this basic object scheme, all other object schemes like programming (C++, Smalltalk, Eiffel, etc.), database (O2, etc.), actors, analysis and design, etc. could be directly derived. We know today that there are plenty of similar object schemes and that they are all different. A Smalltalk scheme has the concepts of instances, classes and explicit meta-classes, with classes grouped in categories, methods grouped in protocols, etc. A Java scheme has the concepts of class and interface, with single inheritance for classes, multiple heritance for interfaces and an implements relation between interfaces and classes. An Eiffel scheme proposes a client relation between classes and pre-conditions and post-conditions for methods. A UML structural scheme, UML collaboration or sequence scheme, a pattern scheme, a use case scheme, an O2 scheme, a workflow scheme, a JavaBeans scheme, are all different schemes that bear some similarities but that remains essentially different.

Twenty years ago the engineer used to work with only one scheme at a given time. The Smalltalk programmer for example was using the Smalltalk scheme only. Nowadays, it is more and more frequent to work with multiple schemes. As a typical example the engineer will work with use cases, collaboration diagrams, UML classes, Java interfaces and Java classes. He/she may transform one scheme into another one. As a consequence it is more and more necessary to be able to handle these various object schemes with accuracy, taking full account of their differences more than their similarities. Of course, we need to invent the tools that will allow dealing with these subtle differences in semantics, to work simultaneously with UML and Java artifacts and to express with the higher possible precision how to map the elements of one scheme on elements of the other one.

In the 70's, structured programming has much improved the level of quality and productive software production. Object technology has then considerably raised this level again. Today we need a new technology able to handle multiple aspects of software systems and this is model technology.

3. MODELS EVERYWHERE

The definition and wide acceptance of UML (Kobryn, C.) acted as a trigger in the move from objects to models. Initially intended to describe only object-oriented software artifacts, UML was rapidly put to work in many different areas. It was even used for self-description and the outcome of this was the UML meta-model (a description of UML in UML). Of course it was rapidly noticed that only a small part of UML had been used in this exercise of self-description. This part (the CORE of UML) was then promoted to a higher modeling level and became known as the MOF (Meta-Object Facility), a so-called meta-meta-model (Dirckze, R. & Iyengar, S.). From then, it became clear that the MOF could also be used to define many other meta-models as well. On the same level than UML, many other proposals exist like the SPEM (Software Process Engineering Model), the CWM (Common Warehouse Metadata), etc. and many more are currently being defined.

The MOF is then a language to define meta-models. A meta-model is a simple form of ontology. A meta-model is composed of three parts: terminological, assertional and pragmatics. The terminological part defines the relevant concepts and the relations that may hold between them. The assertional part associates first order logic statements to concepts and relations when more precision is needed. The pragmatics part includes all the information that could not be easily included in the previous descriptions such as how a given concept should be represented in printing form (round-angle rectangle, etc.).

The result of this work is the four-level modeling stack (Figure 1), at the center of the MDA. In the example of Figure 1, we have deliberately mentioned a Java and a C# meta-model on the same level than UML to show that this is really a framework for handling abstract syntax definitions.

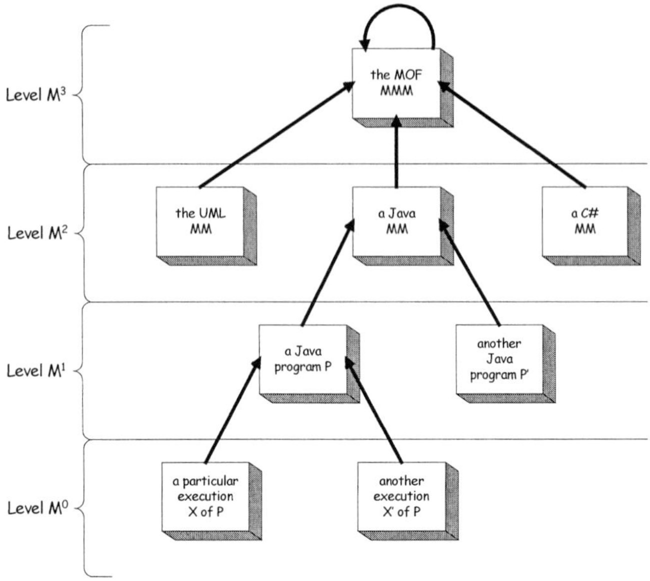

Figure 1: The four-level architecture

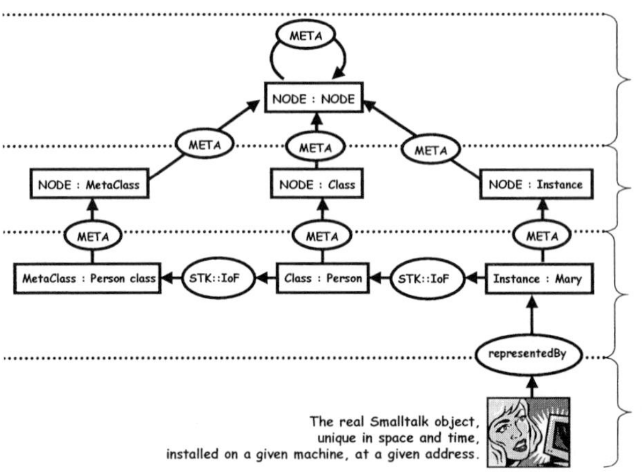

Figure 2: A Smalltalk program (M1), between meta-model (M2) and execution space (M0)

In Figure 2, we present a detail of the Smalltalk meta-model borrowed from (Bézivin & Gerbé 2001). This has the advantage of showing the orthogonal relations between meta-modeling (vertical axis) and meta-programming (horizontal axis). On the represented fragment of the Smalltalk meta-model, one can see that the relation between an instance and a class is the same than the relation between a class and a meta-class, in the Smalltalk context. Obviously this has no signification in a Java or C# model.

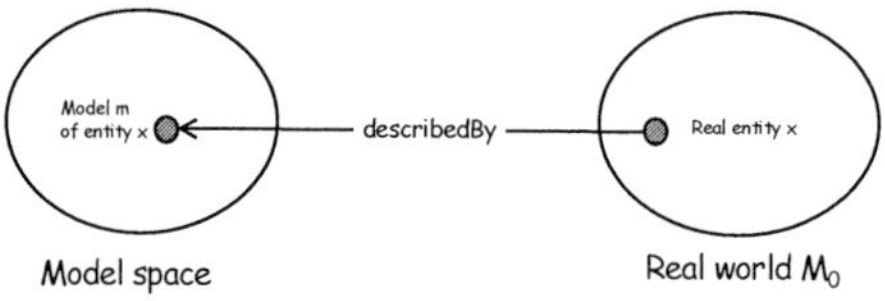

Figure 3: Real World vs. Model Space

The whole domain of concern is divided in two parts: the real world and the model world. The real world, called M_0 in MDA parlance, contains real objects. In some cases these are computer objects, installed and running on real machines. The model space is at the hearth of the MDA and "describes" the real world. So the three upper levels in Figure 1 are modelling layers and the bottom one (M0) is the real world layer. This distinction between the real world and the model world is central to the soundness of the approach. The real world contains entities like *x* that are unique in time and space. The model world contains images of these entities like *m*. Model world entity *m* is a *description* of real world entity *x*. As an example, *x* could be the student *Paul*, enrolled in the academic year 2001-2002 in the computer science master program of the University of Nantes. The model world entity *m* could be *Paul:Student*, the UML instance description of *Paul*, pertaining to the UML model package describing the study organization at the University of Nantes.

A model is a description of a system. It represents only some of the aspects of a system. The particular aspects of a system represented by a given model are specified by a meta-model. A meta-model is thus a specification of a conceptualization, with ontological agreement.

This may be rendered by Figure 4. A model is supposed to be able to answer some specific questions in place of the system it represents, and the answer should be similar to the answers that would have been given by the system itself (principle of limited substitutability). Now there are different kinds of systems. Some are static (like a population census snapshot). The majority of systems are dynamic, i.e. evolving in time. On the contrary, the majority of models are static, i.e. they don't evolve. A self-modifying program is a dynamic model, but most programming languages today don't allow this kind of behavior. A StateChart is a static model of a dynamic system. A simulation program execution is a dynamic model.

There are plenty of other different kinds of models. As discussed in (Breton & Bézivin 2001) for example, a Petri net is a composite model made of two parts: the place and transition graph is a static model while the token marking model is a dynamic model.

A UML model is composed of nine static sub-models. The "Action Semantic" initiative will allow associating executability schemes to a UML model. This is because a UML model is not executable by construction. There is no such notion of an "UML universal virtual machine". On the contrary some

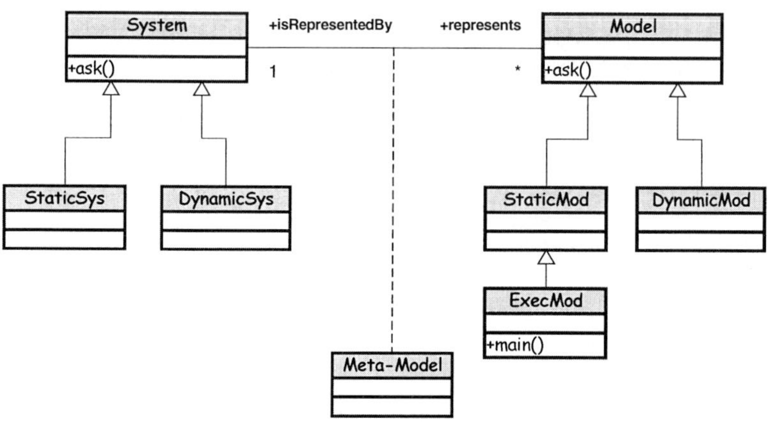

Figure 4: Various kinds of models

other models are executable by definition. A Java program for example may be executed by calling the *main* static method of an identified class. As suggested by Figure 4, the notions of dynamicity and executability are different properties of a given model.

Models have many other properties. The main idea of the MDA is based on the possibility to define and maintain platform independent models (PIMs). There are also models of platform like the Corba Model of Components (CCM). A PIM may be bound to a particular technological platform and then it becomes a PSM (Platform Specific Model). Platform independence is becoming a growing concern. A given company or organization will be able to maintain neutral PIMs and to use generation tools to produce complete or partial implementations on middleware platforms like Corba/OMA, EJB/J2E, COM+, MS DotNet, SOAP/XML, etc.

Models are the basic tool to deal with increasing complexity, increasing evolutivity and to beat technological obsolescence. Models allow capturing the many aspects of software systems. Models are constantly elaborated to answer new problems and new technological solutions. They are able not only to deal with present object and component technology but also with the emerging service-based organization (Web services, UDDI, WSDL, etc.). They allow progressive introduction of non-functional aspects associated with these services (performance, reliability, security, etc.). They also allow dealing with legacy systems (e. g. relational databases, SADT specifications, Cobol programs, etc.).

4. HOPES AND DANGERS OF MODEL TECHNOLOGY

We have already mentioned the difficulties in understanding the executability properties of models. When these notions are well mastered, they may provide very powerful tools to animate, transform, evaluate or perform any kind of pertinent operations on models. They can also be wrongly interpreted and produce undesirable effects in the software production and maintenance chain.

Another example of problem that frequently arises is the confusion between models of problems and models of solutions. Many tools are providing round-trip engineering facilities, allowing producing a UML model from C++ code for example or the reverse way. Using such a reverse engineering tool will only produce a model of the solution with its design decisions, good or bad. In no case it can produce a model of the problem that could be used to derive a solution.

As a final example, we examine the potential power of model transformation and insist on the lack of understanding of model merging.

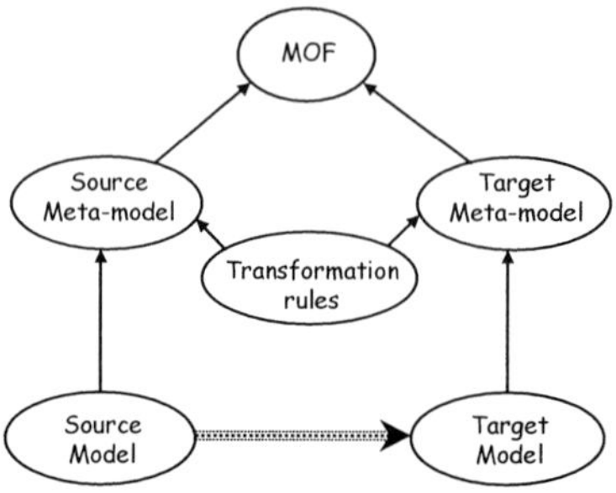

Figure 5: Meta-model based model transformation

Meta-model based model transformation is a very powerful technique that is starting to gain wide acceptance. In (Peltier & al.), a solution for generating XSLT code from a transformation rule program is described. The source and the target models are expressed in XMI, a standard OMG serialization format based on XML and the MOF.

In practice we need even more complex operations. In the classical Y software development cycle, a PIM (business model) should be merged with a platform model (like the Corba Component Model) to produce a PSM. How the merging of the two branches of the Y could be performed is still an open question. The merging process should probably be driven by some kind of pattern model. The precise way to apply this operation needs further investigations.

5. CONCLUSIONS

Moving from code-centric to model-centric approaches to software development means that models and meta-models will become the key artifacts, like objects and classes in the present mainstream object-oriented software development methods.

Raising one step the abstraction level will help to solve many problems like the independence from the middleware and generation towards these platforms. It will also raise an important number of new challenges that will take time to be met. The OMA has taken more than ten years to reach stability. It is very likely that the MDA will need at least as much time and probably more to deliver the promises it is making today.

ACKNOWLEDGEMENTS

I would like to thank Richard Lemesle, Erwan Breton, Mikael Peltier, Olivier Gerbé and Nicolas Ploquin for many exchanges of ideas on the subject of this paper.

REFERENCES

Atkinson, C, Supporting and Applying the UML Conceptual Framework, *In UML'98, Beyond the notation, J. Bézivin & P.A. Muller (eds.), Mulhouse, 1998, Springer Verlag LNCS #1618.*

Bézivin, J. & Gerbé, O. New Trends in Applied Model Engineering *In ASE'2001, Automated Software Engineering, San Diego, November 2001.*

Bézivin, J. From Object Composition to Model Transformation with the MDA TOOLS'USA 2001, Santa Barbara, August 2001, *In Volume TOOLS'39, IEEE publications, Los Alamitos, California, http://computer.org, ISBN 0-7695-1251-8, pp. 346-354.*

Dirckze, R. & Iyengar, S. A Metamodel-Based Approach to Model Engineering Using the MOF, *In First International Workshop on Model Engineering, Nice, France, (June 13, 2000), available at www.metamodel.com*

Kobryn, C. UML 2001: A Standardization Odyssey. *Communications of the ACM, V.42, N.10, 1999*

Soley, R. and the OMG staff Model-Driven Architecture. *OMG document available at www.omg.org November 2000.*

Breton, E. & Bézivin, J. Towards an Understanding of Model Executability *In Proceedings of the Second International Conference on Formal Ontology in Information Systems (FOIS-2001), Ogunquit, Maine, USA, October 2001.*

Peltier, M. Ziserman, F. & Bézivin, J. On levels of model transformation, *In XML Europe Conference, Paris, France, June 2000*

Kikzales, G. & al. Aspect-Oriented programming *ACM Computing Surveys, 28, 4, (Dec. 1996)*

BIOGRAPHICAL NOTE

Jean Bézivin is a professor of Computer Science at the University of Nantes, France. He got his Master degree from the University of Grenoble and PhD from the University of Rennes before spending several years, as an assistant professor, at the University of Brest. He also spent a year as a research fellow at the Queen's University of Belfast (Northern Ireland) and one year at the Concordia University of Montreal (Canada).

He has been very active in Europe in the object-oriented community, starting the ECOOP series of conference (with Pierre Cointe), the TOOLS series of conferences (with Bertrand Meyer) and more recently the <<UML>> series of conferences (with Pierre-Alain Muller). He also organized several workshops at OOPSLA and ECOOP conferences like in 1995 on "Use Case Technology" and more recently in 1998 and 2000 on "Model engineering". He started in 1979 at the University of Nantes, one of the first Master programs in Software Engineering entirely devoted to Object Technology (Data Bases, Concurrency, Languages and Programming, Analysis and Design, etc.).

He is an industrial consultant in the fields of object-technology, analysis and design, model engineering, etc. He published numerous papers on various subjects related to concurrency, software engineering, simulation, object technology, etc. He also presented tutorials on related subjects at several international conferences. His present research interests include object-oriented analysis and design, product and process modeling.

AGENTS AND ELECTRONIC COMMERCE, HYPE AND REALITY

Frank Dignum
Institute of Information and Computing Sciences
Utrecht University
P.O.Box 80089, Utrecht,
The Netherlands
email: dignum@cs.uu.nl
tel: +31-30-2539109, fax:+31-30-2513791

1. INTRODUCTION

In recent years electronic commerce has been at the centre of interest of many companies and also of many researchers. See the International Journal on Electronic Commerce (IJEC) for current research topics and e.g. (Kalakota and Whinston 1996, Kalakota and Robinson 2001) for an overview. However, after a period of a growing world economy in which electronic commerce was advocated as one of the motors of the new economy, at the moment we experience a set back that makes many people doubt the true value of electronic commerce for the economy. In fact what we are experiencing is the maturing of a new way of doing business based on new paradigms. In order to assess the role of IT, and especially software agents, in this development it is paramount to have at least some understanding of this new way of doing business. If electronic commerce is seen only as a way to use the Internet as a new channel through which products can be traded then the role of IT is quite limited. It should provide efficient means to build websites that are secure and robust and that can be connected to the back-office in order to process the incoming orders.

The role of intelligent systems, such as software agents, in this scenario is usually limited to that of searching the Internet for the user in order to find the best bargain. Good examples of this use of agents are (Jango (http://www.jango.com/) (Doorenbos et.al., 1996) and Bargainfinder (http://bf.cstar.ac.com), etc.).

A more interesting way to employ agents, however, is to actually have them execute the transaction on electronic marketplaces where agents can buy and/or sell goods. Some good examples are Kasbah (Chavez & Maes 1996), the Fishmarket project (Rodriguez 1997) and AuctionBot (Wurman 1998). Although the agents in the first case play a role in electronic commerce their actual role is that of searching the Internet in an intelligent way. These types of agents are not supposed to interact with agents at the selling side and strike bargains with these agents. The scenario assumes that prices are fixed and can be found by searching the WWW.

In the scenario of the electronic marketplaces, both sides play an active role. This is a good example of current developments in business and also opens new perspectives for the use of agents. In most cases the selling agents advertise their products in the market. They indicate a price, but this price does not have to be the final selling price. In case of an auction model the price indicated by the seller is the reserved price. It will not sell its products for less than that price.

In these electronic marketplaces the agents have the task to "bargain" about the price of the products and try to find the best deal. An easy way to organize the bargaining is by way of auctioning the products. This way of bargaining is very structured and can easily be done automatically. Of course, the strategies of the participating agents are not trivial and much work is done in trying to find so-called "dominant" strategies for certain types of auctions (see e.g. Varian 1995; Huberman & Hogg, 1995; Rosenschein & Zlotkin 1994; Sandholm 1996). These strategies are guaranteed to give the best result no matter what the other agents do.

In this paper we will first discuss some of the more fundamental developments in electronic commerce and the consequences of these developments for electronic markets. In section 3 we will look at the role of electronic institutions in electronic commerce. The role of agents in electronic commerce and their interactions with electronic institutions will be discussed in section 4. Some examples of the current use of agents in electronic commerce are given here as well. In section 5 we will look at the future roles that agents can fulfil in electronic commerce transactions and

J. Filipe et al. (eds.), Enterprise Information Systems III, 22–35.

which research questions are of interest in this context. Some conclusions will be presented in section 6.

2. DEVELOPMENTS IN ELECTRONIC COMMERCE

2.1 From operational excellence to customer intimacy

Although IT is an important component of electronic commerce, the biggest mistake that many companies have made is that they expected huge benefits from just implementing new IT components that support electronic commerce, without changing their organisational structure. A very similar situation is visible in traditional commerce already. There are mail-order companies that sell their products through the mail by means of (paper) catalogs. However, although this opportunity is open for every company, not all companies choose to use this selling channel. In order to reap full benefit of selling by mail the company has to have a certain structure and do business in a way that does not fit with all existing companies. For instance, these companies often give the possibility to pay for products, like clothes, in monthly installments. This is very unusual for companies that sell their clothes through shops. Also mail-order companies have a huge department that handles returns. Something that is of small importance to most companies that sell their products through shop outlets.

Electronic commerce (or electronic business as some now prefer to call it) should also be seen in this perspective. It is primarily a new way of relating to customers and suppliers. In general it means a transformation from a company that is geared towards production excellence or innovative excellence into a company that is geared towards customer intimacy. (See (Treacy and Wiersema, 1997) for a more thorough description of this development).

A company, that is operational excellent, tries to organize its production process as efficient as possible. This has been the case since the 19th century when Taylor proposed the division of the production process into simple tasks, each performed by a different person. The latest developments on Enterprise Resource Planning and Just In Time production are also part of this strive for operational excellence. Operational excellent companies usually focus on the product that the company delivers. The contacts with the customers are mainly through the sales department. That is where the orders come in and where payments are received. The contacts with the suppliers are mainly through the purchasing department that sends orders based on the current production planning.

In a company, that strives for customer intimacy, the focus shifts from the product delivered by the company towards the customers of the company. The company tries to find out as good as possible what the wishes are of its customers. Knowing your customers and producing those products that have the highest added value for the customers is the most important. One of the consequences of this shift is that the company has to have close contacts with its customer base. Contacts do not only go through the sales department, but customers also have direct access to data concerning the production planning in order to find out the status of their order. They might have contacts with the R&D department to influence the design of new products, etc.

Most of these customer contacts can all be directed through the website of the company. However, the website is no longer just connected with the ordering system, but should be connected to various systems of different departments. As a consequence, these systems should also be integrated in order to have a consistent contact with the customer. One of the main consequences of this development is that several heterogeneous IT systems throughout the organization should be coupled and a secure customer view on the data should be available. I.e. the customer should be able to check the data on production planning, but in only in so-far it pertains to its own order and only the information that is necessary to check its status. Also the communication channels between the departments should be shortened in order to update information about the customers. Usually this is established by using an intranet.

On the supplier side the organization also usually tightens its relations in order to adapt as quick as possible to demands of the customer.

In general, the above developments lead to tighter relations with a fixed number of suppliers and a relative fixed customer base. For the IT support it means loosely coupling many heterogeneous systems, which also become more "open" (i.e. are coupled with systems outside the organization and can be inspected and/or updated from outside the organization).

2.2 Transaction costs theory

A second perspective on developments in commerce and the role of IT comes from the theory on transaction costs. Economic transactions can be organized through two mechanisms: hierarchy or market (see also (Malone 1987) for an analysis). In the hierarchical mechanism the buying and selling party have a "special" (usually longstanding) relationship. This can be because they are part of the same company or because they have a frame contract that covers the transaction. In this situation the negotiation phase (price discovery) can be skipped during the individual transaction. All negotiation is done at the time the parties enter into the frame contract. The situation is relatively static and most suitable for EDI applications. One of the big advantages of this mechanism is that it is possible to make a tight integration between the production processes of the buyer and seller. Something that is very important in just-in-time production in e.g. the car manufacturing industry. A disadvantage is the dependence on a few suppliers and/or buyers. If one of the suppliers fails to deliver (or goes bankrupt) it immediately creates a problem in the production line.

The second mechanism to organize transactions is the market mechanism. The main idea is that there are many providers of a product and many clients that want to purchase the product. The parameters of the transaction (like the price of the product) are not fixed for a long period of time, but determined for each single transaction. In general it holds that the coordination costs for this mechanism are higher than that of the hierarchy mechanism. However, because of the economy of scale and growing competition the production costs are usually lower. Tight coupling of production processes is harder using the market mechanism, because of the fact that suppliers will change regularly.

In general one could say that there is a trade-of between the coordination costs and the production costs (see table 1). If a complete product is manufactured within one company the coordination costs are very small and optimal logistics can be achieved because all is under control of one party. However, the production itself is more expensive because some parts could be produced much more efficient by other parties. If on the other hand the manufacturing and assembly of all parts of a product are out-sourced then maximal efficiency can be achieved in the production processes. However, the costs of coordinating these different parties are much higher.

Table 1: Trade-of between production and coordination costs

	Production costs	Coordination costs
Markets	low	high
Hierarchy	high	low

The introduction of ICT support in performing business transactions (introducing electronic commerce) seems to favour the use of the market mechanism for the transactions. The use of ICT can reduce the coordination costs drastically (easy search, comparison, etc.). Therefore both the production costs as well as the coordination costs will be low and the overall costs will be lower than when a hierarchical mechanism is used. Of course, this is a generalization, but the overall feeling is that the introduction of electronic commerce in a certain industry area will favour the use of markets as a means to coordinate.

2.3 Electronic markets

The developments sketched in the previous two sections seem to point in opposite directions. According to section 2.1 the industry should move to tight connections with long lasting relations, while according to section 2.2 companies should perform their transactions through markets where relations can change for each transaction. In this section we will discuss some more points that are of influence on the use of transaction mechanisms and conclude with the current trend for electronic markets as seen in practice.

Some characteristics of products also influence the decision on whether the products should be traded through a hierarchy mechanism or through a market mechanism. The first characteristic is the asset specificity of a product. For instance, if a product is very location specific (i.e. produced only at a specific place and relatively difficult to transport) then it will be more difficult to trade the product through a market mechanism because it is more difficult to choose freely between different producers (or consumers). A good example is the car manufacturing industry. Because this industry is very competitive they try to lower costs as much as possible. One way to achieve this is by reducing stocks. In order to accomplish this the factories only start manufacturing a car after it has been ordered. Moreover they only want the parts to arrive when they are needed in the production process. As a consequence the factories depend on the fact that their suppliers are located in the vicinity of the manufacturing plant such that parts can be reliably delivered just-in-time. In this situation a hierarchy mechanism is more efficient than a market mechanism. The extra costs that are incurred because the company is tied to a few suppliers are easily outweighed by the benefits of the just-in-time delivery.

Another example of asset specificity is the fact that a product can be related to a specific type of customers and/or producers. For example, if a symphony orchestra is needed for a concert than the quality of the orchestra is very dependant of the people playing in it. One cannot easily substitute one orchestra for another. On the other hand some products are completely geared towards a small market, like operation tools for surgeons. Also for these types of products a hierarchical model is usually preferable to a market model.

Also products that are difficult to specify are not so easily traded through a market mechanism, because it is hard to compare products from different producers. So, it is not about the complexity of a product but about how easy it is to specify. E.g. a car is very complex, but is relatively easy to specify, because most parts are standardized. However, a business insurance policy is very difficult to describe accurately, because there are no standards at all.

Other characteristics of products that determine how they are purchased are: the impact of the product on the company result, the supply risk for the product, whether the product is used in control and management or for production, and the way the products are sourced (systematic vs. spot sourcing). The so-called routine products (see (Kraljic, 1983)) are products with a low supply risk and little impact on the financial result of a company . Office supplies form a good example. These products only account for a small part of the purchase value, but usually cause a major part of the procurement costs. The main goal in electronic procurement for these products will therefore be cost reduction of the procurement process. So, they can best be traded through electronic purchasing tools with a few fixed suppliers. For the products that have a low risk in supply but a high impact on company results, the so-called leverage products, a company might look at using electronic markets. For these products price/quality ratio is more important than transaction costs. Good examples of these products are commodities that are part of the end product of a company. E.g. most of the components of PC's are of this type. The products that carry both a high risk in supply and have a high impact on the company results (the strategic products) can also be purchased electronically. However, these products are usually purchased directly through an EDI connection from the ERP system. Good examples are the car parts for a car manufacturer. The delivery of these parts has to be in line with the own production, while there is only one (or a few) possible suppliers of that part.

The last type of products are the bottleneck products that have a low impact on company results and a high supply risk. The fastening products of e.g. Borstlap are a good example of this category. There are only a few suppliers in this market, but the products have a low impact on the end product of the customers (like car manufacturers). For this type of products no readily available solutions are on the market. Most companies experiment with combinations of EDI and web-based ordering.

To conclude, it can be said that there are products for which the market mechanism is the obvious choice. E.g. commodities like books and CD's. There are also products and markets where the hierarchical mechanism seems natural. E.g. specialized tools for industries with only a few (but large) companies. However, there is also a whole range of products and markets for which the choice is not obvious. For this area it can be said that the use of information technology reduces the coordination costs in all cases and therefore more products in these markets will be traded through some form of market mechanism.

The effect of the development sketched in section 2.1. (towards customer intimacy) is that the markets will not be completely open. Although a market mechanism is used to perform the transactions the players on the market are fixed and usually known to each other. A good example is the market organized for the automotive industry. All suppliers for the major car manufacturers have to compete through this market, but only a limited number of companies qualify as supplier and can enter the market. The latter ensures that suppliers and manufacturers still know each other (and each other's requirements) quite well.

3. MARKETS AND INSTITUTIONS

In this section we will look at the role of institutions in (electronic) transactions. Although the transactions can have many different forms, in general they all follow the following pattern (see also e.g. Kalakota & Whinston, 1996)):

- determine needs
- exchange information on products and companies
- negotiation / price discovery
- establish (legal) contract
- contract fulfillment
- guarantee and feedback

Depending on the type of market (product and participants) there will be more emphasis on one or the other phase. The role of institutions is to facilitate the transactions. An institution only is useful if it improves the performance or quality of the transactions in some sense. In (van Heck 1997) it is argued that an (electronic) institution is only viable if the stakeholders have converging interests in using the institution. I.e. if both buyers and sellers have some advantage in using the institution and the intermediary that manages the institution also has some benefit. This can be the quick fixing of decent prices, enhancing trust in partners (through securities), opening new markets, preventing information asymmetry, etc.

Our main interest lays in how the transactions can be supported when they are performed electronically. Especially of interest is the role of (electronic) institutions to support the transactions. In general one might say that institutions play two roles in this context:

1. They enhance the efficiency of the transaction between the partners
2. They enhance the trust that the parties have in a proper performance of the transaction.

The efficiency of the transaction is enhanced by providing e.g. an efficient price discovery mechanism and a standard transaction protocol.

The role of enhancing trust in the transaction is often underestimated. In many cases though institutions have evolved from in order to remedy a lack of trust in the market. The institution can enhance trust e.g. by providing trusted information on potential partners (Like Chambers of Commerce). They can also provide regulations for the behaviour of the parties during the transactions and ways to enforce that behaviour. They can enforce for instance guarantees of the parties on payment and/or credit. Often the institutions also provide a legal back up for the contracts that are closed within the institution. E.g. in the form of standard legal contracts that cover all transactions within the institution.

The emphasis on which role is played will be different when market transactions are supported and when hierarchical transactions are supported. In case of hierarchical transactions the institution can play a role in establishing a relationship between the parties (the contracting phase), but usually the negotiation phase is far more complicated and involves much more than just price discovery. During the fulfillment phase of the contract, the role might be in monitoring the workflow and assisting in case of disputes. In case of the use of a market mechanism for the transaction the role of the institution will be to structure the way buyers and sellers can interact on the market. E.g. by providing an efficient means for price discovery (like an auction mechanism).

Institutions are determined by two things. First the infrastructure that they provide and secondly the type of interactions that are supported by the institution (see also (Tsvetovatyy 1997)). E.g. an institution might provide both an auction as well as a shopping mall.

3.1 Infrastructure

The infrastructure for electronic institutions should at least contain banking facilities, communication facilities and an ontology. In any transaction at some stage one party has to pay the other party. This can be done very simple by giving a credit card number or very complicated by setting up some letter of credit or other financial security. An institution should provide different ways of payment such that the parties can always find a common way to pay. It is very awkward if a whole transaction is concluded but a payment cannot be made because one side can only pay with a Visa card and the other party only accepts Digital cash. Preferably the institution has some back-up such that it can convert itself between different methods of payment.

Of course the payment should be safe and guaranteed. This means e.g. that credit cards should be checked but also that the communication of the credit card number is encrypted in a secure way.

The communication facilities have two aspects. The first is that the communication should be confidential, integrity should be guaranteed, authentication of messages possible and repudiation of messages impossible. These are all measures of security that should be taken such that parties that do business through the institution can communicate in a secure and reliable way. The second aspect of the communication facilities is the provision of protocols and languages that can be used during the (formal) interaction between the parties. A good example is an auction protocol like the descending bids protocol. Finally there should be a common ontology available for the parties in the institution. This is needed such that they can check whether they are referring to the same objects when they use specific terms. E.g. it might state that a "monitor" refers to a 14" color monitor unless specifically stated otherwise. Also it might state that a "contract" refers to a legally binding contract according to a certain statute of the law.

3.2 Transaction types

The transactions that are performed between two parties can be performed either directly or through some broker. In the case that the transaction takes place through the hierarchy mechanism the transaction is almost always performed direct. This means that the contacts are between the parties themselves directly and no third party plays an intermediary role.

However, the most common example of direct trading is "shopping". Producers expose their products in some way and customers can compare by entering several shops. After the customer makes a choice the transaction is performed directly with the shopkeeper. Another good example of direct trading is the use of classified ads. Of course the cases where the parties enter into a direct negotiation without interference of an arbitrator is also an example of direct trading.

The most common example of indirect trading are the auctions. In that case the producers deliver their products at the auction house and the consumers can buy the products using some predefined auction mechanism. In this case the broker brings buyer and seller together and helps the market to set a fair price. Another way of indirect trading is through distributors, which actually buy the products themselves first and later on resell it to the customers.

Although this is not the place to present a detailed analysis of the roles of the broker in indirect trading (see e.g. (Choi 1997)), it is good to at least sketch some of its functions. Although it might seem that brokers and institutions are the same (namely intermediaries in the trading process) we want to stress that they have different functions. An institution is facilitating the trading process and is usually not seen as an extra link in the supply chain. A broker is an extra link in the chain between supplier and customer.

Brokers can have many functions. First of all they might have information about products and/or companies that are not easily available to the potential customers. In that case they can play a role in matching the interests of customers and suppliers.

Usually brokers do not actually provide a mechanism for price discovery. However, they can be involved in price discovery in at least two ways. First of all they can provide information about current (and/or fair prices) to customers and suppliers, therewith in effect influencing that price if the market is quickly changing (e.g. stock brokers) or very opaque (e.g. house brokers). Secondly, they can operate as distributor, thus first buying the products from the suppliers and later on selling them to the customers. By operating this way, the broker actually determines a price together with the suppliers and customers. This can be beneficial for both sides because of the economy of scale that a distributor can realize. Therefore it can claim a lower prize than normal customers from the supplier. The difference in price is usually large enough such that the customers also profit from the intermediary and still can get a lower price.

A third function of the broker is that of organizing the logistics more efficient. This can e.g. be done through keeping stock in a central place.

Another function of a broker is as trusted party in the contracting phase. The broker can organize the contract and validate it against industry standards. Also the broker might have specific knowledge about procedures that should be followed in the process.

In general it can be said that the function of the broker is to provide knowledge for those phases of the transaction where it is not economical for the parties to obtain that knowledge themselves and to provide economies of scale in those cases where that is profitable for both suppliers and customers. See (Moss 1998) for an economical analysis of the profitability of establishing a broker in a market.

There seem to be at least two cases in which direct trading is the most profitable way of trading. First is the case where there is a "good market". I.e. a market with many buyers and sellers, which can easily get into contact and which have enough information to compare parties and products. A good example are the commodity markets. In these markets the existence of brokers is usually not profitable. The second case where direct trading is the most profitable is where direct contact between buyer and seller is important. This can be important because the contract is complicated and very personal, but also because the product is "personalized" or feedback on the products is very important.

3.3 The role of institutions

The role of the (electronic) institution in direct transactions is naturally smaller than in indirect trading. Because in direct trading the contacts are directly between supplier and customer, the institution has little control over the content of the contract and the transaction. However, the institution can provide facilities to the parties to support their contact. E.g. it can provide payment methods, standard contracts, common ontology, etc. One of the main roles of an institution in direct trading will be to reduce the costs and time of the coordination during the establishment of the hierarchy. However, another important role will be to establish the necessary trust between the parties in order to conclude the transaction. This can be achieved by providing securities to the parties with respect to the information they get (e.g. through certificates on data), providing standard internationally recognized contracts, providing settlement constructions, etc.

In the indirect trading the role of the institution will be an intermediary between the two parties. In fact it will support many of the functions that were described for brokers as well. From this role it follows that the institution has more power to control the whole transaction. It can determine the protocol through which the interaction takes place.

These tighter control possibilities make it easier to automate parts of these brokered transactions. For instance, an auction protocol can be implemented . It is easy to write software that can operate with the auction protocol and automatically sell or buy products. This situation is different for the direct transactions. It is more difficult to automate a free negotiation than an auction mechanism. Of course many aspects can be supported in direct transactions as well. E.g. the information exchange and even price discovery can be supported by shopping agents and shopping malls.

4. SOFWARE AGENTS AND ELECTRONIC COMMERCE

In this section we discuss the roles that agents might have in electronic commerce and more specific how they can be combined with the use of electronic institutions. Before going into this discussion we will reiterate the key properties of agents and indicate which type of tasks agents are particularly suitable for.

4.1 Agents

A commonly used definition of intelligent agents states that they are software systems that should be autonomous, pro-active, reactive and sociable (Wooldridge 1999).

The first property (autonomousness) means that the agents should be relatively independent in executing their functions. It means that agents will not be dependent on input of the user for every decision they have to take. In the other hand an agent cannot be controlled in the way objects are controlled. When sending a message to an object this will evoke a method of the object that is executed whenever the message is of the right type and the sender had the right authority (the center of control lays with the requesting object). In the case of agents, the agent will determine itself when it receives the message whether it will respond to the message or not (the center of control lays with the receiving agent).

The last property (sociability) has as consequence that an agent should be able to communicate with its environment and is able to cooperate with it (including other agents). This means that an agent is not completely autonomous, but can be influenced by other agents and the user.

The property of pro-activeness means that agents have their own (in-built) goals that they try to achieve. Therefore they do not rely on explicit commands of a user to start operating.

Finally, the reactiveness of agents means that they can react to changes in the environment. This property balances the pro-activeness somewhat. It prevents that agents only try to achieve a certain goal without looking whether the goal is still achievable, whether the current plan is the best one, etc.

Some other properties that agents can have are mobility and learnability. The first indicates that agents might move themselves from one machine to another (instead of sending messages) and the second indicates that agents can adapt their behavior on the basis of their experiences.

Unfortunately the practical, implemented agents of today do not have all the properties sketched above. However, we will use these properties to see for what type of tasks agents can be most useful.

The first task that comes to mind is that of collecting and filtering information. Agents can move over networks to gather information, compare it and filter the best information based on the past appreciation of the user.

A second type of task that agents are good in is to negotiate in simple ways over resources and other tasks to be performed. A good example is the use of the Contract Net protocol to divide tasks among a set of agents. This feature is very usefull when many heterogeneous systems have to be connected (such as is increasingly the case in organizations where electronic commerce is used). Instead of having to define one fixed overall model in which all systems fit, we can have the agents negotiate the way the systems have to be connected.

A third task that agents can do very well is to distributedly solve a complex problem. This also fits very well with a situation where electronic commerce requires different systems in a company to cooperate in finding the answer to a problem of a customer.

A last task that agents can perform well is to guide and monitor longterm processes that need frequent attention and have a life span of several hours to several months. This feature makes agents very useful to monitor order processes of customers and sending automatic alerts whenever an interesting event (such as completion of production, or late delivery, etc.) occurs.

4.2 Agents and electronic commerce

Agents can play several roles in the (electronic) commerce transactions. At least one should distinguish a role of agents where they support one or both parties in the trading process and a role of the agent as representative of a party in the trading process. There are several examples of agents supporting one of the parties in the transaction. For instance, the already mentioned, shopping agents that compare prices. Another support function is monitoring and signaling an auction in which a user is participating. Instead of the user having to follow the auction, the agent will do this and signal the user whenever an interesting point is reached. The agent can also bid on behalf of the user up till a certain amount and signal the user whenever this amount is reached.

Agents will only be used as user representative if the benefits of using an agent are high and the trust that an agent will realize them are high enough. Practically this means that agents will most likely be used in situations that are characterized by the following aspects:

1. *Interactions are very fast.* For instance for bandwidth trade. There is no time to go back to the user between trading rounds.
2. *Interactions are repeated* with either (a) high communication overheads, or (b) the domain is limited, hence learning by the agent about the user behaviour is effective. Many B2B areas fall within this category.
3. *Each trade is of relative small value.* If each transaction is of relatively small value it is possible to monitor the process and stop the automatic trade after some time without significant losses. It is important to stress the importance of *relatively* here. A small value for a company is completely different from a small value for a private consumer. This implies that most likely we will first see AMEC in business to business settings.
4. *The process is repeated over long times.* The reason for this is two-fold:
    a. There must be a significant gain in order to justify investments in software, hardware, and/or training.
    b. Automatic agent learning of customer preferences is highly desirable as explicit preference elicitation is a very time consuming business.
5. *The product is relatively easy to specify.* A number of traditional difficult computer science problems pose major difficulties to negotiations over complex objects. Such problems are mainly related to semantics of the communication. This is also related to preference elicitation. It is simply too time consuming to tune huge numbers of different parameters.
6. *The procedure is well defined.*If the user knows exactly which steps are followed, the user will more easily trust that an agent will get an optimal deal.

However, even when the process steps are clear the process itself might still be vague. First of all the product might be difficult to specify. In that case the consumer or supplier might want to start with a vague (or incomplete) description and fill it in during the negotiation. This uncertainty about the actual product makes it very difficult to delegate the trading to an agent, which needs a clear goal to operate reliably. A second major problem is that the user does not always know on forehand what he will accept as a good deal. It is clear that a consumer wants the price to be as low as possible if he negotiates about price only. However, when negotiations are performed over multiple attributes, the relative importance of the attributes is usually not fixed at the start. E.g. when negotiating about price and guarantee a customer can indicate that it finds price very important and guarantee hardly (say they get an importance mark of 90 vs. 10%). However, he might find during negotiation that whenever the price drops below a certain level no guarantee can be given at all. Although it might be that the utility, calculated on the basis of the scales and relative importance he gave earlier, is maximal at that price he still wants some guarantee on the product and decides to go for a sub-optimal price. The main point here is that people usually do not foresee the consequences of their choices for the utilities of the attributes on the final outcome.

Besides the above points that prohibit an easy delegation of the trading process to agents, it might also be that the trading process itself is either not very clear or very complex and context dependent. E.g. if the negotiation is very complex with several parties at the same time or about many interrelated issues, it is not very likely that a customer will delegate this task to an agent.

The representative role is most likely to occur when market mechanisms are used for trading. For the market mechanism there are at least a number of cases where the trust needed is relatively low, the procedures are quite simple and clear and thus the advantage of delegating this task to an agent can be high.

In the other hand setting up a hierarchical relationship is a complicated process that requires the building up of trust between the parties. This will not easily be delegated to a piece of software. However, also in a hierarchy agents can have an important role. First of all the agents can be used to assist in setting up the hierarchy. In the past this was a complicated process, where many agreements had to be made. However, with the advent of "virtual enterprises" where different independent organizations form a company for a specific project or purpose, it becomes more easy to couple several organizations into a hierarchical relation. In cases where the interactions between different organizations are well defined this might be automated using agents (something that is not feasible at this moment yet, due to the fact that exactly those interactions between organizations are usually not formally defined).

Agents can also be used to support the logistics in a hierarchical relation (see Nissen 1999). Of course one could think of using a traditional ERP package like SAP or Baan, or a Work Flow Management package to streamline the logistics. However, these software packages start from the idea that all the logistics is controlled through one organization. It means that the control of the logistics process is centralized as well. In the case of a hierarchical relation between companies this is not (always) the case. Each company is at least to some extend autonomous. Therefore resource allocations as made in the traditional Work Flow Management and ERP packages cannot be made in this case. The use of autonomous agents to represent departments and organizations might solve this problem. Instead of just allocating a task to a resource, the allocation is done through a request that can be negotiated by the agents.

As said before the role of agents is most clear in case a market mechanism is used to perform the transactions. In this case agents can be used to compare products of several producers and help to find the best bargain, but they can also be used to perform the actual transaction. Only in the last case do we speak of actual agent mediated electronic commerce. If a direct trading procedure is followed, agents of producers and consumers should negotiate the deal and inform their users. In case the negotiation is very simple (or not existing as in the case of fixed price markets) this can be done without the use of an institution. E.g. an agent can buy a CD at CD-now, because the transaction is completely specified and simple. However, in most cases a certain context is needed in which the transaction can be performed. This context can be formed by an institution. In the next section we will discuss what role institutions can play when agents are used for electronic commerce.

4.3 Agents and institutions

The institution determines the way that the parties can conduct the transaction and provides an infrastructure to do it. Therefore the institution provides the standard for the agent interactions, which simplifies the agents that only have to cater for one ontology and protocol instead for a different one for each agent they interact with. Good examples are Kasbah and AuctionBot, market places where agents can buy and sell goods. They give a predefined structure for specifying the product and also facilitate the negotiation process (about the price of the product).

As said before, in the case of indirect trading there exists a natural institution in the form of the broker that mediates in the transaction. In case of an auction, this is the auction house. The auction house determines the procedure through which products can be delivered at the auction as well as an auction mechanism that determines the way products can be bought.

In all cases holds that the more elements of a transaction protocol are determined by the institution the more efficient the transaction can be performed. That is, the interaction between the agents is more determined and thus the communication complexity reduced. However, it also holds that the more elements of the transaction protocol are determined by the institution the less flexibility there is to "negotiate" a deal. E.g. in an auction every item is traded separately and basically on price only. It is not possible to buy a whole package of products at once for a lower price.

Institutions that employ very rigid and well-defined protocols for the interactions are the best context for the use of agents in electronic commerce at this moment. First of all the users can trust the agents more easily if the procedures are well defined and rigid. Also the agents that enter the institution can be very simple in terms of communication. The ontology with which products, that are traded, are described is fixed by the institution. This means that matching supply and demand is greatly simplified. Also the model of the outside world can be limited to those elements that are relevant for the protocol and they do not have to adjust to unexpected events in the outside world (all events are determined by the rigid protocols). All the intelligence can be put in the modules that determine the best strategy under the fixed protocol for the transaction process. Therefore the trust of the user in the delegation of the task to the agent is bigger.

One of the disadvantages of institutions that employ rigid protocols for the trading procedure is that many current procedures cannot be captured in that rigid way (yet). In fact one of the few procedures that can easily be formally modeled and implemented is the auction model. For each of the auction types one can very precisely and formally define the procedure to which the participants must adhere. This is one of the main reasons why auctions became a popular form of electronic commerce.

One way of extending the use of institutions and agents is to formalize richer trading procedures such that they can also be handled in the same way as auctions. For instance, multi attribute auctions are an example, as well as multiple linked auctions. Although some first attempts are made in these directions (see e.g. Gutman 1998; Matos 1998, Preist et.al. 2001, Shehory 2001), little formal theory is available to make adequate models for the protocols needed in these situations and especially for the strategies that should be used for the agents in these situations.

5. FUTURE ROLES OF INSTITUTIONS AND AGENTS IN ELECTRONIC COMMERCE

Although the section above already indicates a number of useful roles of institutions and agents in electronic commerce, we feel that the potential of agents and institutions is much bigger.

It is possible to look at institutions that do not fix the entire transaction procedure, but only give some boundaries or support. For instance, it is well known that the negotiation process itself is very complicated. However, the institution might support (or enforce) certain types of negotiations that are still feasible for agents. The main question is, how to extend the negotiation possibilities. Which type of products are traded that need these types of negotiations? If these products are mainly traded through the hierarchy mechanism it might not be very useful to develop such a market mechanism.

Another way of extending the use of institutions is to just let them give support to the trading process without having them dictate the protocol used. E.g. in the negotiation phase the institution might keep track of all commitments that are made so far and that cannot be reneiged. It can also set the boundaries in between which negotiation can take place, such that the negotiation is fair for both sides. This can be achieved by indicating the norms that both parties have to adhere to while interacting through the institution. These types of extensions are also useful in the cases where the parties are trading directly, but need a trusted third party to secure the trading process.

Two things have to be done for these types of extensions of institutions to work. First, the institutions should be described formally. Whenever institutions adhere to strict protocols like the auction mechanism, the description of the institution can be given in terms of several finite state machines that are linked. One finite state machine describes the auction itself, the others describe the payment procedure, entering the institution, etc. Finally one finite state machine describes how one gets from one "scene" to another. E.g. from registration to auction and subsequently to settlement or exit.

However, when the protocols within the institution are not that rigid, it is also not possible to define the working of the complete institution as a set of protocols anymore. What is needed is a normative description of the boundaries of the behavior of the participants within the institution and possibly the penalties incurred when those norms are violated. One way of achieving this is through the use of deontic logic as used in e.g. (Dignum 1999; Meyer & Wieringa 1993)

The second element to be adjusted are the agents that operate within these institutions. Because the protocols are not all fixed anymore, it is important that the agents know what protocol they are following when interacting with other agents. So, the agents must also have a representation of different types of protocols to be used and their abilities to follow those protocols. E.g. there might be agents that can only negotiate about prices using a common haggling protocol of alternating bids that converge to a compromise. Other agents, however, might negotiate about the price using arguments for each bid. Or agents might negotiate over many aspects of the product at the same time. There should at least be a "uniform" way to specify the abilities of the agents to handle all types of different protocols.

The next question is how to develop the institutions and agents together to make it really work. The agent should know both the protocol of the institution, which can be still very precisely specified and definite as well as the possible protocols that can be used within the different phases of the trading procedure.

The ideal situation would be an institution where all types of agents could trade their products. The "simple" agents only accept a very simple transaction protocol. They might miss the very best bargain, but could be very efficient. The "complex" agents can accept both the simple as well as the complicated protocols and can thus trade with simple agents but also try to conduct real negotiations with other complex agents. This means that the protocols for negotiation should be built in a modular version where each module can be seen as an extension of the basic module.

Although we discussed the use of protocols and the composition of protocols as if it is already possible to do this, in reality there are many problems to be solved in this area. First of all, the problem to verify whether the actual protocol used by an agent conforms to the formally specified protocol is undecidable (Wooldridge, 2000). Although this might seem trivial, experience has shown that many small variations emerge of standard protocols and it is not at all clear whether these variations are compatible.

The next problem is to determine whether two protocols used by different agents can be coupled consistently for an interaction. E.g. can different types of Contract net protocols be combined? If this types of combinations are allowed, can we prove that the resulting interaction does not deadlock or continues infinitely?

5.1 Trading agents

All of the above actually assumes that there is one institution where all agents meet. But in an open environment there will be many different institutions. So, for the future it seems important that agents are able to move to different institutions and compare the products and processes at those institutions. E.g. some auctions may use a descending bidding protocol while others use an ascending bidding protocol. How should an agent determine in which auction to participate to get the best bargain? Is it possible to participate in both auctions in parallel and use that as an advantage? Although the institutions give a context in which to perform a transaction, the existence of multiple institutions creates new possibilities and problems for agents again.

Of course, it does not seem very feasible for user agents to know how to choose the best institution and trading procedure. This requires specialized "trading" knowledge, which cannot be required from the agents at the user sites that actually just want to buy or sell a product and only have specialized product knowledge. One way to remedy this problem is through the development of specialized "trading agents" that have knowledge how best to trade in certain institutions. If an agent wants to buy a product it will give a description and a price limit to a trading agent. This trading agent will find the best institution to suit your needs and negotiate the best deal within that institution. Although there is a general tendency in electronic commerce to abolish intermediaries, it seems that this is a viable area for a new type of intermediary!

A possible architecture of such a trading agent is given in the following figure. It is based on (Tsvetovatyy, 1997; Verharen, 1997; Dignum et.al., 1997; Norman et.al., 1997).

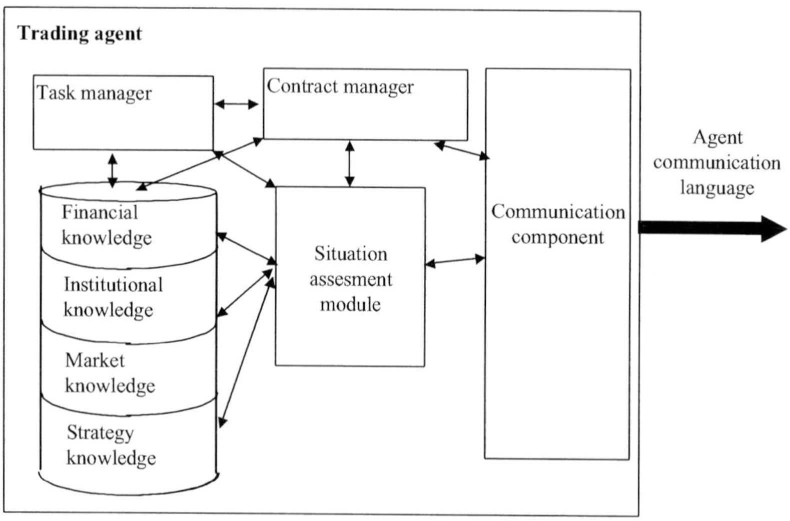

The knowledge base consists of several parts: the financial knowledge (about ways of payment), institutional knowledge (about the protocols and norms of institutions), market knowledge (about the type of market that is suitable for which type of product) and strategy knowledge (about strategies for interacting most profitable within an institution).

The communication manager takes care of all communication with other agents within and outside institutions. It also receives all messages from other agents and sends it to the most appropriate module. It incorporates some knowledge on communication protocols that it should follow (outside institutional protocols). Messages can be anything from bidding on a product, to a payment order to the bank.

The contract manager has control over the negotiation phase in the sense that it keeps track which negotiation strategy is followed, how successful it is and finally which commitments (contracts) have been made. Once a contract has been made, the contract manager keeps track of the fulfillment of the contract. I.e. it will initiate payment at the right moment, check delivery, etc.

The situation assessment module is the decision module of the agent. In this module all knowledge of the agent is consulted and a decision is made about where to sell or buy a product, when to start, when to quit negotiations, etc. This module also contains the goals of the agent as set by the clients. E.g. sell this product as quick as possible, but not below a certain price.

The task manager is a module that plans all actions of the agent. It schedules the actions based on all commitments and resource availability.

6. CONCLUSIONS

Although many people see electronic commerce as a technology driven development, we have shown in this paper that it is an (important) part of some more fundamental developments in doing business. It is important to have some understanding of these developments to understand the main importance of electronic commerce for business. It should never be forgotten that technology has a supporting role for business. Therefore any technological development (such as the use of software agents and electronic institutions) should be judged from the perspective of how it can advance business in the end.

Agents can be used in many ways in the electronic commerce process. In order to use them as mediators it is almost always necessary to create a context in which the trading of the agents takes place. Only when the procedures of the trading are well defined it is feasible to delegate the actual trading to an agent. This context can be provided in the form of an institution. So, institutions can function in two ways. They can be instruments for intermediaries and used to support the function of the intermediary party in the trading process (indirect trading). Institutions can also be used to create a trusted and well-defined environment for direct trading parties.

At the moment agents are mainly used in the indirect trading processes, because in those processes there are well defined protocols and institutions that are dictated by the intermediaries of the trading process (the most famous one being the auction houses). In order to use agents in more complex trading processes, the institutions should be extended to allow more types and more flexible protocols. Only when these can be formally defined and the boundaries of the behavior of agents within the institutions is clearly defined can agents successfully be employed in these more complex trading processes.

The institutions should be flexible enough to provide different types of scenarios. Depending on the type of product and market situation a certain type of trading can be chosen. This means that agents should be able to select the proper (most efficient or profitable) trading procedure for the case in hand. If the chosen procedure allows some freedom within the interaction (e.g. negotiating in different ways) the agent should agree with the other party on a common acceptable way of interacting. One cannot expect all agents to have the same capabilities, therefore agents should be designed in such a way that they can deal with both simple and complex agents in the context of the same institution.

A new challenge will be to design trading agents that function as intermediaries for the trading procedure. They have specialized knowledge on strategies and trading protocols, such that the agents of the trading parties only have to have product and market knowledge and can leave the burden of finding the suitable trading procedure to the trading agent.

Some other more general challenges that have to be faced in order to deploy software agents in electronic commerce have to do with the development of agent technology as a whole. Although agents are being build for industry already, there is no general accepted methodology for designing and implementing multi-agent systems yet. Until some industry standard is set many companies will not venture to use agents for their software systems due to the risks in maintaining such systems.

The last challenge we want to mention is the lack of a comprehensive agent theory. Although there are formal theories for several parts of agents there is no (generally accepted) theory that can describe all aspects of agents in a multi-agent system. (Even the widely quoted BDI theory is far from complete and leaves many choices for the implementation).

REFERENCES

Chavez, A., and Maes, P. 1996. Kasbah: An agent marketplace for buying and selling goods. In *First Int. Conf. On the Practical Application of Intelligent Agents and Multi-Agent Technology,* London, UK, 1996

Choi, S-Y., Stahl D. and Whinston, A., 1997. *The economics of electronic commerce*, MacMillan Technical publishing, Indianapolis, USA, 1997.

Dignum, F. 1999. Autonomous agents with norms. In *AI & Law*, vol.7, pp.69-79, 1999.

Dignum, F., Verharen, E. and Bos, S. 1997. Implementation of a cooperative agent architecture based on the language-action perspective. In M. Singh et.al. (eds.) - *Proc. Of the fourth Int. workshop on Agent Theories, Architectures and Languages (ATAL-97),* Providence, USA, 1997.

Doorenbos, B., Etzioni, O. and Weld, D. 1996. A scalable comparison-shopping agent for the World Wide Web. *Technical report TR96-01-03*, University of Washington, 1996.

Heck, van E., Damme, van E., Kleijnen, J. and Ribbers, P. 1997. New entrants and the role of information technology; Case-study: the tele flower auction in the Netherlands. In *Proceedings of the thirtieth Hawaii International Conference on System Sciences (HICSS'30)*, 1997.

Huberman, B. and Hogg, T. 1995. Distributed computing as an economic system. In *Journal of Economic Perspectives* 9(1): 141-152, 1995.

IJEC, International Journal on Electronic Commerce

Kalakota, R. and Whinston, A., 1996. *Frontiers of electronic commerce*, Addison Wesley, 1996.

Kalakota, R. and Robinson, M., 2001. *e-Business 2.0*, Addison Wesley, 2001.

Kraljic, P. Purchasing must become supply management, *Harvard Business Review*, september 1983.

Malone, T., Yates, J. and Benjamin, R. 1987. Electronic markets and electronic hierarchies. In *Communications of the ACM,* vol. 30, nr. 6: 484-497, 1987.

Matos, N. and Sierra, C. 1998. Evolutionary computing and negotiating agents. In *Proceedings of the first international workshop on Agent Mediated Electronic Trading (AMET'98)*, pp. 91-112, Minneapolis, 1998.

Meyer, J.-J. and Wieringa, R. 1993. *Deontic logic in Computer Science*. John Wiley & Sons, Chichester, 1993.

Moss, S. 1998. The Cost of Rational Agency. Technical report 51 of the Centre of Policy Management, Manchester University, http://www.cpm.mmu.ac.uk/cpmrep51.html.

Nissen, M. and Mehra, A. 1999. Some intelligent software supply chain agents. In *Proceedings of the third international conference on autonomous agents (Agents'99)*, pp.374-375, Seattle, 1999.

Norman, T., Jennings, N., Faratin, P. and Mamdani, E. 1997. Designing and implementing a multi-agent architecture for business process management. In J. Müller, M. Wooldridge and N. Jennings (eds.) *Intelligent Agents III - Proc. Of the third Int. workshop on Agent Theories, Architectures and Languages (ATAL-96),* LNAI-1193, Springer-Verlag, Heidelberg, 1997.

Preist, C., Bartolini, C. and Phillips, I. 2001. Algorithm Design for Agents which Participate in Mulitple Simultaneous Auctions. In Dignum, F. and Cortės, U. (eds). *Third International Workshop on Agent-Mediated Electronic Commerce (AMEC-III),* LNAI-2003, pp. 139-154, Springer-Verlag, Heidelberg, 2001.

Rodriguez, J.A., Noriega, P., Sierra, C. and Padget, J.A. 1997. FM96.5 A Java-based Electronic Auction House. In *Second International Conference on the practical application of intelligent agents and multi-agent technology: PAAM'97*, pp. 207-226, London, 1997.

Rosenschein, J. and Zlotkin, G. 1994. Designing conventions for automated negotiation. *AI Magazine*, fall-1994, 29-46.

Sandholm, T. 1996. Limitations of the Vickrey Auction in Computational Multiagent Systems. *Second International Conference on Multiagent Systems (ICMAS-96)*, Keihanna Plaza, Kyoto, Japan, December, pp. 299-306, 1996.

Shehory, O. 2001. Optimality and Risk in Purchase from Multiple Auctions. In Klusch, M. and Zambonelli, F. 2001. Fifth International Workshop on Cooperative Information Agents (CIA-V), LNAI-2182, Springer-Verlag, Heidelberg, 2001.

Tsvetovatyy, M., Gini M., Mobasher, B. and Wieckowski Z. 1997. MAGMA: An agent-based virtual market for electronic commerce. In *Journal of Applied Artificial Intelligence*, 11:501-523, 1997.

Treacy, M. and Wiersema, F., 1997. *The Discipline of Market Leaders*, Perseus Press, 1997.

Varian, H. 1995. Economic mechanism design for computerized agents. In *USENIX workshop on Electronic Commerce*, New York, 1995.

Verharen, E. 1997. A Language-Action perspective on the design of cooperative information agents. Ph.D. thesis, Katholieke Universiteit Brabant, Tilburg, 1997.

Wooldridge, M. 1999. Intelligent Agents. In G. Weiss (ed.) *Multiagent systems: A modern approach to distributed artificial intelligence*, pp. 27-78, MIT Press, 1999.

Wooldridge, M. 2000. Semantic Issues in the Verification of Agent Communication Languages. In *Int. Journal of Autonomous Agents and Multi-Agent Systems*, Vol.3, nr.1, pp. 9-32, March 2000.

Wurman, P., Wellman, M. and Walsh, W. 1998. The Michigan Internet AuctionBot: a configurable auction server for human and software agents. In *Proceedings of the second international conference on autonomous agents (Agents'98)*, pp. 301-308, Minneapolis, May 1998.

BIOGRAPHICAL NOTE

Dr. Frank Dignum is an associate professor at the Intelligent Systems group of the Institute of Information and Computing Sciences from the Utrecht University.

His main interests are in the area of formal specification of reliable and flexible communications between autonomous systems. A major area in which autonomous systems are used is that of software agents. Another area where this is very important is electronic commerce. He is involved in both areas as well as in their intersection. He is interested in formal specification of systems as a way to better understand how they have to be implemented; to achieve that, in his research, he uses some form of dynamic logic that incorporates both deontic elements as well as communication actions.

He has organized several workshops, mainly in the area of agent communication and agent mediated electronic commerce. He was the technical coordinator of the ESPRIT project MEMO, which aims at providing integrated support for electronic commerce for small and medium sized enterprises.

MUST A COMPUTER HAVE A USER?

Anatol Holt
Milan University
Email: aholt@est.ips.pt

Abstract: Must a computer have a user? My personal answer to this question is "yes" - even though I think that, to my culture, this is no longer clear; that is: people-in-general see no particular difference between the functions which a computer can perform and the "functions" of use. I believe this trend has been encouraged by Science-in-general and by Computer-Science-in-particular - and most especially by AI.
Science-in-general has refused to see a difference between the "functions" of Life, and the "functions" of inanimate matter. Computer-Science (and AI in particular) have carried this indifference a step further in regarding the computer, not as a tool in the hands of man, but as a new form of "artificial" being that can "improve" on human performance in various respects.
I, on the other hand, continue to regard the computer as a tool in the hands of man. I am in the midst of developing a theory which asserts that a necessary aspect of all action is responsibility, and that the user – a human-being-in-society, a living being - is the only possible carrier of responsibility as regards computer-supported action. For, the carrier of responsibility must be capable of rewards and punishments - the key attribute that no "artificial being" can have.
Is it too long? Is it too anything-else?

1. INTRODUCTION

A This paper is out of the ordinary – as you can see by the following: (a) it would not have been written 30 years ago; (b) it addresses issues which are about as "timeless" as issues ever become; (c) at least *I think* that the issues – which have mattered for generations past – matter to us as professionals *now*.

The possible answers to the title question that might be of interest seem to me are as follows.

1.1 No (a computer *must not* have to have a user) but:
  1.1.1 It *can* have a "user" which:
    1.1.1.1 *might be* another machine (such as a suitably programmed computer)
    1.1.1.2 *might be* a person
  1.1.2 It is impossible that it have a user
1.2 Yes (a computer *must have* a user) and this user:
  1.2.1 *must be* a person

No one in his right mind believes 1.1.2 – and not many people (certainly with my exception) believe 1.2 any more. Here the 'historical right' and personal interest happily fall together. Of course I am mainly interested in presenting you with my point of view; of course I want to hold your interest and for this purpose the timeliness of the question (the 'historical right') is useful.

Mr. Everyman has tended to believe:

1.3 Computers *do* have *users*.
1.4 These *users* are usually people (and/or their organizations) – and it is they who take responsibility - for machine maintenance, for starting and stopping its operation, and for what it does while it is "on".
1.5 It is becoming more and more unclear (to Mr. Everyman) whether the functions which these *users* perform are different-in-principle from those performed by the machine. This unclarity has been aided and abetted by the "profession" (of computer science in the USA and informatics in Europe).
1.6 Computers not only *do* have *users*; they *must* have *users* – now and forever; exactly like every machine (as well as every "symbolic machine").

(Since Mr. Everyman's vision was always very important, this paper would never have been writ-ten 30 years ago.) My personal position is a variant on the common-sense "classical" attitude of Mr. Everyman:

1.7 The *users are always* people (and/or their organizations) – now and forever – and it is *they* who take responsibility for *everything*

J. Filipe et al. (eds.), Enterprise Information Systems III, 36–40.

in which *any* machines participates; of course this includes computers because they are nothing but machines, and therefore share in every important machine property.

1.8 Taking responsibility for an action is part of *every* action, but is not an action in its own right. This applies to machines-in-general, and computers-in-particular.

2. AN ADEQUATE THEORY: HOW SCIENCE GETS IN THE WAY

If it is true that taking responsibility is part of every action? And if it is true that people-and-only-people can take responsibility, then it is also true that computers without users *can do nothing*. We as a community are in desperate need of a *theory* which says this (among other things) – a *theory* which (a) is as *practically* potent in the field of computer use as any theory now in existence, and (b) has the recognition of – and the respect of – the relevant professional community. This would have to be a theory which (c) is based on my beliefs 1.6 – 1.8, and (d) dares to oppose very popular ways of thinking and communicating. In my judgement:

2.1 There is no theory on the horizon which satisfies the requirements stated in 1.7-1.8.

2.2 The reason for this lack is – above all – Science, which has dominated nearly everything for several hundreds of years – including *all* fields connected with computing) (since Science was indeed indispensable to the development of computer hardware).

Why do I seem to "blame" Science? The Scientific Revolution (now some 400 years old) began by abjuring everything related to motives/interests/responsibilities as an accepted and acceptable explanatory principle. Of course this did not mean abjuring motives/interests/responsibilities as *subject matter* – like every other scientific subject matter; (and of course it could not be recognized *scientifically* that motives/interests/responsibilities play an important role in the conduct of science – in other words, that motives/interests/responsibilities *underlie* the entire scientific enterprise, rather than merely being a small part of its subject matter).

But I claim: the scientific point of view as described above cannot be maintained in constructing a new theory of computer use consistent with 1.6 - 1.8.

I feel the need to say a few words to you about my view of 'theory'. I do not think like most Americans – and the world at large – about 'theory'; Americans – for the most part – despise 'theory' and adore 'practice'; but I think that practice without theory is not much good; theories that are worth learning, yield – above all – an accurate communication mechanism about a practice; therefore theories usually depend on a pre-existent, non-specialized language. So I think: (a) computer use is a field (of ever increasing importance); (b) it is a field which cannot get along without a theory (which allows people to communicate *accurately* about computer use); (c) much of what ails us today is that "the theory" of computer use is too much influenced by Science – as is true of most accepted theories today – and it is too fragmented.

A new theory of computer use must begin with well-reasoned answers to a few initial questions:

2.3 Of *what use* are computers? (to which "general purpose" is *not* an answer), and

2.4 *Who* is the user?

The theory I favor says: the user is always: a *person* fulfilling an *organizational function* (answer to 2.4); and *the use* of the computer *always* makes his life easier-and-better in the handling of *information* (answer to 2.3).

There are two connections between organized activity and "information": first, is the fact that "information" (in the sense of computers) is a theoretical idea that first finds its home in the context of "organized (human) activity"; secondly: much of the effort involved in carrying on organized activity can be placed on the handling information; this means (if I am right) that computers can be *very* useful to the fulfilling of organizational functions.

In respect to the question raised in 2.4, the answer is the same for all machines: the user must *always* be a person who fulfils an *organizational function*; this means – among other things – that the person must speak a language; therefore the person must be a member of a group. Of course "the user" has to be a person (for only a person is *interested* in being helped).

People have wondered (perhaps because Question 2.3 has seemed so hard to answer): are computers really of *ANY use*? Many smart people have decided (for one reason or another) that Question 2.3 is "wrong headed"; "computers" these people say "are not 'useful'; they are a new form of being – different from other machines; capable of exhibiting all the properties of Life. I am not one of these; I think a computer is no different than a crane or an airplane; according to me, it is a machine (like other machines) which has currency because it is *useful* – to people. Because of the computer's many-sidedness it is not easy to say *clearly* wherein its utility consists.

Much of the argument above rests on a supposition, namely:

2.5 Computers cannot carry responsibility

Is this really "true"? After all: carrying responsibility *is* an effort – and a highly rewarded one at that. The computer has eased (or substituted for) many other human efforts; why not this one? I think the following.

2.6 A part of the issue is political. For now, people do not assign responsibility to computers; they do not put computers in jail or deprive them of life; and I for one hope that the world remains that way.

2.7 What is more: I think that responsibility is not an action-in-its-own-right, but a part of *every* action. I think that computers can help reduce the effort involved in all actions in which "information" is involved, and therefore it can also help with the carrying of responsibility – but this is not the same as saying that a computer can carry responsibility; indeed: I think that a computer can *do nothing* by itself;

It must always have an interested-and-responsible human user!!

3. COMPUTERS AS USED TODAY

Obviously computers are already used extensively today without the benefit of the theory which is the topic of the previous section. How come? If I am right, practices usually cannot get along with *no* theory. So what is the present-day theory which supports the present-day practice (world-wide)? And is it true that this practice can be greatly improved by the introduction of a more appropriate theory?

The present-day "theory" consists in fragments based on practical considerations which arise from the historical accidents of well-established practices, and informed by the spirit of science-and-mathemics – which pervades everything. Accordingly, present-day theory does not consider the user and his organization as an *inevitable* part of ongoing computer use; (The "use" of anything is not a "scientific" idea – since "use" leans on "interest" which is not a notion at the base of science either).

The function of the user and his organization is assumed exhausted in delivering so-called "requirements" to the software writers; these "requirements", once made explicit, are assumed to be "objective" – like the computer. (Present-day theory is useless to figure out what "requirements" are reasonable, and which ones are not).

Present-day theory does not take the role of every-day language seriously. Of course not. Naturally it is best if "requirements" are stated in formalized "requirement languages" – for this is "more scientific", and, besides computers are "exact" machines. But: since requirements are "objective", a change of language can change the exactness with which requirements are expressed, but not affect the essence.

The art of producing "good" software is (assumed to be) the art of "correctly" translating the requirements into a language that the computer "understands". (Of course it would be best if the computer would "understand" expressions of requirements directly, in this way eliminating the need to "translate" from requirements to software. But – alas – this has never been quite achieved).

There is a connection between the tendency of present-day theory *not* to address the quantity of effort that a step takes, and its fundamental disregard of languages. *Theoretically*, one computer language is as good another, provided only that all relevant considerations (relevant to requirements) can be expressed. But the fact of the matter is this: a tool (or anything else) will only be used insofar as it *saves effort*. Therefore the extent to which computer languages are, or are not, adapted to expressing plans whose performance involve many people *does* matter. For the less effort is necessary to express plans *and their changes* relative to computer implementations, the more likely it is that computers will be used for these purposes. But: computers began as tools that were supposed to help engineers. Present-day theory can neither understand nor explain this shift in interest. It can only be used to check the "correctness" of the translation of requirements into software (and hardware) – and this "correctness" covers little that matters. A more adequate "theory" can cover more.

4. EXAMPLES

The above leads to "funny" conclusions – which in their turn, lead to "funny" technical considerations, as illustrated by the following examples

4.1 Did Kasparov play chess against Deeper Blue? The above analysis would say "no". Deeper Blue is only a computer and therefore cannot play chess. But Deeper Blue could be fielded against Kasparov by a team of hardware and software builders who play him *via computer*. This analysis is confirmed by the following: if Kasparov had won he could have received a purse. But Deeper Blue could not receive a purse

– even though the team that fielded Deeper Blue might have.

If the consequences of responsibility (such as the purse) were important to the Kasparov/Deeper-Blue encounter, it would have been *computer-technically* necessary to keep track of the team that fielded Deeper Blue against Kasparov. As things stand, this is not considered relevant to the computer's function in "playing chess".

4.2 Did Robots sent to Venus select and bring back rock samples from the surface of that planet? The above analysis would again say "no". Again: it would have been the team who – via the robot – selected and brought back rock samples for local laboratory analysis.

One difference between 4.1 and 4.2 is this: the team that fielded Deeper Blue could have played Kasparov directly (although perhaps not as well); 4.2 would have been impossible without the robot; but – according to me – this distinction leaves the essential matter unchanged.

4.3 Does putting in a computer system necessarily *decrease* the number of persons involved in fulfilling a function? In 1966 I published an article called 'On the Importance of not Treating a Computer as a Person'. In that article I argued that the mental habit of thinking of computers as *acting* without persons could lead to a failure of the *technical* imagination for computer use. In that article I constructed the following example.

Consider a large company which builds a product sold to many clients. Such a company must be prepared to handle customer complaints. Complaints require many different kinds of response; some are based on simple misunderstandings to be cleared up; some require changes in documentation; some suggest changes in the product; some have legal implications; some imply changes in advertising; some involve several of these – and therefore, probably, coordination among several company functions.

Under this circumstance, a computer could be efficiently used to (a) multiply and format the complaint in various ways for the benefit of different recipients; (b) route these re-formated copies to their recipients; (c) augment the complaint for different recipients from stored information; (d) if appropriate, the complaint could also be formatted and routed to a human coordinator and/or decider about where else the complaint should be sent.

Looked at from the point of view of the 1966 paper, this computer use – though eminently natural and feasible – is unlikely to have been conceived because, relative to the whole of "handling customer complaints" this design is too modest. What is more, it involves functions which are natural enough when a computer is employed, but are not natural without it.

Looked at from the point of view of the present paper the persons involved in the performance of standard functions must remain, though perhaps with a reduced burden; the "new" functions (such as coordinating and deciding) must be assigned to persons who – before computer use – had no reason for existence.

And so we see: in this example the number of persons employed in "handling customer complaints" with computers could be *larger* than the number of persons employed previously (but of course there should be a net gain in human effort).

5. CONCLUSIONS

The long and short of all this is as follows.

5.1 Without full awareness – while knowing the answer to the title question to be "yes" – we are drifting in the direction of "no".

5.2 This "drift" has been set in motion by the Scientific Revolution some 400 years ago, and has been furthered in our own day by AI. According to AI, computers are not ordinary machines; AI regards computers – especially computers equipped with AI software – not as a machine like all other machines, but as a new type of being that can perform *in place of* people – and "better". This AI thought is greatly encouraged by noticing that automation can eliminate human workers, and not noticing that the same is true of cranes. The resulting "drift" is wide and deep.

5.3 In a sense, the purpose of this paper is to make you conscious of the drift, and to make you aware of the fact that there are other ways of looking at the world; these "other ways" have unexpected *technical* consequences for computer design and construction.

5.4 If the main thesis of this paper is right, there is no computer action without a user.

> This means that "informatics" should concentrate as much on users as on computers.
> Should one say the same of every other engineering discipline? No. But one *should* say this about computer science and informatics *precisely because the purpose of a computing machine is hard to understand,* while the purpose of other machines – such as airplanes – are easy to understand. What is more, the purpose of computers – involved as it is with "information" – is more profoundly related to what it means to be a human being than is true of *all* other present-day machines.

I hope you will overcome your sense of outrage at a paper as deviant as this one, and take its message seriously.

BIOGRAPHICAL NOTE

Dr. Anatol Holt's first two degrees were in Mathematics (Harvard and MIT) and, a decade later, a PhD in Descriptive Linguistics from the University of Pennsylvania. In 1953, together with the late William J. Turanski, he developed the world's first programming environment (known as "Generalized Programming"); it ran on UNIVACs I and II. In the '60s and early '70s he helped to develop and promote Petri nets. In 1979, together with Paul Cashman, he developed the world's first "coordination system"; it ran on the ARPANET to support military software development. Anatol Holt has engaged in many R&D activities, sponsored by the Airforce, ARPA, and industry. More recently, in Milano Italy he has been teaching and writing books: "Organized Activity and Its Support by Computer" (Kluwer Academic Publishers, Dordrecht Holland), and "Ripensare il Mondo - il Computer e Vincoli Sociali" (Dunod/Masson, Paris).

RESOURCE ALLOCATION IN LARGE SCALE SYSTEMS, A DECOUPLING APPROACH

Nuno C. Martins, Saligrama Venkatesh, Munther A. Dahleh
Massachusetts Institute of Technology
Rm 35-415, 77 Mass. Ave., Cambridge MA 02139, U.S.A.
Email: nmartins@mit.edu

Keywords: Resource allocation, large-scale, decoupling, optimization

Abstract: In this paper, implementation and design issues are broached for a class of resource allocation problems. The idea of decoupling is used as the main tool to achieve great simplification and complexity reduction. Linear input flow constraints are also considered. One example of application illustrates the main ideas on the paper.

1 INTRODUCTION

In this paper, we propose the use of system decoupling to design and implement resource allocation decision systems with specific structures, including hierarchical. Greater simplification is achieved for the classes of large-scale systems described in section 3. Controller structures can also be adopted that facilitate the design in the presence of linear flow constraints at the input.

Some theorems are presented that state the main results in the paper. Although proofs are not provided, they can be easily carried out from the context or derived from the references.

The paper is divided into 5 sections. In section 2 we formulate the resource allocation problem in the presence of an adversary. Section 3 gives a compact introduction to the theory of spatial decoupling of linear systems. The design of allocation decision systems is broached in section 4. In the last section, we describe an example of application.

2 PROBLEM STATEMENT

We model resource consumption and interaction by facing the overall environment as a system. The specific dynamics of this system determines how supplies affect the quantity of resources.

In general such system is a mapping

$$\mathcal{S} : \mathbf{f}^s \mapsto \mathbf{r}^s, \tag{1}$$

where $\mathbf{f}^s$ and $\mathbf{r}^s$ are vectors of functions:

$$\mathbf{f}^s(t) = \begin{bmatrix} f_1^s(t) \\ \cdots \\ f_p^s(t) \end{bmatrix}, \mathbf{r}^s(t) = \begin{bmatrix} r_1^s(t) \\ \cdots \\ r_p^s(t) \end{bmatrix}$$

that represent the evolution of supplies and resources, respectively, as functions of time. It is important to stress that, for notational simplicity, we assume that $f_i^s(t), r_i^s(t) \in \mathbb{R}$, but that need not be the case. This formulation can be extended by means of the Kronecker product to the most general case when $f_i^s(t) \in \mathbb{R}^k$ and $r_i^s(t) \in \mathbb{R}^m$

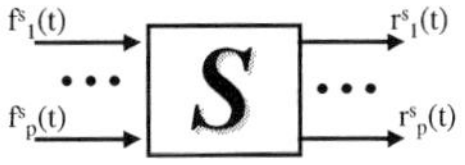

Figure 1: Graphical representation of the type of systems considered for resource allocation.

In this setup, the space is partitioned into p regions associated with each of the elements of $\mathbf{f}^s$ and $\mathbf{r}^s$ (see figure 1).

2.1 Introducing an intelligent adversary

By extending the previous modelling concept we introduce a *competing system* $\mathcal{C}$ which will interfere with $\mathcal{S}$. We assume $that \mathcal{C}$ is in every aspect similar to $\mathcal{S}$ so that the setup is the one described in figure

J. Filipe et al. (eds.), Enterprise Information Systems III, 41–48.

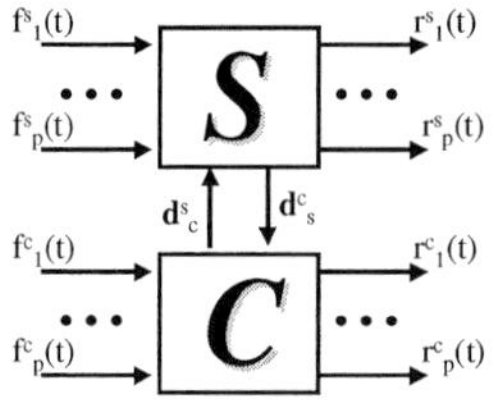

Figure 2: Interconnection scheme comprising two competing systems.

2. The interaction between $\mathcal{S}$ and $\mathcal{C}$ is represented by a disturbance input in each system. Those are indicated by the vectors of functions $\mathbf{d}^s_c$ and $\mathbf{d}^c_s$. Although the nature of the problem may dictate otherwise, we consider $\mathbf{d}^s_c$ and $\mathbf{d}^c_s$ as functions of $\mathbf{r}^c$ and $\mathbf{r}^s$, respectively. The idea of introducing an intelligent adversary was explored in a similar resource allocation setup by (Ravuri, 2000).

2.2 Optimization paradigm

The setup specification is completed by the following assumptions:

1. $\mathbf{r}^c$ and $\mathbf{r}^s$ can be measured.
2. the decision variable is $\mathbf{f}^s$, while $\mathbf{f}^c$ is considered as unknown.
3. $\mathbf{f}^s$ and $\mathbf{f}^c$ are contained in sets F^s and F^c that depend on the problem and are associated with constraints, such as requiring that the total flux of supplies, for each t, is constant.
4. There is an objective function $\overline{J}(\mathbf{f}^c, \mathbf{f}^s, \mathbf{r}^c, \mathbf{r}^s)$. Although $\overline{J}$ is a function of $\mathbf{f}^c, \mathbf{f}^s, \mathbf{r}^c$ and $\mathbf{r}^s$, it can be rewritten as a function J of only $\mathbf{f}^c$ and $\mathbf{f}^s$, since $\mathbf{r}^c$ and $\mathbf{r}^s$ are themselves functions of $\mathbf{f}^c$ and $\mathbf{f}^s$.

The optimization paradigm is stated as follows: *Find the allowable policies* $\mathbf{f}^s = \mathcal{P}^*_s(\mathbf{r}^c, \mathbf{r}^s)$ *and* $\mathbf{f}^c = \mathcal{P}^*_c(\mathbf{r}^c, \mathbf{r}^s)$ *that minimize* $J(\mathbf{f}^c, \mathbf{f}^s)$. It can also be stated as:

$$\mathcal{P}^* = \arg\min_{\mathcal{P}\in P} J(\mathcal{P}(\mathbf{r}^c, \mathbf{r}^s))$$

where $\mathcal{P}(\mathbf{r}^c, \mathbf{r}^s) = (\mathcal{P}^*_s(\mathbf{r}^c, \mathbf{r}^s), \mathcal{P}^*_c(\mathbf{r}^c, \mathbf{r}^s))$ and P is the set of allowable policies, in particular, it must be such that $\mathcal{P}^*(\mathbf{r}^c, \mathbf{r}^s) \in F^c \times F^s$.

Using a H_∞ kind of an argument, it is also possible to modify J to produce a min-max optimization so that $\mathcal{P}^*_s$ is computed for the *worst* possible $\mathcal{P}^*_c$ (Ravuri, 2000). In general this is a very hard problem with complexity highly dependent on J, the model and the types of resources.

Satisfactory solutions can be found for setups comprising linear models, linear flux constraints and quadratic J.

2.2.1 Linear flux constraints and resource allocation

In section 4 we suggest a solution to the optimization paradigm for a setup with linear constraints and linear models.

A variety of situations with practical importance can be modelled by means of linear constraints. Constraints such as:

$$\sum_{i=1}^{p} f^s_i(t) = \upsilon^s(t), \sum_{i=1}^{p} f^c_i(t) = \upsilon^c(t) \qquad (2)$$

establish fixed values $\upsilon^s(t)$ and $\upsilon^c(t)$ for the total flux of resources over space. Since the total flux is fixed, this is clearly a resource allocation problem.

3 LARGE-SCALE LINEAR SYSTEMS

Using the notation introduced in (1), a linear system $\mathcal{L}: \mathbf{f}^L \longmapsto \mathbf{r}^L$ satisfies:

$$\mathcal{L}(\alpha_1 \mathbf{f}^L + \alpha_2 \mathbf{g}^L) = \alpha_1 \mathcal{L}(\mathbf{f}^L) + \alpha_2 \mathcal{L}(\mathbf{g}^L)$$

where α_1 and α_2 are in $\mathbb{C}$.

The assumption of linearity allow us to extend, to the *system space,* the representation of vectors in $\mathbb{C}^p$ as linear combination of elements of a base. This is particularly useful when p is very large and we can decouple the original system into a linear combination of systems *less complex.* In various cases of interest, such representation enables the decomposition of the optimization paradigm cast in section 2.

3.1 Decoupling of linear systems

The fundamental concept leading to the decomposition of a large-scale system is that of a spatial eigenvector.

Definition 3.1 *A vector* $\mathbf{v} \in \mathbb{C}^p$ *is a spatial eigenvector of* $\mathcal{L}$*, provided that:*

$$\mathcal{L}(\alpha(t)\mathbf{v}) = \beta(t)\mathbf{v}$$

where $\alpha(t)$ *and* $\beta(t)$ *are functions taking values on* $\mathbb{C}$.

The following proposition shows how spatial eigenvectors can be used to decouple a large-scale system.

Proposition 3.1 *If a linear system* $\mathcal{L}$ *has a complete set of* p *linearly independent spatial eigenvectors* $\{\mathbf{v}_1, ..., \mathbf{v}_p\}$*, then*

$$\mathcal{L}(\mathbf{f}^L) = \sum_{i=1}^{p} \mathcal{L}_i(\alpha_i(t))\mathbf{v}_i \qquad (3)$$

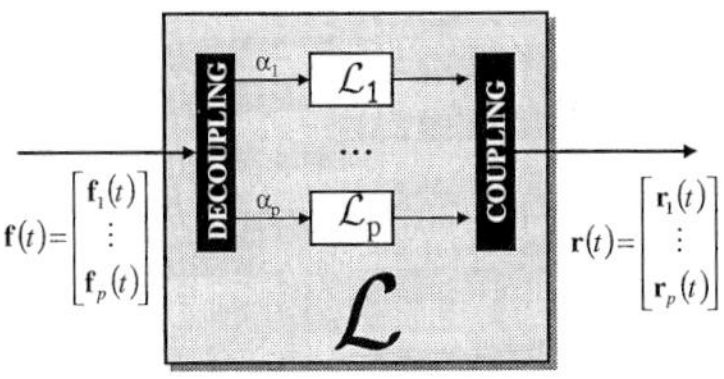

Figure 3: System representation, using decoupled systems.

where $\alpha_i(t)$ *and* $\mathcal{L}_i(.)$ *are such that:*

$$\begin{aligned} \sum_{i=1}^{p} \alpha_i(t)\,\mathbf{v}_i &= \mathbf{f}^L \qquad (4) \\ \mathcal{L}_i(\alpha(t))\,\mathbf{v}_i &= \mathcal{L}(\alpha(t)\,\mathbf{v}_i) \end{aligned}$$

This shows that $\mathcal{L}$ can be decomposed into a linear combination of *simpler* systems that operate over functions instead of vectors of functions. Consequently, $\mathcal{L}$ can be reconstructed by means of the block diagram of figure 3, where the coupling and decoupling blocks stand for (3) and the computation of α_i in (4) respectively.

It is important to mention that this theory can be extended to more general systems that operate over *infinite vectors* of functions indexed in space by a countable set or a compact subset of $\mathbb{R}^n$. For a presentation on linear systems decoupling, in a more general context , please refer to (Bamieh, 1998).

3.2 Spatial Eigenvectors of Shift-Invariant Systems

A major difficulty of spatial eigen-decomposition techniques is the process of finding the eigenvectors of a linear system. In this subsection we explore an approach for finding those spatial eigenvectors based only on input-output invariances under certain permutations.

A spatial permutation Γ acts on a vector of functions $\mathbf{f}^L$ permuting its elements:

$$\Gamma : \mathbf{f}^L \mapsto \mathbf{g}^L,\, g_i^L(t) = g_{\sigma(i)}^L(t)$$

where σ is a permutation over a finite set. For vectors of functions with finite elements, Γ can be represented as a matrix $\mathbf{\Gamma} \in \mathbb{C}^{pxp}$. In this case, $\mathbf{g}^L$ can be computed from $\mathbf{f}^L$ as

$$\begin{bmatrix} g_1^L(t) \\ \vdots \\ g_p^L(t) \end{bmatrix} = \mathbf{\Gamma} \begin{bmatrix} f_1^L(t) \\ \vdots \\ f_p^L(t) \end{bmatrix}$$

and can be indicated in a compact form as:

$$\mathbf{g}^L = \mathbf{\Gamma}\mathbf{f}^L$$

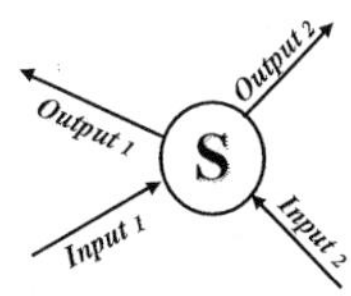

Figure 4: System used as a building block in example 3.2

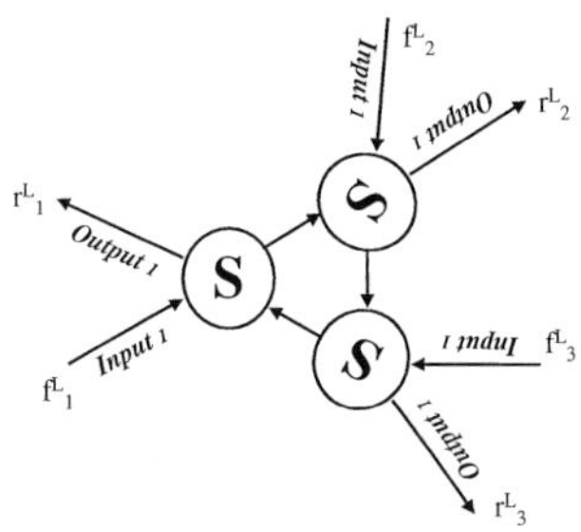

Figure 5: Shift invariant system used in example 3.2.

Example 3.1 *Consider* $p = 3$ *and that* σ_s *performs a cyclic shift* $\{\sigma_s(1), \sigma_s(2), \sigma_s(3)\} = \{2, 3, 1\}$, *then* $\mathbf{\Gamma}_s$ *is given by:*

$$\mathbf{\Gamma}_s = \begin{bmatrix} 0 & 1 & 0 \\ 0 & 0 & 1 \\ 1 & 0 & 0 \end{bmatrix}$$

A permutation $\mathbf{\Gamma}$ is just an invertible linear tranformation. Consequently, we can investigate whether a system $\mathcal{L}$ is invariant under $\mathbf{\Gamma}$ just by checking if $\mathcal{L}$ commutes with $\mathbf{\Gamma}$.

Definition 3.2 *A system* $\mathcal{L}$ *is invariant under a linear transformation* $\mathbf{\Gamma}$ *if*

$$\mathcal{L}\left(\mathbf{\Gamma}\mathbf{f}^L\right) = \mathbf{\Gamma}\mathcal{L}\left(\mathbf{f}^L\right)$$

for any arbitrary $\mathbf{f}^L$ *in the domain of* $\mathcal{L}$

This way, a system is invariant under a permutation Γ provided that applying Γ at the input leads to the same permutation at the output.

Example 3.2 *Consider the system depicted in figure 4. By using this system as a building block we construct the shift invariant system (invariant under* $\mathbf{\Gamma}_s$*) of figure 5. Figure 6 describes a different structure that may not be shift invariant.*

This type of invariance is often easy to detect and may be helpful on the determination of spatial eigenvectors as the following theorem describes. In fact, this is the theory behind the use of Fourier Series to find solutions of certain partial differential equations.

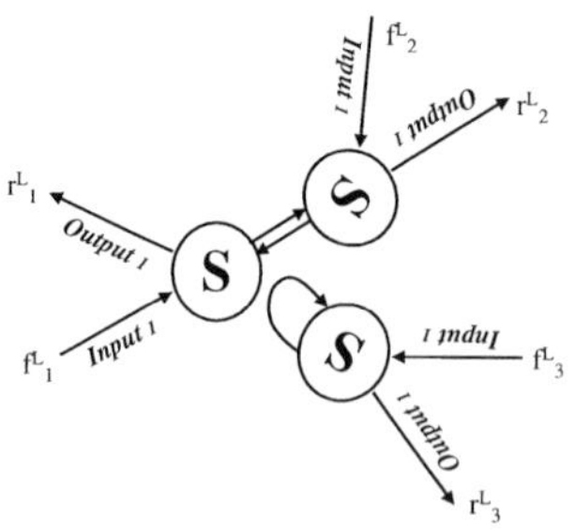

Figure 6: System without shift invariant properties, used in example 3.2.

Theorem 3.2 *Consider a linear system $\mathcal{L}$ invariant under Γ. If $\{\mathbf{v}_1, ..., \mathbf{v}_p\}$ are eigenvectors of $\mathbf{\Gamma}$, then $\mathcal{L}(\alpha(t)\mathbf{v}_i) = \beta(t)\mathbf{u}_i$, where $\mathbf{u}_i$ is also an eigenvector of $\mathbf{\Gamma}$. In particular, if $\mathbf{\Gamma}$ has distinct eigenvalues, then $\{\mathbf{v}_1, ..., \mathbf{v}_p\}$ are spatial eigenvectors of $\mathcal{L}$.*

As an example of application, the previous theorem can be used to infer that the eigenvectors of $\mathbf{\Gamma}_s$ (of example 6) are the spatial eigenvectors of the system sketched in figure 5. Using these vectors and proposition 2, the system in figure 5 can be decomposed as the sum of 3 scalar systems.

3.3 Haar functions and Hierarchical Decision Structures

In this section, we explore a special type of spatial eigenvectors inspired on Haar functions (Adams, 1996).

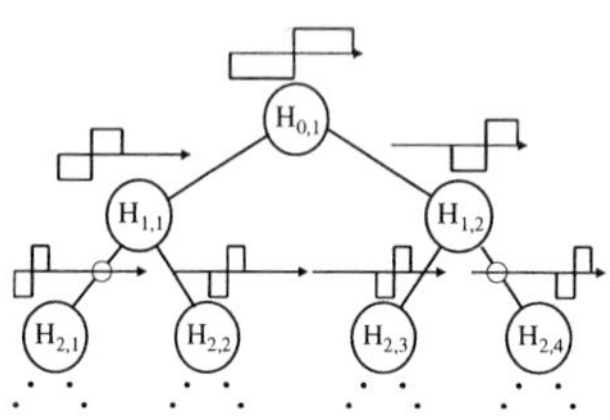

Figure 7: Tree-like structure of the Haar functions on the unit interval

Definition 3.3 *The Haar functions on the interval $[0, 1]$ are defined as:*

$$H_{0,0}(x) = 1,\ 0 \leq x \leq 1$$

$$H_{n,k}(x) = \begin{cases} -2^{n/2} \text{ for } \frac{k-1}{2^n} \leq x \leq \frac{k-\frac{1}{2}}{2^n} \\ 2^{n/2} \text{ for } \frac{k-\frac{1}{2}}{2^n} \leq x \leq \frac{k}{2^n} \\ 0 \text{ elsewhere} \end{cases}$$

Haar functions have the following properties:

- they form a complete set in $\mathbf{L}^2([0,1])$, meaning that every function in $\mathbf{L}^2$ can be represented as a countable linear combination of Haar functions.
- Haar functions form an orthogonal set of variable *resolution*, in particular, as n increases $H_{n,k}(x)$ is nonzero for smaller intervals.
- they can be arranged as in the graph of figure 7. Each node (Haar function) has two siblings, one for each sub-interval where it is non-zero and constant. Those two sibling Haar functions are nonzero on those sub-intervals.

Haar functions can be constructed in similar way for any compact subset of $\mathbb{R}$. We also define a sampled version of the Haar functions on the unit interval, which we designate as Haar vectors:

Definition 3.4 *The following defines a collection of Haar vectors of dimension $p = 2^N$:*

$$\mathbf{h}_{n,k} = \begin{bmatrix} H_{n,k}(0) \\ \vdots \\ H_{n,k}\left(\frac{p-2}{2^N}\right) \\ H_{n,k}\left(\frac{p-1}{2^N}\right) \end{bmatrix}, \text{ for } n \leq N$$

Haar vectors inherit all of the Haar functions' properties, in particular, they are an orthonormal set in $\mathbb{R}^{2^{N+1}}$ which can be arranged as in the graph of figure 7.

The importance of this discussion is that if the Haar vectors are the spatial eigenvectors of a linear decision policy $\mathbf{f^L} = \mathcal{P}(\mathbf{r^L})$ then it can be implemented hierarchically. The reasoning behind this argument is that $\mathcal{P}$ can be decomposed (according to proposition 2) into subsystems, each one associated with its corresponding Haar spatial eigenvector.

In order to describe the implementation of such hierarchical decision structure, consider the following decomposition of $\mathcal{P}$:

$$\mathbf{f^L} = \mathcal{P}(\mathbf{r}^L) = \sum \mathcal{P}_{n,k}(\beta_{n,k}(t))\,\mathbf{h}_{n,k}$$

where $\beta_{n,k}(t)$ and $\mathcal{P}_{n,k}(.)$ are such that:

$$\sum \beta_{n,k}(t)\,\mathbf{h}_{n,k} = \mathbf{r}^L \quad (5)$$

$$\mathcal{P}_{n,k}(\beta(t))\,\mathbf{h}_{n,k} = \mathcal{P}(\beta(t)\,\mathbf{h}_{n,k}) \quad (6)$$

and $\{\mathbf{h}_{0,0}, ..., \mathbf{h}_{N,2^N}\}$ are the Haar spatial eigenvectors of $\mathcal{P}$.

The implementation of $\mathcal{P}$, using the subsystems $\mathcal{P}_{n,k}$, needs to follow the scheme outlined in figure 3. In general, the complexity of the information network required to construct the decoupling and coupling blocks increase exponentially with p. This may translate in high costs of implementation, more so if the spatial regions, that index the elements of $\mathbf{f^L}$ and $\mathbf{r}^L$, are physically distant. More specifically, in (5) (decoupling block), the computation of each one of the $\beta_{n,k}$ requires complete knowledge of $\mathbf{r}^L$. Similarly, the computation of the decision variables in (6), for a specific region $f_i^{\mathbf{L}}$, requires the knowledge of all $\mathcal{P}_{n,k}(\beta_{n,k}(t))$.

An efficient structure can be achieved by taking advantage of the *hierarchical* nature of the Haar vectors $\{\mathbf{h}_{0,0},...,\mathbf{h}_{N,2^N}\}$. The following proposition gives the details on the implementation of the decoupling block.

Proposition 3.3 *The decoupling block can be implemented using:*

$$\beta_{n,k}(t)=\begin{cases}\gamma_{n+1,2k}-\gamma_{n+1,2k-1}\,for\ (n,k)\neq(0,0)\\ \gamma_{1,2}+\gamma_{1,1},\,for\ (n,k)=(0,0)\end{cases}$$

where $\gamma_{n,k}$ are obtained through the backward recursion:

$$\gamma_{n,k}(t)=\begin{cases}\gamma_{n+1,2k}+\gamma_{n+1,2k-1},\,for\ 1\leq n<N\\ r_k^L(t)\,,\ for\ n=N\end{cases}\tag{7}$$

From (7) it is clear that the flux of information flows upwards in a graph identical to the one in figure 7. Similarly, the coupling block (6) can be implemented in such a way that information flows downwards the same graph as described by the following proposition:

Proposition 3.4 *The coupling block (equation (6)) can be implemented as follows:*

$$f_k^{\mathbf{L}}=\eta_{N,k}$$

where $\eta_{N,k}$ is obtained through the forward recursion:

$$\eta_{n,k}=\begin{cases}(-1)^k\,\mathcal{P}_{0,k}(\beta_{0,k}(t))+\mathcal{P}_{0,0}(\beta_{0,0}(t))\\ (-1)^k\,\mathcal{P}_{n,k}(\beta_{n,k}(t))+\eta_{n-1,\lceil k/2\rceil for\ N>n>0}\end{cases}$$

Notice that these equations reveal the advantage of having such hierarchical structure. By inspection, we notice that if the overall system operates as:

$$\mathcal{L}:\mathbb{R}^p\longrightarrow\mathbb{R}^p$$

then each node receives information and generates decision variables through channels of dimension 1. Every node sends information *up* the structure which is the fusion of the measurements of the two nodes bellow. There is loss of information on this operation, but the eigenstructure of $\mathcal{L}$ is such that it does not impact the overall performance of the decision system.

3.4 On issues of complexity

One might think that it is a consequence of decoupling that the resulting sub-systems are less *complex*. In spite of that, such conclusion relies on the definition of system complexity.

In (Bamieh, 1998), it is shown that decoupled systems may be approximately *localized* in space. Such result implies that we can partition the space and identify its associated subsystems. This may be interpreted as complexity reduction provided that our measure of complexity is the number of space partitions associated with a given system. Another measure of complexity is the order of a finite dimensional system. As it is shown in (Martins, 2001), spatial decoupling of linear finite and time-invariant systems may lead to order partitioning, i.e., a system of order Mp being decoupled in p systems of order M.

4 DECISION SYSTEM DESIGN

In this section, we discuss the design of linear resource allocation decision systems. At this point, we assume that the environment is modelled as described in section 2. For notational convenience, we will designate the interconnected setup of figure 2 as $\mathcal{L}_{sc}$ and the vector concatenation of the supplies and resources as $\mathbf{f}^{sc}$ and $\mathbf{r}^{sc}$ respectively. We will restrict our attention to large-scale, linear systems $\mathcal{L}_{sc}$. In order to work with such systems, we also assume that $\mathcal{L}_{sc}$ has a complete set of spatial eigenvectors so that it can be decoupled into subsystems $\mathcal{L}_{sc_i}$.

4.1 Decomposable objective functions

According to the problem statement presented in section 2, the decision policy is the argument of the minimization of an objective function J. In section 3, we described how a large-scale system can be *decoupled*. It is desirable that decoupling can be extended to the design process.

Definition 4.1 *We call J decomposable, provided that there exist functions J_i and sets P_i satisfying:*

$$\min_{\mathcal{P}\in P}J(\mathbf{f}^c,\mathcal{P}(\mathbf{r}^{sc}))=\sum_{i=1}^{p}\min_{\mathcal{P}_i\in P_i}J_i(\alpha_i,\mathcal{P}_i(\beta_i))\tag{8}$$

where

$$\begin{aligned}\sum\beta_i(t)\,\mathbf{v}_i&=\mathbf{r}^{sc}\\ \sum\alpha_i(t)\,\mathbf{v}_i&=\mathbf{f}^{sc}\\ \sum\mathcal{P}_i(\beta_i(t))\,\mathbf{v}_i&=\mathcal{P}(\mathbf{r}^{sc})\end{aligned}\tag{9}$$

and $\{\mathbf{v}_1,...,\mathbf{v}_p\}$ is a complete set of spatial eigenvectors of $\mathcal{L}_{sc}$.

If the decomposition (8) exists, then the design of the overall decision system reduces to independently optimizing $\mathcal{P}_i$ for each of the subsystems $\mathcal{L}_{sc_i}:\alpha_i\mapsto\beta_i$.

One can easily construct meaningful functions satisfying (8) - (9). The following proposition suggests that quadratic objective functions can be tailored to be decomposable.

Proposition 4.1 *Consider the quadratic cost function:*

$$J\left(\mathbf{f}^c, \mathcal{P}\left(\mathbf{r}^{sc}\right)\right) = \int_0^T \left\|\mathcal{P}\left(\mathbf{r}^{sc}\right)\right\|_Q^2 + \rho \left\|\mathbf{f}^c\right\|_Q^2 + \left\|\mathbf{r}^{sc}\right\|_Q^2 dt$$

where

$$\begin{aligned} \|\mathbf{x}\|_Q^2 &= \langle \mathbf{x}, \mathbf{x}\rangle_Q \; for\, \mathbf{x} \in \mathbb{C}^p \\ \langle \mathbf{x}, \mathbf{y}\rangle_Q &= \mathbf{x}^T \mathbf{Q} \mathbf{y} \; for\, \mathbf{x}, \mathbf{y} \in \mathbb{C}^p \end{aligned}$$

and $\mathbf{Q}$ *is a symmetric positive semidefinite matrix. If* $\{\mathbf{v}_1, ..., \mathbf{v}_p\}$ *is a complete set of spatial eigenvectors of* $\mathcal{L}_{sc}$ *such that*

$$\left\langle \mathbf{v}_i, \mathbf{v}_j \right\rangle_Q = 0 \; for\; i \neq j$$

then J *is decomposable in the form (8).*

4.2 Linear Flux Constraints

In this subsection, we assume that $\mathcal{L}_{sc}$ can be decoupled in a way such that flow constraints can be isolated in one of the decoupled subsystems $\mathcal{L}_{sc_i}$. This simplifies the design process by restating the original paradigm as $p-1$ unconstrained optimization problems for the remaining subsystems. The following proposition summarizes the details and conditions under which this can be done.

Proposition 4.2 *Consider* $\mathcal{L}_{sc}$, *a complete set of spatial eigenvectors* $\{\mathbf{v}_1, ..., \mathbf{v}_p\}$ *and a decomposable objective function* J. *If the set* P *of allowable policies is such that there is a flux constraint that can be expressed as:*

$$\left\langle \mathbf{v}_m, \mathcal{P}\left(\mathbf{r}^{sc}\right)\right\rangle_Q = \zeta(t), \tag{10}$$

then the optimization of each of the J_i *in (8)-(9) is not constrained by (10), except for* J_m.

The example given in (2) falls in the above class provided that:

$$\begin{bmatrix} 1 \\ ... \\ 1 \end{bmatrix} \in \{\mathbf{v}_1, ..., \mathbf{v}_p\}$$

This proposition can also be cast geometrically, by requiring that the constraint is aligned with one of the spatial eigenvectors and orthogonal to the others.

5 EXAMPLE OF APPLICATION

In this example we do resource allocation for a linear system with input flow constraints. We consider a finite dimensional time-invariant model, so that the design process is heavily based on standard techniques of linear control theory. The problem statement for this example is the following:

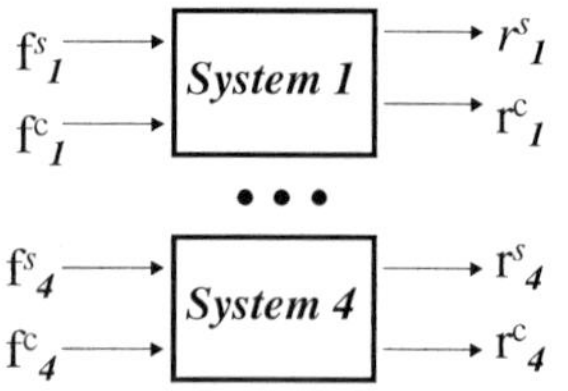

Figure 8: Schematic representation of the systems associated with 4 independent space partitions considered in the example of application

5.1 Problem statement

Consider the system as sketched in figure 8. All of the four systems are identically described by the following state space equations:

$$\begin{cases} \dot{\mathbf{x}}_i = \mathbf{A}\mathbf{x}_i + \mathbf{B}\begin{bmatrix} f_i^s \\ f_i^c \end{bmatrix} \\ \begin{bmatrix} r_i^s \\ r_i^c \end{bmatrix} = \mathbf{C}\mathbf{x}_i \end{cases}$$

where

$$\begin{aligned} \mathbf{A} &= \begin{bmatrix} \mathbf{A}_f & \mathbf{A}_{fe} \\ \mathbf{A}_{ef} & \mathbf{A}_e \end{bmatrix}, \mathbf{B} = \begin{bmatrix} 0 & 0 \\ 1 & 0 \\ 0 & 0 \\ 0 & 1 \end{bmatrix} \\ \mathbf{C} &= \begin{bmatrix} 1 & 0 & 0 & 0 \\ 0 & 0 & 1 & 0 \end{bmatrix} \end{aligned}$$

and the interaction dynamics is given by:

$$\begin{aligned} \mathbf{A}_f &= \mathbf{A}_e = \begin{bmatrix} -.01 & .03 \\ -.1 & 0 \end{bmatrix} \\ \mathbf{A}_{ef} &= \mathbf{A}_{fe} = \begin{bmatrix} -.1 & 0 \\ -.1 & 0 \end{bmatrix} \end{aligned}$$

Such fourth order systems should be interpreted as independent sectors that comprise two rival second order subsystems, labeled as friendly and enemy. The two state variables of each subsystem represent the amount of "primary resources", which is also the output, and a "secondary resource". As can be inferred from the equations, the following effects are modelled:

1. Primary resources natural decay
2. Primary resources consume secondary resources
3. Secondary resources boost up primary resources
4. Friendly's primary resources destroy enemy's primary and secondary resources and vice versa.

5. The decision variables are $f_i^s, i = 1,..,4$. They act as an external flux of secondary resources for the friendly subsystems in each sector. The same role is played by f_i^c over the enemy subsystems, and, as such, it is considered as an unknown disturbance.

Regarding the decision system design, the problem is stated as to design a controller with the following characteristics:

1. Satisfy the input flow constraint $\sum_{i=1}^{4} f_i^s = 0$. Only transferring resources among neighboring sectors is allowed. We assume the same constraint for the enemy $\sum_{i=1}^{4} f_i^c = 0$.
2. Minimize the following cost:

$$J = \sup_{\left|\vec{f}_i^c\right|^2 = 1} \sum_{i=1}^{3} \left|\vec{r}_i^s - \vec{r}_i^c\right|^2 + \sum_{i=1}^{3} \delta_i \left|\vec{f}_i^s\right|^2$$

where $\vec{f}_i^s$, $\vec{f}_i^c$ are the flux of secondary resources from sector i to i+1 for the friendly and enemy's systems, respectively, and δ_i is the distance between sectors. It should be noted that the functions $\vec{f}_i^s$ completely determine f^s and vice versa, provided that the input flow constraint is satisfied. By minimizing J, we choose the strategy that allows the friendly sub-systems to engage the enemy and at the same time account for transportation costs.

5.2 Controller design

The above is one of the simplest cases, where the decoupling vectors $\{\mathbf{v}_1, ..., \mathbf{v}_4\}$ can be chosen to be any linearly independent set. The right choice according to the specifications is:

$$\{\mathbf{v}_1, ..., \mathbf{v}_4\} = \begin{bmatrix} 1 & -1 & 0 & 0 \\ 1 & 1 & -1 & 0 \\ 1 & 0 & 1 & -1 \\ 1 & 0 & 0 & 1 \end{bmatrix}$$

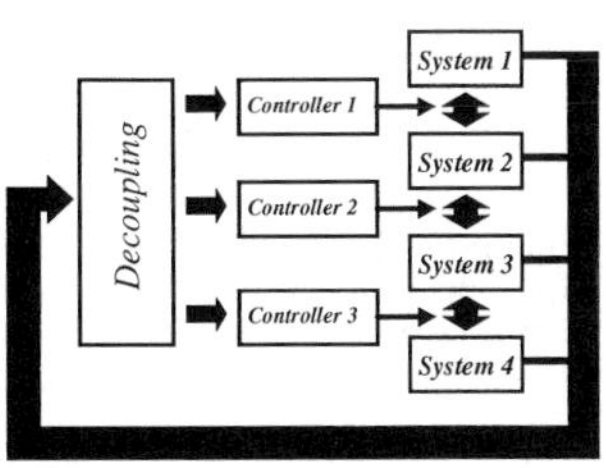

Figure 9: Structure of the decision system.

Each of the resulting four decoupled systems determine the behavior of the total system along their respective $\mathbf{v}_i$. The motivation behind this choice can be easily understood by viewing each $\mathbf{v}_i$ in the following way:

1. $\mathbf{v}_1$ is colinear with the flux constraint and is orthogonal to the remaining $\mathbf{v}_i$. This allow us to isolate the flow constraint so that controller design is unconstrained for the remaining decoupled systems.
2. The output of the controller for the decoupled system associated with $\mathbf{v}_2$ is the required flux of resources from sector 1 to 2. The same principle can be used to explain that $\mathbf{v}_i$ ($i > 1$) is associated with the flux of resources from sector i-1 to i.

Since the flux constraint is aligned with $\mathbf{v}_1$ and perpendicular to $\{\mathbf{v}_2, ..., \mathbf{v}_4\}$, we only need to design 3 controllers. Each controller is designed for a system of dimension 4 (instead of 16).

5.3 Controller structure and implementation

The structure of the final controller is the one shown in figure 9. It has the advantage of having a completely decentralized coupling block. The output of the controller i is the flux of resources $\vec{f}_i^s$ between neighboring systems i and i+1.

5.4 Simulation results

The results for a simulation are plotted in figures 10-12, where we decided to present time plots instead of frequency plots in order to illustrate resource transfers easily.

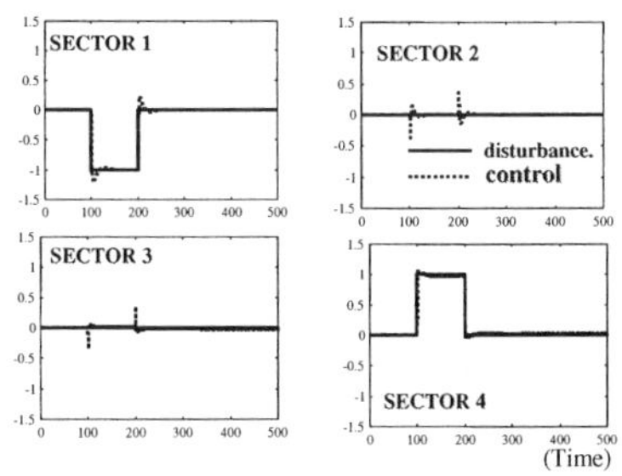

Figure 10: Control and disturbance plots.

We excited the system by means of the disturbance depicted in figure 10. The shape of the disturbance indicates the enemy's intent of moving resources from sector 1 to sector 4. As can be expected from the model symmetry, the friendly's allocation (control action - plotted in figure 10) tracks the enemy's action. The output (primary resources) is plotted for each sector in figure 11. Figure 12 shows the output

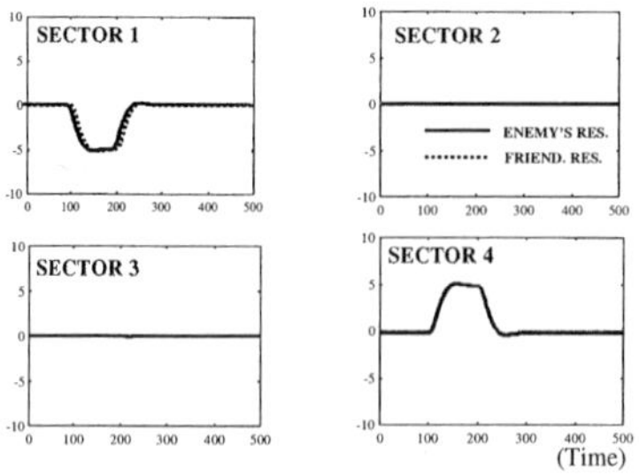

Figure 11: Output plots.

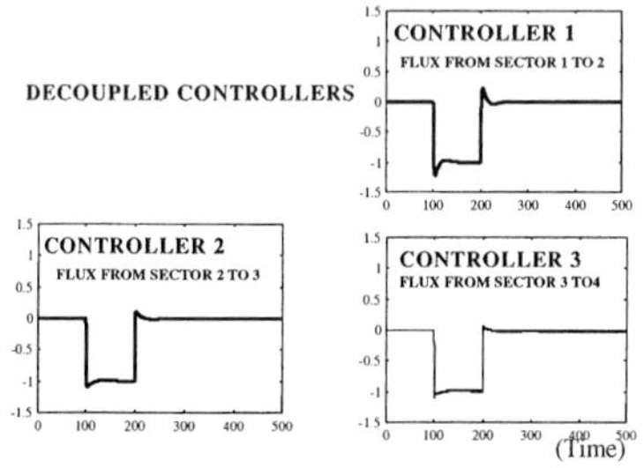

Figure 12: Outputs of the decoupled controllers.

of each of the 3 decoupled controllers. By inspecting this plot, one can recognize that the optimal strategy is to shift resources at once to match enemy's allocation. This transfer is done between neighboring sectors at the same time, so that sectors 2 and 3 do not accumulate resources. The slight difference among the plots for controllers 1 through 3 is a result of having assigned different distances between neighboring sectors. Sectors 1 and 2 are closer than sectors 3 and 4, so that controller 1 is allowed to be more aggressive.

ACKNOWLEDGEMENTS

This work was supported by DARPA grant 6890161. The first author is partially supported by the Portuguese Foundation for Science and Technology PRAXIS XXI/BD/19630/99. The authors would like to thank Prof. Eric Feron, at M.I.T., for his support during this project.

REFERENCES

Adams, M. and Guillemin, V.(1999). In *Measure Theory and Probability*. Birkhauser.

Bamieh, B., Paganini F., Dahleh M. (1999). Distributed Control of Spatially-Invariant Systems. Preprint

Martins N. C., Venkatesh S., Dahleh M. A. Controller Design and Implementation for Large-Scale Systems, a Block Decoupling Approach *Proceedings of the American Control Conference*

Ravuri M., Kao C., Megretski A. Hierarchical Optimization in the Presence of an Intelligent Adversary - an H-infinity Approach *39 th IEEE Conference on Decision and Control*

PART 1

Databases and Information Systems Integration

IODBCON: AN INTEGRATED OBJECT-ORIENTED DATABASE SYSTEM FOR INTEGRATING INFORMATION ABOUT ARCHITECTURE DESIGN AND CONSTRUCTION PROCESSES

Farhi Marir and Yau Jim Yip
School of Informatics and Multimedia Technology, North London University, Holloway Road, London, UK
Email: f.marir@unl.ac.uk, j.yip@unl.ac.uk

Keywords: Construction Object Database, Model-Based CAD System, CORBA, IFC, IODBCON, UML, and VRML

Abstract: This paper presents IODBCON (Integrated Object Database for Construction), an interactive system for integrating CAD and construction related applications to address the problems of design fragmentation and the gap that exists between construction and design processes. It provides a vehicle for storing architectural design information in an integrated construction object-oriented database that can be shared by a range of construction applications. The IODBCON model uses the object-oriented modelling approach to establish standard models for architectural design that comply with Industry Foundation Classes (IFC) for common interpretation of construction design objects and with CORBA (Common Object Request Broker Architecture) for distribution of the objects amongst the construction applications.

1. BACKGROUND

A great deal of work has been carried out in the area of information modelling to support the sharing of information across participants in a construction project (Bohms et al. 1994, Dubois et al. 1995, Björk, 1994 and Aouad et al. 1977). Currently, there exists no accepted way of sharing information between the different software applications used in a construction project. An architect may use a CAD package to produce a set of drawings. A quantity surveyor (QS) will then use these drawings to produce costing information. A construction planner will also use the drawings to produce a set of construction activities in the form of a network or Gantt chart. In some cases information is exchanged in electronic form. For example, QS may also use a CAD system to simplify take-off quantity from the architect's drawing. However, this type of data exchange takes place at a very low level (e.g. AutoCAD DXF files) with each participant having to reinterpret the data for his or her own purpose. This approach, although well established, does have a number of disadvantages. Information lag between participants, errors when re-entering data, difficulty in gathering an overall view of the project for management purposes, and difficulty in integrating software packages due to the lack of a common conceptual information model.

The integration of software in the construction industry has occurred mostly through the development of links between stand alone commercial packages. For instance, integrated planning/estimating and integrated planning/CAD systems have been developed by several researchers (Tah et al. 1991 and Howard 1991). Another form of integration has been achieved through product modelling undertaken in Scandinavia, France, USA, The Netherlands, and the UK (Bjork and Wix, 1991). Integration through the establishment of standards for data exchange (EDICON, AEC STEP Committee, Bjork and Wix, 1991; Brandon, 1993). Also a group of software companies and users have formed the Industry Alliance for Interoperability to define specifications for a set of Industry Foundation Classes (IFC) and to deliver them promptly to end users, incorporated into commercial products (IFC, 1997).

In the last few years, researchers and practitioners have started to develop interfaces between CAD systems and relational and object-oriented databases that support the design process (Kartan 1994, Alashawi 1996 and Gorti et al. 1996).

Most of the research projects mentioned above have developed a user interface in AutoCAD to capture building component data and then use different approaches to translate the CAD representations into an object building product

J. Filipe et al. (eds.), Enterprise Information Systems III, 51–58.

model. This product model has been used as an input to other computer-based applications.

However, several problems can be enumerated within most of these systems. Some of the systems are developed to be fully dependent on a specific CAD system and this limits the possibility for reuse and therefore requires the rewriting of most of the CAD functions of the system to suit a different display environment. Also, most of the systems keep translating drawing data from specific CAD databases into the object-oriented product model they provide. This process of generating the necessary input for other construction-related activities from AutoCAD is expensive and complicated, requiring several transformations and involving several computer languages (Ito 1991). Some of them are designed around the concept of the AutoCAD "blocks" that is defined for each type of design element, e.g. wall, door, column etc., and the user of the CAD system builds up the design using instances of these blocks. This approach faces problems when it comes to representing the relationships between design elements, such as the connection of one wall to another, or the appearance of a window in a wall. Also, to support data-exchange between different computer applications, most of the above systems are developed based on CAD standards like IGES, and DXF for graphical data. However, both of these standards impose restrictions on the data types and formats that they can exchange. This restriction is an obstacle to the integration process and encourages direct exchange of graphical data via customised one-to-one interfaces that requires tedious manual re-entry of data across diverse applications. Finally most of the existing integrated systems concentrate mainly on the problem of integrating applications via data sharing and none provides distribution of objects among the different applications.

This paper presents another approach for integrating information about architecture design and construction processes to addresses the design fragmentation problems and provide a vehicle for storing architectural design information in an integrated object-oriented database shared across a range of construction processes.

The content of the paper is organised as follows. The second section is devoted to the description of the features of the IODBCON system. The third and fourth sections present application sharing information stored in the integrated object database. The last section presents the conclusion.

2. IODBCON

The IODBCON model adopts a top down approach based on a hybrid information and object-oriented approach to establish the principles for integration. This integration is based on applications independent, object-oriented database and architecture for providing access to that database through a variety of common and proprietary application software packages. IT adopts a model-based approach to capture graphical and textual information about building components and directly storing them into an object-oriented database, rather than the complex and ill-structured CAD databases. This approach avoids the expensive process of translating drawing data from the CAD database into an object-oriented database. Moreover this approach is enhanced with the concept of separation of the design data from the specific CAD package used to manipulate it. A consequence of this is that new CAD products will be much easier to incorporate and also other non-CAD applications can have direct access to the design data from such a database. In addition, IODBCON models were designed to comply with the IFC (IFC, 1997) to facilitate data exchanges between construction-related applications and to allow common interpretation of the design objects amongst the applications in a consistent and interoperable manner. Concerning project data interchange, the IODBCON system does not only concentrate on the problem of integrating applications via data sharing but goes further into sharing and inter-working between objects distributed amongst applications by complying with CORBA standards (CORBA, 1995).

2.1 IODBCON Architecture Design Model

Modelling design information is the most debatable aspect of designing the product model. It involves dealing with graphical and non-graphical data and many complex issues such as representing form, function, topology, appearance and many other aspects. Major efforts have been undertaken by researchers in the STEP community and outside it in order to define a generic model that can describe a building (Pentilla, 1989, Svensson et al. 1997).

None of these models has a universal acceptance. This is due to the fact that a data model must be readily accessible to all construction-related applications and users. It must also be compatible with systems across AEC and other industries (Froese et al. 1994). As a result, the Industry Alliance for Interoperability has defined specifications for a set of Industry Foundation

Classes (IFC, 1997) as an industry standard object model for construction integrated systems. The aim of the IODBCON system is not to recommend another design model but to derive classes from the IFC Generic classes and enhance them with knowledge about the detailed design stage that can be shared with other applications, such as cost and time planning. The detailed design model is a description of the design components and their specifications with very limited topological properties incorporated. The model (subset shown in Figure 1) offers the representation of several structural members such as foundation, slab, columns, beams, walls, roof, and non-structural members, such as windows and doors.

2.2 The Architecture of the IODBCON System

The IODBCON Architecture adopts the Client/Server approach. The server is composed of the IODBCON objects. Two kinds of objects are provided. Objects that reflect the database schema of the IODBCON architectural design model where instances of the design component are stored and a set of abstract design classes, which provide abstractions that the design model classes can use to render themselves in a given display environment.

2.2.1 The IODBCON Distributed Design Objects

AEC CAD systems date back to the early 1960's (Port 1989). However, after many years of research and development, these systems are still considered as drafting rather than design packages. This is also the case in the construction industry, where most available AEC CAD systems are used as drafting tools. Regular CAD drawings are usually simple graphic representations of projects. They are collections of points, lines, and other primitives that visually portray project components and have no meaningful information associated with them. These drawings, however, have the advantage of offering maximum drawing flexibility. Primitives can be easily copied, deleted, stretched, or edited in a variety of ways. Taking the advantage of drawing flexibility, the IODBCON adds meaningful information by grouping these drawing primitives into objects with architectural design information associated to them. The objects are encapsulations of a set of operations, which are invoked externally from custom applications using the IODBCON model. They allow the existence of two different views of the drawing. The graphic view, which is the usual three-dimensional CAD drawing, and the textual view which is the collection of all design information. These objects required by the detailed design stage revolve mostly about concepts, such as components and component specifications. The component specifications within a design model play a major role in defining design information and ultimately in generating cost and time data. Also, as objects, design components are handled as single entities, making them direct representations of the elements being symbolised. Besides making the association of design information possible, objects offer the potential for speeding up the design process, particularly in the later stages, since they can be made readily available to the user by the suppliers of building products, or by third party software suppliers.

At present, the data model of object-oriented systems are dictated by their underlying languages, databases, or programming environments. However, several major object-oriented data model standards currently are being developed. These standards provide all the characteristics needed to support integrated systems, and most commercial object-oriented databases are likely to adopt these standards as their fundamental data models. The IODBCON adopts ODMG (Object Data Management Group) and CORBA standards, to allow database portability and also inter-working between object-oriented software components within networked computing environments.

2.2.2 The IODBCON Abstract Design Class

The IODBCON model is designed to be generic and abstract enough to allow separation between the design model and the specific implementations of commercial CAD tools. For this it uses the Abstract Factory Design Pattern which provides an interface for creating families of related objects without specifying their concrete classes (Gamma et al. 1994). The IODBCON system defines three main classes. An Abstract ShapeFactory class, which declares the interface for creating each basic type of design element. An Abstract Design Class (IfcBuildingElement) which represents an abstraction for each kind of architectural design element and provides abstractions that the IODBCON design model classes can use to draw and render themselves in any CAD environment. A set of Concrete Subclasses of the ShapeFactory class, which implement the design elements for a specific CAD or graphical display environment. These classes can be used by the model classes to 'draw' themselves without knowing which application is actually doing the drawing. In IODBCON application the AutoCAD_Drawer and VRML_Drawer are the concrete classes designed specifically for the AutoCAD and VRML applications respectively, and finally a set of client classes that encapsulate the commands the users want to issue. Instances of these classes can then be used to implement command functionality in an environment independent manner.

The ShapeFactory's interface has an operation that returns a new design object for each Abstract Design Class of the design component. The client class (from the user application) uses the IfcBuildingElement Abstract Design Class, which calls operations to obtain instances of a design element and draw themselves without being aware of the Concrete Classes they are using. In other words, the client class has to commit to an interface defined by the Abstract Design Class, not to a particular Concrete Class.

In practice, all classes in the IODBCON design model inherit from the base class *IFCBuildingElement* that defines a common interface. This interface includes a *draw()* operation which is redefined in subclasses to allow instances of the design classes to draw themselves in a given display environment. The *draw()* operation passes a pointer to the ShapeFactory (or Drawer) object which encapsulates a set of simple 3D drawing operations as virtual member functions. These functions are implemented in the ShapeFactory concrete subclasses *i.e. AutoCAD_Drawer* and *VRML_Drawer*, to display the drawing in specific environments. As a result of this modelling approach the design of building components stay independent of the prevailing CAD and other display environment and the AutoCAD and the VRML applications discussed below become graphical front ends for the instances of the IODBCON architectural design model.

3. THE AUTOCAD APPLICATION

The IODBCON Application is an AutoCAD Application Development System (ADS) prototype, which is loaded by a user of an AutoCAD session. It allows the user to create and manipulate architectural components of a building. The created components are stored as instances of classes of the IODBCON design model in the IODBCON object database through which they are made available to other AEC computer-aided applications in computer-interpretable and standard form.

The application provides a simple environment for designing building components. The design primitives are walls, windows, doors, columns, beams, foundations etc. As design objects are created through the AutoCAD interface, corresponding objects are created in the object-database. The information that is used to draw these objects on the AutoCAD screen via an instance of the *Drawer* class comes directly from the instances in the database. This ensures that the screen reflects the design database. This also means that changes in a design can be immediately propagated to other areas of the project database. For instance, if an on-line project-planning package were accessing the database then it would be possible to change a part of the design and immediately see the impact these changes would have on the project schedule. The prototype provides the following functionality: creation and manipulation of foundations, walls, windows, doors, floors, stairs and roofs, creation of Space Diagrams and expansion into building elements, creation of specifications and specification sets for application to a design, and texture mapping of building elements based on component specifications and finishes

The prototype is being developed using Microsoft Visual C++ v4.0 on the PC under Microsoft Windows NT. The database is implemented using the ObjectStore OODBMS in conjunction with the Rationale Rose case Tool. It is designed on top of AutoCAD 13 which provides tools for manipulating low level drafting primitives and for producing realistic 3D views of designs by the use of hidden line removal and shading. It provides two main programming environments for implementing such applications. AutoLISP, which is an interpreted language accessible from the AutoCAD, interface itself, and AutoCAD Developers System (ADS) which is a C language library that provides an Application Program Interface (API) for manipulating AutoCAD and its internal database from a C or C++ program. ADS applications are loaded by issuing a command from the AutoCAD interface. As the IODBCON system uses the ObjectStore object database, which provides a persistent storage mechanism for C++ objects, it was more appropriate to use the ADS C library to build a demonstration application.

3.1 User Interface

A command driven model of interaction was chosen for the application. This is the standard way of implementing an AutoCAD application, with extra sets of menus being added to the standard AutoCAD menu hierarchy to invoke the new commands. These menus as shown in Figure 2 provide commands to create and manipulate building elements such as walls, windows, foundations etc. Levels have been defined for the design components so they can be drawn at the locations specified by the user. The user has the option to draw in 2D or 3D. Editing facilities have also been provided. For instance the user can move junctions, delete and copy objects and any changes made to the design is reflected in the IODBCON object database.

When the application is started it opens the ObjectStore database for storing the design data. As various commands are called to add design elements, each command invokes a function in the application which starts a transaction on the database, prompts the user for parameters and positioning of the design element and creates an instance of the element in the database. The display is then updated to reflect this addition, and the transaction is committed to the database. The graphical representations of the building elements are displayed in the AutoCAD drawing, with the user still having access to all the usual AutoCAD commands for changing the viewpoint, zooming, performing hidden line removal etc. Thus the user creates a design using design elements instead of creating a drawing using low level drawing primitives such as lines and 3D-faces. The advantage of this approach is that the application, and indeed the database objects themselves, can contain knowledge about how buildings are designed and can thus aid the designer during the design process. An example of this kind of knowledge built into the IODBCON database is that a column, which is supporting a beam, will be moved automatically if we stretch the beam. This knowledge is actually built into the database itself (in the implementations of the operations on beams) and so does not have to be programmed directly into any CAD applications that manipulate beams.

When the user leaves the application, the database is closed and the current drawing is discarded. There is no need to save the drawing as a standard AutoCAD file, because the next time the application is started it will recreate the drawing from the IODBCON object database.

3.2 The Concrete Design Class: The AutoCAD_Drawer

The part of the application that is responsible for displaying the design information through the Abstract ShapeFactory (or Drawer) class makes use of the concept of a AutoCAD_Drawer. An Auto*CAD_Drawer* is an application level class. It is responsible for displaying a part of the database design via an instance of the Abstract Design Class for a given CAD package. It may perform its task by itself, or delegate it to one or more sub-drawers. In the case of the AutoCAD building design application the Auto*CAD_Drawer* class is at the root of the hierarchy with classes such as *Wall_CADDrawer*, *Door_CADDRawer* being further down. Each of these *concrete design classes* contains a reference to the part of the database for which it is responsible for presenting, and updates the CAD representation when this information changes. A *concrete design class* may use more than one drawing primitive by performing multiple calls to the Auto*CAD_Drawer* operations. The AutoCAD_Drawer maintains the set of IDs returned by these functions so that it may update the associated drawing primitives.

3.3 Accessing and Populating the IODBCON Object Database

From the IODBCON architecture design model, a set of C++ classes defining design components e.g. slab, wall, door and window, are generated. The code that implements the operations defined on these design classes is then compiled into a library.

Most of the previous research on design-construction integration uses CAD database facilities, such as AutoCAD Block structures to store design information and also provide expensive and specialised interfaces to decode and transfer this information into an object-oriented database. The same process is repeated when the user performs any manipulation on the drawing. The difficulty with block structure is more apparent when performing an operation that involves more than one building element. For instance, to model the intersections between building elements, it is unavoidably necessary to explode the blocks, perform the editing task and then use the block facility once again. For complex projects, such as buildings, the use of blocks is not appropriate as the layout, orientation, shape, geometry, etc. of a building is not well defined. The IODBCON system avoids these complex and expensive interfaces. It uses exclusively the object-oriented database directly to store design information and to display the associated drawing in a CAD environment. To achieve this the IODBCON provides an alternative to block structure is used. An ID protocol is used to refer to objects previously created in the CAD environment. Each operation, which creates or updates a drawing entity, takes an ID string as a parameter. If this string is empty the operation creates a new drawing entity and returns a unique ID string for that entity. The ID string may then be used as a parameter to the same operation in which case the previously created entity is updated.

4. THE VRML APPLICATION

This application is a web-based application using VRML (Virtual Reality Modelling Language). It is used as a means of remotely interrogating information stored within the integrated database and allowing the user to visualise and manipulate the design components in a 3D environment. VRML is a developing standard for describing interactive three-dimensional scenes across the Internet. Based on the design information stored in the IODBCON object database, the VRML_Drawer generates a program for the VRML environment. The generated programme includes nodes such as WWW anchor (which allows links to web pages), material, rotation, and cube and is used by the VRML browser to create a 3D environment that can have links to web pages containing information about the design components. The VRML standard allows links between different worlds to be established on the web. Links are anchored to specific objects, such as walls, beams, etc. By clicking on an anchored object, you request information from other worlds using a URL (Universal Resource Locator) that specifies the address of a file on the web. Worlds loaded from the Internet are delivered by the web server, which is running on the remote host at the remote Internet site. In our case, the URL specifies a CGI script, which is a C++ program to run on the remote host under the control of the web server. The CGI program returns information about objects being queried in the VRML browser.

In IODBCON, VRML is not only used as a visualisation tool, but as a user interface as well. For instance, the user could interact with a 3D column in VRML rather than a column in a traditional database environment. This will allow the construction practitioners better access to information, which will motivate them to use integrated databases. Figure 3 shows a screen shot taken from the IODBCON VRML application of a house and its related schedule from a VRML representation generated by the IODBCON database. The user can navigate inside the building clicking on design objects and retrieving information about their properties, which include geometric, cost and time data.

5. CONCLUSION

The IODBCON research described in this paper attempts to overcome the limitations of the previous research development in the area of design-construction integration. This is by using a model-based approach whose emphasis is on capturing graphical and textual information about building components and directly storing them into an object oriented database rather than the complex and ill-structured CAD database. This approach will avoid the expensive process of translating drawing data from the CAD database into the object-oriented database. Moreover, this approach allows the separation of the design data from the specific CAD package that is used to manipulate it. A consequence of this is that new CAD products will be much easier to incorporate and also other none CAD applications can have direct access to the design data from such a database. In addition, the IODBCON model classes compliance with the IFC and OMG will facilitate data exchanges between construction-related applications and allow common interpretation of the design objects amongst the applications in a consistent and interoperable manner.

REFERENCES

Alshawi M., 1996, 'SPACE: integrated environment'. *Internal Paper*, University of Salford.

Aouad, G et al. 1997, 'Developing a conceptual model for an integrated database', *Proceedings of intelligent information systems, Bahamas, December, pp 316-320.*

Bjork B-C. and Wix J., 1991, 'An introduction to STEP'. *VTT and Wix Mclelland* Ltd. 1991.

Bohms M., Tolman, F. and Storer G. 1994,' ATLAS, a STEP Towards Computer Integrated Large Scale Engineering', Revue international de CFAO, Vol. 9, No. 3, 325-337.

Booch G., 1994, 'Object-Oriented Analysis and Design with Applications', 2nd ed. Addison-Wesley.

Carrera G. and Y. Kalay (eds.) 1994, 'Knowledge-Based Computer-Aided Architectural Design', Butterworths-Heinemann Press, N.Y.

Cattel R.G.G. ,1991,'Object Data Management: Object-Oriented Extended Relational Database Systems', Addison-Wesley Reading, MA.

Cooper G.S. 1995, 'Object-Oriented Databases from an Information Technology Viewpoint: Knocking Down Some Walls, in Object Technology and its Application in Engineering *Conf. on Object Technology and its Application in Engineering, Glasgow, DRAL (1995*).

CORBA 1995, 'The: Common Object Request Broker: Architecture and specification'. Revision 2.0.

Dubois, A.M., et al. 1995, 'Conceptual Modelling Approaches in the COMBINE Project', presented in the COMBINE final meeting, Dublin. http://erg.ucd.ie/combine/papers.html

Gamma, E. et al., 1994, 'Elements of Reusable Object-Oriented Software'.

Gorti, S. et al. 1996, 'From Symbol to Form: A Framework for Conceptual Design', Journal of CAD, Vol. 28, No. 11, 1996.

Froese T. and Paulson B. 1994, 'OPIS: An object model-based project information system'. Microcomputers in Civil Engineering, 9, pp 13-28.

Howard H.C. 1991, 'Linking design data with knowledge-based construction systems'. *CIFE Spring Symposium.*

IFC (Industry Foundation Classes). 1997, release 1.0,Vol 1-4.

Ito K. 1991, 'Design and construction integration using object oriented project model with multiple views'. *In Proceedings of the Computer-Integrated Design and Construction Symposium, Construction Congress II*, Cambridge, MA.

Logcher R.D. and Sriram D., 1990, ' CAE techniques for distribution design'. CIB90, March, *University of Technology Sydney.*

OMG 1995, ' The Common Object Request Broker: Architecture and Specification', OMG. http://www.omg.org/corbask.htm

Penttila H.,1989, '.A Scenario for The Development and Implementation of A Building Produce Model Standard'. *CIFE(Center for Integrated Facility Engineering-Stanford University) Symposium Proceedings.*

Port S. 1989, 'The management of CAD for construction'. *BSP Professionals.*

Rumbaugh J., Blaha M., Premerlani W., Eddy F. and Lorensen, W., 1991, ' Object-Oriented Modelling and Design'. Englewood Cliffs, New Jersey: Prentice-Hall.

Svensson K. and Aouad G., 1997, 'Developing standardised architectural building product models for spaces and space enclosures'. Automation in Construction Journal.

Tah J., Thorpe A.and McCaffer A.1991, 'Decision making within large computer based construction management systems'. *SERC Report GR/E76957/E.*

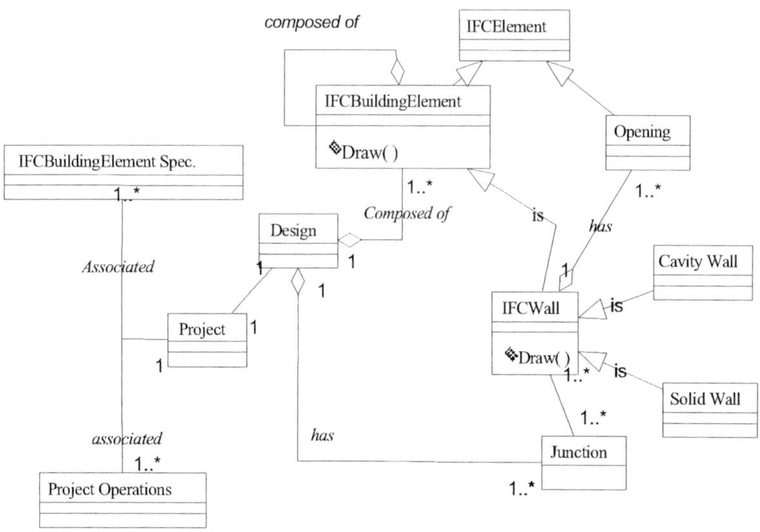

Figure 1: A subset of the IODBCon Object Model

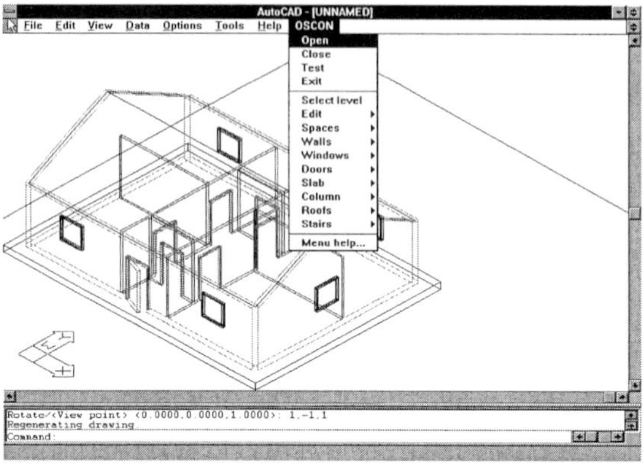

Figure 2: Accessing the IODBCon Object Database through AUTCAD13

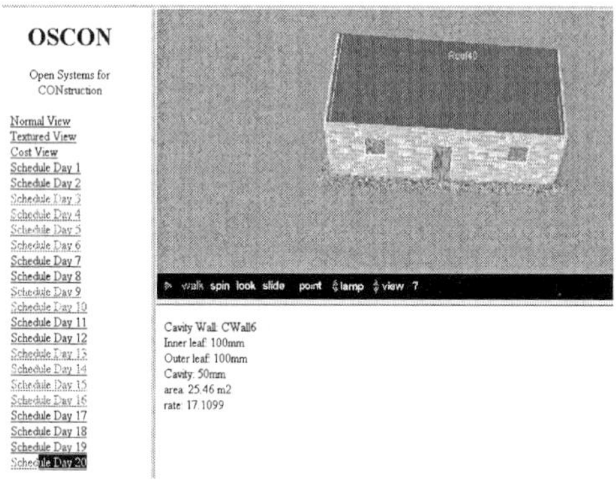

Figure 3: Accessing the IODBCon object Database through the Web

OBJECT EVOLUTION MECHANISMS IN OBJECT DATABASES:
Requirements, Optional Features And Comparison

Slimane Hammoudi
Ecole Supérieure d'Electronique de l'Ouest
4, Rue Merlet de la Boulaye , BP 926
49009 Angers, France
e-mail: slimane.hammoudi@eseo.fr

Keywords: object-oriented database systems - object evolution - object migration - rôle-oriented modeling

Abstract: Nowadays, most Object Oriented Database Systems (OODBs) display serious shortcoming in their ability to model the evolving and multifaceted nature of common real world entities. While researcher in knowledge representation systems have been aware of this problem for some time, database systems represent an environment in which this problem is particularly severe. OODBs store objects over longer periods, during which the represented entities evolve. The intimate and permanent binding of an object to a single type (class) inhibits the tracking of real-world entities over time. In recent years, various mechanisms for supporting many-faceted and evolving objects in the context of OO data models have been proposed in the literature. This paper examines in a first part the semantics associated with object evolution and explores the implications of these semantics on object oriented concepts. In a second part, we discusses features regarding the functionality's of various object evolution mechanisms proposed in the literature in the context of OODBs and finally compares four representatives and more recent works in this area.

1. INTRODUCTION

Over the last two decade, the need for data modeling features capable of capturing the evolving and multifaceted nature of real world entities has been pointed out by many researchers and from different areas: Knowledge Representation Systems (Bobrow et al. 1977), Programming Language (Carré 1989; Ferber 1989) and more recently Object Oriented Database Systems (OODBs) (Atkinson et al. 1989; Bertino et al. 1998; Fishman et al. 1987; Gottlob et al. 1996; Papazoglou et al. 1996; Pernici 1990; Richardson et al. 1991; Stein et al. 1990).

The most commonly and obvious example of this kind of multifaceted and evolving entity is a person. During his life, a given person may become a student. After graduation, that person ceases to be a student, and becomes an alumnus. In the meantime, he may also be an employee, a department manager, a club member, etc. Throughout his life, a person gains and loses many roles. It is important to note that many kinds of entities other than persons have roles that change over time; so do office documents, object in CAD applications, products in production lines etc. While researcher in knowledge representation systems have been aware of this problem for some time, database systems represent an environment in which this problem is particularly severe (Zdonik 1990). Databases are concerned with data that will survive for a very long time. They store objects over longer periods, during which the represented entities evolve.

Nowadays, most OODBs display serious shortcoming in their ability to model the evolving and multifaceted nature of common real world entities. The intimate and permanent binding of an object to a single type (class) inhibits the tracking of real-world entities over time. This represents more than an inconvenience; in fact, it is a critical problem, since one is forced to model entities that evolve dynamically with objects that cannot. If one simulates such entities with a collection of individual objects, then there is no longer a direct correspondence between conceptual entities and objects. Currently various mechanism for supporting many-faceted and evolving objects in the context of OO data models exist in the literature. A consensus, however, on exactly what functionality these mechanisms should support and, in particular, how they could be implemented in OODBs, has not been reached so far. Therefore, the goals of this paper are to:

J. Filipe et al. (eds.), Enterprise Information Systems III, 59–67.

- Examine the semantics associated with object evolution and explore the implications of these semantics on object oriented concepts such as inheritance, object identity and message processing.
- Provide a catalogue of features[1] regarding to various object evolution mechanisms proposed in the literature in the context of OODBs.
- Analyze and compare four representative and recent approaches taking into account the features that have been identified.

The paper is organized as follows. The next section presents an example, which is used throughout this paper, examines some of the semantics associated with object evolution and explores the implications of these semantics on OODBs. In section 3, we will present the features that future OODBs should support to manage evolving objects. Section 4 give an overview of several object evolution mechanisms that have been proposed for object-oriented database systems, and compare four more recent works in this area. Section 5 concludes the paper.

2. SEMANTICS, PROBLEMS AND ISSUES OF AMBIGUITY

Figure 1 shows a class hierarchy that models in a very simplified manner people in a university. Classes are depicted by rectangles and subclass relationships by solid arrows pointing from the subclass to the superclass. For simplicity, only instance variables of classes are depicted; instance methods are not shown. The class hierarchy expresses that students and staffs are persons. The class Person defines two instance variables *name* and *phoneNo* (private phone of a person). These are inherited by the subclass Student, which defines the two additional instance variables *level* and *phoneNo.* The class Staff allows to group three types of university employers distinguishing them by the value of their attribute *profession.* The technicians (profession:=TE), the teachers assistants (profession:= TA) and the professors (profession:=PR). From the class Staff, the class Professor is defined explicitly with the attributes *skills* and *responsibilities.* Finally, the class Salaried-student allows to represent students that are also teaching-assistants at the university. We suppose here that some students (eg. Good graduate student) may occupy also the position of teaching-assistant, thus playing the two roles. Note that in this example, a given salaried-student has three phone number, a personnel one defined in a class Person, and two others in Student and Staff roles respectively.

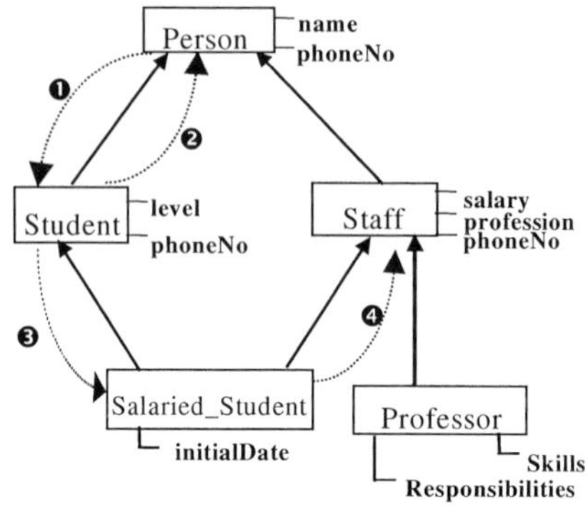

Figure 1: A class Hierarchy

2.1 Semantics of Object Evolution

To describe all possible cases for the evolution of an object in a hierarchy of classes, we distinguish two scenarios:

- Evolution of an object from a class A to another class B located in the same inheritance path (IS-A related classes)
- Evolution of an object from a class A to another class B not related by an inheritance path (Independent classes)

2.1.1 Evolution Through IS-A Related Classes

In this first scenario, basically an object may evolve from a given class A to a class B more specialized or more general. By taking into account a multiple inheritance situation four cases are distinguished here for a possible object evolution in a classes hierarchy (cf. figure1):

- During his life a given person X becomes a student and thus acquires a new representation in the class Student while retaining its representation in the class Person. This situation corresponds to an evolution from a Person class to a Student class.
- During his life a given person X finishes his studies and thus looses its representation in the class Student, while retaining its representation in the class Person. Here there is an evolution from a Student class to a Person class.

[1]We will distinguish the mandatory features from the optional features.

- In a multiple inheritance situation, a given graduate student X doing his PhD may apply to teaching-assistant position and gets it. In this case, the student X will be represented in the class Salaried-Student while playing the two roles Student and Staff (as a teaching assistant).The student X has evolved from a Student class to a Salaried-student class. Note that moreover the role Staff acquired by a student, all the superclasses of Staff are new roles for a student X.
- In a multiple inheritance situation, a given salaried-student X finishes his Ph.D and then looses his representation in the class Student and subsequently in the class Salaried-student. He retains its representation in the class Staff (as a teaching assistant) while loosing all the roles defined by the superclasses of the Student class. This situation will be considered as an evolution from the class Salaried-student to the class Staff[2].

In general, in the case where it is necessary that an object evolve to two or more direct superclasses, two solutions are possible: create a subclass of these superclasses and bind the object to this common subclass, or bind the object directly to each superclass using an appropriate mechanism. Depending on the application to represent, the administrator may choose one of these two solutions.

2.1.2 Evolution Through Independent Classes

In the second scenario, an object may evolve from a given class A to another class B such as A and B are independent. Here we suppose that this evolution is semantically meaningful and tolerated by the administrator of the application. We will comment more on this issue in the next section. Two cases may be considered here. A non-exclusive evolution in which an object evolves from the class A to the class B without loosing its representation (role) in the class A. An exclusive evolution in which the object looses its role in the class A and acquires a new role in the class B. To illustrate these two cases we consider the example in figure 1 without the class Salaried-Student defined through multiple inheritance. When considering the evolution of a given student from a class Student to a class Staff, the two cases could happen whether the university rules accepts or not that a student may occupy a teacher-assistant position. With an exclusive evolution a given student looses its representation in the class Student (he finishes the graduation), and acquires a new representation (role) in a class Staff. With a non-exclusive evolution a given student acquires a new role in a class Staff (teaching-assistant) while continuing to be student.

2 Note that due to the meaning of the common subclass, never an object evolve to all the superclasses at once

2.2 Problems and Issues of Ambiguity

As we have already mentioned in the introduction, representing and maintaining *evolving objects* using OODBs class hierarchies that requires an object to be classified into a single class is a tedious task. Entities need to be reclassified whenever they evolve. The problem is even more cumbersome if an entity can take several roles independently. Having described the semantics under which meaningful object evolution can occur, this section explores the implications of these semantics on future OODBs aiming to support the evolving and multifaceted nature of real world entities.

2.2.1 The Object Identity Problem

The support for object identity (Abiteboul et al. 1989; Ling et al. 1995) is a key feature of most object-oriented database systems. It provides a means to distinguish among objects, even those with similar attribute values. Object identity has a profound impact on the means by which objects are accessed, providing a flexibility not found in relational database systems. The OIDs are system generated, logical and immutable. An object's OID is durable in the sense that it is independent of changes to attributes values of the objects. From the possible representation for OID in object oriented systems (Ling et al. 1995), two only conform to the spirit of the original proposals for using OIDs and that offers reasonable representation (Papazoglou et al. 1996). These are:

- *untyped surrogates* and *typed surrogates.*

In the presence of object evolution, using a classical mechanism of object instantiation[3] in OOS, the two representations may compromise the desirable OID properties of immutability and uniqueness. Using a typed OIDs, an object may adopt another OID when it realizes an exclusive evolution, thus violating the immutability property of OID. Further, as a consequence of object evolution, an object can be an instance of multiple classes in the hierarchy, possibly adopting multiple OIDs either using typed or untyped representation for OID. This violates the uniqueness property of OID.

[3] An object is an instance of a unique class in the system

2.2.2 The Ambiguous Message Interpretation.

Under the classical OO approach to message processing, if a message is dispatched to an object of a class X, the definition for class X is searched to see if there is a method defined for X that matches the signature of the message. If found, the method is executed. Otherwise, a search up the class hierarchy is initiated until either a method is found or the search returns a failure. The underlying assumption here is that the class associated with the object is the most specific class. This assumption may not be true in the presence of object evolution since a real world object may be an instance of multiple classes, and there may be a more specific instance of the object which has to be considered to process the message correctly. Furthermore, as pointed out in previous works (Abiteboul et al. 1989; Ling et al. 1995; Papazoglou et al. 1996), selecting one subrole from several possible ones often gives undesired semantics.

2.2.3 Authorization Constraints for Object Evolution

Two cases may be distinguished here. First if we think how objects evolve in the real world, we notice clearly that some transition cannot occur. For example, it is not possible to evolve an object from a class Person (or one of its subclasses) to a class Plants (or one of its subclasses). Secondly, in the same hierarchy of roles while some evolution could appear more natural (e.g. from a Student role to the Teaching Assistant role) they may be tolerated or not depending from the constraints of the application. For example the same example of figure1 may represent people in two different universities where the constraints for acquiring a Teaching-assistant position are different. One university tolerates that some students (e.g. good graduate student) apply to the teaching-assistant position, while the other university tolerates only persons that have completely finished their graduate studies for applying to a teaching-assistant position. In one case, a given graduate student may play two roles (Student and Teaching-Assistant), while in other case one role at once (Student or Teaching-Assistant). We argue that a system should offers mechanisms to specify constraints for controlling evolution. An administrator defines the constraints as a part of an application schema, and they are automatically taken in account by the system.

3. REQUIREMENTS AND OPTIONAL FEATURES

Having explored some problems regarding evolving objects in OO systems, we discuss now characteristics of mechanisms for supporting evolving objects in the context of OODBs . Various proposals to support the evolving and multifaceted nature of real world entities in the context of OODBs exist. However, it is important to agree now on the functionality's that should be offered. As a first step towards this goal, this paper provides a catalogue of criteria regarding the functionality's of various role mechanisms in OODBs literature. The requirement definition can serve as a checklist for assessing whether a given proposal meets the requirements. Note that in this section we are strictly constrained on discussing what an object evolution mechanism for OODBs should accomplish. Issues dealing with the how (i.e. possible implementations of object evolution mechanisms in OODBs), are not considered in this paper.

3.1 Mandatory features: the requirements

Analyzing the dynamic nature of entities and their ability to play various roles, and in accordance to various object evolution mechanisms proposed in the literature, object evolution mechanisms for OODBs are expected to support:

- PRESERVING OBJECT IDENTITY AND ENCAPSULATION

An OODBs that aim to support object evolution should first of all preserve the useful features of an OODBs(Bertino et al. 1998). Thus an object evolution mechanism should assure the two following features:

unchangeable identity, objects retain their identity during their life no matter which evolution are operated and independently of the point of view through they are observed.

encapsulation, the process of acquisitions of roles for an existing object should not have direct access to its private data.

To preserve the OIDs properties while supporting object evolution and multiple roles representation, all the proposals extend the earliest hypotheses of object creation in object oriented systems:

"Each Object is associated with a single class" (Gottlob et al. 1996; Stefik et al. 1986).

All the proposals extend these hypotheses by making a clear distinction between an object and its potentials representations. A general idea is that an object has a unique identity and a set of roles that it acquires and loses over time. Each role is a representation of the object in a class. An object is not manipulated directly, but always through one of its roles, so that we either say that messages are sent to roles. At the instance level, roles answer to messages while objects essentially retain the identity of a set of roles. Note that in order to manage the different roles of an object, a naming mechanism is proposed in various works for referencing roles and to distinguish the set of roles that an object acquire.

- EXPLICIT OBJECT EVOLUTION AND a Linguistic framework

The system should offer the possibility to represent different roles of an object without using multiple inheritance. In a classical class hierarchies every object need to be represented as an instance of a single class. In this case, one must use multiple inheritance to model objects that have many roles at once. Besides the problems it introduces (Pernici 1990), the multiple inheritance does not assure any independent context since all the object roles are gathered in the same class. Note that we do not argue here that in all cases one should avoid multiple inheritance. The system should offer the two mechanisms and an administrator adapts the more suitable mechanism for his application. This feature is shared by all the proposals for supporting evolving objects in OODBs, since it is a main feature. What is required is a linguistic framework, which allows us to selectively seed new functionality to a distinguishable set of objects within a given class at runtime. This linguistic framework should provide a set of operators for tracking evolving object as easy as possible and with flexibility. Hence, we argue that the following operators are crucial to fully exploit the richness of a multiple role object model supporting evolution:

- *roles acquisition and dropping*

If an existing object acquires a new role, a new instance of the respective role class is created and added to the set of roles of the object. If the object abandons a role, its instance of the respective role class is deleted. A system should offer here very simple and flexible operations for acquiring and demoting roles along the hierarchy of classes. The user has not to write any program to manage the evolution of an object. For example regarding the example of figure1, a promotion of a given teaching assistant to a professor position should involve a single step. Similarly when a given student graduate, demoting it from a class student involve a unique operation. The system should here take into account the problem of dropping roles discussed previously in section 3.4. In Fibonacci (Albano et al. 1993) a contraction operator permits to drop explicitly roles while offering mechanisms that would cause an exception whenever a program tried to refer to the deleted role. To reduce the impact of deletion on unsuspecting programs, the Malampus system (Stein et al. 1990) allows programmers to specify when aspects are dropped. In (Khosafian et al. 1990) a message *abondon* permits to remove all internal references to the receiver.

- *Roles naming:*

A naming mechanism should be offered to reference each new role of the object. This mechanism will bound a newly created role of an existing object to a given name attributed by the programmer. For example, if a person John is a student and a teacher-assistant, the variables JohnS and JohnT are created to reference John in each one of its roles. These references are role identities for a programmer and in contrast to the object identity here each role may be referenced by several role identities attributed by a programmer.

- *Roles Comparison:*

As an object may have different roles and each role may be referenced by different names we need at least two operators for comparing roles. For example, in the Melampus system, the = = operator means "are equivalent roles" and holds only for references for the same role of the same object. In our previous example the expression: JohnS = = JohnT is false since they are two references for two different roles. The @= operator means "are references to same object" and is true for references to any two roles of the same object.

- *Roles Casting and Roles Inspection:*

A system here should offer operators that allow one test object roles and to navigate freely in the role graph of an object observing all its possible roles and behaviors. Role inspection permits to test if a given object has a certain role. Fibonacci uses the predicate isAlso to fulfill this feature. For example, the expression *"JohnS isAlso Teacher-assistant"* will return the value true. In (Khosafian et al. 1990) the Smalltalk method " existAs : aRoleType" achieves the same function. Role Casting allows one to coerce an object to one of its possible roles. The operator will fail if the object does not have the specified role. In Fibonacci, the operator as permits to switch between roles. The expression x as T will be well typed if T and the type of x belong to the same role type family of an existing object. If we consider as previously variable JohnS that reference a Person John in his Student role, someone can select the private phone number of John using the following expression: (JohnS as Person) phoneNo ;

- A COHERENT MESSAGE INTERPRETATION

As shown in the section 2.2, in the presence of object evolution, a message dispatched to an object could be ambiguous because it can be for any of the classes that an object is an instance of. One basic solution (Albano et al. 1993) for avoiding potentials ambiguities is to offers at least two mechanisms for message interpretation: A *normal interpretation of messages* which corresponds to the classical late binding mechanism, and a *strict interpretation of messages* called a strict binding to allow the programmer choose really what he wants. Basically, with a normal interpretation when a role receives a message it first checks whether any of its descendants has its own method (not inherited) to reply to the message. If such descendant is found, then it is delegated to answer the message. The descendants are tried in reversal temporal order, i.e. the last acquired descendant is tried first. If no delegate is found, the receiver searches an implementation for the message inside itself. If this is not found, then the receiver looks for an implementation for the message in the ancestor role from which the corresponding property is inherited. With a strict interpretation of message one can observe the behavior of an object in a certain role without taking into account possible specializations of that role.

- AUTHORIZATION CONSTRAINTS FOR EVOLUTION

As discussed in the previous section, we argue that a mechanism to control evolution of objects in a hierarchy of classes is a key feature of future OODB systems supporting evolving objects. This mechanism will allow modeling the fact that not every sequence of role acquisitions or role dropping is admissible. To address this problem few works have been proposed. In (Richardson et al. 1991) integrity rules permit to specify constraints in the description of the object and transitions rules describe the evolution of the object from a set of roles to another ones. In (Zdonik 1990), the concepts of essential types and exclusionary types are introduced to characterize the properties of types in an ISA hierarchy. An essential type is a type that cannot be lost through object evolution. For example, an object of type Person still retains that type when the object becomes an Employee instance and, later on, a Manager instances. Person is therefore an essential type for that object. An exclusionary type is a type acquired when the object is created, but can be removed as a result of object evolution. Once an exclusionary type is removed, it can never be regained. For example an object of type Child can evolve to a type Teenager, thereby loosing its Child type. The object cannot regain its Child type subsequently. More recent work (Atkinson et al. 1989)while responding to most of the features defined here, they do not address this important problem.

We think that the four features defined here are really mandatory for supporting object evolution in OODBSs. We expect that these functionality's would be used as a straw man, and that others will either invalidate or confirm the points mentioned here.

3.2 Optional Features: the goodies

Moreover the mandatory functionality's, others features can be added to make the system better but which are not mandatory in our view. We consider here two features that have been discussed and implemented in some systems: *Qualified Roles, and Implicit Object Evolution.* We present briefly hereafter each one of these features:

Qualified Roles.

This feature discussed in (Gottlob et al. 1996), permits that an existing object may be represented several times in the same class of role. Occurrences of the same object are distinguished by the value of a special instance variable named *qualifier.* As an example, we consider the class ProjectManager that represents a qualified role where the qualifier takes on the Project supervised. Mr. Jones, who manages two projects, "CAD/CAM" and "OODB", is represented by two instances of ProjectManager. Each instance models Mr. Jones as project manager of one of these two projects. Mr. Jones has different responsibilities in each of them. He is responsible for "reuse management" in the former and for "quality assurance" in the latter.

Implicit Object Evolution.

Object evolution mechanisms that we are discussing in this paper are considered as explicit in the sense that users invoke them explicitly using commands. Implicit object evolution mechanisms support indeed a form of automatic, dynamic classification of objects, based on their run time value, state, or other user-defined properties. In Chimera (Bertino et al. 1998). they use the concept of predicate class, whose extent is implicitly specified by some predicates, called *population predicates.* All instances of a class C that verify the population predicate of some subclass of C are automatically migrated to this subclass. Finally, several techniques that have been developed for active databases are useful for the support of implicit object evolution.

4. MULTIPLE AND EVOLVING REPRESENTATION MECHANISMS FOR OODBS

We have explored the implications of the semantics of multiple and evolving object representation on object-oriented concepts. We have also described the requirements and optional features regarding object evolution mechanisms in OODBs. In this section we review briefly various approaches that have been proposed in the state of the art, and after we will compare four of the most recent works in this area.

4.1 Approaches of object evolution mechanisms in OODBs

The IRIS mechanism (Fishman et al. 1987) for changing types provided the original inspiration in the context of OODBs. IRIS allows an object to belong to several types and to gain or lose types during its lifetime, retaining its identity; but is not possible to observe an object from different perspectives; indeed, despite type multiplicity an object in a fixed instant of its life always exhibits a uniform behavior. Consequently, two roles of an object may not have different methods of the same name.

Stein and Zdonik (Stein et al. 1990) propose a mechanism called *clovers* which allows to model entities with multiple and independent roles. The language that supports this mechanism has provision for strong type-checking a subtyping. Coercion operators are provided for moving among the various views of an object that exist at a particular time.

Richardson and Schwartz (Richardson et al. 1991) propose a model based on the concept of aspect to support modeling of roles in strongly typed object-oriented database systems. They use a model in which type implementations and type interfaces are defined separately without any explicit relationship. A particular type implementation belongs to a type interface if it *conforms* to it. An aspect is defined by a special type implementation that extends the Abstract data type of a root object. Any object conforming to the Abstract data type of a root object may acquire on the aspect, i.e., takes on the role modeled by the aspect. While flexible, this model does not consider inheritance and has not explicit operators for switching between roles. Furthermore the mechanism of conformance may lead to some semantically meaningless aspects being acquired. In Albano et al. (Albano et al. 1993), they have developed an object data model with roles and have implemented this model in a new strongly typed object oriented database programming language called Fibonacci. A novel aspect of Fibonacci is the coexistence of late-binding and multiple inheritance with role multiplicity and dynamic object extension in a framework with strong type-checking and subtyping. An important contribution of Fibonacci, is to show how the role concept can be supported in a new language built from scratch.

In Gottlob et al. (Gottlob et al. 1996), they use Smalltalk to demonstrate how existing object-oriented programming language can be easily extended with roles without modifying the semantics of Smalltalk. The characteristics of this model are the possibility of an object to appear repeatedly in the same type of role ("Qualified Roles") and the possibility to combine object classes and role types orthogonally. We will refer to this approach as **Smalltalk$^+$** in the next section.

The ORM approach (Papazoglou et al. 1996), add more modeling power and flexibility to the object-oriented approach by capturing different kinds of objects dynamics. They do so by being based either on conditions which apply to an individual object, groups of objects from a class, or an explicit/implicit inter-object relationships. They control the forms of object evolution in accordance with application semantics, while respecting the structural and behavioral consistency of the typed objects.

Finally, Bertino &al. (Bertino et al. 1998) present one of the most recent works in this area. They propose an object-oriented, deductive, active data model developed as part of an ESPRIT Project, designed by Chimera. The object-oriented model introduces different kinds of evolution for objects. Explicit evolutions are realized through the invocation of commands while implicit evolutions arise because Chimera supports predicate classes. Constraints between classes could be expressed to control object evolutions in the hierarchy of classes.

4.2 Discussion

Table 1 gives a feature by feature (mandatory and optional) comparison of object evolution mechanisms as discussed in this paper of four of the most recent work. In general, it can be noted that all proposals preserve the object identity while allowing it to change behavior and structure. Hence, this mandatory feature is not presented in the table 1 as it is fully supported by all the proposals.

By comparing these four proposals, we note that only the Chimera system that responds to all the mandatory features that we have proposed in this paper. Moreover, it supports implicit object evolution through derived classes and active capacities.

Table1: Comparison of object evolution mechanisms

	Features \ Mechanisms	**Fibonnacci** (Albano & al.)	**Smalltalk**$^{+}$ (Gottlob & al.)	**ORM** (Papazoglou & al.)	**Chimera** (Bertino & al.)
MANDATORY	linguistic framework and explicit object evolution	yes, evolution limited to the same role family	yes, evolution limited only to subclass & superclass	yes, evolution limited only to subclass & superclass	fully supported
MANDATORY	constraints for object evolution	not addressed	not addressed	mutually exclusive roles	fully supported using disjoint extension and rules
MANDATORY	type safety	only for object dropping problem	not addressed	assured by using type conformance relationship	assured by the propagation of updates
MANDATORY	message interpretation	late and strict binding	my lead to improper behaviors	not addressed	preferred class and argument specificity approaches
GOODIES	implicit object evolution	not addressed	not addressed	yes, using triggers	yes, using derived classes
GOODIES	qualified roles	no	yes	no	no

5. CONCLUSION

One of the major challenges in the engineering of large-scale software systems is to provide mechanisms that allow for evolution and change (Zdonik 1990). This change can take many forms. Modern programming languages and environment (Stefik et al. 1986) has addressed some aspects of this problem. Database systems represent an environment in which these problems are particularly severe. OODBs store objects over longer periods, during which the represented entities evolve. Nowadays, most OODBs display serious shortcoming in their ability to model the evolving and multifaceted nature of common real world entities. The intimate and permanent binding of an object to a single type (class) inhibits the tracking of real-world entities over time. In recent years, various mechanisms for supporting many-faceted and evolving objects in the context of OO data models have been proposed in the literature. However, there is no consensus concerning the fundamental features of evolution mechanisms in the context of OODBs. As a first step towards this goal, we have provided in this paper a catalogue of criteria regarding the functionality' s of evolution mechanisms proposed in the literature. We have also reviewed and compared four of the most recent proposals in this subject.

REFERENCES

Abiteboul, S., Kanellakis, P. C., 1989, "Object identity as a query language primitive", R. T. Altaïr 29-89.

Albano, A., Bergamini, R, Ghelli, G and Orsini R, 1993, An Object data Model with roles. In Proceedings of the International Conference on Very Large Data Bases. VLDB, Saratoga, Calif, 39-51.

Atkinson, M., Bancilhon, F., 1989, The Object Oriented database System Manifesto, Proceeding of DOOD Conference Kyoto, 40-57.

Bertino, E., Guerinni, G., Rusca, L., 1998, "Object Evolution in Object Database", Research Report, University of Genova.

Bobrow, D.G, Winograd, W., 1977 , "An overview of KRL, a Knowledge Representation Language", Cognitive Science, 1(1).

Carré, B., 1989 "Méthodologie orientée objet pour la représentation des connaissanccs, Concepts de Point de vue, de représentation multiple et évolutive d'objets", Ph.D Tesis, Université de Lille, (France).

Ferber, J., 1989, "Objets et agents: une étude des structures de représentations et de communication en Intelligence Artificielle", Ph.D Tesis, Université Pierre et Marie Curie, Paris (France).

Fishman, e al. 1987, IRIS. An Object Oriented Database Management System . ACM Trans Off Inf Syst vol 5, N°1, pp 48-69.

Goldstein, J. P., Bobrow D. G., 1980, "Extending Object Oriented programming in Smalltalk". Conference Record of the LISP Conference, Standford (USA).

Gottlob, G., Sherffel, M., rock, B., 1996, “Extending Object-Oriented Systems with Roles” ACM, Trans. On Informations Systems, volume 14 number 3.

Khosafian, S., Copeland, G., 1990, Object Identity, Proc OOPSLA, Portland Oregon.

Ling, T.W, Teo, P.K, 1995 , “Object Migration in ISA Hierarchies” Proc. Of International Conference DASFAA, Singapore.

Papazoglou, M.P, Kramer, B.J, 1996, A Database Model for Object Dynamics. The VLDB Journal.

Pernici, B., 1990, Object With Roles. ACM/IEE Office Information Systems in SIGOIS Bulletin, 11(2-3): PP 205-215,.

Richardson, J., Schwartz P., 1991, "Aspects: Extending objects to support multiple, independent roles", Proceedings of the ACM-SIGMOD Conference on Management Data, Denver, Colorado,.

Stein, L.A, Zdonik, S.B. 1990, "Clovers: The dynamic behaviour of types and instances. Tech Rep, Brown Univ, Providences, R.I. 1990

Stefik, E. M., Bobrow, D. G. 1986, "Object-Oriented Programming: Thèmes and Variations", The AI Magazine, Vol. 6, no 4, pp. 40-62, AAAI, inverno.

Sciore, E., 1989, “Object Specialization”. ACM Trans on Inf Sys, 7(2): pp103-122.

Zdonik, S., 1990, "Object-Oriented type Evolution”. Advances in Database Programming languages, Bancilhon F., Buneman P., Editors, ACM Press.

MODELLING DATA INTEGRATION IN AN OBJECT BASED GEOGRAPHICAL INFORMATION SYSTEM

Maria Luisa Damiani
Department of Computer Science, University of Milan, Via Comelico 39, Milan, Italy
Email: eldami@iol.it

Keywords: Geographical Information Systems, Data Integration, Process Modelling

Abstract: The integration of geographical data from multiple and heterogeneous sources is a complex process generally performed in an incremental way. Current GIS systems provide a wide range of services to support at least *physical* data integration. A critical point in the development of a GIS application is the design of the integration process. Such a design is necessary to plan out the integration operations which are to be performed to achieve an effective database. Integration process modelling can simplify both the analysis and the documentation of the database construction. In the paper a possible and general approach to the problem is discussed. A case study of spatial data integration in the nautical field is finally presented.

1. INTRODUCTION

The integration of geographical data from multiple and heterogeneous sources is a major task in the development of a GIS (Geographical Information System) application. The technological advances in Earth data acquisition as well as the increasing availability of off-the-shelf data sets in digital georeferenced format open up new possibilities for the development of advanced geographical applications. In this context, spatial data integration is a fundamental issue.

The general problem of heterogeneous data integration has been extensively investigated in Computer Science, especially in the database and cooperative information systems fields (Bertino 2001), (Calvanese 1998), (Damiani 1994). A basic distinction, which can be easily transposed in the geographical context, is between *semantic* and *physical* heterogeneity. Semantic heterogeneity occurs when there is a disagreement about the meaning, interpretation or intended use of the same or related data (Shet 1990); an example in the spatial domain are data acquired at different resolutions (Timpf 1997). Conversely physical heterogeneity occurs when different types of data structures are used for coding the information in the computer. An example in the spatial domain are spatial data represented in different formats and/or data models.

A *GIS system* is a set of tools for geographical data management. Commercial GIS systems provide a number of services to support physical integration such as coordinate transformation functions, format conversion services, etc..; the standardisation initiatives, such as those promoted by the OpenGis Consortium (OCG 1999) and Iso/Tc 211, (the latter summarised in (Brodeur 2000)) aim at overcoming the current heterogeneity of spatial database structures by defining a common data model embracing the *object oriented* paradigm.

Nevertheless in the actual practice, even when no semantic inconsistencies occur, the construction of an integrated database remains a complex task and the effectiveness of the operation mostly depends on the skill of the database designer ('integrator'). The integrator must be aware of the semantic content of the heterogeneous data sources and how data are logically and physically organised; moreover he/she is to be familiar with data conversion tools that may be spread in different commercial systems, or to be implemented from scratch; finally he/she must be able to smartly extract the semantic fragments from the sources and compose them in the integrated database.

Integration of geographical data is a stepwise process which resembles the construction of a puzzle and is performed in an incremental way. The process is complex and we believe it should be formally modelled to simplify analysis and documentation.

Current GIS literature on spatial database modelling (Fonseca 2000), (Parent 1999), (Renolen 1997), (Brodeu 2000), (FDGC 1995) is mostly concerned with the definition of conceptual models for the final databases, i.e. the databases resulting from data integration. As far as we know, the problem of

J. Filipe et al. (eds.), Enterprise Information Systems III, 68–74.

modelling the integration phase is generally underestimated.

In the paper we propose a few guidelines to describe the process of data integration into an object based spatial database:

- In our view, the integration process is to be modelled at different levels of abstraction, to distinguish the meaning of the integration, i.e. "what" has to be done, from the system-dependent operations, i.e. the "how". A *conceptual* plan is opposed to a *logical* and *physical* plan. In the paper we focus on the former.
- The incremental aspect of the process is to be explicitly represented. We propose a notation based on a state transition graph. The graph is directed and acyclic.
- The integration process is to be decomposed in atomic integration operations. To that extent a few abstract operators have been devised to describe the integration flow at a conceptual level.

The paper is structured as follows. First some initial assumptions are introduced; next the general approach to integration process modelling is presented; finally a case study in the nautical field is illustrated.

2. THE INTEGRATION PROCESS

2.1 Assumptions

The user is supposed to interact with the heterogeneous sources through a *geographical integration system*, which provides an integrated view of the distributed information as a homogeneous spatial database. Note that in general these integration functionalities are embedded in GIS systems. At this stage we prefer the term *integration system* because more general. The initial assumptions regard:

- the data model of the spatial database
- the functionalities of the integration system

2.1.1 The spatial data model

The spatial data model specifies how spatial data are logically organised in the database. We assume an entity-based conceptual view of the world (Burrough 1998). Accordingly the reality consists of discrete entities having a well defined geometric shape and position.

The data model for the discrete entities is *feature* based (OCG 1999). The intensional representation of a set of homogeneous entities constitute the *feature class*. A class is identified by: a name, a set of one or more *alphanumeric attributes* and (for simplicity) a unique *spatial attribute* One of the attributes is assumed to univocally identify the feature.

In the paper we consider only spatial objects embedded in the Euclidean plane R^2 and for simplicity we consider three domains: the set of simple polygons; the set of simple polylines; the set of points R^2. These domains constitute the *spatial domains* of the spatial attribute. Feature classes are of either point, line or polygon type, depending on the domain of the spatial attribute. A *spatial database schema* can be defined as a set of feature classes while a *spatial database instance* denotes a set of feature instances with a specific geometric shape and position.

2.1.2 The integration system

We adopt the classification proposed in (Calvanese 1998) in the context of the intelligent information systems, to introduce some basic assumptions on the geographical integration systems in use.

- *Read vs. read/write access* to external sources. Data integration may in principle be used both to read and to update the external sources. In this paper we assume the external sources cannot be modified, i.e. the integration system is seen as a 'client' of the sources and cannot interfere with their operations.
- *Virtual* vs. *materialized views.* In general data integration can be either virtual or materialized. In the first case, the integration system acts as an interface between the user and the sources. Queries are generally expensive because the heterogeneous data are to be directly accessed; in the second case, the system maintains a replicated view of the data at the sources. In this case queries are more efficient, because sources need not to be accessed whereas maintaining the materialized view is costly.
  In GIS, the typical approach to external data sources integration is known as 'data import', i.e. data is read from external sources and properly transformed into materialized view of the external data compliant with the data model of the spatial database; virtual data integration is relatively recent. In the paper we assume that both types of integration can be realised.

- *Procedural vs. declarative approach.* Commonly, in the procedural approach the integration is realised by ad hoc software components such as *wrappers* which encapsulate data sources and *mediators* (Bertino 2001) which integrate data from wrappers and dispatch requests among them; in the declarative approach the idea is to maintain a declarative description of the data at the sources. In the paper we assume – coherently with GIS trends - that external sources are accessed in a procedural way.

2.2 The approach to integration modelling

2.2.1 Abstraction levels

The goal of the integration process is to merge the heterogeneous data sources in a geographical database that the user perceives as a whole independently of how it is implemented (*integrated database*).

Because of the complexity of the process, a *plan* seems desirable to conveniently approach the integration task. In general a plan splits the task in a sequence of actions leading to a *goal*.

The objective of the *integration plan* is to extract the relevant semantic content from the existing sources and compose the knowledge fragments in the integrated database. The plan is splitted in a number of *integration steps*. We model each step as a transition from a dataset into a different dataset. The initial datasets are the external sources while the final dataset, i.e. the goal of the plan, is the integrated database. The overall process can be described as a stepwise composition of the final database.

In our view, the integration planning may be approached distinguishing three major levels of abstraction, in a way that resembles the standard modelling levels in databases (i.e. conceptual, logical, physical). At the highest level of abstraction, a *conceptual plan* describes the integration strategy, i.e. the abstract coarse grained operations to be performed; the *logical* plan maps the conceptual plan into a sequence of system-dependent operations; finally, the *physical* plan describes in details the single actions and the tools which are used to perform each logical step.

2.2.2 The conceptual plan

The three planning levels are introduced to separate the "what" from "how", i.e. the meaning of the integration from the system dependent functionalities.

We consider here the conceptual plan. It specifies "what" has to be done and ultimately the way the integrated geographical database is built. To describe the conceptual plan we use a notation based on a state-transition diagram, we call *Model Transition Graph* (Fig. 1).

A *state* of the diagram corresponds to a dataset. States are classified as follows:

- *Initial, intermediate, final* states
  The initial states are used to identify the external sources. The intermediate and the final states denote homogeneous spatial databases: their data model is compliant with the integrated database model and each data set has a schema and an instance. The goal result from the integration of these partial databases.
- *Virtual, materialized* state.
  Except for the initial ones, the states can be either virtual or materialized. Virtual states describe data sets which are not explicitly stored and that cannot be directly modified by the user; a virtual state is used to provide a read-only view of some external sources as well as of some other dataset; a virtual state generalizes the notion of database *view*. A materialized state describes a dataset which is explicitly stored and can be updated

A transition is a mapping of a state into a different state because of some operation. To exemplify, the addition of a new feature class to a dataset generates a new state. In this case the transition is due to a change of the database schema.

The graph is directed and acyclic. In the paper, we use a simple graphical representation for the graph. States are circles labelled with a state identifier. Note that this representation may be not fully adequate in practice. A more extended description of the content of the dataset would be useful, in the form for example of either a database schema or a semantic model. This aspect is of little relevance for the discussion, therefore we adopt a simpler notation.

Transitions are graphically represented by labelled arrows. Labels denote the operations triggering the transitions.

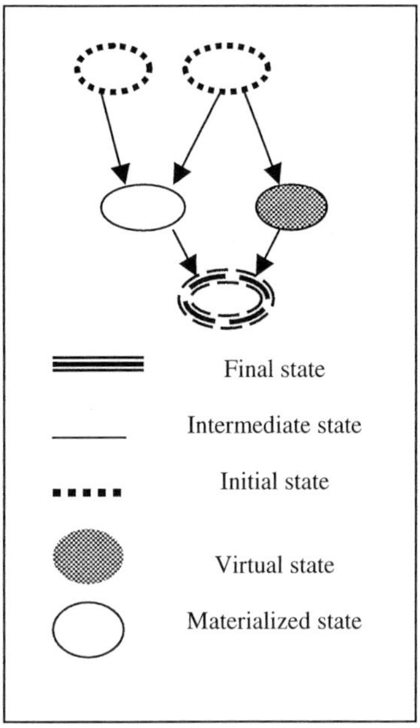

Figure 1: Model Transition Graph

2.2.3 Integration operations

A transition describes an integration step. The action/s which are performed at each step can be summarised in an atomic, high level *integration operation*. A critical issue is to find a set of abstract operators which can properly model the process.

We have devised a possible set of operators, which although not complete, can be useful for this purpose. These operators are partial functions defined and ranging over the set of states. Here the meaning of the operators is presented in an intuitive way:

- *wrapping*: the operator can be applied to the initial states representing the external data sources. The result of the operation is a virtual state. This operator is applied when data sources are to be encapsulated through a wrapper to provide a readable and feature-based view of the external data.
- *import* : the same as wrapping except that the result is a materialized state.
- *virtualize*: the operator maps a not-initial state into a virtual state. In practice the operation is accomplished through a *query*. The operation is used to select a subset of a dataset. The subset selection criteria may be added as an additional parameter.
- *materialize*: as above but the operator returns a materialized state.
- *merge*: it maps one or more states into one state. The operator is used as a union-set operator to combine two or more states in a single one. The operator can generate either a virtual state, or a materialized state
- *schema update* : this operator can be further specialised to precise the kind of schema change, such the addition, removal, update of attribute and/or feature types. For simplicity we consider a unique operator, although the resulting expressivity is low. It can be applied only to materialized states.
- *instance update:* the attribute values of feature instances are modified and/or feature instances are added. As above, although the operation could be further specialised, we consider a unique operator. It can be applied only to materialized states.

The meaning of a transition is ultimately determined by the integration operation. The point is now to understand the adequacy of these operators for the modelling of the conceptual plan.

For better understanding the application requirements and prove these ideas, we have developed a case study.

3. A CASE STUDY

The case study regards the construction of a GIS-based interactive nautical chart (Manghi 2000). Normally, nautical charts are released by authorised national and international organisations and are available at different scales. When in digital form, cartography consists generally of CAD (Computer Aided Design) drawings. Because of the limits of the cartographic product, we have built the prototype of a geographical database integrating existing cartography plus accurate data of the sea ground and additional information with a thematic content.

Two main sources of data have been integrated in the prototype. The first is a large scale digital chart covering a limited area. The cartography is available as a CAD drawing, therefore the geometric information is stored in a file managed by the operating system and coded as sequence of records in a proprietary format (*dgn* format). The second source of data contains sensor-data acquired by a hydrographic survey boat. The source contains a list of points and the depth value at each point. Data is stored in a text file.

3.1 Integration steps

First, we consider in more detail the integration of the CAD dataset. The semantically meaningful objects are :

- the coast line: the coast is geometrically represented as a set of connected lines.
- bathymetries: each bathymetry (i.e. equal sea depth line) is geometrically represented as a set of connected lines. The depth value is specified a part as a label, which is a separated graphical object.

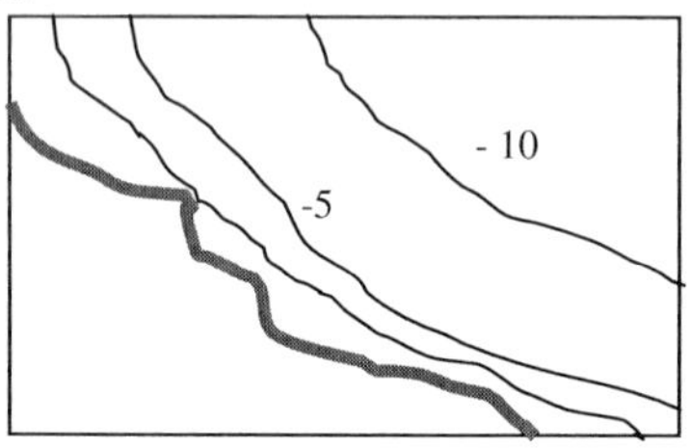

Figure 2: The CAD dataset

In the CAD data model, the above entities are represented by graphic elements of type 'line'; the semantics is not explicit, rather it is indirectly expressed through graphic attributes: colour, patterning etc..

The relevant integration steps are:

1. At first, we need to envelope the graphic elements into semantically meaningful objects. For example , the lines of colour green are to be mapped into coast lines while the lines of colour grey onto bathymetries. The operation to be performed simply extracts or recognises objects but does not alter the thematic and geometric content of the CAD elements. The *wrapping* operator can be used. The result is a virtual data set containing the same objects but represented as features.
2. As second step, we need to represent explicitly the semantics of objects. In the example, the depth value of the bathymetric line - which is originally expressed as a graphic label - is to be added as an attribute. In this way the attribute can be used later on in queries.
   The database schema is to be modified because of the additional attribute and the related instances are to consequently updated. Because this operation is possible only on materialized views, we have to materialize first the current virtual data set. The process is as follows (for sake of brevity the detail of states is omitted) :

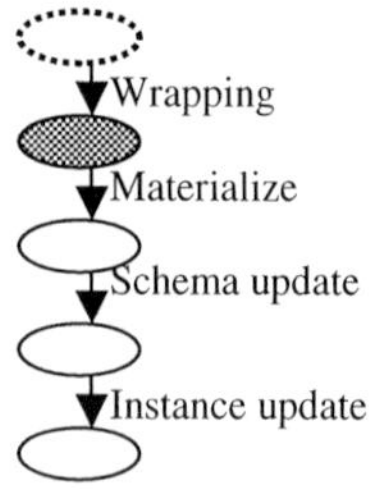

Figure 3: Integration steps

3. One more step is needed to adequate the geometric shape of spatial objects. In the example the coast is geometrically represented as a linear element; it may convenient to represented the object as a polygon.

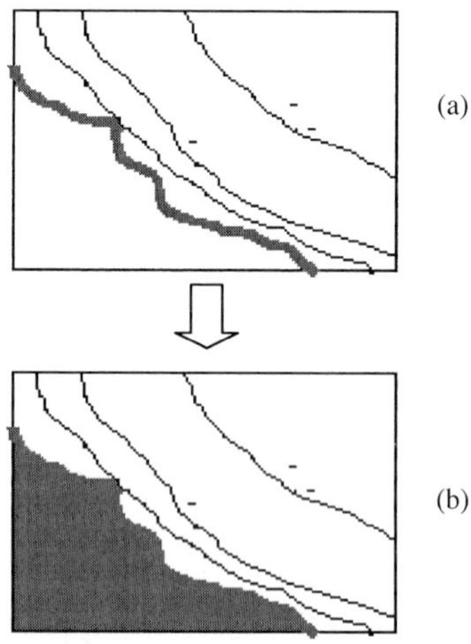

Figure 4: Change of geometry

The database schema is to be modified to account for the new feature class of polygon type, say 'coast land'; next the database instance is to be updated because the new coast object depicted in Figure 4(b) is to be added to the database. Note that in this case the processing is not trivial because several fine grained operations are to be performed such as: editing the coast geometry, checking the geometry consistency, generating polygons from closed lines. At conceptual level the operation could be synthetically modelled by two transitions respectively of type 'schema update' and 'instance update'. The partial outcome of the integration process is an intermediate state we label 'CAD-based dataset'.

Now we consider the integration of the second source of data - a text file of point coordinates and depth values which have been acquired by the hydrographic survey boat. The conceptual plan is augmented with an additional external state.

In this case the integration strategy is to enter the external data into a new separated data set. In this way the integration of the two data sources can proceed in parallel at least to a certain extent.

In principle the integration can be performed through either a 'wrapping' or 'import' transition. Nevertheless, in practice the choice is constrained by the functionalities of the geographic integration system in use. In our case the simplest way to enter data from a text file is to apply an 'import' operation, which generates a materialized data set consisting of point features (say 'Description-based dataset'). The point features have a unique relevant attribute, i.e. the sea depth at each point.

At this stage two intermediate and independent datasets are built. The last step is to put all data together. The final integration step composes the two above states, i.e. the 'CAD-based dataset' and the 'Description based data set' into a unique one, the *final state*. The 'merge' operator is used to accomplish this.

The result is a homogeneous geographic database of point, line and area features, embedded in the same coordinate space, that the user perceives as a whole. Finally integration has been a major step of a larger process that has led to the generation of a DTM (Digital Terrain Model) (Burrough 1998) of the sea ground.

4. CONCLUSION

GIS systems can provide essential support to the integration of spatial data. What, in our view, is missing is a methodological guideline which can suggest how to combine the available operators and perform an effective integration. In this paper we have discussed the definition of a state transition graph based notation for modelling the relevant integration steps at a high level of abstraction. The notation can be used for supporting the application analysis as well for documentation purposes.

A critical point of the approach may the mapping of the *conceptual plan* onto a *logical plan*. The goal of the mapping is to turn the integration steps into a sequence of operations to be performed in the target GIS or integration system. Is this mapping always possible? Of course it depends on the target integration system. In our view the best way for approaching the integration plan is first to assess the capabilities of the integration system and next find a matching of these with the available integration operators.

We have used this approach for integrating the data of the case study into a commercial GIS (Intergraph, Geomedia Professional) (Limp 1998). The GIS system has a set of powerful integration functionalities. However consider that:

- Some abstract operators, for example the 'materialize' operator does not have any direct correspondence with a GIS operation. They can be realised instead through a number of general purpose actions. In the case of the previous operator, by copying ("outputting") selected features in new feature classes inside the same database or a newly created one.
- The GIS operations which are apparently in correspondence with 'import' and 'wrapping' are not atomic and generally performed in a number of steps. The operator at conceptual level instead is an abstract operator which allow technical details be hidden.
- The usage of some abstract operator is constrained by the GIS system working rules. For example the entering of CAD type data can be performed only by a 'wrapping' operation while points data in textual form can be only 'imported'.

Ultimately the proposed operators offer a more concise description of the integration process focused on the semantics aspects rather than on the implementation and technical details.

Future work includes: a) operators refinement. The current operator set is incomplete. For example, we need to model the integration of different spatial reference systems as well as the integration of raster data; b) Formalisation of the operators and further validation.

REFERENCES

Bertino, E., et al, 2001, 'Intelligent Database Systems', *Addison Wesley, ACM Press.*

Brodeur, Y, et al., 2000, 'Modelling Geospatial Application Database using the UML-based repositories aligned with international standards in Geomatics', *Proceedings of the Eigth ACM Symposium on Advances in Geographic Information Systems*,pag. 39-46.

Burrough, P., et al., 1998, 'Principles of Geographical Information Systems', *Oxford University Press.*

Calvanese, D., et al., 1998, 'Information Integration: Conceptual Modeling and Reasoning Support', *CoopIS'98, Proceedings of the 6th International Conference on Cooperative Information Systems.*

Damiani, M., 1994, 'An Intelligent Information System for Heterogeneous Data Exploration', *ISOOMS '94, Proceedings. of the International Symposium on Object-Oriented Methodologies and Systems*

FGDC 1995, 'GIS Development Guide: Conceptual Design of the GIS', *Newsletter*

Fonseca, F, et al, 2000, 'Ontology-Driven Information Integration', AAAI-2000 *Proceedings of the Workshop on Spatial and Temporal Granularity.*

Limp, F. et al., 1998, 'Inside Geomedia', *OnWord Press.*

Manghi, M., 2000, 'Un Sistema Informativo Geografico per la Gestione di Dati Nautici', *Thesis, University of Milan, in Italian*

OCG, 1999, 'The OpenGIS™ Abstract Specification, Topic 5: Features , Version 4', http://www.opengis.org.

Parent, C., et al., 1999, 'SpatioTemporal Conceptual Models: Data Structures + Space + Time', *GIS99, Procedeeings. of the 7th ACM Symposium on Advances in Geographic Information Systems.*

Renolen, A., 1997, 'Conceptual Modelling and Spatiotemporal Information Systems: How to Model the Real world', *ScanGis97.*

Sheth, A., et al., 1990, 'Federated Database Systems for Managing Distributed, Heterogeneous and Autonomous Databases', *ACM Computing Surveys: Special Issue on Heterogeneous Databases.*

Timpf, S., 1997, 'Cartographic in a multi-scale data structure', *Geographic Information Research: Bridging the Atlantic, (Craglia, M & Couclelis,H., eds), Vol 1, Taylor&Francis.*

DATA WAREHOUSE STRIPING: IMPROVED QUERY RESPONSE TIME

Jorge Bernardino
Instituto Superior de Engenharia de Coimbra, Dept. de Engenharia Informática e de Sistemas
Quinta da Nora, Apartado 10057, 3030-601 Coimbra, Portugal
Email: jorge@isec.pt

Henrique Madeira
Universidade de Coimbra, Departmento de Engenharia Informática
Pólo II, Pinhal de Marrocos, 3030-290 Coimbra, Portugal
Email: henrique@dei.uc.pt

Keywords: Data Warehousing, Online Analytical Processing, Query Performance

Abstract: The increasing use of decision support systems led to an explosion in the amount of business information that must be managed by the data warehouses. Therefore, data warehouses must have efficient Online Analytical Processing (OLAP) that provides tools to satisfy the information needs of business managers, helping them to make faster and more effective decisions. Improving query response time in such an environment is very difficult and can only be achieved by a combination of different approaches, in particular the use of materialized views, advanced indexes and parallel query processing. However, achieving quick response times with complex OLAP queries is still an open issue. This paper is an extension of our previous work (Bernardino et al. 2000), where we proposed a novel approach to this problem. In this paper, we analyse the scalability performance of data warehouse striping system (DWS) system using different environments. DWS is experimentally evaluated with Oracle 8 as back-end DBMS, for the most typical OLAP operations using different types of queries and it is shown that an optimal speedup and scale-up can be obtained. A new technique to process subqueries is also proposed and experimentally evaluated.

1. INTRODUCTION

Data warehouses integrate massive amount of data from multiple sources, which is primarily used for decision support purposes. This information is historical in nature and can include detailed transaction information from operational databases, legacy systems, or even external data sources. These large data volumes bring significant challenges to database engines, requiring high level of query performance and scalability. Data warehouses must have efficient Online Analytical Processing (OLAP) tools to process complex analytical queries satisfying the information needs of business managers and helping them to make faster and more effective decisions.

Typical warehouse queries are very complex and *ad hoc* in nature and generally access huge volumes of data and perform many joins and aggregations. Therefore, to handle this demanding in data and processing a highly scalable architecture is vital in a warehouse environment.

In this paper, we build upon our previous work (Bernardino et al. 2000) where a horizontal data partitioning of the fact table specially designed for relational data warehouses based on a star schema was proposed. This approach, called data warehouse striping (DWS), takes advantage of the specific characteristics of star schemas and typical data warehouse queries profile to guarantee optimal load balance of query execution and assures high scalability. In DWS the fact tables are distributed by an arbitrary number of computers and the queries are executed in parallel by all the computers, guarantying a nearly linear speedup and significantly improve query response time.

This paper presents an experimental evaluation of the speedup and scaleup of the proposed technique based on an implementation with three,

J. Filipe et al. (eds.), Enterprise Information Systems III, 75–82.

five and ten computers. We also investigate a technique to deal with subqueries. In this type of queries, the independent calculation of partial results required for nearly optimal speedup is obtained through estimation of some steps of the query. However, it will be shown that the error introduced this way in the final result is negligible for most of the cases.

The remainder of the paper is organized as follows. In the next section, we review related work and discuss the problems associated to the manipulation of large amounts of data in data warehouses. Section 3 describes the proposed approach and section 4 discusses experimental results. The final section contains concluding remarks and future work.

2. RELATED WORK

The most common strategies to improve query response times in warehousing environments are the precomputation of data in the form of materialized views (Chauduri et al. 1997, Agrawal et al. 2000) and the use of special indexes structures (Wu et al. 1998, Srinivasan et al. 2000). Although necessary to tune a DW for speed, these techniques have clear limitations and in the end cannot avoid some very time consuming queries. The precomputation strategy needs to anticipate queries so that it can materialize them in the data warehouse. However, OLAP queries are most frequently of an *ad hoc* nature, which restricts the precomputation to the imagination of the DW administrator. Users might query on dimensions that are not materialized in views. The indexing structures provide faster access to the data stored in the warehouse, but increases the size of the tables stored in that data warehouse. One can say that the strategies presented provide faster query processing, but they may not be fast enough as perceived by the user. Additionally, they require constant care from the DW administrator.

Parallel processing techniques have been applied to relational database systems (Lu et al. 1994, DeWitt et al. 1992) to speedup queries. The basic idea behind parallel databases is to carry out evaluation steps in parallel whenever possible, in order to improve performance. Although some vendors support parallel data warehousing to various degrees, e.g. Oracle8 (Oracle 1997) and Red Brick Warehouse (RedBrick 1998), the fact is that parallel query processing in data warehouses has received little attention in research community.

Most of today's OLAP tools require data warehouses with a centralized structure where a single database contains all the data. However, a large centralized data warehouse is very expensive because of the great setup costs and it is not very flexible due to its centralized nature. The fact that data warehouses tend to be extremely large in size (Chauduri et al. 1997) and grow quite fast in many cases means that a scalable architecture is crucial to the success of these systems. A truly distributed data warehouse can be achieved by distributing the data across multiple data warehouses in such a way that each individual data warehouse cooperates to provide the user with a single and global view of the data. In spite of the potential advantages of distributed data warehouses, these systems are always very complex and have a difficult global management (Albrecht et al. 1998). On the other hand, the performance of many distributed queries is normally poor, mainly due to load balance problems.

In this context the data warehousing striping approach is more flexible because is a distributed implementation of a centralized data warehouse. The data warehouse striping is inspired in both the distributed data warehouse architecture and in classical round-robin partitioning techniques. The data is partitioned in such a way that the load of query execution is uniformly distributed by the available computers. Normally, a partial result is computed in each computer in a pure independent way. For the queries that need communication among computers during query execution we propose a solution that maintain these type of queries execution independent of the others.

3. QUERY PROCESSING USING DWS

In this section, we review the data warehouse striping approach (Bernardino et al. 2000). In particular, is explained how the queries are processed using the DWS system. First, we give some background on data schemas used in data warehouse environments. Then, we present strategies for rewriting queries that cannot be executed independently in each computer.

3.1 Background and DWS

A data warehouse is organized, in logical terms, according to the multidimensional model. This model consists of a set of dimensions and a set of measures (facts), where each dimension is typically arranged in a hierarchy. All dimensions have some attributes, describing a different perspective for the analysis of business. For instance, in the classical example of a chain of stores business, some of the dimensions are Products, Stores, and Time. In this simple three-dimension example, we have a cube (see Figure 1) where each cell within the multidimensional structure contains measures (typically numerical facts) along each of the dimensions. For example, a single cell may contain the total sales for a given product in a given store in a single day.

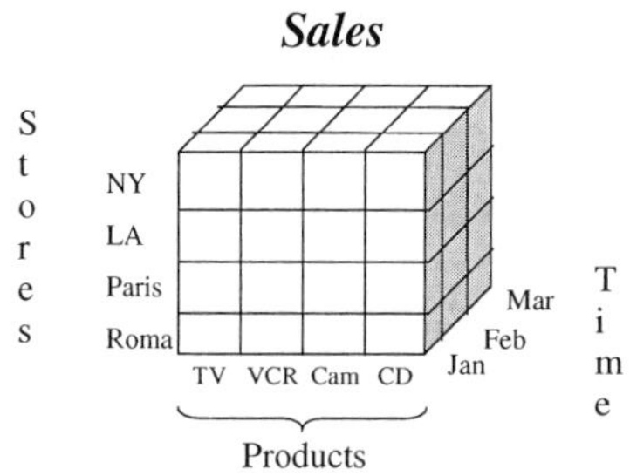

Figure 1: The multidimensional schema

The conceptual multidimensional data model can be physically realized in two ways, (1) by using trusted relational databases (star schema) (Chauduri et al. 1997) or (2) by making use of specialized multidimensional databases.

In this paper, we assume that a multidimensional database is a relational data warehouse in which the information is organized as a star schema (Kimball 1996). It offers flexibility, but often at the cost of performance because more joins for each query are required. A star schema models a consistent set of facts (aggregated) in a central fact table and the descriptive attributes about the facts are stored in multiple dimension tables. The equivalent star schema of the example of a chain of stores presented before is shown in Figure 2. The fact table is Sales and the dimensions are Products, Stores and Time.

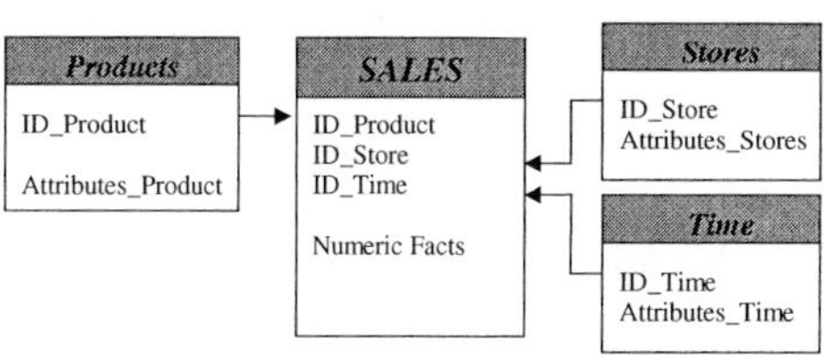

Figure 2: Star Schema

The size of fact table is much bigger than the size of dimension tables. The size of dimension tables could be hundreds or thousands of rows while the fact table could be millions of rows (Kimball 1996). Queries tend to use aggregations and joins on two or more tables, have often a large computation time, and are mainly *ad hoc* in nature.

Taking in account these characteristics of data warehouses our approach replicates the dimensions of star schema and distributes evenly the rows of fact table by the computers that form the DWS system.

All the computers that comprise the DWS system have the same star schema structure, equivalent to the centralized version. The dimension tables are replicated in each computer and the fact rows are distributed by the fact tables of each computer using a row-by-row round robin partitioning approach as illustrated in Figure 3.

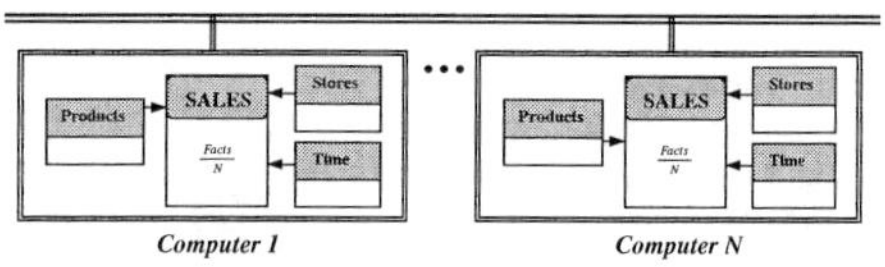

Figure 3: Data Partitioning in DWS

Using DWS, the number of fact rows stored in each computer is about the same, meaning that each computer has a fraction of the fact rows (Facts/*N*), with *N* being the number of computers. In the next section, we explain how the queries are executed in the DWS system.

3.2 Processing Queries with DWS

In DWS, typical OLAP queries are transformed into *N* partial queries that are executed in parallel in each of *N* computers that represent the DWS system (see Figure 4), avoiding the need of communication between computers during query execution. The parallel execution of a query by the available computers maintains the best load balance because the number of fact rows stored in each computer is about the same and the row distribution is random.

The Query Distribution and Processing (QDP) is a DWS layer responsible to receive the original query from the client application, rewriting it if necessary, and distribute this "modified" query by all computers. After the execution of these partial queries, the QDP layer merges these partial results and sends the final result to the user.

Most of the queries over a star schema can be transformed into *N* independent partial queries just because of the nature of the queries (and because the fact rows are partitioned in a disjoint way: i.e., the fact rows stored in a computer are not replicated in the other computers). For some queries, the computation of the partial result in one computer needs to access data stored in the other computers of the DWS system (i.e., needs a truly distributed query). However, in most of these cases it is possible to accurately estimate the partial result that need to access the data stored in other computers by an estimation calculated from the local data, avoiding the need of a truly distributed query. Even though this is only possible because we are working with aggregation functions.

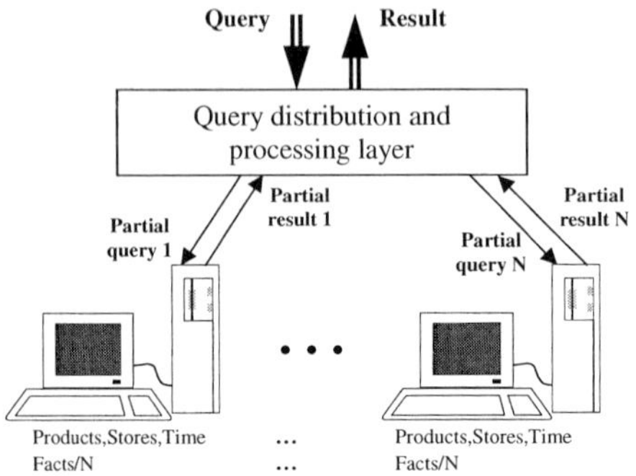

Figure 4: Query Processing in DWS

In reality, processing some queries in a DWS system could need to access intermediate results computed from all the computers. Thus, in a DWS system concerning the need of communication among computers during query execution, typical queries can be divided in two groups:

Independent queries: queries that can be independently executed in each computer, with no need of communication among computers during the execution of the query. In this case the global result can be computed very quickly from the partial results.

Dependent queries: queries that need communication among computers to compute the final result. In these queries the computation of the partial results in each computer need to access data stored in others computers. In this case, the execution of queries is dependent of partial results calculated over the data in all the computers of the DWS system. We designate the number of times that is necessary to access the data in all the computers as number of executions.

In a DWS system the ideal speedup is equal to the number of computers (*N*) used in a DWS system. Independent queries are distributed by the available computers in a DWS system in such a way that each computer needs to execute only one partial query (number of executions=1), which corresponds to the nearly optimal linear speedup.

On the other hand, dependent queries raise several problems concerning the speedup of DWS, as it is not possible to attain the optimal speedup, because the nodes must compute intermediate results that are required in additional steps to compute the partial and final results.

An example of dependent query is a query containing subqueries, where we use the results of one query as part of another query. In the DWS system, this means that we must access the data stored in the others computers to compute the results of subqueries. For example to calculate the number of units sold for all products whose sales price is greater than the average sales price. Using the star schema of Figure 5 (that will be explained in next section), this query corresponds to the following SQL statement:

```
Q0:  select sum(unitssold)
     from actvars
     where dollarsales >
          (select avg(dollarsales)
          from actvars)
```

During the execution the inner query that computes the average dollarsales is executed first. The result of this subquery is used in the main query. The problem with this type of query when DWS is used is that the original query must be partitioned and reformulated, resulting into new partial queries. This means that the distribution of subqueries requires two phases:

Phase one: The innermost subqueries are send to all the computers and the results are computed. The intermediate results are made available for all computers.

Phase two: The main query is rewritten taking into account the intermediate results and it is sent to all computers. If the deep level of the query is greater than two levels these subqueries must be executed sequentially from the innermost query until the main query.

In our example, the original query Q0 gives origin to the following two queries that must be executed in sequence (but each one is executed in parallel in all the available machines):

```
Q0.1:     select sum(dollarsales),
               count(dollarsales)
          from actvars

Q0.2:     select sum(unitssold)
          from actvars
          where dollarsales>
               average_dollarsales
```

The first query, Q0.1, computes the product average sales price and the result can be stored in the auxiliary variable *average_dollarsales*. The second query, Q0.2, computes the units sold for revenues greater than the value computed by Q0.1 (*average_dollarsales*). DWS does not achieve optimal speedup with this type of query because it requires the value of the subquery to be computed first.

A solution to the problem of dependent queries could be the use of an approach similar to materialized views where we store aggregation values like sum, count or average. But this solution has the typical problems of materialized views: we do not know a-priory all the values needed by the user because we are working essentially with *ad hoc* queries.

Instead, we propose another approach that uses the estimation of aggregation values. When a business manager is "digging the data", s/he usually wants to find data trends, extracting important information to future decisions. In this way, the most important action is to explore the data quickly, even if the results are only approximate. This form of working with DW is well suited to DWS technique because this way we can transform dependent queries into approximate independent queries, producing a final result that is an estimation of the exact value but that is obtained much more quickly.

In short, in dependent queries we propose the elimination of the first step by estimation of the aggregation value locally. This means that we transform all dependent queries in independent ones. Using this approach with our example, we use the local average of each computer as an estimate of the global average. In the next section, we analyze more deeply the proposed approach and the errors introduced in the final result with queries that aggregate groups with different number of elements. As we will see later on, the error introduced in the final result is negligible in most cases.

4. EXPERIMENTAL STUDY

The main goals of this study are to show typical speedup and scaleup characteristics of the DWS approach, to illustrate the independent execution of subqueries, and to demonstrate the small error obtained in this case.

All the experiments are conducted in a Windows NT environment, where all the computers have the same hardware characteristics, using Intel Pentium Celeron 466 MHz CPU, with 6.4 GB IDE hard disk and 64 MB of main memory. The computers use Oracle 8, release 8.0.5 as back-end DBMS and are linked together in an Ethernet network at 100 Mbps.

To evaluate the performance of the proposed technique we used the data set of the Analytical Processing Benchmark-1, Release II (APB 1998), that simulates a realistic OLAP business situation.

4.1 Experimental testbed

Figure 5 shows our star schema based on the APB-1 benchmark. The schema provides a typical sales analysis environment with one fact table, ACTVARS (24,786,000 rows) and four dimension tables PRODLEVEL (9,000 rows), CUSTLEVEL (900 rows), TIMELEVEL (24 rows) and CHANLEVEL (9 rows). As usual for star schemas, dimension tables are denormalized to reduce join overhead. The fact table ACTVARS holds the measuring attributes *UnitsSold*, *DollarSales* and *DollarCost* for calculating aggregations.

In order to have a baseline reference for the experiments we apply our technique to one computer, simulating a centralized data warehouse and denote it as CDW (Centralized Data Warehouse). DWS-3 corresponds to the DWS technique applied to three computers. DWS-5 and DWS-10 correspond to data warehouse striping applied to five and ten computers, respectively.

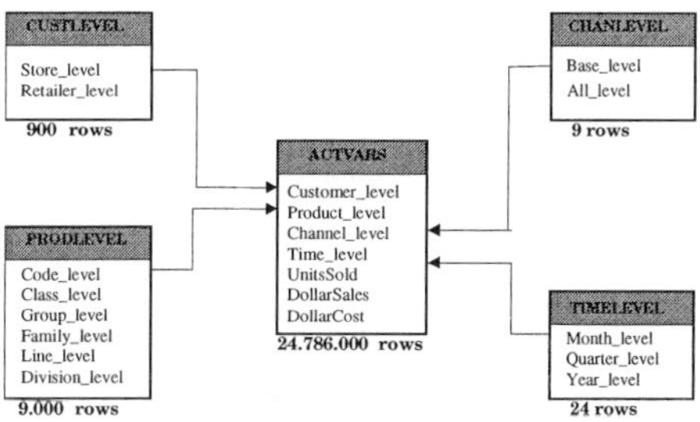

Figure 5: Simplified star schema of APB-1 benchmark

Typical OLAP queries use aggregation functions (SUM, COUNT, MAX, MIN, AVG, STDDEV and VARIANCE) as operators that aggregate a large number of rows in the fact table and return few rows as result. Accordingly, our experiences are simple queries that use these aggregation functions and return only one row. Another type of usual operation of OLAP queries is the join of the fact table with one or more dimensions, which is one of operations computationally most expensive. The objectives of these experiences are the evaluation of the speedup and scaleup of DWS using queries that use aggregation functions and joins.

The vast majority of queries, using the DWS approach, can be converted into queries that compute partial results, independently obtained in the different computers, and the global result can be computed very fast from these partial results. However, for some queries, the independent calculation of partial results is obtained through estimation of some steps. This is another important objective of these experiences, quantifying the error introduced this way in the final result.

4.2 Performance study

4.2.1 Aggregation performance

In order to evaluate the speedup of DWS using aggregation functions, the experiments are made with a simple type of queries, expressed in SQL:

```
select aggregate_function(unitssold)
from actvars
```

Different aggregation functions are used (SUM, COUNT, MAX, MIN, AVG, STDDEV, VARIANCE and ALL functions simultaneously) in order to evaluate the impact of the aggregation function in the query response time. The results query response time using the different aggregate functions are illustrated in Figure 6, for the centralized data warehouse (CDW), using three computers DWS-3, five computers DWS-5, and ten computers DWS-10.

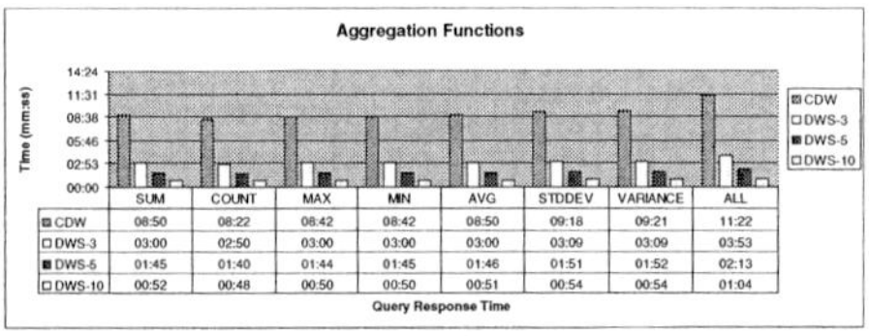

Figure 6: Query response time using aggregates

For each DWS environment the query response time does not depend significantly on which aggregation function is used because the same amount of rows have to be fetched and I/O dominates the response time. The execution times of STDDEV or VARIANCE functions are slightly larger, due to the increased complexity of the operations, and that of ALL aggregation functions simultaneously is about 30% larger in CDW.

The speedup is measured by adding more computers to the DWS system, but keeping the database size constant. Dividing the query response time of CDW by the corresponding time of DWS-X (where X denotes the number of computers) achieves a theoretical speedup of X. For instance, we could determine the speedup of the results from Figure 6 by taking the query response time for the centralized version (CDW) and dividing it by the query response time obtained with three, five and ten computers (DWS-3, DWS-5, DWS-10). The Figure 7b shows the speedup correspondent to query response time of Figure 7a when we are using ALL aggregation functions simultaneously.

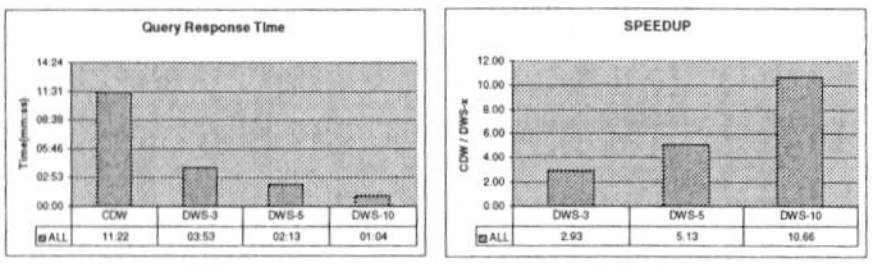

(a) (b)

Figure 7: Speedup using all aggregation functions

The most surprising result is that we obtained a speedup of 5.13 and 10.66 for DWS-5 and DWS-10 respectively, which is greater than the theoretical speedup, suggesting a super linear speedup of DWS when we distribute the data by more computers. As we see, this phenomenon is not present when we use DWS-3 because the workload in individual computers was approaching the memory limits. This result also emphasizes the scaleup advantages of DWS, as distributing the fact table over a larger number of smaller machines allows DWS system to cope with very large DW data.

4.2.2 Join performance

We have also tested DWS with queries that join the fact table with all the dimensions of the star schema of Figure 5. Four queries have been used in the experiments that join the fact table (ACTVARS) with the dimensions PRODLEVEL, TIMELEVEL, CUSTLEVEL and CHANLEVEL, which corresponds to 1-Join, 2-Join, 3-Join and 4-Join, respectively. For example, the 4-Join query corresponds to the following SQL statement:

```
select sum(unitssold)
from actvars, prodlevel, timelevel,
     custlevel, chanlevel
where < join conditions >
```

The other queries used in the experiments are similar to this one. Figure 8 shows the query response times for these four join queries. These experiments show that queries that take about 11 minutes in the centralized version (CDW) are executed in less than 4 minutes in DWS-3, about 2 minutes using DWS-5 and 1 minute using DWS-10.

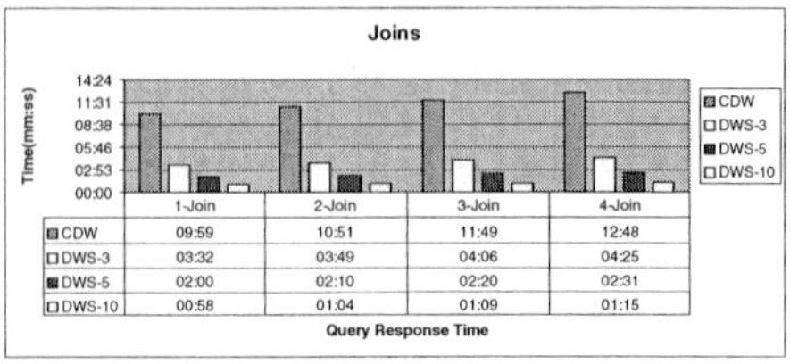

Figure 8: Query execution time with joins

Figure 9a shows the execution time and Figure 9b the corresponding speedup for the 4-Join query. This query that takes 12:48 minutes in CDW is executed in 4:25 minutes using DWS-3, 2:31 minutes using DWS-5 and only 1:15 minute using DWS-10, correspond to speedups of 2.9, 5.09 and 10.24, respectively.

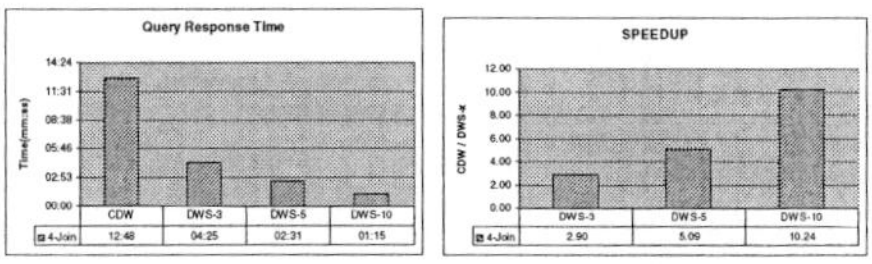

(a) (b)

Figure 9: Execution time and speedup using the 4-Join query

These results confirms our hypothesis of optimal speedup of DWS when the computers are not running near the memory limits as is the case of DWS-5 and DWS-10. Thus, for computers with the same characteristics, how much bigger is the data warehouse better speedup we will obtain using DWS. This is due to the fact the data set we are working on is distributed in more manageable data sets that could be more easily computed using computers limited by memory space.

4.2.3 Evaluation of dependent queries (DQ) with estimation procedures

In these experiments we quantify the error introduced by the estimation of intermediate results in subqueries, which restrict very much the number of rows that are selected.

Our experimental set-up is composed of the CDW, which calculates the exact result and both DWS-3 and DWS-5 systems. In the experiments we use the query Q0, defined in the previous section. A more restrictive query than Q0 is also defined, which computes the total number of units sold for a product whose sales are greater than the averages sales of the same product. We denote this as query Q3 and use it in the experiments with different product names. The SQL statement for query Q3 and product name 'GTMO4OPZVEDI ' is:

```
Q3:  select sum(unitssold)
     from actvars where
     product_level ='GTMO4OPZVEDI' and
     dollarsales >
          (select avg (dollarsales)
          from actvars where
          product_level ='GTMO4OPZVEDI')
```

This query selects 1,464 rows out of 24,786,000 from ACTVARS fact table. However, the query Q3 is modified to restrict even more the number of rows selected by the aggregation function, inserting an additional time level restriction. In the query Q4 (not shown) the time level restriction is inserted only in the subquery, while query Q5 also inserts the time level restriction in the main query, as illustrated by the following SQL statement:

```
Q5:  select sum(unitssold)
     from actvars where
     product_level ='GTMO4OPZVEDI' and
     time_level ='199506' and
     dollarsales >
          (select avg (dollarsales)
          from actvars where
          product_level ='GTMO4OPZVEDI'
          and time_level ='199505')
```

Query Q5 is a very selective query that only selects 103 rows from the fact table. Table 1 shows the results for the experiments done with the different queries. The columns in Table 1 show the names of the different products used by the queries, the number of rows that are selected by each query and the corresponding selectivity. The CDW column shows the correct final result of the query and the other columns DWS-3 and DWS-5 show the result using DWS with three or five computers and the relative error contained in these results.

The results show that when the selectivity of the query is very high, as Q0, the result of the query is estimated with very small error (0.06% for DWS-5 and no error for DWS-3). Using queries with very low selectivity, the error was always less than about 5% with DWS-5 and less than 1.2% with DWS-3.

4.3 Scalability of DWS

To analyse the scaleup we keep a constant hardware configuration and increase the data warehouse size. In this experiment we increased the data size 20 times and we measured the increase in the query response time. If the configuration can scaleup by a factor of 20 then the query response time will not increase more than 20 times. As comparison, we use again ALL the aggregation functions simultaneously, and the query response time is shown in Figure 10 (a) and (b) using a CDW and DWS-5, respectively.

Table 1: Error for the different queries when Dependent Queries (DQ) are executed as Independent Queries (IQ)

Query	Product	No. of rows sel.	Selectivity	CDW result	DWS-3		DWS-5	
					result	Error	result	error
Q0	All	8956764	36.13%	90955602	90955602	**0.00%**	91009415	**0.06%**
Q3	GTMO4OPZVEDI	1464	0.0059%	15416	15323	**0.60%**	15729	**2.03%**
Q3	JNVFUDO2QKIE	1397	0.0056%	14223	14110	**0.79%**	14155	**0.48%**
Q4	GTMO4OPZVEDI	1359	0.0055%	14445	14489	**0.30%**	15178	**5.07%**
Q4	JNVFUDO2QKIE	1345	0.0054%	13839	13813	**0.19%**	14022	**1.32%**
Q5	GTMO4OPZVEDI	103	0.0004%	1060	1049	**1.04%**	1039	**1.98%**
Q5	JNVFUDO2QKIE	100	0.0004%	979	968	**1.12%**	973	**0.61%**

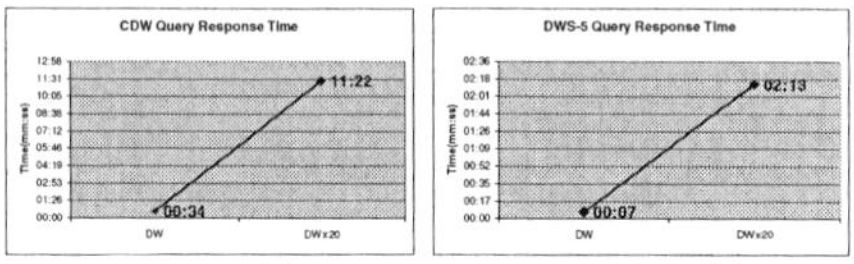

(a) (b)

Figure 10: Scaleup effect when the DW increases 20 times using CDW (a) and DWS-5 (b)

Calculating the respective scaleup, we obtain a scaleup of 20.06 for the CDW and 19.00 for DWS-5. For the CDW this value of scaleup means that when we increase the size of the DW the query response time is always slightly bigger than this increment. Using five computers (DWS-5) we see an interesting effect because the increment is only 19 times; less than then the theoretical increment of 20 times. This confirms our hypothesis of "the bigger is better" as increasing the size of the DW and distributing it by more computers the gain is even better.

5. CONCLUSIONS

The experimental results using aggregation and join queries show an optimal or even super linear speedup and also sow that DWS is scalable. This is due to the fact that, when we distribute the data, we are working with more manageable amounts of data that do not stress memory and computing resources so much. The manipulation of subqueries in an independent way is also possible with an error that can be negligible in most of the cases.

We believe that our modular approach can be incorporated into a commercial relational DBMS with little effort. However, there are still some open questions: one of the identified problems is big dimensions. Typically, dimensions are small in size but there are exceptions to this rule. In that case the space overhead of the strategy becomes more significant. Another future direction is to solve the problem of momentarily unavailability of one or more computer in a DWS.

REFERENCES

Agrawal, S., Chaudhuri, S., Narasayya, V. R., 2000, 'Automated Selection of Materialized Views and Indexes in SQL Databases', *Proceedings of VLDB'2000*, Cairo, Egypt, pp. 496-505.

Albrecht, J., Gunzel, H., Lehner, W., 1998, 'An Architecture for Distributed OLAP', *Int. Conf. on Parallel and Distributed Processing Techniques and Applications,* PDPTA'98.

APB-1 Benchmark, Olap Council, November 1998. Available at www.olpacouncil.org.

Bernardino, J., Madeira, H., 2000, 'A New Technique to Speedup Queries in Data Warehousing', *2000 ABDIS-DASFAA Symposium on Advances in Databases and Information Systems, Proceedings of Chalenges*, Prague, Czech Republic, September 5-8, pp.21-32.

Chauduri S., Dayal, U., 1997, 'An overview of data warehousing and OLAP technology', *SIGMOD Record*, 26(1), March, pp.65-74.

DeWitt D.J., Gray, J., 1992, 'Parallel Database Systems: The future of high performance database systems', *Communications of ACM*, 35(6), June, pp.85-98.

Kimball, R., 1996. *The Data Warehouse Toolkit*, Ed. John Wiley & Sons, Inc.

Lu, H., Ooi B., Tan, K., 1994. *Query Processing in Parallel Relational Database Systems.* IEEE Computer Society.

Oracle 1997, 'Star queries in Oracle 8', White paper, Oracle.

RedBrick 1998, 'Star Schema Processing for Complex Queries', White Paper, Red Brick Systems, Inc.

Srinivasan J., et al., 'Oracle8i Index-Organized Table and Its Application to New Domains', *Proceedings. of VLDB'2000*, Egypt, pp.285-296.

Wu, M., Buchmann, A., 1998, 'Encoded Bitmap Indexing for Data Warehouse', *Proceedings of the 14th International Conference on Data Engineering* (ICDE), Orlando, pp.220-230.

EVALUATION OF A VISUALISATION DESIGN FOR KNOWLEDGE SHARING AND INFORMATION DISCOVERY

Luis Borges Gouveia[1], Feliz Ribeiro Gouveia
CEREM University Fernando Pessoa, Pr. 9 de Abril, 349 P4249-004. Porto, Portugal
lmbg@ufp.pt , fribeiro@ufp.pt

[1]*PhD student, Computing Department, Lancaster University, Lancaster LA1 4YR England*

Keywords: visualisation, knowledge sharing, information discovery

Abstract: This paper presents a tool using a 3D interactive visualisation system that allows knowledge sharing and information discovery. The tool proposes a visualisation design using direct manipulation techniques to convey information about a structure for knowledge sharing. The structure describes a knowledge theme described as a set of concepts. The set of concepts provides a particular context description about the knowledge being shared. The application tested and presented in this paper uses the set of concepts to direct searches in the World Wide Web. The visualisation design is briefly presented and preliminary evaluation results are reported. These results show that the system tends to be better supporting people with some knowledge expertise about the knowledge being shared even if they have little World Wide Web expertise. These results seem to show some potential for the visualisation design as an interface for both knowledge sharing and information discovery. In particular, for people that has already some knowledge expertise about a given theme, but usually suffer from information overload or lack of knowledge about the structure of large information spaces, such as the World Wide Web.

1. INTRODUCTION

There seems to be general agreement that 3D visualisation offers a more convenient and natural way for people to interact with information spaces (as distinct from environments that are naturally 3D) (Tufte, 1990) and (Benedikt, 1992). Work of the type reported here is important in order to find out whether this is true and how (Gouveia, 1999). We must consider that to date there is not much evidence to support it, other than in cases where the information has a natural spatial component (Hubbold et al., 1995). A key problem for using a spatial layout which reflects potentially dynamically changing information is the user sense of position that can be lost if the layout changes (Ingram and Benford, 1995).

One application for testing the visualisation design is information discovery to support user efforts to find relevant information within a given knowledge domain (Gouveia, 1998) and (Li-Jen and Gaines, 1998). In this case, providing a means for users setting up a context, a query generation tool and an Information Visualisation (Card et al., 1999) allows users to have context and information about a particular data source for analysis and comparison.

This application will serve as *proof-of-concept* that based on a given context, shared as a 3D interactive visualisation, users can be assisted to retrieve information and analyse it — information discovery (Baeza-Yates and Ribeiro-Neto, 1990). The integration between the shared visualisation and data source information is made possible by using an information visualisation integrated with the visualisation design.

A number of systems have already taken advantage of 3D facilities. Two examples are (Benford et al., 1995) who proposed a virtual environment to support the co-operative browsing and filtering of large document stores, and (Chevalier and Verlhac, 2000) who present a 3D graphical representation of search results. (Chen, 1999) provides a discussion on Information Visualisation and Virtual Environments, and (Hearst, 1999) discusses user interfaces for communication between human and information retrieval systems.

J. Filipe et al. (eds.), Enterprise Information Systems III, 83–89.

The evaluation was conducted using a prototype that implements (Gouveia, 1998):

- a concept space as a 3D interactive visualisation;
- a visualisation design composed by two distinct visualisations: a concept space, representing the structure, and a criteria space that allows spatial positioning by specifying up to three criteria;
- data source integration by using an Information Visualisation within the criteria space visualisation;
- displaying of results using a search engine (the *AltaVista Search Personal eXtension 97*).

The rest of the paper is organised as follows: section 2 presents the goals of the system, section 3 describes the system, section 4 discusses the evaluation, section 5 analyses the results we obtained, and in section 6 we give our concluding remarks.

2. GOALS AND RATIONALE

The 3D interactive visualisation goal is to convey information about a structure for knowledge sharing. By knowledge sharing we mean activities that allow the dessimination of knowledge as the case of collaboration, repositories, training and context exploring (Clare and Detore, 2000). The proposed application focus on how to represent a context considering a given knowledge theme.

To test how this visualisation design could support knowledge sharing a system has been developed with one specific application in mind: give support to users in information discovery. The proposed system helps users to build their own queries by using a textual search engine based on information from the structure for knowledge sharing. It also allows the visualisation of data source information within the visualisation design and displaying of results using an HTML browser. The advantages of a tool like the one described are greater when data sources do not have an underlying structure and a query returns a vast amount of results as is the case of the World Wide Web.

The tool is based on a shared interactive representation of a knowledge theme that can be used to construct queries and compare a data source with the domain representation, using a 3D interactive visualisation. To allow reuse of each user efforts in information retrieval, a basic support for collaboration is implemented within the system to share the knowledge domain representation and to enhance it.

3. DESCRIPTION OF THE SYSTEM

The system uses a 3D interactive visualisation based on a structured description of a domain based in concepts and weighted keywords — the set of concepts is defined here as a *concept space*. In order to support sharing of these concept spaces, a user with proper rights can add new concepts and keywords, and modify the weights of the keywords. The tool implements a voting facility to support collaborative decision for each proposal.

Table 1 presents a partial structure for knowledge sharing with 5 concepts, defining the theme *Information Management*. Each concept is defined by a set of keywords that characterises it.

Table 1: A partial example of a structure for knowledge sharing about *Information Management*

[1] **Techniques** List of keywords (name, weight) Indexing 0.6 Pull 0.4 Push 0.4 Reading 0.6 Scanning 0.4 Textmining 0.8	[4] **People** List of keywords (name, weight) interpretation 0.7 knowledge 0.7 people 1.0 skills 0.6
[2] **Information** List of keywords (name, weight) Architecture 0.6 Cost 0.6 Information 1.0 Management 0.8 Meaning 0.8 Overload 0.6 Quantity 0.6 Resources 0.6 System 0.8 Value 0.8	[5] **Transformation** List of keywords (name, weight) cost 0.5 optimisation 0.6 people 0.6 planning 0.6 strategy 0.6
[3] **Management** List of keywords (name, weight) Information 0.8 Management 1.0 Organisation 0.8 People 0.8 Planning 0.6 Procedures 0.7 Strategy 0.7	

The exact number of keywords varies, as each concept can need more or less keywords to be described. Later, more keywords can be added to the concept. Each keyword consists of a word that can be used for searching, and an associated weight. The weight can also be modified later by users. The keyword weight is a value between 0.0 and 1.0 and can be understood as a membership value of the relation between the keyword and the concept. The sum of all weights for a given concept does not have to equal 1, since weights are not probabilities.

In this example, shown in Table 1, five concepts were defined, each one with a different number of keywords. Some of the keywords exist in more than one concept. For example, the *strategy* keyword exists in the concepts *Management* and *Transformation* with weights of 0.7 and 0.6 respectively. This may be used to detect a relationship between the two concepts based on the number of common keywords in each concept and on their weights.

The components of this structure (concepts, keywords and weights) were used to build a 3D interactive visualisation which also allows to visualise the relationships, if any, between the concepts. Users can more easily analyse the structure and its content by using the 3D interactive visualisation. The visualisation uses colour and virtual world style user navigation to take advantage of the visualisation design. Each concept is represented as a sphere with size and colour computed based on the concept keywords. The relationship between two concepts is visualised as colour coded lines. The colour code results from computing the keyword degree of similarity taking into account the common keywords and their weights in the two concepts. This visualisation is named a concept space. Figure 1 shows one possible concept space perspective.

The spatial position of each sphere is given by the user who proposes the new concept. After that, the spatial position remains constant. The constant spatial position for each concept (sphere) allows the construction of spatial references that can be recalled for the virtual world navigation. It also allows the creation of a visual image for the structure being shared and the opportunity to externalise the knowledge context for discussion and enhancement by a group of users.

Each user interacts with this shared visualisation — the concept space — and can produce a second visualisation from it for personal use, not to be shared. The second visualisation supports each user organisation of search and browse tactics allowing the creation of a criteria space using the existing concepts.

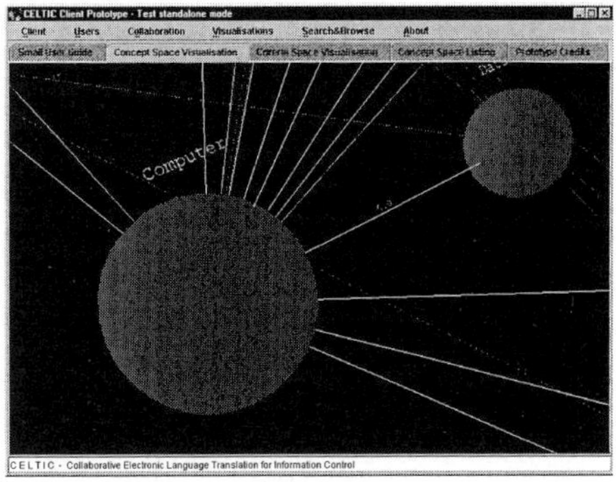

Figure 1: A perspective of the concept space visualisation

Figure 2 presents an example of a criteria space created by a user. As the criteria space is a three-dimensional space, the user can enter three criteria that are used to compute the spatial position of each concept based on its keyword weights.

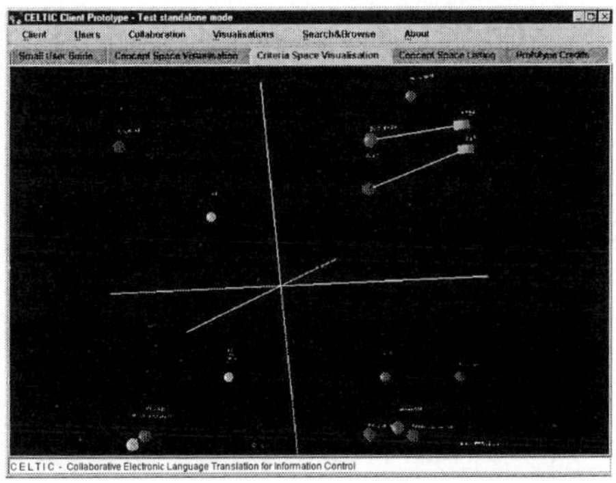

Figure 2: A perspective of a criteria space visualisation

The spatial position for each concept is calculated from comparing the criteria with existing keywords on the concept and using the keyword weight as a co-ordinate value for the criteria. If the criterion does not exist for a particular concept, a co-ordinate value of –1 is given to the concept for the corresponding criteria dimension. The resulting criteria space produces a visualisation of eight possible quadrants resulting from the three criteria combination of three dimensions.

In the criteria space visualisation, the placing of each concept depends on the weight of concept keywords. Each one of the eight quadrants represents a combination of the criteria — no criteria, c1, c2, c3, c1 and c2, c2 and c3, c3 and c1, c1 and c2 and c3 — being c1, c2 and c3, the first, second and third criteria.

The criteria space can be integrated with a data source. Using an Information Visualisation to compare concepts of the criteria space from the first quadrant — the one that contains all the concepts where all three criteria exist. The Information Visualisation symbols are green cylinders linked to the related concepts by lines — see figure 2. Figure 3 presents the results displayed in an HTML window after using the tool to generate the search query.

Figure 3: The HTML windows with query results

4. EVALUATION

System variables are set by scripting commands or are determined by the information your enter when you set up a Dial-Up Networking connection. System variables are read-only, which means they cannot be changed within the script.

The evaluation was conducted using the approach defended by (Shneiderman, 1998) for virtual environments. Work from (Cohen et al., 2000) concerning education issues was also considered for the evaluation design. (Sebrechts et al., 1999) claim in their study that there were high interface costs for the visualisation of search results, although those costs decrease substantially with user experience. An evaluation study conducted to research Web search behaviour of Internet experts and newbies uses as performance evaluation factors web expertise and knowledge domain expertise (Holscher and Strube, 2000). This study allows to verify that both factors were important although deficits in one or the two factors led to compensatory behaviour been knowledge expertise the most difficult to work since internet skills can with easy be trained for learning how to use search engines (Holscher and Strube, 2000).

To evaluate the proposed system we selected eleven undergraduate students from Fernando Pessoa University. The subjects were volunteers and no payment has been made for their participation. The knowledge domain was *Information Management*. The subjects were asked to use the prototype in the following six activities:

1. use the concept space and describe its meaning, by filling with words empty spaces in a set of sentences;
2. use the criteria space to relate the existing concepts giving the three criteria: *information*, *management* and *cost*;
3. choose the concept *Computer* and analyse its relation with other concepts;
4. try to create a criteria space where the *Knowledge* and *Enterprise* concepts would be related;
5. perform a search based on the *Information* concept;
6. perform a search based on the *management* criteria.

4.1 Evaluation script

The evaluation test was designed to have a one-hour and half and was composed of the following activities:

- subject fills a pre-experiment questionnaire (5 minutes);
- subject is given a general overview of the tool functionality (10 minutes demo);
- subject undertakes a lab training period (10 minutes);
- break (5 minutes);
- continuous session for performing the described six activities (50 minutes);
- subject fills a post-experiment questionnaire (10 minutes).

The test was repeated for each subject.

4.2 Evaluation factors

The evaluation was conducted based on a reduced number of variables. For organising data gathering a number of evaluation factors were considered:

- Asking each student:
  - what they have *learned* (as measured by a multiple-choice questionnaire);
  - how they think the system *helped* them (with a like/dislike rating);
  - what is their *opinion* about using the system(with a like/dislike rating);
- taking the *time to complete* of the six activities;
- performance is examined taking into account students opinion for rating as low or high their own expertise considering:
  - the Web expertise
  - the Knowledge domain expertise (*Information Management*)

4.3 Gathered data

Table 2 summarises the data collected during the evaluation test. The eleven subjects were considered and the values for each of the evaluation factors were collected into Table 2. At the bottom of each column, the value range of each of the evaluation factors is shown.

Table 2: Evaluation data

Subject	Learn	Help	Opinion	Complete	Time to complete	Web expertise	knowledge expertise
1	7	4	6	6	34	5	5
2	5	5	5	6	41	4	4
3	6	2	4	6	44	7	4
4	6	6	3	6	32	7	5
5	9	6	6	6	39	6	6
6	8	7	5	6	41	5	6
7	7	4	6	4	50	4	5
8	3	4	2	5	45	3	3
9	6	5	5	6	30	6	3
10	5	6	4	5	50	2	2
11	4	1	3	4	50	2	2
	0 - 10	1 - 7	1 – 7	1 - 6	0 - 50 mm	1 - 7	1 - 7

Learn ten test questions
Help value 1-7 low/high
Opinion value 1-7 low/high
Complete 1 to 6 situations
time to complete minutes
web expertise value 1-7 low/high
knowledge expertise value 1-7 low/high

5. ANALYSING THE RESULTS

5.1 Statistical analysis

The first step is to consider *learn*, *help*, *opinion* and *time to complete* as the independent variables. The dependent variables are Web expertise (*webexp*) and knowledge expertise (*knowexp*). The normalised data table for statistical treatment is presented in Table 3.

The variable *learn* keeps its values between 1 and 10. The variables *help* and *opinion* were dichotomised. These value were dichotomised by grouping the values 1, 2, 3, and 4 converted to 0, and the values 5, 6, and 7 converted to 1.

The *complete* variable was also dichotomised converting the values 4 and 5 to 0, and the value 6 to 1. In this case, the variable reports subjects that accomplished all the proposed tasks.

Dependent variables *web* and *knowledge* expertise where also dichotomised converting the values 1, 2, 3, and 4 to 1, and values 5, 6, and 7 to 2.

We used the Binomial model for *learn*, *help* and *opinion* variables. For the *time to complete* variable (taking into account the *complete* variable), the Cox proportional hazards model was selected.

The statistical software package was *Glim 4*, version 8 from the Royal Statistical Society, running in a Sun SPARCstation. The statistical tests were conducted with the help of the Centre for Applied Statistics at Lancaster University.

Table 3: Normalised data

Subject	Learn	Help	Opinion	Complete	time to complete	Web expertise	knowledge expertise
1	7	0	1	1	34	2	2
2	5	1	1	1	41	1	1
3	6	0	0	1	44	2	1
4	6	1	0	1	32	2	2
5	9	1	1	1	39	2	2
6	8	1	1	1	41	2	2
7	7	0	1	0	50	1	2
8	3	0	0	0	45	1	1
9	6	1	1	1	30	2	1
10	5	1	0	0	50	1	1
11	4	0	0	0	50	1	1

5.2 General observations

Using Table 3 for the statistical tests, the following observations can be made.

About the *learn* variable (test questionnaire):

- *web* expertise has significance at a 5% level;
- *knowledge* expertise has significance at a 1% level;
- both *web* and *knowledge* expertise are significant but with *knowledge* subject being more significance. No important interaction between both variables has been reported.

About the relation between *web* and *knowledge* experience:

- in the presence of *knowledge* expertise, the *web* expertise is no more significant at a 5% level;
- in the presence of web expertise, the *knowledge* subject expertise is approximately significant at a 5% level.

About the *help* variable (low/high help for the users):

- there is no evidence of meaningful effects with *web* and *knowledge* expertise;
- with both *web* and *knowledge* expertise together there is also no effects.

About the *opinion* variable (low/high help for the users):

- *web* expertise is not significant;
- *knowledge* expertise is approximately significant at a 10% level;
- with both *web* and *knowledge* expertise there are no effects.

About the *time to complete* variable (taking into account the subjects that have completed all the tasks):

- *web* expertise is significant at 1% level;
- *knowledge* expertise is significant at 5% level;
- both *web* and *knowledge* expertise do not have any relation (there's no reason to change the above statement).

6. CONCLUDING REMARKS

Based on the statistical analysis it is possible to make several observations concerning the experiment.

People *learn* more when they had already some expertise in the *knowledge* area (in this case, *Information Management*). The importance of using the *web* before was moderate although not so important as the *knowledge* expertise to explain the questionnaire results (*learn*).

The users feeling about how the system *helps* them has not any impact from their *web* or *knowledge* expertise. When considering the user *opinion* about the system, then *knowledge* expertise seems to have some importance, regardless of the web expertise.

Operation of the system seems to be influenced by the users *web* expertise in a very important way. The *knowledge* expertise also assists users in system operation.

Overall, the system tends to be better supporting people with some *knowledge* expertise and little *web* expertise. This seems to show some potential as an interface to access information for people that have already some *knowledge* expertise. However more evaluation is needed in more knowledge domains and with more people using the system.

The use of visualisation techniques can improve the interface by supporting familiar cues to the user perception and thus convey information for knowledge sharing.

People were able to use the visualisation design which allowed them to take advantage of context information about a given knowledge theme (*Information Management*). The proposed system shows that a user can take advantage of sharing knowledge to support information retrieval by representing it as a 3D interactive visualisation context.

REFERENCES

Baeza-Yates, R. and Ribeiro-Neto, B. (1999). *Modern information retrieval.* Addison Wesley.

Benedikt, M. (1992). Cyberspace: Some proposals. In Benedikt, Michael. Cyberspace, first steps. Third printing. MIT Press, pp 119-224.

Benford S. and Snowdon D. and Greenhalgh, C. and Ingram, R. and Knox, I. and Brown, C. (1995). VR-Vibe: A virtual environment for co-operative information retrieval. Computer Graphics Forum, 14(3), pp C349-C360.

Card, S. and Mackinlay, J. and Shneiderman, B. (1999). Readings in Information Visualization. Using Vision to Think. Morgan Kaufmann.

Chen, C. (1999). Information Visualisation and Virtual Environments. Springer.

Chevalier, M. and Verlhac, M. (2000). ISIDOR: A Visualisation Interface for Advanced Information Retrieval. Proceeding of ICEIS 2000, 2nd International Conference On Enterprise Information Systems, pp 414 - 418, 4-7 june, Stafford, UK.

Clare, M. and Detore, A. (2000). Knowledge Assets. Harcout Brace.

Cohen, L. and Manion, L. and Morrison, K. (2000). Research Methods in Education. 5th Edition. Routledge Falmer.

Gouveia, L. (1998). End of first year report. PhD first year assessment. CSEG Group, Computing Department. Lancaster University. Internal Report, September.

Gouveia, L. (1999). Shared Visualisation and Virtual Environments for Co-operative Learning. ECSCW'99 conference. Doctoral Colloquium. 12-16 September. Conference proceedings supplement, pp. 70-72.

Hearst, M. (1999) User Interfaces and Visualization. In (Baeza-Yates and Ribeiro-Neto, 1999). Modern Information Retrieval. Addison Wesley.

Holscher, C. and Strube, G. (2000). Web search behavior of Internet Experts and newbies. 9th International World wide Web conference WWW9, Amsterdam.

Hubbold, R. and Murta, A. and West, A. and Howard, T. (1995). Design Issues for Virtual Reality Systems. In Gobel, M (ed.) Virtual Environments'95. Springer, pp 224-236.

Ingram, R. and Benford, S. (1995). Improving the Legibility of Virtual Environments. In Gobel, M (ed.) Virtual Environments'95. Springer, pp 211-223.

Li-Jen, L. and Gaines, B. (1998). Modelling and Supporting Virtual Cooperative Interaction Through the World Wide Web. In Sudweeks, F. et al. (eds) Network & Netplay. MIT Press.

Sebrechts, M. and Vasilakis, J. and Miller, S. and Cugini, J. and Laskowski, S. (1999). Visualisation of search results: a comparative evaluation of text, 2D and 3D interfaces. 22nd Conference on Research and Development in Information Retrieval ACM SIGIR, Berkley, pp 3-10.

Shneiderman, B. (1998). Designing the User Interface. Strategies for Effective Human-Computer Interaction. Third Edition. Addison Wesley.

Tufte, E. (1990). Envisioning Information. Graphics Press.

NOVEL DATA VISUALISATION AND EXPLORATION IN MULTIDIMENSIONAL DATASETS

Nikolaos Kotsis, George R. S. Weir, John D. Ferguson, Douglas R. MacGregor
Department of Computer Science, University of Strathclyde, Richmond Street, Glasgow G1 1XH, UK
Email: n.kotsis@stefi.gr , gw@cs.strath.ac.uk , jf@cs.strath.ac.uk , douglas@cs.strath.ac.uk

Keywords: Data visualisation, multi-dimensional data, OLAP.

Abstract: Commonly, decision support systems require large-scale data analysis facilities for efficient decision-making. While OLAP tools provide multidimensional analysis, traditional visualisations prove inadequate as means of viewing and exploring complex relationships across multiple dimensions. Commercial databases often support a variety of two or three dimensional visualisation facilities, including bar charts, scatter diagrams, data plots, and cross tabulations. In this context, the present paper describes a novel approach to the problem of access and visualisation for data in complex hierarchical datasets. The approach integrates a novel browsing technique, which affords user navigation in several levels of summary information, with a modified scatter projection of the measure of interest. A prototype implementation of the proposed approach has been developed. This is described and advocated as a multidimensional interface for OLAP that addresses several significant issues in visualisation and exploration of multidimensional datasets.

1. INTRODUCTION

A natural progression of technology into business realms occurs wherever innovation affords a commercial edge. There is reasonable expectation that technological advance brings cost savings through greater efficiency, less obvious are the potential benefits from enhanced decision-making. Fundamental to any decision making process is the assimilation of relevant information, the identification of trends, location of exceptional circumstances, and estimation of likely impact from anticipated decisions. Since many contexts are highly complex, accurate historical perspectives are often invoked to support such decision-making. Historical database systems afford means of storing and analysing such data, but there is continuing need for facilities to aid assimilation of patterns, exceptions and to enable predictions. One trend is the use of visualisation techniques that aim to support end-users in data exploration and discovery. Allied to this is the increasing use of multidimensional and hierarchical datasets attempting to do justice to the complexity of decision making contexts.

In the following, we suggest that traditional visualisations prove ill suited as windows on complex relationships across multiple dimensions. As aid to this conjecture, we must understand the underlying nature of the data and relationships that such systems support. Thereafter, we will consider the scope and limitations of such systems in contrast to the interface technique that we advocate here.

2. FROM RELATIONAL TO MULTIDIMENSIONAL MODEL

Currently, most database management systems are built upon the relational data model (Codd, 1970). The central data construct in this model is a *relation* that is a set of *records,* each record has the same number (and type) of *fields*. A *database* is a collection of one or more relations. A description of data in terms of a data model is called a *schema.* In the relational model, the schema for a relation specifies its name, the name of each field (or *attribute* or *column)* and the *domain* (type) of each field. For example, 'Product' is a relation with the following schema:

Product (Product_ID: integer, Type:string,Date: string)

J. Filipe et al. (eds.), Enterprise Information Systems III, 90–96.

The above schema signifies that each row in the Product relation has three fields, with field names and types as indicated. An example instance of the Product relation is shown in Figure 1:

Product_ID	Type	Production_Date
234	Shampoo	10/3/97
677	Soap	10/5/98
854	Conditioner	12/7/98

Figure 1: Example of the Product relation

Using the Structured Query Language (ANSI, 1992), we may pose a query on the Product relation such as 'Give me Products produced in 1998'. In SQL this query may be expressed as:

Select P.Product_ID
From *Product*
Where P.Production_Date=1998

The need to represent and manipulate more complex data structures is addressed in OLAP systems. Such systems provide multidimensional data analysis by computing summaries and breakdowns along mant dimensions. They are designed for decision support where historical, summarised data are more important than detailed individual records.

OLAP tools typically analyse multidimensional or hierarchical data by aggregating data values along many dimensions. The aggregation functions are relational operators; they consume and produce relations (Graefe, 1993). (Klug 1982) presents aggregation expressions by extending the relational algebra and relational calculus. OLAP systems can be based upon relational data structures (ROLAP), multidimensional data structures (MOLAP) of Hybrid OLAP (HOLAP).

In the first instance, ROLAP employs the star schema which comprises a fact table and several dimension tables (Schneider, 1997). An example of a fact table may be the relation Sales with the following schema:

Fact Table:

Sales*(Product_ID:integer, Store_ID:integer, Time_ID:integer, Quantity:integer)*

Dimension Tables:

Products *(ProductID, Type)*
Store *(StoreID, City, Country, Continent)*
Time *(TimeID, Month, Year)*

Here, the measure of interest is QUANTITY, which is dependent on several attributes (dimensions), *viz.* PRODUCT, STORE, and TIME (in Months). Each dimension may have a set of attributes denoting the hierarchy in this dimension. A simple example of a hierarchy is the StoreID in the Store dimension schema, in which City belongs to Country and Country belongs to Continent. The hierarchy is illustrated below:

StoreID > City > Country > Continent

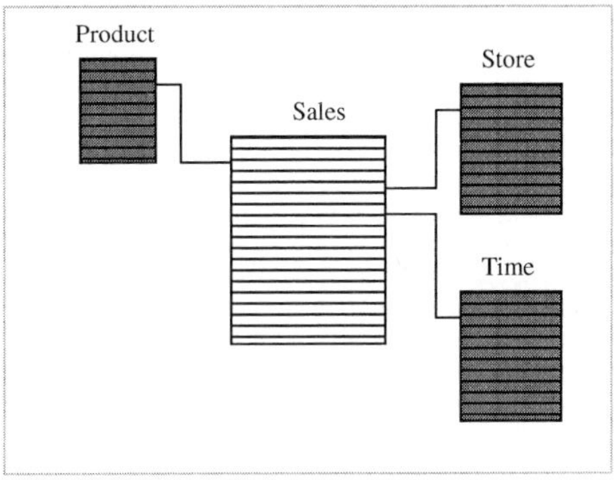

The Star Schema

This relationship between dimensions and measures can be realised as a multidimensional cube (Figure 2).

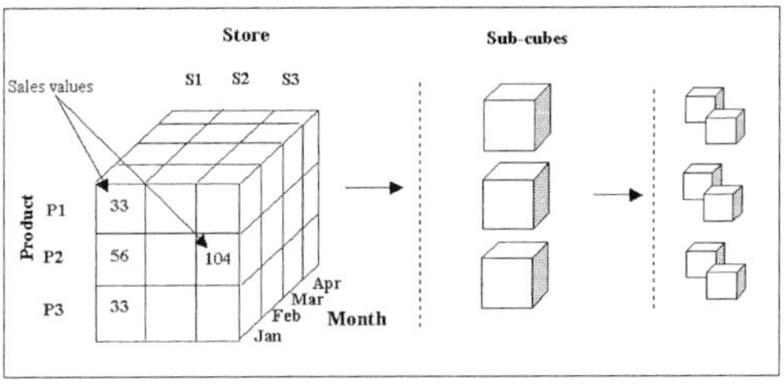

Figure 2: Multidimensional data cube

In principle, multidimensional analysis is supported by graphical user interfaces and differs from traditional querying in requiring no SQL skills. Manipulation of the Cube is completely graphical and operations are straightforward. OLAP tools support graphical interaction to analyse 2-D, 3-D, or even higher-dimensional sub-cubes. The user can *drill-down* by first looking at the total sales per quarter of the year and then total sales per month in that quarter. The opposite process is called *Roll-up*. *Slice* amounts to an equality selection and *dice* amounts to a range selection. *Rotate* applies when the view is rotated 90 degrees clockwise without any rearrangement of the data. In a comparable relational environment this new view would require a complex query or sort.

3. APPROACHES TO VISUALISATION

Traditionally, interfaces to database systems present the database from a system's view, providing the user with a means to gain access to its functionality. From this basis, many tools have been developed in support of user interaction with the database, allowing them to perform the variety of required functions.

The development of database interfaces has migrated over time from a textual format, such as SQL, to a forms based approach, such as QBE, and on to diagrammatic and iconic representations, such as CQl. Along with this migration there has been a move from single to multi-paradigm approaches, and to techniques employing graphical data browsing with multi-dimensional visualization techniques (Goldstein & Roth, 1994).

Database systems enable users to make selections from available data classifications and view the resultant values in one or more graphical realisations. A key requirement for any visualisation is the ability to display both the selected classifications (dimensions) and the resultant data set (cross tabulation). This allows the user to view the data in conjunction with the selection criteria. The simplest two-dimensional method is a cross-tab (e.g., Figure 3).

	Jan	Feb	Mar	Apr	May
Item1	56	234	45	30	56
Item2	34	50	546		78
Item3	06	43	90	80	67
Item4	10	08	56	34	75
Item5	76	34		30	89

Figure 3: A cross-tab approach to data visualisation

Multidimensional datasets prove awkward for visualisation. Hypercubes may be employed as three-dimensional conceptualisations for such datasets. This approach can map sets of hypercubes (each of three dimensions) on to cuboid sections of a more complex multidimensional data space (cf. Figure 2, above).

Clearly, attempts to display multidimensional data by means of a 'hypercube' representation are a progression beyond two-dimensional tabulation of data. In principal, users can manipulate a cube representation to slice a 3D section of data from any multidimensional dataset. The hypercube has superior visualisation properties when compared to conventional display methods but is limited by its very nature when applied to datasets of four and more dimensions. No manipulation of a cube can simultaneously display more than three dimensions of a dataset. Furthermore, the rotational cube display invariably obscures some data dimensions. A further limitation of the hypercube as a display mechanism is the need for real-time three-dimensional rendering. This may impose severe performance demands on the display facility.

Among the wide variety of data visualization techniques that have been devised over the years, approaches can be classified under the following headings (Keim, 1997):

1. Geometric techniques

Such approaches make use of geometric transformations and projection of the data. Examples here include Scatterplot-matrices (Cleveland, 1993), Landscapes (Wright, 1995), projection pursuit techniques that find meaningful projections of multidimensional data (Hubert, 1985), Prosection views (Su et al, 1995), Hyperslice (van Wijk & van Liere, 1993) and Parallel coordinates (Inselberg & Dimsdale, 1990).

2. Pixel-orientated techniques

In these techniques, each attribute value is represented by one coloured pixel and the values for different attributes are shown in different windows. This approach subdivides into either query independent techniques (Keim, Kwiegel & Ankerst, 1995) including space-filling and recursive pattern techniques or query dependent techniques (Keim & Kriegel, 1994) such as spiral, axis and circle segment techniques.

3. Icon-based techniques

In this approach, different data values are visualized as features of icons. Examples include Stick Figures (Picket, 1970), Colour Icons (Keim & Kriegel, 1994) with arrays of colour icons representing different attribute values and TileBars with small icons representing the relevance feature vectors in document retrieval.

4. Hierarchical techniques

Here, data visualization is accomplished by hierarchical partitioning into subspaces. Dimensional stacking (LeBlanc et al, 1990),

Treemaps (Johnson, 1993), Cone Trees (Robertson et al, 1991), World-within-Worlds (Feiner & Beshers, 1990) and the InfoCube (Rekimoto & Green, 1993) utilizing 3D visualization of hierarchical data with transparent boxes, are all examples of this class.

5. Graph-bases techniques

A number of approaches here range from simple basic graphs with lines, polylines, etc., to more specific graphs – Directed Acyclic, Hypergraphs, etc., to systems such as SeeNet (Becker, Eick & Wilks, 1995) and Hy+ (Consens et al, 1994).

6. Hybrid techniques

This final class integrates the use of multiple techniques to enhance the effectiveness of the visualization. An example is the use of scatter plots of icons in Starfield Displays (Ayers & Stasko, 1994) with dynamic zooming and mapping in IVEE (Ahlberg & Wistrand, 1995).

4. THE POLYDIM APPROACH

The approach that we recommend in this paper is a Hybrid Technique called 'PolyDim'. PolyDim combines the use of scatter plots, dynamic zooming and direct schema exploration with more orthodox two-dimensional data display, in support of effective user-driven visualisation.

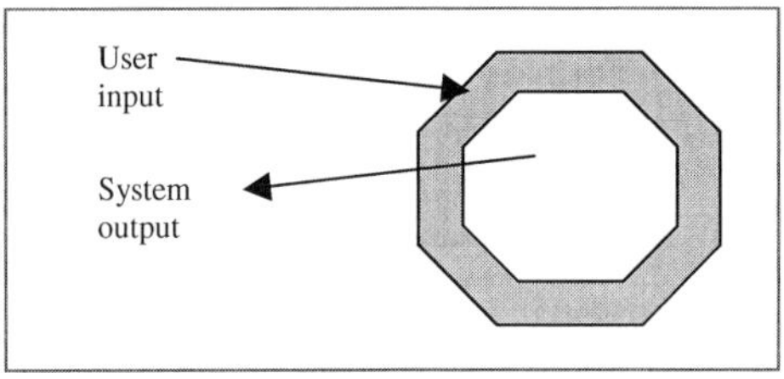

The Polydim Approach

PolyDim is motivated in part, by the belief that OLAP applications should enable the end user to navigate in the database schema. The database schema is the structural characteristics of the data. Any user query must locate data with reference to the existing schema. Consequently, applications that explicitly represent the schema to the user can provide better-directed query facilities. The complexity of multidimensional databases greatly increases the difficulty of explicit schema representation. This is often due to the presence of hierarchies within the multiple dimensions (Kotsis, 2000).

In a data warehouse application fronted by an OLAP system, the data warehouse keeps summarized information, called materialised views. The number of materialzed views depends upon the schema of the dataset and increases by 2^n (where n is the number of dimensions) (Gray et al, 1995). Essentially, two strategies exist for querying multidimensional database. One is the traditional SQL approach and the other is the graphical multidimensional approach. The multidimensional model supports the operators drill-down, roll-up, rotate and slice.

The primary visualisation requirement for multidimensional data is a facility to display datasets drawn from any combination of dimensions. In turn, the interface must readily enable users to select the desired conjunction of dimensions and, where appropriate, levels of hierarchy. PolyDim addresses both of these needs in a single integrated facility. The first innovative feature of the PolyDim interface is its use of a polygon structure in which each side represents a separate data dimension.

PolyDim is a multi-form interface with regard to the number of dimensions it can handle. When handling two dimensions, PolyDim adopts the traditional spreadsheet structure. For three dimensions, PolyDim forms a triangle and in four dimensions forms a rectangle. Beyond four dimensions, PolyDim adopts a polygon shape (Figure 4).

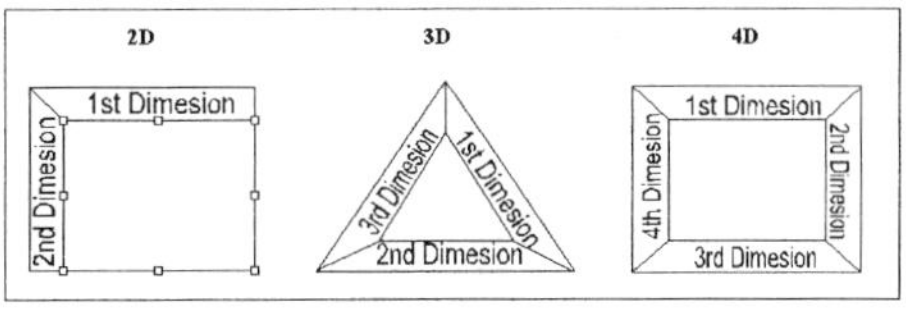

Figure 4: Transition from 2 dimensions to 4 dimensions using the *PolyDim* approach

In turn, these dimensions can be expanded to portray underlying hierarchical structure. Thereby, the interface makes the user aware of the available dimensions and their constituent hierarchies.

For instance, we may have an eight dimensional dataset (Figure 5a) in which each of the dimensions can be expanded into separate hierarchical components (see Figure 5b). Selection of any subset of the data cube and any level of the hierarchy is achieved by simply clicking the mouse on the desired area of the middle and outer polygon.

4.1 Interaction

A novel feature of PolyDim is that it combines multidimensional schema exploration with data visualisation, and direct manipulation, thereby providing efficient interactive navigation through the traditional summary tables.

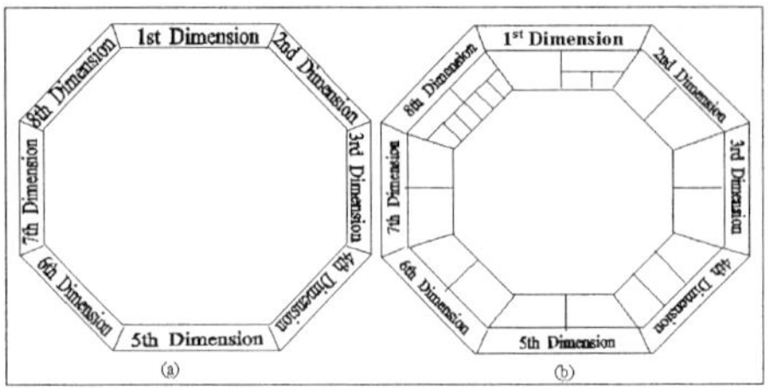

Figure 5: PolyDim interface for an eight dimensional dataset (a) without hierarchies and (b) with hierarchies

PolyDim explicitly and simultaneously represents multiple dimensions and their hierarchical structure and supports direct input that enables the user to explore freely any combination of dimensions and hierarchies in the database schema. Additionally, further refinement is afforded through direct selection of any displayed data points. Significantly, all of these features are integrated within a single direct manipulation interface.

The polygonal structure represents the database shema, wherein the dimensions of the polygon correspond to attributes of the fact table in the multidimensional model. This outer 'containment ring' of the PolyDim display provides the available choice of schema dimensions with their hierachies. Users indicate required dimensions (or their hierarchical components) by directly selecting these items from the PolyDim interface. As a result, the system projects the corresponding tuples in the 'inner circle' of the PolyDim display. Thus, Figure 4 represents equivalence between the eight dimensions selected by the user on the PolyDim control band and the corresponding database fact table. Note that there is a direct mapping between the two modes, with the sides of the polygon corresponding to attributes in the fact table and the data projection of Sales in the inner ring of the PolyDim display.

4.2 Generating PolyDim queries

Given the fact table (in Figure 6, above) and the query 'give me Sales from Glasgow in Shampoo for the year 1999', if the corresponding dimensions for Glasgow, Shampoo and Year are the 1st, 2nd and 3rd dimensions respectively in our fact table, the aggregate would be the table shown below (Fig. 7).

1st	2nd	3rd	4th	5th	6th	7th	8th	Sales
D1	D21	D31	D41	D51	D61	D71	D81	90
D1	D21	D31	D41	D52	D61	D72	D83	60
D3	D23	D32	D42	D51	D62	D73	D84	40
D2	D24	D34	D43	D51	D64	D74	D85	35
D1	D25	D34	D43	D51	D65	D75	D86	20
D2	D24	D34	D41	D53	D63	D76	D87	50
D1	D24	D33	D41	D51	D63	D76	D88	70
D4	D22	D33	D42	D51	D62	D77	D89	55
D1	D24	D34	D42	D51	D65	D77	D82	100

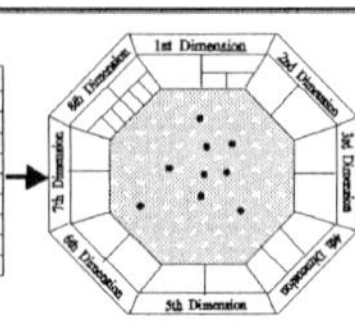

Figure 6: Transition from 8-attribute fact table to the 8-dimension *PolyDim* with hierarchies

In this case, the mapping between dimensions in the table to the PolyDim display is a triangle. During the query stage the user indicates the appropriate dimensions by pointing to (mouse clicking) the appropriate side of the polygon. As a result, the data projection shows the aggregate values for Sales.

Any change in the shape of the PolyDim poses a new query in the database. If the query is a materialised view then PolyDim simply displays this view or else invokes an aggregation to the database. In this manner it is a complete interface between the user and the database.

1st	2nd	3rd	Sales
D1	D21	D31	150
D3	D23	D32	40
D1	D25	D34	20
D2	D24	D34	85
D4	D22	D33	55
D1	D24	D34	170

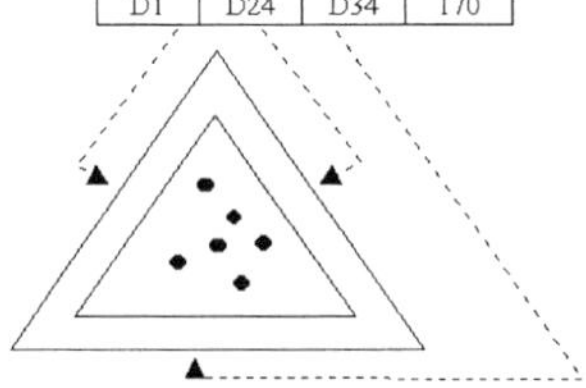

Figure 7: Aggregation in three dimensions within the PolyDim

4.3 Data projection and pattern discovery visualization form

The data values that are selected as a result of user manipulation of the PolyDim control interface are 'projected' in the inner ring of the PolyDim display. Additionally, users can generate an equivalent table of values (part of PolyDim's hybrid nature) and may select individual data points from within the display for further information on the scale or source of that data point. While individual data points may be of user significance, our approach emphasises the 'shape' of data sets (as projected by PolyDim). This is intended to support pattern recognition as a basis for data discovery.

Two novel features for visualizing the measure of interest have so far been implemented in PolyDim. Both follow the principle of projecting the measure of interest from the sides to the centre

The first display feature uses a technique called a *spider*. In this case, straight lines to the corresponding dimensions and hierarchies link to any user-selected data point. Thereby, the user can readily determine the origin of any measure.

The second display feature is called a *Grid*, wherein circles are displayed for every level in the unit of the measure. This resembles a radar chart (as described in Microsoft Excel). Each category has its own value axis radiating from the centre point. Lines connect all the values in the same series. A radar chart compares the aggregate values of a number of data series.

Comparing Polydim with traditional OLAP visualization techniques we note its conveniency in both multidimensional navigation and data visualization.

Navigating through multiple dimensions in Polydim is simply a matter of choosing a side of the outer polygon. Selecting dimension hierarchies is achieved by picking the appropriate sides of the middle polygon.

In data projection, the ability of both the spider and radar charts in visualising large number of data points is significant. Traditional spreasheet tools limit the number of records projected in a page, typically less than 80 lines. In contrast PolyDim displays records as data points, thus allowing more data to be displayed.

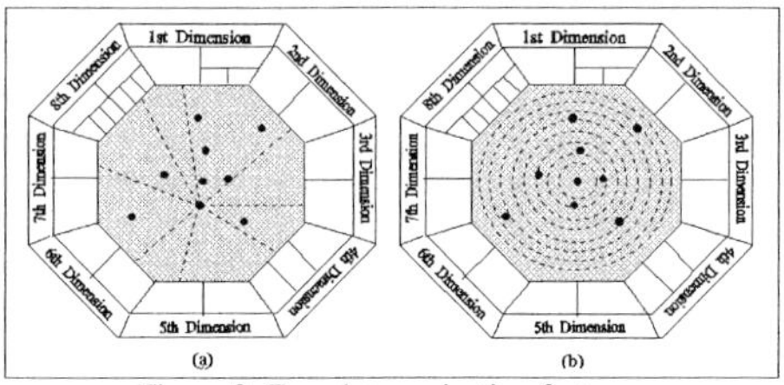

Figure 8: Two data projection features (a) Spider and (b) Grid

5. CONCLUSION

PolyDim is designed with a view to efficient schema browsing, data navigation and visualization across several levels of summary information. Since the number of multidimensional aggregates in a data cube is 2^n combinations of dimensions, a fact table with ten dimensions presents the user with 1,024 group-bys. Such exponential increase in multidimensional aggregates can be difficult to handle with traditional displays since the user can only see two dimensions at a time.

PolyDim provides a unique way to navigate through large numbers of aggregates simply by selecting dimensions in the polygon (n-dimensions). The user may easily apply multidimensional data operators, such as drill-down and roll-up, by pointing and clicking the mouse on the hierarchy of interest. The user may also select dimensions or dimension hierarchies from the sides of the polygon and by pressing a button start aggregation. The aggregation results are projected into the display facility, located within the polygon. Displaying records as data points in PolyDim allows large number of records be accomadated into the projected area.

A prototype version of the PolyDim interface has been implemented in java. This serves as a test bed for experimentation and validation of the approach described in the present paper. Future work includes the improvement of the current implementation and user's feedback for the validation of PolyDim. We anticipate that forthcoming results will further endorse our view that PolyDim affords an amenable and powerful interface for multidimensional data exploration and visualisation.

REFERENCES

Ahlberg C., Shneiderman B., 'Visual Information Seeking: Tight Coupling of Dynamic Query Filters with Starfield Displays', *Proc. Human Factors in Computing Systems CHI '94 Conf.*, Boston, MA, 1994, pp 313-317.

Ayers E.Z., Stasko J.T., 'Using Graphic History in Browsing the World Wide Web', *Proc. 4th World Wide Web Conf.*, Boston, MA, 1995.

Ahlberg C., Wistrand E., 'IVEE: An information Visualization and Exploration Environment', *Proc. Int. Symp. on Information Visualization*, Atlanta, GA, 1995, pp 66-73.

ANSI, SQL Standard, 1992.

Becker R.A., Eick S.G., Wilks A.R., 'Visualizing Network Data', *Trans. on Visualization and Computer Graphics*, Vol. 1, No. 1, 1995.

Cleveland W.S., *Visualizing Data*, AT&T Bell Laboratories, Murray Hill, NJ, Hobart Press, Summit NJ, 1993.

Codd E.F., Codd S.B., Salley C.T., 'Providing OLAP (On-Line Analytical Processing) to User Analysts: An IT Mandate', URL link: 'http://www.hyperion.com/whitepapers.cfm'.

Consens M.P., et al., 'Architecture and Applications of Hy+ Visualization System', *IBM Journal*, Vol. 33, No. 3, 1994, pp 458-476.

Feiner S., Beshers C., 'Visualizing n-Dimensional Virtual Worlds with n-Vision', *Computer Graphics*, Vol. 24, No. 2, 1990, pp 37-38.

Graefe G., 'Query Evaluation Techniques for Large Databases', ACM Computing Surveys 25(2):73-170, June 1993.

Gray J., Bosworth A., Layman A., Pirahesh H., *Data Cube: A Relational Aggregation Operator Generalizing Group-By, Cross-Tab, and Sub-Totals*, Technical Report MSR-TR-95-22, Microsoft Research, Redmond 1995.

Goldstein, Jade and Roth, S.F. Using Aggregation and Dynamic Queries for Exploring Large Data Sets, *Proceedings of Human Factors in Computing Systems* '94, (April 24-29,1994 Boston MA), pp.23-29.

Hubert P.J., 'Projection Pursuit', *The Annals of Statistics*, Vol. 13, No. 2, 1985, pp 435-474.

Inselberg A., Dimsdale B., 'Parallel Coordinates: A Tool for Visualizing Multi-Dimensional Geometry', *Visualization '90*, San Francisco, CA, 1990, pp 361-370.

Johnson B., *Visualizing Hierarchical and Categorical Data*, Ph.D. Thesis, Department of Computer Science, University of Maryland, 1993.

Keim, D.A., 'Visual Data Mining', Tutorial in the 23rd International Conference on Very Large Databases, (26-29 August 1997 Athens, Greece), pp 229-290.

Keim D.A., Kriegel H.P., 'VisDB: Database Exploration using Multidimensional Visualization', *Computer Graphics & Applications*, Sept. 1994, pp 40-49.

Keim D.A., Kriegel H.P., Ankerst M., 'Recursive Pattern: A Technique for Visualizing Very Large Amounts of Data', *Proc. Visualization '95*, Atlanta, GA, 1995, pp 279-286.

Kotsis N., 'Multidimensional Aggregation in OLAP hSystems', PhD thesis, Department of Computer Science, University of Strathclyde February 2000.

Klug A., 'Equivalence of relational algebra and relational calculus query language having aggregate function. In Journal of the ACM, 29(3):69717, 1982.

LeBlanc J., et al, 'Exploring N-Dimensional Databases', *Visualization '90*, San Francisco, CA, 1990, pp 230-239.

Picket R.M., *Visual Analyses of Texture in the Detection and Recognition of Objects, Picture Processing and Psycho-Pictorics*, Academic Press, New York, 1970.

Rekimoto J., Green M., 'The Information Cube: Using Transparency in 3d Information Visualization', *Proc. 3rd Annual Workshop on Information Technologies & Systems (WITS'93)*, 1993, pp 125-132.

Robertson G.G., et al, 'Cone Trees: Animated 3D Visualizations of Hierarchical Information', *Proc. Human Factors in Computing Systems, CHI'91* Conf., New Orleans, LA., 1991, pp 189-194.

Schneider D., The Ins and Outs (and everything in between) of Data Warehousing. Tutorial in the *23rd International Conference on Very Large Data Bases.* Pages 1-31. Athens 1997.

Su H., et al, *An Interactive Visualization Tool for Tolerance Design*, Technical Report, Imperial College, London, 1995.

Van Wijk J.J., van Liere R.D., 'Hyperslice', *Proc. Visualization '93*, San Jose, CA, 1993, pp 119-125.

Wright W., 'Information Animation Applications in the Capital Markets', *Proc. Int. Symp. on Information Visualization*, Atlanta, GA, 1995, pp 19-25.

SUPPORTING DECENTRALISED SOFTWARE-INTENSIVE PROCESSES USING ZETA COMPONENT-BASED ARCHITECTURE DESCRIPTION LANGUAGE

Ilham Alloui and Flavio Oquendo
LLP/CESALP Lab - University of Savoie at Annecy
B.P. 806 - 74016 Annecy Cedex – France
E-mail: alloui@esia.univ-savoie.fr , oquendo@esia.univ-savoie.fr

Keywords: Decentralised software-intensive processes, Component-based Processes, Architecture Description Language, Intentional Interactions, Interaction Management.

Abstract: Software engineering is nowadays moving towards an architecture-based development where systems are built by composing or assembling existing components that are often developed independently. This paper presents Zeta component-based approach to build software-intensive processes that are characterised by their complexity, heterogeneity and decentralisation. Indeed software-intensive processes are no longer monolithic as parts of it referred to as processlets may exist and run separately from the others. ZETA is an interaction-based architecture description language intended to design the "software glue" that connects processlets so that their interactions can be managed at runtime. ZETA addresses the contents of interactions through an intentional approach where interactions are guided by intentions that are revoked/maintained given some defined conditions. The underlying theory of the proposed approach is logic-based. The industrial relevance in a decentralised context, is currently being demonstrated based on case studies from the automotive industry within the framework of an ESPRIT IV LTR Project.

1. INTRODUCTION

Nowadays software-intensive process support environments have to cope with new requirements, in particular, those resulting from enterprise decentralisation and the use of enabling technologies like Internet as a means for inter-operating. Indeed the classical managerial hierarchy is generally replaced by a flatter network of commitments that conducts to the modelling and management of interactions (and associated shared goals) being one of the main requirements to be met.

In such a context, the role of software architecture in the engineering of distributed software-intensive applications has become in the last decade more and more important and widespread. The underlying idea is that better software systems can be achieved by modelling the software application high level organisation at design time and refining it to implementation (Garlan and Shaw 1993). Furthermore, rather than starting from scratch, software systems are built by composing or assembling existing software components that are often developed independently. However even if the technology of component-based systems is quite well established, well-defined techniques, notations and architectural support are still needed in order to understand, specify, design, develop, test and evolve component-based software systems.

In this paper we focus on the particular case of software processes that are characterised by their complexity, heterogeneity and decentralisation (Alloui et al. 2000a). A software-intensive process is no longer monolithic since parts of it may exist and run separately from the others, possibly on distinct sites. Those parts we refer to as processlets[1] must be considered as the building blocks that are often complex, time consuming and in particular designed independently from the other processlets. As such they require an ADL (Architecture Description Language) that enables description of processlet interactions at a high level of abstraction as the only way to put together existing processlets is to be able

[1] A processlet is a software-intensive process element to be enacted by a personal process engine, like an applet is a Java program element to be executed by a browser's Java Virtual Machine.

J. Filipe et al. (eds.), Enterprise Information Systems III, 97–106.

to describe why and how they interact. Semantics of interactions must be clearly defined by the ADL so that they can be managed and guarantied at runtime, i.e. during process enactment.

This paper presents ZETA, an interaction-based architecture description language for building software-intensive processes starting from existing processlet. ZETA is intended to be used by process engineers in order to design the "software glue" that connects processlets so that their interactions can be managed and/or controlled at runtime under the responsibility of a process manager.

Furthermore ZETA enables an intentional connection of processlets based on a logic-based formal theory (Cohen and Levesque 1990, Alloui and Oquendo 1999). When a processlet requests an information or a service from another processlet, it needs to be aware of the results, to manage the state of the request processing. In particular, it needs to know whether the goal behind the request has been achieved or not, if has been withdrawn, etc. (other goals probably rely on these results). For instance, it may become no more possible to perform an activity because a resource is not available, required condition is not satisfied, etc. It may also happen that an interaction becomes useless, i.e. the goal to be achieved is no longer necessary as it has already been achieved by another processlet.

The paper is organised as follows. Section 2 describes the key features and concepts of ZETA ADL. The language is introduced through examples. Section 3 shows how interactions defined at design time are managed at runtime. Section 4 presents some details on the implementation issues. Section 5 presents related work. The conclusion summarises the ZETA main features and presents ongoing work.

2. APPROACH AND CONCEPTS

2.1 General Concepts

The ZETA ADL is used to describe different interaction-based architecture models for software-intensive processes founded on the concepts of *Interaction Interface, Interaction, Message, Port, Attachment* and *Container* (see Figure 1). The main idea behind these concepts is that processlets are seen as black boxes that can interact using some interaction interfaces and that the concept of interaction is a kind of connector that routes messages that are sent/received through interaction interfaces. Messages contain intentions that motivate their sending as well as information to be asserted when they are received. A port represents an interaction point and serves as a message box to send/receive messages.

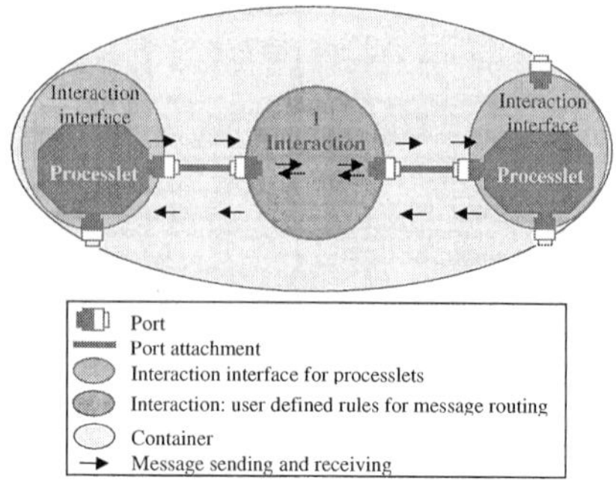

Figure 1: ZETA concepts

An interaction interface defines for a processlet its interaction capabilities. An interaction defines the rules for message routing in terms of ordering constraints when they are exchanged between processlets. Both interaction interface and interaction contain ports that must be attached to each other before any message exchange. A container attaches two or more interaction interfaces through an interaction. It defines a configuration for processlets' interactions.

It is worth noticing that it is possible to change the routing strategy of messages between processlets only by changing the interaction without affecting their interaction interfaces. It is also possible to reuse an interaction within other containers.

In the following ZETA concepts and language are introduced through examples. The scenario called "Hood & Headlight" used for illustration purpose is provided by an industrial partner and comes from the automotive industry. It deals with the study of a car variant design that causes a "deviation process" to be put in place (Pie 1999). A clash report has been issued as the car variant headlights do not fit the hood. A recovery process is then defined with two alternatives: studying a new version for the hood or looking for new headlight procurement. Actually the different processes cited above are processlets being performed on decentralised sites and have not necessarily been designed to work together.

2.2 Zeta Adl

In this section, ZETA concepts are presented through type definitions as the purpose is to provide architecture models for decentralised software-intensive processes. Inheritance is represented by the 'extends' keyword and means all properties of a type definition are inherited by its sub-types.

2.2.1 Interaction Interface

An interaction interface type is defined by its name and expresses interaction capabilities of a processlet in terms of the list of artefact types it can use/manipulate, list of activity types it is able to perform, list of port type declarations that can be used in order to send/receive messages as well as the list of protocols that define ordering constraints that should be respected at those ports. A port type declaration defines a typed port name.

```
interaction interface <ii-type-name>
            [extends <ii-type-name>]
{
  [artefact interface <artefacts>,]
  [activity interface <activities>,]
  [port interface <port-declarations>,]
  [protocol interface <protocole-types>]
}
```

As example, *RecoveryProcessInteractionInterface* is defined by a port *p-recov-prt* of type *P-recov-prt* and by a protocol interface called *RecoveryProcessProtocolInterface*. It describes the interaction interface of a processlet named *RecoveryProcess*:

```
interaction interface
   RecoveryProcessInteractionInterface
{
  port interface p-recov-prt: Recov-prt,
  protocol interface
  RecoveryProcessProtocolInterface
}
```

In the following it is assumed that the *Hood* artefact type belongs to the artefact interface while *HoodDesignStudy* activity belongs to the activity interface. *Hood*, *HoodDesignStudy*, examples of message types, *P-recov-prt*, *RecoveryProcessProtocolInterface* definitions are given next.

2.2.2 Artefact Interface

An artefact interface of an interaction is defined by a list of artefact types. An artefact type defines the structure of an artefact in terms of attributes and relationships. An ODMG/ODL (Object Description Language) sub-language is used. For more details, see (Odl 1997). For instance:

```
artefact Hood extends HH-Artefact
{
  attribute enum hoodState {isNew,
  to_be_approved, approved} status,
  relationship list <HoodCAD> cad
  inverse HoodCAD::is_cad_of,
  relationship list <HoodSketch> sketch
  inverse HoodSketch::is_sketch_of
}
```

defines an artefact type named *Hood* as inheriting from another artefact type *HH-Artefact*. A *Hood* instance has an attribute called *status* (enumeration values) and is linked to a list of *HoodCAD* instances through *cad* relationship and to a list of *HoodSketch* through *sketch* relationship. Reverse links are named *is_cad_of* and *is_sketch_of* respectively.

2.2.3 Activity Interface

An activity interface of an interaction interface is defined by a list of activity types. An activity type is defined by its name, a list of input and output (produces) parameter types defining respectively which artefact types are provided to the activity and those furnished by it, a precondition, i.e. a necessary condition for starting its enactment, a goal i.e. a condition that should be satisfied in terms of artefacts and service production. For instance:

```
activity HoodDesignStudy (hoodCAD:
     HoodCAD, clashReport: ClashReport,
     hoodSketch: HoodSketch)
  extends HH-Activity
  produces (revisedHoodCAD:
             RevisedHoodCAD)
{
  precondition true
  goal     (revisedHoodCAD.isNew)    and
     (revisedHoodCAD.status = revised)
}
```

defines an activity type called *HoodDesignStudy* that inherits from *HH-Activity* activity type. An instance of *HoodDesignStudy* has typed input parameters *hoodCAD* of type *HoodCAD*, *clashReport* of type *ClashReport* and *hoodSketch* of type *HoodSketch*. It produces an output parameter *revisedHoodCAD* of type *RevisedHoodCAD*. As the precondition has *true* as value, the activity can be started at any moment provided that its input parameters are available. The goal of the activity is that a new artefact *revisedHoodCAD* is produced and its *status* has *revised* as value.

2.2.4 Message Types

A message type is defined by its name, a set of typed input parameter declarations, its intention (*intends*), a maintenance condition for the intention (*while*) and the facts that are asserted by the message type (*asserts*).

```
message <message-type-name>
```

```
                (<input-declaration>)
{
  [intends <intention-expression > ,]
  [while <maintenance-expression> ,]
  [asserts <assert-expression>]
}
```

A message intention expresses a goal to be achieved by the message destination. At runtime, an intention persists as long as its maintenance condition is evaluated to true. If this condition becomes false or if the intention is achieved or if it fails or it appears that is impossible to achieve, revision is performed (see section 3.). The *asserts* clause in a message definition is used to add new information (asserts new facts) to the receiver.

Intention, maintenance and assertion expressions are logical expressions based on UML/OCL (Object Constraint Language) (Ocl 1997). The symbol *§* is used to refer to the intention contained in a message.

An example of message type definition is:

```
message  EngineeringOrder   (headlight:
        Headlight,      hood:      Hood,
        clashReport: ClashReport)
{
  intends exists(headlight.cad, hood.cad
       |    headlight.cad.fits   includes
       hood.cad)
}
```

EngineeringOrder has as input parameters three typed artefacts: *headlight* of type *Headlight*, *hood* of type *Hood*, *clashReport* of type *ClashReport*. The intention of an *EngineeringOrder* message is that it exists a headlight CAD that fits a hood CAD. Notice that as expressed, the intention is honoured the first time such artefacts exist.

RequestForStudyNewHeadlightDesign contains the intention that a new headlight CAD is created and that it fits the hood CAD hoodCAD given as parameter:

```
message
RequestForStudyNewHeadlightDesign
   (headlight: Headlight, hood: Hood,
   clashReport: ClashReport,
   hoodCAD: HoodCAD)
{
  intends (headlight.cad.isNew) and
  (headlight.cad.fits includes hoodCAD),
  while not §EngineeringOrder
}
```

This intention is honoured once such headlight CAD is produced. If not honoured yet, it persists while *not §EngineeringOrder* (i.e. the intention of *EngineeringOrder*) is true. This way dependency between intentions of different messages is expressed by the user (i.e. process engineer).

Another example is *HeadlightCAD* message that asserts the fact that a new headlight CAD is created and that it fits the hood CAD given as parameter:

```
message HeadlightCAD
  (headlight: Headlight, hood: Hood,
  hoodCAD: HoodCAD,
  clashReport: ClashReport,
  hoodSketch: HoodSketch,
  headlightCAD: HeadlightCAD)
{
  asserts (headlightCAD.isNew) and
(headlightCAD.fits includes hoodCAD)
}
```

Theoretical foundation of ZETA sub-language for message logical expressions is a first-order modal logic based on the formal theory of rational action (Cohen and Levesque 1990). The semantics of these constructs are given using possible-world semantics.

2.2.5 Port Interface

A port interface of an interaction interface is expressed in terms of a list of typed ports. A port type is defined by its name, the set of messages types that it can send ('*!*' symbol is used) or receive ('*?*' symbol is used) possibly under certain conditions expressed as a precondition that is necessary but not sufficient. Preconditions define conditions that must be fulfilled by messages parameters.

The unit:

```
port type Recov-prt
{
   (message ?EngineeringOrder
       precondition clashReport.isNew),
  message
  !RequestForStudyNewHeadlightDesign,
  message
  !RequestForStudyNewHoodVersion,
  message ?RevisedHoodCAD,
  message ?HeadlightCAD
}
```

defines a port type called *Recov-prt* that can receive instances of *EngineeringOrder*, *RevisedHoodCAD*, *HeadlightCAD* message types and can send instances of *RequestForStudyNewHeadlightDesign*, *RequestForStudyNewHoodVersion* message types. Receiving messages of type *EngineeringOrder* is subject to the condition that its parameter *clashReport* is newly created.

2.2.6 Protocol Interface

A protocol interface is defined by a set of protocol types. A protocol type expresses a set of constraints on the ordering of message types that can be sent/received by ports by the interaction interface.

A constraint may be named or not and contains a message expression where operators are used to constraint the ordering of message sending/receiving. Among binary operators are: sequential (->), alternative (|) or concurrent (||).

The basic kinds of message expressions are: the sending (*!*) or receiving (*?*) of a message type by a port type; successful termination (*$*); reference to a named ordering constraint.

In the example of *RecoveryProcessProtocolInterface* introduced so far (see Section 2.2.1.), the protocol interface contains a protocol named *rec* that defines constraints on the ordering of message receiving or sending by ports:

```
protocol interface
        RecoveryProcessProtocolInterface
{
 protocol rec =
 (p-recov-prt?EngineeringOrder ->
  (p-recovprt!
  RequestForStudyNewHeadlightDesign
  || p-recov-prt!
  RequestForStudyNewHoodVersion)
  ) ->
 ((p-recov-prt?HeadlightCAD
  -> p-recov-prt!HeadlightCAD) |
  (p-recov-prt?RevisedHoodCAD
  -> p-recov-prt!RevisedHoodCAD)
 ) -> rec
}
```

In *rec* an example of constraint is that sending a *RequestForStudyNewHeadlightDesign* message and *RequestForStudyNewHoodVersion* can be done concurrently in any order from the same port *p-recov-prt* but after receiving an *EngineeringOrder* message at that port. *Rec* recursively applies.

2.2.7 Interaction Types

An interaction type is defined by its name, a set of typed ports and a set of constraints on message orderings called routing rules.

As protocols express constraints on interaction interface messages and ports, interaction routing rules express constraints on messages and ports of interactions. For illustration purpose, a *StudyAlterStudyAlternativesRequest* interaction type has been defined by four typed ports, respectively *i-stalt-prt0*, *i-stalt-prt1*, *i-stalt-prt2* and *i-stalt-prt3* and by a routing rule named *stalt*.

The routing rule *stalt* expresses constraints on ordering of the messages that are received/sent by the four interaction ports:

```
interaction StudyAlternativesRequest
{
 port i-stalt-prt0: Stalt-prt0,
 port i-stalt-prt1: Stalt-prt1,
 port i-stalt-prt2: Stalt-prt2,
 port i-stalt-prt3: Stalt-prt3
 routing stalt =
 i-salt-prt0?EngineeringOrder ->
 i-salt-prt1!EngineeringOrder ->
 (i-stalt-prt1?
 RequestForStudyNewHeadlightDesign
 -> i-stalt-prt2!
 RequestForStudyNewHeadlightDesign)
  ->
 (i-stalt-prt1?
 RequestForStudyNewHoodVersion ->
 i-stalt-prt3!
 RequestForStudyNewHoodVersion)
 ->
 ((i-stalt-prt3?RevisedHoodCAD ->
 i-stalt-prt1!RevisedHoodCAD) |
  (i-stalt-prt2?HeadlightCAD ->
   i-stalt-prt1!HeadlightCAD)
 ) -> stalt
}
```

Interactions in ZETA are first class entities. They contain information required for routing messages with possibly different strategies between interaction interfaces of processlets.

2.2.8 Container Types

The way ZETA concepts are constructed enables the definition of interaction interface types and interaction types independently from each others. In order that an interaction can take place between interaction interfaces, interaction interfaces' ports must be attached to interactions' ports. This is defined using the concept of container.

A *container* type is defined by its name and a set of *containee* types. A containee type is either an interaction interface declaration (*interaction interface*), an interaction type name (*interaction*) or a port attachment (*attachment*). An interaction interface can be either an interaction interface type name or a sequence of interaction interface types. Port attachment is synchronous i.e. if a message is sent through a port, this latter blocks until the attached port receives the message.

As example, *StudyAlternativesRequestContainer* (see Figure 2) is defined relating four interaction interfaces of type *ManagementProcessInteractionInterface*, *RecoveryProcessInteractionInterface*, *HoodDesignStudyInteractionInterface* and *HeadlightDesignStudyInteractionInterface* respectively to one interaction of type *StudyAlternativesRequest*. Interaction interfaces and interactions are related to each others through port attachments.

```
container
StudyAlternativesRequestContainer
{
  interaction interface mngtProcess:
  ManagementProcessInteractionInterface,
  interaction interface recovProcess:
  RecoveryProcessInteractionInterface,
  interaction interface hoodesProcess:
  HoodDesignStudyInteractionInterface,
  interaction interface headesProcess:
  HeadlightDesignStudyInteractionInterfa
  ce,
  interaction StudyAlternativesRequest,
  attachment p-mngt-prt to i-stalt-prt0,
  attachment p-recov-prt to i-stalt-
  prt1,
  attachment p-hoodes-prt to i-stalt-
  prt2,
  attachment p-heades-prt to i-stalt-
  prt2
}
```

When refined to implementation, a ZETA architecture description can be instantiated and enacted in order that processlet interaction management becomes effective.

Regarding the "Hood & Headlight" scenario, ZETA has been used to model an architecture that connects a number of processlets in order to achieve the recovery process goals. The next section details how at runtime, the ZETA underlying intentional semantics operates carried out by a dedicated intention management system (IMS).

3. INTERACTION MANAGEMENT

Management of processlet interactions at runtime can be either at a syntactic level, i.e. related to ordering constraints on message exchange or on a semantic level, i.e. related to the state of achievement of the intention that motivated a message sending. Examples are when a processlet requests a service from another processlet, the process manager might need to know if the intention behind the request has been achieved or not. As other intentions may rely on these results, support is needed to be informed of all consequences on the ongoing interactions. Therefore at runtime, ZETA/IMS uses a graph of intention dependencies. This may be compared to a truth maintenance system (TMS) (Doyle 1979) where graphs are constructed starting from the underlying logic theory and from user-defined rules that are supplied at system customisation time. An example is:

```
(achieved(A) and achieved (B)) -:
                    nolongerequired(C)
```

where the user expresses that *C* is no longer required if achievement of both *A* and *B* are true. In addition, predicates to express goal states are defined as facts: *achieved(I)*, *failed(I)*, *nolongerequired(I)* and *impossible(I)*. *A*, *B*, *C* and *I* are logical expressions.

Each time a fact is added or a conclusion is inferred, truth values are calculated. Results of such revision are sent to the concerned processlets through predefined messages (see Table 1).

Concretely to each interaction interface instance is associated an intention base containing the intentions to be achieved, their maintenance conditions and the facts to be asserted.

Table 1: ZETA/IMS predefined messages

Predefined message	Semantics
ZETA-achieved(I)	*I* is satisfied.
ZETA-failed(I)	*I* has failed.
ZETA-nolongerequired(I)	*I* is no longer required.
ZETA-impossible(I)	*I* is impossible to achieve.

In the "Hood & Headlight" scenario, the deviation process consists in launching two alternative processes: headlight procurement and new hood design. Due to time constraints, the goal is to wait for the one which accomplishes first.

One question we may ask is how could all people involved both in the procurement process and the new hood design be automatically aware that one alternative succeeded?

The proposed answer to these questions is to define already at design time the desired properties of the enacting process, in our case, we can link intentions to each other to reflect their dependency. For instance, we have defined the two message types *RequestForStudyNewHeadlightDesign* and *RequestForStudyNewHoodVersion* with as maintenance condition for their intentions the negation of the intention of *EngineeringOrder* (i.e. *while not §2*). This way if the intention behind the engineering order has been honoured through one alternative process, the maintenance condition of *RequestForStudyNewHeadlightDesign* and *RequestForStudyNewHoodVersion* becomes false and consequently this information causes revision.

The message exchange sequence shown in figure 2 illustrates a possible conversation that starts with sending a message of type *EngineeringOrder* from *ManagementProcessInteractionInterface* and ends when receiving a message of type *HeadlightCAD* by *RecoveryProcessInteractionInterface*. Actual parameters are given at runtime.

Table 2 summarises the different steps performed by messages including ports through which they transit as well as the intentions, associated maintenance conditions and information that are added to interaction interfaces' intention bases all along the conversation.

According to what has been defined in the architecture model, tests can be performed at each port on the message to see whether it conforms to the defined port type or not, and, if ordering constraints defined by the protocols and by the routing rules are respected.

Each time a new information is asserted to the intention base, ZETA/IMS revises all intention bases that are involved within the current conversation. For instance when receiving the message *RequestForStudyNewHeadlightDesign* numbered *4*, its associated intention (*§4*) together with its maintenance condition (*not §2*) are added to the receiving interaction interface's intention base.

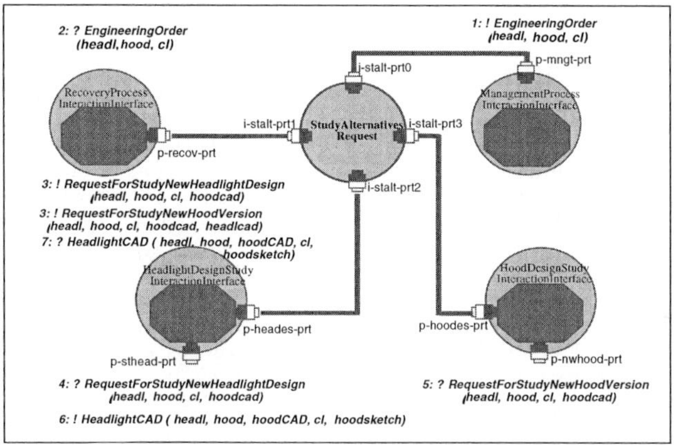

Figure 2: Example of conversation within a container

Table 2: Intention management during a conversation

Message	Interaction interface intention base		
	Intends	**While**	**Assert**
*1: p-mngt-prt ! **EngineeringOrder (headl, hood, cl)***			
*2: p-recov-prt ? **EngineeringOrder (headl, hood, cl)***	exists(nheadlightCAD: HeadlightCAD, nhoodCAD: HoodCAD | nheadlightCAD.fits includes nhoodCAD)		
*3: p-recov-prt ! **RequestForStudyNewHoodVersion (headl, hood, cl, hoodcad, headlcad)***			
*3: p-recov-prt ! **RequestForStudyNewHeadlightDesign (headl, hood, cl, hoodcad)***			
*4: p-heades-prt? **RequestForStudyNewHeadlightDesign (headl, hood, cl, hoodcad)***	(headlightCAD.isNew) and (headlightCAD.fits includes hoodCAD)	not §2	
*5: p-hoodes-prt ? **RequestForStudyNewHoodVersion (headl, hood, cl, hoodcad, headlcad)***	(nhoodCAD.isNew) and (hoodCAD.status = revised) and (nhoodCAD.fits_too includes headlightCAD)	not §2	
*6: p-heades-prt ! **HeadlightCAD (headl, hood, hoodCAD, cl, hoodsketch)***			
*7: p-recov-prt ? **HeadlightCAD (headl, hood, hoodCAD, cl, hoodsketch)***			§4

Table 3: ZETA revision messages

8 !ZETA-achieved(§4) to *p-recov-prt (§4 implies §2)*	marks *§4* as achieved for the *RecoveryProcessInteractionInterface*
9 !ZETA-achieved(§2 to *p-mngt-prt (not §2 false)*	marks *§2* as achieved for the *ManagementProcessInteractionInterface*
10 !ZETA-nolongerequired(§5) to *p-recov-prt*	marks *§5* as no longer required for the *RecoveryProcessInteractionInterface*
11 !ZETA-nolongerequired(§5) to *p-hoodes-prt*	marks *§5* as no longer required for the *HoodDesignStudyInteractionInterface*

When receiving the message numbered *7*, a new information is asserted expressing that *§4* has become true. Therefore ZETA/IMS sends a message *ZETA-achieved(§4)* to *p-recov-prt* and revises all the intention bases involved in the conversation as this is shown in Table 3.

As *§4* (intention of message 4) implies *§2* (intention of message 2) and *§4* has been achieved, this implies that *§2* has also been achieved. Then as *not §2* is false, the maintenance condition associated to *§5* no longer holds, consequently *§5* is no longer required. ZETA/IMS sends a message *ZETA-nolongerequired(§5)* to the concerned interaction interfaces.At the end of this conversation, all intentions contained in intention bases are labelled either as achieved or failed or no longer required or impossible to achieve. This way, people involved both in the procurement process and the new hood design can be automatically aware of the results of both headlight procurement process and new hood design process alternatives.

4. IMPLEMENTATION

Implementation of ZETA is based on the refinement of ZETA descriptions to process-centred environments in both Java and ProcessWeb/PML (Warboys et al. 1999) target implementation languages. The interaction with the user is done via a graphical interface and the communication with the other components (including processlets) is done via a communication layer founded on JMS (Java Message Service).

5. RELATED WORK

Several architecture description languages (ADLs) have been proposed for modelling architectures both within a particular domain and as general-purpose architecture modelling languages. Among them: ACME (Garlan et el. 1995), Aesop (Garlan et al. 1994), C2-SADL (Medvidovic 1996), Darwin (Magee and Kramer 1996), MetaH (Binns et al. 1995), Rapide (Rapide 1996), SADL (Moriconi et al. 1995), UniCon (Shaw et al. 1995), Wright (Allen and Garlan 1994) and π-SPACE (Chaudet and Oquendo 2000). The latter results from our investigations on algebraic approaches and their contribution to the software architecture domain. As for ZETA, it results from our work on logical approaches.

According to the classification and comparison framework for ADLs proposed in (Medvidovic and Taylor 2000), ZETA formalises the semantics of interactions in the context of decentralised, heterogeneous and adaptive software architectures. It offers means for explicit specification of interaction interfaces, interactions and containers (i.e. components, connectors, and architectural configurations respectively). As it is an implementation independent ADL, a framework is provided for refining abstract to concrete specifications that constraint descriptions for generating/reusing code[2].

The most important feature of ZETA is that connectors are considered as the main concept as they contain the semantics of components' interactions. They are explicitly modelled and can be sub-typed, reused and modified. Unlike in Rapide, MetaH and Darwin, connectors are first class entities with a powerful semantics that enables definition of very complex interactions. Rapide and MetaH connections are modelled on-line and cannot be named, subtyped, or reused. Connectors in Darwin are bindings and are also specified in the context of a configuration only.

ACME, Aesop, UniCon, and Wright refer to connector interface points as roles. In ZETA, connector interfaces are named, typed, and described in the same way as component ports. This allows for analysis of compatibility between connected

[2] The refinement framework is based on a process-centred approach. The target implementation languages are currently Java and ProcessWeb/PML persistent reflective language (see Section 4.).

component (interaction interface) and connector (interaction) ports.

Architecture-level communication may need to be expressed with complex protocols. To abstract away these protocols and make them reusable, ADLs should model connectors as types. Only those ADLs that model connectors as first class entities distinguish connector types from instances. This excludes languages like Darwin, MetaH, and Rapide. ZETA, π-SPACE, ACME, Aesop, C2, and Wright base connector types on protocols. ZETA interaction routing rules semantics is expressed in terms of constraints on ordering of messages.

In other respects, a contract-based approach has been adopted on information system development in-the-small by (Andrade and Fiadeiro 1999). Contracts externalise interactions between objects and to some extent they are comparable to ZETA interactions as they contain semantics for controlled coordination of interacting objects. However ZETA differs from this approach mainly by its logic-based intentional approach that provides powerful formal semantics to interactions, its applicability to large-grained software architectures and its ability to connect components that were not designed to work together such as legacy systems.

6. CONCLUDING REMARKS

In the context of architecture-based engineering of distributed applications on local or wide-area networks, the ZETA ADL offers high-level abstractions to define large software-intensive processes starting from existing processlets that are long-time consuming, possibly decentralised and heterogeneous. Semantics of interactions are formally expressed using the underlying logic theory at design time to manage/control them at runtime. The proposed intentional approach where interactions are guided by intentions enables on-line and active guidance to complex and time consuming processes through intention revision. As a formal language interaction properties can be studied and analyses performed during design to verify whether the enacting system conforms to what is expected from it or not. The industrial relevance in a decentralised and heterogeneous context is currently being demonstrated based on case studies within the framework of both ESPRIT IV LTR Project (Alloui and Oquendo 2000, Alloui et al. 2000b, Alloui et al. 2001) and E-ALLIANCE regional project on information technologies for supporting electronic business-to-business applications.

REFERENCES

Allen, R. and Garlan, G., 1994, 'Formalizing Architectural Connection', in Proceedings of the Sixteenth International Conference on Software Engineering, Sorrento, Italy.

Alloui, I. and Oquendo, F., 1999, 'Decentralised Software Processes: Modelling and Supporting Interactions among Processlets', Proceedings of the International Workshop on Process support for Distributed Team-based Software Development (PDTSD'99) World Multi-Conference SCI/ISAS'99, Orlando, Florida.

Alloui, I. and Oquendo, F., 2000. Definition of the process interaction language. D3.04 Deliverable, PIE LTR ESPRIT IV Project No. 34840.

Alloui, I. et al., 2000a, 'Alliance: An Agent-Based CASE Environment for Enterprise Process Modelling, Enactment and Quantitative Control', in Enterprise Information Systems, Joaquim Filipe (Ed.), KLUWER ACADEMIC PUBLISHERS.

Alloui, I. et al., 2000b, 'Advanced Services for Process Evolution: Monitoring and Decision Support', Proceedings 7th European Workshop on Software Process Technology (EWSPT 7). Lecture Notes in Computer Science, Vol. 1780, pp 21 - 37, Springer Verlag.

Alloui, I. et al., 2001, 'Monitoring Software Process Interactions: a Logic-based Approach', Proceedings of the 8th European Workshop on Software Process Technology (EWSPT 8). Lecture Notes in Computer Science, Springer Verlag. (to appear)

Andrade, L.F. and Fiadeiro, J.L., 1999, 'Interconnecting Objects via Contracts', in UML'99 – Beyond the Standard, R. France and B. Rumpe (eds.), LNCS 1723, Springer Varlag.

Binns, P. et al. 1995, 'Domain-Specific Software Architectures for Guidance, Navigation, and Control', in International Journal of Software Engineering and Knowledge Engineering.

Chaudet, C. and Oquendo, F., 2000, 'π-SPACE: A Formal Architecture Description Language based on Process Algebra for Evolving Software Systems', Proceedings of ASE'2000 International Conference on Automated Software Engineering, Grenoble, France.

Cohen, P. R., Levesque, H. J., 1990, 'Rational interaction as the basis for communication. Intentions' in Communication. P.R. Cohen, J. Morgan, and M.E. Pollack (Eds.), M.I.T. Press, Cambridge.

Doyle, J., 1979, 'A Truth Maintenance System', Artificial Intelligence, No. 12.

Garlan, D. and Shaw, M., 1993, 'An introduction to software architecture' in Advances in Software Engineering and Knowledge Engineering. Volume I, World Scientific Publishing Company.

Garlan, D. et al. 1994, 'Exploiting Style in Architectural Design Environments', Proceedings of SIGSOFT'94: Foundations of Software Engineering, New Orleans.

Garlan, D. et al., 1995. ACME: An Architectural Interconnection Language, Technical Report, CMU-CS-95-219, Carnegie Mellon University.

Magee J. and Kramer, J., 1996, 'Dynamic Structure in Software Architectures, Proceedings of ACM SIGSOFT'96: Fourth Symposium on the Foundations of Software Engineering (FSE4), San Francisco.

Medvidovic, N. and Taylor, R. N., 2000, 'A Framework for Classifying and Comparing Architecture Description Languages', in IEEE Transactions on Software Engineering.

Medvidovic, N., 1996, 'ADLs and Dynamic Architecture Changes', in A. L. Wolf, ed., Proceedings of the Second International Software Architecture Workshop (ISAW-2), San Francisco.

Moriconi, M. et al. 1995, 'Correct Architecture Refinement', IEEE Transactions on Software Engineering.

Ocl, 1997. UML Object Constraint Language Specification version 1.1, 1.

Odl, 1997. Object Database Standard: ODMG 2.0, Cattell and Barry (Eds), San Francisco. M. Kaufmann Publishers, Inc.

Pie, 1999, 'User requirements - consolidated version Deliverable', PIE LTR ESPRIT IV Project No. 34840.

Rapide, Design Team, 1996. Rapide 1.0 Language Reference Manual. Program Analysis and Verification Group, Computer Systems Lab, Stanford University.

Shaw, M. et al. 1995, 'Abstractions for Software Architecture and Tools to Support Them', IEEE Transactions on Software Engineering.

Warboys, B. C. et al., 1999. Business Information Systems: a Process Approach. McGraw-Hill.

THE DECOR TOOLBOX FOR WORKFLOW-EMBEDDED ORGANIZATIONAL MEMORY ACCESS

Andreas Abecker, Ansgar Bernardi
German Research Center for Artificial Intelligence (DFKI), P.O. Box 2080, D-67608 Kaiserslautern, Germany
Email: aabecker@dfki.de , bernardi@dfki.de

Spyridon Ntioudis, Gregory Mentzas
Information Management Unit, National Technical University of Athens, 9, Iroon Politexniou Str., 15780 Zografou, Greece
Email: dioudis@softlab.ntua.gr , gmentzas@softlab.ntua.gr

Rudi Herterich, Christian Houy, Stephan Müller
DHC Dr. Herterich & Consultants GmbH, Landwehrplatz 6-7, D-66111 Saarbrücken, Germany
Email: herterich@dhc-gmbh.com , houy@dhc-gmbh.com , mueller@dhc-gmbh.com

Maria Legal
PLANET ERNST & YOUNG, Apollon Tower, 64 Louise Riencourt, Gr-115 23 Athens, Greece
Email: mlegal@planetey.com

Keywords: organizational memory, ontology, workflow

Abstract: We shortly motivate the idea of business-process oriented knowledge management (BPOKM) and sketch the basic approaches to achieve this goal. Then we describe the DECOR (Delivery of context-sensitive organisational knowledge) project which develops, tests, and consolidates new methods and tools for BPOKM. DECOR builds upon the KnowMore framework (Abecker et al 1998; Abecker et al 2000) for organizational memories (OM), but tries to overcome some limitations of this approach. In the DECOR project, three end-user environments serve as test-beds for validation and iterative improvement of innovative approaches to build:

(1) knowledge archives organised around formal representations of business processes to facilitate navigation and access,

(2) active information delivery services which - in collaboration with a workflow tool to support weakly-structured knowledge-intensive work - offer the user in a context-sensitive manner helpful information from the knowledge archive, and

(3) methods for an organisation analysis from the knowledge perspective, required as supporting methods to design and introduce the former two systems.

In this paper, we present the basic modules of the DECOR toolkit and elaborate on their current status of development.

This paper describes the two-years EC-funded RTD project DECOR (Delivery of Context-Sensitive Organisational Knowledge, Grant IST-1999-13002). The DECOR consortium consists of the following partners: German Research Center for Artificial Intelligence DFKI, Kaiserslautern, Germany; Planet ERNST & YOUNG S.A., Athens, Greece; Sema Group Belgium, Brussels, Belgium; DHC Dr. Herterich & Consultants GmbH, Saarbrücken, Germany; IKA Social Security Institute, Athens, Greece; The National Technical University of Athens; Greece.

J. Filipe et al. (eds.), Enterprise Information Systems III, 107–114.

1. MANAGING KNOWLEDGE AND BUSINESS PROCESSES

Business Process Management (BPM) and Business Process Reengineering (BPR) (Hammer & Champy 1993; Malhotra 1998) have been predominant business trends from the mid eighties til the nineties, and are now evolving from a hype towards "serious tools". In the decade from the mid nineties on, the most "fashionable" trend seems to be Knowledge Management (KM) (Davenport et al 1996; Davenport & Prusak 2000).

Although both topics, BPR and KM, are usually discussed independently, there are important obvious similarities: both aim at similar economic targets, like quality or efficiency improvements; both require a clear organisational take-up and strategic planning at the begin; both need an integrated suite of motivational, organisational and technological tools; technological support for both approaches builds upon comprehensive enterprise models (organizational structure, business processes, information systems structure, ...); etc. Both approaches are expensive, difficult and risky. So it makes sense to combine both in order to exploit synergy effects, thus getting "two for one".

Other reasons are, for instance, that BPR is already a well-known term which makes it easier to enter an organization with than with the more "esoteric" KM issue; or the fact that consultants are already familiar with BPR/BPM terminology, methods, and tools which makes it easier to start a KM initiative from this solid ground than totally from scratch. Now the question is what "Business Process Oriented Knowledge Management" (BPOKM) can mean concretely. Basically, promising integration possibilities exist on three levels:

(1) System Design:

Both KM and BPM initiatives start with an elaborated analysis and planning phase. These should be shared between BPM and KM projects. Further, BPM methodology could "drive" (give the rough framework and sequence of activities) for doing the KM specific work.

(2) System Use:

Operationalization of BPM normally means running a workflow tool. Now, if the workflow engine and the KM infrastructure interoperate, this can lead to a higher degree of overall system services. The first three items below show an increasingly closer coupling, and realize increasingly "smarter" information support for the user who solves a knowledge-intensive problem (the context of which is given by the workflow around). The latter two ideas foster filling the knowledge archive and evolving its content during use:

(a) Process-Oriented Knowledge Archive: If business process models are used for organizing knowledge archives, e.g., representing one view in a company or community knowledge portal, they can be used for manual browsing. In particular, it is easy to couple an information system with the actual workflow enactment such that for a given business process activity the respective set of information objects, associated with this activity in the archive index, can be accessed easily. There are several tools in the market realizing this idea (Goesmann & Herrmann 2000; DHC 2001; Fillies et al 2001).

(b) Active Information Delivery: If a workflow engine enacts a business process model, it is possible to attach information need specifications to each activity; then, the workflow system, when starting a specific activity, can automatically pose a query to the knowledge archive according to the attached information need, and proactively offer the results as information support to the user.

(c) Dynamic Process Context: If the approach above is extended in such a way that not only fixed, predefined information needs are attached to business tasks, but information needs are parameterised by variables to be filled by the running workflow instance, an even better, context-specific information retrieval can be performed, which takes into account instance-specific information. This idea has recently been investigated in several research projects (Abecker et al 2000b; Staab & Schnurr 2000). It is the basis of the DECOR approach.

***(d) Contextualized Information Storage*:** If the concrete workflow context of a document being created is known to the KM system at storage time, this creation context (in terms of details of the actual business process instance) can be archived together with the document. This information can be used for a better retrieval in other, similar business situations, or can be used for assessing the quality of the knowledge contained (Who created it? Was the embedding project successful? Is there other important background information related with this process instance? Etc.). This aspect of coupling workflow and KM systems is often neglected, up to now.

(e) Context-Embedded Discussions: If a context-dependent information delivery service actively provides background information for a running business process instance, this can also stimulate discussions about content and quality of the information objects retrieved. According to the reflection-in-action paradigm (Sumner et al 1999), the user should have easy possibilities to make comments, attach discussions, send e-mails to authors or knowledge managers, etc. if a running activity gives rise to critique some information object.

(3) System Evolution:
In the spirit of continuous process improvement, it should be tried to continuously feed back experience and change requests coming from new insights / requirements or changed environment factors to the process design unit in the organization, thus steadily keeping up-to-date the formalized process models with the best practice about how to enact them. This continuous improvement process is a KM process itself.

For all three integration levels discussed above, it was already sufficient to have a conventional, fixed business process model. However, a deeper analysis of knowledge work (Buckingham Shum 1998) shows that knowledge-intensive processes tend to be characterized by dynamic changes of goals, information environment, and constraints, or by highly individual and ad-hoc communication and collaboration patterns; this makes it difficult to plan in detail the work on a knowledge-intensive task in advance. The easy way to deal with this observation (which preserves all benefits achievable with the KM-workflow integration in the section above) is to model the related business process just quite roughly and embed the knowledge-intensive subtasks in black boxes without further details.

We propose a more fine-grained description in order to achieve more of the usual workflow benefits like process documentation, automated document routing, planning support, etc. To this end, a promising way was shown by (Wargitsch et al 1998): (i) below the level of granularity which can be fixed in advance, compose case specific workflows from archived skeletons or process fragments, (ii) enact and adapt the so-configured workflow at runtime, and (iii) evolve the skeleton repository by reflection-in-action, discussing the pros and cons of certain fragments when using them.

In the DECOR project, we concentrate on the first three items of the list above (regarding the system use phase): process-oriented archive structuring, active knowledge delivery, and dynamic process context. In order to systematically build such solutions in business practice, it is further required to investigate the system design phase.

2. AN OVERVIEW OF DECOR

Starting point is the observation that in a company the organisational knowledge base of explicitly documented knowledge is normally spread out over many different sources of documents, forms, media etc. Furthermore, links and relationships between documents are usually not represented. ***Ontology-based information systems*** (Benjamins et al 1998; O'Leary 1998) acquire from the community of system users the commonly agreed upon domain structures (concepts and definitions, relationships, constraints, axioms) *logically* organising a certain domain of expertise or area of work. Then, a formal representation of these generally accepted domain knowledge structures, the ontology, is the basis for a homogeneous, concept-based (instead of keyword-based) content description of knowledge sources which can be used for knowledge portals to support manual browsing and for information retrieval algorithms evaluating queries against an archive system. In DECOR we employ formally modelled *business processes* as one such ontology which can be used to specify the *creation*, or the potential *usage context*, or both, for a given knowledge item. This leads to the idea of a ***process-oriented structured archive***, a meta information system providing conceptual structures to access the underlying legacy systems.

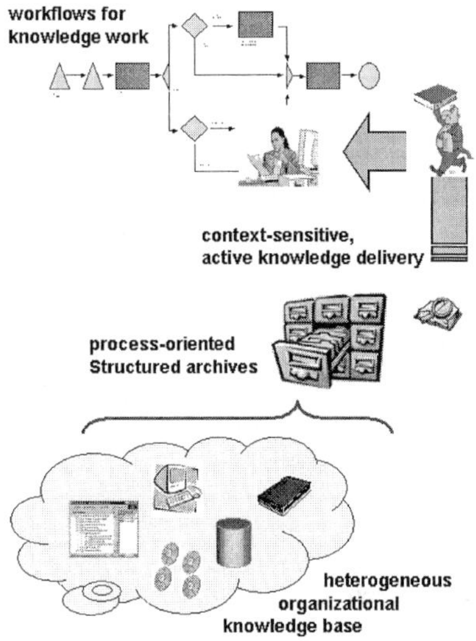

Figure 1: Overall Scenario forActive Knowledge Delivery

On the other hand, users are engaged in their daily work routines; they don't want to spend much time in searching for information or storing expertise. What they would need is an ***active, context-sensitive knowledge delivery*** service which "knows" what the user is actually doing and uses this information for autonomous information management services at the desktop. To achieve this goal, DECOR employs a workflow management system as the host system which is aware of the specific tasks to be performed by each user at a given point in time. We consider *weakly-structured workflow models for representing knowledge-intensive work routines* which are usually not so strict and predetermined as, e.g., administrative workflows. *Enriched workflow models* describe information flow between and information needs for specific tasks. An ***information assistant*** observes the running workflow and interprets modelled information needs to offer active support from the process-oriented structured archive; further it maintains a notion of information *retrieval context* using the additionally modelled information flow variables which allows for more precise queries to the archive. Task context can also be used for information storage to describe the creation context of a given knowledge item.

Altogether, existing knowledge sources are used and extended in a more efficient and more consistent way throughout the company. Figure 1 illustrates the several system parts playing together at system usage time.

However, the above scenario is based upon a number of non-trivial (and not so cheap) organisation analysis and modelling steps. (1) Business process maps and other domain ontologies for knowledge organisation and content description, (2) weakly-structured workflows for knowledge-intensive business processes, and (3) information flow and information needs for workflow enrichment, must be acquired and maintained over time. The overall approach must be introduced in a company in the larger context of a comprehensive Knowledge Management (KM) or Business Process Management (BPM) initiative. All required steps should be carried out by "normal consultants" in a "normal organisation" at reasonable costs and with a predictable result. Recapitulating, we need a structured approach for running Business-Process Oriented KM projects which supports all necessary project steps with appropriate methodological guidance and modelling tools.

3. THE DECOR TOOLBOX

Figure 2 below shows the modules of the DECOR toolbox which support design and implementation of a system which can then be used as described in the previous section.

We discuss the several complementing modules in some more detail:

(1) DECOR Business Knowledge Method

DECOR's Business Knowledge Method provides a methodological approach for running BPOKM projects. Its main elements include:

Identification of knowledge-intensive processes
Process analysis
Domain ontology construction
Analysis of task-specific knowledge needs
Dealing with weak workflow structures

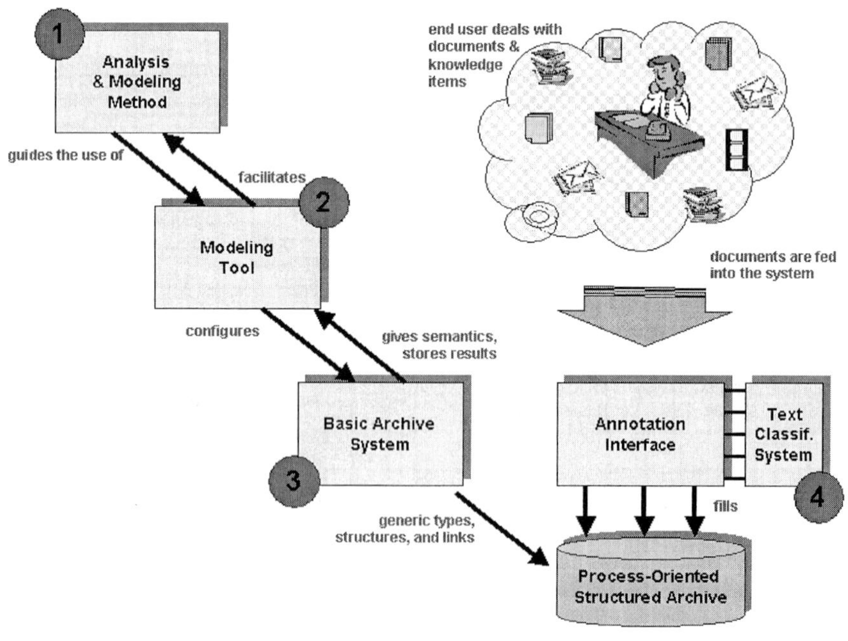

Figure 2: DECOR Modules for System Building

The current draft comprises process analysis and domain ontology construction. It amalgamates elements taken from CommonKADS (Akkermans et al 1999; Schreiber et al 1999) and IDEF5[1]. Figure 3 sketches the relationships of the first three analysis steps. The draft method has already been tested in our three case studies and is subject to further improvements.

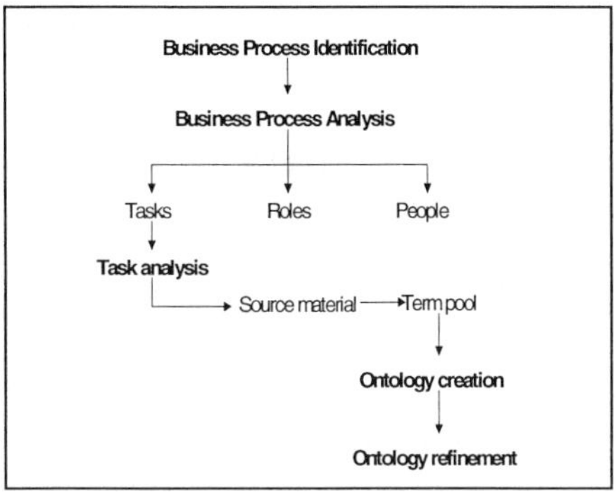

Figure 3: Business Knowledge Method: From Process Analysis to Ontology Design

(2) Business Knowledge Modeling Tool

The DECOR Modeling Tool will support in an integrated manner all modeling activities related to the method described above: (weakly-structured) processes, task-specific information needs, domain knowledge structures/ontologies, process specific context variables etc. In contrast to many existing ontology modeling tools, it shall primarily address users without a specific AI (Artificial Intelligence) background. It will be oriented towards existing BPM tools (like ARIS™ or ADONIS™) and build upon widespread ontology modeling formalisms (like topic maps or the IDEF graphical modeling primitives). The DECOR Modeling Tool is currently under development. It is being realized as a set of related modeling methods for the commercial Microsoft VISIO® 2000 visualization tool. This ensures a wide usability of the software basis and a good familiarity of non-expert users with the overall look-and-feel. The VISIO® interface actions will be coupled by a dynamic link to the DECOR Basic Archive System (see below). So, modeling activities at the user interface directly lead to the respective effects in the configuration of the underlying knowledge networks: new concepts or links are inserted in the ontologies, business process models are extended, or indexing concepts added to document models. This dynamic link to the Basic Archive System allows to equip the graphical modeling interface with a semantic foundation: e.g., only reasonable links are possible, links which do not respect the value restrictions of the represented relationship can directly be rejected. A first demonstrator of this dynamic link between VISIO® and the DHC CognoVision® tool (the software basis for the DECOR Basic Archive System) has already been implemented by DHC. Besides the possibility of directly storing modeling results in CognoVision®, an ASCII based interface for information exchange with third-party tools will be provided based upon upcoming ontology representation standardisation approaches like OIL.

(3) Basic Archive System

The Basic Archive System stores knowledge items (documents and links to documents or tacit knowledge) plus metadata and links between knowledge items. Metadata are represented in terms of underlying ontologies designed with DECOR modules (1) and (2). Business process models are one of many possible structuring criteria. Manual navigation in hierarchical indices extracted from index ontologies is allowed, as well as querying the archive by XML retrieval messages which combine retrieval constraints formulated over links and metadata. Software basis for the DECOR Basic Archive System is the CognoVision® product offered by DHC GmbH (Müller & Herterich 2001). CognoVision® allows to represent arbitrary knowledge networks built from attributed objects (structure elements) and attributed links, and to link information objects to structuring elements. Information objects encapsulate (i) logical content entitities like the set of all documents with the same content, but in a different language, and (ii) the related metadata. These powerful mechanisms allow to express arbitrary indexing ontologies and the related document models plus the link to the original (multimedia) documents.

(4) Annotation Interface

In order to fill the archive system, we need a software for easily attaching semantic categories (in terms of modeled ontologies) to knowledge items, or, in terms of CognoVision®, link information objects to structuring elements. In this way, documents are fed into the process-oriented structured archives and indexed, and the required links are established. This DECOR module is still to be designed. Since indexing is a well-known bottleneck for ontology-based KM systems (indeed, for all document management systems), we are building a generic interface of the annotation tool to an automatic text classification software. Currently we test two such classification systems, the learning text classification workbench (TCW) developed at DFKI (Junker 2000), and

[1] See http://www.idef.com/

the MindAccess® API provided by insiders information management GmbH. MindAccess® is an extensible multiple-paradigm tool which employs a number of state-of-the-art algorithms.

So far, we characterised the DECOR modules required for designing and installing a process-oriented structured archive and for filling it with annotated knowledge items. Returning to Section 2 (which discussed the system behaviour at runtime dealing with operative business processes, Figure 1), we can add the following DECOR solution modules:

(5) Weakly-structured workflow tool

The DECOR Weakly-Structured Workflow (WWF) Support provides modeling support and enactment machinery for flexible and adaptive workflow. In (Schwarz et al 2001) we analyzed requirements for such a workflow support coming from the characteristics of knowledge intensive work (see Figure 4, cp. (Davenport et al 1996)). We described a prototype with the following properties:

- A process archive contains process templates which later are converted to process models
- Task specifications and process logic are defined separately
- Task specifications are hierarchically decomposed into sub-tasks
- Sub-tasks may contain "black boxes"
- Black boxes may be defined at runtime (late modeling)
- MS Visio® 2000 integrated with CognoVision® as the basis for process modeling

Although there exist already prototypical implementations of specific parts, the DECOR WWF support is still in its design phase. Important features are the interfaces to retrieval agents and structured archive. The feasibility of the basic idea has been shown in the KnowMore project (Abecker et al 2000; Abecker et al 2000b). Strong requirements from our three DECOR case studies are the seemless embedding of a conventional strong-structure workflow approach as a proper subset and a comfortable system interface usable by "normal end users".

- Unique and of low volumeVariability in performance across individuals and time
- No strong sequential order
- Frequent exceptions and changesUncertainty in inputs and outputsUnstructured work rules and routines
- Involves personal judgement and

Figure 4: Knowledge-intensive Work

(6) Context-aware knowledge agents

The purpose of the DECOR Context-aware Knowledge Agents is to co-operate with workflow engine and modeled information needs, thus proactively offering information from the process-oriented structured archive to the user in charge of a certain task. The feasibility of the principal idea has also been shown in KnowMore. Implementation details in DECOR have to be clarified, the implementation will presumably be based upon a FIPA[2] compliant software agent platform like JADE[3].

4. RELATED WORK AND PROJECT STATUS

The main distinctive feature of the DECOR project is the idea of a ***total solution*** to context-aware, workflow-embedded information retrieval for knowledge-intensive tasks. So, the main advantage above research prototypes like KnowMore or work at AIFB (Staab & Schnurr 2000) which were mainly concentrated on intelligent techniques in the centre of information retrieval, ontology-based document representation, or context representation, is the completion of this technology-focussed scenario by appropriate analysis methods, modeling support, and introduction and maintenance advice. The descripion of the overall system design and the play-together of different toolkit elements was the main concern of this paper.

Another project focus is the ***technological consolidation*** of research ideas using (de facto) standards (FIPA, RDF/S, Topic Maps, CommonKADS, IDEF), commercial software (CognoVision®) and widespread tools (Visio®, JADE) wherever possible in the scenario.

Regarding the several individual elements of the overall framework, the statements about the status of our work (product, demonstrator, design phase) differ considerably and are also discussed above in the respective parts. The related work for several modules is quite different, too.

The idea of ***knowledge-oriented organization analysis*** is not fundamentally new, so our method is deeply grounded in existing work. However most existing approaches (cp., e.g. (Goesmann & Herrmann 2000; Mertins et al 2000)) do not lead to such far-reaching technical innovations as our project. The idea of BPOKM is also a main topic of the EU project PROMOTE (Karagiannis & Telesko 2000) which has similar analysis goals and methods, but

[2] http://www.fipa.org

[3] http://sharon.cselt.it/projects/jade

relies on a conventional strongly-structured workflow paradigm.

The idea of ***context-aware information retrieval*** is sometimes interpreted in a not workflow-related way: Often, highly knowledge-intensive processes are not formally modeled because they are too complex or because they are too much ad-hoc. *Attentive systems*, e.g. personal information agents like WATSON (Budzik & Hammond 2000), try to detect the task a user is actually performing, and use this knowledge to retrieve context-oriented information. In this way, in contrast to our process-embedded scenario, only the *local work context* can be obtained (e.g., the application a user utilizes). Thus, relevant knowledge from preceding tasks is hardly available to better specify the information need. In the long-term, a combination of both interpretations of work context could be promising. The EU project CoMMA (Perez et al 2000) comes very close to our scenario in many points. However, they focus more on matters of individual user profiles. (Klemke 2000; Elst & Abecker 2001) show the way to a comprehensive context modeling as a unifying view for all these approaches.

The requirements for ***weakly-structured workflow*** systems to support knowledge-intensive work, are seldom discussed in the literature. However, (Macintosh 1999) comes to similar results as DECOR. Interestingly, (Lenk & Traunmüller 2000) recently identified very similar characteristics as typical for many business processes in the new area of "electronic government".

Concerning the ***basic archive system***, the CognoVision® tool is at least as powerful as technologically similar competitors. However, the integration of a method-supported modeling tool and an automatic classification facility seems unique.

Currently, the described method and software modules are under development as described. The DECOR work is organised around the development of three pilot systems in the medical and social security sector:

One pilot is being installed at IKA, the Greek Social Security Institute. The system supports the process of granting full old age pension to insured people which - as part of a normal administrative workflow - contains few central, knowledge and document intensive steps for finding a decision. These steps must be legally checkable, they are often done with uncertainty, are influenced by many legal regulations, and they are central for the correct result of the process. The DECOR pilot will improve a consistent, high quality of service for these decision steps.

One pilot is placed at the interface between a most important Brussels hospital and CPAS, the body of each city that has to deal with people who are in social, financial, ... trouble. In the workflow of accomplishing the patient file and sending administrative and accounting data to CPAS, there are often delays and wrong decisions made due to missing information, knowledge and experience (which is available in other steps of the process) which leads to heavy financial losses.

One pilot is being built for a subsidiary of the German Red Cross, which deals with the acquisition, transport, storage, and processing of blood and blood plasma donors. In this highly sensitive application area, all software systems employed, and in particular the company's SAP R/3 installation must be validated according to national and international laws and regulations. The process of making changes to this SAP R/3 system while keeping the validation status is document and knowledge-intensive and will be supported by our pilot system.

Altogether, the DECOR project develops (and continuously tests in the three pilot sites) a practice-driven, total solution for business-process oriented knowledge management. Long-term goals for extending the scenario concern context-enriched *storage* of documents, and evolution of process knowledge as a knowledge management process intertwined with workflow execution.

REFERENCES

Abecker, A., et al, 1998, 'Towards a Technology for Organizational Memories', IEEE Intelligent Systems, 13(3), May/June.

Abecker, A., et al, 2000, 'Context-Aware, Proactive Delivery of Task-Specific Knowledge: The KnowMore Project', *Int. Journal on Information System Frontiers, Kluwer, 2(3/4).*

Abecker, A., et al, 2000b, 'Information Supply for Business Processes – Coupling Workflow With Document Analysis and Information Retrieval', *Knowledge-Based Systems, Elsevier, 13(5): 271-284.*

Akkermans, H., et al, 1999, 'Hot Issues and Cool Solutions in Knowledge Management: An Industrial Case Study', *KAW'99, Banff, Canada.*

Benjamins, V.R.,et al, 1998, 'Knowledge Management Through Ontologies', *PAKM-98, Basel, Switzerland.*

Buckingham Shum, S., 1998, 'Negotiating the Construction of Organisational Memories, In Borghoff, U.M. and R. Pareschi, R., eds., *Information Technology for Knowledge Management.* Berlin, Heidelberg, New York: Springer-Verlag, pp. 55-78.

Budzik, J. and Hammond, K.J., 2000, 'User Interactions with Everyday Applications as Context for Just-in-time Information Access', *Proc. Intelligent User Interfaces 2000. ACM.*

Davenport, Th., et al, 1996, 'Improving Knowledge Work Processes', *Sloan Management Review, Reprint Series, 37(4), Summer.*

Davenport, T.H. and Prusak, L., 2000, *Working Knowledge*, Harvard Business School Press.

Elst, L. v. and Abecker, A., 2001, *Integrating Task, Role, and User Profiles for Context-Specific Information Delivery in Organizational Memories.* Draft under evaluation.

Fillies, C. et al, 2001, 'Prozessmodellierungswerkzeuge und das Semantic Web', *In (Müller et al 2001).* In German.

Goesmann, T., and Herrmann, Th., 2000, 'Wissensmanagement und Geschäftsprozeßunterstützung am Beispiel des Workflow Memory Information System WoMIS'. *In Herrmann, Th., et al, eds, Verbesserung von Geschäftsprozessen mit flexiblen Workflow-Management-Systemen, Band 4,* Heidelberg: Physica-Verlag. In German.

Hammer, M., and Champy, J.,. 1993, *Reengineering the Corporation: A Manifesto for Business Revolution*, New York: HarperBusiness.

Junker, M., 2000, Heuristisches Lernen von Regeln für die Textkategorisierung, Dissertation, Fachbereich Informatik. Universität Kaiserslautern. In German.

Karagiannis, D., and Telesko, R., 2000, 'The EU-Project PROMOTE: A Process-Oriented Approach for Knowledge Management', *In Reimer, U., ed, PAKM 2000, Third Int. Conf. on Practical Aspects of Knowledge Management*

Klemke, R., 2000, 'Context Framework - an Open Approach to Enhance Organisational Memory Systems with Context Modelling Techniques', *In Reimer, U., ed, PAKM 2000, Third Int. Conf. on Practical Aspects of Knowledge Management*

Lenk, K., and Traunmüller, R., 2000, 'Perspectives on Electronic Government', IFIP WG 8.5 *Conference on „Advances in Electronic Government", Zaragoza.*

Macintosh, A., 1999, *Adaptive Workflow to Support Knowledge Intensive Tasks*, Working Paper, Artificial Intelligence Applications Institute (AIAI), Edinburgh, Scotland.

Malhotra, Y., 1998, 'Business Process Redesign: An Overview', *IEEE Engineering Management Review, 26(3).*

Müller, H.-J., et al, eds, 2001, *WM`2001-Workshop „Geschäftsprozeßorientiertes Wissensmanagement", Baden-Baden.*

Müller, St. and Herterich, R., 2001, 'Prozessorientiertes Wissensmanagement mit CognoVision', *In (Müller et al 2001).* In German.

Mertins, K., et al, 2000, *Knowledge Management: Best Practices in Europe*, Berlin, Heidelberg: Springer-Verlag.

O`Leary, D., 1998, 'Using AI in Knowledge Management: Knowledge Bases and Ontologies', *IEEE Intelligent Systems, May/June, pages 34 - 39.*

Perez, Ph., et al, 2000, 'Corporate Memory Management through Agents', *The eBusiness and eWork Conference, Madrid.*

Schreiber, G., et al, 1999, *Knowledge Engineering and Management: The CommonKADS Methodology.*, MIT Press.

Schwarz, S., et al, 2001, 'Anforderungen an die Workflow-Unterstützung für wissensintensive Geschäftsprozesse', *In (Müller et al 2001).* In German.

Staab, S., and Schnurr, H.-P., 2000, 'Smart Task Support Through Proactive Access to Organizational Memory', *Knowledge-Based Systems, Elsevier, 13(5), pp. 251-260.*

Sumner, T., et al, 1999, 'Moving from On-the-Job Training towards Organisational Learning', *12th Banff Knowledge Acquisition Workshop.*

Wargitsch, C., et al, 1998, 'An Organizational-Memory-Based Approach for an Evolutionary Workflow Management System – Concepts and Implementation', *HICCS`31, Vol. 1, pp. 174-183.*

PART 2

Artificial Intelligence and Decision Support Systems

MULTI-AGENT DYNAMIC SCHEDULING AND RE-SCHEDULING WITH GLOBAL TEMPORAL CONSTRAINTS

Joaquim Reis
Dpt. Ciências e Tecnologias de Informação, ISCTE
Avenida das Forças Armadas, 1600 Lisboa, Portugal
e-mail: Joaquim.Reis@iscte.pt

Nuno Mamede
Dpt. de Engenharia Informática, IST
Avenida Rovisco Pais, 1049-001 Lisboa, Portugal
e-mail: Nuno.Mamede@acm.org

Keywords: Scheduling, Multi-Agent Systems, Supply-Chain Management.

Abstract: A co-ordination mechanism is proposed for multi-agent production-distribution co-operative scheduling problems, based on a purely temporal perspective. This mechanism is based on communication among pairs of client-supplier agents involved in the problem, and allows agents to locally perceive hard global temporal constraints. By exchanging limited specific information, the agents are able to recognise non over-constrained problems and, in that case, rule out non temporally-feasible solutions and establish an initial solution. The information is then used to guide re-scheduling and repair the initial solution and converge to a final one.

1. INTRODUCTION

This article describes an ongoing investigation that developed from work being published on the subject of multi-agent scheduling in production-distribution environments (see (Reis 1998), (Reis 1999a), (Reis 1999b), (Reis 1999c) and (Reis 2000)).

The specific logistics context of the supply-chain/Extended Enterprise (EE) (O'Neill 1996) is considered for short-term scheduling. The EE is usually assumed to be a kind of Virtual Organisation, or Virtual Enterprise, where the set of participant agents is relatively stable (for concepts, terminology and classification see (Camarinha-Matos 1999)).

Scheduling is the allocation of resources over time to perform a collection of tasks subject to temporal and capacity constraints. For a general introduction to classical/Operations Research (OR) approaches to scheduling problems see (Blazewicz 1994). For Artificial Intelligence (AI) based approaches see (Zweben 1994).

Planning and co-ordination of logistics activities has been, in the areas of OR/Management Science, the subject of investigation since the sixties (Graves 1993). Scheduling in this kind of environments has had, recently, a more dedicated attention (*e.g.*, see (Fox 1993), (Arnold 1997), (Kjenstad 1998) or (Rabelo 1998)).

The scheduling problems we consider are:

a) Highly dynamic - Solution development is an on-going process during which unforeseen events must always be accommodated for;
b) Multi-agent co-operative - Each agent has its own local perspective of the scheduling problem, can optimise its own scheduling preferences, but it must co-operate so that it won't invalidate a feasible scheduling solution.

The following sections present: the multi-agent scheduling environment (sec.2), the general approach proposed (sec.3), the initial scheduling step (sec.4) and the re-scheduling (sec.5), both from an individual agent perspective, and finally, future work and conclusions (sec.6). Secs. 4 and 5 are presented with examples based on simulations done.

J. Filipe et al. (eds.), Enterprise Information Systems III, 117–123.

2. THE SCHEDULING ENVIRONMENT

As scheduling resources are managed by individual, geographically decentralised and autonomous entities (enterprises, organisations) we adopted the AI Multi-Agent Systems paradigm (see, for instance, (ICMAS 1996) or (O'Hare 1996)). In the past work already referred, we have proposed a model of the EE/production-distribution based on an *agent network*, with each agent managing an aggregated scheduling resource (representing a production, a store, or a transportation resource) and linked through client-supplier relationships. A scheduling resource is just an individual node of a network of resources, termed a *physical network*, and accommodates the representation of the agent tasks scheduled and the available capacity along a certain scheduling temporal horizon. Ordinary network agents are termed *capacity agents*, because they are responsible for managing the capacity of a resource. A special *supervision agent*, with no resource, plays the role of an interface with the outside, and can introduce work (*i.e.*, new scheduling problems) in the agent network.

Among capacity agents communication is *local* in the agent network, which means that only pairs of client-supplier agents can communicate. This can occur by the exchange of messages of product request (client to supplier), request acceptance or rejection (supplier to client), re-scheduling request, re-scheduling acceptance, re-scheduling rejection and cancellation of a previously accepted request (both ways), and satisfaction of an accepted request (supplier to client, sent when the time of due-date comes). Request messages contain product, quantity of product and proposed due-date information. Some of the above types of messages convey also specific information for co-ordination of scheduling activity. The supervision agent can only communicate with agents playing the roles of retail and raw-material agents, *i.e.*, the agents located at the downstream and the upstream end of the agent network (these are pure clients and pure suppliers for the network) respectively.

At supervision level, a scheduling problem is defined by a *global product request from the outside* of the agent network (*i.e.*, a request of a final product of the network), the global due-date DD, and the global release date RD. These two dates are the limits of the scheduling temporal horizon and are considered the hard global temporal constraints of the problem. The supervision agent introduces a new scheduling problem by communicating a global product request from outside to the appropriate retail agent;[1] later, after the capacity agents have propagated among them, upstream the agent network, the necessary *local product requests*, the supervision agent will collect *global product requests to outside* from raw-material agents. A scheduling problem will cease to exist in the network when the time of the last of the local due-date comes, or if some local requests are rejected, or accepted and then cancelled (the supervision agent knows this as messages of satisfaction, rejection and cancellation will be propagated to retail and raw-material agents and then communicated to it).

In order to satisfy a product request from a client a capacity agent must schedule a task on its resource. A task needs a supply of one (in the case of a store or transportation agent), or one or more products (in the case of a production agent and depending on the components/materials for the task product). For those supplies the agent must send the appropriate product requests to the appropriate suppliers (and there is always a unique supplier for each supply product). The task consumes a non-changing amount of resource capacity during its temporal interval. The duration of the task depends primarily on the product, the quantity of product, the characteristics of the resource, and additional parameters. The details of these latter parameters are omitted here to allow simplicity of explanation, and we will assume a non-changing duration for all tasks.[2]

Although tasks are private to the agents (only the communication messages are perceived by more than one agent), we can view the set of tasks that some agents of the network schedule to satisfy a global product request from outside, as whole, as being a *network job* (see example in Figure 1). This is a just an analogue of the concept of job used in classical production scheduling problems.

[1] Because our networks can be multi-product, the set of products deliverable can depend on the retail agent.

[2] In our model, the duration of a task can be externally imposed, in the case of a store agent, and will depend also on the per time unit capacity amount invested, in the case of a production or transportation agent. Capacity constraints are represented by a value of maximum capacity, possibly varying along the temporal horizon. This value corresponds to a quantity of product for store agents, and to a rate (*i.e.*, quantity per time unit) for production and transportation agents.

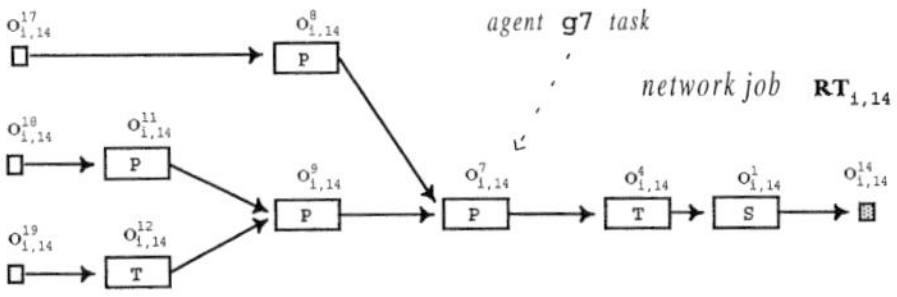

Figure 1: A network job. The task of an agent g_k for the ith global request to retail agent g_r is denoted by $o^{k}_{i,r}$

A *solution* for a scheduling problem is a set of product requests agreed by pairs of client-supplier agents and agent tasks necessary to satisfy the global product request given by the problem. A *feasible solution* has nor temporal nor capacity conflicts, *i.e.*, it respects both all temporal and all capacity constraints. For capacity constraints to be respected, no capacity over-allocation must occur with any task of the solution, in any agent, at any moment of the scheduling temporal horizon. For temporal constraints to be respected, all local product requests of the solution must fall within the global release date and global due-date of the problem; also, for each agent, the interval of its task must fall in between the due-date agreed for the client request and the latest of the due-dates agreed for the requests made to suppliers, and the latter due-date must precede the former. Temporal constraints can be summarised in the temporal precedence of specific points in time.

More details on the resources and the physical network are given in (Reis 1998), (Reis 1999b), and (Reis 1999c); about the agent network and inter-agent communication see (Reis 1999a), also (Reis 1999b), and (Reis 2000).

3. THE PROPOSED APPROACH

Classically, scheduling is considered a difficult problem (Garey 1979). Generally, solutions for a scheduling problem have to be searched for and the search space can be very large. Additionally, for a multi-agent scheduling problem, a part of the searching effort is invested in co-ordination of the agents involved which, in our case, means sharing information through message exchange. Message exchange is considered costly so, methods of pruning the search space for finding at least a first feasible solution with minimal co-ordination efforts are considered satisfactory.

In our approach we consider two special sets of solutions: the set of *time-feasible solutions*, which respect all temporal constraints, and the set of

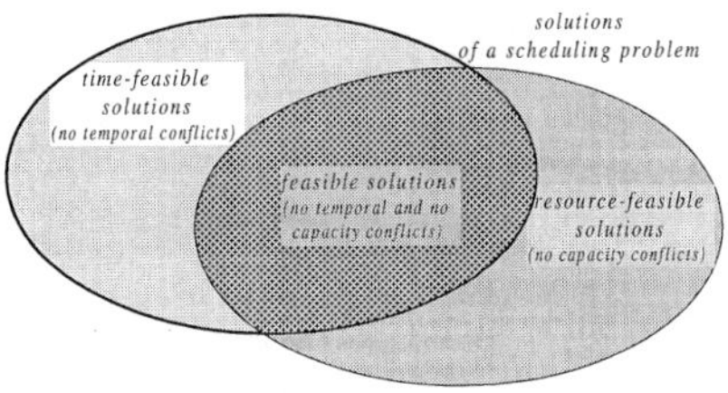

Figure 2: Solutions of a scheduling problem

resource-feasible solutions, which respect all capacity constraints. As Figure 2 shows, the set of feasible solutions is the intersection of those two sets, *i.e.*, a feasible solution is one that is both time-feasible and resource-feasible. A problem is termed *temporally over-constrained* if the set of time-feasible solutions is empty, and is termed *resource over-constrained* if the set of resource-feasible solutions is empty. If a problem has both non-empty time-feasible and resource-feasible solution sets and their intersection is a non-empty set, then the problem has feasible solutions. Now we propose an approach using the following procedure steps for each individual capacity agent:

1. Acceptance and initial solution - Detect if the problem is temporally over-constrained, and if it isn't, establish an initial solution, and proceed in the next step. If it is, terminate the procedure by rejecting the problem, for having no feasible solution;
2. Re-schedule to find a time-feasible solution - If the established solution is time-feasible proceed in the next step. If it isn't, re-schedule to remove all temporal conflicts;
3. Re-schedule to find a feasible solution - For a resource-feasible solution terminate the procedure. In the other case, try to re-schedule to remove all capacity conflicts without creating temporal conflicts, resorting to cancellation, with task un-scheduling, as a last choice, if necessary.

As some approaches in the literature, this procedure starts by establishing one initial, possibly non-feasible, solution which is then repaired in order to remove conflicts (see, for instance, (Minton 1992)). Steps 1 and 2 of the procedure are oriented for a temporal scheduling perspective and concern only to a single scheduling problem of the agent. Step 3 is oriented for a resource scheduling perspective and can involve all scheduling problems of the agent at step 3, as all tasks of the agent compete for the same resource capacity.

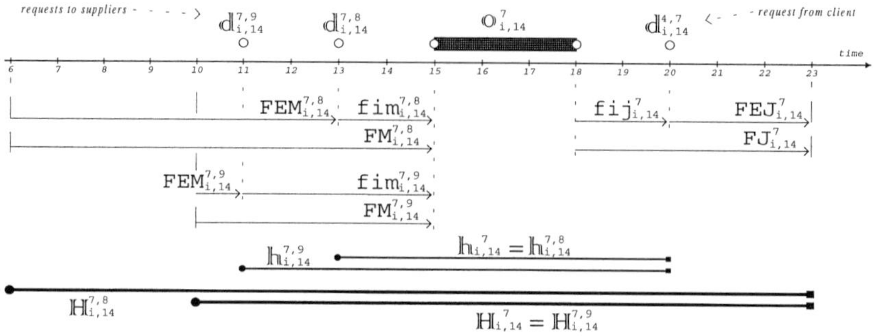

Figure 3: Temporal slacks for agent g_7 task $o^{7}_{i,14}$

The problem rejection referred in step 1 is accomplished through request rejection and cancellation messages. In step 2, the initial solution, if not temporally-feasible, is repaired. The re-scheduling activity referred can involve re-scheduling the requests and/or the task. The re-scheduling requests are agreements on new client and/or suppliers due-dates for the existing product requests. These are accomplished through re-scheduling request, and corresponding acceptance and rejection types of messages, and must have high priority because scheduling for a time-feasible solution is at stake. This is possible, as the problem was previously recognised as not temporally over-constrained. In step 3, the idea is to repair the present solution by restricting the search for a better one to the set of time-feasible solutions, and search for a solution that is not only time-feasible, but also resource-feasible. The re-scheduling activity referred can involve re-scheduling the requests and/or the task; as a last choice there can be request cancellation with task un-scheduling (a drastic last choice, but still an effective one).

4. STEP 1: SCHEDULING AN INITIAL SOLUTION

We show, through an example, how an agent can locally recognise a temporally over-constrained problem, and contribute to establish an initial solution in the case this is possible (step 1).

Suppose g_7 identifies a production agent having the task $o^{7}_{i,14}$ of network job in Figure 1. In Figure 3 a possible situation for this task is represented on a timeline. As agent g_7 has two suppliers for the task, two requests to two suppliers are shown, $d^{7,8}_{i,14}$ and $d^{7,9}_{i,14}$, besides the request from the client, $d^{4,7}_{i,14}$. Temporal slacks and derived intervals (denoted by h and H symbols) are also shown in Figure 3. Symbols fij, fim, FEJ, FEM, FJ and FM denote, respectively, the *internal downstream slack*, *internal upstream slacks*, *external downstream slack*, *external upstream slacks*, *downstream slack* and *upstream slacks*. For each kind of upstream slacks there is one per each supplier. Slacks are represented by arrows.

By definition:

$$FJ^{7}_{i,14} = FEJ^{7}_{i,14} + fij^{7}_{i,14}$$

$$fij^{7}_{i,14} = TIME(d^{4,7}_{i,14}) - ENDTIME(o^{7}_{i,14})$$

$$FM^{7,j}_{i,14} = FEM^{7,j}_{i,14} + fim^{7,j}_{i,14}$$

$$fim^{7,j}_{i,14} = STARTIME(o^{7}_{i,14}) - TIME(d^{7,j}_{i,14})$$

(the last two for $j=8,9$)

Internal slacks are inserted locally, and by the initiative of the agent, when scheduling the task and making requests to suppliers; external slacks are imposed by the other agents of the network. We will assume that, in any case, *the agent will maintain positive internal slacks*. Each of the h's are intervals between one of the supplier due-dates and the client due-date (13 and 20, and 11 and 20, in Figure 3); the H's are intervals between one of the earliest start times and the latest finish time for the task (6 and 23, and 10 and 23, in Figure 3). The temporal end points of the most restrictive H interval are hard temporal constraints of the problem (10 and 23 in Figure 3), in particular for the task. Let us denote these by $\mathtt{RD}^{7}_{i,14}$ and $\mathtt{DD}^{7}_{i,14}$, for the upstream and downstream point, respectively.

It is easy to see that, in order for a solution to be time-feasible, the interval of the task must be contained in the most restricted $\mathtt{h}$ interval, and each $\mathtt{h}$ interval must be contained in the corresponding (same supplier) $\mathtt{H}$ interval (and this must also hold for every capacity agent involved in the network job). For this to hold, no temporal slack can be negative. Also, if the duration of the most restrictive $\mathtt{H}$ interval is less than the task duration, the problem is temporally over-constrained, and the agent can reject it.

We propose that product request messages from the client, additionally to product request information, *carry the value of the* `FEJ` *slack*; also, request acceptance messages from suppliers will *carry the value of the respective* `FEM` *slack*.[3]

In our example, agent g_7 would then calculate the $\mathtt{DD}^{7}_{i,14}$ and $\mathtt{RD}^{7}_{i,14}$ values by:

$$\mathtt{DD}^{7}_{i,14}=\mathtt{TIME}(\mathtt{d}^{4,7}_{i,14})+\mathtt{FEJ}^{7}_{i,14} \text{ and}$$

$$\mathtt{RD}^{7}_{i,14}=\underset{j=8,9}{\mathtt{MAX}}(\mathtt{RD}^{7,j}_{i,14})$$

where:

$$\mathtt{RD}^{7,j}_{i,14}=\mathtt{TIME}(\mathtt{d}^{7,j}_{i,14})-\mathtt{FEM}^{7,j}_{i,14} \quad (j=8,9)$$

When the agent receives request $\mathtt{d}^{4,7}_{i,14}$ from the client, it will, guaranteeing non-negative `fij` and `fim` values, schedule the task and make requests $\mathtt{d}^{7,8}_{i,14}$ and $\mathtt{d}^{7,9}_{i,14}$ to suppliers, passing them also the (supplier `FEJ`) value:

$$\mathtt{FJ}^{7}_{i,14}+\mathtt{fim}^{7,j}_{i,14} \quad (j=8,9)$$

When the agent receives all the request acceptances from the suppliers, verifies first if the problem is temporally over-constrained, by testing if:

$$\mathtt{DD}^{7}_{i,14}-\mathtt{RD}^{7}_{i,14} < \mathtt{DURATION}(\mathtt{O}^{7}_{i,14})$$

If this is true the problem must be rejected. Otherwise, the agent will send the acceptance message to the client, passing it also the (client `FEM`) value:

$$\mathtt{FM}^{7}_{i,14}+\mathtt{fij}^{7}_{i,14}$$

where:

$$\mathtt{FM}^{7}_{i,14}=\mathtt{STARTIME}(\mathtt{O}^{7}_{i,14})-\mathtt{RD}^{7}_{i,14}.$$

If the step 1 concludes with a non temporally over-constrained problem, agent g_7 will internally keep the tuple:

$$< \mathtt{DD}^{7}_{i,14},\ \{\mathtt{RD}^{7,8}_{i,14},\mathtt{RD}^{7,9}_{i,14}\},\ \mathtt{d}^{4,7}_{i,14},\ \{\mathtt{d}^{7,8}_{i,14},\mathtt{d}^{7,9}_{i,14}\},\ \mathtt{O}^{7}_{i,14} >$$

as its own local perspective of the network scheduling problem and its initial solution.

5. STEP 2: RE-SCHEDULING FOR A TIME-FEASIBLE SOLUTION

We now show how, starting from an initial solution with temporal conflicts, can an agent locally contribute to obtain a time-feasible solution (step 2), following the same example.

Clearly, for the local situation represented Figure 3, all slacks are positive: all slack arrows point to the future side of the time line. So, the solution is seen as temporally-feasible by agent g_7, and g_7 will do nothing, unless it receives any re-scheduling request, which it could accept provided non-negative internal slacks can be maintained (this must also always hold in the following).

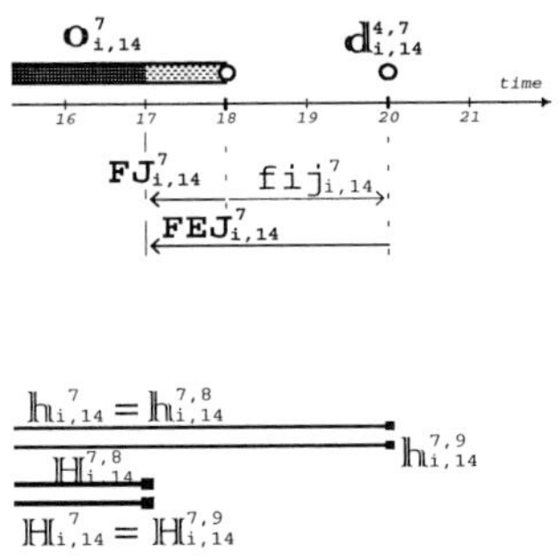

Figure 4: Re-scheduling case 1

We now pose four kinds of different scenarios were, at least agent g_7 must take the initiative of some re-scheduling actions. These are described by the re-scheduling cases 1, 2, 3 and 4, in Figure 4,

[3] For a retail agent, the `FEJ` value can be pre-specified (*e.g.*, 0). For a raw-material agent the `FEM` value will be the difference between the due-date of the agent global request to the outside and the global `RD` date.

Figure 6, Figure 6 and Figure 7, respectively. Cases 1 and 2 *must be tested for first.*

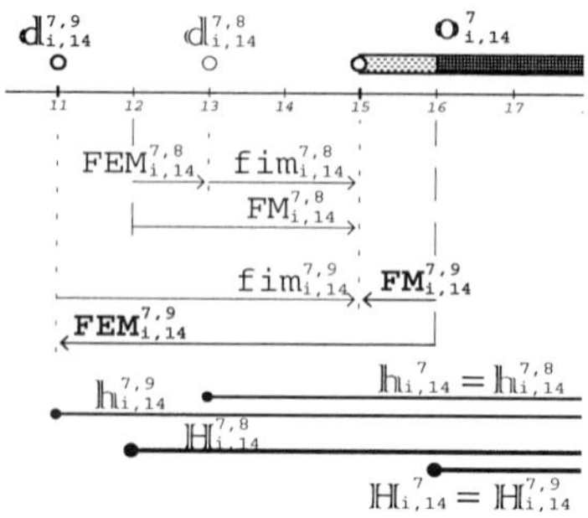

Figure 5: Re-scheduling case 2

Case 1 occurs if $\mathtt{FJ}^{7}_{\mathtt{i,14}}<0$ *and* $\mathtt{FEJ}^{7}_{\mathtt{i,14}}<0$ (the task and the client request violate the hard temporal constraint downstream, 17 in Figure 4). The detection of case 1 must be followed by the appropriate task re-scheduling and client request re-scheduling to earlier times. The re-scheduling of some requests to suppliers can then be necessary to maintain non-negative internal (`fim`) slacks.

Case 2 occurs if $\mathtt{FM}^{7,j}_{\mathtt{i,14}}<0$ *and* $\mathtt{FEM}^{7,j}_{\mathtt{i,14}}<0$, for some $\mathtt{j=8,9}$ (the task and some requests to suppliers violate hard temporal constraints upstream, 16 in Figure 5). The detection of case 2 must be followed by the appropriate task re-scheduling and the re-scheduling of the offending requests to suppliers to later times. The re-scheduling of the client request can then be necessary to maintain a non-negative internal (`fij`) slack.

After handling cases 1 and 2, cases 3 and 4 are handled.

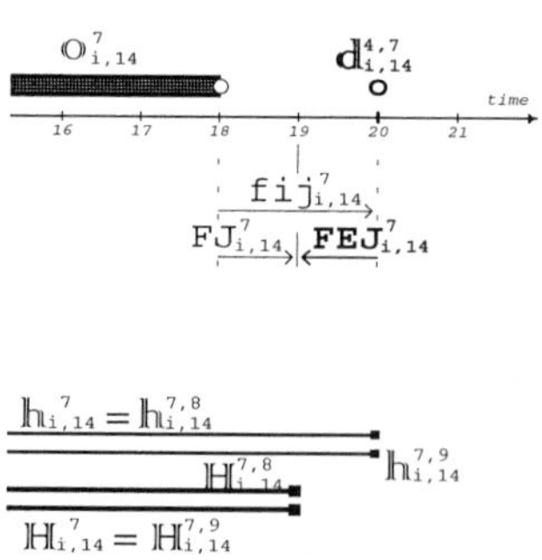

Figure 6: Re-scheduling case 3

Case 3 occurs if $\mathtt{FJ}^{7}_{\mathtt{i,14}}<0$. (the client request violates the hard temporal constraint downstream, 19 in Figure 6). The detection of case 3 must be followed by the appropriate client request re-scheduling to an earlier time.

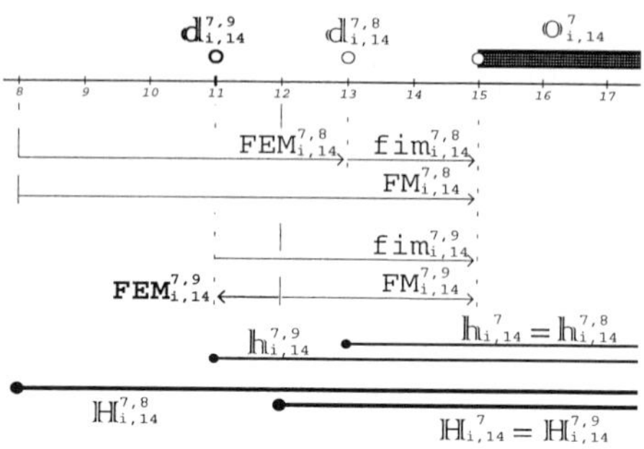

Figure 7: Re-scheduling case 4

Case 4 occurs if $\mathtt{FEM}^{7,j}_{\mathtt{i,14}}<0$, for some $\mathtt{j=8,9}$ (some requests to suppliers violate hard temporal constraints upstream, 12 in Figure 7). The detection of case 4 must be followed by the appropriate re-scheduling of the offending requests to suppliers later times.

6. FUTURE WORK AND CONCLUSION

We described an approach for multi-agent co-operative scheduling based on a three step procedure for individual agents. Step 1 allows agents to detect locally if the problem is temporally over-constrained and, in the case it isn't, schedule an initial, possibly non time-feasible solution. By locally exchanging specific temporal slack values, agents are able to locally perceive the hard global temporal constraints of a problem, and rule out non time-feasible solutions in the subsequent steps. Each of the slack values exchanged in step 1 corresponds, for a particular agent, to a sum of slacks, downstream and upstream the agent network, and so, they cannot be considered private information of any agent in particular. In step 2, if necessary, agents repair the initial solution to obtain a time-feasible one.

The procedure is very general with respect to its step 3. This step can be refined to accommodate additional improved co-ordination mechanisms for implementing certain search strategies, based on capacity/resource constrainedness (*e.g.*, see (Sycara 1991) or (Sadeh 1994)), leading the agents on a fast convergence to specific feasible solutions. For instance, feasible solutions satisfying some scheduling preferences or optimising some criteria, either from an individual agent perspective, or from a global one, or both. This is a subject of our future work.

REFERENCES

Arnold 1997, Arnold, Jörg, et al, 1997, *Production Planning and Control within Supply Chains*, ESPRIT project 20544, X-CITTIC.

Blazewicz 1994, Blazewicz, J.;Ecker, K.H.;Schmidt, G.;Weglarz, J., 1994, *Scheduling in Computer and Manufacturing Systems*, Springer Verlag, 1994

Camarinha-Matos 1999, Camarinha-Matos, Luís M.; Afsarmanesh, Hamideh, 1999, *The Virtual Enterprise Concept*, in Infrastructures for Virtual Enterprises, Camarinha-Matos, L.M. and Afsarmanesh, H. (eds.), Kluwer Academic Publishers, Dordrecht, The Netherlands, 1999, 3-14.

Fox 1993, Fox, Mark S., et al, 1993, *The Integrated Supply Chain Management System*, Department of Industrial Engineering, University of Toronto, Canada.

Garey 1979, Garey, M.R.; Johnson, D.S., 1979, *Computers and Intractability: A Guide to the Theory of NP-Completeness*, W.H. Freeman and Co., New York.

Graves 1993, Graves, S.C.; Kan, A.H.G. Rinnooy; Zipkin, P.H., (Eds.), *Logistics of Production and Inventory*, Handbooks in Operations Research and Management Science, Volume 4, North-Holland, Amsterdam, 1993.

ICMAS 1996, ICMAS 1996, 1996, *Proceedings of the Second International Conference on Multi-Agent Systems (Contents)*, ICMAS-96, AAAI Press, Menlo Park, California, 1996.

Kjenstad 1998, Kjenstad, Dag, 1998, *Coordinated Supply Chain Scheduling*, PhD. Thesis, Norwegian University of Science and Technology, Trondheim, Norway.

Minton 1992, Minton, Steven, et al, 1992, *Minimizing Conflicts: a Heuristic Repair Method for Constraint Satisfaction and Scheduling Problems*, Artificial Intelligence 58, 1992, 161-205.

O'Hare 1996, O'Hare, G.M.P.; Jennings, N.R., 1996, *Foundations of Distributed Artificial Intelligence*, John Wiley & Sons, Inc., 1996, New York, USA.

O'Neill 1996, O'Neill, H.; Sackett, P., 1996, *The Extended Enterprise Reference Framework*, Balanced Automation Systems II, Camarinha-Matos, L.M. and Afsarmanesh, H. (Eds.), 1996, Chapman & Hall, London, UK, pp 401-412

Rabelo 1998, Rabelo, Ricardo J.; Camarinha-Matos, Luis M.; Afsarmanesh, Hamideh, 1998, *Multiagent Perspectives to Agile Scheduling*, Basys'98 International Conference on Balanced Automation Systems, Prague, Czech Republic, 26-28/08/98.

Reis 1998, Reis, J.; Mamede, N.; O'Neill, H., 1998, *Ontologia para um Modelo de Planeamento e Controlo na Empresa Estendida*, Proceedings of the IBERAMIA'98, Lisbon, Portugal, October 5-9, 1998, Helder Coelho (Ed.), Edições Colibri, Lisbon, Portugal, pp. 43-54 (in portugese).

Reis 1999a, Reis, J.; Mamede, N.; O'Neill, H., 1999, *Agent Communication for Scheduling in the Extended Enterprise*, Proceedings of the IFIP TC5 WG5.3/PRODNET Conference on Infrastructures for Virtual Enterprises, Porto, Portugal, October 27-28, 1999, Camarinha-Matos, L.M., Afsarmanesh H. (eds.), Kluwer Academic Publishers, Dordrecht, The Netherlands, 1999, pp 353-364.

Reis 1999b, Reis, J.; Mamede, N., 1999, *What's in a Node, Nodes and Agents in Logistic Networks*, Proceedings of the ICEIS'99, 1st International Conference on Enterprise Information Systems, Setúbal, Portugal, Mars 27-30, 1999, Filipe, J. and Cordeiro, J. (Eds.), pp. 285-291.

Reis 1999c, Reis, J.; Mamede, N., 1999, *Task Modeling in a Multi-Agent Logistic Domain*, Proceedings of the ICEIS'99, 1st International Conference on Enterprise Information Systems, Setúbal, Portugal, Mars 27-30, 1999, Filipe, J. and Cordeiro, J. (Eds.), pp. 769.

Reis 2000, Reis, J.; Mamede, N., 2000, *An Agent Architecture for Multi Agent Dynamic Scheduling*, Proceedings of the ICEIS'2000, 2st International Conference on Enterprise Information Systems, Stafford, UK, 4-7 July, 2000, Sharp, B., Cordeiro, J. and Filipe, J. (Eds.), pp. 203-208.

Sadeh 1994, Sadeh, Norman, 1994, *Micro-Oportunistic Scheduling: The Micro-Boss Factory Scheduler*, Intelligent Scheduling, Morgan Kaufman, 1994, Chapter 4.

Sycara 1991, Sycara, Katia P.;Roth, Steven F.;Sadeh, Norman;Fox, Mark S., 1991, *Resource Allocation in Distributed Factory Scheduling*, IEEE Expert, February, 1991, 29-40.

Zweben 1994, Zweben, Monte; Fox, Mark S., 1994, *Intelligent Scheduling*, Morgan Kaufmann Publishers, Inc., San Francisco, California, 1994.

AN INTELLIGENT AGENT-BASED ORDER PLANNING FOR DYNAMIC NETWORKED ENTERPRISES

Américo L. Azevedo[1,2], César Toscano[2], João Bastos[1,3]
[1]*Faculdade de Engenharia da Universidade do Porto, Rua Roberto Frias 4200-465 Porto, Portugal*
[2]*INESC Porto - Rua José Falcão 110, 4050-315 Porto, Portugal*
[3]*Instituto Superior de Engenharia do Porto - Rua Dr. António Almeida, 4200-072 Porto, Portugal*
email: aazevedo@inescporto.pt, ctoscano@inescporto.pt, jbastos@inescporto.pt

Keywords: Distributed Enterprises, Supply-Chain Management, Multi-Agent Systems, Decision Support Systems

Abstract: There is currently an increasing interest in exploring the opportunities for competitive advantage that can be gained by reinforcing core competencies and innovative capabilities through networks of industrial and business partners.

This paper firstly identifies some of the gaps that exist within current information systems that claim to support eBusiness and eWork in networked enterprises and describes some of the general requirements of distributed and decentralised information systems for companies operating in networks. It goes on to cover some principles for the design of a distributed IS providing an advanced infrastructure to support general co-operation, particular methodologies for co-operative and collaborative planning and guidelines for network set-up and support.

The present work is one of the areas currently being delivered as part of the European IST consortium called Co-OPERATE. A distributed and decentralised information system, based on an architecture of agents and extensively using the internet, is being designed and implemented as a means to provide new and more powerful decision support tools for networked enterprises.

1. INTRODUCTION

New and more demanding needs in terms of product innovation and market responsiveness raised the concept of agility and led many enterprises to improve their organisation and structure. This is often achieved through the establishment of temporary production networks, as an attempt to satisfy both customer expectations and long term enterprise goals and viability. Agile, market responsive supply-chains must not only deal with a rather volatile demand, but also cope with this variability through frequent chain reconfigurations and the implementation of new methodologies or business processes.

Within a given network, the needs of each entity will vary depending on the primary focus of the collaboration and on the nature of the product or service provided.

Traditionally, in a supply-chain, each chain member is a separate entity that may be highly integrated internally but with rigid and linear business processes, when viewed from outside. End-user orders are passed up the chain through each partner and products then flow back down to the end customer in an opposite sequence.

There is a clear conceptual difference between the virtual enterprise model and the vertically integrated model. The virtual enterprise represents, in a certain way, one hybrid or intermediate form of organisation between the concepts of market and hierarchy. In fact, it combines features of a fully market-oriented organisation, such as legal independence of the entities and specialisation of functions, with features of hierarchical forms such as close collaboration with the integration of information and trust between the participating entities.

In this context, we are looking at organisations that are formed on networks of enterprises structured at different levels of a complex chain.

Current IS systems (such as ERP and SCM commercial packages) do not provide the necessary support for networked and distributed organisations, and are clearly insufficient with regards to planning and co-ordination activities required within that environment.

An enterprise network can be made up of many different entities and relationship types according to their relative position within the supply chain, and

J. Filipe et al. (eds.), Enterprise Information Systems III, 124–131.

consequently may have several passive or active interaction forms working simultaneously. Interaction among participants in the network, their co-ordination and their access to knowledge are becoming increasingly important. Setting up a network and managing it in an optimised way, whilst balancing customer needs with increased performance along the whole chain, may be a key factor for the competitiveness of a specific company and in overal the entire network.

In this paper, we begin to identify the gaps and limitations that exist within current available systems that claim to support eBusiness and eWork in networked enterprises. The outcome of the present analysis has resulted in a set of IS requirements for new ways of working and doing business. We therefore go on to a new concept and approach to the development of a distributed IS, addressing the basic requirements of co-operativeness, configurability and efficiency in enterprise networks.

This work is currently being delivered under the scope of the IST project Co-OPERATE. The consortium aims to provide an advanced information and communication infrastructure to support co-operation in networked and distributed organisations. A distributed and decentralised information system, based on an architecture of agents, and extensively using the internet is being designed and implemented, as a means to provide new and more powerful decision support tools for this type of environments.

2. GAPS AND LIMITATIONS OF PRESENT SYSTEMS

Networked and "virtual" enterprises are becoming a new organisational paradigm, creating challenging opportunities in terms of management. In particular, production planning and control is generally regarded as a key area for improving global enterprise performance.

In global environments, operations and logistics management differs in several key aspects from the case of an isolated and domestic enterprise. The traditional business paradigm does not adequately consider the fact that a company is in general part of a much broader matrix of business systems composed of customers, suppliers, products and global information. Moreover, traditional principles for enterprise management, based on an environment tailored for mass production and stable markets, are no longer sufficient. As a recent general trend, companies are focusing on their core competencies, with a large recourse to subcontracting, resulting in more complex links in terms of information systems.

Optimally scheduling production in a local plant or a global manufacturing operation requires real-time knowledge of the status of the resources, availability of manufacturing lines, current inventory, etc. Presents systems don't provide real-time flow of information between the plant and the supply chain systems.

In fact, currently available information systems do not satisfy the distributed planning and control needs, as they lack support for co-ordinated production within networks and for enterprise wide business processes. Moreover, those systems are based on some premises that are no longer valid (particularly MRP based systems) and the need for supply chain management implies fundamental changes in the design of information systems for planning and control (Azevedo and Toscano, 1999).

In order to address this present limitations of the current IS systems, the work we present offers a new approach to overcome this independency and deficiency in co-operation.

3. REVIEW OF RELATED RESEARCH WORK

In recent years, there has been an enormous research interest in topics such as decentralised production management systems (Richards et al., 1997), network organisations (Ching et al., 1993; Sauer and Bruns, 1995), supply-chain management systems (Fox et al., 1993; Thomas and Griffin, 1996) and decision support systems for order planning (Kingsman et al., 1993; Leachman et al., 1996). On the other hand, a number of projects, worldwide, have been addressing different aspects of virtual/extended, distributed, dispersed or networked enterprises. Examples are: X-CITTIC (EU) where the main goal was the design of an enterprise-wide production planing for semiconductor enterprises and PRODNET (EU) which aims at designing and developing a reference architecture and an open platform to support VE, with special focus on small and medium size enterprises (SME).

4. THE CO-OPERATE PROJECT

Co-OPERATE is a project supported by the European Commission, that aims at developing solutions to enhance the entire supply network, providing an advanced information and communication infrastructure to support general co-operation, as well as particular methodologies for co-operative planning and for network set-up and support. The project started in January 2000, and involves two academic groups, a consultancy firm and several industrial companies.

Business processes have been identified and a conceptual framework and methodologies for aggregate planning are being tested and tailored in the pilot companies. Hopefully they will be extensively applicable and easy to adapt to other industries.

The project aims at developing solutions to enhance the entire supply network, from the OEM manufacturer to the original material supplier. It will provide an advanced information and communication infrastructure to support co-operation in dynamic enterprise networks, as well as a methodology for co-operative planning, and a set of mechanisms to enable real-time monitoring of the supply-chain. Moreover, tools to support a fast and effective reconfiguration of manufacturing networks will be made available.

The project has the following strategic objectives aimed at improving the performance of networked enterprises:

- co-operation and supply chain integration;
- higher responsiveness;
- lead time reduction throughout the supply chain and reduced inventory levels;
- improved flexibility in the supply chain;
- increased capability to solve unexpected problems in the supply chain.

In order to achieve these goals a number of "business solutions" (or general functionalities) have been defined, that will focus on the network aspects of the business processes and will try to accommodate and support the current internal tools and processes of companies. These business solutions are the following:

Long term business planning for the network. This business solution will improve the long term planning process in the whole supply network. The goal is to generate long-term plans for the network by synchronising forecasts and plans, and by promoting early communication of changes and feedback about feasibility.

Standard operational order and planning processes. This business solution will support the short and medium term operational order and planning processes. This includes order generation and transmission, synchronised planning, monitoring and status information. This business solution should provide a strong basis for real-time order promising and exceptions handling.

Feasibility studies for new order or change requests across the network. This business solution will support the request for new orders or large order changes across the network and will support and co-ordinate the feasibility checks at the individual companies within the shortest possible time. This includes checking of capacity and materials from suppliers.

Exception handling process. This business solution will include methodologies to detect, as early as possible, problems in the network such as peak orders, capacity shortages or part availability problems.

Multi sourcing co-ordination. This business solution will optimise the allocation of work to the different suppliers, based on a defined set of rules and fast negotiation methodologies with the suppliers. It includes a negotiation process on capacities with feedback from the suppliers.

Process visibility. This business solution will develop methodologies to make the progress of orders in the supply network.

Performance management information. This business solution will provide management information about the performance of the network processes. It includes the identification of key performance indicators and provides the methodologies to collect and present them.

5. GENERAL APPROACH

We have been investigating and designing general methodologies and tools for improving supply chain management through distributed production planning. In contrast to centralised planning systems, a decentralised approach naturally partitions global complex planning problems into smaller specific problems, which are tackled by (local) independent organisational units. Along this line, one key objective of our research is to perform a comprehensive evaluation of the benefits of a distributed approach, based on a framework of multiple agents that communicate through 'speech acts' of advanced languages. Multi-agent systems, due to their nature, seem to be well suited for modelling networks, as they naturally provide a set of features that make the implementations and the operation of complex distributed systems easier (Azevedo and Oliveira, 1999). Critical notions about multi-agent systems can be found in Sycara (Sycara,

1998), organised around the concept of problem-solving coherence.

A global approach to these types of problems is proposed. It includes a collaborative planning methodology supported by an information system architecture based on several autonomous units: one for each node in the network. These units are able to perform a set of activities and to anticipate the consequences of their actions, within the scope of their commitments. Each unit is modelled as a set of agents, owning a set of key features that are of major importance for the effective management of a co-operative and distributed manufacturing environment: autonomy, proactivity, sociability and responsiveness.

A software agent is stated as a system situated within and a part of an environment that senses that environment and acts on it, over time, in porsuit of its own agenda and so as to effect what it senses in the future (Franklin and Graesser, 1996).

In fact, having a set of agents communicating and co-operating with each other, allows us to address richer and more complex problems, and to increase both the functionality and the efficiency of the planning processes. Moreover, a natural support is provided for the whole life-cycle of the enterprise network, especially in what concerns: its set-up, in a static or in a dynamic way; the propagation of information through the chain (e.g. the announcement of customer orders); negotiation between units, leading to a global production plan; and distributed control and "tracebility" of manufacturing orders throughout the chain.

In the Co-OPERATE system each agent in a node plays one or more roles. Adding or removing an agent results in the reconfiguration of the roles played by a node. This leads to an easiness of addition or deletion of roles in each node without any disturbances in the network (no changes are needed for the other nodes). The basic functionality for effective agent co-operation will be directly implemented in an infrastructure that provides the basic services for that co-operation.

In summary we might say that, concerning order negotiation and planning in a highly dynamic supply-chain or enterprise network, the agent-based approach should allow us to set the right ground for: higher levels of autonomy and proactiveness; new communication and expression paradigms, to promote delegation and co-ordination; new planning methodologies and algorithms, based on negotiation and co-operation; and some level of "intelligence" integrated into management applications, the basic components to improve the necessary support for networked and distributed organisations.

5.1 Basic architectural principles

We consider a software agent based system, structured around the following basic architectural principles:

- each business unit in the network of companies is served by a set of agents;
- each of these sets forms a "node" in a community of agents distributed by the several "units" in the network;
- in each node, the agents co-operate to achieve local goals;
- in each node, each agent performs one or more functions, and co-ordinates its decisions with the other agents in the node;
- different nodes in the network co-operate to achieve global or local network goals; co-operation between nodes is carried out through the interactions of the individual agents in the different nodes;
- the functionality across the network or supply-chain is achieved through the interaction of the different nodes;
- the number and types of agents present in each node is variable, i.e. we can have all kind of agents or only some of them.

Some of the agents inside a node have external visibility, thus interacting with agents in the other nodes of the network, whilst some agents have a local scope inside a node being limited to accomplish local goals. Agents belonging to different nodes and carrying out direct conversations between each other give support to the global network planning procedures.

Organisation of the network of nodes is dynamic; nodes may be inserted or deleted from the network during a re-configuration of the supply chain.

These principles define a direction for the design of the agent based system, and they adopt a "corporate" social interaction between agents. This means that local goals have priority over the network goals, when co-operating with other nodes, the agents in a node will act in a way that do not conflict with local goals. The alternative would be a "global" social interaction where each agent acts according to the network goals that are decomposed into individual goals. This means that local goals (roughly, the business unit goals) are secondary when compared with the network goals.

5.2 Structure of a network node

A first analysis of the identified requirements had the purpose of developing an understanding of the system and its structure. Specifically, the organization of each node in the network, defined as a collection of roles standing in certain relationships to one another, and taking part in systematic and institutionalised patterns of interactions with other roles (Wooldridge et al., 2000), was the main objective. Basically, the design of the system was viewed as a set of roles that:

- interact with each other according to some protocol;
- have responsibilities, which in a direct or indirect way determine the functionality inherent to that role;
- have a set of permissions, which identify the "rights" associated with the role, and subsequently identify the resources that are available to that role when its responsibilities are placed into practice;
- perform local computations or activities (local in the sense that no interactions are carried out with any other role in the system).

These abstract entities were used to derive more concrete entities, in terms of the agent types that make up the system, the services required to realise the agent's role and the required acquaintances or patterns of communication between the different agent types. Table 1 identifies the agent types to support the organisation of each node in the network. Basically, an agent type corresponds to a certain combination of roles. This may be a one-to-one correspondence (a very unusual case) or a many-to-one mapping. This is the normal case, where a set of roles is attached to a single entity, being this allocation driven by a number of different types of requirements.

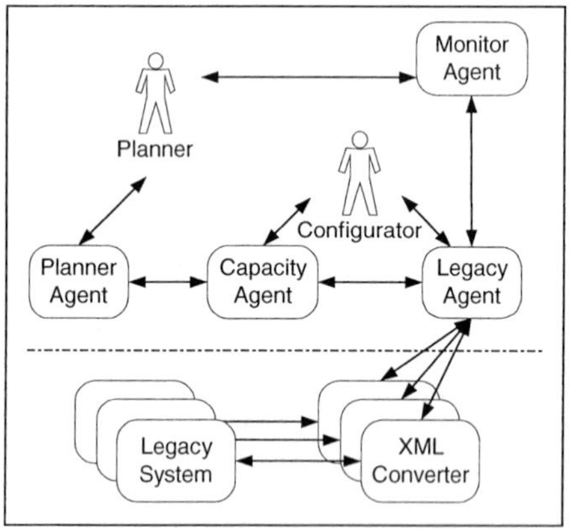

Figure 1: Organisation of Agents in a network node

The basic agent architecture for the network node is represented in figure 1. Necessarily, these agent types are instantiated into agents for each site implementation, requiring the necessary interface with the human agents, namely the planner and the configurator.

Table 1: Types of Agents

Legacy Information Integrator	-Provides an information service; -Collects and aggregates information supplied from different legacy sources; -Propagates information to other required agent types.
Facilitator	-Acts as an organisational agent and is responsible for providing support to other agents; it provides, for example, services to find the location of external agents of a given type or having certain specific skills or properties.
Co-operative Planner	-Co-operates with other planners in other nodes, in order to develop plans that achieve the network goals -Interacts with the local Capacity Agent;
Capacity Agent	-Dynamically evaluates the availability of the business unit for order requests; -Integrates a local Capacity Model with tailored algorithms; -Interacts with the Co-operative Planner and the Legacy Information Integrator.
Monitor	-Acquires and aggregates the network or supply-chain state variables; compares current state variables with target values; -Identifies deviations or disruptions, e.g. resource failure (loss of production capacity), logistics problems (transport delays), quality issues; -Propagates warnings to other agent types.

The Monitor agents of each network node establish ongoing conversations between each other in order to support the propagation of events detected locally. Similarly, the insertion of a new order in the system is accomplished by negotiations carried on between the correspondent Planner agents in the network. Facilitator agents, located in certain places of the system, help to establish conversations and negotiation tasks between the Planner and Monitor Agents.

5.3 Legacy Systems Integration

One of the main reason to concern when designing solutions to heterogeneous companies organised in supply chain networks is the need to make some type of integration interfaces with the management systems running on those companies.

Due to the lack of competencies and the heterogeneous universe of legacy systems existing on each site, the traditional way to design a specific interface with each system is unbearable.

Since the Co-OPERATE project aims to conceive an advanced information and communication paradigm to support co-operation between companies within a business network, a generic integration interface infrastructure was designed. This infrastructure must be deployed on top of the existing systems or infrastructures and should give support to the network processes of co-operation between the companies, in a complementary and independently way from the processes managed by the existing systems.

In order to build meaningful high level data models, it is necessary to import data from existing legacy systems within a network node. For example, aggregated high-level data models, reflecting the actual production availability of a certain unit, must be build by the Capacity Agent, given the data managed by the manufacturing execution system inside the unit.

In the single node context, integration with the existing legacy systems is divided in two phases. The first phase, the most basic one, tries to solve the more critical questions about the connectivity between the different systems. For each legacy system, a software program is envisaged, with the objective of converting raw data, presented in a specific and usually proprietary format, in a general and standard format. The protocol language chosen at this level is the XML, mainly because it is currently recognised as an official (or standard) language to describe data in the Internet environment and also because there are some ongoing efforts by specific segments in the industry trying to develop specific XML applications (RosettaNet, ebXML, Microsoft BizTalk, etc). This approach delimits the original integration problem, into a more specific problem of converting data coded in different formats into generic and recognizable conceptual data.

The Legacy Agent accomplishes the second phase of the integration. Its purpose is to collect, process and assemble the raw data managed by the legacy systems (such as ERP and MES systems) and provide high-level conceptual data, required by the agents to perform their tasks. Normally, the low-level raw data is too detailed to be directly used by the agents in the system. Additionally, data coming from different sources may be insuficcient and/or originate conflicts in the subsequent aggregation of the high levels data models. Development of apropriate abstractions and aggregations in the low level data is the main functionality of this layer. Further, the Legacy Agent mechanisms should be prepared to deal with inconsistencies, conflicts and inaccuracy in the data that is provided by the legacy systems. Due to these limitations, the Legacy Agent must provide the necessary interface with a human expert analyst, in order to validate and set the necessary values regarding the parameters configuration.

5.4 Capacity Models Integration

In order to each local Capacity Agent perform their task and cooperate with the other agents, it is required the existence of a Capacity Model. The Capacity Model is a software component that tries to capture the specificity and singularity of each site, to model it and to provide a capacity checked mechanism for inquiries and order insertions.

This software component interacts at the upper level with the ERP system and on the lower level with the MES system. Mainly, these interactions provide the Model with a time based resource availability data. This interface with the refereed systems is provided by the Legacy Agent using the previously refered XML communication format.

However, the Model isn't only a repository of dynamic data, it also has flexible and user configurable algorithms. These algorithms range from very simple mathematical models to specific implementations, such as cycle time analysis (Leach and Ristic, 1998) or bottleneck detection mechanisms (Bastos and Sousa, 1998). The algorithms itself, dictate the way the model behaves. Since the production systems in question are very heterogeneous and could be modelled in different degrees of detail, a generic solution applicable with success to all cases is very unlikely. Therefore, in order to make the Capacity Model structure flexible, a dynamic instantiation mechanism of algorithms was designed and implemented. The use of dynamic instantiation mechanism of algorithms offers several advantages. With it the user is able to design several different algorithms, and depending on the characteristics of the production system, he can instantiate dynamically the best-qualified algorithm (after evaluation) to that specific system.

The main idea behind the architecture of the Capacity Model was to construct a generic and flexible software component that could be used in very different types of industries and in very different units of the supply chain network with the necessary flexibility. However, an important role is played by the expert user (configurator) in order to configure the Capacity Model. His knowledge is indispensable to capture the specific production system singularities and translate them to the Capacity Model.

The models' performance is intrinsically dependent on the complexity degree used in their configuration. Namely there are two measures to evaluate the models performance. The first one is related with the setting up time, which is the time required to start running the model. This time is only dependent on the volume of legacy data in the unit. The second measure of performance is the time required for the Capacity Model to respond to requests from the other components, namely the Co-operative Planner Agent. This time is obviously dependent on how detailed the model is. If the user has configured a very rough capacity model, the responses are very fast, but not so accurate. On the other hand, if the model is more detailed, the responses become much more accurate, but they take a much longer time to be produced. Obviously, each user has to take into account these facts, when configuring the Capacity Model.

The present structure of the Capacity Model is totally independent of the environment and the respective implementation, providing flexibility in the use of this application. The integration with the Capacity Agent is obtained by encapsulating the Capacity Model and its functionalities. The outcome is a generic capacity agent, able to negotiate order insertions and changes in a multi-agent environment and a specific Capacity Model able to able to model the unit production availability.

6. PROTOTYPE

A first prototype of the multiagent system described in the previous section was developed, and is being subject to evaluation and testing by the end users of the consortium.

The development work was done on top of the FIPA-OS framework (Poslad et al., 2000). This is an open agent platform, originating from Nortel Networks, that provides a FIPA (Aparicio et al., 1999) compliant framework and that intends to promote the uptake of FIPA specifications by agent developers.

In order to facilitate and accelerate the deployment of the prototype in the end users's installations, a set of HTML pages was developed. In fact, these HTML pages encapsulate the multi-agent system and allow a distributed and easy access to their functionality through the Internet environment.

7. CONCLUSIONS

The interaction among participants in a network of companies, their co-ordination and their access to knowledge are becoming increasingly important. Moreover, setting up the network and managing it in an optimised way, balancing customer needs with increased performance along the whole chain, may be a key factor for the competitiveness of a company. Particularly important is the support to co-operation and collaboration, as well as the definition of a methodology for planning and customer order negotiation business processes.

The work being done under the scope of the European project Co-OPERATE approaches these questions by providing an advanced information and communication infrastructure to support co-operation in networked and distributed organisations. A distributed and decentralised information system, based on an architecture of agents, and extensively using the internet is being designed and implemented, as a means to provide new and more powerful decision support tools for this type of environments. The general process and framework for the development of this system have been briefly described in this paper.

In this paper we have addressed the problem of planning an incoming customer order on a distributed production system. The problem was approached in a hierarchical way, by considering two levels for decision making: there is a global network planning procedure, and a set of local capacity models associated to the different production units reflecting their particular features.

In this paper, some general requirements of distributed and decentralised information systems for companies operating in this new environments have been identified. We have also presented a global approach to these problems, based on an architecture of agents, and extensively using the internet, that is being designed and implemented in the currently running European project Co-OPERATE. We have highlighted the types of agents used, their basic functionality, and the main processes of co-operation they use. This system will hopefully provide new and more powerful decision support tools to be used in distributed and virtual enterprises.

The general process and framework for the development of this system was briefly described in this paper, but obviously further research is needed in understanding the mechanisms of decision-making for networked enterprises. On another direction, we are currently working on collaborative and negotiation planning procedures for improving network co-ordination, namely on dynamic interpretative rule based systems, and as well on the complex multi-criteria decision-making processes involved in this context.

Finally it should be noted that the capability of networked enterprises to dynamically change the type and strength of relationships between companies is a key requirement of information systems. But this is not a trivial issue in terms of design or implementation, and deserves therefore further research.

REFERENCES

Aparicio, Manuel; Chiariglione, L.; Mamdani, E; McCabe, F.; Nicol, R.; Steiner, D and Suguri, H (1999). "FIPA – Intelligent agents from theory to practice", Telecom 99, Geneva.

Azevedo, A. L., and Toscano, C. (1999). "An Information System for Distributed Manufacturing Enterprises." *ICEIS 99 - First International Conference On Enterprise Information Systems*, Setúbal, Portugal, 15-22.

Bastos, João A.; Sousa, Jorge P. (1998). "Capacity Modelling for Virtual Enterprises", *Proceedings of the Tenth International IFIP WG 5.2/5.3 Conference*, PROLAMAT 98.

Ching, C., Holsapple, C. W., and Whinston, A. B. (1993). "Modeling Network Organisations: A Basis for Exploring Support Coordination Possibilities." *Journal of Organizational Computing*, 3(3), 279-300.

Flores-Mendez, Roberto (1999). "Towards a Standardization of Multi-Agent System Frameworks", *ACM Crossroads Student Magazine.*

Fox, M. S., Chionglo, J. F., and Barbuceanu, M. (1993). "The Integrated Supply Chain Management System.", Department of Industrial Engineering, University of Toronto.

Franklin, Stan; Graesser, Art (1996). "Is it an Agent, or just a Program?: A Taxonomy for Autonomous Agents", *Proceedings of the Third International Workshop on Agent Theories, Architectures, and Languages*, Springer-Verlag.

Kingsman, B., Hendry, L., and Wilson, E. (1993). "A Decision Support System For The Dynamic Planning of Customer Order Intake and Capacity Resources For Make-To-Order Companies." *APMS'93 - International Conference on Advances in Production Management Systems*, Athens - Greece, 133-141.

Leach, Nick; Ristic, Mike (1998). "Capacity Models for Scheduling the Virtual Enterprise", X-CITTIC project.

Nwana, Hyacinth S. (1996). "Software Agents: An Overview", *The Knowledge Engineering Review Journal*, 11(3).

Nwana, Hyacinth S.; Lee, Lyndon C.; Jennings, N. R. (1996). "Co-ordination in Software Agent Systems", *BT Technology Journal*, 14(4).

Parunak, H. Van Dyke (1998). "Practical and Industrial Applications of Agent-Based Systems", Industrial Technology.

Parunak, H. Van Dyke; Baker, Albert D.; Clark, Steven J. (1999). "The AARIA Agent Architecture: From Manufacturing Requirements to Agent-Based System Design", *Conference Proceedings, Integrated Computer-Aided Engineering.*

Poslad, Stefan; Buckle, Phil; Hadingham, Rob (2000). "The FIPA-OS agent platform: Open Source for Open Standards", *Proceedings of the 5th International Conference and Exhibition on the Practical Application of Intelligent Agents and Multi-Agents*, 355-368.

Richards, H. D., Dudenhausen, H. M., Makatsoris, C., and Rider, L. d. (1997). "Flow of orders through a virtual enterprise - their proactive planning and scheduling, and reactive control." *Computing & Control Engineering Journal*(August 1997), 173-179.

Sauer, J., and Bruns, R. (1995). "Intelligent Multi-site Coordination and Scheduling." *Improving Manufacturing Performance in a Distributed Enterprise: Advanced Systems and Tools*, Edinburgh, Scotland.

Sycara, Katia P. (1998). "Multiagent Systems" *AAAI AI Magazine.*

Thomas, D. J., and Griffin, P. M. (1996). "Coordinated supply chain management." *European Journal of Operational Research*(94), 1-15.

Wooldridge, Michael; Jennings, N. R.; Kinny, David (2000). "The Gaia Methodology for Agent-Oriented Analysis and Design", *Int. Journal of Autonomous Agents and Multi-Agent Systems.*

THE EFFECTS OF DIFFERENT FEATURE SETS ON THE WEB PAGE CATEGORIZATION PROBLEM USING THE ITERATIVE CROSS-TRAINING ALGORITHM

Nuanwan Soonthornphisaj and Boonserm Kijsirikul
Machine Intelligence & Knowledge Discovery Laboratory
Department of Computer Engineering
Chulalongkorn University,
Phathumwan, Bangkok, 10330, Thailand.
Email : nuanwan@mind.cp.eng.chula.ac.th , boonserm@mind.cp.eng.chula.ac.th

Keywords: Web page categorization, Iterative Cross-Training, Feature sets

Abstract: The paper presents the effects of different feature sets on the Web page categorization problem. These features are words appearing in the content of a Web page, words appearing on the hyperlinks, which link to the page and words appearing on every headings in the page. The experiments are conducted using a new algorithm called the Iterative Cross-Training algorithm (ICT) which was successfully applied to Thai Web page identification. The main concept of ICT is to iteratively train two sub-classifiers by using unlabeled examples in crossing manner. We compare ICT against supervised naïve Bayes classifier and Co-Training classifier. The experimental results show that ICT obtains the highest performance and the heading feature is considerably succeed in helping classifiers to build the correct model used in the Web page categorization task.

1. INTRODUCTION

Nowadays, there is a massive increase of Web pages in the Internet. An ideal search engine should have the most updated information of all Web pages to provide the best search result for the user. Therefore, it should have an effective Web robot which crawls the Web and automatically classifies Web pages into categories, since Web page classification task is a tedious job and time consuming process if it is done by human. Thus, we want it to be automatic with a reliable classification result.

The problem of text classification has been explored by many researchers with variety of learning algorithms (Cohen & Singer, 1999; Jochim, 1998) When we give a sufficient set of labeled training examples, supervised learning is the most effective method for the classification. However, the construction of hand-labeled data must be done by a human and thus this is a painfully time-consuming process.

Though it is costly to construct hand-labeled data, in some domains it is easy to obtain unlabeled ones, such as data in the Internet. Therefore, we propose a new learning algorithm called incremental iterative cross-training (incremental-ICT) in order to utilize the available unlabeled data.

Our incremental-ICT is based on the ICT algorithm that has been successfully applied for identifying Thai Web pages (Kijsirikul et al., 2000). ICT employs two sub-classifiers to iteratively train each other by using unlabeled examples in crossing manner. ICT is based on the assumption that one of the sub-classifiers has some knowledge about the domain. However, this assumption is violated on some domains where we cannot give domain knowledge to the classifier. In such a problem, ICT does not perform well. In this paper, we propose a new algorithm, called incremental-ICT, which requires no such assumption.

To evaluate the robustness of our algorithm, we apply it to a more difficult problem than Thai Web page identification. The problem we are interested in is the classification of Web pages into course or non-course pages. Since the concept of ICT needs two classifiers, we build each classifier based on different feature sets using naïve Bayes classifiers.

We run experiments to evaluate the effectiveness of our method and to see the contribution of each feature set. In the experiments, we compare our method with the *Co-Training* algorithm (Blum &

J. Filipe et al. (eds.), Enterprise Information Systems III, 132–138.

Mitchell, 1998) and a supervised learning algorithm which uses a naïve Bayes classifier as a classification mechanism. The results show that incremental-ICT gives better performance than the other classifiers.

The paper is organized as follows. Section 2 presents feature sets used in the experiments. Section 3 describes our learning algorithm, and gives the details of a naïve Bayes classifier. Section 4 and 5 describes other learning methods used in our comparison. Section 6 describes the experimental results. Finally, Section 7 concludes our work.

2. FEATURE SETS

For the classification problem, the classifier's performance usually depends on the classification mechanism with the support of feature sets. The appropriate feature sets will help the classifier to enhance its classification correctness. Therefore we try to investigate the possible feature sets to see their contribution on the precision and recall of the classifier. Feature sets that we study are as follows.

2.1 Hyperlink

The Web page in the Internet is a special document. It has a unique characteristic which makes it different from other plain text documents. Most Web pages have hyperlinks that act like a pointer pointing to other pages and also have links from other pages pointing to them. In our case, we use the hyperlink which link to the page to be the first feature set.

2.2 Content

The content of a Web page provides information to the user in detail. We extract all words in the content to be the second feature set.

2.3 Heading

The heading phrase normally represents the main idea of the following content. We use this opportunity to extract all headings in the page in the hope that they could represent the main concept of a Web page.

3. INCREMENTAL ITERATIVE CROSS-TRAINING

The architecture of our learning algorithm consists of two naïve Bayes classifiers, each of which learns from different features of a Web page. For the ease of explanation, we will use the concrete example of feature sets which are words on hyperlinks linking to the page (hyperlink-based) and words on the page (content-based). Starting with a small number of labeled data, each classifier estimates its parameters and uses the learned parameters to classify unlabeled data for the other as shown in Figure 1. The classification for unlabeled data is done in incremental way, i.e., the algorithm incrementally labels a small number of data. The training data is duplicated into two sets: *TrainingData1* for training the hyperlink-based classifier and *TrainingData2* for training the content-based one. The concept of our algorithm is that if we could obtain reliable statistical information from the first classifier, it should be useful in classifying training data for the second classifier. After receiving training from each other, the parameters of the classifiers should be more reliable every iteration.

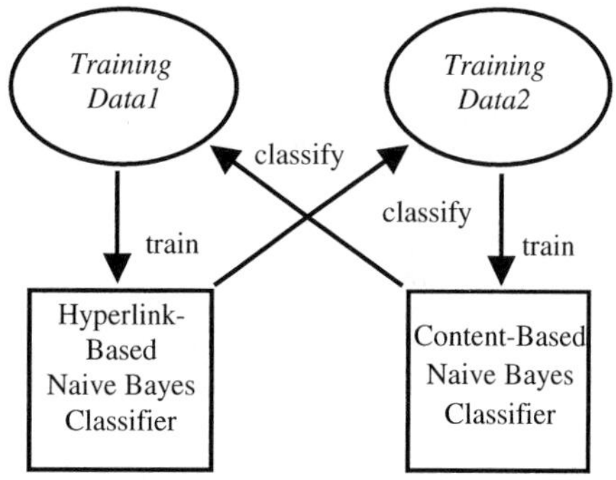

Figure 1: The architecture of iterative cross-training

The training algorithm of incremental-ICT is shown in Table 1. As shown in the table, the training process starts with the parameter estimation of both classifiers, i.e. hyperlink-based and content-based, using initial labeled data. For each round of iteration, the content-based classifier with the current parameter, θ_c, will classify training data into positive and negative examples. Then it will ask for the confirmation from the hyperlink-based classifier that considers another view of each example to make decision about which class the example should be. If both classifiers agree with the same classification result, the most confident p positive and n negative examples will be labeled.

Table 1: The Incremental-ICT algorithm

Given:

- Two training sets: *TrainingData1* of hyperlink-based data and *TrainingData2* of content-based data (*TrainingData1* and *TrainingData2* both contain U labeled examples).
- Use labeled data in *TrainingData1* to estimate the parameter set θ_h of the hyperlink-based classifier.
- Use labeled data in *TrainingData2* to estimate the parameter set θ_c of the content-based classifier.
- Loop until all data are labeled.
  - Use the content-based classifier with current θ_c to classify *TrainingData1* into positive and negative examples.
    - Check consistency of the classification with the hyperlink-based classifier. Label the class for the most confident p positive examples and most confident n negative examples.
  - Train the hyperlink-based classifier by the labeled examples in *TrainingData1* to estimate the parameter set θ_h of the classifier.
  - Use the hyperlink-based classifier with current θ_h to classify *TrainingData2* into positive and negative examples.
    - Check consistency of the classification with the content-based classifier. Label the class for the most confident p positive examples and most confident n negative examples.
  - Train the content-based classifier by the labeled examples in *TrainingData1* to estimate the parameter set θ_c of the classifier.

The hyperlink-based classifier is then trained by the labeled examples in *TrainingData1* to estimate the parameter set θ_h. With this current θ_h, the hyperlink-based classifier will classify *TrainingData2* into positive and negative examples. Then the consistency checking process is performed again to ask for the agreement from the content-based classifier. The most confident p positive and n negative examples will be labeled. The content-based classifier starts again with parameter estimation by using labeled examples in *TrainingData1*. These processes will be repeatedly done until all data are labeled.

The classification mechanisms of these two classifiers ar the same which use the naïve Bayes algorithm. This algorithm is a well-known approach and is considered to be one of the most effective way for text classification (Mitchell, 1997) The algorithm employs *bag-of-words* to represent the document. The method is described below.

Given a set of class labels L = $\{l_1, l_2,\ldots, l_m\}$ and a document d of n words $(w_1, w_2,..,w_n)$, the most likely class label l^* estimated by naïve Bayes is the one that maximizes $Pr(l_j|w_1,\ldots w_n)$:

$$l^* = \underset{l_j}{argmax}\ Pr(l_j|w_1,\ldots,w_n) \quad (1)$$

$$= \underset{l_j}{argmax}\ \frac{Pr(l_j)Pr(w_1,\ldots,w_n|l_j)}{Pr(w_1,\ldots,w_n)} \quad (2)$$

$$= \underset{l_j}{argmax}\ Pr(l_j)Pr(w_1,\ldots,w_n|l_j) \quad (3)$$

For our data set, L is the set of positive and negative class labels which are course homepage and non-course homepage, respectively. $Pr(w_1,\ldots, w_n)$ in equation 2 can be ignored, as we are interested in finding the most likely class label. As there are usually an extremely large number of possible values for $d = (w_1,w_2,\ldots,w_n)$, calculating the term $Pr(w_1,\ldots,w_n|l_j)$ requires a huge number of examples to obtain reliable estimation. Therefore, to reduce the number of required examples and improve reliability of the estimation, assumptions of naïve Bayes are made. These assumptions are (1) the conditional independent assumption, i.e. the presence of each word is conditionally independent of all other words in the document given the class label, and (2) an assumption that the position of a word is unimportant, e.g. encountering the word "subject" at the beginning of a document is the same as encountering it at the end (Mitchell, 1997). Equation 3 can be rewritten as:

$$l^* = \underset{l_j}{argmax}\ Pr(l_j)\prod_{i=1}^{n} Pr(w_i\,|\,l_j,w_1,\ldots,w_{i-1}) \quad (4)$$

$$= \underset{l_j}{argmax}\ Pr(l_j)\prod_{i=1}^{n} Pr(w_i\,|\,l_j) \quad (5)$$

The probabilities $Pr(l_j)$ and $Pr(w_i|l_j)$ are used as the parameter sets θ_h and θ_c, and are estimated from the training data. The prior probability $Pr(l_j)$ is estimated as the ratio between the number of examples belonging to the class l_j, and the number of all examples. The conditional probability $Pr(w_i|l_j)$, of seeing word w_i given class label l_j, is estimated by the following equation:

$$Pr(w_i|l_j) = \frac{1 + N(w_i, l_j)}{T + N(l_j)} \qquad (6)$$

Where $N(w_i,l_j)$ is the number of times word w_i appears in the training examples from class label l_j, $N(l_j)$ is the total number of unique word in the training set. T is the number of class. Equation 6 employs Laplace smoothing (add one to all of word counts), to avoid assigning probability values of zero to words that do not occur in the training examples for a particular class.

To evaluate our method, we will compare it with the other two techniques that are the Co-Training and the supervised naïve Bayes classifiers. These classifiers are described in the following sections.

4. CO-TRAINING CLASSIFIER

The Co-Training algorithm explicitly uses the split of the features when learning from labeled and unlabeled data. Its approach is to build the naïve Bayes classifier for each of the distinct feature sets. Each classifier is initialized using a few labeled documents. Then every round of Co-Training, each classifier chooses the most confident p positive and n negative labeled examples to add to the labeled set of documents. The documents selected are those that have the highest posterior class probability, $Pr(l_j|d)$. Then, each classifier rebuilds from the augmented labeled set and the process repeats (Blum & Mitchell, 1998).

Table 2: The Co-Training algorithm

Given:
A set *LE* of labeled training examples
A set *UE* of unlabeled examples
Create a pool *UE'* of examples by choosing *u* examples at random from *UE*.
Loop while there exist documents without class labels:

- Use *LE* to estimate θ_h of the hyperlink-based classifier using the hyperlink portion of each document.
- Use *LE* to estimate θ_c of the content-based classifier using the page portion of each document.
- Allow the hyperlink-based classifier with current θ_h to label p positive and n negative examples from *UE'*.
- Allow the content-based classifier with current θ_c to label p positive and n negative examples from *UE'*.
- Add these self-labeled examples to *LE*.
- Randomly choose $2p+2n$ examples from *UE* to replenish *UE'*.

5. SUPERVISED NAÏVE BAYES CLASSIFIER

The basic concept of *supervised learning* for building a classifier is that it requires a set of examples with predefined classes. The classifier is then try to find some common properties of the different classes in order to make correct classification for unseen data. Thus, this kind of classifiers need a large number of labeled examples to correctly model the characteristic of the class during learning process. Labeling must be done by human to train the classifier accurately. In our experiment, we employ the naïve Bayes classifier as a supervised learning algorithm. The algorithm of the naïve Bayes is the same as one described in Section 3, except that it is trained by hand-labeled data.

6. EXPERIMENTAL RESULTS

In order to test the robustness of the incremental-ICT algorithm and to investigate the effectiveness of feature sets , we set up experiments on the problem of course/non-course Web page classification, and compare the performance of incremental-ICT to the other classifiers, i.e., the Co-Training algorithm and the supervised naïve Bayes classifier.

6.1 Data Set

The data for our experiments is obtained via ftp from Carnegie Mellon University (The World Wide Knowledge Base Project). It consists of 1,051 Web pages collected from Computer Science department Web sites at four universities: Cornell, University of Washington, University of Wisconsin, and University of Texas. These Web pages have been hand-labeled into two categories. We consider the category "course home page" as the positive class and the other as the negative class. In this dataset, 22% of the Web pages were course homepages and the rest were non-course homepages.

In this data set, the two Web categories are actually closely related which make the classification more difficult. A course home page gives information about the subject such as the course outline, the class schedule, reference books. A non-course homepage is an instructor homepage or department Web page.

6.2 Experimental Setting

We have 230 course Web pages and 821 non-course Web pages. Each sample is filtered to remove words which give no significance in predicting to the class of the document. Words to be eliminated are auxiliary verbs, prepositions, pronouns, possessive pronouns, phone numbers, digit sequences, dates and special characters. The training set contains 172 course Web pages and 616 non-course Web pages.

Three positive examples and nine negative examples were randomly selected from the training dataset to be initial labeled data. Therefore, each data set contains 12 initial labeled examples, 776 training examples and 263 testing examples. We then used 3-fold cross-validation (Mitchell, 1997) for averaging the results. Three positive and nine negative samples are used as the initial labeled data for the incremental-ICT and the Co-Training algorithms. The parameters p and n in Table 1 and Table 2 is set to 1 and 3, respectively.

6.3 The Results

Standard precision (P), recall (R), accuracy (A) and F1-measure (F1) are used to evaluate the performance of the classifiers. These are defined as follows.

$$P = \frac{\text{no. of correctly predicted positive examples}}{\text{no. of predicted positive examples}}$$

$$R = \frac{\text{no. of correctly predicted positive examples}}{\text{no. of all positive examples}}$$

$$A = \frac{\text{no.of correctly predicted examples}}{\text{no. of all examples}}$$

$$F1 = \frac{2PR}{P+R}$$

6.4 Experiment using content and hyperlink features

For the first experiment, we use words appearing in the content of a Web page as the feature for the first classifier. The second classifier uses words appearing on the hyperlink as a feature set. The results are shown in Table 3.

Table 3: Performance of content-based and hyperlink-based classifiers using 3-fold cross-validation: P = Precision, R = Recall, A = Accuracy, F1 = F1-measure.

Classifier	P(%	R(%	A (%	F1
I-ICT (content)	94.04	80.46	94.55	86.72
S-Bayes (hyperlink)	85.34	63.22	89.48	72.61
I-ICT (hyperlink)	67.54	72.41	85.17	69.89
Co-Training (content)	81.52	54.08	87.32	65.03
S-Bayes (content)	99.05	42.20	87.25	58.97
Co-Training (hyperlink)	75.92	44.83	84.28	56.37

In Table 3, I-ICT (content) and I-ICT (hyperlink) stand for the content-based and hyperlink-based naïve Bayes classifiers of the incremental-ICT, respectively. Co-Training (content) and Co-Training (hyperlink) are content-based and hyperlink-based naïve Bayes classifiers of the Co-Training algorithm, respectively. S-Bayes (content) and S-Bayes (hyperlink) are supervised naïve-Bayes classifiers, which classify Web pages based on words in Web pages and words in hyperlinks, respectively.

As shown in the table, I-ICT (content) gives the best performance followed by S-Bayes (hyperlink), I-ICT (hyperlink), Co-Training (content), S-Bayes(content) and Co-Training (content), respectively. The reason that I-ICT (content) gives better performance compared to S-Bayes is because I-ICT (content) cooperates with I-ICT (hyperlink) while S-Bays uses single classifier. The performance of I-ICT (hyperlink) is not as good as that of I-ICT (content). This is because hyperlinks contain fewer words and thus are less capable of building the accurate classifier. The training technique of I-ICT is also an effective way, as its performance is better than that of Co-Training, which uses a different training technique.

6.5 Experiment using content and heading features

In order to see the impact of the heading feature on the categorization problem, we did experiments using heading-based classifier with various learning algorithms.

As shown in Table 4, I-ICT (content) and I-ICT(heading) stand for the content-based and heading-based naïve Bayes classifiers of the incremental ICT algorithm. S-Bayes (heading) and S-Bayes (content) are supervised naïve Bayes classifiers based on heading and content features, respectively.

Co-Training(heading) and Co-Training (content) are the heading-based and content-based naïve Bayes classifiers of the Co-Training algorithm.

Table 4: Performance of heading-based and content-based classifiers using 3-fold cross-validation: P = Precision, R = Recall, A = Accuracy, F1 = F1-measure.

Classifier	P(%	R(%	A (%	F1
I-ICT (content)	98.12	78.66	95.05	87.32
S-Bayes (heading)	96.51	77.58	94.43	86.02
I-ICT (heading)	80.72	89.65	92.65	84.95
Co-Training (heading)	79.71	74.71	90.24	77.13
Co-Training (content)	82.49	43.68	85.93	57.11
S-Bayes(content)	99.05	42.20	87.25	58.97

The best performance belongs to the content-based naive Bayes classifier of I-ICT followed by the supervised naïve Bayes classifier based on the heading feature, the heading-based of I-ICT, the heading-based of co-training, the content-based of co-training and the content-based of the supervised naïve Bayes classifier.

7. DISCUSSION AND CONCLUSION

In this paper, we have demonstrated the concept of the I-ICT algorithm and investigate the impacts of feature sets to the classification correctness. From the experimental results, the performance of S-Bayes (heading) is much higher than that of S-Bayes (hyperlink). It means that the heading feature has more potential than the hyperlink feature in helping the classifier to build the correct model used in categorization task. This is because the detail of the Web page is usually organized into sub-sections with the headings, which represent the main idea of the following content. Thus the structure of all headings in a page should give some common properties that is useful to identify its category. In the contrary, the words in the hyperlink, which links to the page could not provide enough information to identify the class of the page. This is not surprising because normally the hyperlink phase contains just few words referring to the page. For the worst case, the hyperlink might contain only a proper noun that is not sufficient in classifying that referring page.

According to the F1-measure, we obtained only 58.97% accuracy for S-Bayes using the content feature. It implies that the content feature alone could not help much in Web page classification because the two Web categories actually have high relevance in detail. Therefore the naïve Bayes classifier could not find the exact model for each category using all words appearing in the page.

Considering all classification mechanisms, we found that our I-ICT algorithm provides the highest correctness in both experiments. This is because I-ICT combines two classifiers based on different feature sets and these two classifiers cooperate with each other during the training process. The I-ICT algorithm has been proved to be robust under new assumption that each example can be viewed in two different views using different feature sets. With the consistency checking process, which is used to compensate the lack of domain's knowledge of the classifiers, our algorithm outperformed the supervised naïve Bayes algorithm, and Co-Training algorithm.

ACKNOWLEDGEMENT

This paper is supported by the Thailand Research Fund and National Electronics and Computer Technology Center.

REFERENCES

Kijsirikul, B., Sasipongpairoege, P., Soonthornphisaj, N. and Meknavin, S., 2000, 'Supervised and Unsupervised Learning Algorithms for Thai Web Pages Identification', *Proceeding of the Pacific Rim*

International Conference on Artificial Intelligence (PRICAI-2000), 690-700.

Blum, A. and Mitchell, T., 1998, 'Combining Labeled and Unlabeled Data with Co-Training', *Proceeding of the Eleventh Annual Conference on Computational Learning Theory*.

Cohen, W. and Singer, Y., 1999, 'Context-sensitive learning methods for text categorization', *ACM Transactions on Information Systems*, 17(2): 141-173.

Joachims, T., 1998, 'Text categorization with support vector machines: Learning with many relevant feature', *Proceedings Tenth European Conference on Machine Learning*, Springer Verlag.

Nigam, K., McCallum, A., Thrun, S. and Mitchell, T., 2000, 'Text classification from labeled and unlabeled documents using EM', *Machine Learning*, 39(2/3): 103-134.

Apte, C., and Damerau, F., 1994 'Automated learning of decision rules for text categorization', *ACM TOES*, 12(2): 233-251.

Mitchell, T., 1997, *Machine Learning*, McGraw-Hill. New York, 180-184.

The World Wide Knowledge Base (web-kb) project, http://www.cs.cmu.edu/afs/cs.cmu.edu/project/theo-51/www/co-training/data/course-cotrain-data.tar.gz, Carnegie Mellon University, U.S.A.

DATA REDUCTION TO IMPROVE KNOWLEDGE EXTRACTION

Maria de Fátima Rodrigues
Polytechnic Institute of Porto, School of Engineering
Rua Dr Antonio Bernardino de Almeida, 4200-072 Porto, Portugal
Email: fr@dei.isep.ipp.pt

Pedro R. Henriques
University of Minho, DI/gEPL
Campus Gualtar, 4710-057 Braga, Portugal
Email: prh@di.uminho.pt

Keywords: Knowledge Extraction, Data Reduction, Attribute Discretization, Rough Sets

Abstract: Knowledge Discovery in Databases (KDD) is a challenging machine learning application, because it must be a very efficient process with yet high understandability and reliability requirements. First, the learning task shall find all valid and non-redundant rules (rule learning). Second, the datasets for learning are very large. When learning from very large databases, the reduction of complexity is of highest importance. We highlight the advantages of combining attribute value discretization with rough set theory to find a subset of attributes that lets the KDD process discover more useful patterns. We present the evaluation of such approach by providing results from the application of a classification algorithm to various public domain datasets.

1 INTRODUCTION

The term Knowledge Discovery in Databases was coined in 1989 by the academic community (Frawley *et al.* 1995), (Fayyad *et al.* 1996) to refer the broad process of finding knowledge in data and to emphasize that the "high level" application of particular Data Mining (DM) methods is only one step in this complex process. Most of the previous work on KDD has focused on the development of DM algorithms aimed solely at extracting patterns from raw data, but KDD is an overall process which includes pre-processing and post-processing of data, as well as interpretation of the discovered patterns as knowledge.

This paper focuses in the pre-processing phase, on which we consider two phases: attribute discretization and data reduction. In data discretization we perform the aggregation of attribute values using knowledge about concept hierarchies and relevance of data. In data reduction phase, Rough Set theory (Pawlak1991) is applied to compute the minimal attribute set with respect to a mining goal.

Fast algorithms have been developed that generalize attribute values and find dependencies between attributes. The APRIORI and APRIORITID (Leo *et al.* 1984) find association rules that determine subsets of correlated attribute values. Attribute values are represented such that each attribute value becomes a Boolean attribute indicating whether the value is true or false for a certain entity (Agrawal *et al.* 1993). Other fast learning algorithms exploit given hierarchies and generalize attribute values by climbing the hierarchy (Michalski1983), merging tuples that become identical, and drop attributes with too many distinct values that cannot be generalized. The result are rules that characterize all tuples that have a certain value of attribute A in terms of generalized values of other attributes (Cercone *et al.* 1992). Similarly, the KID3 algorithm discovers dependencies between values of two attributes using hierarchies from background knowledge (Piatetsky-Shapiro and Frawley1991).

However these learning algorithms are tuple-oriented algorithms, they examine data tuple by tuple and perform generalization based on comparison of tuple values with the intermediate generalization results. Since the number of possible tuple combinations is exponential on the number of tuples in the relevant dataset, the worst case complexity of the generalization process is exponential on the size of the relevant datasets.

Our method integrates the generalization and reduction processes and thus eliminates undesirable tuples in the generalization process and removes irrelevant or superfluous attributes in the reduction process. This is very important as most discovery algorithms can achieve a linear scalability with respect to the number of tuples, but as we know, they are non-

J. Filipe et al. (eds.), Enterprise Information Systems III, 139–145.

linear with respect to the number of attributes in the dataset. For this reason, in order to select the relevant attributes, Rough Set theory is applied; the cause effect relationships among the condition and decision attributes are analysed and the irrelevant attributes to the discovery task are eliminated without lost of information of the original database system. The Rough Set theory provides the necessary tools to analyse the set of attributes globally.

We have been applying those techniques successfully to various public domain datasets collected in UCI repository (Merz and Murphy1996) to obtain some comparative figures. From those exercises we chose two examples, Tae and Abalone datasets to illustrate our approach and also because each dataset is a particular case and the data pre-processing techniques applied must also be particular to each one. After discussing these two cases, we will present in one table the results obtained with all datasets.

This paper is organised as follows: in section 2 we introduce some data treatment methods, explain the principle of data discretization and present basic notions about Rough Set based data reduction. Next, in section 3, two DM exercises are described to show the advantages of combining attribute value discretization with Rough Set data reduction. Finally, concluding remarks are presented.

2 DATA PRE-PROCESSING

The data collected and stored in databases has not been produced and originally recorded for knowledge extraction purposes; that explains why previous to any DM process it is indispensable a pre-processing phase that includes data cleaning and data reduction. The main purposes of data cleaning are:

- consistency checking
- error correction
- null values filling or elimination
- outliers remotion

Data cleaning methods are inherently application-domain dependent, and the participation of the end-user is crucial. Also, due to the large volume of databases, the selection of specific subsets of tuples is crucial.

Very often data stored in databases needs to be generalized in order to get meaningful or useful information. To achieve this, discretization of attributes is performed using knowledge about concept hierarchies and relevance of data; this task greatly reduces the number of tuples that must be examined. In the next subsection these ideas will be illustrated.

2.1 Attribute Discretization

Conventionally, discretization has been defined as the partitioning of the range of a continuous-valued attribute (called base or independent variable) into intervals which capture the behaviour of a related discrete-valued attribute (called goal or dependent variable). An attribute is discretizable if there are a large number of distinct values in the relation but there exists a concept hierarchy for the attribute (i.e. there are higher level concepts which subsume these attribute values). Otherwise the discretization is undesirable (Michalski1983). Some of the applications of discretization are:

- *Summarization:* it provides a high-level view of the relationship between the base and the goal without overwhelming the user with detail
- *On-Line Analytical Processing (OLAP):* tools pre-compute aggregations based on the values that an attribute can take on (for example, sales by geographical region). Extending this ability to continuous-valued attributes requires them to be discretized into a smaller, finite number of intervals.

We refer the reader to (Dougherty *et al.*1995), for an excellent survey of the work on discretization. Discretizing one continuous attribute based on a discrete goal attribute so as to minimize entropy was proposed in (Fayyad and Irani1993). They use the minimum-description-length principle to determine the appropriate number of intervals. Kerber suggests that intra-interval similarity should be maximized and inter-interval similarity should be minimized (Kerber1991). He uses the χ^2 metric to determine similarity. Maass provides an efficient algorithm that minimizes classification error (Maass1994). They also suggested the use of interactive visualizations to situate the user in an appropriate context and then allow further experimentation. Catlett describes a supervised dynamic discretization method (Catlett1991) that recursively selects cutpoints, maximizing Quinlan's gain (Quinlan1993) until a stopping criteria, based on a set of heuristic rules, ends the recursion.

In the context of our application area, pre-processing of DM, we consider two extensions to this conventional model of discretization:

1. discretization of a discrete unordered attribute, which normally take one of many possible, non-hierarchical values, e.g. "fruit" could take one value on a vast set of possibilities "apples, oranges, ...". Note that discretizing an ordered discrete attribute is very much the same as discretizing a single continuous attribute. At first sight, one might consider it redundant to discretize a discrete attribute. However, for reasons of simplicity and

readability, there is an advantage in grouping the values into mutually exclusive and exhaustive sets. For example, the village to which a person belongs could take hundreds of values in any country. Using such a variable as a decision node in a decision tree makes difficult to understand rules since it would have an out-degree of many values. Instead, one might wish to "discretize" the attribute "village" into fewer groups, while retaining the ability of the groups to discriminate the behavior of a related "goal" attribute. So, we must aggregate these values into groups accordingly to its semantic (Rodrigues *et al.*1999). The transformed attribute now takes as value one of these groups (significantly fewer in number).

2. simultaneously discretization of real attributes, which normally allows a better characterization of the behaviour of the goal attribute than independent discretizations would allow. Discretization of continuous attributes has been motivated by the need of simplicity and the fact that many classification algorithms work better with categorical data than continuous data. Discretizing real attributes simultaneously sometimes allows a better characterization of the behaviour of the goal attribute than independent discretizations would allow (Parthasarathy *et al.*1998).

2.2 Rough Set Data Reduction

It is difficult to know exactly which features are relevant to a given discovery task. Our goal applying this theory is to find a minimal subset of interesting attributes that keeps essential discovery information and simplifies the final relation enabling the discovery of more concise rules. For that it is necessary to perform a comprehensive analysis of properties of attributes prior to the generation of rules.

The most important issue addressed in the Rough Set theory is the idea of imprecise knowledge. In this approach, knowledge is imprecise if it contains imprecise concepts. It turns out that imprecise concepts can be however defined approximately in the available knowledge by employing two precise concepts called their *lower* and *upper approximation*.

Let $S = \{U, A, V\}$ be an information system, where

U is a finite set of objects, $U = \{x_1, x_2, ..., x_n\}$,

A is a finite set of attributes $A = \{a_1, a_2, ..., a_n\}$,

$V = \bigcup_{p \in A} V_p$ is a finite set of domains for attribute p.

The attributes in A are further classified into two disjoint subsets, `condition attributes C` and `decision attributes D`, $(A = C \cup D, C \cap D = \emptyset)$.

The next definition introduces the concept of `indiscernibility relation`. If such a relation exists between two objects, it means that all their attribute values are identical with respect to the attributes under consideration, and thus can not be discerned (distinguished) regarding the considered attributes.

With every subset of attributes $B \subseteq A$ in the information system $S = \{U, A, V\}$, an equivalence relation $IND(B)$ is associated, called `indiscernibility relation`, which is defined as follows:

$$IND(B) = \{(x, y) \in U^2 \mid a(x) = a(y) \text{ for every a} \in B\}$$

By $U/IND(B)$ is meant the set of all equivalence classes in the relation $IND(B)$.

The lower approximation $\underline{B}X$ and the upper approximation $\overline{B}X$ of a set of objects $X \subseteq U$ with reference to a set of attributes $B \subseteq A$ (defining an equivalence relation on $U - U/IND(B)$) may be defined in terms of the classes in the equivalence relation, as follows:

$$\underline{B}X = \cup\{\, E \in U/IND(B) \mid E \subseteq X \,\}$$
$$\overline{B}X = \cup\{\, E \in U/IND(B) \mid E \cap X \neq \emptyset\}$$

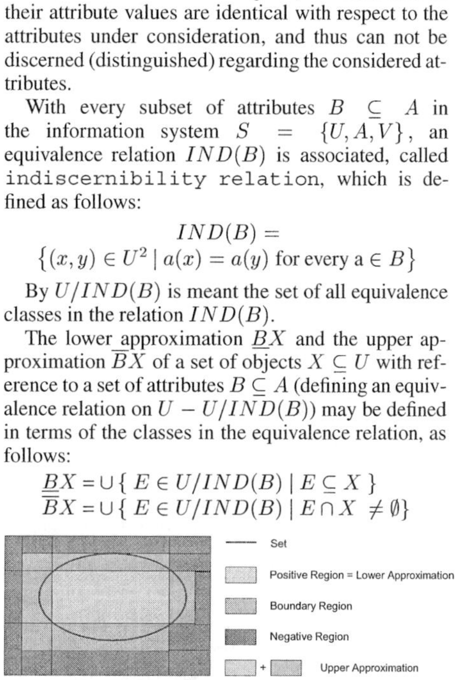

Figure 1: Rough Approximation

The *lower approximation* of a concept ($\underline{B}X$ *or* $POS_B(X)$ - B – *positive region of* X) consists in all objects which surely belong to the concept whereas the *upper approximation* of the concept $\overline{B}X$ consists in all objects which possibly belong to the concept in question. The difference between the *lower* and *upper* approximation is a *boundary region* ($BN_B(X) = \overline{B}X - \underline{B}X$) of the concept and consists in all objects which can not be classified with 100% certainty (figure 1).

In many problems of DM we want to identify classes of objects based on values of the discovery task, and define these classes in terms of features of their corresponding condition attributes. In most cases, classes are determined by a few attributes. Rough Set theory provides a tool to deal with this. `Core` and `reduct` are two fundamental concepts of Rough Sets. A `reduct` is part of an information system which keeps essential information of the original information system. A `core` represents the common parts of all reducts.

A positive region B ($B \subset C$) in $U/IND(D)$, $POS_B(D)$, is defined as

$$POS_B(D) = \cup\{\underline{B}X \mid X \in U/IND(D)\}$$

The positive region $POS_B(D)$ includes all objects in U which can be classified into classes of $IND(D)$ without error, just based on the classification information in $IND(B)$.

An attribute $p \in B$ is superfluous in B with respect to D if $POS_B(D) = POS_{B-\{p\}}(D)$; otherwise p is indispensable in B with respect to D.

A superfluous attribute in the information system can be removed without changing the dependency relationship of the original system. An indispensable attribute carries essential information about objects and should be kept to avoid changing the original system´s dependency relationship.

If every attribute of B is indispensable with respect to D, then B is indispensable with respect to D.

The set of all indispensable attributes in C with respect to D is called the `core` of C and is denoted by $CORE(C, D)$.

$$CORE(C, D) = \{a \in C \mid POS_C(D) \neq POS_{C-\{a\}}(D)\}$$

The concept of the `core` can be used as the starting point for computation of reducts.

$B \subset C$ is defined as a reduct in S if B is independent with respect to D and $POS_C(D) = POS_B(D)$.

Usually C may have more than one reduct. The selection of which reduct is the best depends on the existence of a cost function associated with the attributes; for example, some attributes are much more expensive to obtain than others. Other approach is to select the reduct with minimal number of attributes and if there are two or more reducts with the same minimal number of attributes, then the reduct with the least number of combinations of values of its attributes is selected (Cercone *et al.* 1992).

3 EXPERIMENTS

In the context of machine learning and statistical communities, there is much current research on algorithms for decision tree classifiers (Lim *et al.* 1999). Often the emphasis is on the accuracy of several decision tree algorithms compared against some non-decision tree algorithms on a large number of datasets. Recently, comprehensibility of the tree structures has received some attention. Comprehensibility typically decreases with the increase in tree size and complexity. If two trees employ the same kind of tests and have the same prediction accuracy, the one with fewer leaves is usually preferred. The purpose of combining attribute discretization with Rough Set data reduction is to improve both the prediction accuracy and the interpretation of rules. We have downloaded from the Repository of Machine Learning Databases (UCI - University of California, Irvine) (Merz and Murphy1996) some public domain datasets to perform on them a comparative study applying C5.0 decision tree algorithm (Quinlan1993), first without any data treatment, and then using discretization and reduction. From this exercise, we have chosen two examples to present in this paper in order to illustrate the proposed approach.

3.1 First dataset

Teaching Assistant Evaluation (TAE). This dataset consist of evaluations of teaching performance over three regular semesters and two summer semesters of 151 teaching assistant (TA) assignments at the Statistics Department of the University of Wisconsin-Madison. The scores are grouped into three roughly equal-sized categories ("low", "medium" and "high") to form the class attribute. In order to achieve a better train and test time we have encoded the attribute values as shown in Table 1.

Table 1: Attributes from the TAE dataset

Attribute	Values	Evaluation Correlation	Value Codification
Speaker	English, Non_Eng	-0.0255	English -1, Non_Eng -2
Instructor	1, ..., 25	0.075	
Course	1, ..., 26	0.143	
Semester	Summer, Regular	-0.283	Summer - 1, Regular - 2
Class size	3, .., 66	-0.036	
Evaluation	Low, Med, High		Low - 1, Med - 2, High - 3

The first mining process was carried out using directly the initial dataset without any previous data treatment, and the accuracy was 63,2 %.

The attributes Instructor, Course and Class Size besides they present too many values their range is much greater than the other attributes, so they can be dominants. To avoid that we have normalized these attributes. We have used Min_max, Zscore and Sigmoidal normalizations (Lippman *et al.* 1997). The results obtained with these new datasets are 62,5%, 63,2% and 65% respectively. The Zscore normalization has conducted to better results than the others, because this dataset presents isolated values for Class and Course attributes that may be dominant, for example, in the Min-max normalization.

In the next iteration we have discretized the class attribute based on its semantics and/or expected forms of generalized rules. For example, the attribute class has been discretized according to the next criteria:

$$\text{Class}\begin{cases} 3-15 & Small = 1 \\ 16-30 & Medium = 2 \\ 31-45 & Large = 3 \\ 46-66 & Very\ Large = 4 \end{cases}$$

The generalization is performed replacing lower-level (discrete) attribute values by the concepts in the desired level of the hierarchy. The other attributes have not been discretized because we didn't identify a semantic associated with them. The classification accuracy obtained with this new dataset was 70,6%

Unless data sets are small, Rough Set data analysis can only be performed with the assistance of suitable computer programs. There are only a few such systems available; the known RoughSet_analysers are listed in (Soft-links1998).

To perform Rough Set analysis in the TAE dataset, we have used Rosetta (Ohrn1988) to compute the reducts. The general problem of finding all reducts is NP-hard (Ziarko1991). In most cases it is not necessary to find all reducts. Rosetta calculates the reducts finding in each step those attributes with the largest significant values. If the user prefers some particular attributes, Rosetta finds the user's minimal attribute subset including the attributes the user emphasizes.

We have obtained the reduct - {Instructor, Course, Class}to characterize the attribute "Evaluation". The classification accuracy obtained using the reduct above was 71,4%.

3.2 Second Dataset

Abalone (Abal). The aim of this exercise is predicting the age of abalone from its physical measurements. The age of abalone is determined by cutting the shell through the cone, staining it, and counting the number of rings through a microscope – a boring and time-consuming task. Other measurements, which are easier to obtain, are used to predict the age. Further information, such as weather patterns and location (hence food availability) may be required to solve the problem. The attributes consider under this dataset are described in Table 2.

Table 2: Attributes from the Abalone dataset

Attribute	Data Type	Values
Sex	nominal	M, F, and I (infant)
Length	continuous	Longest shell measurement
Diameter	continuous	perpendicular to length
Height	continuous	with meat in shell
Whole weight	continuous	whole abalone
Shucked weight	continuous	weight of meat
Viscera weight	continuous	gut weight (after bleeding)
Shell weight	continuous	after being dried
Rings	integer	+1.5 gives the age in years

From the analysis of class distribution we have seen that the classes 1, 2 and bigger than 24 (24..29) don't have a significative number of instances, so they will not be considered in this study.

In the first C5.0 execution we have used the initial dataset, without any previous data treatment, and we have obtained 60.6% Classification Accuracy.

The value to predict - number of rings - has too many values, so we have discretized this discrete attribute in data intervals with 3 rings. After that this attribute takes 7 distinct values -> 3-5, ..., 21-23. With this new dataset the Classification Accuracy has significantly improved 77.1%.

In order to achieve better results we have considered new datasets from the previous, with all attributes discretized, except the attribute sex, because this one only has three distinct values. The discretization that we made was for the numeric attributes. This one consists in dividing their domains into ten equal data intervals and to each data interval associated a number. For example if the length of abalone is between 0.075 and 0.149 the value in the second dataset will be 1. Table 3 shows the value discretization made for all numeric attributes.

Table 3: Attribute discretization

	Length	Diam	Height	Whole	Shucked	Viscera	Shell	Rings
Min	0.075	0.055	0	0.002	0.001	0.001	0.002	1
Max	0.815	0.65	1.13	2.826	1.488	0.76	1.005	29
Mean	0.524	0.408	0.14	0.829	0.359	0.181	0.239	9.934
SD	0.12	0.099	0.042	0.49	0.222	0.11	0.139	3.224
Correl	0.557	0.575	0.557	0.54	0.421	0.504	0.628	1
	0.074	0.0595	0.113	0.2824	0.1487	0.0759	0.1003	
1	0.149	0.1145	0.113	0.2844	0.1497	0.0769	0.1023	
2	0.223	0.174	0.226	0.5668	0.2984	0.1528	0.2026	
3	0.297	0.2335	0.339	0.8492	0.4471	0.2287	0.3029	
4	0.371	0.293	0.452	1.1316	0.5958	0.3046	0.4032	
5	0.445	0.3525	0.565	1.414	0.7445	0.3805	0.5035	
6	0.519	0.412	0.678	1.6964	0.8932	0.4564	0.6038	
7	0.593	0.4715	0.791	1.9788	1.0419	0.5323	0.7041	
8	0.667	0.531	0.904	2.2612	1.1906	0.6082	0.8044	
9	0.741	0.5905	1.017	2.5436	1.3393	0.6841	0.9047	
10	0.815	0.65	1.13	2.826	1.400	0.76	1.005	

With this generalization the number of distinct tuples has been reduced 66% and the accuracy has also been significantly improved - 79.2%.

In order to get rules more concise and simple we will reduce the dataset by calculating the reducts relative to rings.

From the list of reducts obtained we select the reduct with minimal number of attributes - {Whole weight, Shucked weight}. With this reduct the classification accuracy (78.4 %) is little less than the one obtained with all attributes discretized (79.2 %), but is superior than that obtained with atomic values (60.6 %).

3.3 Summary

The next table (4) summarizes the accuracy for both the experiments, before and after data pre-processing.

Table 4: Summary results

Dataset	C5.0 Accuracy	
	TAE	Abalone
Initial Values	63.2%	60.6%
Attributes Discretized	70.6%	79.2%
Reduct	71.4%	78.4%

From the results achieved we can see that value discretization always implies a gain in accuracy. Attribute reduction not always conduces to a new gain in accuracy (sometimes we have detected a minimal loss). However, both techniques are a valuable DM approach as a simplification mechanism making the produced rules easier to understand.

We have also done analogous mining exercises with other datasets from the UCI Repository and we have achieved the accuracy described in Table 5.

Table 5: Accuracy after Data Discretized and Reduced

Dataset	C5.0 Accuracy	
	Atomic Data	Discretized and Reduced Data
Contracep. Met. Choice	76.8%	78.6%
Pima Indians Diabetes	80.4%	90.1%
Wisconsin Breast Cancer	99.1%	100%
Automobile	80%	87.3%
Echocardiogram	——	60%
Protein Localization Sites	76%	91.3%
Flag	76.9%	84.2%
Glass	70.3%	81.1%
Hepatitis Domain	82.4%	90.6%
Wine Recognition Data	92.3%	100%

4 CONCLUSION

While discretization has been conventionally used to partition a continuous value attribute into intervals, we have shown that even discrete attributes can benefit from grouping their outcomes when the number of outcomes is large.

Databases usually contain undesirable, irrelevant or unimportant fields for a given discovery task. Identifying relevant fields is very useful for all phases of KDD process. In this paper, Rough Set theory was used to compute the minimal attribute set, or reduct, in order to select the relevant attributes with respect to a decision attribute. Each reduct can be used instead of the entire attribute set without loss of any essential information.

The results obtained substantiate our point that there is much simplicity to be gained from the combination of attribute discretization with Rough Set data reduction and usually an accuracy improvement.

As future work we intend to apply the approach to other classification algorithms as well as to different kind association and clustering algorithms.

REFERENCES

R. Agrawal, T. Imielinski, e A. Swami. Data Base Mining : A Performance Perspective. Special issue on learning and discovery in knowledge - based systems, 1993.

J. Catlett. On changing continuos attributes into ordered discrete attributes. In *Proc. European Working Session on Learning*, 164–178, 1991.

N. Cercone, J. Han, e Y. Cai. Knowledge Discovery in Databases An Attribute-Oriented Approach. In *Proc. 18th Very large Databases (VLDB), Vancouver, Canada*, 335–350, 1992.

J. Dougherty, R. Kohavi, e M. Sahami. Supervised and unsupervised discretization of continuos features. In *Proc. 12th Int. Conf. Machine Learning*, 194–202, 1995.

U.M. Fayyad e K.B. Irani. Multi-interval discretization of continuos valued attributes for classification learning. In *Proc. 14th International Joint Conf. on Artificial Intelligence IJCAI-93*, 1022–1027, 1993.

U. Fayyad, G. Piatetsky-Shapiro, P.J. Smith, e R. Uthurasamy. From data Mining to Knowledge Discovery: An Overview. In *Advances in Knowledge Discovery and Data Mining*, 1–34. AAAI/MIT Press, 1996.

W.J. Frawley, G. Piatetsky-Shapiro, e C. Matheus. Knowledge Discovery in Databases: An Overview. technical report, 1995.

R. Kerber. Himerge: Discretization of numeric attributes. In *Proc. 10th National Conf. on Artificial Intelligence*, 123–128, 1991.

Breimann Leo, Jerome H. Friedman, Richard A. Olshen, e Charles J. Stone. *Classification and Regression Trees*. Wadsworth International Group, 1984.

Tjen-Sien Lim, Wei-Yin Loh, e Yu-Shan Shih. A Comparison of Prediction Accuracy, Complexity, and Training Time of Thirty-three Old and New Classification Algorithms. *Kluwer Academic Publishers*, 1–27, 1999.

Richard P. Lippman, Ruby L. Kennedy, Yughun Lee, Benjamin Van Roy, e Christopher D. Reed. *Solving Data Mining Problems through Pattern Recognition*. Prentice Hall PTR, 1997.

W. Maass. Efficient agnostic pac-learning with simple hypotheses. In *Proc. 7th Anual ACM Conf. on Computational Learning Theory*, 67–75, 1994.

C.J. Merz e P.M. Murphy. UCI Repository of Machine Learning Databases. http://www.ics.uci.edu/ mlearn/MLRepository.html, 1996.

R.W. Michalski. A theory and methodology of indutive learning. 111–161, 1983.

Aleksander Ohrn. ROSETTA Technical Reference Manual. technical report, Dec 1988.

S. Parthasarathy, R. Subramonian, e R. Venkata. Generalized Discretization for Summarization and Classification. In *Proc. 2th International Conf. on the Practical Application of Knowledge Discovery and Data Mining*, 219–240. Practical Application Company Ltd, 1998.

Zdzislaw Pawlak. Rough Sets and Fuzzy Sets, Fuzzy Sets and Systems. Institute of computer sciences reports, Warsaw Technical University and Fudamenta Informaticae, 1991.

G. Piatetsky-Shapiro e W. J. Frawley. Discovery, analysis and presentation of strong rules. In *Knowledge Discovery in Databases*, 229–248. Cambridge AAAI Press, 1991.

J.R. Quinlan. *C4.5: Programs for Machine Learning*. Morgan Kaufmann Publishers, 1993.

F. Rodrigues, C. Ramos, e P. Rangel Henriques. An Intelligent System to Study Demographic Evolution. In *Proc. on Data Mining and Knowledge Discovery: Theory, Tools, and Technology*, 161–170. SPIE - The International Society for Optical Engineering, 1999.

EBRSC Rough Set Soft-links. Rough Set Community. World Wide Web page - http://www.cs.uregina.ca/ roughset/software.html, 1998.

Wojciech Ziarko. *The Discovery, Analysis, and Representation of Data Dependencies in Databases in KDD G. Piatetsky-Shapiro and W.J. Frawley*. (eds) Menlo Park, CA AAAI/MIT, 1991.

DESIGNING INTELLIGENT TUTORING SYSTEMS: A BAYESIAN APPROACH

Hugo Gamboa
Escola Superior de Tecnologia de Setúbal, Campus do IPS
Estefanilha, Setúbal Portugal
Email: hgamboa@est.ips.pt

Ana Fred
Instituto de Telecomunicações, Instituto Superior Técnico
Lisboa Portugal
Email: afred@lx.it.pt

Keywords: Intelligent Tutoring Systems, Bayesian Networks, e-Learning.

Abstract: This paper proposes a model and an architecture for designing intelligent tutoring system using Bayesian Networks. The design model of an intelligent tutoring system is directed towards the separation between the domain knowledge and the tutor shell. The architecture is composed by a user model, a knowledge base, an adaptation module, a pedagogical module and a presentation module. Bayesian Networks are used to assess user's state of knowledge and preferences, in order to suggest pedagogical options and recommend future steps in the tutor. The proposed architecture is implemented in the Internet, enabling its use as an *e-learning* tool. An example of an intelligent tutoring system is shown for illustration purposes.

1 INTRODUCTION

Intelligent tutoring systems (ITSs) are software programs that give support to the learning activity. These systems can be used in the normal educational process, in distant learning courses, either under the form of CDROMs or as applications that deliver knowledge over the Internet. They present new ways for education, which can change the role of the human tutor or teacher, and enhance it.

Computers have been used in education sincefor over 25 years (Beck et al., 1996). First developments towards the introduction of software programs as auxiliary tools in the learning process were formalized in the area of computer aided instruction (CAI). These programs used a decision tree to guide the student from one content page to another depending on his/her answers (Urban-Lurain, 1996). These programs didn't consider the diversity of students and their particular needs, background or history. CAI programs failed to adapt to the specific way of acquiring knowledge a student had, and couldn't give the individualized attention that a human tutor provides (Bennett, 1997).

Recent research developments in Artificial Intelligence led to a new application field, named Intelligent Tutoring Systems (Burns and Capps, 1988). The basic underlying perspective is to consider every student as being unique. This paradigm is based on the creation of a user or student model (VanLehn, 1988) that keeps records on user preferences and progress during the knowledge acquisition process.

The main characteristic that increases effectiveness to the task of teaching with an ITS, is the adaptability to the student. Assessing the user state of knowledge and profile requires uncertainty reasoning. Artificial Intelligence has addressed this problem in various ways (Nilson, 1998) such as certainty factors in knowledge representation (Buchanan and Shortliffe, 1985), probability theory or fuzzy logic (Zimmerman, 1991). Bayesian Networks (BNs) (Pearl, 1998)(Frey, 1998) are a most actual approach to uncertainty modelling. This technique combines the rigorous probabilistic formalism with a graphical representation and efficient inference mechanisms (Jensen, 1997).

Examples of ITSs (Brusilovsky et al., 1996) (Frölich and Nejdl, 1997) (Schulze et al., 2000) present various ways of dealing with the problem of tutoring using the computer, suggesting different approaches to the user model.

A typical ITS architecture separates domain application dependent parts—including a knowledge base which stores course contents—from generic parts which are independent of the knowledge to be taught. The same approach has been adopted in the field of expert systems (Buchanan and Shortliffe, 1985)(Fred, 1994)(Russel and Norvig, 1995), according to which the set of all domain independent parts of the system

J. Filipe et al. (eds.), Enterprise Information Systems III, 146–152.

is called a *shell* (an empty knowledge base, inference mechanisms and eventually a design interface). This generic part in intelligent tutoring systems is sometimes called *authoring tool*. This structure is being used to accelerate the developing process of new applications (Fleming and Horwitz, 1996)(Murray, 1999).

The potentialities that the Internet provides, makes it the best place to locate an ITS for distance education or as an *e-learning* tool (Ubell, 2000). By scanning the literature on ITS, one can identify three main classes according to the systems main goal (Murray, 1999): (a) problem solving guidance (Schulze et al., 2000); (b) curriculum sequencing (Brusilovsky et al., 1996); (c) device/process simulation. No global solution has yet been proposed covering the several aspects.

In this paper we propose a model and an architecture for the creation of ITSs under a Bayesian approach supported.

The global model is decomposed in interactive submodels explicity addressing user modelling, knowledge design and Bayesian inference. This approach provides modularity to create tutors in different contexts with the same architecture. The shell, the part of the tutor that is teaching domain independent, is divided into five parts: user model, knowledge model, adaptation module, pedagogical module and presentation module.

The ITS shows the contents to be learned via an Internet browser that, through a set of content specialized pages, interacts with the student and suggests pedagogical options. A Bayesian Network combines the contents structure with the user profile and learning style to suggest pedagogical directions.

Section 2 gives a brief introduction to BNs in the context of user modelling; in section 3 the design model for ITSs is proposed; section 4 describes the architecture; implementation aspects are treated in section 5; and section 6 illustrates the use of the proposed architecture and model a draft of an ITS ia a topic of *Pattern Recognition*.

2 BAYESIAN NETWORKS

A Bayesian Network is a graphical description of a probability distribution that permits efficient probability propagation combined with a rigorous formalism. A BN for a given domain represents the joint probability distribution, $p(x)$, over the set of random variables, X, of the domain, as a set of local distributions combined with a set of conditional independence assertions. This joint probability is computed from expression 1,

Figure 1: A Bayesian Network.

$$P(x_1, x_2, \ldots, x_n) = \prod_{i=1}^{n} P(x_i \mid \Pi_i) \qquad (1)$$

where, for each variable x_i, $\Pi_i \subseteq \{x_1, \ldots, x_{i-1}\}$ is a set of variables of which x_i is conditionally dependent.

The BN structure encodes the assertions of conditional independence as a directed acyclic graph such that: (a) each node corresponds to a variable; (b) the parents of the node corresponding to x_i are the nodes associated to the variables in Π_i. The pair formed by the structure (graph) and the collection of local distributions, $P(x_i \mid \Pi_i)$, for each node in the domain, constitutes the Bayesian Network for that domain. Figure 1 plots a sample Bayesian Network where variables **B** and **D** are independent, variable **C** is only dependent of **D**, and variable **A** is conditionally independent of the variable **D** given **B** and **C** variables.

Exploring conditional independence between variables, this formalism provides a compact description of the joint distribution, explicitly representing local dependence; this characteristic is explored in the design of efficient inference algorithms.

In the context of ITSs, Bayesian Networks have been applied to user modelling (VanLehn et al., 1998) in a diagnostic perspective: given a student action (symptom) the network provides the most likely state of knowledge (diagnosis). In our work, BNs are used to model the user, the structure of knowledge and pedagogical options. The values related to student status are taken from the user interaction with the tutor, further described in section 3.3.

3 THE DESIGN MODEL

Our design model presents a unified solution for the creation of ITSs based on Bayesian Networks.

This model is developed taking into account two phases of the ITS life cycle: the *design* phase of ITSs, where we focus on the modularity and rapid development of systems; the *usage* phase as an auxiliary tool, directed towards the adaptability to the user.

A student will use an ITS to receive a specialized learning orientation, on a given domain, tuned to the user unique learning style and state of knowledge.

We envisioned the design of an ITS system by decomposing it in three conceptual modules: one associated to the user; another concerning the contents related to the knowledge representation; and finally, an inference mechanism which form the core of the system, linking the other modules. This conceptual design will be further explored in a modular architecture implemented as a *shell.*

3.1 User Modelling

To model the user learning style and state of knowledge we define a set of variables both generic (associated with the learning style) and content specific (associated with the state of knowledge). These variables will be part of a BN (see section 3.3) to infer conclusions about the student.

Generic user related variables (learning style variables) include:

- mean time per page—indicates the average time a student spends on a page.
- superficial scan—identifies a student preference in passing the contents in a shallow way.
- answers—indicates if a user answers to questions.

For each topic exists the list of variables include (state of knowledge variables):

- spent time—specifies the time spent by the user reading/interacting with the specific topic.
- topic deepness level—refers to the tendency of a user to deepen a topic.
- wrong answers—number of questions not answered correctly.
- right answers—number of correct answers.

These variables keep information about the user interaction with the ITS and are used to adapt the presentation of contents to the user profile.

3.2 Knowledge Design

The repository of knowledge stored in the *knowledge base* is structured as: (a) a set of *topics* that represent atomic content parts (b) *knowledge map* that describes the interdependence between *topics*. Each *topic* is composed by: (a) a hypertext page including text, pictures and other multimedia items; (b) a set of questions.

Steps towards the construction of the *knowledge base* are as follows: *knowledge map* definition; topic creation; design of individual topic text, pictures and multimedia items.

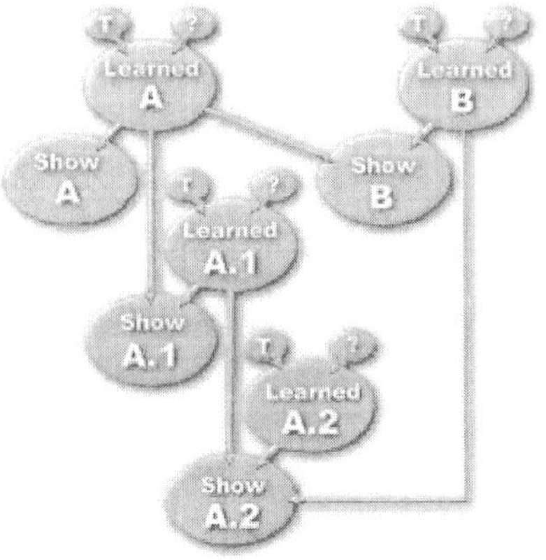

Figure 2: Bayesian Network from a sample knowledge base.

3.3 Bayesian Inference

Our model of ITS is completed with the definition of a BN that relates the *knowledge map* with *topic* related variables and integrate the learning style of the user with the pedagogical options.

Consider an ITS with the following topics:

- Topic A
  - Subtopic A.1
  - Subtopic A.2
- Topic B

In this example, a dependence relation exists between Topic B and Topic A.2, meaning that in order to entirely understand topic A.2 it is necessary to learn topic B.

A simplified Bayesian Network for the previous example is shown in figure 2. The **learned** nodes represent the degree of belief that a certain topic has been learned. These belief values are dependent on the time spent on the corresponding topic (**T** in figure 2) and on the answered questions (**?** in figure 2).

We define each **T** and **?** in equations 2 and 3 respectively.

$$\mathbf{T} = \frac{Time\ in\ topic}{Standard\ time\ in\ topic} \tag{2}$$

$$? = \frac{Right\ answers - Wrong\ answers}{Number\ of\ question} \tag{3}$$

Each **show** node specifies the degree of belief in that the related topic should be learned. These nodes depend on its **learned** parent nodes and on the **learned** node of the same topic.

Figure 3: Bayesian network for the pedagogical actions.

The student learning style is inferred through a set of BNs using user related variables. Figure 3 shows a subset of this BN illustration *deepen* topic and *review* topics.

4 THE INTELLIGENT TUTORING SYSTEM ARCHITECTURE

According to the previous design model the proposed ITS architecture adopts a modular structure composed by five basic blocks (figure 4), namely: (a) **User Model**; (b) **Knowledge Base**; (c) **Adaptation Module**; (d) **Pedagogical Module**; (e) **Presentation Module**. The internal structure of these modules is independent of the tutor specific content, thus equal for all the ITS implemented using this approach, constituting a *shell*. Implementation aspects of this *shell* are detailed in section 5.

The **User Model** is the part of the ITS where the variables defined in section 3.1 are kept. This module retains user information from the interaction with the tutor.

The content subjects to be taught are kept in the **Knowledge Base** structured as a *knowledge map* and a set of *topics*. This is the unique module in a working ITS that is dependent of the contents, producing the desired separation between the domain application dependent part and the generic part, the *shell*.

User assessment is performed in the **Adaptation Module** which combines information from the Knowledge Base with user data (from the user model) in a BN, inferring the user state of knowledge.

The **Pedagogical Module**, also supported in BNs, uses the data provided by the three last modules and creates a set of suggestions of what the student should do next.

The result of the ITS reasoning process is the page composed and shown in the **Presentation Module**. It collects the topic and respective questions to present,

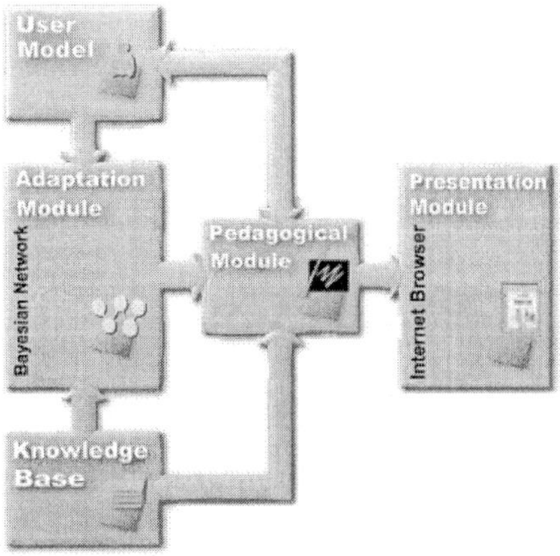

Figure 4: Intelligent tutoring system architecture.

the pedagogical suggestions and the most likely step to be taken.

This architecture serves to isolate the different parts of the system defining their functionalities and specifying the implementation directions.

5 THE ITS SHELL IMPLEMENTATION

The proposed architecture is implemented in *Java* and *JavaScript* being accessible through an Internet browser. BNs structure and their respective inference algorithms are built using the *JavaBayes* (Cozman, 1998) (Dechter, 1996) program also implemented in *Java*.

- User model

  The user model is kept in a *Java* data structure that has a set of general variables and a set of variables related to the topics from the knowledge base.

- The Knowledge base

  The internal structure of the knowledge base is developed under an object oriented approach, and for each content part that is present in the ITS, exists an object associated with an html page, a set of questions and variables.

  The structure of this `Page` object is as follows:

```
Page{
  Title
  Html File

  Questions List
```

```
    Number Of Questions
    Wrong Answers
    Right Answers

    Time Spent In Page
    Visited Page?
    Standard Page Time

    Parent Pages List
    Number Of Parents
}
```

Where `Questions List` is a list of objects of the type `Question` with the following items:

```
Question{
    Question Text
    Help In Case Of Error
    Correct Answer
    Used Question?
}
```

The *html* page is composed in a separate program and the questions are designed to be answered with yes or no choices. Information in the `Page` structure is passed to the other modules of the system.

At each user action these variables are updated in order to have this information available for the other modules.

- The Adaptation Module

  From the structure of the knowledge base, a BN is automatically built to infer if each topic is learned and infer the next topic to be learned.

- Pedagogical module

  The role of the pedagogical module is to choose between one action over the current topic and the decision of showing a new topic: (a) deepen a topic; (b) shallow scan; (c) review previous topic; (d) show a new topic.

  These options are defined using the BNs in figure 3; the propagated probabilities of possible actions are compared with the probabilities of the **show** nodes in the adaptation model. The highest probability node is selected using equation 4.

$$action = arg\max \left\{ \begin{array}{l} P(\mathbf{deepen\ topic}) \\ P(\mathbf{shallow\ scan}) \\ P(\mathbf{review}) \\ \max_i[P(\mathbf{show_i})] \end{array} \right\} \quad (4)$$

If the decision is **deepen topic** the tutor presents the descendent page of the actual page. In case of **shallow scan**, the next page in the index is presented. The **review** decision selects the parent page most likely to be shown (the parent page with the highest **show** node probability).

With this structure the ITS enables a guided navigation through the topics, and adapts the path to the student learning style.

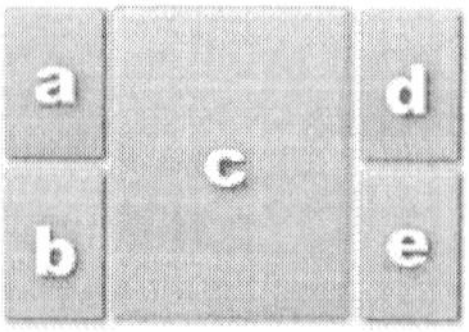

Figure 5: Presentation module parts: (a) navigation; (b) questions; (c) topics (d) suggestions (e) index.

- The Presentation Module

  The user interacts with the ITS through the presentation module, the system part that composes the information to be shown, using the information generated by the previous modules. The presentation module enables the user to accept the guidance of the ITS or directly select a topic.

  The interface consists of a screen divided into five parts (figure 5): (a) *navigation*; (b) *questions*; (c) *topics*; (d) *suggestions*; (e) *index*.

  The *navigation* part has three buttons: the *next* button leads to the presentation of the next page according to the pedagogical direction (formula 4); the other buttons follows to the *last* subject accessed or jumps to a parent subject so that the user can *review* related subjects.

  The area of the screen dedicated to *questions* is dynamically changed, drawing user attention. These questions are optional, but if answered they produce information that enables the tutor to better guide the user.

  The *topic* is displayed in an *html* page positioned at the center of the browser.

  The *suggestions* displayed are the three higher probability decisions taken from the pedagogical module.

  In the *index*, the ITS presents a conventional structure, like in a book, that enables the user to freely navigate through the topics. Every user action is sent to the user model, so that the variables related to the user are updated.

6 ILLUSTRATIVE EXAMPLE

In this section we show an example of an ITS, developed using the previously described *shell*, in the area of *Pattern Recognition*.

In the design phase the contents were produced using available tools to create *html* pages and graphics. We added a set of questions for each topic, and the interdependence among the different topics were identified and mapped into the tutor.

After the design phase the system was used as an auxiliary tool. Figure 6 shows a typical screen of the

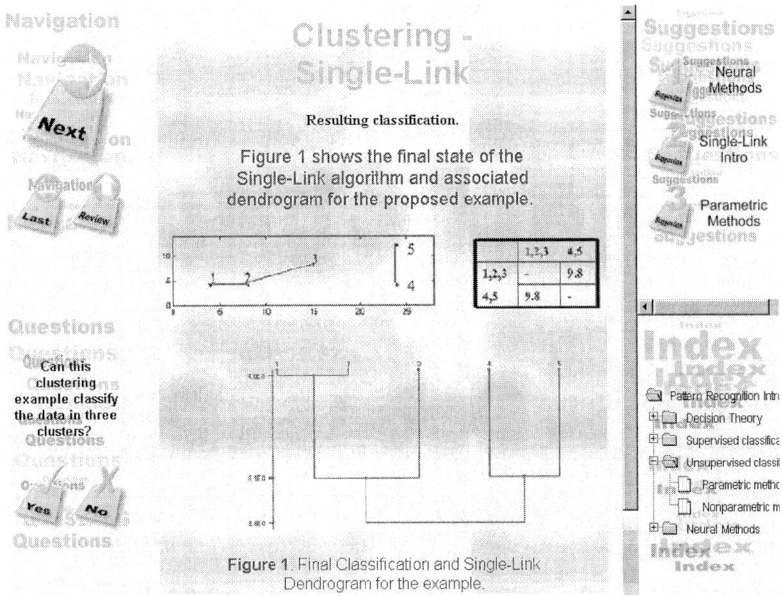

Figure 6: Interface of the illustrative example.

system in the topic related to *clustering algorithms*.

When the user starts using the tutor, he/she is asked to do a short test to assess his prior knowledge in the subjects to be taught. This test will initialize variables in the BN. The ITS then starts showing the topics, making question and suggesting paths. It acquires information about the user via the interaction with the browser in the presentation module. At the end of the tutor usage, an evaluation test will compare the first results with those of the final test.

7 CONCLUSIONS

In this paper we proposed a modular architecture for the design of ITS, under a Bayesian approach. Adopting Bayesian Networks as the basic formal device for modelling and reasoning under uncertainty, two main goals were pursued: personalization and adaptation of the system to student profiles and state of knowledge; facilitate the design process of ITS.

Contributions towards these objectives included:

- definition of a global ITS model resulting from the integration of specialized models, namely: the user model, the knowledge base and the Bayesian inference.
- providing these models with learning capabilities by means of probabilistic inference based on Bayesian Networks.
- mapping of this conceptual model into a modular architecture clearly separating domain application blocks from generic knowledge representation and inference mechanisms common to all applications, implemented as a *shell*.

The implementation of the *shell* using *Java*, extends the usage of the ITS as an *e-learning* tool.

Structuring knowledge as atomic knowledge pieces hierarchically organized according to precedence rules in an interdependence *knowledge map*, *html* files were chosen for the design of content pages enabling the incorporation of a versatile set of multimedia publishing resources.

An example of the application of the proposed methodology and *shell* in the domain of Pattern Recognition was shown illustrating the design and final usage phases of an ITS.

Ongoing work includes refinement of the present model, and special attention is given to the adaptability of the model to produce internet programs to be introduced in existing *e-learning* tools.

REFERENCES

Beck, J., Stern, M., and Haugsjaa, E. (1996). Applications of AI in Education. In *Proceedings of the Third Inter-*

national Conference on Intelligent Tutoring Systems.

Bennett, F. (1997). *Computers as Tutors: Solving the Crisis in Education.* First Monday. http://www.firstmonday.dk/issues /issue6/intro/index.html.

Brusilovsky, P., Schwarz, E., and Weber, G. (1996). Elm-art: an intelligent tutoring system on world wide web. In C. Frasson, G. Gutier, A. L., editor, *Intelligent Tutoring Systems, ITS'96*, pages pp. 261–269.

Buchanan, B. G. and Shortliffe, E. H. (1985). *Rule-Based Expert Systems: The MYCIN Experiments of the Stanford Heuristic Programming Project.* Addison-Wesley.

Burns, H. L. and Capps, C. G. (1988). Foundations of Intelligent Tutoring Systems. In Polson, M. C. and Richardson, J. J., editors, *Foundations of Intelligent Tutoring Systems*, chapter 3, pages 55–78. Lawrence Erlbaum Associates.

Cozman, F. (1998). Javabayes version 0.34, bayesian networks in java usermanual. http://www.cs.cmu.edu/ ~fgcozman/home.html.

Dechter, R. (1996). Bucket elimination: a unifying framework for several probabilistic inference algoritms. In *Twelfth Annual Conference on Uncertainity in Artificial Inteligence.*

Fleming, J. L. and Horwitz, C. (1996). Applications of the Rapid Intelligent Tutoring System Development Shell (RIDES). In *ITS'96 Workshop on Architectures and Methods for Designing Cost-Effective and Reusable ITSs.*

Frölich, P. and Nejdl, W. (1997). A Database-Oriented Approach to the Design of Educational Hyperbooks. In *Proceedings of the workshop: Intelligent Educational Systems on the World Wib Web, 8th World Conference of the AIED Soceiety.*

Fred, A. (1994). Expert systems: Conceptual, methodological and management aspects. Technical Report Project HC 1014, European Neurological Network.

Frey, B. (1998). *Graphical Models for Machine Learning and Digital Communication.* MIT Press.

Jensen, F. (1997). *An Introduction to Bayesian Networks.* Springer.

Murray, T. (1999). Authoring intelligent tutoring systems: An analysis of the state of the art. *International Journal of Artificial Intelligence in Education*, 10: pp. 98–129.

Nilson, N. (1998). *Artificial Intelligence: A New Synthesis.* Morgan Kaufmann.

Pearl, J. (1998). *Probabilistic Reasoning in Intelligent Systems: Networks of Plausible Inference.* Morgan Kaufmann.

Russel, S. and Norvig, P. (1995). *Artificial Intelligence: a modern approach.* Prentice Hall.

Schulze, K. G., Shelby, R. N., Treacy, D. J., Wintersgill, M. C., Vanlehn, K., and Gertner, A. (2000). Andes: An intelligent tutor for classical physics. *The Journal of Electronic Publishing, University of Michigan Press.* http://www.press.umich.edu/ jep/06-01/schulze.html.

Ubell, R. (2000). Engineers turn to e-learning. *IEEE Spectrum*, 37(10): pp. 59–63.

Urban-Lurain, M. (1996). Intelligent tutoring systems, an historic review in the context of the develpment of artificial inteligence and educational psychology. Technical report, Department of Computer Science and Engineering, Michigan State University. http://aral.cse.msu.edu/ Publications/ITS/its.htm.

VanLehn, K. (1988). Student Modeling. In Polson, M. C. and Richardson, J. J., editors, *Foundations of Intelligent Tutoring Systems*, chapter 3, pages 55–78. Lawrence Erlbaum Associates.

VanLehn, K., Niu, Z., Siler, S., and Gertner, A. (1998). Student modeling from convencional test data: A bayesian approach without priors. In Goettl, B. P., Halff, H. M., edfield, C. L., and Shute, V. J., editors, *Intelligent Tutoring Systems, 4th International Conference, ITS'98*, volume 1452. Springer.

Zimmerman, H. J. (1991). *Fuzzy Set Theory.* Kluwer, 2nd edition.

QUALITATIVE REASONIG FOR SOFTWARE DEVELOPMENT PROJECT BY CONSTRAINT PROGRAMMING

Antonio J. Suárez, Pedro J. Abad
Department of Electronic Engineering ,Computer System and Automatic.University of Huelva
E-mail: asuarez@uhu.es, abadhe@uhu.es

Rafael M. Gasca, J. A. Ortega
Department of Computer Languages and System. University of Sevilla
E-mail: gasca@lsi.us.es, jaortega@lsi.us.es

Keywords: Qualitative Reasoning, Software Development Project, Constraint Programming, Constraint Satisfaction Problem

Abstract: This paper presents a new approach on the problem of the estimation and planning in the software development projects (SDP). Therefore, a qualitative simulation of a part of the dynamic system of Abdel-Hamid, (subsystem of human resources) will be carried out. We will model this subsystem like a CSP (Constrains satisfaction problem), that is, it will be modelled as a set of restrictions that should be full satisfied. Next, the associated program will be generated under the constraint-programming paradigm. This will simulate the dynamic subsystem and will give as result all its possible behaviours. This way we achieve to improve and to concrete the qualitative information that we can get to obtain of such a subsystem.

1. INTRODUCTION

1.1 Abdel-hamid and manick dynamic system

The concept of using models to represent engineering systems doesn't have anything essentially new. In fact, engineering software project managers use mental models in an intuitive way when they make decisions. They select among different alternatives according to the different effect they produce. The relationship that connects the possible actions with its effects, is the system model. We will use model of Abdel-Hamid (Abdel 1991), which is composed by four subsystems: Software production, Control, Planning and human resources. The relationships among them are shown in the figure 1.

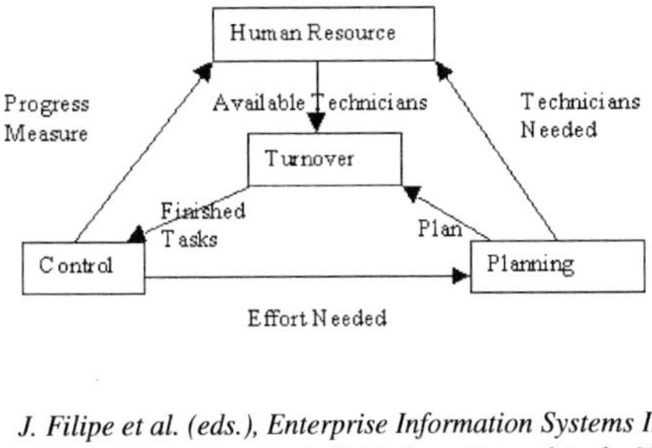

The software production subsystem takes charge of the basic activities. These activities consist on the assignment of effort, development, quality and tests. On the other hand, the control subsystem takes charge of measuring the progress of the project and making the comparisons with the planning subsystem. The planning subsystem carries out the function of revising and modifying the initial estimation of the project and this is done according to the information that the system gets from control subsystem. The human resources subsystem, object of our study, is responsible for recruiting, training of selected staff and transfer of human resources among projects. This subsystem is shown in figure 2. Technicians are divided in two groups: callow technicians and experienced technicians. This division is necessary for several reasons: Training, productivity, needed effort, rotation.

Training. New members in the project require a period to adapt. Along the period, productivity shows to be low. At the same time, senior staff gives training and company knowledge to recent comers. This show to be expensive for the company as seniors are not hundred per cent producing.

Productivity. Main issue is that the fact mentioned above affects the whole team. The decision to measure the need of effort is taken on an intuitive base.

J. Filipe et al. (eds.), Enterprise Information Systems III, 153–160.

Necessary effort. To determine the necessary total effort, or what is the same thing, the number of necessary technicians, the project management should consider many factors. Factors to be considered are: effort level needed to complete the project inside the planned limits, remaining tasks and production stability. It is always necessary to keep in mind the phase of the project in which we are. At the end of the project it is more difficult to incorporate personal, although the time and the perceived effort imply this incorporation, This fact would mean longer training time for the organization and the work environment than the project live itself

Rotation. More than a project at a time are normally carried out in software development companies. The rotation of senior from a project to another, plus the need of training for junior by seniors, reduce the ratio of technical full time equivalence senior force.

Remaining time, human resource stability and training requirements will affect the quantity of new human resources that we are looking for.

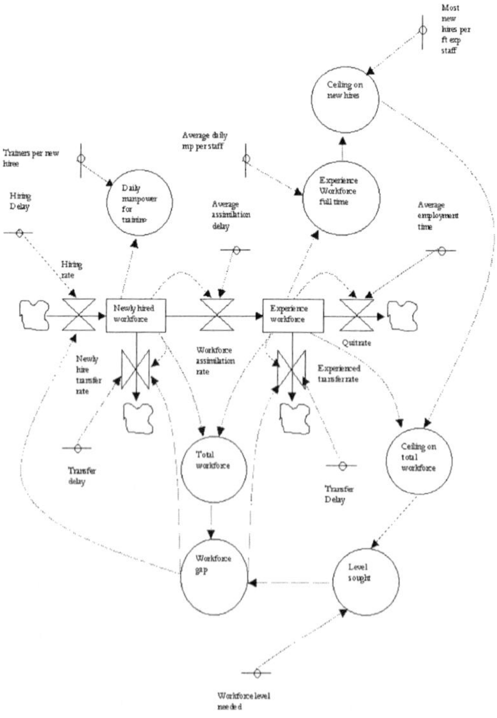

Figure 2: Human resources subsystem

1.2 Constraint satisfaction problem. (CSP)

Constrains satisfaction problems are those in which you have a set of variables; each of them to be instantiated in an associated domain and a set of Boolean constrains which limit the set of allowed values for these variables.

A constrains satisfaction problem(CSP) is characterised as follow: a set V of n variables $\{v_1, v_2, ..., v_n\}$, and a domain D_i of possible values associated with each variable v_i. On some specified subsets of these variables, there are constraint relations, given that there are subsets of the Cartesian product of all the given variable domains such that each n tuple in that set satisfies all the given constraint relations. One may be required to find the entire set of solutions or one member of the set or simply to report if the set of solutions has any member. If the set of solutions is empty, the CSP is unsatisfiable.

1.3 Qualitative simulation

Qualitative simulation is specially useful when we don't have enough quantitative information to simulate a dynamic system, This is our case.

Qualitative reasoning is considered as one of the discipline of the artificial intelligence. It aims to provide a technique to carry out designs, diagnosis, analysis and simulation where knowledge that we have of the system is little. Qualitative reasoning tries to incorporate the observations coming from the common sense or the intuition, and it gives qualitative explanations of the behaviour of a system based on qualitative descriptions of the possible situations of the real world.

A qualitative simulation for a real system can be carried out when a qualitative change of the characteristics of the system takes place along the time. These changes can take place due to variations in the parameters, in the structure or in the behaviour models.

For a qualitative simulation, based on a quantitative model, to be well defined we should detail corresponences between:

the quantitative model and the qualitative one,
the quantitative solution and the qualitative one,
the qualitative solution and the quantitative one,
the set of qualitative values
and the algorithm used to solve the model.

1.4 Constraint programming

Within constrains programming, a problem is represented in terms of it unknowledge, that is, on base of its variables and constrains to be satisfied by these variables. In other words, the unknowledge of a problem is represented as constrained variables. Thus, for any given problem, the problem representation consist of declaring the variables and define the constraints on them.

Solution for the problem consist of finding a value for each variable that fulfill and satisfy all the constraints. We mean this activity as the search for the solution. This is because when we begin work on a problem, we do not always know beforehand whether there is a solution that satisfies all the constrains of the problem.

Constrains programming thus entails two relatively different activities: Problem representation and solution search. A problem representation consist of the declaration of the unknowledge and the constrains of the problem. To solve the problem we have to select a set of values in the domain of each constrained variable, so that all the constrains are satisfied.

Constrains programming provides us some advantages when we apply dynamic systems, among which it is necessary to highlight:

1. Constrains programming gives a very natural and declarative form of specifying problems like this.
2. we can re-use a set of search techniques of new information by means of a great quantity of efficient and parametric algorithms.
3. The possible variations in the model are carried out in a very comfortable way

2. DESCRIPTION OF THE PROBLEM

For a long time the development software has been an art in hands of the improvisation of the project managers. These projects were carried out taking in account the technical considerations, leaving on a second plane the considerations that had to do with the administration. These administration activities (estimation and planning), were sometimes considered, at the beginning of the project, as a protocol act; with few hopes that they were fulfilled. For project development, the estimation, planning, follow-up and control were carried out without a minimum rigor, most of it was blindly left to the full trust on the intuition and the project managers's experience. Through the techniques that we expose in the present work, these activities will now have a technological support, since we will apply the above mentioned techniques.

When the projects were of medium complexity and you could take advantage of the market fever, the enormous deviations in cost and time with regard to initial estimates were considered as something worthless to avoid in a software project.

All software development projects assumed the fact that final cost and timing of delivering the final product were something difficult to compromise.

Projects were more and more complex when the power of the hardware increased and it lowered its cost This caused that the price of the software began to be important in the total cost For these reasons they need more reliable estimates and planning

Putnam (Putnam 1996) defined the estimate of software development like the activity that responds to the questions: how much will it cost? and how long will it be?. Therefore the estimate in software projects consists on predicting the time of the project and the cost that the project will have when it finish.

3. SOLUTION. APPLICATION OF THE CONSTRAINS PROGRAMMING TO THE DYNAMIC SYSTEM OF ABDEL-HAMMID. SUBSYSTEM OF HUMAN RESOURCES. QUALITATIVE MODEL IN ORDERS OF ABSOLUTE MAGNITUDE

To solve the outlined problem we will treat the subsystem of human resources of the dynamic system of Abdel - Hamid (Abdel 1991) as a constrains programming problem. We will make a treatment to the system in a qualitative way to obtain qualitative information of the variables of state of the system.

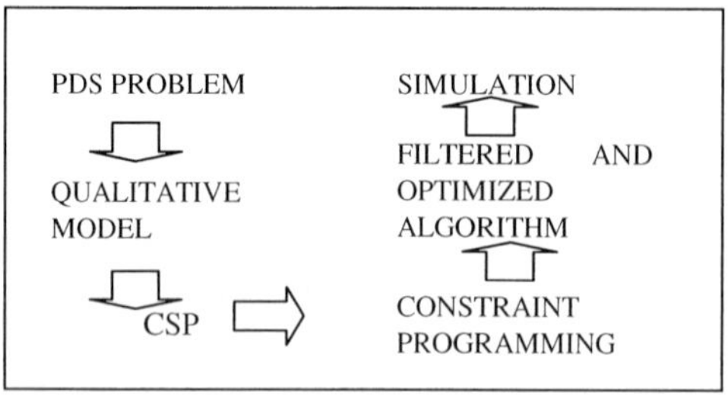

3.1 System equations

The equations that serve as base are obtained starting from the Forrester diagram of the Abdel-Hamid model (Abdel, 1991)

```
Celnwh = ftexwf * mnhpxs
Celtwf = wfexp + celnwh
Wfgap = wfs – totwf
Ftna = - wfgap
Fc = wfgap
Fea = -wfgap and do not exist wfnew
Wfnew = wfnew + fc – fatnp – ftna
Wfexp = wfexp + fatn – fea –frte
Totwf = wfexp + wfnew
```

In this group of equations we can distinguish 3 different types of variables:

- ✓ State Variables. For our case, they will be named as wfexp and wfnew. These variables are those that interest us in the study of our system. The result of our actions will rebound in this variables.
- ✓ Flow Variables. They will determine the variations in the state variables. They represent the actions taken in the system. In our case they will be named as: ht, etr, etl, cta and ctl
- ✓ Auxiliary Variables. They will be the rest of variables of the system. They are used to calculate the flow and state variables. Some of them will come imposed initially and other they are calculated starting from these variables .

Besides of the information in form of equations that we can obtain of the Forrester diagram of the Abdel-Hamid model, an additional knowledge exists on this model (Abdel 1991) necessary to incorporate. We will consider this group of basic equations and the rest of conditions as a constraint satisfaction problem.

The resulting equations will be the following ones:

```
totwf = wfnew + wfexp
ftexwf = wfexp @ admpps
celnwh = ftexwf @ mnhpxs
celtwf = wfexp + celnwh
wfs = min(celtwf,wfneed)
wfgap = wfs - totwf
wfnew~ = wfnew + ht~ - cta~ - ctl~
IF wfgap<=0 THEN ht~ = 0
IF wfgap>0 THEN ht~ = wfgap @ rs~
IF wfgap>=0 THEN cta~ = wfnew @ asntp~
IF wfgap<0 THEN cta~ =(wfnew – ctl~) @ asntp~
IF wfgap>=0 THEN ctl~ = 0
IF wfgap<0 THEN ctl~ = min(|wfgap|,wfnew) @ asct~
wfexp~ = wfexp + cta~ - etr~ - etl~
etr~ = wfexp @ rset~
IF wfgap>=0 OR |wfgap| <= wfnew THEN etl~ = 0
IF wfgap <0 AND |wfgap| > wfnew AND |wfgap| -wfnew
   >= wfexp – etr~ THEN etl~ = wfexp @ aset~
IF wfgap <0 AND |wfgap| > wfnew AND |wfgap| -wfnew
   < wfexp – etr~ THEN etl~ = (|wfgap| - wfnew) @
   aset~
```

As we can see now, the flow variables, that are those that modify the state variables, don't belong together with the defined ones in the original equations. This has been made this way to be able to introduce the conditions required for the calculation of these variables. The new flow variables will be here named as ht, cta, ctl, etr and etl. These variables will contain the number of technicians that modify the state variable values wfexp and wfnew.

The flow new variables depend of others that indicate the *speed of change* of flow variables.

The *speed of change* indicates the speed with which the technicians are incorporate to the project or they abandon the project. These variables of *speed of change* will be called here: rset, asntp, rs, asct and aset. When we calculate the flow variables to modify the state variables we will keep in mind that speed.

We have implemented a new operator, here called *adapts* (represented for @), With it we can to be able to generate concrete values starting from speed change values. *adapt* takes two operands. The first one will be the variable on which it is necessary to act and the second will be the change speed for this variable. This way *adapt* generates a new flow value for the following time step depending of the change speed of the second operand.

Next we will shortly describe the meaning of each one of the variables of the model.

State Variables

wfexp Experienced WorkForce. It indicates the number of experienced technicians, that there are in the project for each time step. In the initial instant this variable should have a value, because we need to know the number of experienced technicians assigned to the project in a first moment.

wfnew Newly Hired Workforce. It indicates the number of callow technicians involved in the project. In the initial instant this variable should have a value, because we need to know the number of callow technicians assigned to the project at the beginning

Flow variables

ht Hired technicians. They will be the number of new technicians that are hired when we need workforce.

etr Experienced technicians that rotate. They are the technicians that are assigned to other projects.

etl Experienced technicians that abandon the project. It will be the number of experienced technicians that should abandon the project. It is not eliminated of the project any experienced technician if there are callow technicians that can be eliminated.

cta Callow technicians that are adapted. They will be the callow technicians that after a time in the project will be considered experienced technicians.

ctl Callow technicians that abandon the project. They will be the number of callow technicians that abandon the project when in the project there are a number of technicians greater than we need.

Auxiliary variables

wfneed Workforce level needed. It comes of another subsystem. It is incorporate to the model in each time step. It provides information of the technicians that we need in that moment for diverse reasons.

mnhpxs Most new hires per full time expert staff. It depends of the number of callow technicians that the experienced technicians can train It will stay stable along of the project lifetime

admpps Average Daily MP per staff. In all organization the norm is that the technicians don't have exclusive dedication to a project. They will have to dedicate part of his time to training, to another projects or to other tasks not related with the project.

rset Rotation Speed of experienced technicians. It indicates the speed to which the experienced technicians change of project.

asntp Adaptation Speed of new technicians to the project. It indicates the speed with which the callow technicians become experienced technicians

rs Recruiting speed. It indicates the velocity with which the technicians are hired. Bureaucratic problems cause that the incorporation of new technicians is never immediate. It will depend on each organization

asct Abandon Speed of the callow technicians. It will indicate the speed with which the callow technicians will abandon the project.

aset Abandon Speed of the experienced technicians. This parameter will indicate us the speed with which the experienced technicians will abandon the project If all the callow technicians have abandoned the project or if none exists is necessary to reduce experienced technicians.

ftexwf Full Time Equivalent Experienced Workforce. Technicians don't usually have total dedication for different causes. This variable contains the equivalent full time technicians with the current technicians dedication.

celnwh Ceiling on new hires. It will be the maximum number of callow technicians that we can incorporate to the project. It will depend on the maximum limit that the experienced technicians can train.

celtwf Ceiling on Total Workforce. This variable indicates us the maximum number of technicians in the project. It is calculated as the addition of the experienced technicians and the maximum number of technicians to hire.

wfs Workforce level sowght. It is calculated as the minimum of the maximum number of technicians in the project and the number of necessary technicians. Although we need more technicians, we cannot have more technicians than the possible ones.

wfgap Workforce gap. If it is positive we will incorporate technicians to the project, otherwise we should fire to them totwf Total Workforce. It contains the addition of the state variables wfexp and wfnew

3.2 Qualitative values election

The information that we have of the system is insufficient and quite ambiguous most of the times. In those cases a quantitative treatment of the system is not possible. With the same information, we can achieve a qualitative treatment in most of the cases.

We need a correspondence of natural values with qualitative values to treat the system in a qualitative way. This causes a necessary division of the natural numbers. To carry out this division we won't select a fixed value in the natural numbers. We will simply choose qualitative values and to impose them an order relation. This way any expert will have an idea of what are each one of the qualitative labels for him, without necessity of providing a concrete value for each one of them. A complete study on the treatment in absolute magnitude order can be found in (Agell 1998).

It is necessary to assign a correspondence of magnitude among the qualitative labels if we don't want to associate quantitative values to the qualitative labels. The qualitative operators need to know those magnitudes for generating the possible operation results

Decisions taken when selecting the order and magnitudes of the qualitative labels are the following ones:

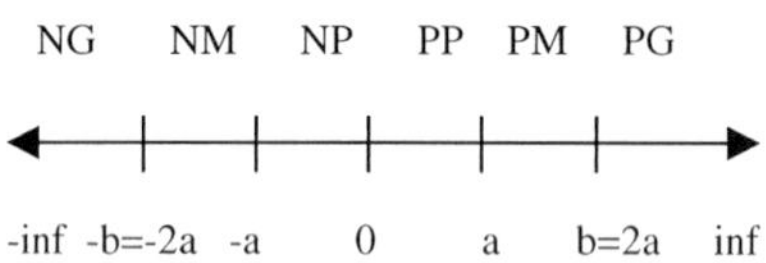

As we can see in this situation, we have chosen a symmetrical partition of the natural numbers. The labels PP, PM, NP, NM take values inside the intervals corresponding to the same magnitude. The labels PG and NG take values in open intervals at right and left respectively.

3.3 Qualitative operators

We need to define the operators of the restrictions in a qualitative way because the values of the operands are qualitative also.

The result of the qualitative operations depends of the intervals that we have defined and of the proportions of these intervals in connection with the other ones.

For the qualitative values that have been chosen the definition of qualitative operators will be:

Sum							
	NA	**NM**	**NB**	**0**	**PB**	**PM**	**PG**
NA	NA	NA	NA	NA	NM NA	-	?
NM	NA	NA	NM NA	NM	NB NM	0 PB NB	+
NB	NA	NM N A	NBN M	NB	NB 0 PB	PB PM	PG PM
0	NA	NM	NB	0	PB	M	PG
PB	NM NA	NB NM	NB 0 PB	PB	PB PM	PM PG	PG
PM	-	NB 0 PB	PB PM	PM	PM PG	PG	PG
PG	?	PB PM PG	PM PG	PG	PG	PG	PG

Substraction							
	NA	**NM**	**NB**	**0**	**PB**	**PM**	**PG**
NA	?	-	NM NA	NA	NA	NA	NA
NM	+	NB 0 PB	NB NM	NM	NM NA	NA	NA
NB	PM PG	PB PM	NB 0 PB	NB	NB NM	NM NA	NA
0	PG	PM	PB	0	NB	NM	NA
PB	PG	PM PG	PB PM	PB	NB 0 PB	NM NB	NM NA
PM	PG	PG	PM PG	PM	PB PM	NB 0 PB	-
PG	PG	PG	PG	PG	PM PG	+	?

Adapts				
	0	**PB**	**PM**	**PG**
0	0	0	0	0
PB	0	PB	PB	PB
PM	0	PB	PB PM	PM
PG	0	PM	PM PG	PG

In the operator *adapts* the rows characterize the variables for *adapt* and the columns characterize the *speed of change* of these variables. We consider for selecting those return values that the *adapts* operator behaves, in a heuristic way, the following performance form:

$$\text{Adapts}(V_i, F_i) = \begin{cases} 1/5 * V_i \text{ for Vi = PP} \\ 1/2 * V_i \text{ for Vi = PM} \\ 1 * V_i \text{ for Vi = PM} \end{cases}$$

3.4 Model operating

We consider a new time step when the values of the state variables change.

For each time step, we need provide the value of the workforce level needed (*wfneed*) because this variable is generated in another subsystem that is not treat here.

We begin with a series of well-known values of certain variables. We consider these variables as initial parameters of the system. The values of initial parameters will stay constant for all remaining time. Values of the rest of variables, in the initial moment, are calculated for satisfying the defined constraint for that time step.

The values of the variable *totwf*, for each time step, is the addition of the two state variables values in that time step.

The difference among the variable workforce level sought (*wfs*) and the variable total workforce (*totwf*) indicates us the necessity of incorporating technicians or firing technicians for the project. If the variable *wfs* is greater than the variable *totwf* we will need to incorporate technicians to the project. If the variable *totwf* is greater than the variable *wfs* we will need to fire technicians from the project. Thus, we can know the difference in the number of technicians.

This will cause a modification in the values of the state variables, what takes us to the following time step. For generating the new value of state variables we need to calculate the values of de flow variables previously. The values of the flow variables depends of the numbers of technicians that we need hire or that we need fire and of the value of the *speed of change* variables for these. Operator *adapts* returns the values of the flow variables according these two operands. With the new values of the state variables we calculate the values of rest variables. These new variables take the values that complete the imposed restrictions. This way we will have the values of all the variables of the model for that time step. We repeat this process to calculate the following time steps again.

We introduce the value of the variable *wfneed* in each new time step. Value for this variable should have been generated in another subsystem.

To represent this performance form we need that each variable of the system have been implemented as a values vector. The index of the vector indicates the time step for each variables. This way the position 0 of the vector of a variable indicates their value in the initial moment, and the position n, their value in the time step n.

4. RESULTS

The constraints have been programmed using the constraint programming tool ILOGSolver 4.4, on a programming language C++. The whole development has been carried out on a Intel Pentium III computer with 64 Mb of RAM memory.

Depending on the initial parameters values and the number of simulation time steps the results can be obtained in a margin between 1 and 3 minutes. This time of simulation allows us to prove multiple performance possibilities.

To see like the model runs we will give an example.

The initial parameters for the example will be:

Variable	Value	Variable	Value
wfnew	PG	Wfexp	PG
asntp	PG	Rset	PG
mnhpxs	PG	Wfnew	PCERO
aset	PG	Asntp	PG
admpps	PG	Rs	PG

Values of the variable *wfneed* are in this example:
For the time step 0: wfneed = PG
For the time step 1: wfneed = PM
For the time step 2: wfneed = PB
For the time step 3: wfneed = PCERO

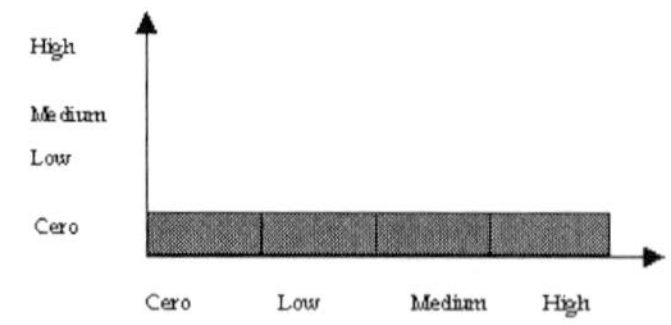

Instant 1

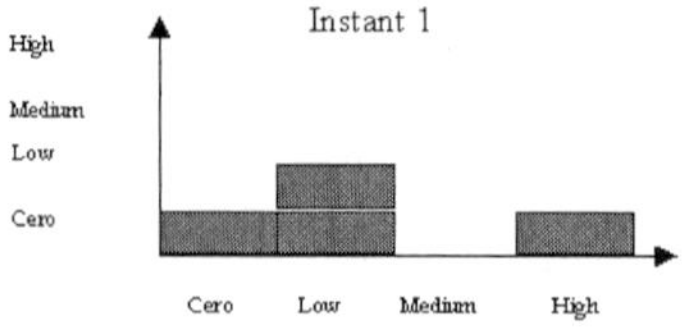

Instant 2

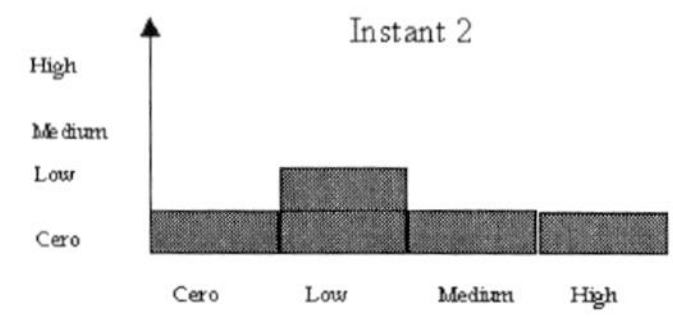

Instant 3

The behaviour of the model is represented like a chart. We will use a chart for each moment. The axis x represent the experienced technicians. The axis y represent the callow technicians

5. CONCLUSIONS AND FURTHER WORKS

With this model we can have a complete qualitative solution, for a software development project dynamic simulation, in the field of human resources administration. Because of the width of qualitative operators and the necessity for the model to be complete, the number of variable values might become too wide. This causes that many of the generated solutions don't belong the real behavior, non valid.. On the other hand, in the group of solutions obtained, we are sure that all the valid solutions are present. The group of non valid solutions can be filtered with the apropiates techniques; but that task escapes from the scope of this paper and they are being analyized for future works.

One of the main advantages that provide the qualitative simulation is that we don't need to know the values of the variables previously, but expert's orientations are enough to make a simulation. On the other hand, this shows us to that the qualitative results are sometimes a bit imprecise, although it offers us a clear idea of the possible behaviors

With this work we just try to show the idea of something that aims to be a wider work. This work will gather not only qualitative information but also available quantitative information. In that way, mixing the available quantitative information with the qualitative information for those variables of that don't have another information, we will have a semi-qualitative model that should be more powerfull and accurate in the results.

On the other hand, the problem estimation of the Software Development Project will include the complete Abdel-Hamid model (Abdel, 1991), not only in the human resources subsystem, but in all the factors playing in a SDP.

ACKNOWLEGMENTS

This work have been partiality financed by the Comisión Interministerial de Ciencia y Tecnología (DPI2000-0666-C02-02) y and the Modelización Matemática Redes y Multimedia investigation group of the University of Huelva.

REFERENCES

Abdel-Hamid T., Madnick, 1991,"Software Proyect Dynamics: an integrated approach"

Putnan L. H., Myers W,1996; "Executive Briefing. Controlling Software Development". IEEE Computer Society Press

Benjamin Kuipers,1994, "Qualitative Reasoning."

Agell Jané, N,1998, "Estructures matematiques per al model cualitatiu D'ordres de magnitud absoluts.

Aracil, J.,1986 "Introducción a la Dinámica de Sistemas"

Ortega Ramírez, J.,2000, "Patrones de comportamiento temporal en modelos semicualitativos con restricciones"

Clancy D., Kuipers B.,1998, "Qualitative simulation as a temporally extended constraint satisfaction problem"

Clancy D., Kuipers B.,1999, "Divide and Conquer: A component based qualitative simulation algorithm"

Coghill, G, Chantler M.,1999, Constructive and Non-constructive Asynchronous Qualitative Simulation"

Ramos Román, I.,1998, "Un Nuevo Enfoque en la Gestión de Proyectos de Desarrollo de Software"

TOWARDS SCALABLE MULTI-AGENT SYSTEMS

Ralph Deters
Depart of Computer Scienc , Campus Dr. 57, Saskatoon, Canada
Email: deters@cs.usask.ca

Keywords: Distributed Multi-Agent System, Scalability, JESS.

Abstract: The multi-agent research community is currently faced with a paradox. While promoting the use of agents as the silver bullet for various software engineering problems, it faces difficulties in presenting successful deployments. Despite the countless multi-agent prototypes that have been developed, the number of actually deployed and in use MAS is at best very small (Gasser 2000). And as long as multi-agent frameworks continue to encounter difficulties in scaling up, it seems unlikely that this will change. This paper has two aims. First, it is an attempt to relate the scalability problem of multi-agent systems with that of executing large numbers of concurrent threads. Second, it evaluates a CORBA/Java middle-ware layer for transparent access to distributed resources. Using such a layer, it is possible, to build multi-agent systems that require large numbers of concurrent threads and significant memory resources.

1. INTRODUCTION

Scalability is an important issue in the successful deployment of modern software artefacts, since performance requirements can change over time. Therefore, it is often expected that the software can be scaled up or down to ensure the desired performance at minimal costs. But unlike mainstream computer science, where scalability is a central design issue, the multi-agent research community is just beginning to realize its importance (Gasser 2000). With the growing interest in *deploying* multi-agent systems, scalability is becoming an issue in multi-agent research.

The focus of this paper is the design and the current experiences in using a thin CORBA/Java based middle-ware layer, which supports the distribution of agents (threads and objects) over multiple machines. By dividing the resources of multiple physical machines into atomic cells (agent runtime environments) with well defined processor, memory and communication resources it becomes fairly easy to distribute the load. The described middle-layer is part of a currently in use agent based help system (I-Help Vassileva 1999), which consists of over 500 agents, each representing a concurrent thread of execution.

This paper starts with a discussion about scalability and multi-agent systems followed by a comparison of different approaches for achieving scalability. Then the concept of using atomic agent runtime environments (called cells) as a means for ensuring scalable agent host is presented. This is followed by a presentation of the proposed agent-framework architecture and its empirical evolution.

2. SCALABILITY

2.1 Defining Scalability

Weak Scalability

"It is the ability of a computer application or product (hardware or software) to continue to function well as it (or its context) is changed in size or volume in order to meet a user need. Typically, the rescaling is to a larger size or volume. The rescaling can be of the product itself (for example, a line of computer systems of different sizes in terms of storage, RAM, and so forth) or in the scalable object's movement to a new context (for example, a new operating system)" (Scalability 2001).

Strong Scalability

"It is the ability not only to function well in the rescaled situation, but also to actually take full advantage of it. For example, an application program would be scalable if it could be moved from a smaller to a larger operating system and take full advantage of the larger operating system in terms of performance (user response time and so forth) and the larger number of users that could be handled" (Scalability 2001).

J. Filipe et al. (eds.), Enterprise Information Systems III, 161–168.

2.2 Scale-Up & Scale-Down

Scaling can be performed either up or down. A program is considered able to scale up, if the adding of certain resources (e.g. memory, processor) will lead to an increase in performance. While scaling up is the most dominant form of scalability, it is important to realize that systems can also scale down. A program can be considered able to scale down if it is possible to remove/reduce the access of certain resources (e.g. less memory, slower processor). Especially with the rise of small and/or mobile computing devices the problem often arises if and how software can be scaled down to run in a more resource-constrained environment.

2.3 Types of Scalability

It seems useful to distinguish between systems that can dynamically adjust at runtime and those that require restarting or even recompiling. Systems that can adjust at runtime have *total dynamic scalability*, ones that require restarting have only *partial dynamic scalability* and those that require recompiling have *static scalability*. From the viewpoint of a multi-agent system developer, total dynamic scalability is of the greatest practical importance, since the load in a MAS is constantly changing.

2.4 Metrics

In this paper, the scalability of the system will be viewed as the ratio between performance and resources. Performance will be measured in completed tasks. If two systems, A and B, are to be compared, A will have a better performance than B, if it either completes more tasks in the same time or completes the same amount of tasks in less time. As the available resources increase, the performance should increase. This rather crude formula ignores many important aspects, like quality of service, but offers the advantage of simplicity. Whenever scalability is measured, typically three types are identified, super-linear, linear (strong scalability) and sub-linear (week scalability). Since super-linear is very rare and sub-linear is of limited practical importance, this paper will limit the discussion to linear scalability.

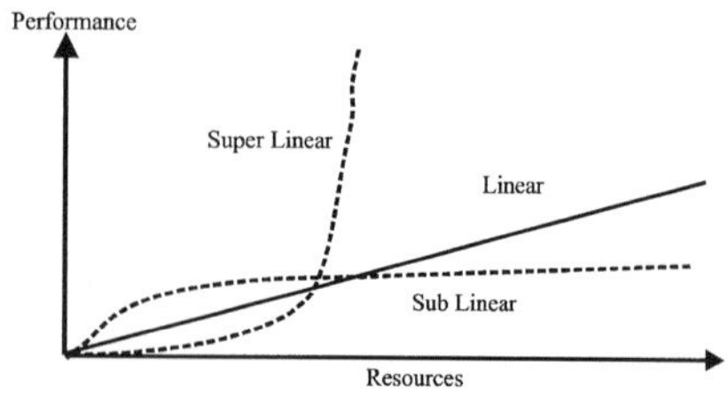

Figure 1: Types of Scalability

3. MULTI-AGENT SYSTEMS & SCALABILITY

In the multi-agent system community there is no commonly shared interpretation of scalability. While scalability can refer to many different aspects like agent complexity or message volume, this paper focuses only on the following three aspects.

Number of Agents in the System/Host

How many proactive agents can be hosted in the multi-agent system and/or any agent host? How many concurrent threads can the multi-agent system manage?

Resource Consumption of Agents

What is the upper limit of resources an individual agent can acquire in a multi-agent system? How large (memory consumption) can the agents become?

Number of Messages

Is it possible to increase the number of messages and still ensure a fast and reliable message routing? What is the limit for the message routing and can it be distributed?

3.1 Factors that impact the Scalability

Two main factors can be identified, that impact the scalability of a multi-agent system: load and complexity. Even a medium sized multi-agent system with only a few hundred agents is already a significant workload, with a large memory footprint and high processor usage. But it is important to note, that the scalability problem of multi-agent systems is not only a question of computational resources - it is also one of software complexity. Fault management (Klein 1999, Kumar 2000) and consequently agent design patterns (Wooldrige 1997, Jennings 1995) are equally important problems that impact the maintainability. While solving the resource problems is crucial for building a larger multi-agent system it seems clear, that without fault management and design patterns these systems would not be maintainable/extendable.

3.2 Scalability Enhancing Techniques

While many different types of multi-agent scalability exist (e.g. number of messages, complexity of agents) increasing the number of agents is by far the most important one. When dealing with large numbers of agents, it is important to distinguish between reactive and proactive agents. A reactive agent will only be executed if it receives a message (and consume processor time only if it computes a response). Therefore increasing the numbers of reactive agents is predominantly a memory (agent storage) problem. Consequently, large multi-agent systems consisting of reactive agents focus on techniques to minimize the amount of agents in the memory. Idle agents are paged out (serialized to file) and agents that received a message are paged in (de-serialized from file). The work of (Yamamoto 2000) demonstrates in an impressive way, that this simple approach can enable the hosting of several hundred thousand agents. The number of agents is therefore limited only by the storage capacity of the used secondary storage devices e.g. hard disk. Unfortunately, purely reactive agents are somewhat less interesting than proactive agents. Unlike their reactive counterparts, proactive agents don't need messages to start actions, they can initiate themselves complex tasks like the discovery of new services. As a result, a system consisting of proactive agents seems more lively and adaptive, making it a more attractive for researchers. But this agility of the proactive agents comes at the price of continuous execution. Each proactive agent is an object with one or more threads of control. Increasing the number of proactive agents leads to an increase in concurrent threads that sooner or later exceeds the possibilities of a single machine. Unlike a multi-agent system using reactive agents, it is not memory but processor power that limits the growth. It comes as no surprise that the distribution of processor load is a central issue in the development of multi-agent systems using proactive agents.

While there are great differences in the various multi-agent frameworks, they typically all consist of an agent-host that offers memory and thread management, as well as some basic message communication mechanism. In addition, there are services like white pages (agent registry) and yellow pages (service registry). To enable the hosting of more agents various approaches are possible.

The most common strategy has been the replication of the multi-agent system as shown in figure 3.

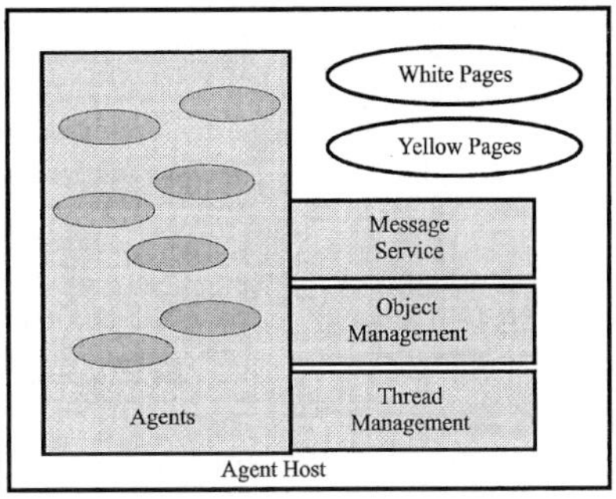

Figure 2: Standard MAS Framework

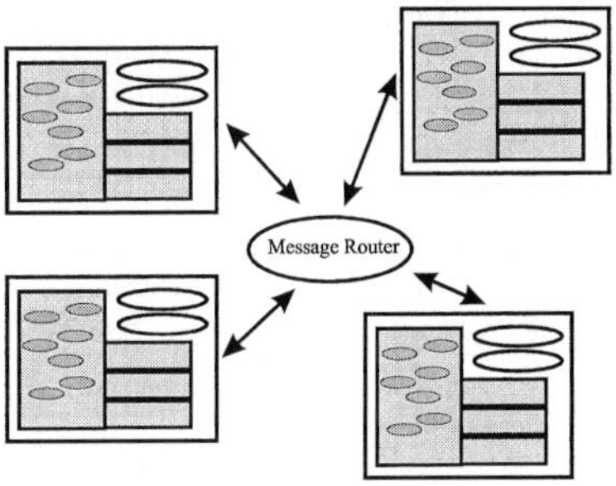

Figure 3: Replicating the MAS Framework

Replicating the agent framework on different machines and providing a message router to connect the different replicates creates uniform architectures. Often the agents in such environments are mobile and can hop from machine to machine in the quest for resources and optimal load balancing. The Hive (Maes 2000) and Agora (Matskin 2000) are recent examples of this approach. While being fairly straightforward to build and deploy, the major drawback of this approach is the waste of resources since services are often unnecessarily duplicated. To avoid this, researchers often begin to distribute the agent frameworks (fig. 4). By hosting the different components on different physical machines each component has more resources available and the framework can scale up. When using a CORBA-ORB (CORBA 2001) as a means for inter-process communication, (to glue the different components together) this approach comes at a minimal overhead.

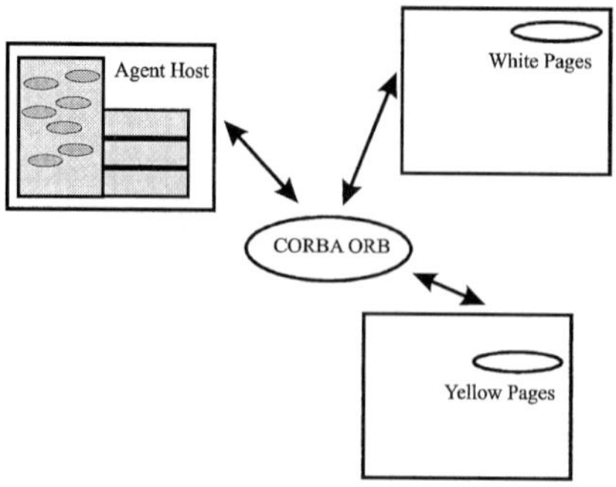

Figure 4: Distributing the MAS Framework

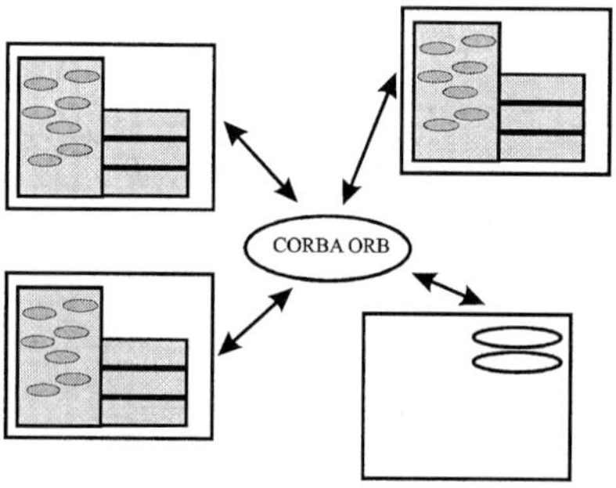

Figure 5: Selective Replication

The FIPA-OS, which consists of several processes, can be easily distributed in this way over several machines since its inter-process communication (IPC) relies on IIOP (CORBA 2001). The main disadvantage of component distribution is the inability to scale components beyond the limits of one physical machine. As an alternative, selective component replication is used (fig. 5). Instead of distributing all the components of an agent framework over many machines, many agent hosts are used. The "federation" of services in FIPA-OS can be seen as an attempt into this direction. By replicating multiple agent hosts and sharing some services the replication costs can be minimized.

The inflation of agent hosts enables the developer to increase the number of agents, but comes at the price of high resource consumption since several host specific services e.g. messaging have to be replicated. As a result the utilization of CPU for agent execution is small. To ensure that the available resources are not wasted for unwanted replication of services, this paper proposes the use of a middle-ware layer that ensures transparent access to resources of multiple physical machines. Using such a transparent access layer, which enables uniform access to resources from different machines, encapsulates the details of location and consequently enables a single agent host to handle large agent societies.

4. THE NEED FOR TRANSPARENT ACCESS

All three mentioned approaches enhance the scalability of a multi-agent system, but fall short of providing a possibility to enable components to scale beyond the limitations of their underlying physical machines. To ensure that all components of the multi-agent system can scale, it is important to ensure that the resources of several physical machines can be accessed by its components. Only if the components themselves, most notably the agent host, have *transparent* access to the distributed resources scalability can be achieved. Ensuring that this access is transparent helps in avoiding additional complexity within the components. Access to resources is transparent, if it hides details like resource location from the requesting component ensuring a simple access and the flexibility to add or remove resource providers without the resource requestors knowing. But what are the resources that are most likely needed by a host? They are threads (processor) and objects (memory). Therefore the transparent resource management layer needs to be able to use/create threads and objects within other processes. As shown in figure 6, a physical machine is viewed as a collection of atomic cells, each representing a container for one object to which one thread of control is associated. The cells are effectively containers for the agents.

The main advantage of using the cells is that machines with different capabilities can be viewed as machines with more or less cells. This uniformity allows for the simplicity and efficiency in accessing the resources of different machines. To be able to view a machine as a collection of cells it is necessary to have at least one process running on the machine. This so-called provider process will create the cells and offer them to the transparent access layer. Provider processes can create all cells in an initialization phase. But it is also possible to dynamically create and destroy cells to adjust to the requests from the transparent access layer. The transparent access layer allows a host to farm out the execution of agents. Only by distributing the load it becomes possible to ensure that a large number of agents reside in a single agent host. Besides being a means to access resources of different machines, cells are also a useful concept ensuring security and safety. The cells are designed to protect the agent from hostile events and to ensure that the agent can access directly system resources. Each cell consists of two containers, one for an agent and one for an environment object.

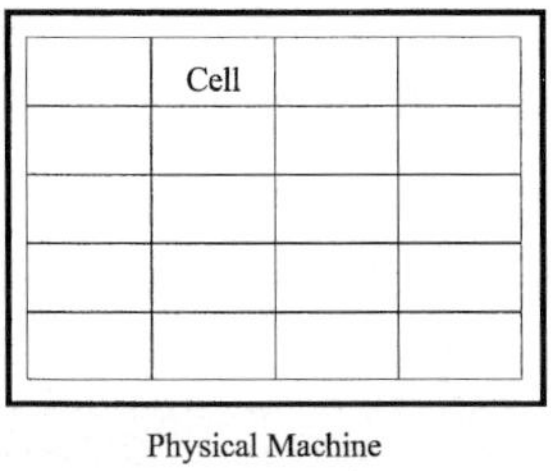

Figure 6: Machine = Array of Cells

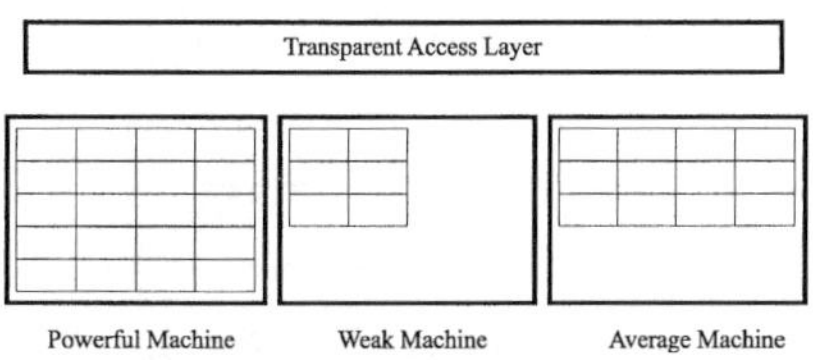

Figure 7: Different Machines = Different Arrays

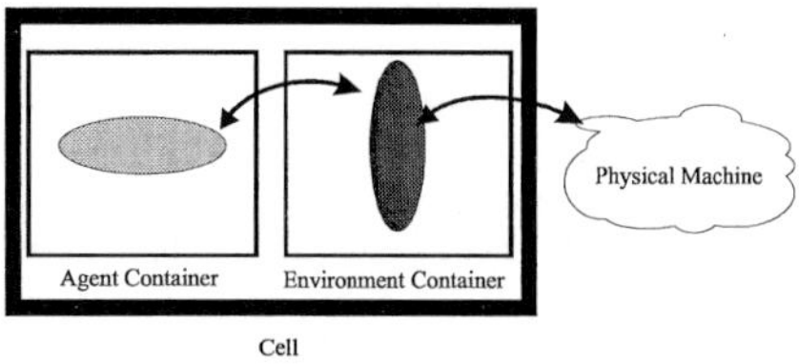

Figure 8: Cell = Agent Sandbox

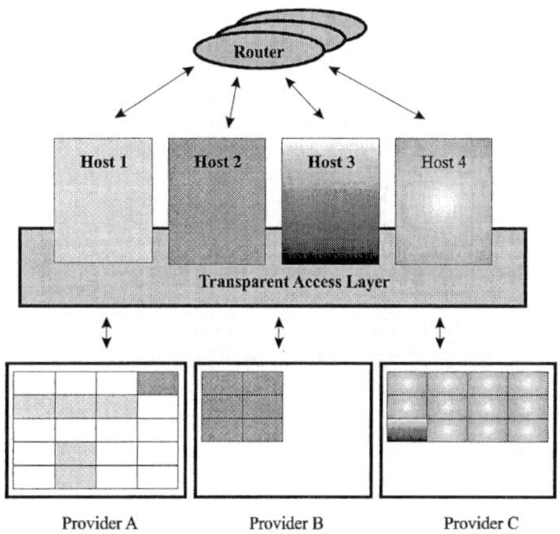

Figure 9: The DICE System

Since the agent is prohibited to directly access any system resources or services it has to use the environment object as a proxy. Only via the environment object the agent is able to send messages or use standard services like the registries. The environment object can therefore be best described as interface that keeps the implementation of its the public methods hidden. The environment object contains a hash-table that can be modified by the higher management functions to allow more or less access or to create a different perception of the system.

By forcing the agent to channel every interaction through the environment object two goals are achieved, *fine-grained control* and *location independence*. Fine-grained control enables the system to completely disconnect troublesome agents or to redistribute sparse resources to agents performing vital services. The environment object also allows for the physical location independence of the agent

The agent interacts with the system only via the proxy and is kept unaware of location details. This allows the system to freely move agents between processes by moving their cells. In addition cells can be linked to any agent host by having the environment object returning references to the services of the same agent host.

5. IMPLEMENTATION

The agent framework is implemented in Java using JDK1.3 and uses the standard Java CORBA tools of that version. Providers, Hosts, Routers are all designed as different processes that communicate via an object request broker, which can be different for every process. Using IIOP a simple cross ORB communication is enabled. The source code for DICE (including the code generated from the IDL) is about 490 KB. The code is available upon request from the author.

6. EVALUATION

The empirical evaluation was performed to answer the three questions.

Can the multi-agent system handle 1000 or more agents?

What is the average response time to incoming messages?

Can provider processes be added or removed during runtime?

6.1 Configuration

The system is implemented in Java jdk1.3 and uses the jdk1.3 CORBA tools to provide IPC. The configuration used in the evaluation consisted of using 10 Sun Ultra 5 machines (128 MB, 64-bit ULTRASPARC IIi 333 MHz), one Sun Ultra II (1 GB, 4 x 64-bit ULTRASPARC II 400 MHz) and one NT Workstation (64 MB, P1, 200 MHz). The 10 Ultra 5 were hosting each a provider process, which contained 100 cells and used 20 native threads to executed them. The Sun Ultra II hosted the ORB, the agent host process and the router process.

Each provider process was configured to create 100 cells and use 20 threads to execute the contained agents in a round robin approach.

6.2 Test Conditions

The experiments were conducted over a period of low machine usage by other users. As a result the observed performance measurements are conservative.

6.3 A few Experiments

Two types of experiments were conducted. The first four experiments were aimed at investigating the behaviour of the system under increasing agent loads. To measure the impact of larger numbers on hosts and agents, up-load time and average response time were measured. The fifth and sixth experiment were used to determine the effects of adding and removing resources at runtime.

6.3.1 Adding thousand Agents

To measure the impact of using a larger agent society on a host four different sets of agents were used. Each experiment uploaded 1000 agents and measured upload time and average response time to a message. Uploading refers to the creation of the agent in a launcher process, and the sending of the serialized agent to the host. The host de-serializes the agent and allocates a cell in which the agent will be placed. As the last step, the host registers the agent in its registry (white pages).

The first experiment (empty-load agents) involved 1000 *empty agents* that did nothing except checking for incoming messages. As soon as a message was detected, it was returned to the sender. These agents represented the simplest type of agents that are possible using the DICE framework and are useful as a reference point for the other experiments.

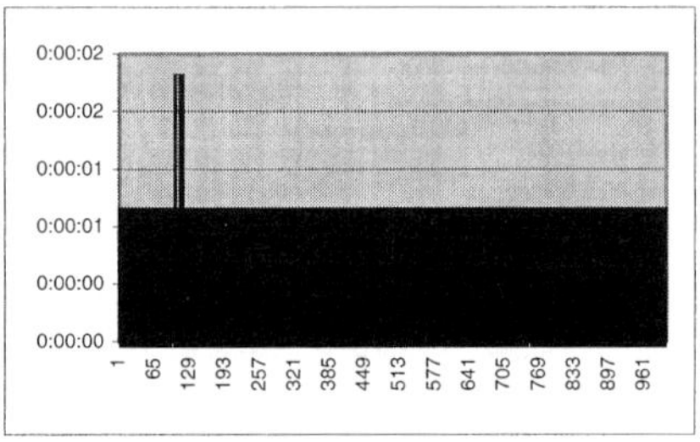

Figure 10: 1000 Empty-Load Agents

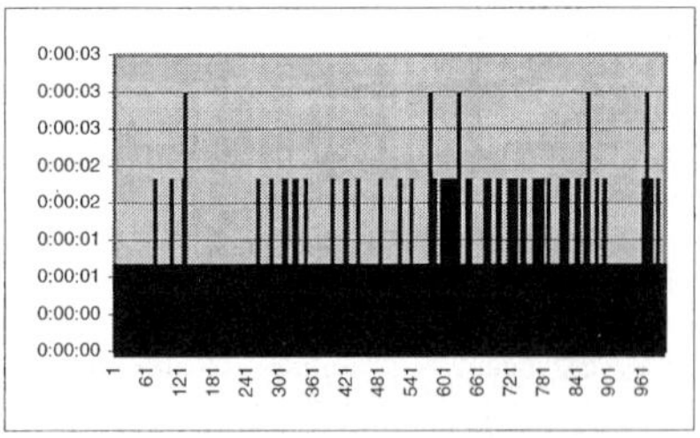

Figure 11: 1000 Mixed-Load Agents

The second experiment (mix-agent-load) was aimed at investigating the impact of more CPU costly agents. To simulate a vivid agent society with varying loads, every agent was now expected to first calculate a randomly selected Fibonacci number between 0 – 30 and then to check for incoming messages. Since the goal of calculating Fibonacci numbers was to simulate different loads, the inefficient recursive approach [fib(X) := fib(X-1) + fib(X-2)] was used. The response to an incoming message was to send it back to the sender. The second experiment was designed to represent a system consisting of simple agents that have varying loads over time.

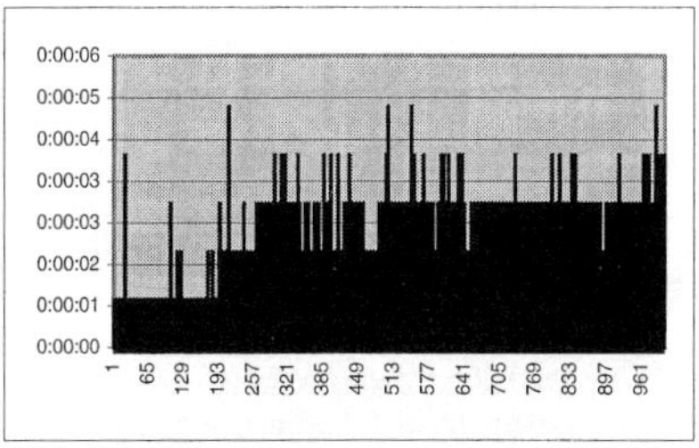

Figure 12: 1000 Heavy-Load Agents

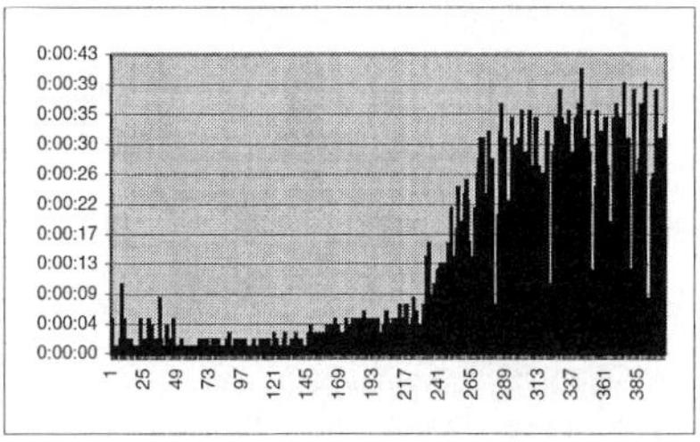

Figure 13: 400 JESS Agents

In the third experiment a heavy constant load for the system was simulated. The agents had to calculate the Fibonacci of 27 prior to responding to messages. While in principle any Fibonacci number could have been selected, 27 seemed a good choice given the available hardware. Figure 10 shows the result for uploading 1000 empty agents to a host. Besides a few unexplainable spikes the time consumption is constant. This graph indicates that the upload time is more or less constant. Each provider process needed about 27 % of its CPU for hosting the agents.

The results of figure 11 show that with agents that create a load (calculating a random Fibonacci sequence) more spikes appear. The average agent needed about 1.5 seconds to calculate the sequence making it a moderate load. Each provider process needed about 87 % of its CPU for hosting the agents. Figure 12 shows the result of uploading the heavy-load agents. Each agent calculated the Fibonacci sequence for 27, which took an individual agent in average more than 2 seconds. Each provider process needed about 96 % of its CPU for hosting the agents.

6.3.2 Sending 1000 Messages to 1000 Agents

After the uploading was completed, 10 processes on different hosts were used to send each 100 messages to each agent. The agents were randomly selected and received a message a time. Each agent provided a timestamp in the return message that allowed for calculating message response averages. Please note that only the time between sending the message and having the agent creating a response is measured.

The results were as follows:

No-Load agents:	average of 1 second
Mixed-Load agents:	average of 2.5 seconds
Heavy-Load agents:	average of 3 seconds

6.3.3 Using Jess in an Agent

After the promising results of uploading agents that were programmed using only Java, an experiment was conducted in measuring the impact of loading 400 agents that each contained the Jess rule interpreter. As seen fig 13, the load of only 400 Jess agents is already significant. As soon as they are up-loaded they begin to consume processor and memory space at a stunning rate. The average memory footprint for a provider hosting 100 jess agents is about 100 MB. Since only simple load-balancing was used, the more powerful machines are "filled up" first. The upload time is already initially significantly larger than for an average Java agent. A Java agent is anywhere between 400 and 800 bytes. The jess agent with only a few rules uses already around 10 K (4.5 KB for the serialized Rete engine alone). Since fewer agents were used the performance for responding to a message was keep to 2.5 seconds.

6.3.4 Adding & Removing Providers

The adding of providers has proven to be simple. Using a command-line Java program new providers can be added at any given moment in time. In the current phase of development the new providers are only used, when agents are uploaded or created. An automatic load-balancing is currently not in use. Removing a provider has to be announced to avoid loss of data. If the provider announces to the hosts that it will go offline, the hosts try to allocate from the other providers additional cells (to use as replacements). The time for moving from one provider to another is equivalent to the already presented up-load times. If a provider goes unexpectedly offline or attempts to allocate new cells from other providers fail, the agents hosted on the provider are lost.

7. DISCUSSION

The results for the first three experiments were more or less predictable. As the load of the individual agents increases, so does the load for the provider processes. That the adding of providers at runtime is without problems and that the removal of providers hosting agents is problematic in case that no notice is given or no alternative cells can be found, is more or less expectable. The interesting feature is that the number of physical machines can easily be scaled up. Other experiments used 32 different machines, 15 Sun workstations, and 17 NT boxes with 256 MB and Atholon 800 MHz. processors. While it was expected that agents using Jess rules to define their behavior were to consume more resources than purely Java coded ones, the number is still surprising. According to the measured results, machines with powerful processors and large memory are needed to run even average size agent communities. In addition, the sudden rise to an upload time of 35 seconds is not very encouraging form a developers perspective. An explanation for this surprisingly high time is the time consuming de-serialization of the Jess rule engine. Since it is only partially serializable the facts have to be saved prior to serialization in a string array and later re-entered into the de-serialized Rete object. As a result the moving of Jess rule engines is slow. Being able to still keep the message response time around 2.5 seconds is a very good achievement since this indicates that given enough "resources" Jess agents can be used in a real world application

8. CONCLUSION

Scalability is a central problem in the deployment of multi-agent systems. Among the many forms of scalability the increase in numbers of agents is the most important one. In this paper a multi-agent framework called DICE was presented that uses atomic agent runtime environments called cells as a means to distribute the load. Hosting the cells on different physical machines and ensuring a transparent access layer enables an agent-host to farm out the execution of agents to different machines thus allowing for easy up-scaling. The evaluation results show that this approach is well suited for handling large numbers of agents by automatically distributing the load.

9. CODE

The code for the DICE framework and the evaluation is available upon request from the author.

REFERENCES

CORBA (2001) http://www.corba.org

Gasser L. (2000) MAS Infrastructure Definitions, Needs And Prospects, in Proceedings of Workshop "Infrastructure for Scalable Multi-Agent Systems" at Agents 2000, Barcelona, 7 pages.

Jennings N., et al (1995) Developing Industrial Multi-Agent Systems, Proceedings of the First International Conference on Multi-Agent Systems ICMAS-95, San Francisco, 423-430.

Klein M.(1999) Exception Handling in Agent Systems, in Proceedings of Agents 99, Seattle, 62-69.

Kumar S., Cohen P.: Towards a Fault-Tolerant Multi-Agent System Architecture, Proceedings Autonomous Agents 2000, Barcelona, 459 –466.

Maes P. et al (2000) Hive: Distributed Agents for Networking Things, in IEEE Concurrency, April-June 2000, 24-33.

Matskin M, et al (2000) Agora: An Infrastructure for cooperative work support in multi-agent systems, in Proceedings of Workshop "Infrastructure for Scalable Multi-Agent Systems" at Agents 2000, Barcelona, 6 pages.

Scalability (2001) What Is Scalability? http://iroi.seu.edu.cn/books/whatis

Vassileva J., et al (1999) A Multi-Agent Approach to the Design of Peer-Help Environments, Proceedings of AIED'99, Le Mans, 1999, 38-45.

Wooldrige M. (1997) Agent-Based Software Engineering, IEEE Transactions on Software Engineering, 144 (1), 26-37.

Yamamoto G., Tai H. (2000) Architecture of an Agent Sever Capable of Hosting Tens of Thousands of Agents, Proceedings Autonomous Agents 2000, Barcelona, 70-71.

PART 3

Information Systems Analysis and Specification

DOMAIN ORIENTED FRAMEWORK CONSTRUCTION

Ivan Mathias Filho
Department of Computer Science, Pontifícia Universidade Católica do Rio de Janeiro, Rua Marquês de São Vicente 225, Rio de Janeiro, RJ, 22453-900, Brazil
Email: ivan@inf.puc-rio.br

Toacy Cavalcante de Oliveira
Department of Computer Science, Pontifícia Universidade Católica do Rio de Janeiro, Rua Marquês de São Vicente 225, Rio de Janeiro, RJ, 22453-900, Brazil
Email: toacy@inf.puc-rio.br

Carlos J. P. de Lucena
Department of Computer Science, Pontifícia Universidade Católica do Rio de Janeiro, Rua Marquês de São Vicente 225, Rio de Janeiro, RJ, 22453-900, Brazil
Email: lucena@inf.puc-rio.br

Keywords: Reuse, Framework, Domain Analysis, UML, XML, Object-Oriented

Abstract: Object-oriented Application Frameworks is a powerful reuse technique that allows the sharing of requirements, design and code among a set of application systems instantiated from an original framework. Nevertheless, little attention has been given to the role of an explicit Domain Analysis phase in the framework construction process. This paper describes an approach where the requirements capture for an entire application family takes a central role in the framework development, thus facilitating verification processes and providing reliable documentation that will assist the instantiation step.

1. INTRODUCTION

The software development process can be seen as a set of steps that produce models of a decreasing level of abstraction up to the code, its ultimate product. These different levels of abstraction bring out what we have called an inter-phase semantic gap, which makes the transition from one phase to the next more difficult. Moreover, in the early stages of development, knowledge is fragmented and incomplete so software engineers have to use a mix of free text and visual models to capture stakeholders' needs.

In the field of framework construction this problem is amplified because the requirements to be collected are not for one application but for an entire family of applications (Parnas, 1976). The design of a framework has to be flexible enough to generate instances, members of the family, in accordance with its own requirements, and to accommodate future needs.

This paper describes an approach that tries to minimize the semantic gap through a series of refinement steps. It begins by making a thorough domain analysis to determine the common and different aspects of an application family with the FODA Method (Kang, K.C. et al., 1993) and Use-cases (Jacobson, 1999), and proceeds in an iterative way until the framework design is accomplished. The framework design is then expressed in a precise notation that clearly separates the hot-spots from the frozen-spots (Pree, 1995).

The models produced during the full process are tied together through adoption of industry standard languages like UML and XMI, which are used as the basis of the representation of the diagrams involved. This common background representation will be of crucial importance for the construction of verification tools that will be used to maintain the consistency among the models and for documentation purposes.

Section 2 describes the approach overview. In Section 3 we describe how domain information is collected. In Section 4 the process for framework

J. Filipe et al. (eds.), Enterprise Information Systems III, 171–179.

construction is depicted. Section 5 reports on a Rental System development used as a case study. In the last section we present our conclusions and future directions.

2. THE APPROACH OVERVIEW

The usual approaches for framework construction do not give the proper support to the requirement elicitation phase of the development process. The consequences are the absence of mechanisms that allows the developers to identify the origins of the hot-spots and the frozen-spots of a framework, and the absence of tools for validation of a framework instance, regarding its set of functional requirements in relation to the set of functional requirements of the application family that originated the framework.

So, our approach begins with the Requirement Analysis Phase, where the functional and non-functional system requirements are collected to represent its main functionality (from the end user's point of view). After that the framework designer moves to the Design Phase to represent the functionality by using an object-oriented representation. In this phase the designer represents the main structures of the system and how they collaborate to achieve the system functionality. Usually, the designer goes back to the first phase to begin another development cycle and to reach the desired level of application representation (Figure 1).

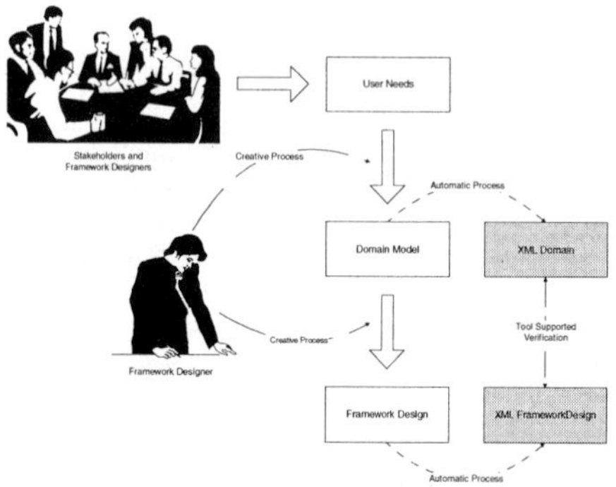

Figure 1: The approach overview

To represent the framework design, we have chosen the Feature Oriented Domain Analysis Method, FODA, in combination with The Unified Modeling Language, UML, to achieve a more precise representation of the framework semantics and provide compatibility with market standards. Since our approach combines O.O. designs, we are particularly interested in the class diagrams and how to obtain them. Naturally, class diagrams are a structural refinement of domain designs that in our approach are obtained by combining an initial conceptual model, Features Diagrams, and Use-cases in a guided way, to provide traceability. The next step is to represent the dynamic aspects of a domain. This will be done by constructing a set of collaborations that realize the domain use-cases, assigning responsibilities to the classes of the domain. The problem now is to obtain a representation of those diagrams that can be manipulated by programs. This can be achieved through the use of a XML representation called XMI. XMI is an acronym for XML Metamodel Interchange, which is an attempt of the OMG/W3C organizations to provide a platform-independent representation of UML designs. In order to do this, they propose a complete representation of UML using the XML format that can be shared among software vendors. The XMI representation of a design can be achieved using case tools like Argo/UML or using the IBM XMI toolkit converter for Rational Rose.

An important point in our approach refers to the initial design boundary. To obtain a high level of reuse we propose that the designer initially should specify the core functionality and structure of his application using Domain Engineering techniques such as Domain Analysis (Prieto-Díaz, 1993) and Domain Design (Arango, 1993). With this approach we tend to isolate the application domain design from the techniques used for framework instantiation, such as inheritance, parameterization and design patterns.

3. OBTAINING DOMAIN INFORMATION

3.1 Domain Analysis

The growing demand for more efficient, cheaper and delivered-on-schedule software systems suggests that software development needs to take place in an environment that allows proven solutions to be modified, combined and adapted for use in new software construction projects (Prieto-Díaz, 1993).

One of the answers provided by Software Engineering to this question can be found in the field of Domain Analysis, which can be defined as the study and organization of the common aspects and variations that exist among various software systems of an application domain. This process will provide a set of models that describe the applications of a domain in a generic fashion, besides the strategies used to construct new software systems from the generic artifacts that are produced.

3.2 The FODA Method

During the late 1980s and early 1990s the Software Engineering community proposed several domain analysis methods. Despite the existing differences between them, these methods are functionally equivalent, invariably exhibiting operations such as aggregation, classification, specialization and parameterization (Arango, 1993).

Because of existing similarities between these domain analysis methods, we have chosen the FODA method (Feature Oriented Domain Analysis) (Kang, K.C. et al., 1993), developed by the Software Engineering Institute (SEI), as the method to be used in connection with our development approach. The choice of FODA can be credited to the vast documentation available, including some case studies (Vici, A. et al., 1998 and Griss, M. et al., 1998) and the tight relationship between the models produced by the FODA method and those found in the majority of the Object Oriented Analysis and Design methods (OOADM). One of the main characteristics of FODA is the process of identification of the more relevant software features of an application domain. In the FODA method, a feature is defined as a user-visible aspect or a characteristic of a software system.

3.3 The Analysis of a Domain

In the FODA method, the domain model is subdivided into three distinct models that represent commonalties and existing differences between applications of a given domain. They are:

- Feature Model – which captures the main user-visible aspects of systems in a domain.
- Information Model – which captures the main abstractions, and the relationships between them, in an application domain.
- Operational Model – which models the functional and behavioral aspects of applications in a domain.

The Feature Model is used to represent common features, and the relationships to each other, in a family of applications. Features are classified as mandatory, alternative and optional. Besides usual relationships, the model also captures structural relationships such as consist of, and generalization/specialization structures.

Compositional rules between features also are represented in the model. For instance, two alternatives features that must simultaneously be present in an application of a domain have to be connected by the **requires** operator; while two other features that cannot simultaneously be present will be connected by the **mutually exclusive with** operator.

The Information Model is used to capture domain knowledge throughout the representation of its main abstractions and relationships. As with the Feature Model, aggregation and generalization/specialization structures will be added to the usual relationships between objects in a domain.

Any tool capable of representing the semantic aspects of data, such as the Entity-Relationship Model (Navathe, S.B. et al., 1992) and the class diagrams of UML can represent the Information Model.

The objective of the Operational Model is to identify existing functional and behavioral variations between various applications of a domain. Tools like State Diagrams and Interaction Diagrams found in UML can be used for this purpose. Nevertheless, such models have to be parameterized to properly represent existing variations.

3.4 Applying Domain Analysis to the Proposed Approach

The objective of this section is to explain how Domain Analysis techniques, especially the FODA method, will be integrated into our framework development approach. The first question that arises is why did we choose the FODA method? First, because it represents the domain knowledge using several complementary models. Second, because its most interesting model, the Features Model, matches well with use-cases, which is important since our approach is object-oriented.

The initial step in developing software systems is to identify the needs of the users and other stakeholders. These individuals have business or technical problems that require our help (software developers) to solve them. So it is our responsibility to understand the problem domain and translate the stakeholders' needs into a set of services, called features, that the system will provide to address those needs (Leffingwell, D. & Widrig, D., 2000).

The features address one or more stakeholders' needs and reside in the solution domain, the land of computers, programming, operating systems, etc. It is beyond the scope of this work to specify how the features are obtained. What concerns us is that once the list of features is available we will structure it like the FODA's Features Model.

The second step is to define more specific requirements that conform to stakeholder needs. These more specific requirements are the software requirements; that is, those things that the software does on behalf of the players who interact with the system.

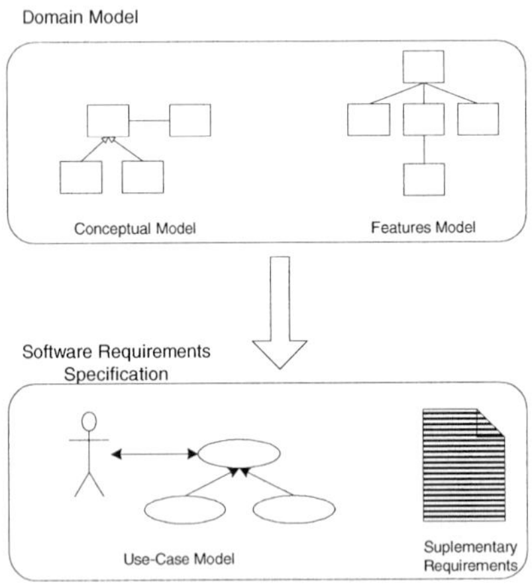

Figure 2: Obtaining Software Requirements Specifications from the Domain Model

At this point it is important to distinguish Features from Software Requirements. While the Features Model captures the desired functionalities provided by the system in a high-level abstraction, the Software Requirements should express these features in a more detailed fashion. That is, the Software Requirement artifacts have to be of a level of abstraction that allows software engineers to lay down the initial design. Nevertheless, despite the differences between the two models there is a mapping that relates features to software requirements (this is explored in more detail in the next section).

3.5 The Relationship between Features, Use-cases and other Artifacts

The Features Model and the Information Model, represented here by a Conceptual Model or a first-cut Class Diagram, constitute the Domain Model of our approach, and is the basis from which the Domain Use-case Model will be generated (Jacobson, 1999). The Domain Use-cases Model expresses the functional requirements of an entire application family, and will play the main role in the Software Requirements Specification (Jacobson, 1999 and Leffingwell, D. & Widrig, D., 2000). Although non-functional requirements are beyond the scope of this work, they can be attached to the use-cases that they concern or kept in a separate document (Supplementary Requirements). Figure 2 illustrates the process of obtaining the Software Requirements Specifications from the Domain Model (Feature Model plus Information Model).

Some features can be associated with use-case or use-case sections, while other features can be associated with the type of players, virtual operations, parameters in objects, target platform, etc. (Griss, M. et al., 1998). Although one feature can be related to only one use-case, use-cases can be traced back to many features.

As stated previously, the objective of an explicit Domain Analysis phase is to capture the common and variable aspects of an application family. Alternative features represent variability that occurs at variation points (Jacobson, 1997). There are many kind of variability mechanisms used to represent variations. Inheritance is the mechanism used when the variation point is a virtual operation, and extensions are the mechanisms used when the variation point is an extension point. When an extension point is located in a use-case, the extensions are others use-cases that are linked to the former use-case through the <<extends>> relationship.

So, some features -- the ones that better expresses alternative functionalities -- will be mapped to extension use-cases (linked to the more abstract use-case through <<extends>> relationships), while other types of alternative features will be mapped to models that can capture abstract structures and abstract behaviors (abstract classes, abstract operations, etc).

Now that the roles of the Features and the use-cases (two closed related concepts) are well established, another question has to be answered: are the Features Model and the Use-Case Model both necessary? The answer is yes, because while the Features Model captures the structural relationships between the features in an easy to understand and concise way, the Use-Case Model describes a subset of those features as a set of actions that will be used later to realize the features as interactions between objects of the Design Model; that is, the Object-Oriented Design of an Application Family or, as it will be seen in a later section, an Object-Oriented Application Framework.

3.6 The Role of Traceability

Traceability is an effective technique that help us understand the relationships between the objects (features, players, use-case, classes, etc.) of our projects, thus permitting verification activity. The verification process helps us maintain the consistency among the models and to discover things that have been missed or are superfluous. Supported by the right tools, traceability permits us, for example, to check if an alternative feature has been mapped to an extension use-case or virtual operation, or if a hot-spot doesn't trace back to any alternative or optional requirement, which would be an error.

Traceability is divided into two categories: implicit and explicit (Leffingwell, D. & Widrig, D., 2000). An implicit traceability may arise naturally from the modeling paradigm and the associated modeling language used. For example, an implicit trace relationship occurs in UML when a player communicates with a use-case or a subclass inherits from its super-class.

On the other hand we define explicit traceability as the development of a relationship that is derived from external consideration supplied by the developers. So, for instance, there is no intrinsic relationship between a feature and a use-case. If such a connection is established, it is based only on the semantic of the constructions.

It is important to state that the use of XML/XMI as the target design description language will reduce significantly our effort in building tools to support traceability. There are many XML tools on the Internet that can be adapted for such a purpose.

4. OBJECT-ORIENTED APPLICATION FRAMEWORKS

4.1 Frameworks as a Reuse Technology

Object-oriented Application Frameworks, hereinafter called frameworks, are an object-oriented reuse technique based on other object-oriented techniques, such as inheritance, polymorphism and design patterns. Frameworks provide a built-in architecture and a set of incomplete methods representing an abstract collaboration model or a pattern of object interaction.

Frameworks can be defined as "a reusable design of all or part of a system that is represented by a set of abstract and concrete classes and the way their instances interact." (Fayad, M. et al., 1999). Another good definition states that a framework is "a system composed of a kernel subsystem, which is common to all applications that may be generated within the framework, and a hot-spot subsystem, which implements the application-specific behavior." (Fontoura, 1999). No matter which definition we choose, one central idea is always present: the reuse of software requirements and complex designs.

By definition, application specific increments, from now on called ASI, are placed in hot-spots, that is, in the framework flexible parts. In our work we use a subset of the Framework Design Language (Fontoura, 1999), FDL for short, for identifying the hot-spots. We have chosen this language for two reasons. The first one is that with FDL we can express three kinds of extension points that, due to our framework development experience (Oliveira et al., 2000) and study of current solutions, can express hot-spots in all dimensions. The three kinds of hot-spots are variation methods, extension classes and extension interfaces.

The second reason for our choice is that FDL provides a complete mapping into UML description using stereotypes and tagged values. This is important because stereotypes and tagged values can be trapped in the UML XMI description to be manipulated by the environment.

Extension interfaces are hot-spots that need the definition of sub-classes to determine the ASIs and can be mapped to a basic class redefinition clause. This means that to obtain ASIs, the framework reuser must provide at least a class name for sub-classing.

Variation methods are methods that have a well-defined signature, but whose implementation may vary depending on the framework instantiation. This hot-spot has no correspondence in basic O.O. instructions, since methods can not have its code “reassigned”. Using inheritance to override the variation method is not possible because the framework is based on the existing class. To solve this problem we use the Strategy Design Pattern (Gamma et al., 1995) to transform this hot-spot into a simple extension interface.

Extension classes are classes whose interfaces can be modified during instantiation. Here we have the same problem of variation methods; that is, traditional O.O.L. does not allow changes to this operation when it is time to compile. The solution again relies on the strategy design pattern.

Variation methods are methods that have a well-defined signature, but whose implementation may vary depending on the framework instantiation. This hot-spot has no correspondence in basic O.O. instructions, since methods can not have its code "reassigned". Using inheritance to override the variation method is not possible because the framework is based on the existing class. To solve this problem we use the Strategy Design Pattern to transform this hot-spot into a simple extension interface.

Extension classes are classes whose interfaces can be modified during instantiation. Here we have the same problem of variation methods; that is, traditional O.O.L. does not allow changes to this operation when it is time to compile. The solution again relies on the strategy design pattern.

FDL distinguishes between ASI made at compile-time and run-time. Compile-time hot-spots should be instantiated statically in code and are defined by the *static* tagged value. In contrast Run-time hot-spots should be instantiated at run time through a reflective mechanism or any mechanism that allows changes into the class structure at run-time.

4.2 Deriving Frameworks from Domain Models

Instantiating a framework is a complex process that does not only deal with the specialization of a generic design. Beyond this, the instantiation process has to deal with the specialization of a generic set of software requirements, those that were specified for an entire application family. So the framework development process has to take into account, as of the early stages of the development, the artifacts produced by the Domain Analysis phase.

The static structure of a framework that is represented by Class Diagrams will be directly derived from the Conceptual Model plus the addition of other design classes. The pattern of interaction among the objects of the framework will be based on the interaction diagrams that realize the Domain Use-cases. Since the Domain Model artifacts are naturally abstracts of the Design Model, the framework obtained by such a process will be equally abstract. The mandatory features will be mapped to the frozen-spots while the variant features, and some optional features, will be reflected in the hot-spots in some way.

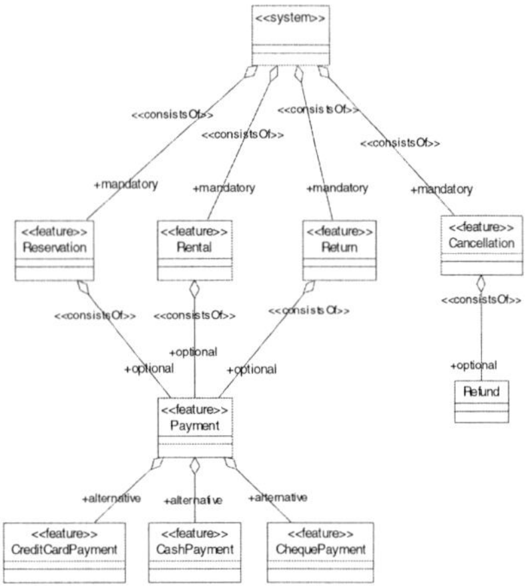

Figure 3: Features diagram of the Rental System

Due to the documentation problem stated in Section 4.1, it is very important that during the instantiation of a framework the developers can trace back to the software requirements that the framework is based upon. Moreover, the application that will be generated has to conform with some of the alternative features and has to include some of the optional features. This process has to be ideally supported by verification tools that can report the existence of inconsistencies in the instantiated application to the developers.

Now the role of the FDL introduced in the previous section became clearer. The FDL precisely and explicitly represents the existence of a hot-spot and its nature. Since the FDL and the Features Model are compatible with each other and are described by the same language -- for example XMI -- the construction of such verification tools will not be a difficult task.

The Case Study introduced in the next section will clarify some of the ideas that were presented so far.

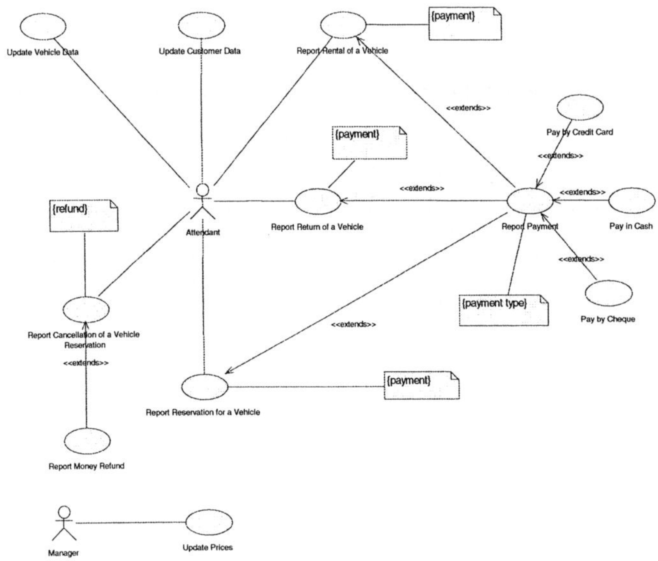

Figure 4: Use-case diagram of the Rental System

5. A CASE STUDY

To provide a complete understanding of the approach, in this section we report about a fictitious case of a Rental System development that was the approach that was first used. The purpose of theRental System is to rent vehicles to users, providing control over the Rental Company's transactions.

According to our approach, the development begins with the creation of a Features Model (Kang, K.C. et al., 1993) where we can represent the system's main characteristics. Figure 3 shows that a payment is accepted at reservation time, rental time or return time. Moreover, credit cards, checks or cash can be used for payment purposes.

The next step is the construction of the Use-case Model (Figure 4). Some functional features trace to whole use-cases while other trace to use-case sections. We can associate extension points with use-cases to represent alternative and optional features in the Use-case Model. For instance, a **payment** is an extension point in the Report

Reservation of a Vehicle, Report Rental of a Vehicle, and Report Return of Vehicle use-cases. Those extension points reflect the fact that the features Reservation, Rental and Return are composed of an optional feature, called Payment.

Another extension point, called **payment type**, is associated with the Report Payment use-case. This extension point is used to represent the three alternative ways of making a payment: through credit cards, checks or cash. All of the three alternatives are represented as alternative features in the Features Model, and are traced back to the Payment feature through the **consistOf** relationship. An extension point is represented as tagged value attached to a use-case through a UML note.

Both Use-case Model and Features Model are important. The objective of the Features Model is to provide a description of the main characteristics of the system. The use-case diagram is a thorough description of the functional requirements of the system and will drive the development process (Jacobson, 1999). The matching of these two diagrams will provide a way to check the integrity of the domain knowledge.

Once the application developer has a satisfactory knowledge of the domain it is time to represent this knowledge in a initial Conceptual Model (Figure 5), represented as a class diagram.

The Conceptual Model will evolve trough the addition of operations and design classes, and will further represent the static view of the framework. The hot-spots are represented as tagged values attached to the classes through UML notes. For example, the fact that the types of vehicles for rent can vary for each framework instance is represented as an Interface Hot-spot.

Although the Class Model is the main model of a framework, it cannot capture all of the variation details embedded in the framework. For example, to better explain the fact that a payment is an optional feature in a reservation process we can construct a sequence diagram that can clarify our understanding. Figure 6 shows such a diagram.

6. CONCLUSION & FUTURE WORKS

This paper describes a thorough and well structured approach to construct frameworks based on domain models. Although the proposed method works well when applied to Information Systems, it is necessary to apply it to other types of systems, especially ones that are not based on user interfaces, to verify if it is a general approach.

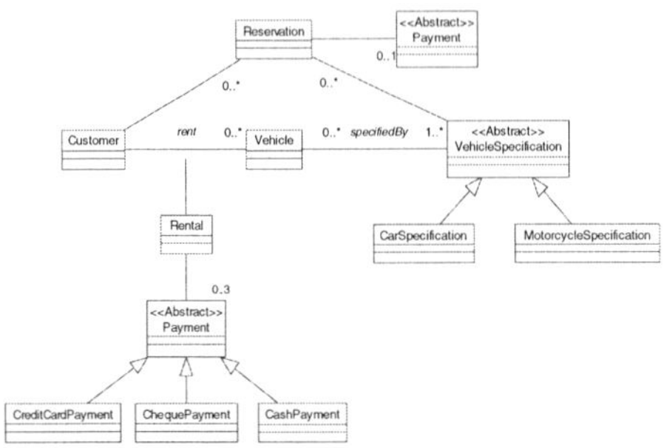

Figure 5: The initial conceptual model

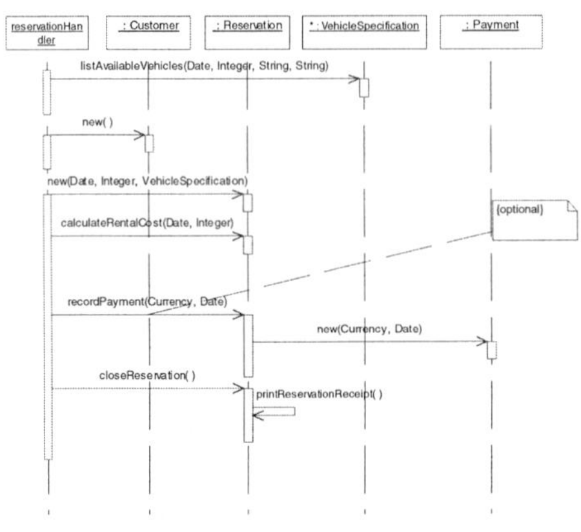

Figure 6: An optional feature represented as an optional operation call

Despite its strengths, a lot of improvements need to be carried out and some tools must be constructed. It is necessary to create a mechanism to support the Features Model in the UML. Although the stereotype mechanism seems to be useful at first sight, perhaps we have to extend the UML Metamodel to accommodate the Features Model. Moreover, we need to be able to express more redefinition points that are not defined as hot-pots or frozen-spots in the frameworks design but rather as an intermediary spot so that the designer is not obliged to define ASI. This is particularly important when the framework provides user interfaces that can be customized. It is also necessary to improve the mechanism used to express the FDL constructions in UML since, for example, it is not possible to use a UML note to attach a tagged value to a specific class operation

Another important extension is the construction of a set of tools to support the verification process based on trace relationships. Such tools will take advantage of the fact that all of the models are represented in XML/XMI.

BIBLIOGRAPHY

Arango, G. (1993) Domain Analysis Methods. IN: Prieto-Díaz, R. Frakes, W.B. eds. Advances in Software Reuse: Selected Papers from the Second International Workshop on Software Reusability. Los Alimos, CA. IEEE Computer Society Press. pp.17-49.

Fayad, M.E. Schmidt, D.C. & Johnson, R. (1999) Application Frameworks. IN: Fayad, M.E. Schmidt, D.C. & Johnson, R. eds. Building Application Frameworks. New York, NY. John Wiley.

Fontoura, M.F.M.C. (1999) A Systematic Approach to Framework Development. PhD Thesis, Department of Computer Science, Pontifical Catholic University of Rio de Janeiro (PUC-Rio).

Gamma, E., Helm, R., Johnson, R. & Vlissides, J. (1995) Design Patterns: Elements of Reusable Object-Oriented Software. Reading, MA. Addison-Wesley.

Griss, M. Favaro, J. & d'Alessandro, M. (1998) Integrating Feature Modeling with the RSEB. IN: 5th International Conference on Software Reuse (ICSR-5), June, Victoria. ACM/IEEE.

Jacobson, I. (1999) The Unified Software Development Process. Reading, MA. Addison-Wesley.

Jacobson, I. Griss, M. & Jonsson, P. (1997) Software Reuse: Architecture, Process and Organization for Business Success. Reading, MA. Addison-Wesley.

Kang, K.C., Cohen, S.G., Hess, J.A., Novak, W.E. & Peterson, A.S. (1993) Feature-Oriented Domain Analysis (FODA) Feasibility Study. Technical Report 21 (CMU/SEI-90-TR-21). Pittsburgh, PA. Software Engineering Institute, Carnegie Mellon University.

Leffingwell, D. & Widrig D. (2000) Managing Software Requirements – A Unified Approach. Reading, MA. Addison-Wesley.

Navathe, S.B. Batini, C. & Ceri, S. (1992) Conceptual Database Design – an Entity-Relationship Approach. Redwood City, CA. Benjamin Cummings.

Oliveira, T.C. Filho, I.M. & Lucena, C.J.P. (2000) A Framework Based Approach for Workflow Software Development. IN: Proceedings of IASTED International Conference on Software Engineering and Application, 6-9 November, Las Vegas. Anaheim, CA, IASTED/ACTA Press. pp. 330-335.

Parnas, D.L. (1976) On the Design and Development on Program Families. IEEE Transaction on Software Engineering, (2) 1 March.

Pree, W. (1995) Design Patterns for Object-Oriented Software Development. Reading, MA. Addison-Wesley.

Prieto-Díaz, R. (1993) Historical Overview. IN: Prieto-Díaz, R. Frakes, W.B. eds. Advances in Software Reuse: Selected Papers from the Second International Workshop on Software Reusability. Los Alimos, CA. IEEE Computer Society Press. pp.1-16.

Vici, A. Argentieri, N. Mansour, A. Favaro, J. & d´Alessandro M. (1998) FODAcom: An Experience with Domain Analysis in the Italian Telecom Industry. IN: 5th International Conference on Software Reuse (ICSR-5), June, Victoria. ACM/IEEE.

MANAGING PROCESSES THROUGH A BASE OF REUSABLE COMPONENTS

Bernard Coulette [(1)], Xavier Cregut[(2)]
(1) UTM-IRIT 5, allées A. Machado F-31058 Toulouse, France
(2) ENSEEIHT-IRIT 2, rue Camichel 31071 Toulouse, France
Email: Bernard.Coulette@univ-tlse2.fr , Xavier.Cregut@enseeiht.fr

Dong Thi Bich Thuy, Tran Dan Thu
Université des Sciences Naturelles 227 Nguyen Van Cu, Q5, Hochiminh Ville, Vietnam
Email: tdt@hcmuns.edu.vn , thuy@hcmuns.edu.vn

Keywords: Software Process Modeling, RHODES PSEE, Reusability, Process Pattern, Process Component Base, Object-oriented database.

Abstract: RHODES is a Process centred Software Engineering Environment (PSEE) that allows to describe software development processes and to control their enactment. To make process reuse efficient in such PSEE, we think that it is necessary to go towards ***an engineering of reusable process components***. To efficiently store and retrieve such components, we have defined a ***Process Component Base*** offering classical database functionalities, especially consistency properties. In this paper, we first describe the RHODES PSEE principle, then we define reusable process components (patterns), and we focus on the definition of component consistency, particularly the ***topological consistency*** based on relationships among constituents of a component. The Process Component Base is implemented over the Jasmine object-oriented database.

1. INTRODUCTION

In the last decade, many development methods were proposed to software engineers, in particular in the field of object-oriented systems : HOOD (Delatte & al. 1996), BOOCH (Booch, 1994), UP (Unified Process, Jacobson & al. 1999; Rumbaugh & al. 1999), etc. Those kinds of method are mainly based on textual/graphical formalisms to model a system, and an informal process to guide the development. To facilitate the work of software developers, CASE tools have been built to support such methods (e.g. STOOD for HOOD, ROSE for UP). In CASE tools, informal and specific development processes are hard coded. However, software developers need more methodological knowledge such as development heuristics (Riel 1996), design patterns (Gamma & al. 1995), and process patterns (Ambler 1998; Bergner & al. 1998; D'souza & al. 1999; Front & al. 1999). They also need flexibility to adapt processes to their particular needs. Because such characteristics cannot be completely hard coded, CASE tools lack methodological assistance. To reduce this deficiency, Process centred Software Engineering Environments (PSEE) have been developed (Derniame & al. 1999), to describe software processes and to control their enactment.

After the first generation of CASE tools and PSEE, a new technology is now emerging: **Component-Based Software Engineering (CBSE)** (Bergner & al. 1998; Pree 1997; Sametinger 1997) is a very promising trend to improve the reusability of software products and processes. At the product level, several industrial standards (COM, SOM, Java Beans) have been proposed for CBSE (Pree 1997). COTS components are being developed and integrated into CASE tools. They are usually based on design patterns such as those of the GoF (Gamma & al. 1995). At the process level, very little work has been done so far in the field of reusable components, as shown in related works (see section 5).

To make process reuse efficient, we think that it is necessary to go towards an **engineering of process components** (Coulette & al. 2000b). To achieve this goal, we have extended our PSEE RHODES (Coulette & al. 2000a; 2000b; Crégut & Coulette 1997) by applying pattern-based approaches to software process modelling. In the first version of RHODES, only elementary components were supported. Now, RHODES manages complex process components able to

J. Filipe et al. (eds.), Enterprise Information Systems III, 180–190.

describe process patterns (Coulette & al. 2000a). Process entities are stored into *a Process Component Base (PCB)* whose aim is to support component process management (storage, retrieval, maintenance), as well as process reuse and evolution.

In this paper, we focus on the PCB, and more precisely on characterising its components. A particular **attention is given to component consistency properties**, especially topological ones, to help process designers build well-formed process components. In section 2, we recall the functional architecture of RHODES and we describe reusable process components. Section 3 is dedicated to the definition of the PCB and to component consistency. In section 4, we give some principles of the PCB implementation. Section 5 discusses related works. Finally, we conclude the paper with a summary of our current and future works (section 6).

2. THE RHODES ENVIRONMENT

RHODES is a PSEE whose goal is to support the description and the execution of software processes. It is based on a Process Modeling Language, initially called PBOOL, allowing process designers to describe elementary components (activities, products, roles, strategies) of their processes, and an execution kernel independent from any application domain. To enact a given process for a specific application domain, one must first produce an instance of RHODES (see figure 1). The second version of PBOOL, namely PBOOL+ (Coulette & al. 2000b; Xavier & Coulette 1997), integrates complex process components as sets of related elementary components. Such complex components meet the following quality factors : *Separation between specification and implementation*, *Self-description*, *Autonomy*, *Evolution*, *Consistency*, and *Multiple description views*. A more detailed description of RHODES is given in (Coulette & al. 2000a).

2.1 RHODES Architecture

Figure 1 illustrates the functional architecture of RHODES with its main constituents : the meta-model, the process component base (PCB), the process component editor, the execution kernel, the PBOOL+ compiler, and executable instances of RHODES corresponding to specific software processes. The first five constituents correspond to the static level of process management whereas the last one expresses the dynamic level.

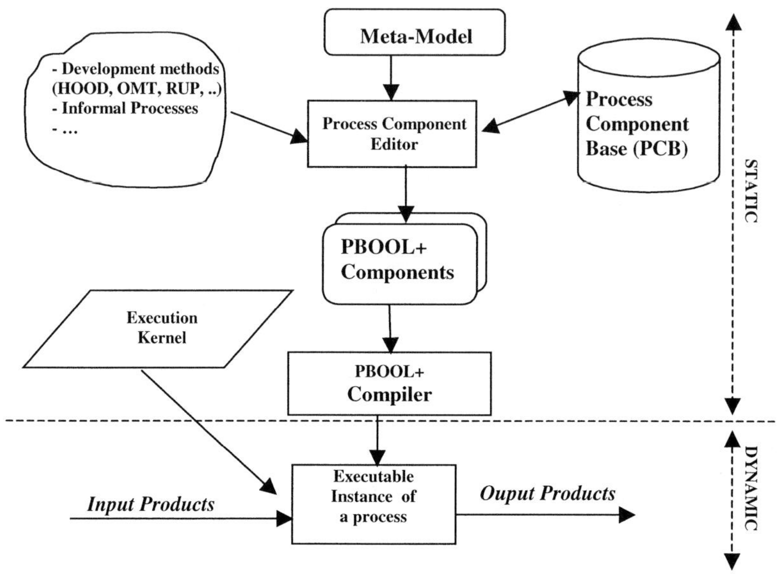

Figure 1: Functional Architecture of RHODES

The meta-model aims to describe the semantics of RHODES components. The process component editor is an integrated tool that comprises a set of features manipulating process components coming from/stored into the PCB. The editor supports different views of process components and facilitates the work of process designers through functionalities such as description, storage, search, update, consistency checking, and versioning.

Software developers use an instance of RHODES to develop software products. Such an instance is produced for a given process by linking the execution kernel with a compiled version of the PBOOL+ process description.

2.2 Process Components model

Figure 2 illustrates the process component meta-model in the UML formalism (Rumbaugh & al. 1999). We distinguish between two levels of process components : elementary components and complex ones. Elementary process components correspond to atomic constituents of a process : activities, products, roles and strategies (Xavier & Coulette 1997) that can be described in the PBOOL language. A software product is modelled by a PBOOL product model. Every product possesses sub-products and operations that are similar to attributes and methods of classes in an object-oriented programming language. A development process is decomposed into activities that fit well together to implement this process. An activity is specified through input and output products, assertions (pre-condition, post-condition, and invariant), and the role of the developers who can perform the activity. The activity implementation describes realisation sketches (each of them is a way to perform the activity) and methodological guidance (to correct inconsistencies).

To put process reuse into practice, we have added a higher representation level based on **complex components.** Such components (Coulette & al. 2000b) are used to group elementary components related to specific process areas (e.g. object-oriented methods). Grouping elementary components is also convenient for searching and extracting components from the PCB. Each component has a specification part and an implementation part. A complex component may have several implementations, each of them corresponding to a given version.

2.3 Reusable Process Components

The main interest of building process components is to facilitate their reuse and thus to improve software process productivity and reliability. Like design patterns for software products, it is worth developing *process patterns* describing pieces of methodological expertise. We have decided to use complex process components to describe such process patterns.

2.3.1 Process patterns definition

A process pattern (Ambler 1998; Bergner & al. 1998; Coulette & al. 2000) is a reusable generic (sub-) process whose goal is to provide a solution to recurring situations occurring in the domain of software process modelling. We have adapted to

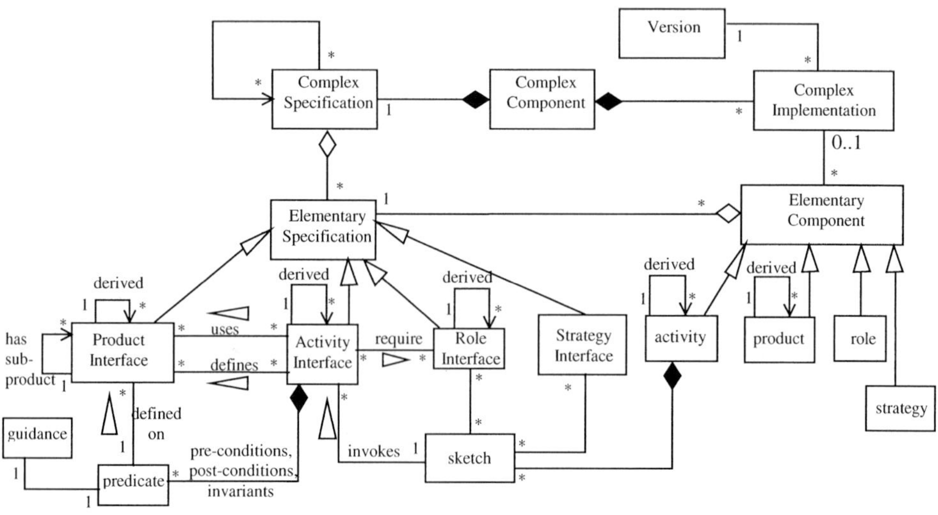

Figure 2: Meta-model of process components

RHODES some properties of existing design patterns (Gamma 1995) and process patterns (Ambler 1998).

A RHODES process pattern is described by *a name*, *an intention*, *a context*, *a semi-formal solution*, *a formalisation*, and *an application clause* as detailed below:

- The pattern *name* identifies in a unique way the process problem to be solved. It is the first criterion for searching the pattern in the PCB;
- The *intention* is an informal description of the problem to be solved by the pattern;
- The *context* describes the context in which this pattern may take place;
- The *semi-formal solution* shows a way to resolve the proposed problem. This solution is represented in a UML-like formalism (Rumbaugh & al. 1999);
- The *formalisation* is a PBOOL+ description of the pattern. It is an executable solution that can be integrated into several processes;
- *The application clause* describes ways of applying the pattern, for example in a given process. Advice to designers may be provided in this application clause.

To enhance the generic property of our approach, we have also introduced the notion of *generic pattern*, i.e. a pattern whose one or several constituents are parameterised by activities. Let us take the example (see figure 3) of a generic pattern: the ***revision*** process. This process describes the revision of any document used during a software development. That process should be frequently reused since a lot of processes include revision activities.

The REVISE activity - the root activity of the revision process - is decomposed into three sub-activities: *read the document*, *make comments*, and *decide to accept or reject it*. The first two activities are described by two generic parameters *A*, *B*. The third activity possesses two sketches ***Accept*** and ***Refuse*** that are two exclusive ways of performing the activity. The parameter *C* corresponds to an activity that improves the rejected document. This activity is enacted whenever the sketch ***Refuse*** is chosen. Notice that the REVISE activity is recursive.

<u>Name</u> : ***REVISION***

<u>**Intention**</u> : The goal of this pattern is to describe the revision process of a document

<u>**Context**</u> : Any situation where a document must be validated, reviewed or updated. It may be a specification document, an analysis/design document, a source code, etc.

<u>**Semi-formal solution**</u> :

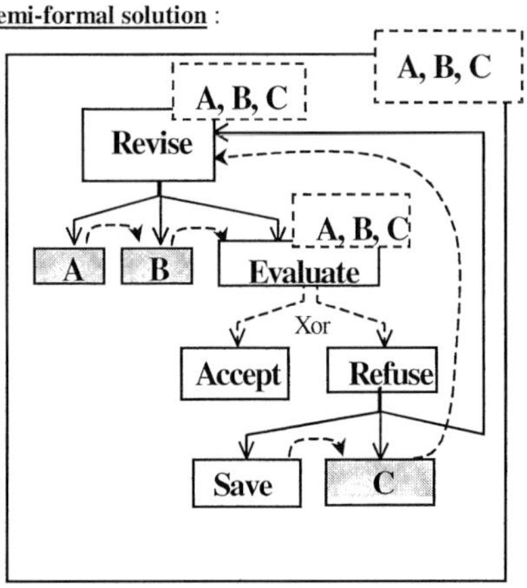

<u>**Formalization**</u> : see PBOOL+ description below

<u>**Application**</u> : Parameters A, B can be instantiated respectively by an activity reviewing the content and an activity producing comments. The parameter C corresponds to an activity editing the document.

Figure 3: The REVISION pattern

2.3.2 Process pattern formalisation

Figure 4 shows the specification and the implementation of the REVISE activity in PBOOL+. Parameters *A*, *B*, *C* are declared in the template clause, and used in the body of the implementation

```
specification activity SPEC_REVISE
  artifact            -- manipulated products
     P: DOCUMENT;
     L: LIST[DOCUMENT];
  use                 -- used products
     P;
  define              -- defined products
     L;
  require             -- preconditions
     P_EXISTED: P.DEFINED;
     P_MODIFIED: P.MODIFIED;
  ensure              -- postconditions
     ACC: not P.ACCEPTED
            implies (L.COUNT > old L.COUNT);
end; -- SPEC_REVISE

template
  <   activity A→SPEC_READ,
      activity B→ SPEC_NOTE,
      activity C→ SPEC_IMPROVE      >
activity REVISE
    implement SPEC_REVISE;
sketch
    refinement sketch DECOMPOSITION is
    do
      call  <A> (P);   -- Read ...
      call  <B> (P);   -- Note ...
      call  EVALUATE <A, B, C> (P, L);
    end;
end; -- REVISE
```

Figure 4: A parameterized activity

part. They are constrained respectively by the activity specifications *SPEC_READ*, *SPEC_NOTE*, and *SPEC_IMPROVE*. It means that, for example, parameter *A* can be instantiated by an activity which is an implementation of *SPEC_READ* or a derived implementation of it (PBOOL+ polymorphism). The preconditions and postconditions are described respectively by the ***require*** and ***ensure*** clauses. The decomposition of the activity is described by the clause ***refinement sketch***.

In PBOOL+, a pattern is described by one or several complex components through a specific clause "component". Figure 5 shows two complex process components of the *Revision* pattern : the *REVISE_CYCLE* process component (a specification and one implementation) and the *PRODUCT_MANIPULATION* product component (specification only).

```
specification component REVISE_CYCLE
    use
            PRODUCT_MANIPULATION;
    ---------------------------------------------------------------------
    specification activity SPEC_REVISE;
    specification activity SPEC_EVALUATE;
    specification activity SPEC_SAVE;
end; -- REVISE_CYCLE

component REVISE_CYCLE_IMP1
                        implement REVISE_CYCLE
  indexing
    version: "1.1"
    date: "29/03/2001"
    ...
  implementation
    activity REVISE <    A→SPEC_READ,
                         B→SPEC_NOTE,
                         C→SPEC_IMPROVE >;
    activity EVALUATE < A→SPEC_READ,
                         B→SPEC_NOTE,
                         C→SPEC_IMPROVE >;
    activity SAVE;
end; -- REVISE_CYCLE_IMP1

specification component PRODUCT_MANIPULATION
    specification activity SPEC_READ;
    specification activity SPEC_NOTE;
    specification activity SPEC_IMPROVE;
end; -- PRODUCT_MANIPULATION
```

Figure 5: Components of the REVISION pattern

3. PCB DEFINITION

The process component base (PCB) of RHODES is a process repository that allows process designers to save and load reusable process entities. It comprises both designer and predefined process components. At the enactment time of a process, the PCB also stores the artifacts manipulated during the software development (for example specification documents, analysis/design documents, source code...) that are instances of product models. Navigation on the PCB is realised through browsing functions of the component editor of RHODES.

3.1 Functionalities of the PCB

The PCB supports four main functionalities: process information storage, process entity retrieval, process entity update, and process entity consistency maintenance. The objective is to favor reuse, evolution, and consistency of software development processes. We have adapted functionalities of databases and software component repositories (cf. Chapter 15, Sametinger 1997) to our PCB.

Process information storage. There are many kinds of process information stored in the PCB: meta-process information, process entities and their relationships, different views of a process entity, status information at enactment time, history information, etc.

Process entity retrieval. Access to process entities must be easy for process designers and fast enough in the case where the process component base grows up. That work is realised by a *component base engine* that is implemented over an object database engine. The component base engine supports functions at the component level. Thanks to flexible queries of an object database system, we have defined component-oriented queries based on query templates of QBE style ("Query By Example"). Moreover, we are also interested in resolving problems of synonymous keywords, pattern matching search, query history marks, and improvement of successive queries.

Process entity updating. It consists of insertion, deletion, modification and adaptation of process entities. Thanks to transaction control capabilities of the object database engine, these operations ensure the integrity and consistency of object data in the component base when executed. To facilitate the work of process designers, the entities updating is visualised through graphic views of the RHODES component editor.

Consistency maintenance of process entities. Process entities are complex objects that have relationships with other ones. Although the transaction control ensures the consistency of every data items, it does not ensure completely the consistency of process entities. Thanks to the persistent storage of component structures, component formal descriptions, and component relationships, the component base engine statically verifies consistency properties. This verification is very important to build high quality components and to reduce inconsistencies during the process enactment.

3.2 Consistency of process entities

The consistency of process component base allows processes to be enacted in a rigorous way. We consider both static consistency (controlled at editing/compiling time) and dynamic consistency (controlled at execution time). Dynamic consistency mainly consists in checking assertions (Coulette & al. 2000a) and *is out of the scope of this paper.* As mentioned above, the static consistency includes topological consistency concerning relationships between process components.

In the following, we **focus on the topological consistency**. Topological consistency properties are presented informally rather than formally since the formalisation of these properties requires some mathematical definitions and proofs that are not in the scope of this paper. These properties are implemented in the component base engine to control the consistency of process components.

We first present some concepts and properties related to topological consistency. Examples of application will be presented in the next section.

3.2.1 Relationships between elementary components

Dependent relationships (or dependencies) of an elementary process component on another one are defined by the semantics of PBOOL+. They are based on the notions of inheritance, decomposition, manipulation, use, and association. We have investigated the following types of relationship:

- *Dependency of an activity on another one.* There are three relations: *decomposition relation* (an activity "A1" depends on an activity "A2" if "A2" is a sub-activity in the decomposition of "A1"), *reuse inheritance relation* (an activity "A1" depends on an activity "A2" if "A1" is derived from "A2" by inheritance of reuse), and *subtype inheritance relation* (an activity "A1" depends on an activity "A2" if "A1" is derived from "A2" by inheritance of subtype);
- *Dependency of an activity on a product.* This is the manipulation relation. A product "P" can be an input product, an output product, or a local product of an activity "A". Then we say that "A" depends on "P" by the use/define relation;
- *Dependency of an activity on a role or a strategy.* It is defined by the association of a role or a strategy with an activity. An activity "A" depends on a role "R" or a strategy "S" by this relation if "R" or "S" is associated with "A";
- *Dependency of a product on another one.* There are three relations: *aggregation relation* (a product "P1" depends on a product "P2" if "P2" is a subproduct of "P1"), *manipulation relation* (a product "P1" depends on a product "P2" if "P2" is a local product or a method parameter of "P1"), and *inheritance relation* (a product "P1" depends on a product "P2" if "P1" is derived from "P2" by inheritance).

3.2.2 Topological structure of complex components

To study topological consistency properties of a complex component, we associate the component with a directed graph whose vertices are its elementary components and whose arcs are dependencies between these elementary components. Every arc of this graph is assigned a dependency type that is also called "a stereotype" of arcs. The set of stereotypes is denoted by STEREOTYPE. In some specific situations, we investigate the graph with only arcs of the same stereotype. For example, to detect cyclic inheritance relations, we consider the graph with arcs that have the stereotype "inheritance". In the following, CC and G(CC) denote respectively a complex component and its associated graph. The figure 6 below illustrates two graphs associated to a complex component: a first one with all arcs and a second one with arcs having the stereotype "Inheritance".

3.2.3 Topological consistency

The topological consistency of complex components is based on properties of their associated graphs. Some consistency properties are mandatory whereas others may be optional. Although stereotypes are not mentioned, the definitions below also work for the case in which we investigate only the same arc stereotypes of G(CC).

The connection properties concern the necessity of linkage every two elements in a complex component. We have studied two properties: *connection* and *weak connection.* A complex component is *connected* if its associated graph is connected: any two of its nodes must have a direct relationship or must be indirectly linked thanks to a sequence of linked successive nodes. A complex component is *weakly connected* if it can be contained in a connected complex component. In other words, two elements in a weakly connected component must be related indirectly by a sequence of intermediate elements that are not necessarily members of the component. For example in figure 6, {5, 6} is a weakly connected component because it is not a connected component but it is contained in {3, 5, 6} which is a connected one.

Cousin properties concern the relative cousins of any two elements in a complex component. We consider four properties, defined as follows:

(Cousin 1a) For all c1, c2 in CC, it exists c in CC such that c depends on c1 and c2;

(Cousin 1b) For all c1, c2 in CC, it exists c in CC such that c1 and c2 depend on c;

(Cousin 2a) For all c1, c2 in CC, it exists c in CC such that c depends indirectly on c1 and c2;

(Cousin 2b) For all c1, c2 in CC, it exists c in CC such that c1 and c2 depend indirectly on c.

There is a logical implication of the weak connection property from anyone of these properties.

The closure properties concern the autonomy of complex components. Three closure properties have been defined:

- The *transitive closure* property is defined as usual: a transitively closed component contains all the nodes on which a node of the component depends. A complex component with this property can be reused independently from other components. However, it is not convenient to satisfy this property in some cases. For example, a component can become very large to satisfy this property.
- The *weak closure* property is used to maintain the relative autonomy of a process component. A complex component CC is a weak closure related to a family of complex components if every element of CC is either independent, or depends on another element of CC, or depends on an element of a component of the family. In this case, the component CC must explicitly declare all of the components of this family.
- The *local closure* property is used particularly for the decomposition dependency of activities. For each element x of a complex component CC, we define *Depend*(x) as the set of all elements on which x depends. The component CC is called a *local closure* if *Depend*(x)$\subset$CC or *Depend*(x)$\cap$CC=$\emptyset$ for each x in CC.

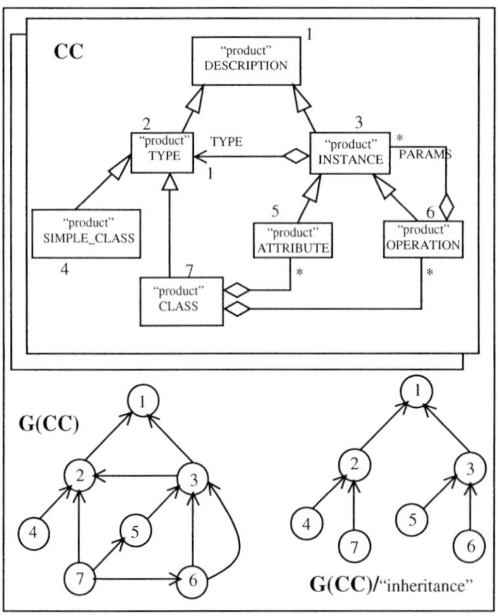

Figure 6: Associated graphs of a complex component

The anti-closure properties concern the dependence of a complex component on extern elementary components. We consider two properties: *property of cutting cycle* and *open property*. A complex component CC is said to be a *cutting cycle* if there is a cycle that is not included in CC but contains at least one element of CC. An *opened* component is a component that contains two terminal elements of a path but does not contain all the elements of the path. A complex component should not possesses these properties, for example, in the case of inheritance relationships.

We have established logical relations between the above properties and studied the maintenance of some properties under *composition* (intersection and union) of complex components. For example, a transitive closure component is also a weak closure and a local closure; it is neither a cutting cycle component nor an opened component. The union of two connected components, such that their intersection is not empty, is also connected.

3.3 Application of topological consistency properties

This section illustrates the interest of applying topological properties to obtain low coupling between complex process components, high cohesion of each complex process component, and to avoid inconsistencies.

First, the system must not accept any cycle in the inheritance relation. It means that for every complex component CC, any cycle of the graph G(CC)/"inheritance" must be detected. In other words, the acyclic property is mandatory in the case of "inheritance" relationships.

The cohesion of a complex component concerns the degree of collaboration between its individual elementary components. Every complex component should have a cohesion degree as high as possible. The above connection properties can characterise the static aspect of the component cohesion. We use these properties to evaluate different levels of cohesion.

Every complex component should have at least the weak connection property when limited to a certain stereotype. Let us consider elementary components in Figure 7 below which illustrates the *Revision* process. It is not very good to make a component as CC1={DOCUMENT,DEVELOPER}. Indeed, CC1 is a weak connection component, but CC1 loses this weak connection property when it is limited to a given stereotype. The link between DOCUMENT and DEVELOPER is established only through relationships that have not the same stereotype. It is more suitable to make a component as CC2={READER, AUTHOR} because the two components READER and AUTHOR are indirectly related by the inheritance relation. In fact, CC2 is weakly connected when limited to the stereotype "role inheritance". In addition, a component such as CC3={DEVELOPER, AUTHOR, READER} has a higher cohesion degree than CC2, because CC3 is connected but CC2 is not. We can deduce the following cohesion degree comparison:

Cohesion(CC3)>**Cohesion**(CC2)>**Cohesion**(CC1).

Cousin properties are also used to characterise cohesion degree of complex components. Each of these properties is stronger than the weak connection one. Let us consider the following components: CC4={READ, NOTE}, CC5={READ, STORE}, CC6={STORE, IMPROVE}, and let us verify the cousin properties. Both CC4 and CC5 have the property "Cousin 1b" for the stereotype "manipulation" since READ, NOTE, and STORE depend on DOCUMENT through the manipulation relation. When limited to the stereotype "decomposition", CC4 possesses the property "Cousin 1a" but CC5 does not. Similarly, CC6 has the property "Cousin 1b" for the stereotype "manipulation" and "Cousin 1a" for "decomposition". We can then deduce the following cohesion degree comparison:

Cohesion(CC4)>**Cohesion**(CC5), and

Cohesion(CC6)>**Cohesion**(CC5).

The *component coupling* concerns the degree of interdependency between components. Process designers should try to get a component coupling degree as low as possible. The closure/anti-closure properties can be applied to characterise the static aspect of the coupling. A component having the transitive closure property is independent from other components. It is the case of CC3={DEVELOPER, AUTHOR, READER}. The possession of anti-closure properties can increase the coupling between components. For example, CC7={READ, NOTE, EVALUATE} is a cutting cycle component because

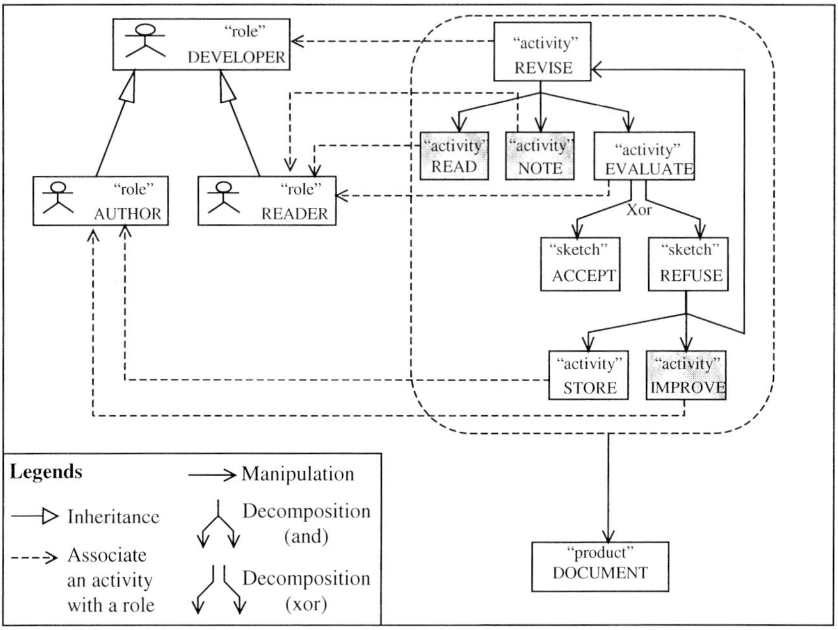

Figure 7: Components of the Revision process

it contains an element EVALUATE but does not contain all the elements of the cycle:

"decomposition" "decomposition"
REVISE————→EVALUATE————→ REVISE.

This situation should be avoided. Any complex component CC containing the element REVISE will have a "double" coupling with CC7 (i.e. a cyclic dependency between CC and CC7).

4. PCB IMPLEMENTATION

We have chosen to implement the PCB in RHODES through Jasmine (Khoshafian S. 1999). Jasmine allows to develop multimedia applications and supports object-oriented database management. Jasmine applications are based on the client-server model. Figure 8 illustrates the implementation architecture of the PCB. The client side comprises two main constituents : the editor and the PCB interface. They are implemented by using VC++ and the Jasmine library. The server side comprises the object database (ODB) server of Jasmine and the PCB engine. The engine is implemented by using an Object Database Query Language (ODQL).

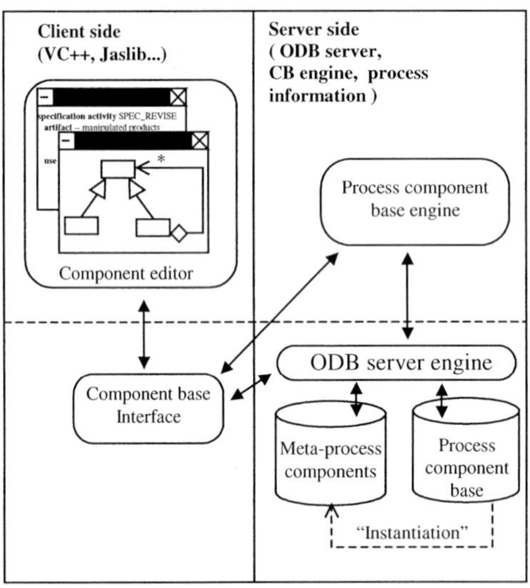

Figure 8: Implementation Architecture of the PCB

4.1 Jasmine & ODQL

A Jasmine database is a repository for defining, administrating, and accessing class definitions and objects. Jasmine supports the definition of class members (properties or methods) both at the class and instance levels. The Object Database Query Language (ODQL) provides complete database access including data definition, data access/update, and method writing. ODQL allows to define and compile classes and methods, to invoke compiled methods, to execute queries, and to manipulate objects. Figure 9 shows an example of method definition in ODQL. It is the class-level method "*find*" of a class named "*Project*". The method looks for the first project whose name nearly matches the string pattern stored in parameter "*s*" (using the "like" function). The definition comprises the method and data declarations, an object query, and flows of control similar to those of C++.

```
defineProcedure Project Project::class:find(String s)
language: "c"
{
    $defaultCF demoCF;
    $Bag<Project> Prjs;
    $Project pr;
    $Prjs=Project from Project where Project.name.like(s);
    $if (Prjs.count ( )==0)
    {
        $return (NIL);
    };
    $scan (Prjs, pr)
    {
        $return (pr);
    };
};
```

Figure 9: Method definition in ODQL

4.2 Meta-process components

The first stage of implementation converts the meta-model of figure 2 (cf. section 2) into classes stored in a Jasmine object database. Such classes are called *meta-process components*. Each class has properties (data members and relationships) and methods implemented by using ODQL. We also use the inheritance and polymorphism mechanisms of Jasmine to implement reusable meta-process components. Every component in the PCB is instantiated from a meta-process component.

4.3 PCB Engine

The implementation of the PCB engine is based on meta-process components (cf. figure 8 above). The engine is also implemented by using ODQL. We distinguish between three groups of functions: *component base functions, query functions*, and *consistency control functions*. There are two kinds of component base functions: manipulation functions (creation, deletion, updating) and administration functions (connection, transfer of data between process component bases, etc.). Query functions includes generic queries, user queries, QBE-based query templates, and query solving motor (to process synonym keywords, query history marks, etc.). The consistency control functions implement functions that verify the topological consistency of the PCB (see section 3.2).

4.4 PCB interface on the client side

The object library of Jasmine version 1.21 (Khoshafian S. 1999) supports only C-API primitive functions to manipulate objects and classes in object databases. These functions are written in C programming style.

To have an homogeneous manipulation of objects and classes at both client and server side, we encapsulate the primitive functions in C++ classes that are organised in the component base interface module. The module maps Jasmine objects into C++ objects. The two design patterns «*Composite*» and « *Template method* » (Gamma 1995) are applied to design and to implement this module.

5. RELATED WORKS

Main representative projects that have introduced process components are **Pynode** (Avrilionis & al. 1996) and **OPC** («Open Process Components», Gary & al. 1998). The Pynode environment distinguishes two levels: the process component level and the process composition level. The composition level is realised dynamically at the enactment time thanks to execution and observation views. The OPC project proposes a 3-layer architecture: the framework layer, the representation layer, and the component layer. These projects focus on the dynamic aspects of process components rather than the static one. Moreover, the pattern-based approach for processes is not covered.

Ambler (1998) defines a process pattern as a collection of general techniques and activities to resolve a specific software process problem. He distinguishes three types of process patterns : task process patterns, stage process patterns, and phase process patterns. Bergner et al. (2000) propose process patterns providing guidelines about the organisation of development process. A process pattern suggests a sequence of development activities which are advisable in the current situation of project. D'souza and al. propose process patterns at the high level to guide development process.

Gzara and al. (2000) propose an approach for developing Product Information System (PIS) by reuse of process patterns. They have elaborated a reference framework specifying the various PIS concepts. The framework is based on a static framework and on a dynamic one. The static framework comprises concepts related to product and process descriptions. The dynamic framework models the behaviour of product concepts in response to a process execution.

Each of the above approaches for process patterns is either at an informal level (Ambler 1998; Bergner & al. 1998; D'souza & al. 1999), or at the methodological study (Front & al. 1999; Gzara & al. 2000) without supporting an environment for defining, reusing and integrating process patterns into executable processes.

The environment **OPC** (Gary & al. 1998) supports the management of process components through an OPC repository. Process management in the environment **Pynode** (Avrilionis & al. 1996) is implemented over an object-oriented database. However, these environments do not provide the control of static consistency for the process component base.

6. CONCLUSION

It is now well recognised that the quality of software processes play an important role in software engineering. So far however, PSEEs (Derniame & al. 1999) were not powerful enough to meet the reuse needs in process modelling, as they did not support process component based approaches. Our purpose is to put process reuse in practice through a process component technology.

We have elaborated the RHODES environment as a PSEE supporting reusable process components, including generic patterns. We have developed PBOOL+, a process modelling language, to describe both elementary and complex process components. Patterns are implemented in RHODES as complex components. To make process components persistent and provide process designers with reuse facilities, we have designed a Process Component Base (PCB).

In this paper, we have emphasised the static consistency properties of process components, especially topological consistency ones. The goal is first to ensure the PCB consistency, second to characterise well formed components. To achieve that, we consider complex components as graphs whose nodes are elementary components and whose arcs are dependency relationships among nodes. We have thus established several types of consistency properties: *connection, cousin, closure* and *anti-closure*. Such properties should be used by process designers to get *low coupling* and *strong cohesion* for components.

The PCB is being implemented through the Jasmine object-oriented database. Meta-process components and the component base interface module are validated. Component base engine functions are being implemented and validated. It is also the case for the dialogue based functions of the component editor. We have also implemented a graphics based prototype of the component editor, but the communication between the prototype and the PCB is not yet completed.

Our future work will be focused on the one hand on the realisation and validation of the second version of RHODES, on the other hand on the building of a library of reusable process patterns, in the field of object-oriented analysis and design methodologies. Afterwards, we will investigate other process application domains.

REFERENCES

Ambler, S. W., 1998. *Process Patterns - Building Large-Scale Systems Using Object Technology.* Cambridge University Press/SIGS Books.

Avrilionis, D., Belkhatir, N., Cunin P. Y., 1996, 'A Unified Framework for Software Process Enactment and Improvement', *ICSP4, 4th International Conference on Software Process*, Brighton, UK.

Bergner K., Rausch A., Sihling M., Vilbig A., 1998, 'A Componentware Development Methodology based on Process Patterns', *PLOP98, 5th Annual Conference on the Pattern Languages of Programs.*

Booch G., 1994. *Object Oriented Analysis and Design with Applications.* The Benjamin/Cummingo Publishing Company.

Coulette B., Crégut X., Tran D. T. and Dong T. B. T., 2000a, 'RHODES, a Process Component Centered Software Engineering Environment', *ICEIS2000, 2nd International Conference on Enterprise Information Systems*, Stafford.

Coulette B., Crégut X., Tran D. T. and Dong T. B. T., 2000b, 'Vers une ingénierie de composants de procédé réutilisables', *ICSSEA2000,13th International Conference on Software & Systems Engineering And Their Applications*, Paris.

Crégut X. and Coulette B., 1997, 'PBOOL - an Object-Oriented Language for Definition and Reuse of Enactable Processes', *Software-Concepts & Tools*, 18(2), June 1997.

Delatte B., Heitz M., and Muller J. F., 1996. *HOOD Reference Manual release 4.* Masson, Paris.

Derniame J. C., Wastell D., and A. B. Kaba (Editors), 1999. *Software Process : Principles, Methodology, Technology.* Lecture Notes in Computer Science, 1500, Springer-Verlag.

D'souza D. F. and Wills A. C., 1999. *Objects, Components, and Frameworks with UML - The Catalysis Approach.* Addison Wesley Longman, Inc.

Front A., Giraudin J. P., Rieu D. et Saint-Marcel C., 1999, Chapitre 4 - Réutilisation et patrons d'ingénierie, *Génie Objet, Analyse & Conception de l'évolution d'objets.* Editions Hermes.

Gamma E., Helm R., Johnson R. and Vlissides J., 1995. *Design Patterns: Elements of Reusable Object-Oriented Software.* Reading, MA: Addison-Wesley.

Gary K., Derniame J. C., Lindquist T., Koehnemann H., 1998, 'Component-Based Software Process Support', *ASE'98, 13th Conference on Automated Software Engineering*, Honolulu, Hawaii.

Gzara L., Rieu D., Tollenaere M., 2000, 'Towards a Dynamic Reference Framework for Product Information Systems: Focus on Engineering Change Process', *IDMME'2000, Conférence Internationale sur la Conception et la Fabrication Intégrées en Génie Mécanique*, Montréal.

Jacobson I., Booch G., Rumbaugh J., 1999. *The Unified Software Development Process.* Addison Wesley Longman, Inc.

Khoshafian S., Dasananda S. and Minassian N., 1999. *The Jasmine Object Database - Multimedia Applications for the Web.* Morgan Kaufmann Publisher, Inc.

Osterweil L. J., 1997, 'Software Processes Are Software Too', Revisited, *ICSE'97, 19th International Conference on Software Engineering*, Boston, MA.

Pree W., 1997, 'Component-Based Software Development: A new Paradigm in Software Engineering?', *Software-Concepts & Tools* (1997) 18: 169-174.

Riel A. J., 1996.*Object-Oriented Design Heuristics.* Addison Wesley Publishing, 1996.

Rumbaugh J., Jacobson I., and Booch G., 1999. *The Unified Modeling Language Reference Manual.* Addison Wesley Longman, Inc.

Sametinger J., 1997. *Software Engineering With Reusable Components.* Springer - Verlag Berlin Heidelberg.

ENTERPRISE INFORMATION SYSTEMS: SPECIFYING THE LINKS AMONG PROJECT DATA MODELS USING CATEGORY THEORY

Michael Johnson, C.N.G. Dampney
Department of Computing, Macquarie University
Sydney, Australia
Email: {mike, kit}@ics.mq.edu.au

Keywords: Enterprise information system, logical data independence, category theory, view update, interoperating systems, data modelling

Abstract: Major enterprise information systems are frequently specified by integrating information models which have been developed in separate divisions of the enterprise. These models, often called project data models, embody the information that needs to be modelled in the enterprise, but they can be difficult to link because when common information is stored in different divisions it is frequently stored in significantly different forms. This paper describes a new technique, based on category theory, that uses the specification of logically data independent views to link project data models. The link mechanism is powerful because the use of views permits data in radically different forms to be linked, and a new solution to the view update problem allows the linking mechanism to be embodied as code, thus allowing the linked data models to be implemented as interoperating information systems. The paper is somewhat theoretical since it describes the foundation for a new technique, but the methods described here are being tested in large consultancies including the enterprise models for a government department, an oil company, and a telecommunications carrier.

1 INTRODUCTION

Major enterprise information systems are frequently specified by integrating information models which have been developed in separate divisions of the enterprise. These models, often called project data models, embody the information that needs to be modelled in the enterprise, but they are often difficult to link because when common information is stored in different divisions it is frequently stored in significantly different forms.

This paper describes a technique that uses the specification of logically data independent views to link project data models. The link mechanism is powerful because the use of views permits data in radically different forms to be linked, and a new solution to the view update problem (Johnson *et al.* 2001), (Dampney *et al.* 2001), allows the linking mechanism to be embodied as code, thus allowing the linked data models to be implemented as interoperating information systems.

The tools that we use are based on category theory. Category theory ((Barr *et al.* 1995), (Mac Lane 1971), (Walters 1991)) is a branch of mathematics renowned for its semantic power, its simple axiom set, and its use of graphical techniques. It has been widely used for specification in computer science in, for example, abstract data types (Goguen *et al.* 1978), (Goguen *et al.* 1977), semantics of programming languages (Scott 1972), (Scott 1982), and functional programming (Asperti *et al.* 1991).

We make extensive use of logical data independence (Ullman 1988). Logical data independence supports views of data with different logical structure from the original model. We argue that this is especially important in specifying links between project data models as it is only rarely that such models include common data in the *same* logical structure. We present below a mathematical treatment of logically independent views in a category theoretic framework and show how it is used to support the linking of project data models to create an enterprise data model.

In summary our technique is as follows. Given two project data models which we wish to link we use category theoretic specification techniques to develop a single logically data independent model of (parts of) each of the project data models. This model, $\mathbb{K}$, is the link. It is a single formal representation of those parts of the original systems that share common data in whatever form. It remains to develop the interoper-

J. Filipe et al. (eds.), Enterprise Information Systems III, 191–197.

ation code.

To develop the interoperation code we need to explore the *transmissibility* of update information from each project data model, "out" to the common submodel $\mathbb{K}$ and back "in" to the other project data model. It turns out that the outward transmissibility (from a project model to $\mathbb{K}$) is guaranteed for formal mathematical reasons. Inward transmissibility on the other hand *cannot* be guaranteed. Instead, inward transmissibility needs to be explored in detail using view updatability, and a novel approach to view updatability is outlined below.

The plan of the paper is as follows. In Section 2 we set the scene with an example illustrating the category theoretic information system specification techniques that we use. In Section 3 we define views in our category theoretic framework. Section 4 explains how for these views the view update problem can be analysed. Finally in Section 5 we show how the theory developed in the earlier sections can be used to link interacting project data models. and in Section 6 we illustrate this using our example specification introduced in Section 2.

2 CATEGORY THEORETIC SPECIFICATION: AN EXAMPLE

In this section we give an example to illustrate some of the category theoretic tools we use in our information systems consultancy work, and we introduce some basic terminology. The main problem that we will consider here is the *specification* of information systems, including particularly the specification of real-world constraints. The example that we have chosen is artificial. It has been constructed so as to illustrate the main constraint specification tools with a minimum of extraneous details. Nevertheless, despite being small it is sufficiently realistic that we will return to it in section 6 to illustrate project data model linking.

We will not review elementary category theoretic notions. Definitions and basic properties of commuting diagrams, limits, and coproducts, can be found in most introductions to category theory, including (Barr *et al.* 1995) and (Walters 1991). We will assume familiarity with ER terminology (Ullman 1988).

The graph shown in Figure 1 is a part of a specification for an e-commerce information system. The graph may be thought of as an ER model: The vertices of the graph represent entities (types), the arrows represent many-to-one mandatory relations (functions or methods), and the arrow with tail ($\rightarrowtail$) represents a sub-entity (subtype or injective function). There is a correspondence between standard ER models and such graphs given by tabulating many-to-many relations and using subentities to eliminate non-mandatory many-to-one relations. For simplicity attributes have not been shown in Figure 1, with the sole exception of Price, but if desired they can be included as arrows from the entity on which they are defined to a node representing their attribute value set, or they can be recorded in a separate data dictionary.

Of course, the specification technique we use also has extra-ER aspects. We specify three further sets of properties: Which diagrams commute, which nodes occur as limits of specified diagrams (via specified cones) defined in the graph, and which nodes occur as coproducts (via specified cocones) of specified nodes of the graph. In our example the extra-ER properties include the specification that the two triangles commute, that the square be a pullback (a kind of limit), and that the Product node be the coproduct of Physical product and Virtual product (electronically available software, music, etc). These constraints ensure that: Deliveries only take place to fill specific Orders (the commuting triangles); All Products, and only those Products, which have a Physical location are Physical products (the pullback); All Products are either Physical products or Virtual products (the coproduct). The Location entity stores both warehouse locations and URLs.

In our technique the quadruple consisting of the graph, sometimes called the *underlying graph*, and the extra-ER constraints (three sets), is called a schema. Formally

Definition 1 A *schema* $\mathbb{E} = (G, \mathcal{D}, \mathcal{L}, \mathcal{C})$ is a directed graph G, a set $\mathcal{D}$ of pairs of paths in G with common source and target, a set $\mathcal{L}$ of cones in G, and a set $\mathcal{C}$ of cocones in G.

(It may be worth noting that the definition uses merely directed graphs — there is no need to decorate some arrows with tails to indicate subentities. This follows from the simple technical result that the property of being a subentity can also be specified as a limit. See for example (Johnson *et al.* 2001) page 539.)

A schema can be thought of as the raw material, the base entities and relationships, for a mathematical abstraction called the *classifying category*. Roughly speaking it is the smallest category containing the schema, satisfying the constraints, and closed under finite limits and finite coproducts. The classifying category has objects corresponding to each of the structural queries that can be applied to the information system (Dampney *et al.* 1992). The classifying category for $\mathbb{E}$ is denoted by $Q(\mathbb{E})$ to remind us that it incorporates all the queries. The category $Q(\mathbb{E})$ is usually infinite, so it is not likely to be very useful in implementations, but because it embodies all the structural queries it has theoretical value as it represents all possible data that can be derived from an in-

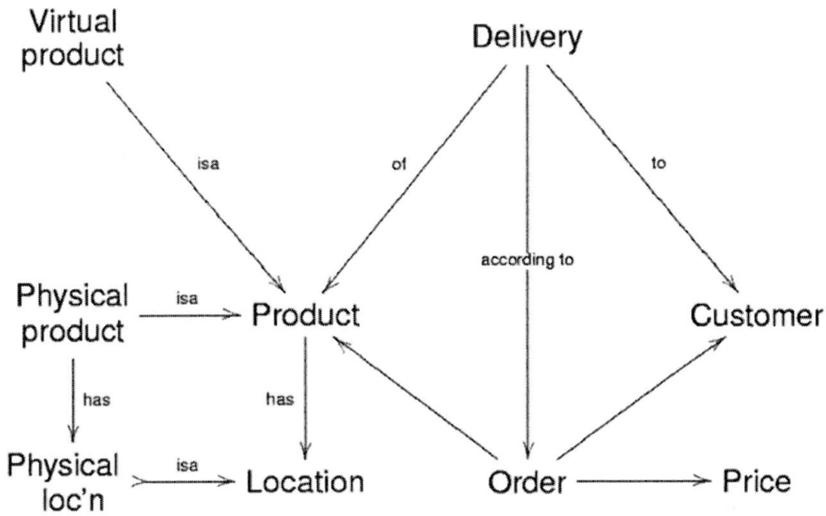

Figure 1: An illustrative example: Part of an e-commerce schema

formation system, and because it is finitely generated it remains tractable.

Schemata can be interrelated using schema maps. A *schema map* is a graph morphism between the corresponding graphs which maps each of the constraints on the first schema to a constraint (already) specified in the second schema. Formally

Definition 2 Consider two schemata $\mathbb{E} = (G, \mathcal{D}, \mathcal{L}, \mathcal{C})$ and $\mathbb{E}' = (G', \mathcal{D}', \mathcal{L}', \mathcal{C}')$. A *schema map* $m : \mathbb{E} \to \mathbb{E}'$ is a graph morphism, also denoted $m : G \Rightarrow G'$ which carries by composition diagrams in $\mathcal{D}$, cones in $\mathcal{L}$ and cocones in $\mathcal{C}$ to respectively diagrams in $\mathcal{D}'$, cones in $\mathcal{L}'$ and cocones in $\mathcal{C}'$.

Sometimes we will speak of a schema map from a schema into a category. In that case we mean a schema map from the schema into the underlying schema of the category: its graph is the underlying graph of the category, and its constraints are all of the constraints that happen to be true in the category — all of the commuting diagrams, all of the limits, and all of the coproducts.

An information system, sometimes called a database state or instance, is an assignment of, for every node in the schema a finite set (the set of instances or values of that entity or attribute), and for every arrow in the schema a function between the corresponding sets (the relationships among the entity instances or the attribute values corresponding to the instances), such that the constraints are satisfied in the category of finite sets. Often we will elide the reference to database and simply refer to a database state as a state. Formally

Definition 3 A *state* E for a schema $\mathbb{E}$ is a schema map $\mathbb{E} \to \mathbf{Set}_0$ into the category of finite sets.

In other words, a state for a given schema is a diagram of (finite) sets and functions which is the same shape as the schema's underlying graph, and which satisfies the constraints.

Now that we have established the context in which we work, we turn to the important question of defining views of schemata.

3 DEFINABLE VIEWS

The question of which views are definable for a particular schema is long-standing, and has generated considerable controversy. The main problem has been that proposals for definable views have frequently been formulated to correspond to those view mechanisms which have been implemented in a particular system.

Instead, we seek to deal with views defined as widely as possible.

One of us has argued (Johnson *et al.* 2001) that truly logically independent views should have the following properties:

1. A logically independent view should be able to contain any data that can be derived from data

stored anywhere in the entire information system. This is sometimes referred to as *the universality principle*. It is so called because it states that the universe of data available from the information system should be available to be included by a designer in a view.

2. A logically independent view should be able to be structured, queried and manipulated as if it were an independent information system. This is sometimes referred to as *the modularity principle* because it states that the view mechanism should produce modules which encapsulate their definition. A user should not be able to distinguish between a module which is an entire information system, and one which is a view of a part of an information system.

Both principles are statements of the power of the view mechanism: System designers should be able to construct a view using any of the data from the information system, arranged in any logical arrangement, and manipulable by a user exactly as if the view were an entire information system.

In terms of the technique that we use, a view should be an arbitrary specified schema (thus an arbitrarily structured information system) which inherits its data from any legitimate queries carried out on the viewed system. Thus we define:

Definition 4 Let $\mathbb{E}$ be a schema. A *view* of $\mathbb{E}$ is a schema $\mathbb{K}$ and a schema morphism $k : \mathbb{K} \to Q(\mathbb{E})$.

The idea is that $\mathbb{K}$ is an arbitrary schema, and it tells us how the view is to be structured as a (virtual) information system, and the schema map k indicates for each node in $\mathbb{K}$ how to find the corresponding data from the information system $\mathbb{E}$. The virtual information system can be structured in any reasonable way, and looks like an ordinary information system (modularity), and it can incorporate data obtained from any query applied to the information system with schema $\mathbb{E}$ (universality).

Naturally the mere existence of k does put some restrictions on the possible structures for the view $\mathbb{K}$. After all a schema map has to carry constraints to constraints. Thus, $\mathbb{K}$ cannot include constraints that have no corresponding constraints in $\mathbb{E}$. But this is no real limitation — of course it isn't possible to require constraints in the view which are not required in $\mathbb{E}$ since the data from $\mathbb{E}$, which might violate those constraints, is just inherited by the view.

Example 5 Returning to Figure 1 we can consider some simple examples of views. The simplest examples of views just include some of the data from the information system. Thus the Sales Department might have a view which includes only Customer, Product, Order, Location, Price and the relationships between them. Even more simply the Software Development Department might have a view of Figure 1 which only includes Virtual product. More interestingly the administrator of a particular warehouse might have a view of Figure 1 which consists of those Products which are located in his or her warehouse, those Deliveries which are scheduled for any of those products, and the Customers who are awaiting those deliveries. Notice that the nodes for the warehouse administrator's data are not present in Figure 1 but rather occur in the classifying category of the schema as pullbacks of Product and of the categorical product of Delivery and Customer over the warehouse location, or equivalently as `select` and `project` queries including a `where` clause specifying the administrator's warehouse. And of course the administrator's warehouse doesn't appear explicitly in his or her view — it is just used in the calculation of that view.

In fact, these examples are slightly oversimplified because attributes have been left out of Figure 1 and they add considerable complexity to views. For example, even the view for the Software Development Department might include or not include each of the attributes of Product and also each of the attributes of Location.

4 BIDIRECTIONAL LINKS

Now that we have a precise definition of view we are in a position to develop links as proposed in Section 1: Given two project data models which we seek to link we will develop a single schema $\mathbb{K}$ together with two schema morphisms which exhibit $\mathbb{K}$ as a view of each of the project data models.

The schema $\mathbb{K}$ is a single formal representation of those parts of the project data models that share common data in whatever form. Thus it might seem that we have achieved our goal since we have identified the common data that needs to be linked, and we have through the schema morphisms identified how that data can be obtained from the project data models. However, thus far we have only a one-way transmission of data "outward" from the project data models to the link schema $\mathbb{K}$. This is insufficient for a link between the project data models since when the common data in one of the models changes, we need it to change in the other project data model. Sure enough the corresponding data in the link model $\mathbb{K}$ will change for formal mathematical reasons (Dampney *et al.* 2001), but without "inward" data transmission from $\mathbb{K}$ to the second project data model there can be no true link.

Therefore, we consider "inward" transmissibility of data changes. For precision, suppose K is the current state of a link model with schema $\mathbb{K}$. If K is a logically independent view of an information system state E, we should be able to insert and delete in K. But in reality K is a view of some of the data derivable from E, so an insert or delete in K must transmit some change to the underlying database state E. This change of the data of E must be arranged so that the change of the *view* of the data corresponds to the intended insert or delete.

Unfortunately, not all view inserts and deletes are transmissible in this way. This is the *view update problem* (Date 1986, Chapter 8) (or (Date 2000) but note that this later version has a much less detailed treatment).

Here is a minimal but real example of the difficulty. Suppose that $\mathbb{E}$ is the schema $\mathsf{Product} \to \mathsf{Location}$ with no constraints. Let $\mathbb{K}$ be $\mathsf{Product}$ (with k the evident inclusion). An insert into $\mathsf{Product}$ in $\mathbb{K}$ is straightforward. But upon transmission to E we find that we cannot decide how to make such an insertion, because we need to specify the product's location too.

That example shows that we sometimes do not know how to transmit data inwards because there are too many choices. There are also examples where there is no possible state E of the project data model which could correspond to the effect of a specific insert in K — there are no choices.

Once again there has been controversy over the view update problem, arguably for the same reason as the controversy over views: People have defined updatability based on what their systems have been implemented to do, rather than seeking a fundamental definition. In fact there is a real difficulty with obtaining a fundamental definition in the usual framework because traditionally people have sought to define updatability for schema. Instead updatability, renamed in this context transmissibility, can be treated as a property of the current *state* of the information system, and transmissible can be defined as follows (based on (Johnson *et al.* 2001)).

Definition 6 Suppose we have a view $k : \mathbb{K} \to Q(\mathbb{E})$ and a current state E for the database corresponding to $\mathbb{E}$. A view insert/delete is *transmissible* if there exists a unique minimal insert/delete in E which achieves the view insert/delete. More precisely a view insert (delete) is transmissible if, among all of the inserts $D \rightarrowtail D''$ ($D'' \rightarrowtail D$) which achieve the view insert, there is one $D \rightarrowtail D'$ ($D' \rightarrowtail D$) which is initial (terminal) in the full subcategory of the slice category under (over) D.

Notice that we do not require a correspondence between the instances inserted into a view, and those inserted into E as a result of the transmission. To transmit a single inserted instance in a view we may need to carry out multiple inserts in various parts of E. We require only that the needed inserts are well-defined in the sense that as a collection they are the unique minimal insert in E which will achieve the intended view insert.

We move now to how we can use transmissibility to support the interaction of project data models along links specified by views.

5 CONSTRUCTING ENTERPRISE INFORMATION SYSTEMS

We now seek to apply the theory developed so far to the construction of enterprise information models from project data models. For simplicity consider two project data models with schemata $\mathbb{E}$ and $\mathbb{F}$.

We may assume that the project data models include some common data (otherwise we can construct the enterprise data model by taking the disjoint union of the project data models). However, it is unlikely that the common data will have the same names, or even share similar data structures. For example, one system might have separate nodes for each of several different types of product, while the other has a single node for all products. Or one system might only store the products which are at a particular location, while the other stores in one node the products from all locations and has an attribute to record their locations.

So we use logical data independence.

In Section 3 we defined a view to be a schema morphism $k : \mathbb{K} \to Q(\mathbb{E})$. Furthermore we noted that $Q(\mathbb{E})$ contains all queries that can be performed on $\mathbb{E}$. So we can construct views that see the coproduct of all of the different types of product, or the subtype of products at all locations obtained by pulling back over the particular location, etc.

In this manner we construct a logically independent structure, a view, which contains matchable nodes from each of $Q(\mathbb{E})$ and $Q(\mathbb{F})$, and schema maps

$$Q(\mathbb{E}) \leftarrow \mathbb{K} \to Q(\mathbb{F}).$$

Next we explore inward state-based transmissibility for each schema map. Consider arbitrary states E and F of $\mathbb{E}$ and $\mathbb{F}$. An insert or delete in E affects directly the state K of $\mathbb{K}$ under the view k. We explore the transmissibility of this change of the state of K to the state F. Frequently we can prove lemmas that assure us that all such changes are transmissible (Johnson *et al.* 2001). In that case we have achieved interoperability, and the schema maps, expressed in say SQL terms, together with the construction used in the proof of the lemmas, provide the algorithms for the interoperability mechanism.

In some cases the failure to prove transmissibility identifies specific cases where interoperability fails, and these can be the subject of negotiations between the divisions involved to determine business rules or model changes that will assure good links with effective interoperability.

6 LINKING FIGURE 1

To provide a more detailed example, we now explore how this linking process could arrive at Figure 1.

We suppose that there are several divisions of the e-commerce organisation and that each has developed its own project data model.

As in Example 5 we may have a Sales Department, a collection of warehouse administrators (one for each warehouse), and a Software Development Department. In addition we would expect to have a Delivery Department which can see the entities Delivery, Product, Location, Order and Customer. And perhaps there are other departments too.

We construct Figure 1 incrementally, incorporating constraints as well as graphs as we link project data models pairwise (of course we could do several at once, but it is easier to explain pairwise linkages).

We can begin by linking the Sales Department's project data model with a project data model belonging to one of the warehouse administrators. Both models include an entity called Product but they are not semantically equivalent because the Sales Department's Products include all of the products that the organisation sells, while the warehouse administrator's Products are merely those products which occur in his or her warehouse. So we seek a common view. Since the warehouse administrator's view includes details about deliveries which are invisible to the Sales Department the common view will have to be a part of the warehouse administrator's project data model. In fact his or her Product, taken as a view of some of the project data model, can also be a view of the Sales Department's project data model by identifying it, via a schema morphism, with the pullback of the Sales Department's product over the warehouse's location (equivalently by the query `select product where location = warehouse-location`).

Customer needs to be treated in a similar fashion.

Similarly the other warehouses can be linked with the resulting model, one at a time.

Interestingly, once all of the warehouses have been linked all of the data is in place for the Delivery Department, but the deliveries corresponding to each warehouse were disjoint from those for the other warehouses, and at this point in the development there are separate delivery entities for each warehouse's products. So, to match the semantics of the Delivery entity for the Delivery Department with something in the cumulative model we need take the view of the cumulative model which exhibits all of the warehouses' deliveries as a single coproduct (disjoint union).

Fortunately Order and Customer have identical meaning between the cumulative model and the Delivery Department's project model, so they may be matched immediately.

But there is yet one more twist: The Delivery Department's Product entity only knows about physical products (because virtual products are delivered electronically). So the common view which amalgamates warehouse deliveries, and preserves customers and orders, needs to link the Delivery Department's Product with the cumulative model's query (another pullback) `select from product where location = location1 or location2 or ...` where each of the locations specified is a Physical location.

Finally the Software Development Department is linked similarly.

Of course at each step it is necessary to prove that view inserts and deletes are transmissible, but fortunately for our example this follows from propositions proved in (Johnson *et al.* 2001), and the proofs of those propositions provide the linking code.

Note that the checks for transmissibility are vital, and if for example the Delivery Department did not include the Location of products in its project data model it would not be possible to transmit updates from the coproduct of the warehouses' deliveries to the individual warehouses' project data models. This would be an example of a need for a negotiation between departments to obtain linkable project data models. Still, in this case it's rather unlikely that that difficulty would arise as it would correspond to the Delivery Department planning the deliveries of products without knowing where they were located!

7 CONCLUSION

This paper has presented a technique for the specification of links between project data models. In essence the technique aids in constructing enterprise models or enterprise information systems by linking project data models.

The technique is founded on a category theoretic data model which has already been used extensively in industrial consultancies. This foundation provides rich representations which aid in the design of interoperable views, and a well-understood mathematical basis which supports both constraint definition and the analysis required to guarantee the transmissibility of updates.

The approach uses fundamentally logical data independence in the new category theoretic sense. We use logical data independence between mathematically specified project data models to link data in those models even when those data are stored in perhaps radically different forms.

The interoperations themselves depend upon the transmissibility of updates between logically independent views. For this use of logical data independence to work it is necessary to mathematically analyse the logically independent views to ensure the required transmissibility.

The techniques described here are currently being tested on the interoperation of very large project data models in industry. Preliminary results have shown the techniques to be very successful, and the development of these case studies (and their important practical use in the organisations) continues.

One interesting limitation that we have found in applying the techniques in industry is that they seek to ensure the transmissibility of all updates in both directions (from project model E to project model F and vice versa). In fact, most interoperating systems we have investigated do need to interoperate in both directions, but updates of many particular data structures only occur in one direction (for example, a branch office changes orders and this needs to be indicated on the central warehouse systems, while the warehouse changes internal charges to accounts and this needs to be indicated on the branch office's systems). Using data communications terms, simplex interoperations (which correspond to the client-server model) are well understood, full-duplex interoperations (as described in this paper) are proving very useful but sometimes require more interoperability than is actually used, and half-duplex interoperations would seem to suffice. We are currently attempting to extend the techniques presented here to support "half-duplex" interoperations.

ACKNOWLEDGEMENTS

The research reported here has been supported in part by the Australian Research Council and the NSW Department of Health.

REFERENCES

A. Asperti and G. Longo. *Categories, Types and Structures: An introduction to category theory for the working computer scientist.* MIT Press, 1991.

M. Barr and C. Wells. *Category theory for computing science.* Prentice-Hall, second edition, 1995.

C. N. G. Dampney, Michael Johnson, and G. P. Monro. An illustrated mathematical foundation for ERA. In *The unified computation laboratory*, pages 77–84, Oxford University Press, 1992.

C. N. G. Dampney, Michael Johnson, and Robert Rosebrugh. View Updates in a Semantic Data Model Paradigm. Proceedings of ADC2001, IEEE Press, 29–36, 2001.

C. J. Date. *An Introduction to Database Systems.* Addison-Wesley, fourth edition, 1986.

C. J. Date. *An Introduction to Database Systems.* Addison-Wesley, seventh edition, 2000.

J. Goguen, J. W. Thatcher and E. G. Wagner. An initial algebra approach to the specification, correctness and implementation of abstract data types. In R. Yeh, *Current Trends in Programming Methodology IV*, 80–149, Prentice-Hall, 1978.

J. Goguen, J. W. Thatcher, E. G. Wagner, and J. B. Wright. Initial algebra semantics and continuous algebras. *JACM*, 24:68–95, 1977.

Michael Johnson and Robert Rosebrugh. Database interoperability through state based logical data independence. *International Journal of Computer Applications in Technology*, in press, 2001.

Michael Johnson and Robert Rosebrugh. View updatability based on the models of a formal specification. Proceedings of Formal Methods Europe, LNCS 2021, 534–549, 2001.

Saunders Mac Lane. *Categories for the Working Mathematician.* Graduate Texts in Mathematics 5, Springer Verlag, 1971.

D. Scott. Continuous lattices. *Lecture notes in Mathematics*, 274:97–136, 1972.

D. Scott. Domains for denotational semantics. *Lecture notes in Computer Science*, 140:577–613, 1982.

J. D. Ullman. *Principles of Database and Knowledge-Base Systems.* Volume 1, Computer Science Press, 1988.

R. F. C. Walters. *Categories and Computer Science.* Cambridge University Press, 1991.

A FRAMEWORK FOR EVALUATING WIS DESIGN METHODOLOGIES

Luca Cernuzzi, González Magalí
Universidad Católica "Nuestra Señora de la Asunción", C.C. 1683, Asunción, Paraguay
Email:lcernuzz@uca.edu.py, maga@conexion.com.py

Keywords: Web based Information System, WIS Design Methodologies, Methodologies Evaluation

Abstract: Nowadays, with the rapid growth of the Internet and the Web-based Information System (WIS), special effort is spent in order to provide a well-defined software production process for WIS. Considering this, it may be very interesting for WIS designers to carry out an analysis or evaluation of the existing methodologies that would be most appropriate to use in each case. This study presents a proposal of a framework for the evaluation process of WIS design methodologies. The proposal, based on previous works, takes into consideration qualitative evaluation criteria employing quantitative methods. In order to clarify the proposal, this framework is also applied to a case study, and some interesting aspects are analyzed from both a qualitative and a quantitative perspective.

1. INTRODUCTION

Web is one of the hypermedia interfaces most used to share data in a network (Internet and Intranet). This kind of interface is becoming a standard platform for almost every possible future application. With the exponential growth of the Web, it has been possible to observe a change in the way it used. The Web has changed from a platform merely for information dissemination; to a platform for Web based Information Systems (WIS) which correspond to Internet interface systems that disseminate and process information to return different kinds of results, taking into consideration the users' objectives. This change implies a higher level of integration that merges concepts of database, interfaces, networks and hypermedia. With these new types of applications the Internet's complexity has grown exponentially. It would, therefore, not be worthwhile to develop a system using a non-structured approach. For this reason it is becoming more and more important to apply engineering techniques to develop these systems (Murugesan, S. et all, 1999).

The three major tendencies in designing and developing WIS applications are:

1. The use of techniques that are known in the area of information systems, such as structured or object oriented analysis and design.
2. The use of techniques that are known in the area of hypermedia, such as RMM (Relationship Management Methodology) (Isakowitz, T. et all, 1995) and OOHDM (Object Oriented Hypermedia Design Model) (Rossi, G., 1996);
3. The use of other techniques more specific to the area of WIS, for example; ARANEUS (Atzeni, P., 1997), USER CENTERED (Gnaho, C. et all, 1999), CWSD (Corporate Web Site Development Methodology) (Chen, L. et all, 1999), WEB ARCHITECT (Takahashi, K., 1997) besides others.

Therefore, a waste range of methodologies is available for WIS designers. Considering this, may be very interesting for WIS designers to carry out an analysis or evaluation of the existing methodology that would be most appropriate to use in each case. However, in the specialized literature, there exist few evaluations of these methodologies. Some possible explanations for this are that it seems to be more natural to evaluate the product (application) than the process, and it is also quite difficult to define the correct steps to evaluate the process (design and development). For this reason, the main objective of the present study is to propose a framework for evaluating methodologies, so that designers may carry out the evaluation and accumulation of experience useful both for their own work and for that of other future works as well.

The rest of the paper has been organized in the following manner: chapter 2 presents the framework for evaluating methodologies; chapter 3 presents the application of the framework to a case study: "SIR (Sistema de Información de la Red Rural,

J. Filipe et al. (eds.), Enterprise Information Systems III, 198–207.

Information System for Rural Network)"; and finally, chapter 4 offers some conclusions and presents some future works.

2. EVALUATING METHODOLOGIES

As previously mentioned, our objective is to find an appropriate form for evaluating methodologies that support the WIS construction process. To this end, the following are some of the main objectives of the process that are to be considered:

- Increased efficiency
- Assurance of a higher quality product
- Provision of appropriate documentation
- Facilitation of the reusability and maintenance of the components of the system.

Some results of the process are reflected in the product quality. We must take into consideration these aspects in the evaluation process, that is, some of the criteria will have to refer to characteristics of the product in order to be able to evaluate the methodology. Important contributions related to the quality of the process may be found in patterns and models like the Capability Maturity Model (Paulk , M. et all, 1996), SPICE (Bamford, R. C. et all, 1999) and ISO 9000-3 (ISO 9003 – 3, 1991). Their purpose is more general, however, and does not adequately cover the need to identify and measure specific criteria in order to achieve a finer perception of the quality of the methodology under study.

Before continuing, it is necessary to clarify the meaning of the term evaluation in this context. Evaluation is considered the comparison between a dimension and a criterion or its indicators. In our case, the main objective is the usefulness of a specific methodology for the design of WIS applications, taking into consideration different dimensions and several criteria or indicators that would help evaluators to verify the objective.

Here we present an evaluation framework based on works carried out by different authors (Basili, V.R et all, 1988) (Cernuzzi, L. et all, 1999) (Fenton N. et all, 1997) (Lowe, D. et all, 1999). The proposal takes into consideration qualitative evaluation criteria employing quantitative methods.

2.1 Definition of a framework for the evaluation of WIS design methodologies

Step 1. Application of the paradigm Goal-Question-Metric GQM (Basili, V.R et all, 1988). The main objective of this stage is to determine exactly what is needed to be measured and which criteria to take into account to reach the prospective objectives.

Objective: The main objective of the evaluation is: "The usefulness of methodologies for the design and development of Web based information systems, considering the dimensions that concern general and specific aspects of the methodologies, as well as their influence with regard to the product or to the process."

Questions: The questions that should be answered beginning with the main objective are: Which criteria are needed to carry out the evaluation of the methodologies? Which criteria affect the product and which the process? Which criteria are general and which specific?

Step 2. Specification of an entity- attributes model (Lowe, D. et all, 1999) (Cernuzzi, L. et all, 1999) (Fenton N. et all, 1997): Beginning with the results of the GQM, a model entity-attributes is created. A summary of the measures and criteria taken into consideration in the paradigm GQM, as well as different perspectives to be evaluated (general and specific criteria that affect the product or the process) are shown in Table 1. This model is the base for measurement in later phases.

Step 3. Definition of the empiric relationships, and evaluation of qualitative and quantitative attributes:

Each attribute to be evaluated is defined and then observations on it are carried out. The observations may correspond to empiric relationships among attributes, qualitative evaluations or quantitative evaluations, depending on the criterion and the type of measurement needed. Hereinafter a guideline (rule) is presented for each criterion.

Rigor and Formality

- The formality of models presented in each one of the stages is measured applying the following formula:

$$F_{fm} = \frac{\sum_{i=1}^{N} f(i)}{N}$$

N corresponds to the total amount of models of the methodology
f(i)=0 if the model *i* is not formally defined
f(i)=0,5 if the model *i* is formally defined syntactically or semantically
f(i)=1 if the model *i* is formally defined syntactically and semantically
F_{fm} is the average of formalization of the models presented by the methodology

- Another formality related criterion to be considered is the formal guide needed to carry out the mapping from a model to the following one. In this case the following formula is used:

$$F_{fg} = \frac{\sum_{i=1}^{N-1} f(i)}{N-1}$$

$f(i)=1$ If $\exists$ guides from the stage i to the i+1
$f(i)=0$ If do not exist guides from the stage i to the i+1
N corresponds to the total amount of stages
F_{fg} is the average of existent formal guides in the methodology

Separation of concerns

- Separation of concerns at the views level: It refers to different contexts for the same domain. It can consider different user types, different navigational paths, etc.
- Separation of concerns in the phases and design activities: The number of phases that a methodology takes into consideration is measured.

Table 1: Entity-attributes model

CRITERIA	General	Specific	Product	Process
Rigor and formality - Formality of the models presented in each stage - Formal guideline to mapping a model to the next one	✓			✓
Separation of concerns - Separation of concerns - view - Separation of concerns in the phases and design activities	✓			✓
Modularity - High cohesion - Low coupling	✓		✓	✓
Abstraction - Abstraction inside each phase - Global structure of the application - Existence of design primitives and high level abstraction mechanisms	✓			✓
Anticipation of change - Model independence - Views, interface and performance	✓		✓	✓
Generality - With regard to the users - With regard to the navigational paths - Generality inside each model	✓			✓
Incrementality - With regard to the design - With regard to the life cycle	✓			✓
Independence from the implementation - Information domain - Application interface - Execution of processes or procedures	✓	✓	✓	✓
Navigability - Definition of healthy navigational structures - Cognitive management during browsing - Links validity		✓	✓	
Reusability support - Modules, views, interfaces	✓	✓	✓	✓
Communication support - Clear and precise models - Simple and elegant transition from the description of abstract models to the design, and later implementation	✓	✓		✓
Information management - Information contextualisation - Information structure - Content validity		✓	✓	
Management of different media - Combination of sounds, images, text		✓	✓	

Modularity

- To determine the degree of cohesion of a methodology the following formula it is applied:

$$F_{fanin} = \frac{\sum_{i=1}^{N} f(i)}{N}$$

fan in represents the number of incoming edges for each model (Ghezzi, C. et all, 1991, pp. 77)
f(i) is the ***fan in*** of each model of the methodology
N represents the total amount of models

- To determine the degree of coupling of a methodology the following formula it is applied:

$$F_{fanout} = \frac{\sum_{i=1}^{N} f(i)}{N}$$

fan out represents the number of outgoing edges for each model (Ghezzi, C. et all, 1991, pp. 77)
f(i) is the ***fan out*** of each models of the methodology
N represents the total amount of models

Abstraction

- Abstraction inside each phase: The methodologies present different stages, each stage uses defined models that take into consideration factors that affect exclusively to this stage.
- Global structures of the application: It measures whether or not the methodology allows modeling of this structure.
- Existence of design primitives and of high level abstraction mechanisms: To determine this factor the following formula is applied to the methodology under study:

$$F_p = \frac{\sum_{i=1}^{N} f(i)}{N}$$

f(i)=1 If $\exists$ design primitives and abstraction mechanisms
f(i)=0 If do not exist well defined design primitives and abstraction mechanisms

Anticipation of change

- Models independence: To analyze this aspect the dependence degree that exists among the models of each methodology is considered.
- Anticipation of change with regard to views, interfaces and performance.

Generality

- Generality with regard to the users: This aspect tries to analyze whether or not the methodology explicitly takes into consideration the types of users that access the system.
- Generality with regard to the navigational paths: The context could have different navigational paths depending on the types of users who access the system.
- Generality in each model: This refers to the expressive capability of each model to reflect aspects that are concerned in the stage in which it is used.

Incrementality

- Incrementality with regard to the design: To determine if the methodology contemplates the design process in incremental form. This is very important to achieve a good design solution, especially for complex and large size applications.
- Incrementality with regard to the software life cycle.

Independence from the implementation

- The independence from the implementation is related to the information domain, the application interface and the execution of processes or procedures. This is interesting because it facilitates the design reuse.

Navigability

- Healthy navigational structures: Allows the evaluation of the degree of navigational flexibility, maintaining consistency with clearly established associative relationships.
- Cognitive navigational management: The use of maps and a consistent structure could help in the implementation of this aspect for two reasons; first, both reduce the cognitive effort required by a user in the understanding of the structure; and second, both help to identify where the individual information item is positioned inside the structure. Therefore, it is possible to affirm that a healthy navigational structure influences this criterion.
- Links validity: Refers to how the methodology allows designers to validate the created links or, if links do not need to be sustained in previously defined associations in the domain.

Support to the reuse

If a methodology fulfills the modularity, abstraction, separation of concerns and anticipation of change criteria it is possible to affirm that it is much more easily reusable. This criterion, therefore, is an indirect attribute and will be measured later, in Step 6.

Support to the communication

- Clear and precise models: this criteria can be evaluated applying the following formula:

$$F_{cp} = \frac{\sum_{i=1}^{N} f(i)}{N}$$

N represents the total amount of models in the methodology
f(i)=0 If the model is not clear nor precise
f(i)=0,5 If model *i* is clear or precise or partially clear and precise
f(i)=1 If the model *i* is clear and precise
F_{cp} is the average obtained in this evaluation

- Simple and elegant transition from the description of abstract models to the design and later implementation: It evaluates the ease, for all the professionals involved in the design and implementation of the WIS, of understanding a model and its translation to an implementation.

Information management

- Information context: Refers to the consistency of the semantic context in the navigation.
- Information structure: Refers to eventual guidelines for the design of the application structure from a global perspective.
- Content validity: Determine whether or not the methodology assures certain control of the validity of the content.

Management of different media

To analyze this approach it is necessary to keep in mind the domain of the information (although in most of the cases the possibility of managing different media is more directly related with the adopted database than with the adopted methodology), the application interface (the possibility of mixing different media in the presentation) and the execution of processes or procedures.

Step 4. Definition of a normalized scale type and rules to carry out the mapping: In the previous step formulas have been identified, that enable quantitative evaluation, and the definition of empiric relationships among attributes as defined in Table 1. In this step, the objective is to define a normalized scale type and a group of rules for mapping the results obtained in Step 3 as they relate to the normalized numeric scale.

A Ratio Scale Type is adopted for the following reasons:

- It preserves the ordering, the size of intervals between entities and the ratios between entities.
- All arithmetic can be meaningfully applied to the classes in the range of the mapping.

Each attribute may be assigned numeric values, in the range of 0 to 10, that may be mapped according to the following rules (the mapping rules should preserve the representation condition (Fenton N. et all, 1997):

- If the relationship contains the possible values 0, 0.5 or 1 then the value 10 is assigned for those that obtained 1; for those that obtained 0.5; and for those that obtained 0.
- If the relationship is <, > or = (greater than, less than or equal to) 10 is assigned to those that had greater value, 5 to those that had intermediate value and 0 to those that had lesser value.
- For those measurements that were carried out starting from absolute values (count) and mathematical formulas, the following formula is applied:

$$M = \frac{V_n \times 10}{May}$$

M represents the mapping result
$\boldsymbol{V_n}$ represents the previously evaluated value
May represents the maximum evaluated value between the methodologies

- The modularity criteria may be mapped in the following way:
  - Cohesion: the simple rule of three is applied (higher cohesion corresponds at 10).

$$C = \frac{V_n \times 10}{May}$$

C represents the mapping result
$\boldsymbol{V_n}$ represents the previously value
May represents the maximum evaluated value between the methodologies

  - Coupling: the inverse simple rule of three is applied (smaller coupling corresponds at 10).

$$A = \frac{Men \times 10}{V_n}$$

A represents the mapping result
$\boldsymbol{V_n}$ represents the previously value
Men represents the minimum evaluated value between the methodologies

OBS: the formulas previously presented are applied because a methodology helps to obtain good modularity if it possesses a high cohesion and low coupling. (Ghezzi, C. et all, 1991, pp.51).

- The independence of the models is also mapped applying the inverse simple rule of three because the measurement carried out captures the degree of dependence of the methodologies. Therefore, to a greater degree of dependence corresponds less independence of the models.

It is important to clarify that the rules previously specified conserve the representation condition, since the results obtained in the empiric relationships are preserved when carrying out the mapping (Fenton N. et all, 1997).

Step 5. Mapping of the relationships to the normalized numeric scale: This allows designers and evaluators to use a comparative analysis and to carry out operations among the attributes that present interesting results.

Step 6. Indirect measurement of other attributes: Starting from the indirect measurement it is possible to infer a latent variable attribute or a more general variable attribute, not directly observable, obtained from the measurement of defined attributes. In Table 1 everything emphasized in bold (Modularity, Abstraction, etc.) is an attribute resulting from an indirect measurement. This step assures a more general vision of how the methodology supports certain aspects.

t is possible to observe that the proposed framework is sufficiently general to grant flexibility to the evaluators and, at the same time it is sufficiently precise in the steps and the conceptual tools that support it, to assure an interesting guide for the evaluation process.

3. APPLYING THE FRAMEWORK TO SIR

In this section a case study is presented with the aim of clarifying the application of the framework. For this purpose the SIR (Sistema de Información de la Red Rural, Information System of the Rural Network) application was designed and implemented, using different methodologies.

3.1 SIR design

The SIR tries to integrate information between different rural area institutions that work to educate and inform people lacking easy access to computer technology. The SIR is composed of different modules: jobs offers and demands, offers and demands of agricultural products, course offerings, information about the agricultural market, newsgroups, information about professionals in rural areas, publications, information about fundable projects of the Rural Net, information about institutions in Paraguay, email, etc.

Table 2: Evaluation of the entities

CRITERIA	RMM	ARANEUS	U-C
Formality of the models presented in each stage	1	1	0,75
Formal guideline to mapping a model to the following one	0,5	1	0,4
Separation of concerns - view	0,5	0,5	1
Separation of concerns in the phases and design activities	3	3	5
Cohesion	28,5	33	28,5
Coupling	29,5	30	26
Abstraction inside each phase	1	1	1
Global structure of the application	1	1	1
Existence of design primitives and high level abstraction mechanisms	1	1	0,75
Model independence (standard deviation)	1	1	1,22
Anticipation of change: views, interface and performances	= Araneus < U-C	= RMM < U-C	> Araneus > RMM
Generality with regard to the users	0,5	0,5	1
Generality with regard to the navigational paths	0,5	0,5	1
Generality inside each model	= Araneus < U-C	= RMM < U-C	> RMM >Araneus
Incrementality with regard to the design	1	0	0,5
Incrementality with regard to the life cycle	0	0	0
Independence of the implementation	< Araneus = U-C	> RMM > U-C	< Araneus = RMM
Definition of healthy navigational structures	1	1	1
Cognitive management during browsing	= Araneus < U-C	= RMM < U-C	> Araneus > RMM
Links validity	= RMM > U-C	= Araneus > U-C	<Araneus < RMM
Clear and precise models	0,67	0,83	0,75
Simple and elegant transition from the description of abstract models to the design, and later implementation	0,5	1	1
Information contextualisation	> U-C = Araneus	> U-C = RMM	< RMM < Araneus
Information structure	1	1	1
Content validity	> U-C = Araneus	> U-C = RMM	< RMM < Araneus
Management of different media	1	1	1

Three different methodologies were used to design the SIR:

- RMM (Isakowitz, T. et all, 1995): A well accepted methodology in hypermedia that uses traditional information systems design techniques for relational databases.
- ARANEUS (Atzeni, P., 1997): Along with RMM and OOHDM, that initially were present for hypermedia applications, ARANEUS is one of the methodologies probably most often mentioned by specialized literacy in WIS applications.
- USER-CENTERED (Gnaho, C. et all, 1999): Methodology that allows designers to define different kinds of users. Also used to represent processes and some other interesting particularities of WIS. This methodology also tries to formalize, in a very interesting way, the user objectives.

3.2 Framework application to SIR design

Steps 1 and 2 are the same as those of the general framework. The results of step 3 are shown in Table 2.

Due to reasons of space, only some examples of how to obtain these results are shown:

- Formality: The RMM methodology presents 3 models semantically and syntactically well defined (Entity-Relationship, Application Diagram and M-Slices). For this reason, the result of the formula applied to this methodology is 1. The ARANEUS methodology also presents 3 semantically and syntactically well-defined models (Entity-Relationship, Navigational Conceptual Model and Araneus Data Model), and the result of the formula applied to this methodology is also 1. The USER-CENTERED methodology presents four models (O*, Way of Navigation, Navigational Semantic Units and Navigational Nodes), but one of these (Navigational Nodes) is not well defined syntactically because its internal structure is not formalized. Thus, the result of the formula applied to the last methodology is 0.75.
- Anticipation of change: The USER-CENTERED methodology considers views and concepts more explicitly, taking into account user profiles and ways of navigation (WoN), which are related to the user profiles. It also considers concepts, like the navigational semantic unit (NSU), related to the user role.
- Link validity: the entity-relationship model (used in RMM and ARANEUS) not only identifies the key entities, it also identifies the associative relationship between the entities. There are many techniques that could ensure that these relationships are valid. Many of the links on the navigational diagram are derived from these relationships, assuring that they would also be correct.
- Content validity: Using the RMM and ARANEUS methodologies, all information of the application must be based on the entities identified during the initial entity relationship analysis. This means that it is less likely to spuriously incorporate irrelevant information into the application, securing the validity of the content. The USER-CENTERED methodology focuses on the determination of objectives. This doesn't ensure content validity, but gives more flexibility on the issue of user interests

Table 3 shows the mapping of the results to the normalized ratio scale as defined in step 4.

The attributes obtained by indirect measurement, mentioned in step 6, were obtained by averaging the attributes related to each indirect measurement shown in Table 1. The results of this average are shown in Table 4.

In Table 5 the results implementing the perspectives of Table 1 are presented. We also calculated the sum and average of the indirect attributes shown in Table 4.

This experience, although it cannot be considered completely significant, shows that none of the studied methodologies is substantially better than the other ones. Nevertheless, it is possible to affirm that the WIS oriented methodologies (ARANEUS and USER CENTERED) obtain better results in the specific and product related aspects.

Table 3: Mapping to the ratio scale

CRITERIA	RMM	ARANEUS	U-C
Formality of the models presented in each stage	10	10	7,5
Formal guideline to mapping a model to the following one	5	10	4
Separation of concerns - view	5	5	10
Separation of concerns in the phases and design activities	6	6	10
Cohesion	8,6	10	8,6
Coupling	8,8	7,8	10
Abstraction inside each phase	10	10	10
Global structure of the application	10	10	10
Existence of design primitives and high level abstraction mechanisms	10	10	7,5
Model independence (standard deviation)	10	10	8,2
Anticipation of change: views, interface and performances	5	5	10
Generality with regard to the users	5	5	10
Generality with regard to the navigational paths	5	5	10
Generality inside each model	5	5	10
Incrementality with regard to the design	10	0	5
Incrementality with regard to the life cycle	0	0	0
Independence on the implementation	5	10	5
Definition of healthy navigational structures	10	10	10
Cognitive management during browsing	5	5	10
Links validity	10	10	5
Clear and precise models	6,7	8,3	7,5
Simple and elegant transition from the description of abstract models to the design, and later implementation	5	10	10
Information contextualisation	10	10	5
Information structure	10	10	10
Content validity	10	10	5
Management of different media	10	10	10

Table 4: Indirect attributes

INDIRECT ATTRIBUTES	RMM	ARANEUS	U-C
Rigor and formality	7,5	10	5,75
Separation of concerns	5,5	5,5	10
Modularity	8,7	8,9	9,3
Abstraction	10	10	9,1
Anticipation of change	7,5	7,5	9,1
Generality	5	5	10
Incrementality	5	0	1,6
Independence from the implementation	5	10	5
Navigability	8,3	8,3	8,3
Reusability support	7,9	7,9	9,3
Communication support	5,9	9,2	8,6
Information management	10	10	6,6
Management of different media	10	10	10

Table 5: Results according to the perspectives

METHODOLOGY	GENERAL	SPECIFIC	PRODUCT	PROCESS
SUM				
RMM	68	47.1	59.5	76.3
ARANEUS	74	55.4	64.7	82.3
USER CENTERED	77.75	47.8	58.3	86.05
AVERAGE				
RMM	6.08	7.85	7.44	6.9
1.1.1.1.1.1.1 ARANEUS	7.4	9.23	8.09	7.5
USER CENTERED	7.75	7.97	7.29	7.8

4. CONCLUSIONS AND FUTURE WORKS

This work proposes a framework for the evaluation of WIS design and development methodologies. The framework corresponds to a refinement of previous works (Cernuzzi, L. et all, 1999) (Lowe, D. et all, 1999) that are mainly based in carrying out a qualitative analysis of the methodologies.

A first important refinement is that the present proposal was defined not just considering heuristic but it was defined employing formal aspects of mensurations and metric presented by Fenton and Pfleeger (Fenton N. et all, 1997). So, it is possible to carry out quantitative evaluations and not just qualitative ones.

A second refinement is centered in the criteria. In (Cernuzzi, L. et all, 1999) criteria for the hypermedia system design are classified as general and specific while in (Lowe, D. et all, 1999) are considered criteria that affect the product or the process. This work presents a synthesis of both proposals introducing finer criteria. In effect, criteria proposed in the previous works have been considered indirect attributes and have been refined by means different criteria that may be directly measured.

This framework contemplates 6 steps:

1. Application of the paradigm Goal-Question-Metric (Basili, V.R et all, 1988) to determine the objective of the evaluation.
2. Specification of an entity/attributes model (Lowe, D. et all, 1999) (Cernuzzi, L. et all, 1999) (Fenton N. et all, 1997) that constitutes the base for measurement process in later phases.
3. Definition of the empiric relationships and evaluation of qualitative and quantitative attributes.
4. Definition of a normalized scale type and rules to carry out the mapping from each mensuration to this scale.
5. Mapping of the relationships to the normalized numeric scale.
6. Indirect mensuration of other attributes inferred from those directly evaluated.

For exemplification purposes, an application of the framework to the case of SIR (Sistema de Información de la Red Rural: available in http://www.redrural.org.py) has been introduced.

One of the main contribution to the methodologies evaluation of our proposal is to explicitly take into account not only qualitative aspects, but also quantitative aspects. In effect, in step 5 all evaluated attributes are converted to a normalized numeric value. This conversion allows WIS designers to carry out operations among the attributes, with interesting results. Another important contribution is the possibility to carry out a comparative analysis among different methodologies. This is facilitated by the numeric value for direct or indirect attributes.

As for future works, at least three possible lines may be seen:

- a better refinement and formalization of the proposed evaluation framework;
- the application of the framework to several cases that cover different types of WIS;
- and finally, a revision of the indicators (attributes) adopted to better cover significant aspects for the evaluation of the quality of a methodology.

REFERENCES

Atzeni, P. Et all , 1997. "*Design and Maintenance of Data-Intensive Web Sites*". In Sixth International Conference on Extending Database Technology. In: http://pincare.inf.uniroma3.it:8080, June 1997

Bamford, R. C. et all, 1999. "*Comparing, contrasting ISO 9001 and the SEI Capability Maturity Model*". Software System Consulting. IEEE Computer, October 1993

Basili, V.R et all, 1988. "*The TAME project: Torwards improvement – oriented software environments*". IEEE Transactions on Software Engineering, SE - 14(6), pp. 758-773, 1988.

Cernuzzi, L. et all, 1999. "*Propuesta de un marco de evaluación para modelos y metodológias de desarrollo de aplicaciones hipermedia*", XXV Conferencia Latinoamericana de Informática - CLEI99 pp.1-12, Asunción: Paraguay, September 1999

Chen, L. et all, 1999. "*A development methodology for Corporate Web sites*". In: http://fistserv.macarthur.uws.edu.au/san/icse99-webe/ICSE99-WebE-Proc, 1999

Fenton N. et all, 1997. "*Software Metrics: A rigorous and Practical Approach*". PWS Publishing Company, 1997

Ghezzi, C. et all, 1991. "*Fundamentals of Software Engineering*". Prentice Hall International, New Jersey: USA, 1991.

Gnaho, C. et all, 1999. "*A User Centered Methodology for complex and customizable Web Application Engineering*". Université Paris. In: http://fistserv.macarthur.uws.edu.au/san/icse99-webe/ICSE99-WebE-Proc, 1999

Isakowitz, T. et all, 1995. "*RMM: A Methodology for Structured Design*". Communications of the ACM. Vol. 36 (8), pg. 34-43, August 1995

ISO 9003 – 3, 1991. "*ISO 9003-3: Quality Management and quality assurance standards-part 3: Guidelines for the application of ISO 9001 to the development, supply and maintenance of software*", 1991

Lowe, D. et all, 1999. "*Hypermedia and the Web: An engineering approach*". Hohn Wiley & Sons Ltd, Chichester: England, 1999

Murugesan, S. et all, 1999. "*Web Engineering: A new Discipline for development of Web based systems*". Australia. In: http://fistserv.macarthur.uws.edu.au/san/icse99-webe/ICSE99-WebE-Proc, 1999

Paulk, M. et all, 1996. "*The continuing improvement of the CMM: Version 2*". In Fifth European Conference on Software Quality, September 1996

Rossi, G., 1996. "*An Objet-Oriented Method for Designing Hypermedia Applications*". PhD Thesis. Departamento de Informática, Pontifícia Universidade Catolica do Rio de Janeiro, Brasil. En http://www-lifia.info.unlp.edu.ar/~fer/oohdm/, 1996

Takahashi, K., 1997. "*Analysis and Design of Web Based Information Systems*". In: http://www.nttlabs.com/~kt/WebArchitect/, 1997

AN INFORMATION SYSTEM VIEW OF CONSISTENCY AND INTEGRITY IN ENTERPRISE OPERATIONS

Yoshiyuki Shinkawa
Systems Laboratory, IBM Japan
Ltd, 1-1, Nakase, Mihama-ku, Chiba-shi, Chiba Japan
Email: yshink@jp.ibm.com

Masao J. Matsumoto
Graduate School of Systems Management, The University of Tsukuba
3-29-1, Otsuka, Bunkyo-ku, Tokyo Japan
Email: mjm@gssm.otsuka.tsukuba.ac.jp

Keywords: Data mining, Association rules, Relational database systems

Abstract: Mining for association rules is one of the fundamental data mining methods. In this paper we describe how to efficiently integrate association rule mining algorithms with relational database systems. From our point of view direct access of the algorithms to the database system is a basic requirement when transferring data mining technology into daily operation. This is especially true in the context of large data warehouses, where exporting the mining data and preparing it outside the database system becomes annoying or even in-feasible. The development of our own approach is mainly motivated by shortcomings of current solutions. We investigate the most challenging problems by contrasting the prototypical but somewhat academic as-sociation mining scenario from basket analysis with a real-world application. We thoroughly compile the requirements arising from mining an operative data warehouse at DaimlerChrysler. We generalize the re-quirements and address them by developing our own approach. We explain its basic design and give the details behind our implementation. Based on the warehouse, we evaluate our own approach together with commercial mining solutions. It turns out that regarding runtime and scalability we clearly outperform the commercial tools accessible to us. More important, our new approach supports mining tasks that are not directly addressable by commercial mining solutions.

1 INTRODUCTION

Recent evolution of the internet technologies have been affecting the ways of business operations. Many kinds of new business styles using those technologies are emerging. They include electronic commerce (e-commerce), Electronic Data Interchange (EDI), Supply Chain Management (SCM), electronic marketplace (e-marketplace), virtual enterprise, and so on (Menasce and Almedia, 2000), (Norris et al., 2000), (Simchi-Levi et al., 2000).

They require rich functionality of information systems in order to deal with complex data flow and control, not only within an enterprise (intra-enterprise), but also beyond enterprise boundaries (inter-enterprise).

Although there are standardized protocols for inter-enterprise data exchange, which define data formats and semantics, e.g. OBI (Open Buying on the Internet), RosettaNet PIPs (Partner Interface Processes) and IFX (Interactive Financial eXchange), we are faced with the following two problems when implementing information systems for enterprise operations.

1. There are no appropriate measures to evaluate validity or correctness of enterprise operations, even in an intra-enterprise environment.
2. The lack of the above measures make the design of information systems difficult , especially in designing exception handling and failure recovery.

Traditional enterprise modeling frameworks, e.g. ARIS (Scheer, 1998), CIMOSA (Kosanke et al., 1999), PERA (Williams and Hong, 1998) or SDAT (Vernadat, 1996), mainly focus on functionality and structure of enterprises, however they refer little to the above issues.

This paper presents a formal approach to modeling intra-enterprise and inter-enterprise operations, which can deal with validity or correctness of them. In addition, it also proposes a way to design exception handling and failure recovery.

The paper is composed as follows. In section 2, we discuss a way to model intra- and inter- enterprise operations, along with a way to define *states* of the enterprise. Section 3 deals with the concept of valid-

J. Filipe et al. (eds.), Enterprise Information Systems III, 208–214.

ity or correctness of the enterprises which are referred to as *consistency*. Section 4 proposes how the consistency is kept in case of exceptions and failures.

We assume all the business processes are carried out by DataBase Management Systems (DBMSs) and Transaction Processing Monitors (TPMs).

2 MODELING INTRA/INTER-ENTERPRISE OPERATIONS

Before discussing validity and correctness of enterprise operations, we first have to define enterprise operations more strictly. Enterprise operations have many aspects, e.g. functional view, organizational view, or logistic view. This paper focuses on more generic business operation view, which is composed of many business processes.

2.1 Modeling Intra-Enterprise Operations

In our definition, an enterprise operation is a set of business processes, and those business processes are defined as a set of (partially) ordered activities which alter the state of the enterprise. A state of an enterprise can be regarded as a status of all the resources, organization, and other constituents composing the enterprise.

If an enterprise operations are automated, or in other words, are controlled by information systems, the status of the above stuff is stored in databases. Since we assume such an automated environment, we define the state of the enterprise as a set of all the database records relevant to the enterprise operations. Those database records are altered by *transactions* controlled by TPMs, therefore each activity can be associated with a transaction.

In order to model business processes composed of databases and transactions, we need some notational method which can express the behavior of a business process along with state transition of the process.

Colored Petri Nets (CPNs) are one of such methods, since they can express the behavior of a system by transition firing sequences, while they can express the state of the system by marking of tokens.

CPN are defined as follows (Jensen, 1997).

CPN=(S, P, T, A, N, C, G, E, I) ,

where

S : a finite set of non-empty color sets,

P : a finite set of places,

T : a finite set of transitions,

A : finite set of arcs $P \cap T = P \cap A = T \cap A = \emptyset$,

N : node function $A \rightarrow P \times T \cup T \times P$,

C : a color function $P \rightarrow \Sigma$,

G : a guard function $T \rightarrow$ expression,

E : an arc expression function $A \rightarrow$ expression and

I : an initialization function :

$P \rightarrow$ closed expression.

Each business process is expressed by CPN in the following way (Shinkawa and Matsumoto, 2000), (Shinkawa and Matsumoto, 2001).

- Each transition represents an atomic transaction (Elmagarmid, 1992) in a TPM.
- Each place represents either an input/output parameter to/from the transaction or a database.
- Each token represents data or a record to be processed.
- Each arc function represents functionality that is performed by the atomic transaction.

In order to distinguish a place for an input parameter from that for a database, we denote the former by single line ellipse, while the latter by double line one. Figure 1 shows an example of a simple business process for a travel agency.

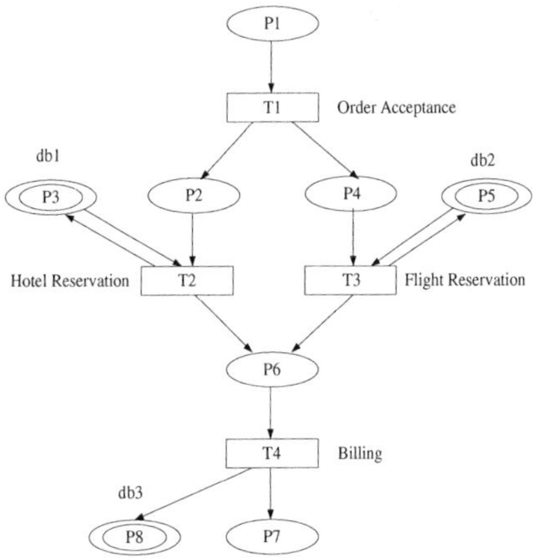

Figure 1: Sample CPN model

Color tokens in a place for a database represent the records in the corresponding database. A state of an enterprise is represented by a set of all the records reside in those databases. When a CPN model including the places for databases $db_1, \ldots, db_l$ is given, the state S is denoted by

$$S = \bigcup_{i=1}^{l} \{\langle r_j^{(i)} \rangle | j = 1, \ldots, n_i\}$$

where $r_j^{(i)}$ is a record in the database db_i, and n_i is the total number of the records in that database. Usually, a database record is composed of several fields (or attributes). We denote the structure of record $r_j^{(i)}$ as

$R^{(i)} = \langle a_1^{(i)}, \ldots, a_{m_i}^{(i)} \rangle$
and each record as
$r_j^{(i)} = \langle x_{j1}^{(i)}, \ldots, x_{jm_i}^{(i)} \rangle \ (j = 1, \ldots, n_i)$
where $x_{j1}^{(i)}, \ldots, x_{jm_i}^{(i)}$ are instance values of the attributes $a_1^{(i)}, \ldots, a_{m_i}^{(i)}$ respectively.

Each record is identified by a key. We assume all keys are put in the first attribute, that is, $x_{j1}^{(i)}$ always represents the key.

Those records are altered (e.g. updated, deleted, or inserted) by transactions corresponding to transitions. Arc functions to the places for databases express how the databases are altered.

2.2 Modeling Inter-Enterprise Operations

Recent evolution of the internet technologies expand the scope of enterprise operations from intra-enterprise to inter-enterprise. Such inter-enterprise operations are often called *inter-enterprise collaboration* .

In the early stage of inter-enterprise collaboration, simple one-way data transmission composes the only interface between two enterprises. Such a form of collaboration is often called Electronic Data Exchange (EDI). Each enterprise can perform its own business processes independently in this form of collaboration because of the simplicity of interaction.

In the next stage, a more complicated form emerged for effective collaboration, which are composed of a series of one-way data transmissions. Such a form of collaboration is referred to as Supply Chain (SC). Even in this form, each enterprise can perform its own business processes independently, since each interface of the above supply chain is as simple as EDI, and those interfaces are activated sequentially. The above two forms of collaboration can be represented by connecting two or more CPN models as shown in Figure 2.

In those models, some transitions are responsible to send data to another CPN model, and denoted by drawing arcs from the transitions of one CPN model to the places of another CPN model (The transition T2 and the place P6 are those ones in Figure 2). Each CPN model represents a business process of each enterprise. The structure of inter-enterprise operations is always fixed in those forms of collaboration. Such inter-connected CPN models can be regarded as a single CPN model. There is another more complex form of inter-enterprise operations, often referred to as *virtual enterprises*. In this form, collaboration is not accomplished by simple message transmission, but by composing a global business processes of participating enterprises.

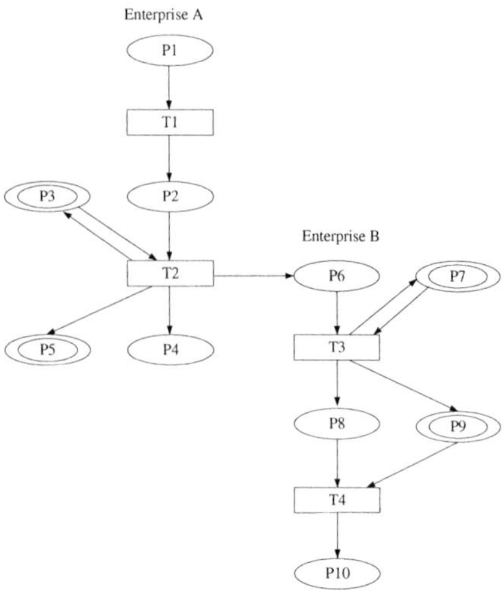

Figure 2: Connecting CPN models

Such global business processes cannot be expressed by CPN in the above way, since each business process could be performed differently every time, depending on which enterprises undertake the process. In many *virtual enterprises*, only high-level global business processes are defined, and an implementation of them is left to each participating enterprise. Those high-level global business processes and their detailed implementations can be expressed by *hierarchical CPN* in the following way.

First, a high-level global business process is depicted as a CPN model, in which each transition represents a part of the business process to be implemented by participating enterprises. Second, each enterprise substitute the CPN models of its own business processes for the above transitions. Each transition could be substituted by different enterprises. Finally, we obtain a set of ordinary (or non-hierarchical) CPN models, which covers all the possible business processes that are the implementations of the above high-level global business processes.

Figure 3 shows an example of high-level global processes and the substitution of a transition. The transitions of the CPN model on the left, which are drawn with broad lines, represent a part of the business process to be implemented by each participating enterprises. On the other hand, the transitions of the CPN model on the right drawn with fine lines, represent actual transactions implemented in the enterprise.

As discussed above, we can build a single CPN model for any forms of inter-enterprise operations, which has the same semantics as an intra-enterprise

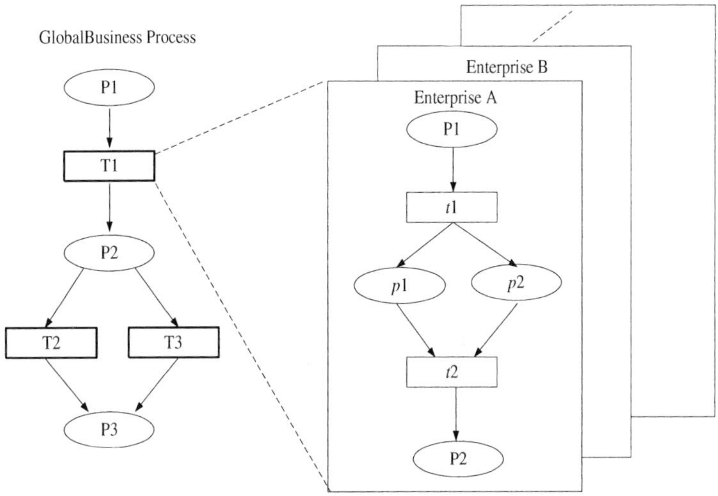

Figure 3: Global business process and its implementation

operation. Therefore, we can define the states of inter-enterprise operations in the same way as intra-enterprise operations.

3 DEFINING CONSISTENCY IN ENTERPRISE OPERATIONS

One of the ways to check validity of a business process is to evaluate the result of it. Since the result is stored in databases in automated business processes, as we assumed, the evaluation can be done by examining the state of the enterprise, that is, a set of all the records in the databases. However, since the values of those records are unknown until the COMMIT time of the associated transaction, it is difficult to determine the states unless all the transactions in the TPM are COMMITed, and there are no active transactions in TPMs (Elmagarmid, 1992), (Krishnamurthy, 1992). Such a situation seems very rare in actual environments.

In addition, the completion of a transaction does not imply the end of some logical unit of work, but only assure the end of a physical operational unit for DBMSs. From application viewpoint, we need state transition by each business process, which is composed of a set of transactions (Molina and Salem, 1987). Figure 4 illustrates this situation intuitively. We need to modify the definition of states to avoid ambiguity. We introduce *overlaid states* for this purpose, which is defined as follows.

1. Let $T_1, \ldots, T_s$ be transactions running concurrently at the time t, which hold the database records

$$H_{T_p} = \bigcup_{i=1}^{l} \{\langle (\rho_{T_p}^{(i)})_k \rangle | k = 1, \ldots, q_{T_p}\} \quad (p = 1, \ldots, s)$$

respectively, where each $(\rho_{T_p}^{(i)})_k \in db_i$ $(i = 1, \ldots, l)$ has the original values when the transaction starts. By LOCK mechanism of TPM, $H_{T_i} \cap H_{T_j} = \emptyset$ $(i \neq j)$ holds.

2. The state overlay operator "$\triangleright$" is defined as $S_1 \triangleright S_2 = S_3$ where

$$S_1 = \bigcup_{i=1}^{l} \{\langle {r'}_j^{(i)} \rangle | j = 1, \ldots, {n'}_i\} = \bigcup_{i=1}^{l} \{\langle {x'}_{j1}^{(i)}, \ldots, {x'}_{m'_i}^{(i)} \rangle | j = 1, \ldots, {n'}_i\}$$

$$S_2 = \bigcup_{i=1}^{l} \{\langle {r''}_j^{(i)} \rangle | j = 1, \ldots, {n''}_i\} = \bigcup_{i=1}^{l} \{\langle {x''}_{j1}^{(i)}, \ldots, {x''}_{{m''}_i}^{(i)} \rangle | j = 1, \ldots, {n''}_i\}$$

and

$$S_3 = \bigcup_{i=1}^{l} (\{\langle {r'}^{(i)_j} \rangle | \forall k \, [{x'}_{j1}^{(i)} \neq {x''}_{k1}^{(i)}]\} \cup \{\langle {r''}_j^{(i)} \rangle\})$$

"$\triangleright$" overlay the old records by the altered new records.

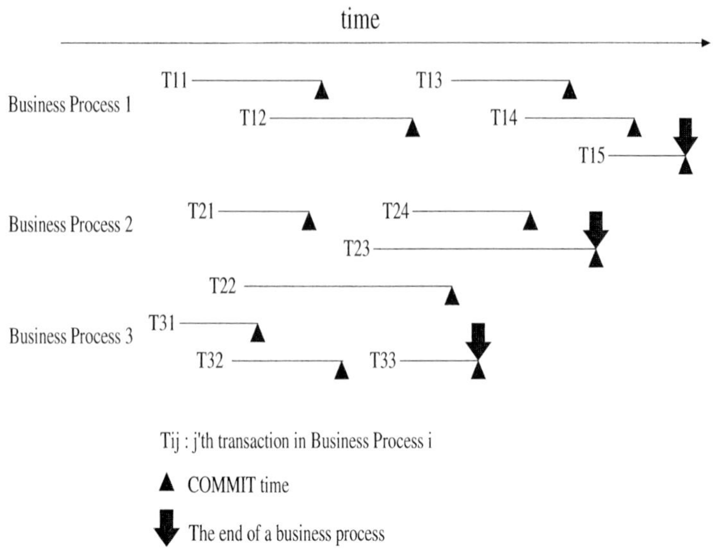

Figure 4: States and transactions

3. Let $F(t) = \bigcup_{i=1}^{l}\{\langle \rho'^{(i)}_j\rangle | j = 1,\ldots,q'_i\}$ be a set of all the free records[1] in db_i. The overlaid state $S(t)_{\mathbf{T}}$ of the transactions $\mathbf{T} = \{T_1,\ldots,T_s\}$ is defined as
$$S_{\mathbf{T}} = F(t) \triangleright (\bigcup_{p=1}^{s} P_{T_p}(t))$$
where $P_{T_p}(t)$ is a set of altered records by the transaction T_p, produced at the COMMIT time.
4. Let $\mathbf{B} = \{B_1,\ldots,B_u\}$ be the business processes running at time t, and $\{T_{ij} | j = 1,\ldots,u_i\}$ be the transactions involved in the business process B_i. The set of overlaid states $\mathbb{S}_{\mathbf{B}}(t)$ as
$\mathbb{S}_{\mathbf{B}}(t) = \{S_{\mathbf{B}}(t)\} = \{F(t)(\prod \triangleright P_{T_{ij}}(t))\}$
where $\prod \triangleright P_{T_{ij}}(t)$ represents one of the possible sequences of transactions completed after t. $S_{\mathbf{B}}(t)$ means one of the possible final state when all the new business processes are suspended at time t, and $\mathbb{S}_{\mathbf{B}}(t)$ is the set of them.

By defining the above overlaid states, we can determine all the instances of database records at any time, and we can discuss consistency in an enterprise based on those states.

Consistency, or consistent states of an enterprise can be roughly defined as the states that all the relevant applications can accept. Those acceptable states are derived from constraints on the states, that is, constraints on the values of each record, on the relationships between attribute values within a record, or on relationships between the records.

In order to deal with those constraints rigorously, we use predicate logic formulas composed of the predicates used in the relevant applications, the variables and the constants representing the values of database records, and logic operators.

For example, in the business process shown in Figure 1, the following constraints would be imposed.

- $P_1 : \forall r^{(1)}_j \in db_1, \exists r^{(2)}_k \in db_2\ [x^{(1)}_{j1} = x^{(2)}_{k1}]$
- $P_2 : \forall r^{(3)}_j \in db_3\ [x^{(3)}_{j2} = x^{(3)}_{j3} + x^{(3)}_{j4}]$

if $x^{(1)}_{j1}$, $x^{(2)}_{k1}$ represent the *order number* and $x^{(3)}_{j2}$, $x^{(3)}_{j3}$, $x^{(3)}_{j4}$ represent *total charge*, *room charge* and *flight fare* respectively.

When constraints are expressed in the predicate logic formulas $P_1, P_2, \ldots$, and P_n, a set of all the possible states
$\mathbb{S} = \{S\} = \{\cup\{\langle r^{(i)}_j\rangle\}\}$
is divided into the subset $\mathbb{S}_C$ and $\mathbb{S}_I$, where $\mathbb{S}_C$ satisfies the formula $P = P_1 \wedge \cdots \wedge P_n$, while $\mathbb{S}_I$ does not.

The above $\mathbb{S}_C$ is the set of consistent states since each state in it satisfies all the constraints.

The completion of each business process should keep the state consistent if the initial state of the busi-

[1]the records which are not LOCKed

ness process is consistent. We define an enterprise is consistent if

1. The initial state $S(0)$ is consistent.
2. At any time t, if $\mathbb{S}_{\mathbf{B}}(t)$ is consistent for any set of business processes, $\mathbb{S}_{\mathbf{B}'}(t')$ $(t' > t)$ is consistent[2].

Our definition can easily expand to inter-enterprise operations, in which business processes spread over the boundaries of enterprises. Under such circumstances, states are defined as set of all records in the relevant databases that each enterprise owns. As discussed in Section 2, inter-enterprise operations are also expressed in CPN model, and the state of the model is determined by the marking of the places for databases. Each states can be evaluated whether it satisfies all the constraints that each participating enterprise provides, and therefore we can define the set of consistent states and that of the inconsistent states in the same way we did for a single enterprise.

4 INTEGRITY OF ENTERPRISE OPERATIONS

As long as every business process proceeds normally, the state of an enterprise (intra- and inter-) keeps consistent, if the conditions discussed above are satisfied. However, once a business process or a part of business process fails, it could cause inconsistent states.

For example, if the transition T_3 (Flight Reservation) of our sample business process fails, e.g. by the reason of sellout, the enterprise gets into inconsistent state, since the state does not satisfies the constraint of

$P_1 : \forall r_j^{(1)} \in db_1, \exists r_k^{(2)} \in db_2\ [x_{j1}^{(1)} = x_{k1}^{(2)}]$,
which was discussed in Section 3.

As shown in this example, some part of a business process CPN model must be dealt with as one unit (like transitions T_2 and T_3 in Figure 1), that is, all the involved transactions must be COMMITed or ABORTed together. Such a unit is often referred to as *sphere* (Leymann, 1995), (Leymann and Roller, D, 1999), or *compensation scope* (Du et al., 1997).

When some of the transactions in a sphere fail, the updates to the databases by the other transactions in the same sphere must be removed. Such removal operations are called *compensation* or *semantic undo* (Du et al., 1997), (Leymann, 1995). The compensation is a user logic to remove the undesired updates, and would be implemented as transactions, called *compensation transactions*.

Those compensation transactions are scheduled after a failure is found, and remove the updates that the associated transactions made. However, the compensation transactions could be scheduled much later after the failure, and the records to be restored could be altered by other transactions.

In order to deal with such situation, we define compensation as follows.

1. Let $\Sigma = \{T_1, \ldots, T_n\}$ be a sphere to be restored, which is composed of two sets of transactions
$\Sigma^{(F)} = \{T_1^{(F)}, \ldots, T_p^{(F)}\}$ which ended in failure and
$\Sigma^{(S)} = \{T_1^{(S)}, \ldots, T_q^{(S)}\}$ which ended in success.
Evidently $\Sigma = \Sigma^{(F)} \cup \Sigma^{(S)}$, and $\Sigma^{(F)} \cap \Sigma^{(S)} = \emptyset$ hold.
2. At any time t after the failure, supposing there are m business processes $\mathbf{B} = \{B_1, \ldots, B_m\}$ at that time, Σ is *compensatable* if there is a consistent state $S'(t')$ at time t' which satisfies
$S'(t') \rhd P_{\Sigma^{(S)}}(t') = S(t)$
and $\mathbb{S}_{\mathbf{B}}(t')$ is a set of consistent states.
3. When the condition 2 is satisfied at any time t after the failure and for any combination of business processes composing $\mathbf{B}$, Σ is *compensatable* sphere.

The above $S(t')$ is the target state to which the current state $S(t)$ is to be restored by compensation transactions. Next, we discuss how the compensation is accomplished.

A state transition performed by a transaction is determined by database update requests from the transaction. Each request, e.g. expressed in SQL, can be regarded as a function

$f : D_f \subseteq \wp(\mathbb{S}) \longrightarrow I_f \subseteq \wp(\mathbb{S})$
where $\mathbb{S}$ is a set of all the possible records in the databases, $\wp(\mathbb{S})$ is the power set of $\mathbb{S}$, and D_f, I_f are subsets of $\wp(\mathbb{S})$ which mean the domain of definition and the image of f respectively. A transaction T is a series of those functions, and can be denoted by

$T = f_1, \ldots, f_n$
from database viewpoint.

Let the transaction $T_i^{(S)}$ be composed of the set of functions $\{f_1^{(i)}, \ldots, f_{p_i}^{(i)}\}$, which belongs to a sphere Σ and ended in success. When the sphere Σ fails at time τ, the state $S(\tau)$ includes

$$\{f_j^{(i)}(H_{T_i^{(S)}}) | i = 1, \ldots, q\ j = 1, 1, \ldots, p_i\},$$

since $\Sigma^{(S)} = \{T_1^{(S)}, \ldots, T_q^{(S)}\}$ is assumed to end in success.

At the compensation time $t (t > \tau)$, the records in $\{f_j^{(i)}(H_{T_i}^{(S)})\}$ could be altered, therefore we are not able to replace $\{f_j^{(i)}(H_{T_i}^{(S)})\}$ by $H_{T_{T_i}^{(S)}}$ for the state restoration. In order to avoid this inconvenience, we introduced a virtual origin state $S'(t')$ for Σ as defined above, which derive the current state $S(t)$ by performing $\Sigma^{(S)}$.

[2]The completion of each transaction does not ensure the consistency, since it does not imply the completion of semantic unit of work

This virtual state $S'(t')$ must include a set of records ${H'}_{T_i^{(S)}}$ $(i = 1, \ldots, q)$ which satisfies

$$f_j^{(i)}({H'}_{T_i^{(S)}}(t')) \subseteq S(t)$$

It implies that if we can identify the inverse function of each $f_j^{(i)}$ which is denoted by

$$(f_j^{(i)})^{-1} : I_{f_j^{(i)}} \longrightarrow D_{f_j^{(i)}}$$

the state $S(t)$ would be changed to $S'(t')$ by the transaction

$$T_{C_i} = \{(f_j^{(i)})^{-1} | j = 1, \ldots, p_i\}.$$

This approach is applicable only when all the functions $f_j^{(i)}$s are *injection*, that is, one-to-one mapping. Otherwise, we can not determine the inverse functions.

The above discussion is based on intra-enterprise operations, however it can be extended to inter-enterprise operations in the same way we did in Section 3.

5 CONCLUSIONS

A formal approach is presented, which deals with consistency and integrity of an intra-enterprise and inter-enterprise operations from information system viewpoint. We define a state of an enterprise as a set of the relevant database records. Those states are changed by business processes expressed in CPN, and carried out by DBMSs and TPMs.

Consistent states are the sets of database records, which satisfy a given set of constraint rules on them, which are expressed in predicate logic. The concept of consistency is expanded to theree styles of inter-enterprise collaboration, that is, EDI style, supply chain style, and e-marketplace style.

Integrity is defined as a mechanism to keep an enterprise consistent. We use compensation, or semantic undo, for the mechanism.

We assume all the functions that represent database updates are *injection*, in order to derive the inverse functions of them. However, the assumption is too restrictive in some cases to design compensation transactions. We need more semantic approach to identify the inverse functions.

REFERENCES

Du, W., Davis, J. and Shan, M.C., 1997, 'Flexible Specification of Workflow Compensation Scopes', *Proc. of the International ACM SIGGROUP Conference on Supporting Group Work : The Integration Challenge*, pp. 309-316

Elmagarmid, A.K., 1992, *Database Transaction Models for Advanced Applications*: Morgan Kaufmann Publishers.

Jensen, K., 1997, *Coloured Petri Nets* Volume 1-3.: Springer.

Kosanke, K., Vernadat, F. and Zelm, M., 1999, 'CIMOSA: enterprise engineering and integration', *Computer Industry*, Vol.40, No.2-3: Elsevier, pp83-97.

Krishnamurthy, E.V., 1992, *Transaction Processing System*: Prentice Hall.

Leymann, F., 1995, 'Supporting Business Transactions Via Partial Backward Recovery In Workflow Management Systems', *Proceedings Databases in Office Engineering and Science*: Springer, pp. 50-70.

Leymann,F. and Roller, D., 1999, *Production Workflow Concepts and Techniques*: Prentice Hall.

Menasce, D.A. and Almedia, V.A.F., 2000, *Scaling for E-Business*: Prentice-Hall.

Molina, H.G. and Salem, K., 1987, 'SAGAS', *Proc. of the ACM SIGMOD Annual Conference on Management of Data*, pp. 249-259.

Norris, M., West, S. and Gaughan, K., 2000, *eBusiness Essentials*: John Wiley & Sons, Ltd.

Scheer, A.W., 1998, *ARIS-Business Process Frameworks*: Springer.

Simchi-Levi, D., Kaminsky, P. and Simchi-Levi, E., 2000, *Designing and Managing the Supply Chain*: McGraw-Hill.

Shinkawa, Y. and Matsumoto, M.J., 2000, 'Business Modeling and Component Mining Based on Rough Set Theory', *Proc. of 6th International Conference on Software Reuse*: Springer, pp. 231-250.

Shinkawa, Y. and Matsumoto, M.J., 2001, 'Identifying the Structure of Business Processes for Comprehensive Enterprise Modeling', *IEICE Trans. on Inf. and Syst*, Vol.E84-D. No.2, pp. 239-248.

Vernadat, F.B., 1996, *Enterprise Modeling and Integration*: Chapman and Hall.

Williams, T.J. and Hong, L., 1998, 'PERA and GERAM enterprise reference architectures in enterprise integration', *Proc. of Design and Information Infrastructure and Systems for Manufacturing*: Kluwer Academic Publishers.

INTEGRATING ORGANIZATIONAL SEMIOTIC APPROACH WITH THE TEMPORAL ASPECTS OF PETRI NETS FOR BUSINESS PROCESS MODELING

Joseph Barjis
Department of Information Systems, Delft University of Technology, The Netherlands.
Tel: +31-15–2785827, Fax: +31-15–2786632
e-mail: J.Barjis@is.twi.tudelft.nl ; http://is.twi.tudelft.nl/~barjis

Samuel Chong
School of Computing, Staffordshire University, Stafford, Beaconside, ST18 0AB, England, UK.
Tel: +44-1785–353509, Fax: +44-1785–353497
e-mail: Y.C.Chong@staffs.ac.uk ; http://www.soc.staffs.ac.uk/~cmrycc

Keywords: Petri Net, Semantic Analysis, Process Modeling, System Analysis

Abstract: This issue of business process modeling has been debated in numerous papers. Despite the widely available source of information, this area of study is still a poorly understood issue. In this paper a methodology is proposed for business process modeling. The methodology introduced in this paper aims to create a more clearer, formalized and comprehensible approach to business process modeling. In this methodology we combine two different methods and modeling techniques in order to propose a more complete approach. These two methods are the well-tested semiotic approach and Petri net modeling method and technique. The aim is to bridge the gap between the precision of capturing business requirements using the semiotic approach with the graphical time sequence of the Petri net method. In order to demonstrate applicability and appropriateness of the proposed approach, the paper considers a real life example. The example case was conducted in the Electro-Medics International b.v. (EMI).

1. INTRODUCTION

The term 'business process' is used to denote the behavior of a business system in operation or the dynamics of a business system. Business process modeling concerns the elicitation and articulation of the business processes in an organization. In order to do this in a rigorous yet structured way, a methodology is needed. Without a well defined and structured methodology, poor analysis and understanding on the very nature of business processes can lead to the inadequate design of a business systems. To this end, the MEASUR approach, founded on the semiotic theory, has proved to be a promising candidate for the task of articulating the business processes (e.g. Liu *et al.* 1995). The MEASUR approach views an organisation from a behavioural perspective; and from the norms that govern the behaviour of the stakeholders. Their behaviour defines the business processes that take place in the organisation. One major drawback of the MEASUR however, is the lack of ability to model concurrency and parallelism of business processes in a structured manner. This clearly represents a gap in the understanding of the occurrence of the business processes in relation to time and sequence. This paper adopts Petri Net to bridge this gap in the MEASURE approach.

The Petri Net (PN) is an instrument for the study of systems. PN theory allows a system to be modeled by a PN, a mathematical representation of the system. Analysis of the PN can then, hopefully, reveal important information about the structure and dynamic behavior of the modeled system (Aalst, 1998; Barjis *et al.*, 2000). This information can then be used to evaluate the modeled system and suggest improvements or changes. The ability to model concurrency, parallelism and to easily combine subsystems modeled as PNs makes the PN model

J. Filipe et al. (eds.), Enterprise Information Systems III, 215–222.

very useful for modeling business systems. Petri nets are currently popular in business process modeling and workflow management (Agostini *et al.*). However, one deficiency with the method is the inability of PN to help the analysts when conducting a preliminary analysis of the business processes. As we can now see, the SAM and PN method adequately and coherently complements each other in their shortcomings.

PNs have several advantages as instruments for modeling and analyzing business systems. The advantage from Petri net are many. Like MEASUR, it is based on a sound and theoretical foundation and have been around for more than three decades, and is well documented in the literature. Petri net have few, but powerful, primitives and is easy to learn. Its graphical representation is intuitively very appealing to a wide audience and easy to understand and grasp. This is due to the fact that Petri net diagrams resemble many of the traditional design drawings (e.g. flowchart) that designers and engineers make while they analyse and develop a system. Furthermore, Petri net has an elaborated set of computer tools that support their drawing, simulation and analysis. These computer tools provide interactive simulation of the system to be built, where results of the simulation of the triggering process between behaviour are shown directly on the Petri net diagram. Furthermore they have been successfully applied to the studying of complex systems. There are different kinds of PN models that can handle processes in business systems, such as synchronisation, concurrency, and parallelism. Last but not least, since MEASUR enables one to construct a business model of the business domain, which is rigorously and formally defined, it should not be too difficult to transform from the MEASUR model to PNs.

The rest of this paper is structured as follows. Section two introduces the MEASUR approach, its theoretical foundation and the methods inherent in MEASUR. Section three provides the problem statement of EMI, in which the case study is conducted. Section four illustrates the application of the semantic analysis method of MEASUR in the EMI case study. Section five exhibits how the analysis can move to the next stage of modeling the business processes using PN in a seamless and coherent way. Section six draws some conclusions about the combined approach and future work.

2. THE MEASUR APPROACH

In the quest for a better approach in order to improve the design of information systems, Stamper (1973) developed a set of semiotic methods for analysing and modelling information systems based on the work by Peirce (1931/35, Locke 1960). This approach is better known as organisational semiotic or the MEASUR approach (Stamper *et al.* 1997). MEASUR is an acronym for *Methods for Eliciting, Analysing and Specifying Users' Requirements.* It fundamentally introduces a new perspective on information system, namely, it regards organisations as the real information system in which technologies such as computer systems have an indispensable role to play in supporting the sign usage in the organisation. Such a perspective therefore helps to keep both the technical and human issues in focus. The MEASUR consists of two main semiotic methods, Semantic Analysis Method (SAM) and Norm Analysis Method (NAM). The MEASUR approach has proved to be very useful in the study of IS-related activities such as business process redesign (Liu *et al.* 1995), agent-based e-commerce systems (Chong & Liu 2000a, 2000b), Legacy systems (Liu *et al.* 1999; Alderson & Liu 2000) and Object Oriented information engineering (Liu & Ong 1999), just to list a few.

In order to understand the MEASUR, the concept of an affordance needs to be understood. Human agents are bombarded with signs from all directions. These signs are known as invariances. They could be sounds, light, smell, echoes, room temperatures, their own movements, and so on. Affordance is the word used by Gibson (1968) for the behaviour of an organism made available by some invariants of the combined structure of organism and its environment. An alternative expression is *patterns of behaviour.* The significance of each of these invariants is what it allows or does not allow one to do. In Gibson's terminology (see Gibson 1968, 1979; Michaels & Carello 1980), each significant invariant represents a state of affairs or situation that affords or makes possible for one to have some patterns of behaviour. Gibson (1968) writes, "the affordances of the environment are what it offers the animal, what it provides or furnishes, either for good or ill". For example, oxygen is dissolved in water, and one of the properties of water is liquid, water hence affords a living environment for a fish. The liquid properties of the water also enable the fish to swim. For the purpose of studying social behaviour, the theory of affordances can be naturally extended into the social world. Human agents perceive the world by detecting the invariants around them. The invariants then trigger off an intrinsic ability of the human agents to behave in certain way. For the human agents in the social world, the invariant is called a norm. In other words, norms make possible the behaviour of the human agents. Based on the social and business norms, the social world of the human agents is socially constructed through their behaviour. For example, a person's ability to use a computer is socially afforded by norms of the society that defines what a computer is capable of doing and what it is not able to achieve. Norms also afford what type of behaviour is allowed or forbidden. Having enough experience in the social world that is governed by norms, a human agent can know which boundaries of behaviour are socially acceptable. This can be expressed as:

AGENT............ invariant............ behaviour

The relationship between the invariants (norms) and the behaviour of the human agents is illustrated in figure 1. However, all knowledge that relies on the behaviour can only refer to the here-and-now. In order to connect the past and future behaviours with the knowledge of here-and-now, the semiotic constructs by which such connection can be made by the knowing subject was introduced. Using signs helps us to establish afforded coordinated actions among members of an organisation. These signs that people create (e.g. invoice, inspection certificate) have meanings assigned to them, and can be used to refer to the future and past. The focus of the analysis is on the behaviour which creates these documents, and not on the documents themselves.

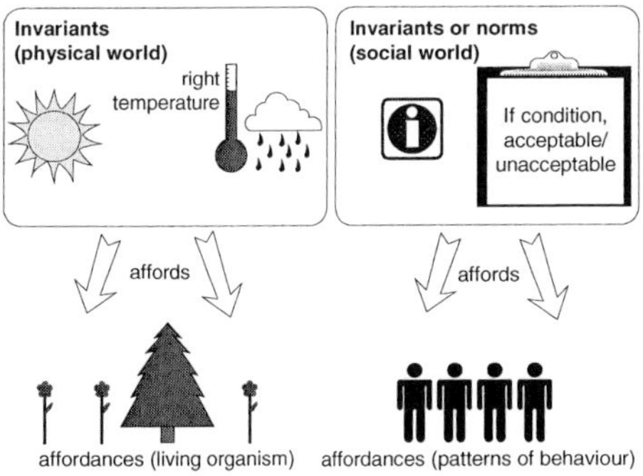

Figure 1: Invariants and affordances of the physical and social world

SAM is a method that analyses the signs that are created by members of an organisation and consists of a four-step approach to conduct the analysis, where the end result is a semantic schema called the semantic model. Since semantic analysis deals with analysing documents and conversation that describe the analysis domain, the first step is for analysts to gather the relevant data and document, which is sometimes called a problem statement, and to understand the problem. The second step is to produce a list of semantic units such as verbs, nouns, adjectives and adverbs that may be used to describe human agents and their respective patterns of behaviour. The third step will allow further analysis of the semantic units by linking then together according to their generic-specific relationship, which is shown graphically from the left to right. The fourth step brings together all the linked semantic units into a coherent whole, which produces a complete semantic model. An example of a simplistic semantic model is shown in figure 2.

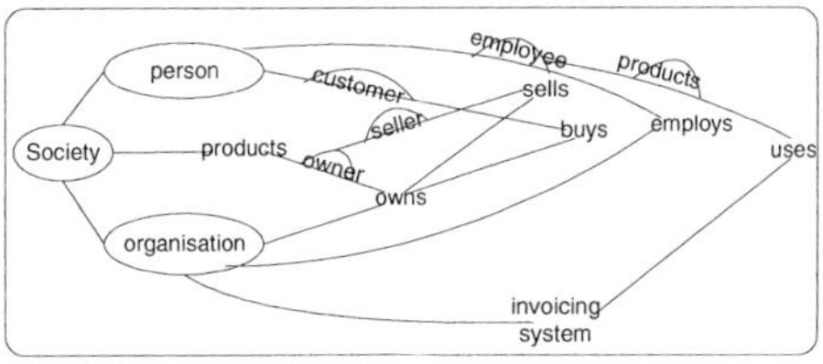

Figure 2: Example of a semantic model

Finally, norm analysis, as a separate method, will be conducted to identify the norms and link the norms with each action in the semantic model. In particular, norm analysis serves to study an organisation from the perspective of norms, which determine the action of the human agents in certain domains. This is because norms allow the human agents to judge the situation and to decide if an action is to be performed. By capturing norms, the concept of time that determines the existence of each action can be made explicit, because norms lead one to identify the human agents that bring about the start and finish of an action. The idea is that for each action, there lies a set of norms that govern their existence, as demonstrated by figure 3. The resulting norm specification can be used for several purposes, including:

- The idea of norms can be imposed on the technical domain as constraints to check that operations that occur in the computer system are not invalid (e.g. a routine should not update the database without proper authority).
- Can be translated into any programming language for in order to act as triggers to prompt action (or behaviour). These actions can be of two kinds. First, they can be used to trigger some automatic computer operations (e.g. compute the leave balance when one has applied for leave). Secondly, they can serve to trigger reminder messages to the human users to perform some action

in the business domain (e.g. reminding them that there are certain number days of leave that are not eligible to be carried forward into the next calendar year).

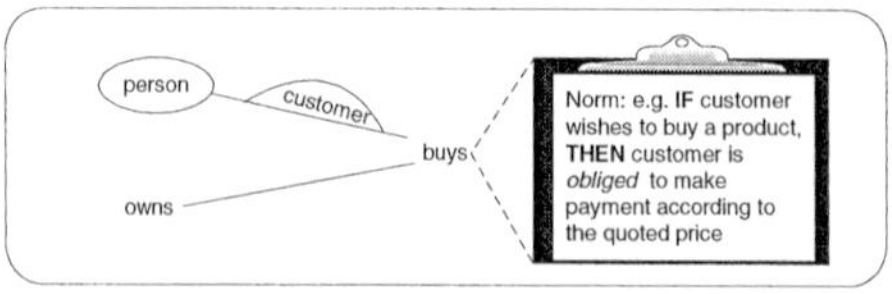

Figure 3: Behaviour and norms

The foundation of SAM and NAM is based on a sound theoretical framework and offers several advantages over other methods for modeling IS. Firstly, the approach makes explicit the concept of time since the realization of each action can be specified by its norm. Secondly, one special feature of the approach is worth mentioning. One has to realize that the existence of a behaviour must be within the existence of its antecedent. Once its antecedent ceases to exist, the lifetime of the dependant behaviour will also come to an end. For example, the dependant 'buys' should not occur when there are no customers. Such an understanding serves two functions when designing computer systems. Firstly, this understanding can be programmed as constraints to ensure that only no illegitimate occurrence of sensitive task can occur when the rightful human agents does not exist. Secondly, if one chooses to adopt an object-oriented approach to develop the system, the generic-specific relationship provides a mapping association to the concept of object inheritance in object-oriented design. Thirdly, by analyzing and comparing the norms that describe the existence of potential actions, it allows one to establish the understanding of the link between action and reality on a more concrete level.

Despite these advantages, one of the obvious drawbacks of the semantic model is that it is 'timeless', in that it does not show the occurrence of the potential behaviour in relation to sequence and this clearly represents a gap in the approach. From the semantic model, it is impossible for one to discern if one behaviour happens serially after another, or if it happens in parallel to other behaviour. Our experience with business process modeling using the MEASUR approach relates that this drawback makes it difficult to fully understand and model the business process of an organization, because in actual business practice, business processes occur in relation to time. To cope with this drawback, we proposed in this paper that the Petri net approach to be used in conjuction with the MEASUR approach. In the next sections, we demonstrate how SAM and PN can be integrated to conduct an analysis from a problem statement to the modeling of business processes in a seamless transition through a case study conducted in Electro-Medics International b.v.

3. PROBLEM STATEMENT OF EMI

Electro-Medics International b.v. (EMI) has been established in response to the growing need for a service company that could create an interface to two different business cultures- the developing countries and the developed countries. Hence, the medical profession in the developing countries is entirely dependent on the importation of such goods and services. However, the constraints on the availability of the hard currency on one hand and impatience of the business world in advanced societies make the conduct of the business a real challenge.

3.1 Basic Stages in EMI

In order to conclude a business deal, there are several stages involved in the entire business process, namely, *Product Awareness*, *Marketing*, *Contract Negotiation* and *Contract Execution*, as shown in figure 4. Due to space restriction this paper only the Contract Execution stage of the whole business process will be investigated in this paper.

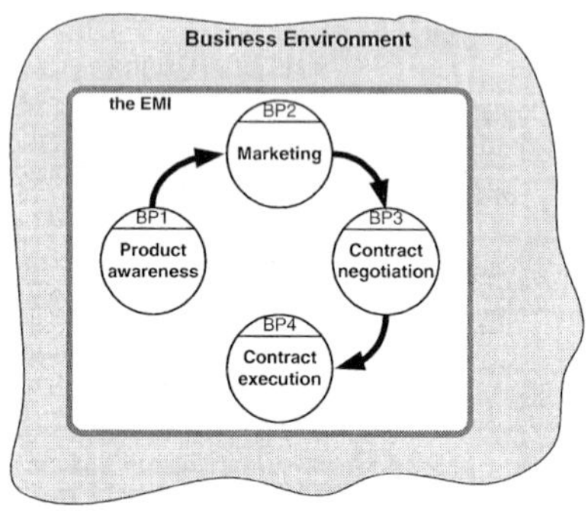

Figure 4: Structural diagram of business processes in the EMI

3.2 Contract Execution

After finalization of the contract and negotiating the financing of the deal it is time to execute the order and deliver the goods. This stage involves as the placing of the order with the supplier by preparing the related documents of shipment of the goods. In this stage each activity requires different inputs.

(a) Placing the order: This requires a close attention about exact description of the goods and pricing. Afterwards, the agreement must be reached with the supplier for the payment, place of delivery and terms of the delivery.

(b) Documents preparation: In most cases the following documents are required:

- Invoice: to be certified by the chamber of commerce and the related embassy.
- Packing list: Identifies the packing with the exact description of the goods contained in the packing.
- Certificate of origin: This document is being issued by the local chamber of commerce and, in most cases, it must be legalized by the relevant embassy
- Inspection certificate: This is the third party verification designed to verify the contents of the shipment by independent authority.
- Airway bill (bill of lading): This document is related to the type of transportation meaning that the goods should be shipped to the customer. With the air transport it must be airway bill and with the land and sea transport it is bill of lading (B/L). This document is being prepared by the transport company and it indicates that the goods are already shipped/en route.

(c) Documents submission to the bank and finalization: The payment process is the last stage of the order execution. This stage is as important as any other stage. Any shortfall whether it is the document or discrepancy in the documents could lead to a fatal mistake. The consequence could be a very late payment or in some cases to the termination of the contract.

(d) Delivery to the customer: At this stage the goods are being cleared from the customs at the destination and are being physically delivered to the customer. This is the final stage where the goods are in the possession of the end-user and they become operational. At this stage the final check takes place and they are being installed, test-run and finally delivered in the operational form to the end-user. In most cases it is part of the contract that the end-user has already been trained or the training takes place at the site. In addition, there is a guarantee/warrantee period varying from one to five years and in some instances up to ten years. It is the responsibility of the supplier to keep the system functional during this period. Additionally, there is a maintenance contract plus the upgrading of the system(s) for its life-time. This includes periodical control of the equipment plus the trouble shooting.

4. SEMANTIC ANALYSIS OF THE EMI CASE

When confronted with the business situation in the problem statement, it is imperative to have an understanding of the key nature of the business processes in the organization. Semantic analysis in the MEASUR approach serves as a valid point of departure for conducting such an analysis. The first step in carrying out a useful analysis of the problem statement study the problem statement carefully and to single out potential semantic concepts that will be helpful in the analysis later on. Examples of useful concepts include verbs, nouns, prepositional verbs, pronouns or articles, which may indicate possible human agents and their potential behaviour. Every word is useful in analysis, so one have to be cautious when a word is going to be ignored. The two semantic units to be identified are the human agents and their potential behaviour. For the sake of brevity, we shall not elaborate on the steps of SAM. The end result of applying SAM on the EMI contract execution stage of their business is depicted as the semantic model shown in figure 5.

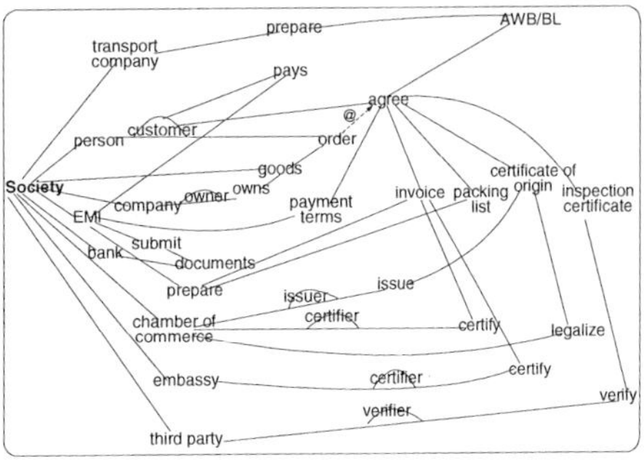

Figure 5: Semantic model of EMI

The above semantic model is explained in the following manner. The semantic model has to be read from the left to the right (otherwise known as the generic-specific relationship). Entities that are on the right are dependent on the existence of the entities on their left to exist. Any entity whose existence is dependent on the existence of other entities is known as the dependant, while the parent entity of the dependant is known as the antecedent. In this model, the roles of the human agents can be identified from the semi-circles. Nodes that represent verbs reflect the potential behaviours (or business processes) that the human agents can perform (e.g. 'order', 'prepare'). Other types of nodes that represent nouns may reflect the atomic activities (e.g. invoice, packing list, inspection certificate, etc) that are associated to its antecedent behaviour. The entities in circles are usually the companies or human agents that are responsible for the realization of the behaviours. The behaviour 'order' leads to the existence of the behaviour 'agree' if the behaviour 'order' is satisfactorily completed. Therefore, a dotted line with an "@" sign is used to indicate that the successful completion of the behaviour 'order' activates the occurrence of the behaviour 'agree'.

The semantic model is useful for identifying the various business processes that go on in the business domain of EMI and the respective stakeholders involve in them (e.g. customer places order) in a formal and rigorous manner. Approaching the task of business process modeling without such an understanding is almost like searching for a needle in a haystack. However, as one can imagine the entire process of the contract execution stage in EMI is very dynamic and, in most cases, there are several behaviour that are running in parallel. Therefore, the modeling of these behaviours in relation to time is very essential. The SAM come as far as helping the analyst to identify the time span of a behaviour, for instance, the behaviour 'buys' ceases to exist when there are no customers. However, there are uncertainties as to the occurrence sequence of the behaviour. In order to deal with that, Petri nets are introduced to bridge this gap.

Due to the scope of the paper, a detailed report of norm analysis for this case study is omitted here. However, one aspect should be noted. Although the semantic model is not capable of capturing the sequences of behaviours, the time span of each behaviour can be captured by a more detailed study of the business norms that govern their existence. For instance, by studying the business norms of EMI, we observe that the time span of the preparation of the documents is determined by the business norm which dictates that if seven days are passed before finishing the preparation of all the documents, then the process has to be suspended. This type of temporal aspect in the business processes will be modeled later on using PN.

5. PETRI NET MODELS OF THE EMI CASE

With the elicitation of the various business processes and their atomic activities from the semantic model, the next step is to single them out and group them according to their occurrence sequence into a coherent whole. Figure 6 represents a process oriented diagram to achieve this end. In this figure the gray roundangle represents the cross stages boundary- boundary between the main stages. It represents the boundary for the contract execution stage. In this step the contract execution stage is represented as a set of core processes e.g. CP1, CP2 etc. So, as shown, the contract execution stage consists of three core processes such as *placing order*, *documents preparation* and *documents submission*. Each core process, graphically represented by a rectangle, is identified by the name of the process and also numbered accordingly. It should be noted that each core process consists of a set of supplementary atomic activities (identified from the semantic model in figure 5). These atomic activities are listed below each core process correspondingly. In this figure the timing listed for CP3 means that there is a time constraint for this core process. It will be explained later in figure 7c. It is clear from figure 6 that the core processes and their atomic activities are identified based on a rational grounding through semantic analysis. This suggests an improvement in current practice which drives one to identify the behaviour on *an ad* hoc basis.

Another feature inherent in the process oriented diagram of figure 6 is that each stage (e.g. contract execution stage) has one beginning point (B) and one end point (E). In its essence, such a presentation makes it possible to represent more complex business structures in very compact notations. For example, each stage can be compacted as network represented by one symbol having the beginning and end points.

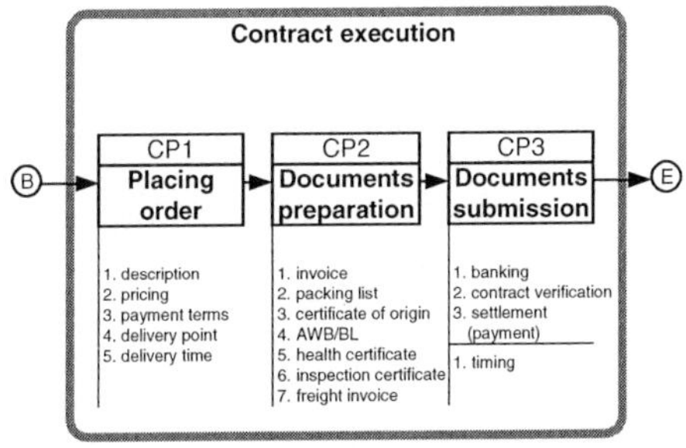

Figure 6: Process oriented diagram of the contract execution in the EMI

The following step in the proposed approach is action oriented modeling of the system under study. In this step we build most detailed model of the system. For the graphical representation of the detailed (action and time oriented) models, a type of Petri net has been used (see figure 7). In order to adapt the proposed type of Petri net for constructing the process oriented models including high risk processes (with time constraint), in particular we added to the standard Petri net elements a new element called a timer (clock). The timer will trigger a timeout behaviour, if the fixed time for the high risk process is reached before completing its execution. To simulate the derived business process one can, e.g., deploy Arena simulation tools. Using these simulation tools, one is able to assign parameter values for the processes such as execution time or costs involved in them. Then the result of the simulation gives some indications and verifications with which analysts can analyze the behavior of the business process for optimizing or redesign it.

A Petri net model captures the sequential and/or parallel processing order of the atomic activities which are contained in the business process. Figure 7a represents a simple place transition Petri net modeling the CP1. In figure 7b (CP2) there are two choice elements within the flow of processing, represented by circles numbered as 2 and 4. The first choice concerns to find out if it is necessary to verify the contents of the shipment by independent authority. The second choice concerns if it is necessary to make freight invoice. Synchronization elements in this figure are used in order to synchronize the end of execution of several activities before proceeding further.

In figure 7b, one new element is represented. This new element (the bold bar) is a fictive (dummy) transition. Fictive because it doesn't have any duration or any activity. It is only included for keeping syntactic correctness of the PN when dealing with optionality.

Figure 7c (CP3) contains two new elements: the timer and subnet (represented by the double line rectangle and identified as CP2). The timer element is introduced in order to model the time span of the process. As mentioned before, the duration for the document preparation process is usually seven days. If seven days are passed before finishing this process, then the timer will trigger a timeout token (signal). The subnet represents the document preparation process (figure 7b) in compact notation. It means, if after contract verification, it is found that some thing is wrong, then the document preparation process has to be repeated again.

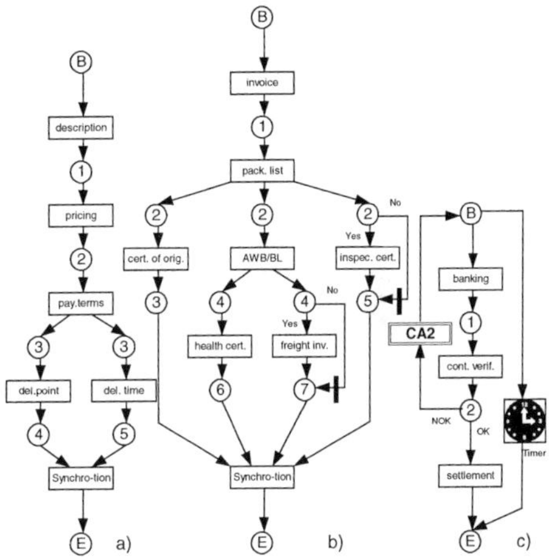

Figure 7: Petri net model of: a) the placing order activity; b) the documents preparation; c) documents submission.

Once, having models in the manner presented in figure 7, it will be a straightforward task to conduct further analysis e.g. simulation of the business system under study. The only necessary value lacking in this model is duration of all the activities. However, in order to study dynamic behavior of the system it is not necessary to have an exact value for duration of all activities.

6. CONCLUSION

As we have pointed out in the introduction, in order to make business process modeling more structured, a thorough, appropriate and precise understanding of the organization is needed. The SAM in the MEASUR approach appears to offer such an understanding. It provides a formal basis for conducting the analysis, which identifies all the business processes (behaviours) and the their stakeholders. The combination of SAM with PN seems appropriate, precise and thorough since they both complement the shortcomings of each other. It is appropriate because it allows one to focus on the essence, thereby abstracting from realization issues. It is precise because the models are appropriate for mathematical analysis. Lastly, it is thorough because both SAM and PNs have a consistent theoretical foundation.

In summary, this paper has demonstrated that the SAM and PN methods jointly provide a complete and rigorous analysis and modeling of organization. The SAM allows the identification for the key business processes (behaviours) and the responsible stakeholders, while PN facilitates the business processes to be modeled in relation to time or sequence, thus providing a mathematical representation of the system. Analysis of the PN can further result into developing new knowledge about the structure and dynamic behavior of the organization. This knowledge can then be used as the basis for the requirements analysis phase of the information system to be developed. Much research however, is needed to improve the approach in order to make it better defined. Evaluation and application of the combined approach in further case studies will be the subject for our future work.

REFERENCES

Aalst, W.M.P. van der, 1998. Finding Errors in the Design of a Workflow Process: A Petri-net-based Approach. In the proceedings of the Workshop on Workflow Management: Net-based Concepts, Models, Techniques and Tools (WFM'98) within the 19th International Conference on Applications and Theory of Petri Nets, Lisbon, Portugal, June 22.

Agostini, A. ; Michelis, G. De. 1998. Simple Workflow Models. In the proceedings of the Workshop on Workflow Management: Net-based Concepts, Models, Techniques and Tools (WFM'98) within the 19th International Conference on Applications and Theory of Petri Nets, Lisbon, Portugal, June 22.

Alderson, A., K. Liu (2000), Reverse Requirements Engineering: the AMBOLS Approach. In Henderson, P. (ed.), *Systems Engineering for Business Process Change*, Springer, London, 196-208.

Barjis, J.; Barjis, I.; Dokht, R.M.; Chitchian, D. A Simulation Methodology for Investigating Business Processes in Small Companies. In the proceedings of the 2000 Summer Computer Simulation Conference (SCSC'00), July 16 - 20, 2000, Vancouver, B.C. Canada.

Chong, S. & K. Liu (2000a) A Semiotic Approach to the Design of Agent-Mediated E-Commerce, in E.D. Falkenberg, K. Lyytinen, A.A.Verrijn-Stuart (eds.), *Information Systems Concepts: An Integrated Discipline Emerging*, Kluwer Academic Publishers, Boston, pp95-114.

Chong, S. & Liu, K. (2000b). A Semiotic Approach for Distinguishing Responsibilities in Agent-Based Systems, in Liu, K., Stamper R., Clarke, R. & Andersen, P. (eds.), *Organisation Semiotics*, Kluwer Academic Press (in press).

Gibson, J. J. (1968) *The Senses Considered as Perceptual Systems*, Allen & Unwin.

Gibson, J. J. (1979) *The Ecological Approach to Visual Perception*, Mifflin Company.

Liu, K., Sharp, B., Crum G. & Zhao, L. (1995) Applying a Semiotic Framework to Re-engineering Legacy Information Systems, *Proceedings of the First International Conference on Organisational Semiotics*, University of Twente, The Netherlands.

Liu, K. & Ong, T. (1999) A Modelling Approach for Handling Business Rules and Exceptions, *The Computer Journal*, 43 (3), 221 - 231.

Liu, K., Alderson, A. & Qureshi, Z. (1999), Requirements Recovery of Legacy Systems by Analysing and Modelling Behaviour, *Proceedings of the International Conference on Software Maintenance*, IEEE Computer Society, Los Alamitos, pp3-12.

Locke, J. (1960) *Essay Concerning Human Understanding*, Unabridged edition 1959, Dover, New York.

Michaels, C.F. & Carello, C. (1980) *Direct Perception*, Englewood Cliffs, Prentice Hall

Peirce, C. S., 1931/35, *Collected Papers of C.S. Peirce (1931-35)*, in Hartshorne, C. & Weiss, P. (eds.), Harvard University Press, Cambridge, Mass.

Stamper, R. K., 1973, Information in Business and Administrative Systems, Second Edition, Basil Blackwell, Oxford.

Stamper, R., K. Liu, M. Hafkamp & Y. Ades, 1997, Signs plus Norms - one paradigm for organizational semiotics. The First International Workshop on Computational Semiotics, Paris.

THE USE OF FORMAL AND INFORMAL MODELS IN OBJECT-ORIENTED REQUIREMENTS ENGINEERING

Linda Dawson
School of Information Management and Systems, Monash University, Caulfield East, Victoria, Australia
email: ldawson@sims.monash.edu.au

Keywords: requirements engineering, object-oriented modelling, case study

Abstract: Little is understood, or reported on the basis of research, of the use of object-oriented models and methods by practising professionals in the production of requirements specifications for commercial or industrial sized projects. This paper describes a research project and the findings from a set of six case studies that have been undertaken which examine the use of object-oriented models in professional requirements engineering practice. In these studies, it was found that the more formal models of object-orientation were rarely used to validate, or even clarify, the specification with clients or users. Rather, analysts tended to use informal models such as use cases or ad hoc diagrams, to communicate the specification to users. Formal models are more often used internally within the analysis team and for communicating the specification to the design team.

1. INTRODUCTION

The move towards the use of object-oriented methods for information system development has led to a need for the development of object-oriented approaches to requirements engineering. Object-oriented methodologies can generally be thought of as having evolved from programming languages and design modelling (Graham, 1994). Most of the commonly used texts emphasise object-oriented design (Booch, 1991, Rumbaugh et al., 1991, Meyer, 1988). Object-oriented analysis and requirements specification is a relatively new addition to most object-oriented development methodologies and many methodologies take a fairly traditional, structured approach to the early phases of requirements specification with the emphasis on deliverables (Booch, 1994, Graham et al., 1997, Jacobson et al., 1999).

This paper presents the findings from a program of research into the use of object-oriented models in object-oriented requirements engineering. The case studies presented here indicate that analysts believe that users or clients cannot understand the more formal models such as Object Modelling Technique (OMT) (Rumbaugh et al., 1991) or Unified Modelling Language (UML) (Booch et al., 1999) diagrams and interaction diagrams and that variations on use cases (Jacobson et al., 1992), ad hoc diagrams or rich pictures are a more appropriate informal models with which to communicate the specification to users.

Section 2 provides background in requirements engineering, object-oriented methods and related work. The research approach is presented in Section 3. Section 4 describes six case studies of practising professional requirements engineers. Section 5 presents the findings and interpretation of those findings. A discussion of the findings is presented in Section 6.

2. BACKGROUND

2.1 Requirements Engineering

Software engineering developed as a discipline to address the need for developing large complex software systems in an organised and structured manner. Requirements engineering (Loucopoulos and Karakostas, 1995, Macaulay, 1996) specifically addresses the problems associated with errors in functional specifications which result in the costly maintenance or failure of software systems (Boehm, 1976, Jackson, 1997, OASIG, 1996). Requirements engineering has now expanded to include more than just software construction (Loucopoulos and Karakostas, 1995, Macaulay, 1996) and is now an

J. Filipe et al. (eds.), Enterprise Information Systems III, 223–230.

accepted term in information systems for defining the process and outcome of systems analysis.

Various definitions of and approaches to the requirements engineering process are suggested in the literature. Loucopoulos and Karakostas (1995) suggest a useful framework. In this framework the requirements engineering process can be broken down into three sub-processes, elicitation, specification and validation, which deal with two external entities, the user and the problem domain. Kotonya and Sommerville (Kotonya and Sommerville, 1998) suggest that

> *"...there is no single [requirements engineering] process which is right for all organisations. Each organisation must develop its own process which is appropriate for the type of systems it develops, its organisational culture, and the level of experience and ability of the people involved in requirements engineering,"* p9.

Macaulay (1996) similarly suggests nine different approaches which *"...vary depending on the interest of the groups from which they originate"*. Pohl (1993) proposes three dimensions of requirements engineering. These three dimensions can be outlined as follows:

Representational issues involve the range of representation methods from informal, natural language specifications to formal specification.

Social domain issues encompass the social process involved in the iterative, co-operative elicitation of information for building requirements. Of particular importance is the aspect of communication between end users and analysts in establishing and documenting system needs within the organisational context.

Cognitive domain issues are concerned with the understanding of the problem itself within the problem domain using various conceptual models.

2.2 Object-oriented Methods

Many claims have been made about the object-oriented paradigm (Booch, 1994, Coad and Yourdon, 1991, Henderson-Sellers and Edwards, 1994, Meyer, 1988). These claims include:

- ease of understanding object-oriented models due to a consistent underlying representation throughout the development process
- the ability to model the behaviour of objects (encapsulation of data and process)
- ease of modification and extensibility of object-oriented models.
- ease of reuse of object components from previously designed systems
- superior data abstraction facilities including inheritance and polymorphism

Object-oriented systems development life cycles are usually based on non-linear cycles such as the spiral model (Boehm, 1988) or the fountain model (Henderson-Sellers, 1997). One of the generally regarded strengths of object-oriented methods is that complexity is reduced because the concept of an object remains the same throughout the development process from analysis to implementation and flow of control is modelled as interactions between objects.

In an object-oriented modelling process several models are usually produced. These models can be loosely categorised as either static models or dynamic models. Static models describe objects, their characteristics and the relationships between them. Some common models are class and object diagrams (Booch, 1994), component notation and templates (Coad and Yourdon, 1991), object models (Rumbaugh et al., 1991), class cards, hierarchies and collaborations (Wirfs-Brock et al., 1990), object/class models (Henderson-Sellers, 1997), object and layer models (Graham, 1994).

Dynamic models define states of objects, state transitions, message passing and event handling. Some common dynamic models are state transition and event diagrams (Booch, 1994), state diagrams (Coad and Yourdon, 1991, Rumbaugh et al., 1991), objectcharts (Henderson-Sellers, 1997), interaction diagrams (Jacobson et al., 1992), rules (Graham, 1994), object communication models (Shlaer and Mellor, 1991). Sequencing is often modelled using use cases (Jacobson et al., 1992), task scripts (Graham, 1994) or scenarios (Henderson-Sellers, 1997, Rumbaugh et al., 1991) defining typical user interaction with the system

2.3 Related Work

Although little is understood about how practising professionals use object-oriented methods and models for requirements determination and few empirical studies have been published which investigate this issue, there is some evidence that untrained users have difficulty in understanding the standard data models and object/class models that many professional analysts use during requirements and system modelling (Vessey and Conger, 1994, Flynn and Warhurst, 1994). Various approaches to representing requirements in a manner that is understandable to untrained users have been suggested often based on use cases and scenarios. Jacobson designed use case models (Jacobson et al., 1992, Jacobson, 1995) as a *"...first system model ...[which must] ... be comprehensible by people both inside the development organisation ... and outside... Object models are too complex for this purpose"*, but also suggests that use cases serve many other purposes as well (Jacobson and Christerson, 1995). Some recent work has looked at scenarios which are described by Kotonya and Sommerville (1998) as *"... stories which explain how the system is used."* Weidenhaupt et al (1998) provide an exploratory study of the use of scenarios in current practice. They found that *"...while many companies express interest in Jacobson's use case approach, actual scenario usage often falls outside what is described in textbooks and standard methodologies."*. They also found different forms of scenarios similar to those found in this study. That is, narrative text, structured text, diagrammatic notations, images, animations and simulations. Graham (1994) suggests the use of task scripts which are *"...roughly similar to use cases"*.

There have been some studies of small groups, usually students in laboratory-type situations where the participants use object-oriented methods for small one-off exercises and problems (Guindon, 1990, Chaiyasut and Shanks, 1994, Boehm-Davis and Ross, 1992, Lee and Pennington, 1994, Morris et al., 1996, Sutcliffe and Maiden, 1992, Vessey and Conger, 1994). But the behaviour of students, even graduate students, cannot be considered to be indicative of the behaviour of experienced professionals without clear justification and/or demonstration. Also, the problems used in these experiments tend to be small and, therefore, not representative of commercial or industrial practice.

3. RESEARCH APPROACH

The research approach used was multiple sequential-case studies which involved taped semi-structured interviews with individual practising professional requirements engineers. An evolving set of categories was used to structure the qualitative data as it was gathered. Firstly, a set of seed categories (Miles and Huberman, 1994, Fitzgerald, 1997, Wynekoop and Russo, 1997) (see Table 1) was formulated and these were used to formulate the initial semi-structured interview script (see sample questions in column 2, table 1). The sequential nature of the case studies meant that although a core set of interview questions remained the same for each case study each case sought to refine the interview script by building on findings from previous cases.

The transcript of each interview was partitioned and distilled into a template structure reflecting the current set of categories. In each interview other categories and sub categories emerged and were incorporated into interview scripts and template for investigation in the following cases. So the number of categories grew as the case studies continued. The final analysis for the findings outlined in this paper were based on the following chain of processes:

Table 1: Research Issues and example questions

Seed categories	**Example questions**
Elicitation How is knowledge elicitation influenced by the use of object-oriented modelling methods?	Is knowledge elicitation explicitly undertaken? Is it seen as object-oriented? Is it seen as sequential or opportunistic?
Modelling When, how and for whom is object-oriented modelling undertaken?	When does modelling begin? Which (how many) models are produced? How are the models used? Who are they produced for? Which models, if any, are shown to the user?
Validation How is validation performed on object-oriented models?	When does the validation process begin? Which models are used in the validation process? When is the validation process considered to be complete?

- **Revelation** of emergent new categories, or sub categories, during an interview
- **Reinforcement** of previously emergent or seed categories by explicit questioning, during an interview
- **Re-examination** of previous interview templates and transcripts to find any further reinforcement of an emerging category

4. THE CASE STUDIES

4.1 Unit of Analysis: the analyst in context

In order to understand the use of object-oriented models by practising professionals we must set the bounds of the research and data collection by determining the unit of analysis - the entity about which we want to gather data and the context of that entity within each case study. Yin (1994) suggests that the unit of analysis defines the "case" in a case study. He suggests five possible units of analysis: individuals, decisions, programs, implementation processes and organisational change.

The choice of the unit of analysis in a study is related to the way the questions and propositions are defined. In one sense, this project is concerned with all of the above categories but the main unit of analysis is the individual experienced requirements engineer or analyst.

4.2 The Participants

As is common with this type of qualitative research, the case studies were opportunistically selected in that the participants were used because they were available and willing to be part of the study. Participants were recruited through industry. Some participants provided contacts for subsequent participants. The lack of available professionals working in the field of object-oriented requirements engineering in Melbourne where this study was undertaken means that there has been no attempt to select participants based on specific background characteristics. The common factor is that all the participants were currently working in the field of object-oriented requirements specification. The contextual information for each consultant interviewed is summarised in Table 2.

4.3 Data Collection Method

Although the core of the data was gathered from taped and transcribed in depth interviews, several other data sources were used. The types of data, sources of data and collection methods are summarised in Table 3

Table 2: Background Information for each consultant

Case	Title	Years in RE	Years in OORE	Client	Project
1	Operations manager	3.5 yrs	0 yrs	Federal Govt	Complex Technical
2	Principal Consultant	15 yrs	10 yrs	State Govt	Web transactions
3	Senior Consultant	12 yrs	4 yrs	Telecommunications	Fault Mgt System
5	Consultant	14 yrs	14 yrs	Software developer	LifeInsurance
6	Technical Manager	12 yrs	5 yrs	Software developer	Stockbroking

Table 3: Types and sources of data and their collection methods

Type of data	Source of data	Collection Method
Overall contextual data	Initial interview	Made by phone and followed up by email to set the context of the project and the participant's role in the project
Background data	Core Interview	First part of taped interview
Qualitative data	Core Interview	Major part of taped interview
Clarification	Followup interview	Further questions in need of clarification which emerged from the transcription process
Final clarification	Summary report	A report submitted to the participant with a final request for comment from participant

5. FINDINGS

For the purpose of discussion we distinguish between formal models and informal models in the following way. *Formal* models are considered to be those models that require training in order to be understood or explained. That is, models that contain specific, often graphical notations such as OMT models, UML models, interaction models or state models. *Informal* models are considered to be models that can be understood and explained without specific training. In this category are natural language models including text descriptions, use case scripts, ad hoc diagrams and interactive demonstration models as often produced for prototypes. Evidence of the use of separate models is shown in Table 6.

Three of the cases used prototypes early in the specification process. One case used coded sections of the system that provided sample screens for discussion with the users. In another case an animation package was used. The other case used a standard presentation package (Power Point) to produce sample screens that were worked through with the users. All but one of the object-oriented analysts produced use case scripts and one also used use case diagrams for informal modelling direct with clients. Some also used ad hoc diagrams and one used rich pictures (Checkland and Scholes, 1990) to explain and communicate the specification to users.

In the case studies there seemed to be these two different kinds of modelling taking place. Firstly, there were the informal models that were used to communicate with the users. Secondly, more formal models were developed which were not shown to the users because it was believed that the users would not understand them. The formal models were developed primarily for design purposes and were kept internal to the analyst or team of analysts. In effect these formal models were the analysts internal version of informal models.

The mapping process of informal models to formal models appeared to be based on using the informal models to clarify requirements with the users and the formal models were refined accordingly. When asked how this mapping process was done most analysts had difficulty describing the process. It was described as being able to think in terms of either type of model depending whom the analyst was talking to at the time. It was also described as "an automatic translation process", going from one model or group of models to the other as appropriate.

Some illustrative quotes (researcher's questions are shown in bold type)

"**Did you show this group [of users] use cases?** *Yes.* **And what about the object models?** *We would have stopped short there.*"

"*We tell them [the users] that the model is technical mumbo jumbo.*"

"*A requirements specification has to be in terms that they understand and those three mechanisms we've already mentioned are the way: the use case, the ad hoc diagrams and the dynamic screen simulations... and the encompassing text too, you don't write your requirements document in use case speak from start to finish.*"

Table 4: Evidence of the separation of models

Case No.	Models shown to users	Models used in design & implementation (not shown to users)
Case 1	Requirements cards that were part of the methodology	Unknown
Case 2	Simplified use case diagrams & dialogues	OMT class & interaction models
Case 3	Use case scripts & prototype	OMT class & interaction models
Case 4	Ad hoc diagrams, a prototype (in PowerPoint) and some use cases	OMT models
Case 5	Text document only	No models – the system was implemented directly from text document
Case 6	Simplified Odell event diagrams, prototype and use cases for exceptions & special cases	OMT class & interaction models

In one case the most important objective was to get the users or clients to sign off on the specification "*...we would have a formal walkthrough with the users where we go through the requirements, generally not the rules as much, but mainly the requirements and probably the prototype and we would get formal sign off*". In this case the prototype was the most used tool for validation and use cases were only used for exceptions or special cases "*...as we were looking at the requirements document we had the prototype running and projected up on a big screen and we actually walked through the prototype in relation to the requirements*".

6. DISCUSSION

There was evidence that the modelling process produced two types of models: informal models in the form of pictures, text and diagrams and/or use cases and prototypes; and formal models in the form of class models, object models and to a lesser extent interaction and event models. The informal models were used in the validation of the specification with the clients and users and the formal models were used internally within the analysis team and passed on to the design phase of the development. There was also evidence of a less well-defined mapping of the informal models to the formal models. This appeared to be a two way process where each group of models were developed in parallel and where each group of models "informed" the other as they were developed by the analysts. The validation subprocess was informal and formal models were not used in this subprocess.

These findings indicate that analysts believe that users or clients find formal models much too complex, both conceptually and technically, to understand and that the use of informal models such as rich pictures, diagrams and use cases, particularly use case scripts which are closer to natural language models, are perceived to be better models for communicating and validating specifications with clients. Further research is necessary to determine the validity of this perception.

The basis for this belief may lie in the concept that the requirements engineering process is fundamentally a social process involving two main groups: the users/clients and the professional consultants. If we believe that the *product* of the requirements engineering process is the specification document on which the design and implementation of the system is based, then this product has to be agreed upon by both parties. That is, the specification needs to be validated as correct from both points of view - the *formal* or consultant's point of view and the client's *informal* point of view. The perception seems to be that for this agreement to take place there needs to be two levels of modelling: informal modelling for communicating the specification to the user for information and validation; and formal modelling for the analyst team to pass on to the design and implementation team.

7. CONCLUSION

The implications for practice in these findings lie in the recognition of the social aspects of the requirements specification process (Urquhart, 1998, Macaulay, 1996). The errors which arise due to inconsistencies, omissions and ambiguities in functional specifications often result in the costly maintenance or failure of software systems (Boehm, 1976, Jackson, 1997, OASIG, 1996, DeMarco, 1982). If, as the findings of this research project suggest, the models used for validation of the specification with the clients are different to the models used in design and implementation, then this may indicate one of the areas where these inconsistencies, omissions and ambiguities might arise. The extension of use case models and concrete scenarios as suggested in Weidenhaupt et al (1998) may assist in addressing these issues.

The findings also present evidence of a recognition on the part of the practising professionals that they had to understand what the users wanted in some diagrammatic terms and that further they had to explain what they were building and specifying back to the users in order to get agreement or sign off on the specification document.

Understanding the way models and methods are used in practice should lead to

- improving existing modelling techniques and tools
- developing new modelling techniques and tools appropriate for a creative and social process
- developing new modelling techniques and tools appropriate for new environments such as electronic commerce

Ultimately, we expect to gain more knowledge of how large real world organisational systems have been specified and developed and which tools and techniques facilitate the successful specification for the design and implementation of useable systems.

REFERENCES

Boehm, B. W. (1976) Software Engineering, *IEEE Transactions on Computers,* 25, (12) pp. 1226-1241.

Boehm, B. W. (1988) A spiral model of software development and enhancement, *IEEE Computer,* 25, (5) pp. 61-72.

Boehm-Davis, D. and Ross, L. (1992) Program design methodologies and the software development process, *International Journal of Man-Machine Studies,* 36, pp. 1-19.

Booch, G. (1991) *Object-Oriented Design,* Benjamin/Cummings, Menlo Park, CA.

Booch, G. (1994) *Object-Oriented Analysis and Design with Applications,* Benjamin/Cummings, Redwood City.

Booch, G., Rumbaugh, J. and Jacobson, I. (1999) *The Unified Modeling Language User Guide,* Addison-Wesley, Reading, MA.

Chaiyasut, P. and Shanks, G. (1994) Conceptual Data Modelling Process: A Study of Novice and Expert Data Modellers, In *Proceedings of First International Conference on Object Role Modelling* Magnetic Island, Australia, pp. 310-333.

Checkland, P. and Scholes, J. (1990) *Soft Systems Methodology in Practice,* Wiley, Chichester.

Coad, P. and Yourdon, E. (1991) *Object-Oriented Analysis,* Yourdon Press/Prentice-Hall, Englewood Cliffs, NJ.

DeMarco, T. (1982) *Controlling Software Projects: Management, Measurement and Estimation,* Yourdon Press, New York.

Fitzgerald, B. (1997) The use of systems development methodologies in practice: a field study, *Information Systems Journal,* 7, pp. 201-212.

Flynn, D. J. and Warhurst, R. (1994) An empirical study of the validation process within requirements determination, *Information Systems Journal,* 4, pp. 185-212.

Graham, I. (1994) *Object Oriented Methods,* Addison-Wesley.

Graham, I., Henderson-Sellers, B. and Younessi, H. (1997) *The OPEN process Specification,* Addison Wesley, New York.

Guindon, R. (1990) Knowledge exploited by experts during software system design, *International Journal of Man-Machine Studies,* 33, pp. 279-304.

Henderson-Sellers, B. (1997) *A Book of Object-Oriented Knowledge,* Prentice-Hall, Upper Saddle River, NJ.

Henderson-Sellers, B. and Edwards, J. (1994) *BOOKTWO of Object-Oriented Knowledge: The Working Object,* Prentice Hall, Englewood Cliffs, NJ.

Jackson, M. C. (1997) Critical Systems Thinking and Information Systems Development, In *Proceedings of Eighth Australasian Conference on Information Systems,* (Ed, D. J. Sutton) University of South Australia, Adelaide, South Australia, pp. 1-20.

Jacobson, I. (1995) The Use-Case Construct in Object-Oriented Software Engineering, In *Scenario-Based Design: Envisioning Work and Technology in System Development* (Ed, J. M. Carroll) John Wiley and Sons, Inc, New York, pp. 309-336.

Jacobson, I., Booch, G. and Rumbaugh, J. (1999) *The Unified Software Development Process,* Addison Wesley Longman, Reading, MA.

Jacobson, I. and Christerson, M. (1995) Modeling with use cases: A growing concensus on use cases, *Journal of Object-Oriented Programming,* 8, (1) pp. 15-19.

Jacobson, I., Christerson, M., Jonsson, P. and Overgaard, G. (1992) *Object-Oriented Software Engineering: A Use Case Driven Approach,* Addison-Wesley/ACM, New York.

Kotonya, G. and Sommerville, I. (1998) *Requirements Engineering: processes and techniques,* John Wiley and Sons, Chichester, UK.

Lee, Y. and Pennington, N. (1994) The effects of paradigm on cognitive activities in design, *International Journal of Human-Computer Studies,* 40, pp. 577-601.

Loucopoulos, P. and Karakostas, V. (1995) *Systems Requirements Engineering,* McGraw-Hill, London, UK.

Macaulay, L. (1996) *Requirements Engineering,* Springer-Verlag, London.

Meyer, B. (1988) *Object-Oriented Software Construction,* Prentice-Hall, Englewood Cliffs, NJ.

Miles, M. B. and Huberman, A. M. (1994) *Qualitative Data Analysis: An Expanded Sourcebook,* Sage Publications Inc, Thousand Oaks, CA.

Morris, M., Speier, C. and Hoffer, J. (1996) The impact of experience on individual performance and workload differences using object-oriented and process-oriented systems analysis techniques, In *Proceedings of 29th Hawaii International Conference on System Sciences* Maui, Hawaii.

OASIG (1996) Why do IT Projects so often Fail?", In *OR Newsletter*, Vol. 309, pp. 12-16.

Pohl, K. (1993) The three dimensions of requirements engineering, In *Proceedings of Fifth International Conference on Advanced Information Systems Engineering (CAiSE'93),* Springer-Verlag, Paris, pp. 275-292.

Rumbaugh, J., Blaha, M., Premerlani, W., Eddy, F. and Lorensen, W. (1991) *Object-Oriented Modeling and Design,* Prentice-Hall, Englewood Cliffs, NJ.

Shlaer, S. and Mellor, S. J. (1991) *Modelling the World in States,* Yourdon Press, Englewood Cliffs, NJ.

Sutcliffe, A. G. and Maiden, N. A. M. (1992) Analysing the novice analyst: cognitive models in software engineering, *International Journal of Man-Machine Studies,* 36, pp. 719-740.

Urquhart, C. (1998) Analysts and Clients in Conversation: Cases in Early Requirements Gathering, In *Proceedings of Nineteenth International Conference on Information Systems,* (Eds, R. Hirschheim, M.

Newman and J. I. DeGross) Helsinki, Finland, pp. 115-127.

Vessey, I. and Conger, S. (1994) Requirements specification: Learning object, process, and data methodologies, *Communications of the ACM,* 37, (5).

Weidenhaupt, K., Pohl, K., Jarke, M. and Haumer, P. (1998) Scenarios in System Development: Current Practice, *IEEE Software,* 15, (2) pp. 34-45.

Wirfs-Brock, R. J., Wilkerson, B. and Wiener, L. (1990) *Designing Object-Oriented Software,* Prentice Hall, New York, USA.

Wynekoop, J. L. and Russo, N. L. (1997) Studying system development methodologies: an examination of research methods, *Information Systems Journal,* 7, pp. 47-65.

Yin, R. K. (1994) *Case Study Research: Design and Methods,* Sage Publications Inc., Thousand Oaks, CA.

ENTERPRISE MODELLING FOR AN EDUCATIONAL INFORMATION INFRASTRUCTURE*

Ing Widya[1], Cees Volman[2], Stanislav Pokraev[3], Italo De Diana[4], and Eddie Michiels[5]

[1,5]Centre for Telematics and Information Technology, Department of Computer Science
University of Twente, PO Box 217, 7500 AE Enschede, the Netherlands
Email: widya@cs.utwente.nl , michiels@cs.utwente.nl
[2]Utopics MultiMedia, the Netherlands
Email: cvolman@utopics.nl
[3]KPN Research, Enschede, the Netherlands
Email: s.v.pokraev@kpn.com
[4]Faculty of Educational Science and Technology
Dept. of Instrumentation Technology, University of Twente
Email: i.p.f.dediana@edte.utwente.nl

Keywords: ODP enterprise modelling, UML educational business models.

Abstract: This paper reports the modelling exercise of an educational information infrastructure that aims to support the organisation of teaching and learning activities suitable for a wide range of didactic policies. The modelling trajectory focuses on capturing invariant structures of relations between entities in educational organisation into Enterprise object models. An Educational Model Space has been introduced to define the problem domain context for the modelling. In this space, educational requirements have been elaborated towards the Open Distributed Processing Enterprise Viewpoint object models expressed in terms of the Unified Modelling Language. Recursive structures, which are uniform for the planning, performance and evaluation activities of education, have been used to capture the dynamic needs of education.

1. INTRODUCTION

Continuous advances in information and communication technology (ICT) boost the intensive and rapid changes in today's service-oriented society. To cope with such changes, people and organisations must continuously and almost instantaneously learn new and appropriate knowledge and skills. Such 'life-time', 'on-demand', and 'just-in-time' learning intensifies the challenge for tele-education, i.e. education that occurs at any time and any place (Collis, 1997). ICT offers appropriate support for (tele-)education by its capability to provide dedicated and adaptable environments for (remote) teaching and learning. However, practice proves that accomplishing organisational environments is a sine qua none for (tele-)education.

A challenge is to develop a (distributed) educational information infrastructure that aims to support the organisation of teaching and learning activities in this service-oriented era and which is sufficiently flexible to address a diversity of educational approaches and didactic policies. This paper describes the outcomes of an exercise in the modelling of such infrastructure using an approach of separations of problem domain and enterprise modelling concerns along together with early feedback from developed infrastructure prototypes.

* This work has been funded by the University of Twente within the project Idylle (http://www.ctit.utwente.nl/~idylle).

J. Filipe et al. (eds.), Enterprise Information Systems III, 231–239.

This paper emphasises on object models of the infrastructure, dynamic data flow descriptions will not be part of this paper.

Educational literature confirms that effective courses represent a class of complex design problems (De Corte et al., 1981), (Romizowski, 1981) and (Reigeluth, 1983). Based on educational objectives, appropriate teaching and learning activities, suitable learning materials and instructional media must be selected. Teachers and learners may be required to work plenary, in smaller groups, or even individually within constraining time frames. In addition, proper evaluation procedures must be selected to assess the progress and (intermediate) results of a course. In case of tele-education, the complexity of instructional design is even higher since communication and information processing capabilities, human factors in distributed systems such as 'tele-presence' awareness, as well as distributed course organisation and logistics have to be additionally accounted for.

Educational processes in progress are typically apt to changes to ensure that instructional objectives are indeed accomplished (Repman, 1993) and (Newman, 1995). The capability of making adjustments depends on the didactic policies adopted. Learners, for example, may be assigned different levels of learner control in respect to course adaptations (Baack, 1995). Tele-education thus appears to be a very dynamic phenomenon and should therefore be designed to enable participants to dynamically plan, perform and evaluate courses in compliance with typical course management policies (Volman et al., 1997).

One may conclude that tele-education courses form a complex and multi-faceted educational landscape, which structure needs to be modelled to become visible. In this paper, we investigate the support for the organisation of the teaching and learning activities, the communication between the participants, and the information involved in the teaching and learning process. In our view, an infrastructure that supports such organisation in a flexible, i.e. adaptable, manner could improve the quality of tele-education courses and assist teachers in organising their courses. The design of such infrastructure should moreover be based on a multi-disciplinary collaboration involving, amongst others, the expertise available in the disciplines of educational and computer science. In this work, we use the Open Distributed Processing (ODP) Enterprise Viewpoints (ISO, 1995) to provide a suitable framework for the collaboration. The Unified Modelling Language (UML) (Fowler, 1997) is used to expressively communicate the models between the two disciplines. An early-developed prototype of the infrastructure has also been used to provide modelling feedback towards the two disciplines.

This paper is structured as follows. The next section describes the early-developed prototype. Section 3 discusses a space used to identify the educational modelling context. The development of the Enterprise models for the infrastructure is explained in Section 4 and Section 5 describes the assignments that link the entities of the model. Finally, Section 6 presents the conclusion of the work.

2. AN EARLY-DEVELOPED PROTOTYPE

In educational research, early feedback is a typical vehicle to evaluate and to improve educational models. Accordingly, a prototype of the infrastructure has been used as a first step to capture structures of relations between education entities. In this section, we briefly introduce the underlying model of the prototype, describe the involved entities and their relations, and briefly report small-scale experiences of users of this prototype.

2.1 The underlying model

A so-called project driven model is applied to combine didactic and process plan-do-check models, which in combination typically describe education. A didactic model is a structural model that organises the major variables in course design, e.g. educational objectives, educational activities, learning resources, media and tools, time schedules, grouping schemes, and evaluation activities (De Corte et al., 1981) and (Romizowski, 1981). The plan-do-check model is an educational process model that organises three classes of activities that are not necessarily consecutive, i.e. course planning, course performance and course evaluation.

Course planning involves educational actors specifying the contents for the design variables in the didactic model, resulting in concrete course plans. Course performance implies educational actors to accomplish educational objectives according the activities described in course plans. The checking part refers to the evaluation of the (intermediate) course results, and may cause the cycle to close by requiring appropriate course plan adaptations.

2.2 The project driven structure

Figure 1 shows the project driven structure of educational entities that details the planning part of education. The 'tasks' entity represents combined educational activities of a course. This structure of the entity offers the possibilities for breaking the work down into composite task structures and including associated leaf-tasks, which comprise information resources required to accomplish a particular task. The 'teams' entity enables the definition of team structures. Team structures comprise sub-teams and educational roles, they allow for structured resourcing in project organisation. The 'flows' entity supports the specification of the permissible patterns of communication and information relations in respect to resources or roles in a particular project. This entity is considered useful to avoid message and information overload during performance of a project. Finally, the 'project' entity, which is the integrating element, links the entity components as assignments. It enables a planner to assign the teams to particular tasks, to set time schedules and to define authorisations (i.e. privileges) in respect to project management.

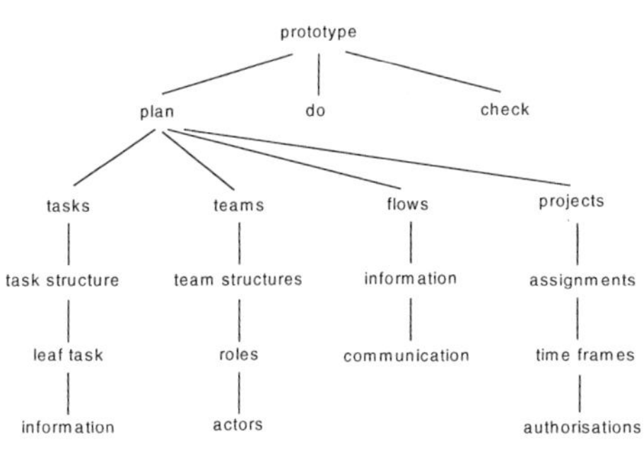

Figure 1: The project driven structure

Together with the 'plan' entity, the 'do' and 'check' entities represent the educational plan-do-check process model. The 'do' entity provides the educational actors access to (authorised parts of) the project plan in order to carry out activities aiming at accomplishing the project objectives. The 'check' option provides access to (authorised parts of) the project plan in order to evaluate (intermediate) project outcomes.

2.3 First experiences with the prototype

The first prototype has been explored in respect to two main questions:

1. Does the prototype provide a usable set of functions for planning, performing and evaluating courses in an efficient, effective and satisfactory manner?
2. Does the logical ordering of the functions comply to user requirements while working with projects?

In a class on courseware design, learners who were not familiar with the prototype were asked to evaluate the prototype. These learners participated in a test to implement a pre-specified course plan in the prototype. Afterwards, they were asked to indicate their general opinion, the usefulness, and the ease-of-use regarding the prototype. Beside this questionnaire, the duration of implementing the plan was measured and this was compared to the performance of an experienced prototype user.

The results suggest that the prototype does not fully meet the requirements of the actors. The prototype shows only one implementation model of the structures of relations between education entities and does not indicate generic and flexible models as discussed earlier. The prototyping approach alone does not provide the means for a systematic design of the intended infrastructure. In our view, the identification of alternative models of these structures in education requires a complementary conceptual approach.

3. THE EDUCATIONAL MODEL SPACE

As expected, the models of the infrastructure depend for a large part on the problem domain context. The evaluation of the prototype described in the previous section also has emphasised the need to identify the type of the model, the scope of the educational organisation under consideration and the level of the modelling details. For this, the Educational Model Space presented in Figure 2 is applied. Three dimensions mark this space, namely the organisational dimension of the problem domain, the ODP viewpoint dimension and the granularity dimension of the modelling domain.

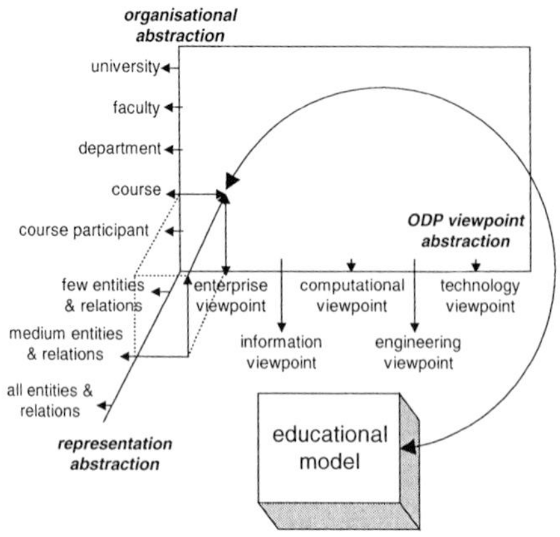

Figure 2: The Educational Model Space

The first dimension involves the scope of the real-life system under consideration, referred to as the *organisational abstraction*. Since the infrastructure is designed particularly for educational environments, such levels of scope are represented as a University, Faculties or Departments, Courses and Tasks.

The second dimension concerns the amount of details involved in a particular model, referred to as the *representation abstraction*. A particular granularity level may reflect all the conceptual entities and their relations as identified in the project driven model discussed earlier.

The third dimension is concerned with ODP Enterprise, Information, Computation, Engineering and Technology Viewpoints. In this paper, the focus will be mainly on the Enterprise Viewpoint. This viewpoint provides the common ground for collaboration between educational science and computer science, among others because no distinction is necessarily to be made between 'system' roles and activities (which can be automated) and the 'user' roles and activities (which have to be performed manually). As an ODP system, the intended infrastructure is viewed as a community constituted to the purpose of accomplishing educational objectives. This community is described in terms of roles, policies and activities for each of the involved educational entities that are considered essential from educational or didactical point of view (Volman et al., 1997).

4. ENTERPRISE MODELS IN EDUCATION

This section describes the design trajectory of the modelling of the educational information infrastructure. Based on a chosen reference point in the Educational Model Space (Section 3), an initial Enterprise model for educational entities will be discussed. This model will then be refined in a stepwise manner yielding an Enterprise model capturing structural educational relations suitable for a wide range of didactic policies.

The chosen design decisions embody our modelling purpose to capture invariant relations between education entities as much as possible in object models. It must be remarked that the object models do not only capture static structural relations identified in the educational problem domain. These models also capture invariance of the dynamics in education, such as the nested plan, performance, and evaluation activities in courses applying so-called 'open' didactic policy, where learners have a high degree of freedom in planning and organizing parts of their courses. Though the followed modelling approach gives the risks in defining models that are possibly too rigid for very specific educational processes, this approach improves clarity of the models and exposes the weak and strong properties of these models better. It also is expected that correct procedures for dynamic educational information processing can then be constructed more easily. Further, the design decisions incorporate the so-called task-oriented educational approach, where educational tasks and their objectives play a central role in education design (e.g. courseware design) (Reigeluth, 1987) and (De Vries, 1996).

4.1 The reference point

Though a reference point as discussed in Section 3 is not immediately necessary for the first (not refined) Enterprise model, an educational context provides a better hook for examples.

In accordance with the prototype, a Course has been taken as the reference value at the organisational dimension of the Educational Model Space. Moreover, the focus will be on the Enterprise models and the granularity of details is selected at the component level of the project driven model discussed in Section 2.

4.2 The applied UML concepts

In this work, we apply UML (Unified Modelling Language) (Fowler, 1997) to express the developed Enterprise models. The visual representation of the UML notation makes our educational enterprise models more accessible for both educational scientists and system engineers. The modelling elements are moreover sufficiently expressive, enabling both groups to reason about the specified models and to provide modelling input in respect to their domain of expertise.

UML concepts that are used in this paper are shown in Figure 3.

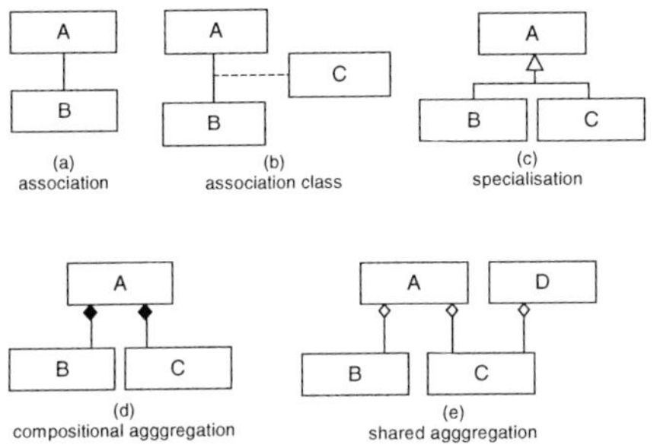

Figure 3: Class aggregations and associations

A box represents a class, which is a set of objects with similar structure, behaviour and relations. Figure 3a shows an association (represented by a line) between class A and class B. Figure 3b shows the concept of 'association class', which is an extension of the concept 'association'. The box with the dashed line represents the class property of the association. For clarity, multiplicity in associations will be omitted in most of the figures.

Figure 3c illustrates the concept of specialization, represented by a triangular symbol. This concept is suitable to express the distinction between the different roles, e.g. teacher's and tutor's roles.

Figure 3d shows a compositional aggregation in which class B and class C are genuine components of class A. This means that deletion of an instance of class A implies deletion of the component instances of class B and class C and that instances of class B or class C may not be shared by compositional aggregation instances other than that of class A. This type of aggregation is represented by a black diamond symbol.

Figure 3e shows a weaker aggregation form, namely a 'shared aggregation', and is visually represented by an open diamond symbol. In this case, deletion of an instance of class A does not necessarily mean the deletion of the component instances of class B or class C. Moreover, instances of class B or class C may be shared by shared aggregation instances, e.g. shared by D.

4.3 The initial Enterprise model

The first Enterprise model (Figure 4) shows an educational entity class as a central entity (e.g. a Course in respect to the previously chosen reference point).

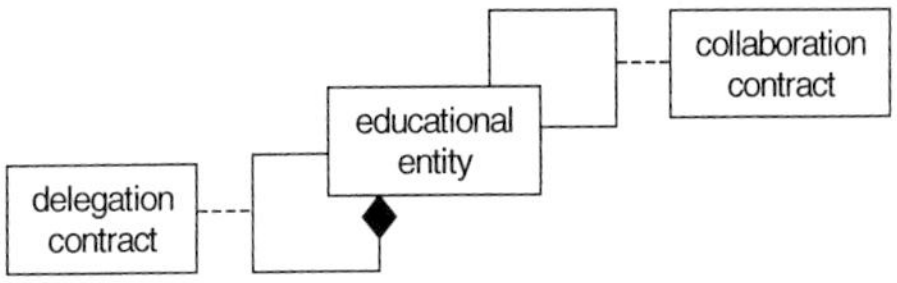

Figure 4: The initial Enterprise Model

The hierarchical relations

The model exposes the relations of the central entity with a higher level as well as lower level entities in respect to the organisational dimension of the educational model space. The relation is modelled as a compositional aggregation with the class 'Delegation Contract' attached to it. In the Enterprise Viewpoint, the combination of a compositional aggregation with an association class is considered expressive in the capturing of hierarchical relations as found in many didactic models (De Corte et al., 1981) and (Romizowski, 1981), for example in mastery learning approaches. In these models, educational entities are strongly coupled with their objectives and are typically hierarchically decomposed in smaller entities, each of them possesses objectives derived from the aggregating entity (e.g. derived learning goals of course lessons). The association class as is applied here elegantly justifies the relations of the course-tasks *in* the course setting. In other learning approaches (e.g. in thematic learning), this dependence relation in the hierarchy is less constrained. This hierarchical top-down and goal directed structure is considered appropriate in Enterprise models. Analogous structures are also found in other fields and are often expressed in a similar way, for example in Hospital Information Systems (Luzi, Ricci & Serbanati, 1997).

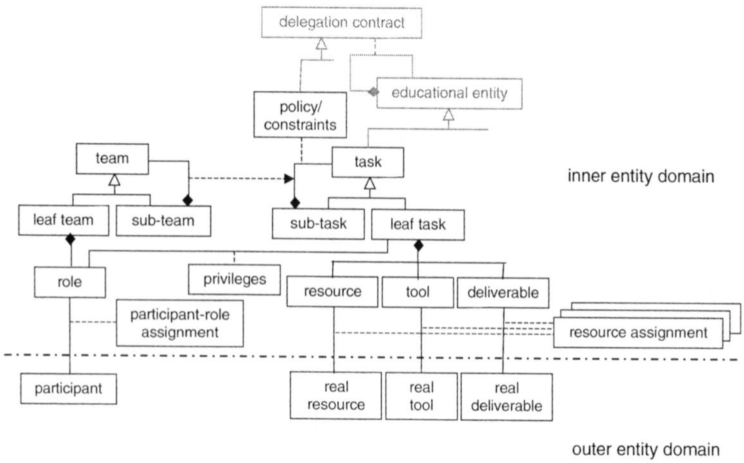

Figure 5: Refined Educational Enterprise Model

Example:

A Course is a compositional aggregation of so-called course tasks. These tasks are related to each other via the association class "Delegation Contract" which for example contain a strict ordering of tasks in the context of a closed didactic policy or a partially ordered task structure in the context of a more open policy. This flexibility supports a wide range of didactic approaches, such as the mastery or the thematic learning approaches.

Complexity of a Delegation Contract depends for a large part on the applied policies of the hierarchically higher-level entities. At universities, some faculties may demand complete micro planning of courses, some others may only require course content lists and learning objectives. Besides structures for course descriptions or micro-plans, a delegation contract at course level often contain structures for incorporating policies for Learners' Control (e.g. learners' authorisation to plan, perform or evaluate a particular educational task), in general, or Learning Control authorisation tables, in particular.

Moreover, likelihood of use of specific educational tools, e.g. ICT applications or the educational information infrastructure reported here, may be improved by formulating the associated Faculty or University mission related to ICT in a Delegation Contract, see for example (Collis & Pals, 2000).

The collaboration relations

On the other hand, a top-down delegation from a higher-level to a lower-level entity, such as the Delegation Contract, is not sufficient in many dynamic and collaborative educational environments. Nowadays, Faculties start to collaborate with sister faculties of other institutes. In tele-education projects, courses may also be organised between faculties of different universities, but typically with maintaining student administrations under local university regime. To facilitate these dynamic inter-faculty collaborations, the educational entity class (e.g. modelling faculties) has a self-referring association with class Collaboration Contract. This structure is also found in other business models (Yates et al., 1997).

4.4 The refined task-oriented object model

As was mentioned earlier, the Enterprise models discussed in this paper have been influenced by the task-oriented educational approach. Accordingly, course tasks have been modelled explicitly and take an important place in these models. It has to be remarked that the task-oriented approach does not constraint the usability of the targeted infrastructure for other types of educational approaches.

Task hierarchy

Figure 5 shows a refinement of a part of the model depicted in Figure 4. A course task, which is a specialisation of the educational entity, is hierarchically decomposed in sub-tasks. Though a sub-task may contain attributes or component objects, e.g. to model task roll-ups, summary of (expected) results (IMS, 2000), these details are not visible at the chosen granularity level.

A leaf element of such tree is called a leaf-task and has a structure that exposes the educational resources (i.e. task inputs), the deliverables (i.e. task outputs), and the tools of this task. Tools represent the utilities and, if appropriate, the logistical means like classrooms, laboratories, network interconnectivity, and computers.

The recursive way of modelling course tasks complies with the different educational practices. Especially open policy courses, in which task decomposition and task classification (i.e. plan, perform, evaluate types) are heavily intertwined (Volman et al., 1997), will benefit from this recursive structure. During the performance activities of these courses, for example, the performing participants (e.g. teachers or authorised learners) usually further decompose these tasks in smaller units themselves.

The association class of the hierarchical relation is a specialisation of the delegation contract described earlier. If a subtask models a test activity in a course, the association class may contain constraints like the prohibition to assign resources to external learning materials (i.e. a closed book examination). This class may therefore be used to guide course planners to detail the test in a way that the leaf-tasks of the test preserve the test objectives.

Tasks and roles

As in many other business organisations, tasks are associated to teams or roles in a homomorphic way. In the planning or performance activities (e.g. during course lessons), planners typically assign tasks to teams or individual learners who have to fulfil specific roles. Accordingly, teams and roles are organised in a homomorphic way to the task hierarchy. In the model, a dashed arrow expresses this.

This homomorphism enables planners to assign the same tasks to different teams, useful for cases where large numbers of learners are enrolled for a course. In the task-oriented educational approach, the task hierarchical structure inherently determines the team structure. These homomorphic structures will guide educational planners to organize the teams and roles (e.g. learners groups, tutors and lecturers) in accordance with the goal directed tasks and task structures, or vice-versa.

Roles that are homomorphically associated to a leaf-task may have constrained access to the task components. This is modelled by the Privileges, which determines the denial or the types of access of the role on the task component. Privileges may be defined in terms like rights to "use", "re-plan", and "extend" tasks. These privileges are therefore derived from the delegation contract, e.g. the Learning Control tables mentioned earlier.

4.5 The problem domain entities

Opposed to the modelling domain entities that in our case represent the educational modelling concepts like tasks and teams, problem domain entities represent the teachers, the enrolled learners, the books or web-pages used in courses. These so-called *outer* entities of the model complement the *inner* (i.e. educational modelling) entities as they provide the necessary hooks to enable instantiation of the model onto real education cases, e.g. a specific course in a specific course year.

Participants and roles

In the planning phase, typically, teams and roles will be assigned to the educational participants (e.g. the learners enrolled for a course in a particular year and the registered tutors or teachers). A many-to-many association has been used to express the relation between the role and participant classes (Figure 5). This multiplicity enables participants to be responsible for several roles and on the other hand, it enables use of shared roles in collaborative work oriented courses. An association class between the two classes makes re-assignment of roles to other participants also possible, for example, in case of re-planning on the fly during performance of courses applying open policies.

Problem domain entities and task components

In analogy to the modelling of roles and participants, problem domain entities, in particular, real education resources, tools and deliverables have to be assigned to the aggregated components of a leaf-task. These associations are also many-to-many; association classes are accordingly used to specify them.

5. ASSIGNMENTS

By their role, course planners (or designers) have the responsibility to specify and plan the course. Optionally in a hierarchical way, these roles may execute their responsibility or delegate (part of) the role to other course participants by appointing some of them to become planners (of part) of the course. Additionally, planner roles have to assign the instances of the earlier mentioned outer entities to the instances of the specified inner entities (Figure 6). For example, after defining teams and team missions, planners may have to assign also the enrolled learners (or, if appropriate, also teachers, tutors, etc.) to these teams. Depending on the applied didactic policy and the followed educational approach (e.g. a mastery learning approach), resources, tools and deliverables may also be assigned by the same planner role, see also Figure 5.

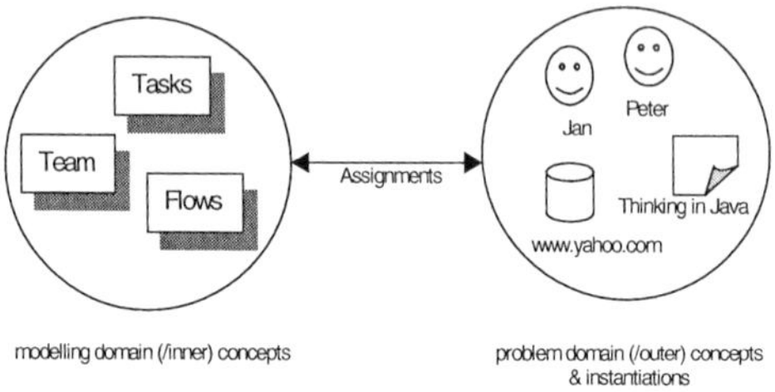

Figure 6: The connections between entities & instances

Assignment is therefore the making of the connections between the educational instances specified in the educational information infrastructure in respect of the planned course. The patterns of the specification and assignment procedures depend on the didactical policy and the educational approach followed by the course participants (which include the course planners).

The second version of the prototype is object based and is implemented as a web-based application using Active Server Pages and a relational database constructed using MS Access. The left and right columns in Figure 7 illustrate a task hierarchy, in which an indented task represents a sub-task. For example, the task "Assignment 1" comprises of six sub-tasks and subtask "Study ABC tool", in turn, comprises of the child tasks "Study tool manual" and "Make examples". The figure represents an activity flow window, which enables a course tutor-planner to assign the possible follow-ups of tasks (illustrated by the arrows) by clicking the appropriate radio and connectivity (symbolized by "<>") buttons.

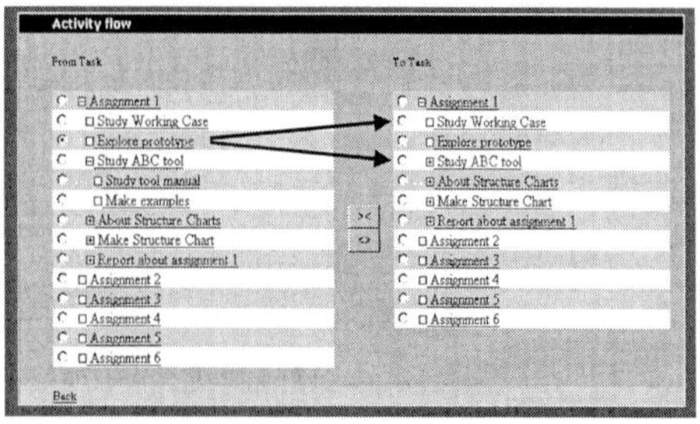

Figure 7: Activity flow represents tasks follow-ups

Some simplifications however have been made in the prototype. Tasks and teams have been implemented in one relational table, which constrains the prototype to support isomorphic team and task structures only. Moreover, real resources, tools and deliverables have been implemented by tables containing string typed attributes, which are sufficient to specify textual descriptions or string references, but URL references are not launchable. Information structures developed in other educational projects, e.g. (IMS, 2000), may be used to extent the prototype.

6. CONCLUSIONS AND FUTURE WORK

This paper described the outcomes of an exercise for the modelling of an educational infrastructure that aims to support the organisation of teaching and learning activities. This exercise has been carried out in a multi-disciplinary collaboration in which ODP Enterprise Viewpoint and UML have shown their value in bridging the conceptual gap between educational scientists and computer science engineers. Nonetheless, feedback provided by the developed prototype has been a complementary necessity, especially to validate the perception of the developed models by the researchers of the different disciplines.

The richness and especially the diversity of educational approaches and models make the modelling of an infrastructure that generically has the ability to support educational processes no matter what the applied didactic policy is is very complex. In fact, this complexity has triggered the capturing of invariance in educational relations, resulting in recursive structures that do not only support the hierarchical structure of a typical educational entity, these structures are also uniformly applicable in respect to the educational plan-do-check model. This enables an infrastructure support for intertwined activities of planning, performance, and evaluation type that are typically not consecutive in open didactic policies.

The Enterprise Viewpoint has been used for its emphasis on justification purposes, which provide a better assurance that hierarchically decomposed education entities as a whole fulfils the educational objectives of the aggregation, a property necessary in many educational environments in general or didactic models in particular. However, these Enterprise models are not directly suitable for implementation of the targeted infrastructure. Further work therefore need to concentrate on the derivation of advanced Information and Computation Viewpoint models that are more suitable for processing of information related to educational organisation. The dynamic models of the infrastructure, in alignment with the previously mentioned object models, will also be needed as well.

Educational courses have proven to be highly dynamic organisations. Expressing and explaining the capturing of invariant relations of dynamic enterprises is also one of the major challenges faced in many business environments. It is therefore believed that the results reported in this paper provide useful feedback concerning the modelling of the dynamics in business enterprises as well.

REFERENCES

Baack, M. (1995) *Remote Learning System, Media Supported Learning via Network/ISDN*, Newsletter, Basel.

Collis, B. (1997) *Tele-learning in a Digital World: the future of distance learning*, London, International Thomson Computer Press.

Collis, B. and Pals, N. (2000) *A Model for Predicting an Individual's Use of a Telematics Application for a Learning-Related Purpose*, Journal of Educational Telecommunications, 6(1), 63—103.

De Corte, E., C.T. Geerlings, N.A.J. Lagerweij, J.J. Peters, R. Vandenberghe (1981) *Beknopte Didaxilogie (in Dutch)* Groningen, the Netherlands, Wolters-Noordhoff.

De Vries, Sj. (1996) *The Design and Use of Adaptable Courseware*, PhD. thesis University of Twente, Faculty of Educational Science and Technology, the Netherlands.

Fowler, M., K. Scott (1997) *UML Distilled: Applying the Standard Object Modelling Language*, Addison-Wesley.

IMS (2000) *IMS Global Learning Consortium Inc.* homepage, http://www.imsproject.org.

ISO (1995) *ISO/IEC 10746 ODP Reference Model Part 1: Overview*, ISO/IEC JTC1/SC21/WG7.

Luzi, D., F.L. Ricci, L. Dan Serbanati (1997) "Extending the Standard Architecture for Healthcare Units: the Guideline Server", *New Technologies in Hospital Information Systems*, J. Dudeck et al. ed., 95-101, IOS Press.

Newman, D. (1995) "Technology's Roles in Restructuring for Collaborative Learning" in *Computer Supported Collaborative Learning*, C.O'Malley ed., Berlin, Springer Verlag.

Reigeluth, C.M. (1983) *Instructional Design Theories and Models: an Overview of Their Status*, Hillsdale NJ, Lawrence Earlbaum.

Reigeluth, C.M. (1987) *Instructional Theories in Actions: Lessons Illustrating Selected Theories and Models*, Hillsdale NJ, Lawrence Earlbaum.

Repman, J. (1993) "Collaborative computer-based learning: cognitive and affective outcomes", *Journal of Educational Computing Research*, (9)2, 149-163.

Romizowski, A.J. (1981) *Designing Instructional Systems, Decision making in course planning and curriculum design*, London, Kogan Page.

Volman, C.J.A.M., V.M. Jones, M.J. van Sinderen, I. Widya, E.F. Michiels (1997) "Tele-education Process Modelling supported by the ODP Enterprise Viewpoint Language", *EDOC'97 Workshop*, Oct. 24-27th, Gold Coast Australia, 2-12;

Yates, M., et al. (1997) *TINA Business Model and Reference Points – version 4.0*, May 22nd, 1997, http://www.tinac.com.

TOWARDS E-MANAGEMENT AS ENABLER FOR ACCELERATED CHANGE

Hugo Lérias
Instituto de Engenharia de Sistemas e Computadores I&D, Lisboa, Portugal
Email: Hugo_Lerias@hotmail.com

João Luz
Instituto de Engenharia de Sistemas e Computadores I&D, Lisboa, Portugal
Email: jpvl@clix.pt

Pedro Moura
Instituto de Engenharia de Sistemas e Computadores I&D, Lisboa, Portugal
Email: pedro.moura@mail.pt

Ana Mendes
Escola Superior de Tecnologia de Setúbal, Portugal
Email: ana.j.mendes@clix.pt

Isabel Teixeira
Instituto Superior Técnico, Instituto de Engenharia de Sistemas e Computadores I&D, Lisboa, Portugal
Email: isabel.teixeira@.inesc.pt

J. Paulo Teixeira
Instituto Superior Técnico, Instituto de Engenharia de Sistemas e Computadores I&D, Lisboa, Portugal
Email: jct@cezanne.inesc.pt

Keywords: Business process reengineering, e-x, process, empowerment, working-environment, integration, distributed systems

Abstract: In a context of permanent change, Process Enterprises (PE) implement flexible mechanisms around processes that make them adequate platforms to deal with the emerging host of critical business problems. Processes are becoming cornerstones of business strategy, which place them among the most valuable assets of a company. However, transition to a PE should not be a traumatic experience. The purpose of this paper is to present a methodology and tools supporting e-management for accelerated change. The goal is, while boosting company effectiveness, to enable smooth and pleasant adaptation of enterprises and employees to change in objectives, strategy, culture, roles and career opportunities. Process Oriented Working Environment (POWER) architecture is proposed, with its architecture and man-machine interface, on which actors have their role and profile dynamically up-dated, as they progress through process completion. As a case study, a University, organized according to a very conservative model, is used as vehicle for ascertaining the proposed solutions.

1. INTRODUCTION

Globalization, merging and e-business have clamped, in our days, to the top of organizations agenda. Sustainable growth of the information society quests for innovative, flexible and robust management models, organization models and cost-effective, timely implementation. Accelerated change is mastering our lives (Rose 1997, Hammer 1996). However, people and their culture, being the key to success, can also represent the "slow lane" of

J. Filipe et al. (eds.), Enterprise Information Systems III, 240–247.

this highway. How can they be motivated to adapt, play new roles and perform tasks in a novel way, in full harmony with a company's vision and purpose?

In this contribution, emphasis is put on the fact that management and engineering sciences must be integrated to identify, formalize, discuss and implement evolving management and organization models. Moreover, implementation needs a stimulating and cost-effective Working Environment (WE), a common ground in which all actors in the process can meet, discuss, generate consensus, perform their work, exchange information and knowledge and produce added value to customers. Information Systems (IS) can perform this role in an profit or non-profit (Druker 1992) organization, if adequately designed, maintained and up-graded. The purpose of this paper is twofold. First, to present a methodology for e-management, adequate to accelerate change. This methodology is illustrated with a Process Enterprise (PE) model, (http://www.hammerandco.com/), which uses Business Process (BP) (Hammer 1993, Hammer 1996) as the core entity of the organization model. Second, to introduce an IS-based WE supporting the methodology, referred as POWER (Process Oriented Working EnviRonment), with its architecture and man-machine interface, on which actors have their *role* and *profile* dynamically up-dated, as they progress through process completion.

The paper is organized as follows. Section 2 highlights the usefulness of the PE management model, and BP as its building block. In section 3, the underlying principles of the methodology and tools required to implement e-management for a process-centered enterprise is proposed. In section 4, the POWER Working Environment and its IS target architecture are presented. Section 5 presents the IS architecture. Section 6 describes a case study, used to ascertain the main features of the proposed methodology. Section 7 summarizes the key conclusions of the work.

2. PROCESS ENTERPRISE

The success of a modern enterprise is mainly, if not entirely, the result of the robustness of its *Purpose*, its *People* and its *Processes*. In fact, purpose sets the road to the future, people are an anchor on the present and processes are the tools that lead people to fulfill the purpose. As a consequence, 3P culture is becoming a paradigm of modern organizations.

Competitive and sustainable enterprises center the focus of concern on customer's satisfaction, even delight. A BP is defined as a set of related tasks that, together, create value to a customer. Processes focus on customer satisfaction. Customer satisfaction means results tuned to their needs and processes are designed to create such results. As a consequence, modern enterprises need to be organized around BP that create the answers to customer requirements.

The new role of human resources (People) in a Process Enterprise (PE) is associated with *peer professionals*, performing diverse roles, according to their core competencies. Managers and doers are peers, sharing different responsibility. The ghost of the boss is replaced by the friendly image of the coach, as an enabler for success. Empowerment is another keyword, as professionals, experts in their own field, are the ones that know best *how* tasks should be carried out, as bricks of a building that needs to be built - the process, and its added value to the customer. Managers, as process leaders, design (by themselves or after peer consultation) the process. Managers become process architects, defining task breakdown, input, output, top-level functionality, and resources, milestones and deliverables, which include making the choice of the most adequate task leader. Thus, *process-centered management* enters the limelight and remains on stage.

Every PE requires a cadre of process masters: individuals with deep expertise and understanding on what a PE is, how it is designed, implemented, and managed. In fact, *process leaders* play critical roles in both transitions to a PE and its subsequent operation. They act as catalysts that persuade the company to undertake this initiative. They plan the transition and its implementation; they play leadership roles on process design teams; they are resources to whom others throughout the company will turn for guidance and counsel. To be sure, everyone in a PE must have a basic understanding of the process concept; managers need in-depth understanding of their new roles and responsibilities.

To process leaders, task interaction is defined according to customer-supplier relationship. When process realization takes place, a process leader acts as enabler, motivator, consensus builder, trouble shooter, and intermediates with the process context - customers, suppliers, the enterprise, etc. Process *team members* concentrate in adding value to the whole, by timely performing their work in such as way that they design *how* tasks will be carried out in a cost-effective way, and taking the lead to deliver valuable results on time.

However, the implementation of a process centered organization model may correspond, for many existing enterprises, to a dramatic change on its culture. If such change is carried out on a context of a quantum step, as is the case with reengineering (Hammer 1996), it may turn out to be a very traumatic experience, since it corresponds to the rupture with an existing culture and the attempt to implement another. People easily accept evolution, hardly revolution, unless they fully identify themselves with its outcome. Nevertheless, culture is not something that can be imposed; instead, it is something that results from practice. Hence, in almost every case, time, patience and persuasion are required for a new way of working to become a culture.

3. METHODOLOGY FOR E-MANAGEMENT

Since *purpose* is associated with the mission of an organization, in this work we focus on the implementation of novel management and organization models adequate to accelerated change, in such a way that people voluntarily and willingly support them. As referred, the management model used to illustrate the methodology is the *process enterprise,* using Business Process (BP) as the core entity of the organization model. Therefore, the proposed methodology aims at process implementation and on methodologies and tools required for helping people to fully participate on process implementation. As this is not a trivial task, an enabler mechanism is required to help enterprises in promoting a new culture, as efficiently as possible, without rising opposition (even without conscience) from its members. It is our belief that this can be achieved by providing people with tools that, while easing their job, promote change in an adequate Working Environment (Fig. 1).

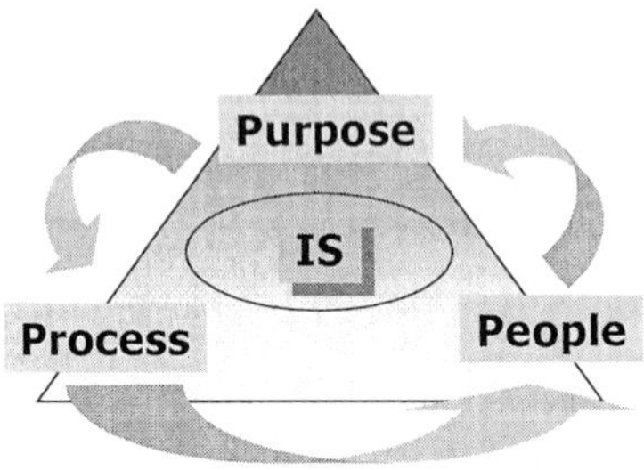

Figure 1: The role of IS (POWER) in the trilogy of the 3 Ps

Hence, the basic underlying principles of the proposed methodology are

(1) *Management* and *engineering* sciences must be combined to clearly characterize company's BP. In particular, it is rewarding to bring the problem solving (and preventing) approach, typical of the engineering sciences, to BP modeling;
(2) The concept of *process* (BP) pervades all the aspects of system organization, productive or non-productive;
(3) In order to exploit people's talent, knowledge and skills and to boost their willingness to support purpose, an *IS-based Working Environment* must be operational to ease communication, work, trust, and continuous improvement. Such WE, supported on Information, Communication Technologies (ICT), is an adequate platform to nest all participating actors - managers, process leaders, team members, even customers and suppliers (fig. 2). We refer as *e-management* the process-centered management designed and operated through an IS-based WE. Moreover, *Internet* has become a commodity and a privileged mean of communication, as time and space are reduced almost to null. So, the IS-based WE must implement the PE organization model around ICTs taking full advantage of the Web. As an example, merging enterprises or easing B2B, B2C and customer-supplier relationship using the Internet may be viewed mainly as *process integration.*
(4) The *IS architecture* is a critical factor of success, since it must be highly flexible and highly resistant to technology evolution. Accelerated change is triggered not only by a continuous shift in market and society context, but also by the dynamic push of hardware (hw) and software (sw) releases. Moreover, economic reasons make mandatory the *reuse* of system parts (either sw applications or hw platforms) as long as possible. The target IS needs to survive and operate under periodic maintenance and repair, as e.g., new OS (Operating Systems), new applications versions or new hw platforms take the stage. Furthermore, in order to increase flexibility in supporting the work of the process team, people's *role* and *profile* should be dynamically defined and up-dated, thus easing communication among process actors. The target IS architecture must support this feature.

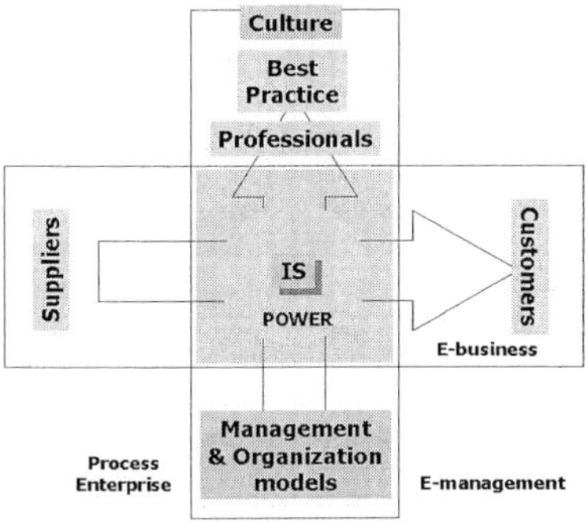

Figure 2: Proposed e-management scenario

In this paper, a Process Oriented Working EnviRonment (POWER) is proposed to be the backbone of a PE, satisfying the above requirements. Working within this environment, any member of the company is connected to the others providing cooperation, workflow, etc. Each member may feel being needed, useful, appreciated, respected, rewarded and may be able to see his (her) own contribution to enterprise success. The POWER Working Environment aims at providing an open avenue for e-management.

4. WORKING ENVIRONMENT

As pointed out before, a culture is not something that we can buy. It takes time to become part of the life of the actors playing any role on the context of that culture. However, time is becoming scarcer every day. Enterprises may have not the time usually required to transform a practice into a culture. In a context of accelerated change, help is needed to reduce this time. For this, a concept that is the basis of almost (if not all) every law that rules the physical world, namely, the concept of *field,* can be used to illustrate the role of the WE. A field may be simply defined as the area of influence of something that is, in fact, the source of this field. Hence, a gravitational field describes the region of influence of a mass over the others, an electric field, the region of influence of an electric charge over the others, etc. Knowing the field laws, the intrinsic characteristics of any actor within a field, and its position in space and time, it is usually possible to predict its position and behavior in the future.

To apply this concept to the universe of enterprise management requires the identification of the entity that can create this area of influence over the playing actors. Modern technology provides this entity. In fact, an Information System that implements a desired enterprise management model, and that is designed with the correct interface among the IS and any of the players, may be regarded as such field of influence that establishes pleasant laws of interaction among the different players. As a consequence, it smoothly models the way of living within the enterprise. It may contribute to standardize working relationships and to promote the desired culture. In this work, this field of influence, created around an adequate IS, is referred as POWER.

The proposed Working Environment takes also into consideration the past of the enterprise by the adequate exploitation of *company legacy*. This legacy includes existing IS, people and previous organization models. Previous (but still operating) IS can be viewed as static legacy actors, while people and organization models can be considered as dynamic actors. The first may not be changed, while the latter are expected to adapt to the new environment. The main objective of the POWER environment is to ease the life of the different human actors. It should provide to everyone the tools and applications that respond to their needs. People need to feel that they actually gain by using the system. As soon as everybody is using the system, a new culture is implemented, 'without pain'.

5. IS ARCHITECTURE

Given its key role on the implementation of the Working Environment, the design of the IS *architecture* is a critical factor of success. The accelerated change pace of knowledge and technology requires extremely high flexibility in the solutions. Moreover, economic reasons make mandatory the reuse of system parts. As a result, acting IS should behave like a living creature on stage. Always under observation and criticism, and always changing. However, like a living *being*, modifications need to take place without shutdown. They progress silently, in the intimacy of the organism. Similarly, the target IS needs to survive and operate under periodic maintenance and repair, as new OS, new applications versions, and new hw platforms take the stage.

Hence, the IS needs to be built with the LEGO concept: standardized parts, easy to plug & play, looking alike and easy to interface. In LEGO, individual components are not equal, instead they share similar boundary characteristics, which allows to plug & play the way the user wants, when he (she) wants, according to his (her) imagination.

Additionally, the role and the performance of people are critical to the success of process realization and consequently to the enterprise. Therefore, if people are unable to fully exploit the features of the tool on their hands, it will fail its purpose of easily implementing a culture. As a consequence, the IS must be flexible enough to deal with different user's expertise, profile and role. Our experience is that the BP concept is also particularly adequate to answer to this requirement. In fact, as it is shown in section 6, actors playing any role on a given process should have their personal Working Area defined according to the corresponding, expertise, profile and role, at any time interval.

These concepts underlie the implementation of a *key feature of the proposed architectural solution, that is, the dynamic definition of man-machine interfaces (Working Areas), according to the role each team member performs in a given process, or in each process to which he (she) is committed.* By using the correct identification, the user has access to a set of functionalities and / or tools. These functionalities are the *touching point* between the user and the processes on which he participates. As in the example within the universe of our case study (section 6), a professor responsible for a given course is responsible for the definition of the corresponding process.

Another important feature is the possibility of on line monitoring the process evolution. In fact, since process realization is based on the use of POWER, any process leader can follow, on-line, the progress of the process he(she) manages. It is straightforward to examine, on-line, each *actor's profile*, i.e., the set of tasks and/or processes to which each team member adds manpower, to check the way they are using (or bringing) their core competencies, being well used or wasted in some tasks, their ability for time management, etc. Process leaders have also the vision of team membership, their comparative role and effort. POWER can thus support decision making.

5.1 Modelling Methodology

A key component of system architecture is the model that describes the BP in terms of playing actors, their role, their interaction and the time. The underlying model (Mendes 2000) is based on the assumption that a Process can be organised as a set of Activities, each one composed of tasks. A task corresponds to the execution of a given functionality. For process modelling, a main primitive construct is the AMM (Activity Management Matrix), generically represented in Fig. 3. The AMM is a graphic representation of the process activities and their assignment to the actors involved in their execution with a time frame as key parameter.

The AMM is one of the most important model primitives, as it can become a key tool to process managers. As depicted in Fig. 3 two fundamental concepts are defined over this matrix. A horizontal cross-section over an activity identifies the *team profile*, as the set of actors responsible for its execution. The process manager and the activity leader can use this information to ascertain the core competencies of the team members, required to perform the activity. A horizontal cross-section over an activity identifies the team profile, as the set of actors responsible for its execution. A vertical cross-section over an actor identifies the activities on which the actor is involved, that is, the actor profile on that process. This set of activities defines the role of the actor on that process, which can be used to evaluate the time-sharing of each actor among the different activities of the process. Furthermore, the set of activities of the actor's profile is used for the automatic and dynamic definition of the user area of this actor in that process.

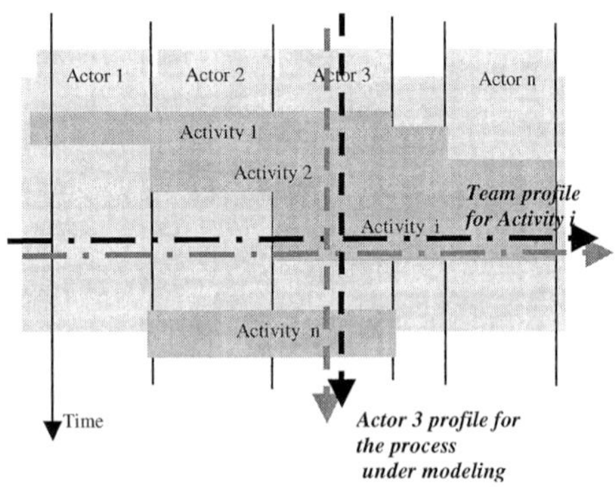

Figure 3: Activity Management Matrix for a Process

5.2 Implementation Details – The Technological Architecture

POWER is implemented as a N-tier architecture that allows a clear separation between the Legacy Systems, Data Storage, Operational Repositories, Business Rules and Presentation Rules tiers (Fig. 4). All these tiers are glued using the now *de facto* XML language and Enterprise Applications Integration (EAI) methodologies (Margenthal 2000). Several XML (Hunter 2000) standards have been defined to normalize communication between the tiers.

This clear separation of tiers leads to some valuable characteristics. In fact, it is possible to wrap legacy systems, turning them into standardized interface business objects and to implement various objects in any tier with any technology that supports XML (like Microsoft (SQL Server and DCOM) and Oracle (9i and EJBs)) (Brown 2000). It supports, virtually, all type of client machines (Web Browser, WAP, client-server, etc), with the separation between the business and presentation rules, with the use of a XSL style sheets to render the information to the various types of clients. Additionally, it enables a modular and incremental development of applications (that map processes), through a LEGO-similar approach. Finally, it allows the development of basic architectural mechanisms, like, for example, support to Workflow-Based Processes, Enterprise-Wide Collaboration, or event-triggered access to tasks (functionalities).

The diagram depicted in Fig. 4 shows the technological and applicational architecture of the POWER system. Horizontal Layers are the technological tiers. Between these tiers are XML standards technology and EAI (middleware), the glue that joins the whole system. In the vertical slots, applicational units are shown.

There is a separation between Operational Applications (management applications, with On-Line Transaction Processing (OLTP) technology), and Analytical Applications, mostly decision-support and analysis applications, (http://www.olapreport.com) implemented using DataWarehousing and On-Line Analytical Processing technology. In our case study, the first corresponds to course management software and the second to the analysis of Course Success rates, through various analysis dimensions. One key aspect of this architecture is the unique and integrated touching point between the user and the various applications (or processes tasks). In this particular case, the business and presentation rules are implemented using Enterprise Java Beans and Servlets technology (Hunter 1998), with XML between these two and the Repository and Legacy tiers. The client technology used is HTML-enabled browsers. An Application Service Provider approach is possible with this architecture, since all the access to the system is made through the Internet. All this architecture is user-role driven. Applications and data accessible to the user are dependent on the corresponding role within the organization. Hence, when a given user is identified by the system, the system checks the applications and data he (she) has access to and presents it in the *User Individual Working Area*.

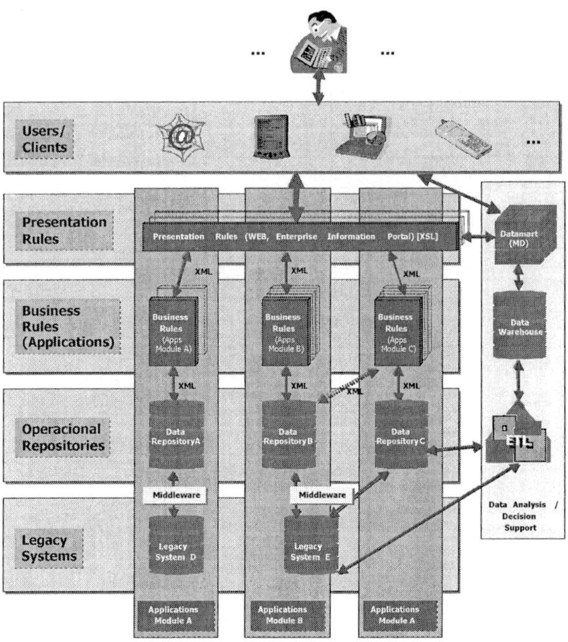

Figure 4: Power Architecture

6. CASE STUDY

As mentioned previously, a Higher Education Institution Case study (CaseHEI) is used to assess the features of the POWER environment. At the CaseHEI, Instituto Superior Técnico, IST, (the School of Engineering of the Technical University of Lisbon), a distributed management system is under development, focusing on two different processes, a 5 year *Programme* and the corresponding *Courses*. 8500 student plus, 1000 academic and 1000 non-academic staff members constitute IST population to cover 17 programmes and 1500 courses.

As almost every University in Portugal, IST management model is centred on Departments. However, since Programmes are the primary service provided by the University to the community, several Departments, responsible for different Programmes, are shifting the focus of their management model from Departments to Programmes. Departments are responsible for providing resources to carry out Programme implementation. By doing so, it is believed that considerable savings on the available resources can be obtained. This corresponds, in fact, to shift the focus of the organisational paradigm from *resource* to *processes* orientation.

Since quality assessment of Programmes is common practice in Portugal, two bottlenecks of Programme management have been identified (Pile 1997): the heterogeneity of data sources and the lack of meeting deadlines by some members of academic staff. In order to overcome these bottlenecks, 2 actions are being carried out. First, the problem solving approach of Engineering Sciences is applied to guarantee consistency and compatibility of data sources. Second, POWER is being used to motivate academic staff to fulfil their administrative activities on time.

POWER is planned to act as a common ground for all programme players and to pave the way to a new culture. This is achieved by providing personal User Areas for the different actors involved on the Programme, namely, academic and non-academic staff and students. Additional, the Programme itself and the courses are treated as autonomous objects. The access to a user area of a course depends on the user's profile. As an example, the professor responsible for the course, the other staff members and finally the students will have access to less and less functionality (Figure 5).

7. CONCLUSIONS

In conclusion, accelerate change, globalisation, customer requirements and technology are irreversibly modifying the way we live, work and do businesses. New management and organisation

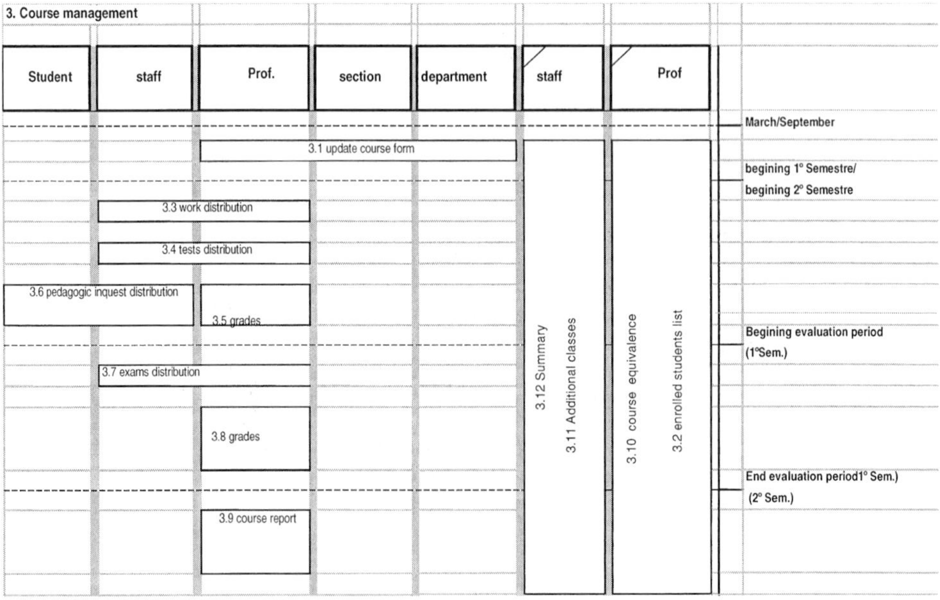

Figure 5: AMM for a Course at IST

models are emerging, and need to be rapidly applied. Enterprises no longer define themselves only in terms of their products and services, but also in terms of their key BPs. The 3P paradigm (Purpose, People and Process) heavily relies on People's talent and willingness to support change. However, people, being the most valuable asset of a company, may also be the "slow lane" of the new highway.

In this paper, it was shown that the path to e-management passes through the implementation of an IS-based Working Environment (WE). It was shown that the use of engineering sciences formalisms, methods and tools can support e-management, aiding to identify, formalize, discuss and implement new management and organization models. Moreover, it was demonstrated that a stimulating and cost-effective WE can be a common ground on which all actors in the process can meet, discuss, generate consensus, perform their work, exchange information and knowledge and produce added value to customers. Therefore, a methodology for e-management, adequate to accelerate change, has been proposed. This methodology is illustrated with a Process Enterprise (PE) model, which uses Business Process (BP) as the core entity of the organization model. The POWER Working Environment has been introduced, with its architecture and man-machine interface, on which actors have their *role* and *profile* dynamically up-dated, as they progress through process completion.

The Activity Management Matrix is used as a basic construct for modeling purpose. The supporting IS architecture is a N-tier architecture where legacy systems, data storage, Operational Repositories, Business Rules and Presentation Rules are separated tiers. XML and EAI methodologies are used as the glue among these tiers. The IST School of Engineering is used as a case study to demonstrate the key features of POWER and of the proposed methodology.

REFERENCES

Brown, B.D., 2000, ORACLE 8i Web Development, Oracle Press, McGraw-Hill.

Drucker, P.F, 1992, "Managing the Non-Profit Organization", HarperBusiness.

Hammer, M., 1996, "Beyond Reengineering - How the Process-Centered Organization is Changing our Work and our Lives", HarperBusiness, HarperCollins Publishers, Inc..

Hammer, M., Champy, J., 1993, "Reengineering the Corporation", HarperCollins Publishers, Inc..

Hunter, D., 2000, "Beginning XML", Wrox Press Ltd.

Hunter, J. Crawford, W., 1998, "Java Servlet Programming", O'Reilly & Associates.

Margenthal, J.P., 2000, "Enterprise Applications Integration with XML and Java" 1st edition, Prentice Hall.

Rose, C., Nicholl, M.J., 1997, "Accelerated Learning for the 21th Century - the 6-Step Plan to Unlock your Master-Mind", Delacorte Press.

Mendes, A. J., Teixeira, I., Teixeira, J.P., 2000, "Process-Centered Information Systems", 1ª Conferência Especializada de Sistemas de Informação.

Pile, M., Teixeira, J. P., Teixeira, I.C., Durão, D., 1997, "Quality Development in Engineering Education at IST", SEFI/CDWG Seminar on "A Tool to Improve the Learning Process – Evaluation and Quality Development in Engineering Education".

EXPERIENCES IN THE DEVELOPMENT OF INFORMATION SYSTEMS IN AN INDUSTRIAL INNOVATION CONTEXT

António Lucas Soares
INESC Porto and FEUP-DEEC University of Porto, R. José Falcão, 110, 4050 Porto, Portugal.
Email: als@fe.up.pt

Waldemar Gaida
WZL - RWTH Aachen, Steibachstraße, 53, D-52056 Aachen, Germany.
Email: w.gaida@wzl.rwth-aachen.de

Christian Schmidt
FIR, Aachen, Pontdriesch 1416 D-52062 Aachen, Germany.
Email: sm@fir-main.fir.rwth-aachen.de

Keywords: Information systems development, industrial innovation projects, teamwork, total quality management.

Abstract: This paper describes the methods and experiences of developing of an information system in an industrial innovation context. The case analysed respects to a system supporting quality management tasks of working teams in industrial companies, developed within a research & development EU funded project. The initial concept of the system is described first, followed by the way how requirements where elicited and structured and the system specified. Next, design and prototyping are analysed , detailing the end-users evaluation approach. Conclusions are drawn on the opportunities and difficulties od R&D involving industrial enterprises.

1. INTRODUCTION

There is an old and recurring dilemma in information systems (IS) development in organisations related with adopting off-the-shelf, packaged systems or to develop from scratch custom-made ones. Most of the times custom-made systems would be the best solution, but time and resource constraints preclude this option. If, alternatively, existing commercial packages or solutions are adopted, it can be the case that a significant amount of resources are spent on the system customisation. Furthermore, the configurability of these packages is most of the times limited in scope and, more frequently than would be desirable, the organisational changes imposed by those limitations are not beneficial to the organisation. In any case, the process and content of change is crucial as well as the methods and tools used to undertake such process.

The challenges and difficulties are even more accentuated when the IS to be developed encompasses a high degree of innovation. In this case, the problem situation is more vaguely defined and the uncertainty about the outcomes is typically high. Furthermore, as the results of such projects are highly uncertain and do not solve immediate problems, the development actors (within the companies) tend to be much less committed towards the success of the project.

The context of the work described here is the later case. It concerns the inception and development of an information system to be used in the support of working teams in industrial enterprises, under a framework of total quality management. The so-called ManTIS - Manufacturing Teams Information System - refers to both the information system and the project that produced it. The project involved a consortium of five industrial and academic partners from four European countries - United Kingdom, Portugal, Germany and Sweden - that played complementary roles in the system development.

J. Filipe et al. (eds.), Enterprise Information Systems III, 248–255.

2. FROM THE IDEA TO THE FIRST SPECIFICATION

2.1 The project plan

The global work effort of the project was about 27 person-year, during 36 months. It was divided in seven work packages (see Figure 1): (1) project management, (2) user requirements definition, (3) IT requirements definition, (4) system prototyping, (5) advanced prototyping, (6) industrial evaluation and validation, (7) exploitation and dissemination. This paper will describe mainly work packages 2 to 6.

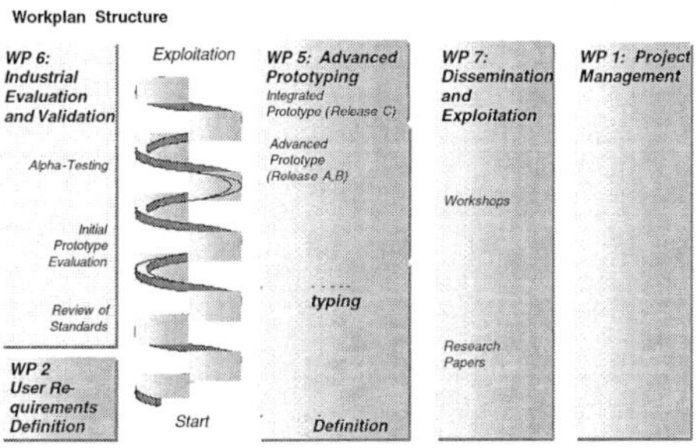

Figure 1: The project structure

2.2 The starting idea

The initial idea of ManTIS was generated (ManTIS, 1996) by a mix of innovation and company requirements. These were brought by the experience of some of the partners that crystallised the idea and structured it in a project proposal.

The goal was to provide manufacturing working teams (in enterprises structured around those forms of organisation) with an information system capable of improving visibly the efficiency and co-ordination. As a more specific rationale, ManTIS information system would support manufacturing working teams in their everyday tasks, following the methods and general guidelines of the Total Quality Management perspective. This would be delivered through two basic sets of functionalities:

1. a toolbox supporting all aspects of the team quality management and co-ordination and,
2. a uniform access to the company data (documents, plans, etc) needed by the group for the everyday operation.

Initially, Seven Team Performance Tools were considered covering: (1) Team Quality Monitoring, (2) Team Process Quality Monitoring, (3) Team Suggestion Book, (4) Team Self-Assessment, (5) Team Communication, (6) Team Co-ordination and (7) Team Training, These tools would hopefully contribute to integrate quality, resources, people and process management aspects of work-groups and would be focused on SME's. The scope of each tool is briefly described below (see figure 2).

Team Process Quality Monitoring

Process monitoring tool focus on the manufacturing processes where the team participates or is responsible for. It encompasses all aspects of processes where direct contact with production exists, particularly providing facilities to register, analyse and manage non-conformities. For that, performance indicators can be defined and graphics generated both for real-time and later analysis. Of most importance is the ability to set up the targets that the team will commit to achieve, and use the previously mentioned graphics to evaluate the team performance.

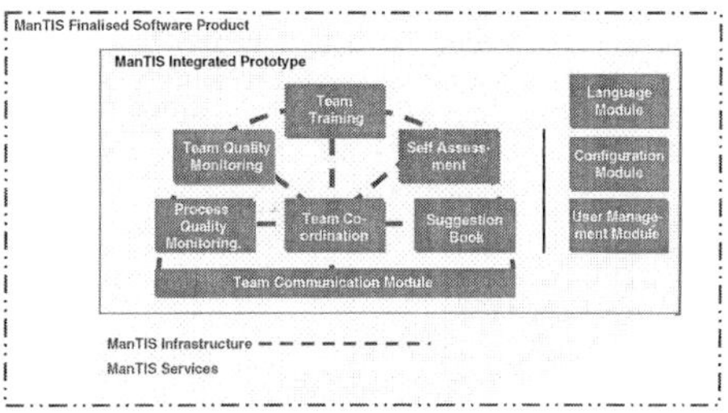

Figure 2: Generic system architecture

Team Quality Monitoring

This tool provides the team with the ability to assess and manage their quality performance as a whole and individually by team member. The team can define team's performance indicators and targets and monitor in real time the evolution of those indicators. Examples are the team's average productivity, average non-conformance ratio, average non-quality costs, etc. The same applies to team members, the only difference being the access to the data: individual performance is only accessed by the owner, while team performance can be accessed by all team members.

Team Co-ordination

Team co-ordination tool provides the team with the facilities to co-ordinate the work of their members and to co-ordinate the work of the team with other teams. Basic functions are the handling of work-lists with sorting, grouping, and filtering facilities, the assignment of people and resources, the flexible management of time (e.g., working shifts), etc. Another important functionality of this tool is the management of the team actions, namely continuous improvement actions. This tool is aimed to be used by the team as a whole (or e.g., by the team-leader).

Team Self-assessment
Team self-assessment is a simple tool to manage the team internal quality audits. It provides functionalities to schedule and register quality audit actions that concern to resources that the team is responsible for. As with the previous tools, targets can be set and graphic representations used to analyse trends. This is a tool to be used for the team as a whole (or e.g., by the team leader).

Team Training
Team training tool addresses the management of the team members' skills. The tool manages information such as training programmes, training schedules, and can provide access to computer based training. Individual members can define their profiles and training plans and register and evaluate the training actions. The group as a whole (or the team-leader) can manage the team skills detecting learning opportunities, managing this way the team skills development more rationally.

Team Communication
Working together as a team requires fast and reliable exchange of all relevant information needed to do the job. This tool enables the notification of events and exchange of information between team members and between the team and external people. It implements a very simple email client to be used with the company's mailing system.

Team Suggestion Book
The last tool provides a way for the team to manage their suggestions. The team members can in a first phase store ideas for improvement and then send the suggestion to the right person. If the suggestion is rejected the team can register the reason why. If it is accepted, the team can register the success or not of the corresponding actions.

The first step in the project was the validation of the general idea for the system. A two-phased approach was adopted, beginning by a general questionnaire and ending in a detailed analysis of selected companies. This is described in the next sections.

2.3 Validating the initial idea

The first phase of the two-phased approach included the completion of a questionnaire by the companies within the user groups in order to get an overview of their current status and further expectations in terms of teamwork, quality and information technology. The results were used afterwards to define subsets of companies for the second phase of the analysis. The survey was sent to 700 companies and the rate of return was 13%. Most of the questionnaires were filled up by a manager or an IT person. It covered a broad range of industrial sectors, all related with discrete production and where 75% of the surveyed companies had less than 200 employees. Approximately 60% of the companies had officially implemented a ISO9000 quality system implementation although only 12% were organised in some variant of team work. Roughly, 50% of the work force were skilled employees.

The second phase consisted in a detailed analysis of a small set of selected companies from the user groups. It was focused on finding detailed requirements for quality management by team work on particular companies, and to generalise those requirements where possible. Furthermore, it was expected that the individual analysis would enrich the research team with valuable practical knowledge regarding relevant technical and organisational issues related with teams and quality at the shop floor. The detailed analysis consisted in a field work in the selected companies, involving meetings, interviews, document analysis and observation.

The guideline for the detailed analysis was the EFQM (European Foundation for Quality Management) model. The EFQM Excellence Model (EFQM, 1999) is a practical tool to help organisations to establish an appropriate management system by measuring where they are on the path to Excellence, helping them understand the gaps, and then stimulating solutions. Considering this model, the ManTIS project addressed mainly people management, resources, and processes, as enablers, and customer satisfaction and business results as results.

For the analysis guideline, 66 questions or issues mainly based on the EFQM model and QS9000 standard were chosen. A sample of those questions is in Table 1.

For each of these questions and for each of the analysed companies the Importance of each issue, the Approach (Results) defined within the company, the Deployment (Scope) of the approach and the Potential Benefit of Computer Support were recorded on the scale 0 (0%), 1 (25%), 2 (50%), 3 (75%), 4 (100%). Eleven SME's from Germany, Portugal, and the UK were analysed.

Table 1 - Extract of the analysis guideline

1.How are teams defined and what are the features of teams?	47.Does the Manufacturing Team apply procedures for handling, storage, packaging, preservation and delivery of product?
2.Does the management document trends in quality, operational performance and current quality levels for key product and service features?	48.Does the Manufacturing Team participate in Quality Planning (Feasibility Reviews, Control Plans, Quality Plan, Process FMEAs)?
....	....
32.Does the Manufacturing Team ensure that processes are carried out under controlled condition?	56.Is the responsibility for review and authority for the disposition of non-conforming product defined?
33.Is the Manufacturing Team supplied with and does it use documented process monitoring and operator instructions?	57.Does the Manufacturing Team report non-conforming purchased products to the purchase department?
....	....

2.4 The QFD approach

For the detailed validation of the Team Performance Tools concept, a QFD-Matrix Approach was applied (Logothetis, 1992). The goal was to link the results of the meetings and interviews to the initial ManTIS concepts, in a structured and systematic way. The outline of the approach is in Table 2.

From points 6 and 7 a set of preliminary requirements can be generated. The questions/ criteria of the detailed analysis are written into the lines of the matrix, the weight of each question and the Seven Team Performance Tools into the columns.

The QFD matrix approach delivered the overall score for each of the Seven Team Performance Tools. The Process Monitoring Tool has the biggest share (30%), followed by the Team Communication Tool (21%), the Team Co-ordination Tool (19%) and the Team Quality Monitoring Tool (14%).

In addition to the detailed analysis, the companies were already asked in the first questionnaire phase how they assess their need for the presented Team Performance Tools. They were asked to rate them using the scale: not needed (0%), useful (33%), needed (66%), indispensable (100%).

In addition to the detailed analysis, the companies were already asked in the first questionnaire phase how they assess their need for the presented Team Performance Tools. They were asked to rate them using the scale: not needed (0%), useful (33%), needed (66%), indispensable (100%).

Table 2: Outline of the QFD based approach

Phase	Step
a. setup the analysis framework:	1.arrange the questions/issues in rows and the Team Performance Tools in columns within a QFD matrix, 2.assign a weight factor to each attribute of a question/issue (importance, approach, deployment, benefits).
b. analysis (from the data collected)	3.correlate the questions/issues with the Team Performance Tools, 4.compute the score for each tool, in each company, 5.consolidate the results of all companies, 6.analyse the overall score achieved by each tool, 7.analyse each tool against the question/issues.

The results obtained until this point, the results from the questionnaire plus the overall score of the tools obtained from the QFD matrix approach, led to some preliminary conclusions:

1.all the seven Team Performance Tools were recognised as useful,
2.except for very general aspects, all questions/issues were covered by the tools.

The detailed analysis of the correlation between the questions/issues and the Team Performance Tools (analysis of the QFD-matrix columns) resulted in a statement of requirements that originated the first specification of the system. This will be described below.

2.5 The first specification

The subject of questions/issues together with the resulting score from the previous analysis provided an implicit statement of requirements for each tool. Thus, by the analysis of each of the QFD matrix columns and grouping the questions/issues in strong, medium and weak correlation results, it was possible to define broadly the functionality of each tool. This was made first by stating the functional requirements and then by describing the input, processing and output of each tool (see Table 3 for an extract of the functional requirements).

From the analysis of the QFD matrix columns, the records of meetings and interviews at the companies and from the experience and knowledge of the project team, a generic "Specification of Team Performance Tools" was produced. An extract is shown in Table 4.

Table 3: Functional requirements

Tool-ReqID	Question/ issue	Requirement
PQMO-R1	Team support: process control	The system must have functions that enable the team to ensure that processes are carried out under controlled conditions (32)
PQMO-R2	Team support: instructions	The system must have functions that enable that the team is supplied with and uses process monitoring and operating instructions (34)
...	...	...
TQMO-R11	Team support: continuous improvement	The system must have functions that enable the team to manage one or more continuous improvement project (30)
TQMO-R12	Management support: trends in quality	The system must have functions that supports management and the group to document trends in operational performance and quality levels for key products and service features (3)
...	...	...

The generic system specification was the starting point for a more complete specification. Two structuring concepts were adopted for the system: the Deming PDCA (Plan-Do-Check-Act) cycle and the Action Workflow Loop (AWL) (see Medina-Mora et al., 1992). The first concept helps to organise the functionality of the tools in a common (pseudo) sequence. The main advantage for the users is to easily learn and mentally organise the system functionality, which is common to all tools. The second concept purports a negotiation perspective into the actions performed by the group, implying a co-ordination of every action. From simple actions (such as signaling an alarm) to complex ones (such as continuous improvement projects) the concept structures those actions in four phases: proposal, acceptance, performance, satisfaction. Having in the background these two concepts, an iterative process for the detailed specification of the system started with the development of an HTML based user interface prototype. This was the instrument both for the users to generate the details through a practical view of the system and for the developers to start to design and build an advanced prototype.

Table 4: Preliminary system specification

Tool	Input (other systems)	Processing
Process Quality Monitoring	Basic SPC data, MRP, process data, other methods and tools, customer feedback data, feedback from management, company goals.	*Local input:* targets/goals set by the team, identification of processes, process changes, evaluation of process changes, preventive action, non-conformities, corrective action, process improvement plans, inspection and test results *Processing:* decision support, application of methods and tools, cost and performance computation, computation of trends in quality. *Local output:* displaying data, productivity and operating efficiency, maintenance of local data base.
...	...	...

2.6 Summary and comments to the specification process

The second phase of the system definition was the most interesting in terms of users involvement. In fact, although the first step - the filling of a questionnaire - returned important aggregate data, it represented the view of a single person in the company, most of the cases a manager.

The detailed analysis in the selected companies was interview based. These were semi-structured interviews because the goal was to let people to express their points freely. In average, 2-3 people with a managerial role and 2-3 people with a manufacturing role (within a team) were interviewed.

The main result of the analysis phase was a detailed requirements framework (ManTIS, 1998), intended to be the comer stone of the software development. The framework was composed by a HTML mock-up of the system together with a description of the required functionality. In general terms, and after the experience of building the first prototype based on the referred outcome, we can say that the result from the requirements specification phase was too generic. In fact, the level of detail present in the framework (both the HTML mock-up and the functionality documentation) was not sufficient to design the system without major questions.

It was concluded that an HTML mock-up of the user interface was not rich enough for the users to understand the proposed functionality and to consequently suggest the details or changes. A "working" prototype should have been built earlier in order to involve the users in a more effective way. Practical questions in the project management precluded this option.

3. DESIGNING, PROTOTYPING, EVALUATION AND SPECIFICATION

For the development of the ManTIS advanced prototype an evolutionary approach was adopted. The requirements specification obtained in the previous phases was intended to drive the implementation of the software. The development of the final prototype was planned in three releases, each of them subjected to validation and evaluation by the user groups. The methods used to help user groups to assess the prototype versions ranged from the registration of subjective, non-structured impressions, to the collection of information through a question catalogue approaching the software operation, revision and transition. Finally, the advanced prototype was assessed in three companies by the end users, in the shop floor working places.

3.1 From specification to detailed design and prototyping

ManTIS adopted a CORBA (Common Object Request Broker Architecture) compliant component based architecture. A component-based information system allows the system to be assembled from binary replaceable parts. In fact, this means that it is possible to design and implement a system, and subsequently make it evolve, by either adding new components or replacing others, without having to rebuild the whole system (Szyperski, 1998).

The distributed object computing technology is well suited for the creation of flexible and easy to maintain client-server systems, mainly because data and business logic are abstracted and encapsulated within objects, the objects being located anywhere inside the distributed system. The main benefits brought by this technology come from the flexibility of the "plug-and-play" capability and from the interoperability across the network. Additionally, systems may be deployed on different platforms, allowing an easy integration with legacy systems. Distributed objects are also able to self-manage and to roam across a network.

The programming language selected to implement ManTIS was the Java language. A discussion of this option is out of the scope of this paper, but the main reason leading to this it was platform independence. In the same way, it had to be chosen a modelling method to support the specification and design of the software. The Unified Modelling Language (UML) was chosen due to the project team previous experience and background, and because the trend is to become an industry standard. Also, well established software engineering techniques such as design patterns and analysis patterns were thoroughly used.

One of the major ideas of ManTIS is to supply Manufacturing Teams with an uniform front-end software. This idea implies two major constraints: one constraint is that ManTIS has to be an easy to learn and equally easy to use software; the other is that ManTIS must generally have the capability to interact and to exchange data with other systems already available on the market and/or in use in the companies. This general but important requirement was stressed (as expected) during the in-depth analysis in the selected user companies. To what extent the interfacing towards other systems is required depends on different factors. One major factor is the size of the company. Small SMEs tend to be less computerised compared to larger SMEs. There, it may be required that ManTIS runs without interfacing to other systems. Larger SMEs, however, are already equipped with some computer-supported systems, such as Materials and Resources Planning (MRP), Shop Floor Control, Shop Floor Data Collection, and Statistical Process Control (SPC).

Prototyping and evaluation activities ran for one year. Three prototype releases were planned, each of them providing a full functional set of tools. First release comprised Process Quality Monitoring, Team Co-ordination and Team Communication tools, the second release added Team Quality Monitoring and Team Training, and finally release three provided Team Self-Assessment, Team Suggestion Book and also the system configuration tool. Each of the releases was evaluated by users in the selected companies. Nevertheless, the main evaluation effort was more concentrated in the final release. The evaluation approach is described in the next sections.

3.2 Walkthrough approach and On-Site Testing

A question catalogue based on software quality characteristics concepts was developed, in order to conduct the testing as comprehensively as possible in the areas system operation, revision and transition. Nevertheless, system revision and transition were considered of reduced importance in the context of a "proof of concept" prototype. Therefore, the evaluation method was adapted in order to deepen the evaluation in the area of system operation and to simplify the evaluation in the area of system revision and transition. These were evaluated through an analysis of the service requirements of the end users (see Figure 3)

The guided walkthrough presented the entire functional scope of the system. The evaluators were team representatives and manufacturing managers. As the basis for this approach a "function tree" of the ManTIS system was developed. Furthermore, a reference process through the system was established in order to make the evaluation process efficient and in order to include dependencies of different areas or modules of the ManTIS system.

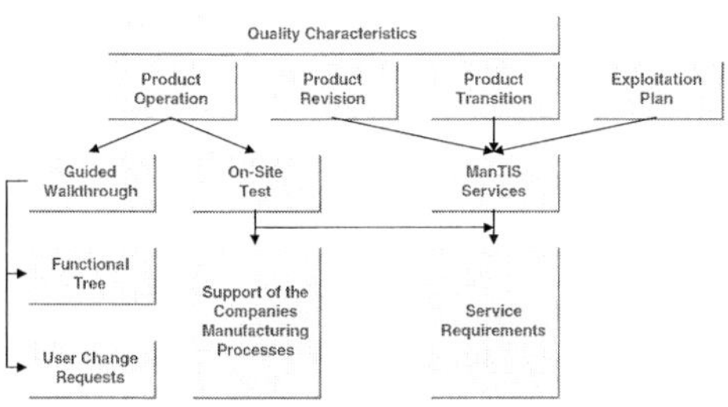

Figure 3: Evaluation scheme

3.3 Results of the evaluation of the advanced prototype

ManTIS prototype releases were extensively reviewed against the user requirements document and the users feedback on the basis of the functional tree and the ManTIS reference process. Each of the system functionalities was assessed by the users, following the above referred reference process.

The results show the highest rate of potential utilisation for the modules Team Training (2,02), Team Co-ordination (2,17) and Team Communication (2,33). This shows the need to support a the single person and an entire team with adequate IT and functionality.

Companies see the Team Training module as key to support the qualification process of their work force. The increase of qualification and the administration of qualification skill profiles are seen as way to decrease production planning errors.

The handling of orders and the assignment of resources to specific operations (e.g. operations with bottleneck capacities) were evaluated as highly beneficial to increase the quality of the production planning process. Also beneficial to the quality of the planning process was the availability of the shift and vacations plans of each team member. The ability to define and to administer team projects was a reason for the high utilisation and the potential to increase manufacturing efficiency.

The Team Communication was immediately accepted as major contribution to reduce information distribution costs and reduce manufacturing lead times.

The Suggestion Book (2,41), the Process Quality Monitoring (2,43) and the Team Quality Monitoring (2,48) are the areas of the ManTIS System with an average rate of utilisation.

The suggestion book was evaluated as application not only to handle improvement proposals, but also as tool to support the process of engineering change requests of the team in communication with the engineering department.

The Process Quality Monitoring was evaluated by the companies without a precise definition of their own processes. Therefore the "Plan"-area of this module was seen as tool to support the initial definition of processes and support the migration of the shop floor teams from a still functional view to a process oriented view.

The evaluation of the Team Quality Monitoring needs to be distinguished in those areas where the entire team is monitored and those where the individual is being addressed. The companies had difficulties with the administration and monitoring of individual data, they rather intended to support the team as a whole.

Self Assessment is the module with the lowest rate of utilisation (2,96) on the operative level. This is due to the fact, that this is rather an indirect, strategic tool, which administers the company, team and individual objectives and supports auditing and TQM assessment at team level.

After the on-site test phase the pilot end users and managers were interviewed not only on the utilisation of ManTIS and the potentials of the software to support Manufacturing Teams but on the services they require for an integrated implementation in the companies.

The fields of services are oriented at the product life cycle of a software product. Beginning with the support for introduction of such a system to the companies and identification of potentials, the phase of implementation and installation including customisation is addressed. The requirements in terms of interfaces are technologically driven but crucial for the success of such a project. The area of training end users as well as troubleshooting or utilisation support are focused on the shop floor worker. The maintenance and documentation of the system as well as the documentation of the implementation project are crucial for the continuous usage of the ManTIS System.

We already referred the HTML mock-up was considered insufficient to a first evaluation of the system by the users, conducting to the detailing of functionalities. Furthermore, even in the preliminary versions of the ManTIS prototype, users were reluctant in being involved deeply because of the incomplete definition of the scope of some tools. As the prototype evolved in detail and scope, the users participation became more effective. The guided walkthrough approach was rather effective in practical terms, giving to the users some guidance for the system evaluation.

Concerning the degree of involvement in the system evaluation, it was evident (as expected) that only when clear benefits from the system are understood the involvement is high. Also, the degree and quality of the involvement reflects the degree of participatory culture in the company. In some cases, team members input only confirmed the anticipated management view, while in other cases team members were rather critical of those views, evaluating and suggesting issues effectively, according to their knowledge and practice.

4. CONCLUSIONS

Information systems research and development involving industrial companies, can be both challenging and frustrating. From one side, the research opportunities are always interesting, but from the other side the difficulties frequently demotivates research works with larger scope and thoroughness.

This particular project was not different regarding these issues. The participating companies were moderately motivated, enabling the validation of the concepts developed throughout the project, but without too much effort in the generation of new ideas. The priority of individual and collective interests was not the ideal to fully support the project work.

Nevertheless, this project brought us useful experience in the development of computer based systems for industrial companies, particularly in the phases of requirements elicitation and system specification. The two phased approach proved to be effective in the structuring of the system analysis. Particularly the in-depth analysis conducted in several companies produced interesting results, both in methodological and in technical terms. The prototyping phase is very crucial. When an high degree of innovation is present it is more difficult for the users to foresee how to use the system and the potential benefits coming from that. Therefore, advanced prototypes, close to the final concept of the system are more effective in the users evaluation. At the end, it revealed that the additional work compensates.

Overall, the approach suffered from some inefficiency, due to the exploratory nature of the project (Soares *et al.*, 2000). However, the methodological outcomes presented here can be of great benefit for similar projects. Further research work using the ManTIS project results can be found in Cruz and Soares (2000).

REFERENCES

Cruz, J., Soares, A. L., 2000, A component based framework for the organisational configuration of information systems for quality management, in: Manufacturing Agility and Hybrid Automation III. T. Marek and W. Karwowski (Eds.).

European Foundation for Quality Management, 1999, EFQM Excellence Model. ISBN-90-5236-360-9.

ManTIS, 1998, ManTIS User Requirements. Deliverable 2.1.

Soares, A., Schmidt, C., Gaida, W., 2000, Reflections on the users involvement in the development of an information system for team centred quality management. Seventhth IFAC symposium on Social Aspects of Automation.

Szyperski, C., 1998, Component Software, Beyond Object-Oriented Programming. Addison-Wesley. ACM-Press, New York.

PART 4

Internet Computing and Electronic Commerce

AN XML-BASED MULTIMEDIA MIDDLEWARE FOR MOBILE ONLINE AUCTIONS

Matthias Wagner, Wolf-Tilo Balke, Werner Kießling
Institute of Computer Science, University of Augsburg, Germany
{wagner,balke,kiessling}@informatik.uni-augsburg.de

Keywords: mobile commerce, online auctions, middleware architectures, pervasive Internet technology, multimedia database applications.

Abstract: Pervasive Internet services today promise to provide users with a quick and convenient access to a variety of commercial applications. However, due to unsuitable architectures and poor performance user acceptance is still low. To be a major success mobile services have to provide device-adapted content and advanced value-added Web services. Innovative enabling technologies like XML and wireless communication may for the first time provide a facility to interact with online applications anytime anywhere. We present a prototype implementing an efficient multimedia middleware approach towards ubiquitous value-added services using an auction house as a sample application. Advanced multi-feature retrieval technologies are combined with enhanced content delivery to show the impact of modern enterprise information systems on today's e-commerce applications.

1 INTRODUCTION

Emerging standards and technologies for mobile Web services promise to create Internet ubiquity. Allowing users not only to carry their data and user profiles with them, but also guaranteeing facilities to interact with online applications anytime anywhere they are expected to overcome today's Internet problems. Users should be provided with a quick and convenient way to shop, pay bills, or find places and products that they want or need. However, the industry is still struggling how to best take advantage of the Internet in the wireless environment: while simple mobile applications like the Short Messaging System (SMS) or e-mail over cellular phones are considered as a success, the recent roll-out of mobile services based on the Wireless Application Protocol (WAP) (Wireless Application Protocol Forum, 1999) by European telecommunication carriers has shown that new mobile commerce applications still lack consumer acceptance. Poor design and information architecture are hampering the usability of WAP sites. The lack of specially adapted multimedia content additionally decreases their acceptance by consumers.

To be a major success mobile services must target users with immediate, context-dependent content and advanced value-added Web services. General services like e-shopping or Internet search engines are less likely to succeed in the mobile environment unless major improvements happen. Mobile devices, be it WAP cellular phones or Internet enabled handheld PCs, might indeed support a broad success of e-commerce applications throughout the public. But, whereas existing WAP or i-mode (NTT DoCoMo Japan, 2001) services are mainly designed as standalone applications we feel that the successful future of m-commerce lies in a truly pervasive approach. This means that existing Web services should be successively expanded to support access for the increasing number of mobile clients. In this paper we will show how to smooth the way from standard Internet services towards value-added m-commerce applications using the example of an online auction house as a value-added Web service enabled for ubiquitous access.

The developments in enterprise information systems and architectures (Melling, 1994) can also be useful in today's e-commerce applications. The main idea of an enterprise information system (Afsarmanesh et al., 1998) is to provide a single, Web-based interface to sometimes incompatible data scattered across a variety of repositories. These sys-

J. Filipe et al. (eds.), Enterprise Information Systems III, 259–269.

Rank	Image	Description	Current Bid
1		**Category: Painting** This beautiful modern oil on canvas painting by Pablo Picasso is entitled 'Woman in an Armchair' and was created in the year 1927. It presents a woman, who occupies an armchair upholstered in a leaf-printed fabric...	$ 3,560
2		**Category: Painting** 'Bottle, Newspaper, Pipe, and Glass' is the title of this painting by Modernist painter Georges Braque. Its unique style is supported by his use of charcoal and various papers pasted on paper...	$ 1,230
⋮	⋮	⋮	⋮

Figure 1: A sample result set for a complex query.

tems thus provide one (possibly personalized) logical view and common query capabilities across different platforms and information sources. The information sources in general are not limited to relational databases, image archives or document repositories, but more sophisticated systems also allow external Web data to be directly integrated into query result sets (R. Goldman, 2000). The ideal goal is 'just in time' information, retrieved and assembled as needed, freely accessible and exchangeable across diverse systems. Though most enterprise systems provide suitable connectors for multi-repository support, especially when it comes to advanced federated searches and the delivery of user-tailored information to mobile devices, even the most modern systems experience major problems. Approaches to advanced federated multi-feature searches (Güntzer et al., 2000; Güntzer et al., 2001) and content delivery (Smith et al., 1999; Wagner et al., 2000) were recently presented in the literature. In this paper we show how these techniques can enrich an XML-based multimedia middleware in our prototypical application.

The rest of this paper is organized as follows. In section 2 we will deal with the demands of online auctions and present an example for user interaction in modern Web-based auction applications. User profiles and usage patterns are recognized as the basis for pervasive applications. By comparison to existing online auctions like Ebay or Yahoo!Auctions the presented system allows auctioneers to search auction catalogs by content-based and fuzzy full-text retrieval methods in addition to standard search criteria. The way our sample auction application is enabled for universal access through an XML-based middleware approach is explained in section 3. Section 4 deals with the nature of federated and multi-feature retrieval capabilities and its benefit for our application. Here we present the application of the Stream-Combine (Güntzer et al., 2001) algorithm to leverage efficient and multi-feature search capabilities in multimedia resources. The delivery of result sets and more general content to a wide variety of possibly mobile clients is finally discussed in section 5. We conclude with a short summary and an outlook on future work.

2 MOBILE ONLINE AUCTIONS

Today's online auction houses like Ebay or Yahoo!Auctions offer a wide variety of categories to choose from. Items are presented together with a short description and a digitized photo. However, the search capabilities of these auction applications only focus on standard attributes like item numbers, categories, keywords and price ranges. More sophisticated search capabilities like weighted searches or visual retrieval are currently not supported.

We claim that the acceptance of e-commerce applications will increase with the development of effective multimedia search facilities allowing users to compose complex queries in an intuitive way. The better customer queries can be composed the more satisfying the retrieval results will generally be. Moreover, anticipating typical usage patterns and user profiles will further help to get a broad acceptance.

query profiles	Frank	Cathy
category	painting	painting
painter	don't care	Picasso
technique	don't care	oil on canvas
style	modern	don't care
average color	brown	brown

usage patterns	user device			frequency	location
browse, choose item	PC	-	-	rare	home
find similar item	PC	PDA	-	rare	anywhere
check, increase bid	PC	PDA	WAP	often	anywhere

Figure 2: Query profiles and usage patterns for different users and devices.

2.1 Query profiles

Let us consider a short example of a next-generation online auction house. Assume that a customer named Frank is interested in buying a modern painting to furnish a new apartment. Using our online auction he will state

- the category 'painting',
- the description of the painting should indicate that the painting is 'modern' art
- and to go well with the wallpaper, carpets and furniture brown or earthen colors should be prevalent.

In this example the auction query engine will have three aspects to satisfy. For each aspect a possibly ranked result has to be computed using possibly different data sources. At the end a few overall best objects matching the different aspects best are calculated and returned to the user as shown in figure 1.

The typical user interaction with an auction system will first provide some query information for the search together with a user profile for the later presentation of the results. The auction system will analyze the query constraints and (depending on the user's profile) decide which sources to query. Having merged all ranked result sets the overall top-scored objects can be returned. Consider for our example two different profiles. Dealing with pieces of art our auction house will have several typical groups of customers. To understand how our architecture deals with their typical profiles let us choose two users Frank and Cathy. Frank is our above user who wants to furnish his apartment and looks for a modern painting which is mainly painted in brown colors. Cathy is a collector who is strongly interested in copies of paintings by Picasso that are oil on canvas technique. To fit in her collection she also would prefer a mostly brown painting, but it does not really matter to her. We will be concerned with these queries more deeply in section 4. For now let us assemble the two different query profiles in the left table of figure 2.

2.2 Usage profiles and mobile access

As wireless technology improves at an ever-increasing rate, mobile devices for every situation and user are being created. Let us focus on two main types of such devices:

Personal Digital Assistants: The personal digital assistant (PDA), e.g. the Palmpilot (Palm Computing, 2001), has become the standard handheld computer. With Internet-enabled PDAs users can have real-time connections to text information and low-resoluted images.

WAP Phones: As the European counterpart to the Japanese i-mode technology (NTT DoCoMo Japan, 2001) the Wireless Application Protocol (WAP) (Wireless Application Protocol Forum, 1999) is designed to create ubiquitous access to Internet resources. Using WAP-enabled mobile phones, users can mainly perform simple text-based tasks.

Of course, for the delivery of the result sets the technical environment of the user has to be taken into account. On one hand users may at home or in the office be connected by a LAN using a high speed PC, on the other hand the user may only use a WAP mobile phone having a rather slow connection being out of home, e.g. riding the train. Users having high-speed access would obviously process a large compound document containing e.g. all the images, whereas users with slow access probably would rather prefer a text-only version of the document or even be satisfied by an abstract of the document. These compound documents not only have to be adequate for the device, but also are more or less useful in different stages of the auction.

Since different tasks may need different modes of access, the right hand side of figure 2 shows typical usage patterns together with the devices needed to perform a task. Tasks may differ in their frequency of performance, the location of the user and the need for more or less advanced technical devices. The most important thing is to enable users to perform frequently needed tasks with preferably small and mobile devices. Thus, these tasks can be integrated into their daily routine with a maximum degree of freedom. Knowing the query profiles, usage patterns and technical restrictions a user profile can be modeled (Cetintemel et al., 2000).

Again consider our above example. To choose a painting from the auction catalog one would definitely prefer to get high resoluted color images and descriptive text. Thus a typical task is browsing catalogs via a Web browser using a PC having fast Internet access. Once having decided to bid for any object it is useful to follow the auction and if necessary to increase the bid. Since online auctions may take a few days time, it is necessary to check the current bid from time to time. However, for this task not all the descriptive and visual information is needed, but only e.g. the catalog number, title or painter. Simple, but frequent tasks like this can thus conveniently be carried out anywhere using a mobile phone or PDA, if only few data has to be exchanged. But advanced mobile devices like PDAs even have the capabilities of performing slightly more complex tasks. For instance if the bids for a chosen object are above a certain limit, users might want to search for objects most similar to the previously chosen one. Suppose for the course of our example that both sample users have access to the Internet via a standard Web browser. In addition Cathy owns a WAP phone, whereas Frank uses a PDA for mobile access.

3 THE XML-BASED MULTIMEDIA MIDDLEWARE

Due to the rapid pace of technological change, emerging standards and the constant evolution of mobile devices, the use of flexible and adaptable technology and methodologies is essential for pervasive applications. We think that content management (Jain, 1998) is paramount for pervasive applications, meaning that application logic, server-side and database-side content as well as delivery formats are to be strictly separated. This section illustrates how we support the virtues of content management.

3.1 XML base technologies

To address the requirements of commercial Web applications and enable the further expansion of Web technology into new domains, the World Wide Web Consortium has developed the Extensible Markup Language (XML) (World Wide Web Consortium, 1998). Aiming at a middleware approach our prototypical implementation builds upon the following XML standards, tools and extensions.

XML (Extensible Markup Language): XML is a subset of SGML (Standard Generalized Markup Language) and basically a markup language for documents containing structured information. XML is currently on the way to become the standard markup language for Internet applications.

XSL (Extensible Stylesheet Language): XSL and XSLT (XSL Transformations) (Kay, 2000) provides a powerful implementation of a tree-oriented transformation language for converting instances of a specific XML document type into basically any document format, like either simple text, the legacy HTML vocabulary, or document formats currently used in mobile applications, e.g. WAP.

XSP (Extensible Server Pages): XSP (Apache Software Foundation, 2001) is a new technology integrated into the Apache Web server for building Web applications based on dynamic XML content. They allow XML developers and designers to rapidly develop and easily maintain dynamic Web pages that leverage XML applications. Related technologies for server-centered computing of dynamic content include Sun's JavaServer Pages or Oracle's XSQL servlet.

Java Technology: The XSP technology connects underlying databases and application modules using the Java programming language. The application logic resides in middleware resources, e.g. database access, database search and the combination of search results is coded in Java and executed in a middle-tier java virtual machine. Furthermore Apache Web server with its servlet engine JServ is used to handle incoming client search requests and to initiated content delivery.

3.2 An advanced multimedia middleware architecture

Figure 3 depicts the conceptual design of our system. How the XML technologies mentioned above come into play is best explored by a short example. Let us consider a sample auction session:

1. Cathy carrying her WAP phone (A) wishes to track several items from the auction catalog. The first step in initiating a database search from any device is to download a search form from the application server. A corresponding client-side request from (A) to the middle-tier application server (B) results in preparing a generic XML form, provided by the Query Manager, for delivery to the client.

2. Therefore the server-side search form is passed to Content Delivery together with a client profile. XSL rendering is then done on the XML form w.r.t. the given profile and results in a client specific search form which is in turn delivered to the device (A).

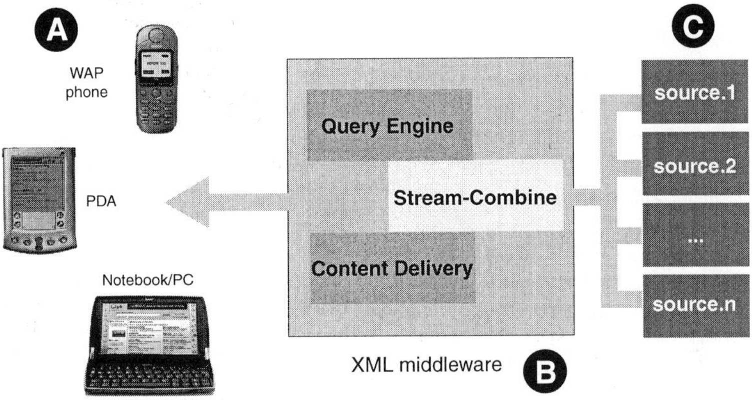

Figure 3: An XML-based multimedia middleware architecture.

3. A search request is issued from the client (A) by completing the search form and sending it back to the Query Manager (B).
4. Complex queries are allowed to be constructed via search forms and are typically restricted to the best k results fulfilling the request. As will be explained in section 4 these complex queries are split into their atomic parts and passed to the underlying data sources (C) for execution. The combining algorithm Stream-Combine (B) takes over and is responsible for the efficient combination of the possibly ranked result streams from the sources.
5. Within the middleware (B) the search result is then encapsulated in a generic XML document and again passed to the Delivery Engine. As with the search form the XML result set is finally transcoded to a format that will satisfy the client and delivered to Cathy's device (A).

The parts of the architecture presented here will be discussed in depth in the following sections.

4 FEDERATED SEARCHES AND MULTI-FEATURE QUERIES

The ability to perform federated searches and multi-feature queries is one of the most demanding in enterprise information systems. The answer sets will generally consist of compound documents involving data of different types collected from different sources. These searches include:

- Conventional full-text searches.
- Fuzzy search capabilities including phonetic search or thesauri.
- Attribute-based queries relying on syntactical attributes, e.g. documents of certain length or images in specific image formats.
- Advanced content-based retrieval relying on semantical attributes, like semantic document retrieval or query by visual example.

Since techniques for multi-feature queries have already shown their usefulness in state of the art information systems (Balke et al., 2000), we will adapt these techniques for the use in our auction system. Our above example will again help us to understand the way federated searches and multi-feature queries can be performed.

For user Frank we have to pose a complex query involving three aspects or features: The category of object is 'painting', the object should be in 'modern' style and the color should mainly be brown. All these query models are essentially different. Whereas the category can be evaluated as an exact match query, the query on the keyword 'modern' will return a ranked result set of descriptions. The query on color even has to be performed using visual retrieval returning a ranked set of documents containing more or less brown images. Using the emerging SQL/MM standard (Cotton, 1999) this query can be expressed as follows:

```
1  SELECT top(5, images)
2  FROM    repository
3  WHERE category = 'painting'
4  RANK BY description CONTAINS 'modern'
5       AND SI_average_color(images)
6            SIMILAR TO (150,120,20)
```

In this sample query statement

- the top five images are retrieved (line 1)
- that belong to the category 'painting' (line 3),
- have a description which contains the word 'modern' (line 4) and
- have an average color close to the RGB-value (150,120,20) which is a shade of brown (line 5).

Since in the expression above no weights are specified, all these parts of the query are considered equally weighted. As commercial database systems currently do not yet support the full SQL/MM standard, in our auction system prototype this statement is further mapped onto the specific implementations of the underlying database management systems. The query result in this case consists of three parts, an exact match part for the category, a ranked result list for the keyword 'modern' in the description, and a ranked result list for the visual retrieval part. Efficiently combining these different result sets to get the overall best objects has been a major performance bottleneck until recently. With Quick-Combine (Güntzer et al., 2000) and Stream-Combine (Güntzer et al., 2001) two efficient combining algorithms are now available.

In our prototypical auction system the Stream-Combine algorithm is used for merging multi-feature result lists within the middleware even from distributed data sources. Stream-Combine guarantees the correct retrieval of the k overall top-ranked results. For score aggregation any monotonic combining function can be used, including weighted queries. Due to its heuristic control flow this algorithm is narrowly self-adapting to the particular score distributions. Top-ranked results can be computed and output incrementally. The way how results are merged obviously is strongly user-dependent. In complex queries the user might want to emphasize some properties, i.e. weighting the query, or use a special combining function. Such functions can be for instance arithmetic means to ensure a certain consistency of performance for the top-scored objects in all query parts or maximum/minimum to find the top performers in any query aspect. Thus not only the query aspects themselves, but also user preferences as emphasis on certain topics or preferred combining functions add semantic information for a relevant search result. Though using the same auction system users having different profiles should generally be allowed to use different combining functions to express their search semantics.

Let us have a short glance at the sample combining functions of Cathy and Frank. The score for any auction item X consisting of an image together with a category and a description can for instance be computed as depicted in figure 4.

We know that Cathy is a collector of paintings by Picasso. Obviously she will assign very high weights to the category and keyword search, and only rather low values to her preferred brown color. She will even be pleased with the evaluation of the category as a hard filter condition like it is provided by today's database systems. Frank on the other hand wants to furnish his apartment. Thus the color and appearance of the painting is of high importance to him. He will probably assign equal weights to all categories. But in his case it might also be sensible to weaken the filter effect of the category. Since he wants to cover a wall, for instance he could also be satisfied by a modern, brown tapestry. Unlike traditional databases our multimedia middleware can easily adapt to these requirements using the Stream-Combine approach.

Related database applications and middleware approaches like GARLIC (Carey et al., 1995) or HERON (Kießling et al., 1998) have already started to use the capabilities of such an advanced retrieval. However, if ranked result sets from several data sources already can be merged within one retrieval system, the combination does not have to take place inside the middleware.

Consider for example Cathy's query. She wants the painting to be an oil on canvas technique by Picasso. Since both keywords are contained in the object's description, those two result sets can already be combined within the text-retrieval engine and passed on to the middleware as a single ranked result set. For those special combining tasks within one retrieval engine the Quick-Combine algorithm (Güntzer et al., 2000) is a prime candidate. Quick-Combine shows the same useful characteristics as Stream-Combine, but is especially efficient inside a retrieval engine or database kernel.

5 MULTI-PLATFORM DELIVERY

Content management for pervasive applications needs to address both the nature of the content and the capabilities of the various client platforms the content is being delivered to. User preferences and technical limitations of the user devices are expressed by user profiles and usage patterns demanding different delivery formats.

Historically, electronic information was expressed, created, stored and transmitted by application-specific formats. Alternatively, with XML all data is structured without taking the later presentational layout

$$\begin{aligned} score_{\text{Cathy}}(X) &= \frac{1}{5}((2 \cdot score_{\text{category='painting'}}(X) + \\ &\quad 2 \cdot score_{\text{description\_CONTAINS\_('Picasso'\_AND\_'oil on canvas')}}(X) + \\ &\quad score_{\text{SI\_average\_color(image)\_SIMILAR\_TO\_(150,120,20)}}(X)) \\ score_{\text{Frank}}(X) &= \frac{1}{3}(score_{\text{category='painting'}}(X) + \\ &\quad score_{\text{description\_CONTAINS\_'modern'}}(X) + \\ &\quad score_{\text{SI\_average\_color(image)\_SIMILAR\_TO\_(150,120,20)}}(X)) \end{aligned}$$

Figure 4: Personalized combining functions for varying user preferences.

```
<page>
  <title>Track Item</title>
  <form action="tracking.xml">
    <select name="category" dname="Category">
      <option value="">All</option>
      <option value="Carpet">Carpet</option>
      <option value="Paintings">Paintings</option>
      <option value="Porcelain">Porcelain</option>
    </select>
    <input name="usr" format="*a" dname="User" value=""/>
  </form>
</page>
```

```
<wml>
  <card id="top" title="Track_Item">
    <p align="left">
      User: <input format="*a" name="name" value=""/>
      Category: <select name="category">
        <option value="">All</option>
        <option value="Carpet">Carpet</option>
        <option value="Paintings">Paintings</option>
        <option value="Porcelain">Porcelain</option>
      </select></p>
    <do label="start" type="accept">
      <go href="tracking.xml" method="get">
        <postfield name="category" value="$(category:noesc)"/>
        <postfield name="usr" value="$(name:noesc)"/>
      </go>
    </do>
  </card>
</wml>
```

Figure 5: A generic XML form and the corresponding WML search form.

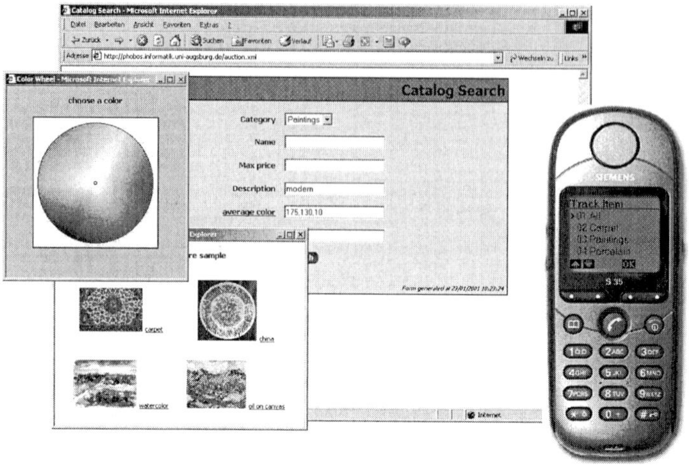

Figure 6: Search request from a Web browser and tracking of bids from a WAP phone.

into account. How our system benefits from the use of XML and XSLT is again best illustrated by our running example. As we have seen in section 4 both Frank and Cathy want to pose somehow similar queries against the auction database. Suppose that one evening, for initially searching the catalog, both use their standard Web browsers at home. The upper listing in figure 6 depicts the search form with enhanced multimedia input facilities for content-based search criteria completed for Frank's initial query. Let us assume furthermore that Frank and Cathy get the same top-scored item from the auction catalog and place a bid. During the next day Cathy follows the auction and occasionally checks the selected item using her mobile phone and increases her bid (cf. second listing of figure 6).

In the middle-tier of our application, generic XML formats are used together with client-specific XSL stylesheets to tailor compound documents for any supported delivery platform. As we know from section 2 tracking of auction items is enabled for all existing usage patterns. Hence, when Cathy decides to check her selected item from her WAP phone she requests a download of the generic XML document displayed on the left hand side of figure 5. Besides a page title this generic XML document defines a search form having two input fields in universal style: the first one named 'category' is defined as a selection on the existing categories whereas the second one named 'usr' defines a text input field to submit the name of an auctioneer. This XML document is basically the same for any enabled platform. But since Cathy's request is issued from a WAP phone the application server will transform this generic search form from generic XML into WML prior to delivery (cf. right hand of figure 5).

Using different client-specific XSL stylesheets the server-side delivery scheme for XML documents is virtually the same for any content: based on the user profiles associated with client requests the middle-tier server will associate specific stylesheets with server-side XML documents and use their formating instructions to output new delivery documents. According to the different usage patterns from figure 2, stylesheets for the creation of WML (WAP phones), restricted HTML (PDAs) and full HTML/CSS (Web browsers) reside in the middle-tier. Considering Cathy's tracking request, the rule-driven transformation of XML content is partially illustrated in figure 7.

Each transformation rule is expressed in the stylesheet as a template rule with a 'match' attribute. Here a rule matching the XML structure 'form' is defined. Once the 'form' tag is found in the XML source the rule fires and results in the execution of the formatting instructions in the rule's body. In this example, XSL instructions necessary to process several selection fields in a generic XML form are displayed. Note that in contrast to HTML the concept of forms is not defined in the current WML standard. Figures 5 and 7 demonstrate a useful way of incorporating this concept into WML and other non-HTML delivery formats.

Let's continue our example. Cathy's bid eventually gets accepted. By noon she owns a new Picasso for her collection. Frank who stopped placing bids during the auction now has to look for a new piece

```
<xsl:template match="form">
  <p align="left">
    <xsl:for-each select="select">
      <xsl:value-of select="@dname"/>:
      <select>
        <xsl:attribute name="name"> <xsl:value-of select="@name"/> </xsl:attribute>
        <xsl:for-each select="option">
          <option>
            <xsl:attribute name="value"> <xsl:value-of select="@value"/> </xsl:attribute>
            <xsl:value-of select="."/>
          </option>
        </xsl:for-each>
      </select>
    </xsl:for-each>
  .
  .
  .
  <do type="accept" label="start">
    <go method="get">
      <xsl:attribute name="href"> <xsl:value-of select="@action"/> </xsl:attribute>
      <xsl:for-each select="input|select">
        <postfield>
          <xsl:attribute name="name"> <xsl:value-of select="@name"/> </xsl:attribute>
          <xsl:attribute name="value"> $(<xsl:value-of select="@name"/>)</xsl:attribute>
        </postfield>
      </xsl:for-each>
    </go>
  </do>
</xsl:template>
```

Figure 7: Transformation of a generic XML form to a WML search form.

of art to furnish his apartment. Using his Palmpilot PDA he queries the auction catalog for similar items. The auction system uses the properties of his primarily selected item to pose a new query and delivers the results to Frank's PDA. Again, prior to delivery the generic XML representation of the search result is transformed. This time a stylesheet for the creation of restricted HTML content satisfying the limited resources of Frank's PDA is used. The most similar item in the result set is a self-portrait of Pablo Picasso. The right hand side of figure 8 shows the display of his PDA. He immediately places a bid for this item and follows the auction at home in the evening again using his Web browser (cf. figure 8). After a few hours he also is the proud owner of a nice Picasso painting.

6 SUMMARY AND OUTLOOK

In this paper we presented a prototypical virtual auction house with ubiquitous access benefiting from modern information system technology. The implementation and evaluation was done using IBM DB2 Universal Database as the database management system for the underlying data sources. In particular DB2 Relational Extender technology (Faloutsos et al., 1994) was used to support fuzzy full-text retrieval and content-based catalog queries. Additionally, due to the open design of the middle-tier application server, other database management systems and general data mediators supporting a ranked query model are easily adaptable.

Complex Internet applications will have to collect data from a variety of sources possibly using several retrieval engines. As we have illustrated in the discourse of this work the retrieval and aggregation strongly depends on user profiles and usage patterns. New efficient techniques like Stream-Combine (Güntzer et al., 2001) will enable efficient federated multi-feature searches w.r.t. specific query profiles. We proposed to build efficient middleware applications for mobile commerce using XML technology together with sophisticated algorithms for merging ranked result lists and pervasive content delivery. The running prototype was already presented at the international computer fair CeBIT 2001 in Hannover (HERON Project, 2001).

Besides, aggregated content is not uniquely accessed through standard Web browsers using high-performance network infrastructure but at a progressive rate through mobile devices. Existing Web applications lack the value added by enabling their services for multiple pervasive devices. Thus, content management and delivery in tune with federated and multi-feature searches promise to leverage future m-commerce applications. An advanced multimedia middleware architecture as presented in this paper efficiently supports these techniques in common Internet environments.

For multimedia delivery the text-based formats like XML, variations of HTML and WML, binary formats for the storage of multimedia data from auction catalogs can be taken into account. Delivery formats are not independent of each other but interrelated by conversion options. Given the diversity of today's image, audio or video formats this is even more true for multimedia content resulting in a large variety of ways to store and deliver multimedia data in various formats. The benefit of techniques for partitioning delivery data into formats that are physically stored in the middle-tier for fast delivery and those that are converted into a specific delivery format on-demand was shown in (Wagner et al., 1999; Smith et al., 1999). Future work should also focus on XML-based standardized query languages, capable of ac-

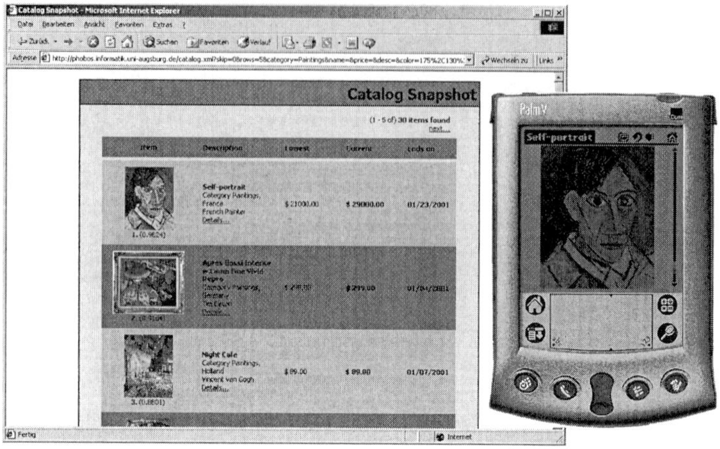

Figure 8: Search result in a Web browser and on the Palmpilot.

cessing relational and object-oriented databases, together with multimedia extensions like SQL/MM or query languages for e-business. Recent XML applications like Motorola's VoxML (Motorola Wireless Resources, 2001) even offer standard capabilities for incorporating speech recognition and synthesis. Enriching the multimedia middleware presented in this paper with such advanced technologies will further improve the acceptance of m-commerce applications.

REFERENCES

Afsarmanesh, H., Garita, C., and Hertzberger, L. (1998). Virtual Enterprises and Federated Information Sharing. In *Proc. of the 9th Int. Conf. Database and Expert Systems Applications (DEXA 1998)*, LNCS Vol. 1460, pages 374–383, Vienna, Austria. Springer.

Apache Software Foundation (2001). The Apache XML Project. http://xml.apache.org/cocoon.

Balke, W.-T., Güntzer, U., and Kießling, W. (2000). Applications of Quick-Combine for Ranked Query Models. In *Proc. of the 1st DELOS Workshop on Information Seeking, Searching and Querying in Digital Libraries*, Zurich, Switzerland. DELOS.

Carey, M., Haas, L., Schwarz, P., Arya, M., Cody, W., Fagin, R., Flickner, M., Luniewski, A., Niblack, W., Petkovic, D., Thomas, J., Williams, J., and Wimmers, E. (1995). Towards Heterogeneous Multimedia Information Systems: The GARLIC Approach. In *5th Int. Workshop on Research Issues in Data Engineering: Distributed Object Management*, pages 124–131. IEEE-CS.

Cetintemel, U., Franklin, M. J., and Giles, C. L. (2000). Self-Adaptive User Profiles for Large-Scale Data Delivery. In *Proc. of the 16th Int. Conf. on Data Engineering*, San Diego, CL, USA. IEEE Computer Society.

Cotton, P., editor (1999). *ISO/IEC FCD 13249-5:1999 SQL/MM SAF-005: Information Technology - Database Languages - SQL Multimedia and Application Packages - Part 5: Still Image*. ISO/IEC.

Faloutsos, C., Barber, R., Flickner, M., Hafner, J., Niblack, W., Petkovic, D., and Equitz, W. (1994). Efficient and Effective Querying by Image Content. *Journal of Intelligent Information Systems*, 3:231–262.

Güntzer, U., Balke, W.-T., and Kießling, W. (2000). Optimizing Multi-Feature Queries for Image Databases. In *Proc. of the 26th Int. Conf. on Very Large Databases (VLDB 2000)*, pages 419–428, Cairo, Egypt.

Güntzer, U., Balke, W.-T., and Kießling, W. (2001). Towards Efficient Multi-Feature Queries in Heterogeneous Environments. In *Proc. of the IEEE Int. Conf. on Information Technology: Coding and Computing (ITCC 2001)*, Las Vegas, USA. IEEE.

HERON Project (2001). Homepage. http://www.uni-augsburg.de/heron.

Jain, R. (1998). Content-based multimedia information management. In *Proc. of the 14th Int. Conf. on Data Engineering*, pages 252–253, Orlando, FL, USA. IEEE Computer Society.

Kay, M. (2000). *XSLT Programmer's Reference*. Wrox Press.

Kießling, W., Erber-Urch, K., Balke, W.-T., Birke, T., and Wagner, M. (1998). The HERON Project — Multimedia Database Support for History and Human Sciences. In *28. Annual Conf. of the GI: INFORMATIK98*, LNCS, pages 309–318, Magdeburg, Germany. Springer.

Melling, W. (1994). Enterprise Information Architectures - They're Finally Changing. In *Proc. of the ACM SIGMOD Int. Conf. on Management of Data*, pages 493–504, Minneapolis, Minnesota, USA. ACM.

Motorola Wireless Resources (2001). VoxML. http://www.motorola.com.

NTT DoCoMo Japan (2001). Homepage. http://www.nttdocomo.com.

Palm Computing (2001). Palmpilot Homepage. http://www.palm.com.

R. Goldman, J. W. (2000). WSQ/DSQ: A Practical Approach for Combined Querying of Databases and the Web. In *Proc. of the ACM SIGMOD Int. Conf. on Management of Data*, pages 285–296, Dallas, Texas, US. ACM.

Smith, J. R., Mohan, R., and Li, C.-S. (1999). Scalable Multimedia Delivery for Pervasive Computing. In *Proc. of the ACM Multimedia '99*, pages 131–140, Orlando, FL, USA. ACM Press.

Wagner, M., Holland, S., and Kießling, W. (1999). Towards Self-tuning Multimedia Delivery for Advanced Internet Services. In *Proc. of the 1st Int. Workshop on multimedia intelligent storage and retrieval management (MISRM'99)*, Orlando, Florida.

Wagner, M., Holland, S., and Kießling, W. (2000). Efficient and Flexible Web Access to Art-Historical Image Collections. In *Proc. of the 15th ACM Symposium on Applied Computing*, volume 2, pages 915–921, Como, Italy.

Wireless Application Protocol Forum (1999). *Official Wireless Application Protocol: The Complete Standard.* John Wiley & Sons.

World Wide Web Consortium (1998). Extensible Markup Language (XML) Version 1.0. W3C Recommendation.

AN ANALYSIS OF B2B CATALOGUE INTEGRATION PROBLEMS

Content and Document Integration

Borys Omelayenko, Dieter Fensel
Division of Mathematics and Computer Science, Vrije Universiteit,
De Boelelaan 1081a, 1081HV, Amsterdam, The Netherlands
Email: borys@cs.vu.nl , dieter@cs.vu.nl
URL: http://www.cs.vu.nl/~borys, http://www.cs.vu.nl/~dieter

Keywords: B2B Catalogue Integration, Content Integration, Document Integration

Abstract: Recent development of the Web opens new possibilities for business-to-business electronic commerce, and enterprise application integration. To employ these possibilities a new transformation technology able to perform content and document integration need to emerge. The enterprises use thousands of different ways to classify their products and to specify business documents, and a number of standards were developed to organize this information, as discussed in the paper. The marketplaces must be able to transform the information presented according to these standards. The large number of standards and their significant complexity make the integration problems non-trivial and require development of special integration architecture. In the present paper we discuss the tasks and the problems, which occur during the content and document integration, and survey possible solutions and available techniques.

1. INTRODUCTION

Nowadays e-business includes thousands of companies, which provide a tremendous number of products for electronic markets. Unlike the traditional markets, the electronic markets allow the participants to easily compare the offers and perform business negotiation faster due to electronic information interchange between the market participants provided by the Business-to-Business (B2B) marketplaces.

Forecasts for the dollar value of B2B EC in the US range between $600 billion to $4 trillion for 2003 (U.S. Department of Commerce 2001). By 2003 some 80 percent of all business-to-business transactions could occur online. Electronic marketplaces for B2B electronic commerce bring together many online suppliers and buyers, which participate in the business interactions (cf. (Fensel 2001) for an overview of the field). The (U.S. Department of Commerce 2001) estimates around 800 B2B marketplaces in early 2000 and other studies estimate around 10,000 B2B marketplaces in the very near future. However, the marketplaces have to deal with the problem of heterogeneity in *product*, *catalogue*, and *document* description standards of their customers. Effective and efficient management of different description styles become a key task for these marketplaces. In addition, a number of serious mapping problems have to be solved to make the B2B area working. Three different types of standards need to interoperate together:

- Different standards for describing product catalogues, which specify the products according to some content standard, and exchangeable business documents like purchase orders, delivery requests, etc. (e.g. xCBL[1] and cXML[2]).
- Content standards, which specify the products with the hierarchy of product categories and their attributes (e.g. UNSPSC[3], ecl@ss[4]).
- Business processes, which specify the order and conditions for creation and distribution of different documents and messages (e.g. mapping private processes to ebXML[5]).

Integration of these standards leads to a number of problems to be resolved. However, a common

---
[1] www.xcbl.org
[2] www.cxml.org
[3] www.unspsc.org
[4] www.eclass.de
[5] www.ebxml.org

J. Filipe et al. (eds.), Enterprise Information Systems III, 270–277.

technology may be developed to resolve these heterogeneous problems.

In the paper we discuss how the above standards must be integrated to facilitate B2B e-commerce. We discuss the content integration task in Section 2, followed by the document integration task discussed in Section 3. The technology for resolving these problems is sketched in Section 4. We finalize the paper with the future research directions and conclusions in Section 5.

2. CONTENT INTEGRATION

The content standards provide hierarchies of product descriptions and define the subclass-of relationship between product categories. Each product from a product catalogue has an attached link to a certain product category, which describes the product. The content standards may be classified into 'horizontal' standards and 'vertical' standards (cf. Figure 1). As shown in the figure, the horizontal standards provide a high-level classification of *all* possible products and cover many domains. Each of the vertical standards provides a deep and narrow classification of a certain limited domain, e.g. the domain of IT devices. Usually, a vertical standard expands several bottom-level categories of a horizontal standard.

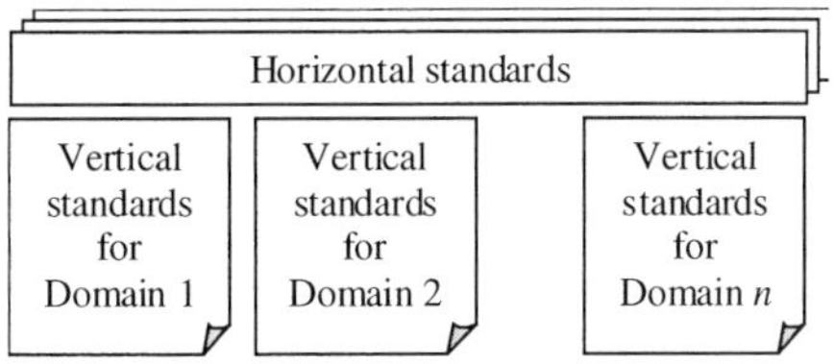

Figure 1: The relation between the horizontal and vertical standards

The most well-known horizontal standard UNSPSC has a 5-level classification scheme with more than 17,000 categories. It is not descriptive, that is it contains no attributes for the products but only a hierarchy of product names and their textual descriptions. Consequently, the next initiative, UCEC[6] extends UNSPSC with attributes. It uses only four top levels of the UNSPSC classification hierarchy and provides a couple of attributes for each category. For example, the category [44-12-15-05] 'Specialty envelopes' has six attributes: type, length, width, weight, colour, and composition.

Another horizontal standard ecl@ss supports the information flow along the supply chain of an industrial enterprise and is mainly used in Germany. It provides the attributes for each of more than 13,000 categories tailored to the needs of industrial customers and their suppliers.

There exist a number of 'vertical' standards. ISO[7] provides many product coding standards specific for certain branches of industry. RosettaNet[8] contains a catalogue of IT products with a categorization, attributes, and mapping of each category to UNSPSC. Large manufacturers tend to develop special product cataloguing schemes, and usually these schemes are reflected in the product coding system used by the company. Finally, the company may have its own focus and therefore require specific product classification scheme.

Hence, the products may be classified in the suppliers' catalogue according to some certain content standard, which may differ from the content standard used by the buyer to specify its needs. In consequence, a B2B mediation system must be able to reclassify a product, already classified once, according to another classification schemas. This product (re-)classification task becomes the bottleneck of efficient content management (Fensel et al. 2001) and hampers its further development.

2.1 Aligning Horizontal Standards

The horizontal standards provide general hierarchies of products, and we can expect many equivalence mappings to appear between them. Sometimes content standard providers publish these mappings as a part of the standard. For example, UNSPSC provides direct one-to-one mapping between UNSPSC and other 'horizontal' standards: CPV, NAICS, and SIC[9].

Despite these published mappings, a number of problems arise in aligning the horizontal standards:

- Only few horizontal standards have officially published mappings, and most of the standards are not related one to each other.
- The standards significantly differ in their classifications because of the absence of a consensus scheme for classifying *all* products. For example, UNSPSC imposes the suppliers' view on the classification, and 'Writing paper' goes together with 'Computer printout paper' under the 'Paper Products' family, and 'Rollerball pens' belong to completely different group 'Office Equipment'. ecl@ss imposes the

[6] www.ucec.org

[7] www.iso.ch

[8] www.rosettanet.org

[9] www.unspsc.org/crosswalk.html

buyers' view according to which 'Writing paper' together with pens belongs to 'Office supplies' (see Figure 2).
- The standards differ in the granularity level in the classifications of each particular group of products. Hence, very often the mappings list as equivalent the concepts with different generality level.
- Textual descriptions of the categories present their main definitions. However, equivalence of the categories is not evident from their descriptions, e.g. NAICS[10]' code [39] 'Miscellaneous Manufacturing Industries' is mapped to the UNSPSC code [73] 'Industrial Production and Manufacturing Services'.

'Rollerball pens' are subclassed in UNSPSC in the following way:

[44] Office Equipment and Accessories and Supplies
[4412] Office supplies
[441217] Writing instruments
[44121701] Rollerball pens
[44121702] Pen or pencil sets
...
[44121711] Felt pen

ecl@ss classifies rollerball pens as Writing material follows:

[24] Communication technology
[24-11] Office Supplies
[24-11-01] Writing and drawing materials
[24-11-01-01] Writing material
[24-11-01-02] Drawing material

Figure 2: The example of mapping two horizontal standards

An example of aligning two horizontal standards is shown in Figure 2. In general, aligning two horizontal standards has the following properties:
- It is based on the published official mappings.
- It contains additional mappings created by the user, which extend the set of official mappings.
- It contains multiple mappings if the pair of standards has overlapping categories.

It is difficult even for a human user to identify these mappings, but due to huge size of the standards they must be identified with a high degree of automation.

[10] www.naics.com

2.2 Linking Vertical and Horizontal Standards

Linking the vertical and horizontal standards differs from the previous case. The vertical standards provide a deep and narrow classification opposite to wide and shallow horizontal standards. Normally a vertical standard expands one or few nodes of a horizontal standard.

For example, consider the mapping of the RosettaNet standard for the electronic component and IT supply chain to UNSPSC. The mapping links only 136 UNSPSC elements out of more than 17,000, most of which belong to the bottom level in the UNSPSC hierarchy, to 445 categories and 2660 attributes of RosettaNet.

The vertical standards are very precise in describing the items they are focused. The same time they are even shallower than the horizontal standards in describing the things, which lay beyond their focus.

Aligning the vertical and horizontal standards requires:
- Mapping a relatively small number of top-level vertical concepts with more general concepts of the horizontal standard.
- Mapping the concepts, which are outside the focus of the vertical standard to the correspondent concepts in the horizontal standard. In this case the vertical concepts may have the same granularity level as the horizontal concepts.

This linking is simpler than the horizontal aligning and it has an evident top-down structure. Hence, technologically it can be treated as a light version of the horizontal mapping and it can be performed with the same technologies.

2.3 Aligning Vertical Standards

Aligning vertical standards requires linking their categories in a similar way as it is done for the horizontal standards. In additional the vertical standards have an extensive set of attributes, which can be even larger than the set of classes, as it happens in the RosettaNet case.

Hence, aligning the vertical standards requires:
- Mapping attribute names and attribute abbreviations.
- Transforming attribute types, e.g. transforming an integer value into a corresponding string representation.
- Mapping the list of possible values for the enumerating types.

```
<IndexItem>
  <ItemDetail>
    <UnitPrice>
      <Money currency="USD">1000</Money>
    </UnitPrice>
    <Description xml:lang="en"> Armada M700 PIII 500 12GB
</Description>
    <UnitOfMeasure>EA</UnitOfMeasure>
    <Classification domain="SPSC"> C43171801</Classification>
    <ManufacturerPartID>140141-002</ManufacturerPartID>
    <ManufacturerName>Compaq</ManufacturerName>
    <URL>http://www.compaq.com</URL>
  </ItemDetail>
  <IndexItemDetail>
    <LeadTime>10</LeadTime>
    <ExpirationDate>2000-06-01</ExpirationDate>
    <EffectiveDate>2000-01-01</EffectiveDate>
    <SearchGroupData>
      <Name xml:lang="en">Notebook</Name>
      <SearchDataElement name="Processor Speed" value="500MHZ"/>
    </SearchGroupData>
    <TerritoryAvailable>USA</TerritoryAvailable>
</IndexItemDetail>
</IndexItem>
```

(a) cXML

```
<CatalogSchema>
    <SchemaVersion>1.0</SchemaVersion>
    <SchemaStandard>UNSPSC</SchemaStandard>
  </CatalogSchema>
    <Product Type="Good" SchemaCategoryRef="C43171801">
    <ProductID>140141-002</ProductID>
    <Manufacturer>Compaq</Manufacturer>
    <CountryOfOrigin>
      <Country><CountryCoded>US</CountryCoded></Country>
    </CountryOfOrigin>
    <ShortDescription xml:lang="en">Armada M700 PIII 500 12GB
</ShortDescription>
    <LongDescription xml:lang="en">This light, ...
</LongDescription>
    <ObjectAttribute>
      <AttributeID>Processor Speed</AttributeID>
      <AttributeValue>500MHZ</AttributeValue>
    </ObjectAttribute>
  <ProductVendorData PartnerRef="Acme_Laptops">
    <VendorPartNumber>12345</VendorPartNumber>
    <ProductPrice>
      <Amount>1000</Amount>
      <Currency>
        <CurrencyCoded>USD</CurrencyCoded>
      </Currency>
    </ProductPrice>
  </ProductVendorData>
</Product>
```

(b) xCBL

Figure 3: Two fragments of product catalogues

- Transforming between the unit scales, e.g. translating length in meters into length in feet.
- Mapping attribute domains: the list of categories from the source standard, to which the attribute applies, must be translated into the list of categories from the target standard. This translation exploits previously defined mappings of the categories.

A non-trivial transformation technology is needed to satisfy these requirements. The existent relevant approaches and recent developments are presented in Section 4.

3. DOCUMENT INTEGRATION

The standards for B2B document exchange contain a large number of different documents to be exchanged between the market participants. For example, the xCBL standard proposes a document infrastructure described with 594 XML DTD's. Other standards define a document infrastructure of a similar complexity (see (Li 2000) for a comparison). Let us consider a fragment of a product catalogue as defined by the cXML and xCBL formats and presented in Figure 3 (a) and (b) respectively.

Both catalogs contain two parts: static catalog information and dynamic information. The static part contains the descriptions, which are not updated frequently, such as product name and description, its UNSPSC code and a manufacturer name. The dynamic part contains frequently modified information, which is sent to the user on request. However, different concepts are regarded as dynamic in xCBL and cXML. According to the xCBL format, product attributes are present in the static part, while the price is regarded as a dynamic part, requested from the vendor (and it appears in the ProductVendorData section). This scenario assumes that the user accesses full descriptions of all the products, while the price can change in time.

cXML expects another implementation scenario partially targeted to the needs of B2B website development. It assumes that the user browses through the descriptions of the first interest, such as product name, content classification, and the price. Additional product details, such as LeadTime, ExpirationDate, etc. are available on request (and regarded as a dynamic part represented in the IndexItemDetail section) together with product attributes, which are treated as the static part in the previous case.

The documents represented in Figure 3 represent the same information, however several differences occur in document formats (see (Omelayenko and Fensel 2001a) for relevant discussion and examples):

- Different terminologies are used, i.e. tag names used to denote semantically equivalent elements (these differences are known as naming conflicts in the database schema integration area). For example, in xCBL the price is marked up with the tag Amount, while cXML uses the tag Money.
- The standards can use either XML attributes or XML elements to represent semantically equivalent information. For example, xCBL uses the XML element CurrencyCoded to encode the currency, while cXML uses the XML attribute currency; in both cases the currencies are denoted in the same way.
- Different value formats and encoding conventions may be used. For example, as shown in Figure 3, the reference to UNSPSC is encoded with the attribute domain in cXML, value domain="SPSC". At the same time the xCBL standard encodes the same link with the element SchemaStandard, value "UNSPSC". Hence, the values of the attributes and elements must be translated in addition to the element mapping.
- Different scales may be used for the values. For example, the price in US dollars has to be scaled for comparison to the price in DM. Unlike the representational differences shown in the previous example, the latter require the scales to be properly verified and timely updated.
- Different natural languages may be used in the *tag values*, as marked up with the XML xml:lang attribute.
- In addition to multi-lingual tag values we can expect that national document standards may use other languages in the *tag names*.

Document integration requires performing both syntactic and semantic transformations, which makes it more complex than the content integration task.

3.1 Single-Layered Integration

Recent years XML becomes a leading standard for enterprise document representation and slowly replaces legacy EDI-based document exchange systems.

The W3C[11] consortium provides the standard architecture for XML document transformation with the XSL-T (Clark 1999) and XPath (Clark and DeRose 1999) languages. Hence, the document integration task can be principally resolved by means of the XSL-T language. This requires development of a set of XSL-T rules able to translate one XML serialization to another one. Direct document transformation with XSL-T rules is discussed in (Omelayenko and Fensel 2001a) and appeared to be a partial solution, and have raised a number of problems. The problems arise from the fact that this approach mixes several independent tasks in a single batch of XSL-T rules:

- Aligning different conceptual models of the documents.
- Aligning different document syntaxes and value encoding agreements.
- Aligning different usage scenarios (e.g. the resulting document may need the source document and some data from another document, implicitly linked from the source)

The problems of the single-layer integration appear because two tasks run together with a single bungle of transformation rules: syntactical translations between different XML representations and semantical mapping between the terminology and granularity level of the representations. Naturally, these two types of transformations belong to different layers of representation.

3.2 Multi-Layer Integration

The layered approach for information representation on the Web was proposed in (Melnik and Decker 2000), where three layers, syntax layer, object layer, and semantic layer are proposed for information modelling on the Web. The syntax layer provides a way of serializing information content into a sequence of characters according to some standard, e.g. XML. The purpose of the object layer is to offer an object-oriented view on the information with the normalized data models of standardized triples. Finally, the semantic layer provides a conceptual model for the information. We use this partitioning to base our integration architecture.

In the multi-layer approach (Omelayenko and Fensel 2001b) we separate three layers of information representation, which are *Syntax layer*, *Data Models layer*, and *Ontology layer*.

The Syntax layer corresponds to the instance documents represented with their XML serialization. The serialization specifies the XML elements and

[11] www.w3c.org

attributes used, and their order. Even semantically equal documents may differ in their serialization.

The Data models layer serves as a bridge between the Ontology layer and the Syntax layer. On this layer the representations are abstracted from the differences imposed by the Syntax layer and the products are represented by object-property-object triples, where the attributes stand for products' attributes. The normalization is done according to the corresponding ontology, which specifies the semantics of the elements at the granularity required for successful element splitting. The terminology used on this layer is defined by the corresponding ontology and generally must coincide with the one used on the Syntax layer.

The most suitable language candidate to encode the triples on this layer is RDF (Lassila and Swick 1999), a W3C standard for describing machine-processable semantics of data represented with the object-attribute-value triples.

The Ontology layer corresponds to the document ontologies used to represent the products. These ontologies specify formal semantics of the elements, the purpose of the documents, and their role in the underlying business process. This semantics is used to specify equivalence bridges between different standards.

4. COMMON TECHNOLOGY

From the technological perspective the content integration task requires conceptual transformation, while the document integration task needs both syntactical and conceptual transformations. Hence, the both tasks need a technology to transform different conceptual models.

RDF Schema (Brickley and Guha 2000) is an emerging W3C standard to represent conceptual models on the Web. It includes resources (instance objects being described), classes of resources, properties of resources, and statements, which assign properties to classes. Basically, it provides a typing system for RDF structures.

Ontologies (Fensel 2001) can be seen as extension conceptual models targeted at knowledge-based representations with rich semantics, axioms, formal reasoning support, targeted for sharing and reuse.

4.1 Ontological Modelling

Content standards form a kind of product ontologies, which specify the hierarchy of product classes and class properties representing product attributes. Ontology instances are then represented with the descriptions of products listed in catalogs. The standards can be easily modelled as ontologies (Omelayenko 2001), and in principle ontology-based editors and inference engines can be used to work with them.

However, huge size of the ontologies creates a performance bottleneck for using the editors and computationally expensive inference engines.

Document standards provide the structures for XML documents, the semantics and the purpose of the documents and their elements, and document usage scenario (which may be linked to a certain business process standard). Because of this, DTDs and other means to model document structure become insufficient to model document standards. Ontology technology provides a way to model them and perform knowledge-level interoperation between the standards. Ontology size is quite limited and semantics of each ontology element is well defined.

The DTDs of the documents must be coupled with RDF annotations which link document elements to the classes and properties of the corresponding document ontology.

4.2 Mapping RDF Schemas

Existing logic-based schema integration approaches like TRIPLE (Sintek and Decker 2001) provide a complete solution of the transformation problem, which, however, does not scale due to high computational complexity of the inference process. Knowledge transformation approaches (Chalupsky 2000) solve similar problems in knowledge-based transformation, but they focus at different technologies and application scenarios and do not employ the full power of XML-based technologies.

Because of this, we are currently developing a new RDF transformation methodology depicted in Figure 4. The methodology assumes that the user maps two RDF Schemas with a mapping tool (in the case of document integration) or with an automatic search tool (which searches for mappings between huge content standards). The manual mapping tool being developed is an extension to a standard ontology editor Protégé (Grosso et al. 2000), and the automatic mapping search engine uses the experiences collected in Chimaera (McGuinness et al. 2000) and PROMPT (Noy and Musen 2000) ontology merging environments.

The mappings, produced by the tool, are described in an RDF Schema mapping language (RDFS-m). RDFS-m provides a mapping ontology, which specifies the structure of bridges between the classes and properties of the ontologies.

RDFS-m expressions may be reused to map other similar ontologies. They are executed by an RDFS-m transformation engine, which receives a source RDF instance document and executes the mappings to create the target RDF document.

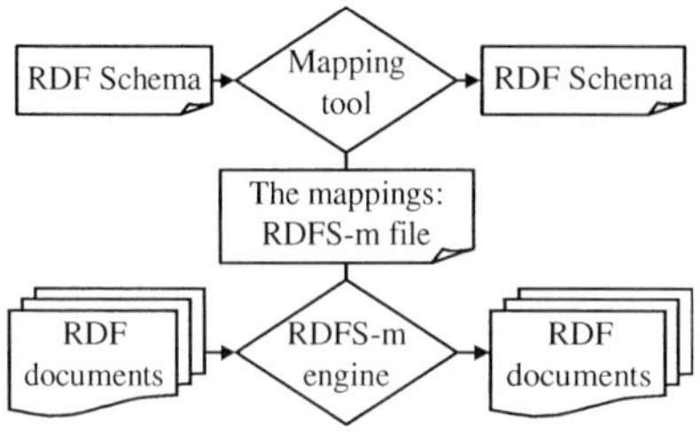

Figure 4: The scheme of RDFS-m

Logical inference engines are computationally expensive because they deal with very expressive logical languages. Only a small fraction of this expressiveness is needed to perform the mappings. RDFS-m has a limited expressiveness sufficient to perform the mappings. This allows building more efficient mapping techniques. In addition, we separate schema-level mapping and instance-level execution of the mappings, making the latter even more efficient.

The RDFS-m ontology, examples of the mappings, and the prototype of the RDFS-m engine are available from the RDFS-m homepage[12].

4.3 Mapping XML - RDF

In addition to the conceptual transformations required for the content integration task, the document integration task need smooth technology to annotate XML documents with RDF annotations. These annotations link XML elements to the underlying ontologies, and provide the information needed to apply RDFS-m mappings to XML instance documents.

The multi-layered information modelling approach discussed in Section 3.2 assumes that the integration is performed at least via two layers: the syntax layer of the actual XML documents and the layer of RDF data models. Accordingly, the integration process passes through three steps: the translation of the source XML catalogue into its normalized data model on the data *abstraction step*, ontology-based translation of a pair of data models on the *transformation step* performed with RDFS-m, and the translation from the data model back into XML according to the target XML format on the *refinement step*.

On the abstraction step the XML catalogues are translated into their normalized data models encoded with the RDF triples. This requires the following transformations:

- The translation of each XML element or XML attribute, which refers to a product feature into an RDF property with the same name (however, the latter may have another namespace).
- The split of a single XML element into two or more RDF triples, if this is required for the integration.
- The combination of multi-file descriptions into a single file, if required.
- Inclusion of the optional XML elements in the RDF triples; the values of the elements are filled with the default value.

During the refinement step all syntactical restrictions required by the target format are restored. The rules must be able to perform the following transformations:

- Each RDF triple is translated into a corresponding XML element, XML attribute, or non-XML entity for a non-XML catalogue.
- The target XML elements are created in a proper order.
- One or more RDF triples have to be merged into a single XML element, if required.
- The XML representation may be partitioned into several files, if required.

XSL-T (probably, with some modifications, improvements, and specialized tool support) seems to be a sufficient technology for the abstraction and refinement steps as discussed in (Omelayenko and Fensel 2001a).

5. CONCLUSIONS

In the paper we discussed two problems, which are quite important for the B2B area: the content integration task and the document integration task. Both tasks require creating, maintenance and efficient execution of a large number of links. Each of the tasks can be solved with an ad-hoc solution. However, an attempt to solve all of them with an ad-hoc technology naturally fails.

Therefore, we developed a B2B information integration framework, which clearly separates several independent subtasks:

- Conceptual mapping of the standards at the schema level.
- Transformation the data models of the instance documents.
- Perform syntactical transformations for the document integration task.

[12] http://www.cs.vu.nl/~borys/RDFT/

Further development of the B2B integration area need to couple with two more integration issues:

- Different exchange protocols, which specify the time and conditions of document creation and utilisation.
- Knowledge-level business models, which specify the role of the documents in the business model of an enterprise.

The integration at this level requires the involvement of ontologies to specify the concepts being linked and the execution of an ontology integration task. As a result the electronic commerce will provide a qualitatively new level of service.

ACKNOWLEDGEMENTS

The authors would like to thank Christoph Bussler, Michel Klein, Ellen Schulten, and Volodymyr Zykov for their comments.

REFERENCES

Brickley, D. and Guha, R., 2000, 'Resource Description Framework (RDF) Schema Specification 1.0', *W3C Candidate Recommendation*; available online at http://www.w3.org/TR/rdf-schema

Chalupsky, H., 2000, 'OntoMorph: A Translation System for Symbolic Knowledge', *In Proceedings of the Seventh International Conference on Knowledge Representation and Reasoning (KR-2000)*, Breckenridge, Colorado, USA, April 12-15.

Clark, J., 1999, 'XSL Transformations (XSL-T)', *W3C Recommendation*; available online at http://www.w3.org/TR/xslt/

Clark, J. and DeRose, S., 1999, 'XML Path Language (XPath)', *W3C Recommendation*; available online at http://www.w3.org/TR/xpath

Fensel, D, 2001, *Ontologies: Silver Bullet for Knowledge Management and Electronic Commerce.* Springer-Verlag, Berlin.

Fensel, D., Ding, Y., Omelayenko, B., Schulten, E., Botquin, G., Brown, M., and Flett, A., 2001, Product Data Integration for B2B E-Commerce. *IEEE Intelligent Systems*; 16(4):54-59.

Grosso, W., Eriksson, H., Fergerson, R., Gennari, J., Tu, S., and Musen, M., 1999, 'Knowledge modeling at the millennium (the design and evolution of Protégé-2000)', *In Proceedings of the Twelfth Banff Workshop on Knowledge Acquisition, Modeling, and Management*, Voyager Inn, Banff, Alberta, Canada, October 16-21.

Lassila, O. and Swick, R., 1999, 'Resource Description Frame-work (RDF) Model and Syntax Specification', *W3C Recommendation*, February; available online at http://www.w3.org/TR/REC-rdf-syntax/

Li, H., 2000, 'XML and Industrial Standards for Electronic Commerce', *Knowledge and Information Systems*, 2(4), p. 487-497.

McGuinness, D., Fikes, R., Rice, J., Wilder, S., 2000, 'An Environment for Merging and Testing Large Ontologies', *In Proceedings of the Seventh International Conference on Principles of Knowledge Representation and Reasoning (KR-2000)*, Breckenridge, Colorado, April 12-15.

Melnik, S. and Decker, S., 2000, 'A Layered Approach to Information Modeling and Interoperability on the Web', In *Proceedings of the Workshop on the Semantic Web at the Fourth European Conference on Research and Advanced Technology for Digital Libraries (ECDL-2000)*, Lisbon, Portugal, September 21.

Noy, N. and Musen, M., 2000, 'PROMPT: Algorithm and Tool for Automated Ontology Merging and Alignment', *In Proceedings of the 17-th National Conference on Artificial Intelligence (AAAI-2000)*, Austin, Texas, July 30 – August 3.

Omelayenko, B., 2001, 'Preliminary Ontology Modeling for B2B Content Integration', In *Proceedings of the First International Workshop on Electronic Business Hubs at the Twelfth International Conference on Database and Expert Systems Applications (DEXA-2001)*, IEEE CS Press, Munich, Germany, September 3, pp. 7-13.

Omelayenko, B. and Fensel, D., 2001a, 'An Analysis of the Integration Problems of XML-Based Catalogues for B2B Electronic Commerce', *In Proceedings of 9th IFIP 2.6 Working Conference on Database Semantics*, Hong Kong, April 25-28, pp. 232-246.

Omelayenko, B. and Fensel, D., 2001b, 'A Two-Layered Integration Approach for Product Information in B2B E-commerce', *In Proceedings of the Second International Conference on Electronic Commerce and Web Technologies (EC WEB-2001)*, LNCS 2115, Munich, Germany, September 4-6, 2001, pp. 226-239.

Sintek, M. and Decker, S., 2001, 'TRIPLE - An RDF Query, Inference, and Transformation Language'. In *Proceedings of the Workshop on Deductive Databases and Knowledge Management (DDLP-2001)*; Tokio, Japan, October 20-22.

U.S. Department of Commerce, 2001, 'Leadership for the New Millennium, Delivering on Digital Progress and Prosperity', *Third annual report the Electronic Commerce Working Group at the US Department of Commerce*, January 16.

A CORBA AND WEB TECHNOLOGY BASED FRAMEWORK FOR THE ANALYSIS AND OPTIMAL DESIGN OF COMPLEX SYSTEMS IN THE OIL INDUSTRY

Carlos Arévalo, Juan Colmenares, Nestor Queipo, Nelson Arapé, Jorge Villalobos.
Applied Computing Institute, Faculty of Engineering, University of Zulia, Maracaibo, Zulia, Venezuela
Email: carevalo@luz.ve, juancol@luz.ve, nqueipo@luz.ve, narape@luz.ve, jorge@ica.luz.ve

Keywords: CORBA, WEB-based Software Engineering, Modeling and Optimization, Reservoir Characterization

Abstract: This paper discusses the design and implementation of a CORBA and WEB technology-based framework for the analysis and optimal design of complex engineering systems. The framework provides an environment for the coupled execution over a network of data analysis, modeling and optimization heterogeneous software using a WEB browser. A framework application is illustrated solving a reservoir characterization problem, critical for devising an optimal strategy for the development of oil and gas fields. The results suggest that the framework can be effectively and efficiently used for solving reservoir characterization problems and holds promise to be useful not only in other areas of petroleum engineering (e.g. hydraulic fracturing design, enhanced oil recovery processes) but also in the solution of complex system design problems found in industries such as electronics, automotive and aerospace.

1. INTRODUCTION

Many problems of interest for the oil industry require the coupled execution of different applications. For example, reservoir characterization involves the use of a reservoir simulator and an optimization program, hydraulic fracturing design implies the cooperative execution of different applications to address issues such as fracture geometry, pre and post fracture production, profitability and optimization, whereas solving enhanced oil recovery process optimization problems requires the use of applications for simulating the process at hand, evaluating the economic benefits and selecting the optimal set of control parameters.

In a typical scenario, an engineer or researcher has several applications for modeling and optimization, which have been written in different languages and run in different hardware/software platforms. The coupled execution of these programs usually requires either to rewrite/recompile them in different platforms or to move data among computers through files or the network. These are time consuming tasks not related to the user's main interest, which result in delays and additional costs in achieving the expected outcome.

During the last decade, technologies such as CORBA (OMG 2001, Vinoski 1997, Henning 1999) and DCOM (Microsoft 1998, Eddon 1998) allow software integration across dissimilar hardware/software platforms. However, the direct use of these technologies for software integration is a time consuming task and may be limited to people with expertise in software development, object oriented programming, and distributed computing. In addition, regarding using interfaces, Web browsers are ubiquitous being the primary point of access to Internet. As a result, it is of primary interest the developing of frameworks that assist the users in the integration of heterogeneous applications for the analysis and optimal design of complex systems across a network with Web browsers as user interface.

There have been limited work in the development of frameworks for modeling and optimization of complex systems and CORBA/Web integration that satisfy the above-referenced requirements (Michelena 1999, Papalambros 1997 and Merle 1996). Michelena et al. and Papalambros et. al. developed a CORBA based framework for the design of large complex systems, which they have used in the design of various mechanical systems, including a pressure vessel, an automotive hybrid power train and a tracked vehicle; this framework have a limitations in the user interface and in

J. Filipe et al. (eds.), Enterprise Information Systems III, 278–286.

supporting services such as session and user management. Merle et al. developed CorbaWeb, a gateway between the World Wide Web and CORBA based on the CorbaScript scripting language (OMG 1996).

This paper presents a framework based on CORBA and Web technology for the integration of software tools typically used for the analysis and design of complex systems and illustrates its application in reservoir characterization, a critical task for the oil industry. The framework has been designed using object-oriented techniques, and includes basic support services (e.g. session, user and project management), a CORBA-WEB gateway, and several modeling and optimization applications. Reservoir characterization addresses the problem of estimating the distributions of permeability and porosity in heterogeneous and multiphase petroleum reservoirs by matching the static and dynamic data available. The remaining sections of the paper discuss the framework overview (Section 2), architecture (Section 3), and its application to the solution of a critical problem in the oil industry (Section 4); conclusions and recommendations are the subject of Section 5.

2. FRAMEWORK OVERVIEW

The objective is to create an environment for the coupled execution of applications (modeling and optimization) deployed over a network using a WEB browser. A single application is executed through the following steps:

- The user enters the framework URL. A welcome page is presented with fields to login to the framework. Once the user has been validated, an HTML page is displayed where he can select an application to work with.
- When the user selects an application, a request is sent to the latter to return its user interface (an HTML page to be displayed in the browser).
- The user fills in the information required by the application and clicks a button to execute it. An execution request is sent to the application including all the necessary information.
- The application performs the requested task and returns an HTML page that displays the results on the browser.

A similar procedure is followed in the case of the execution of several applications. Applications interact dynamically by creating CORBA objects and making them available to other applications through basic support services provided by the framework.

The requests that come from the WEB browser are HTTP requests. On the other hand, the application modules are CORBA objects that use the IIOP protocol. Therefore, the requests must be converted from one protocol to the other. This is achieved by a CORBA-WEB Gateway. Details of the framework components are provided in the following section.

3. FRAMEWORK ARCHITECTURE

With reference to Figure 1, the framework has the following components:

- A **CORBA-WEB Gateway module** that serves as a bridge between the WEB and CORBA.
- A **portal module** that is the entry point to the framework.
- A **session manager module** that provides mechanisms for preserving the state of applications and for accessing objects created by other applications.
- A **user manager module** that handles user access and permissions.
- A **project manager module** that creates and manages user projects.
- A **naming service** that manages a directory of all framework resources and applications.
- **Application modules** that perform specific tasks such as data analysis, modeling and optimization.

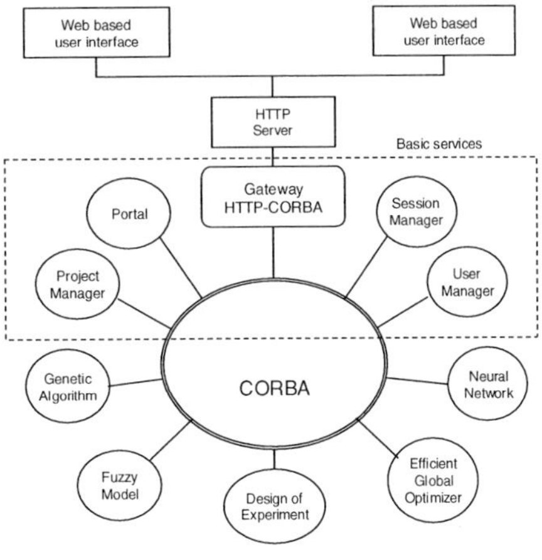

Figure 1: Framework architecture.

3.1 The CORBA-WEB Gateway

A bridge between the WEB and CORBA. It receives HTTP requests from a WEB browser, translates them to CORBA messages, and sends them to the target application module. If necessary, it translates the response into HTML format and ends it back to the client for display.

The Gateway consists of a core object and several Java servlets (Figure 2). The servlets receive requests coming from the WEB client, gather the information needed to execute the request and invoke the core object for execution. The core object performs the following tasks:

- Invoke the naming service to retrieve a CORBA reference for the target module.
- Call the target module to obtain the list of parameters required to make the request.
- Create a dynamic request by means of the CORBA dynamic invocation interface (DII).
- Perform the request, wait for the target application to finish and return the output data to the calling servlet, which in turn returns the data to the client for display.

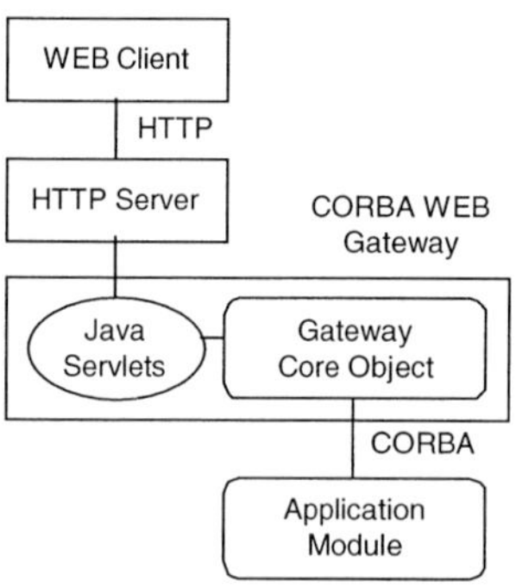

Figure 2: CORBA-WEB gateway architecture.

For each request made by the WEB client, a new thread is created. Since the CORBA request is always made synchronously, the thread will be blocked until the application returns. However the gateway will continue to process requests due to its multithreaded nature.

The gateway module includes the following objects (Figure 3):

- The dispatcher servlets that receive the requests made by the WEB client.
- A core gateway object. This object receives the request from the servlets and coordinates the construction and execution of the dynamic CORBA requests.
- A request builder. This calls the target object to get its interface definition and builds the request.
- A request invoker that executes the request.

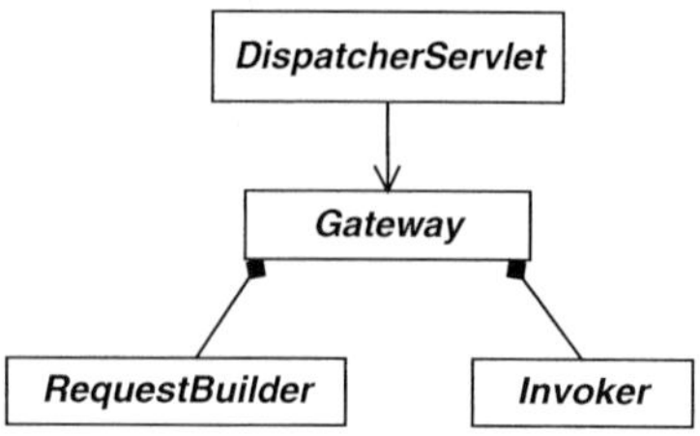

Figure 3: UML class diagram for the CORBA-WEB gateway.

3.2 Portal module

The entry point to the framework. It consists of a CORBA object that returns the HTML login page and the framework main page that contains links to available applications and framework services.

3.3 Session manager module

It consists of two CORBA object types: `Session` and `SessionManager`. The former includes a public container where applications store object references that become available to other applications. It also contains a private container that stores CORBA data types and object references representing the application state. In addition, the `SessionManager` creates and manages user sessions. Hence, this module serves two purposes: i) to provide a way for applications to access objects created by other applications and ii) to provide a mechanism for preserving the state of applications.

Sessions are created by the gateway (through a request made to the session manager) and passed to applications in every request made by a WEB client. The Java session tracking mechanism is used to ensure that all requests coming from the same user during some period of time get the same session object.

3.4 User manager module

A CORBA based user administration tool implemented in Java. It allows an administrator to create and delete framework users, change their properties through a WEB interface, and offers an UNIX-like user authentication service.

3.5 Project manager module

A basic framework service that allows users to create, rename and delete experiments and projects through a WEB interface. An experiment is a persistent entity that stores data related with configuration parameters and results of applications. Experiments are grouped in projects, which are stored in a repository handled by the Project Manager and mapped on a file system, with projects and experiments being directories where application files are stored. In addition, through this module, applications may store results associated with experiments and retrieve configuration data for their execution. The Project Manager Module is implemented in Java using multithreaded programming.

3.6 Naming Service

It manages a directory of all the framework resources with a hierarchical structure similar to the corresponding to the application interface (described in the next section). This service was implemented directly with the CORBA naming service.

3.7 Application modules

These modules are the focus of the user interests and perform not only those tasks related to modeling and optimization but also framework related operations such as returning the HTML pages that make up the module's user interface, initializing user sessions and registering themselves with the framework name service.

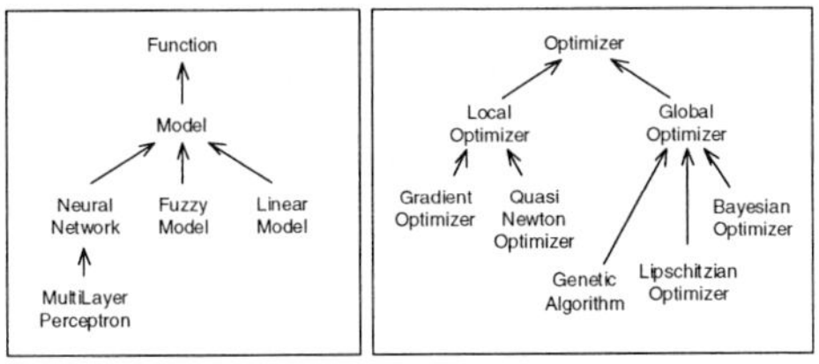

Figure 4: Application Module Interface Hierarchies.

A set of CORBA interfaces has been developed to standardize the call protocol that application clients must use to invoke operations on other objects. The interfaces are organized hierarchically; an example of which is illustrated in Figure 4. This figure presents the CORBA interfaces corresponding to the Function and Optimizer application modules.

An application module may have objects that implement different interfaces. For example, a typical modeling application module consists of a model builder (creational object) that constructs models (core objects) which implements the interface `Model` and. an object that implements the `Application` interface if the module has a WEB based user interface. Below it is shown the IDL code of the `Model` and `Application` interfaces.

```
typedef sequence<double> DoubleVector;
typedef sequence<DoubleVector>
                DoubleMatrix;

interface Application {
  string
  initWorkSession(in Session session);
};

interface Function {
  DoubleVector
  evaluate(in DoubleVector inputData);

  DoubleMatrix
  multiEvaluate(in DoubleMatrix
                inputData);
};

interface Model : Function {};
```

Usually, the first message received by an application module is a request to retrieve its user interface. This is an HTML page that will be displayed by the WEB browser. This page has at least a button to request the execution of framework servlets, and includes the target application and operation names. The operation is executed using the mechanism outlined in Section 3.1. The page may also have several execution buttons; an example of this situation is the case of a neural network application user interface that has a button to train the network and a button to execute it; alternatively, a genetic algorithm application may have a button to create and set the parameters of a GA and a button to run it.

Considering that the applications are responsible for creating dynamically their web pages, an object that facilitates this task have been designed. This object, implemented in Java, is named `UserInterfaceManager`. An application module can create an `UserInterfaceManager` (using a factory object), configure it, and use it to create dynamic HTML pages.

At present the framework has available the following application modules:

- Genetic algorithm. It has a CORBA object that implements the `GeneticAlgorithm` interface. The implementation is based on the

Banda genetic algorithm developed by Brian W. Bush (Bush 2000).

- Direct algorithm. It includes a CORBA object that realizes the method proposed by Jones et. al. (Jones 1993) and implements the `LipschitzianOptimizer` interface (derived from `GlobalOptimizer`).
- Efficient Global Optimization algorithm. This application has a CORBA object that realizes the method proposed by Jones et. al. (Jones 1998) and implements the `BayesianOptimizer` interface (derived from `GlobalOptimizer`).
- Neural network. Implements two CORBA objects, `NeuralNetworkTrainer` and `NeuralNetworkModel`. Allows the creation of multilayer perceptron neural networks with various training algorithms. This module is a wrapper to the Stuttgart Neural Network Simulator (IPVR 1995).
- Fuzzy model. Implements two CORBA objects, `FuzzyModelBuilder` and `FuzzyModel`. It allows the creation of Sugeno type fuzzy models using a fuzzy discretization method and an orthogonal parameter estimation (Wang 1995).
- Linear model. Implements two CORBA objects, `LinearModelBuilder` and `LinearModel`. It can be used to create linear models using classical techniques such as linear regression and stepwise elimination.
- Design of experiment. Creates designs of experiments based on simple random and latin hypercube sampling. It implements the `DesignOfExperiment` interface.

4. CASE STUDY. SURROGATE MODELING-BASED OPTIMIZATION FOR THE INTEGRATION OF STATIC AND DYNAMIC DATA INTO A RESERVOIR DESCRIPTION

The identification of the permeability and porosity parameters that best match the data (static and dynamic) available for a given reservoir is critical for devising an optimal strategy for the development of oil and gas fields. The static data makes reference to those originated from geology, electrical logs, core analysis, fluid properties, seismic and geostatistics; while the dynamic data is represented by field measurements such as, production history, bottom hole pressures from permanent gauges, water-cut, and gas-oil ratio.

Estimating permeability and porosity parameters from available data is difficult because of the following reasons: i) in general, the number of parameters to be estimated are very high, since data is scarce, and the reservoirs are heterogeneous (permeability and porosity have spatial variability), ii) the available data may have very different scope and nature, and, iii) the numerical simulation of the reservoir, necessary to assess how well given permeability and porosity parameters match the available data are computationally expensive.

Queipo et. al. developed a methodology for solving the problem of interest which includes the construction of a "fast surrogate" of an objective function whose evaluation involves the execution of a time-consuming mathematical model (i.e. reservoir numerical simulator) based on neural networks, DACE modeling and adaptive sampling.

The proposed solution approach, called NEGO (Neural-network based Efficient Global Optimization), is an improved version of the EGO algorithm (Jones 1998) for the optimization of computationally expensive black-box functions. It involves the following five steps:

1. Construct a sample of the parameter space using the latin hypercube method. The latin hypercube sampling procedure has been shown to be very effective for selecting input variables for the analysis of the output of a computer code.
2. Conduct mathematical simulations using the sample from the previous step and record the response values associated with static and dynamic data available, and the objective function values.
3. Construct a parsimonious neural network using the data obtained in the previous step. The purpose of this neural network is to capture the general trends observed in the data; no rigorous performance criteria are placed on the neural network. The input variables of the neural network are the permeability and porosity parameters and the output variable is the corresponding objective function value.
4. Construct a DACE model for the residuals, that is, the difference between the observed objective function values, and the neural network responses using the sample data. These models provide not only an estimate of the residual values but also of the respective errors. The surrogate model for the evaluation of the objective function is the sum of the neural network and DACE models.

5. Additional points are obtained balancing the exploitation of the information provided by the surrogate model (where the surface is minimized) with the need to improve the surface (where error estimates are high), until a stopping criterion has been met. This balance is achieved by sampling where a figure of merit is maximized.

As can be noticed, this problem involves the coupled execution of several optimization and modeling tools such as: sampling programs, a reservoir numerical simulator, surrogate models, and optimization algorithms. To implement this methodology using the framework it is necessary to:

1. Design and implement a framework application for optimization based on NEGO.
2. Design and implement a framework application for reservoir numerical simulation.
3. Integrate the two applications using the framework resources.

4.1 Design of application for optimization based on NEGO.

The framework includes an interface hierarchy for solving optimization problems. These interfaces, their implementations and relationships are shown in Figure 5. The general procedure to solve an optimization problem within the framework is:

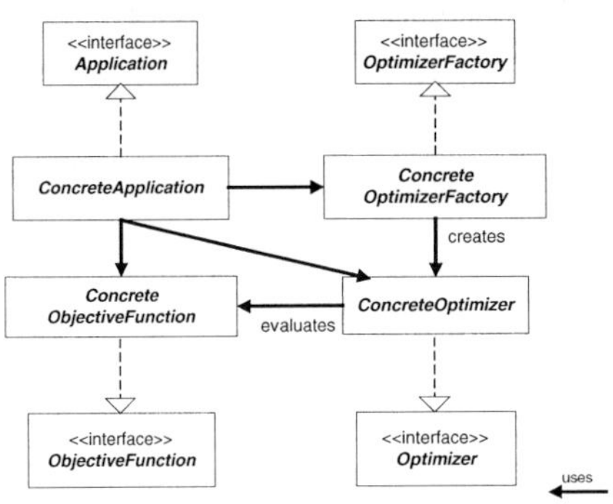

Figure 5: UML class diagram of a optimization application

1. Create a concrete optimizer object by invoking the create operation on the optimizer factory.
2. Obtain the reference to an objective function from the user session and pass it to the optimizer.
3. Invoke the optimize operation on the optimizer.
4. Obtain the optimal value and solution from the optimizer.

The NEGO algorithm falls under the bayesian optimizer category (see Figure 6). Below it is shown a fragment of the framework CORBA interface definitions needed for bayesian optimization applications. Note that there are interface definitions for `Optimizer`, `GlobalOptimizer` and `BayesianOptimizer`.

```
typedef sequence<ConstraintFunction>
        ConstraintFunctionVector;

interface Optimizer
{
  // Exceptions
  struct FaultExceptionDetails {
     string info;
  };

  exception FaultException {
     FaultExceptionDetails details;
  };

  struct BadParamDetails {
      unsigned short numOfBadParam;
      string msg;
  };

  exception BadParamException {
    BadParamDetails details;
  };

  //operations
  void optimize()
    raises(FaultException);

  void
  setObjectiveFunction(in Function
                      objFunction);
  void
  setMaxNumIterations(in ULONG m)
    raises(BadParamException);

  void
  setReportFrecuency(in USHORT
                    frecuency)
    raises(BadParamException);


  void
  defineSearchSpace(in USHORT dim)
    raises(BadParamException);

  void
  defineBoundedSearchSpace(
    in USHORT dim,
```

```
      in DoubleVector upperBounds,
      in DoubleVector lowerBounds)
      raises(BadParamException);

    void defineConstraintedSearchSpace(
      in USHORT dim,
      in DoubleVector upperBounds,
      in DoubleVector lowerBounds,
      in ConstraintFunctionVector
         constraints)
      raises(BadParamException);

    double getOptimalValue();

    DoubleVector getOptimalValues();

    DoubleVector getOptimalSolution();

    void abort();
};

// Global Optimizers
interface GlobalOptimizer : Optimizer {
};

interface BayesianOptimizer :
  GlobalOptimizer {};

interface NEGO : BayesianOptimizer {
  void
  setNeuralNetworkTrainer(
    NeuralNetworkTrainer
    neuralNetTrainer);
};
```

The NEGO application consists of the following CORBA objects:

- NEGOApplication. This object presents the application's user interface. It implements CORBA interface Application (section 3.7).
- NEGOFactory. This object creates NEGO objects.
- NEGO. This object does the optimization. It implements the NEGO strategy outlined in the previous section.

The Figure 6 illustrates UML class diagram of NEGO application where the gray boxes represent objects that are already present in the framework and white boxes represent objects that must be implemented.

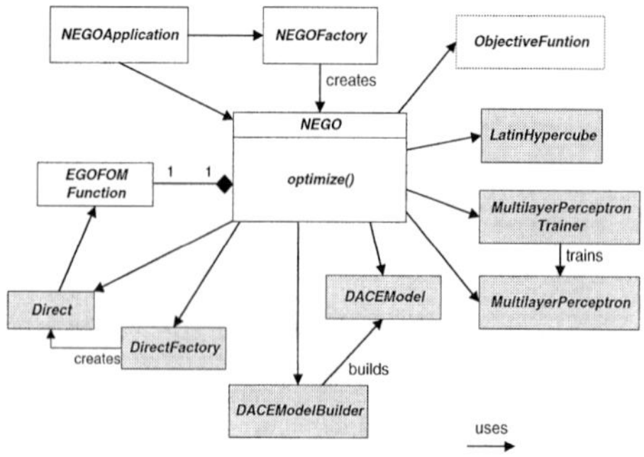

Figure 6: UML class diagram of NEGO application.

4.2 Application for reservoir numerical simulation

This application is developed using an existing reservoir numerical simulation program. In order to use this program within the framework a wrapper must be created. The wrapper is a framework aware object that receives the CORBA requests and executes the simulation program using the facilities provided by the operating system. Data is exchanged between the wrapper and the simulator through files.

The framework reservoir numerical simulation application consists of the following objects:

- ReservoirSimulationApplication. This object presents the application's user interface. It implements CORBA interface Application (section 3.5).
- ReservoirSimulator. This object is a wrapper of the reservoir numerical simulation program. It implements CORBA interface Function and performs the following tasks:
    - Receives the CORBA requests and writes a file formatted for the numerical simulation application.
    - It executes the simulator and waits for it to exit.
    - Finally, it reads the output data produced by the simulator from a file and produces the CORBA response.

The reservoir numerical simulation program reads input data from a file, performs the simulation, writes an output file with the simulation results and exits.

4.3 Coupled execution of created applications using the framework.

The integration of the two applications requires the creation by the user of a reservoir simulator object through the corresponding application. The reference to this object is stored in the user session (section 3.3), then the user executes the NEGO application, selects the reservoir simulator object (wrapper) as the objective function and performs the optimization.

5. CONCLUSIONS

This paper discussed the design and implementation of a CORBA and WEB technology based framework for the analysis and optimal design of complex engineering systems. The framework provides an environment for the coupled execution over a network of data analysis, modeling and optimization heterogeneous software using a WEB browser, and includes the following modules:

- A **CORBA-WEB Gateway module.** Multithreaded and based on Java servlets and CORBA Dynamic Invocation Interface (DII), it serves as a bridge between the WEB and CORBA.
- A **portal module.** It is the entry point to the framework and consists of a CORBA object that returns the HTML login page and the framework main page that contains links to available applications and framework services.
- A **session manager module.** It provides mechanisms for preserving the state of applications and for accessing objects created by other applications. Its functionality is based on the Java session tracking mechanism and CORBA session objects that hold containers where applications store object references that become available to other applications and CORBA data types and object references representing the application state.
- A **user manager module** that handles user access and permissions, and offers an UNIX-like user authentication service.
- A **project manager module** that allows users, through a WEB interface, to create, rename and delete experiments and projects stored in a repository mapped on a file system.
- A **naming service** that manages a directory of all framework resources and applications. It was implemented directly with the CORBA naming service.
- **Application modules.** They are the focus of the user interests and perform not only specific tasks such as data analysis, modeling and optimization but also framework related operations. They implement interfaces developed to standardize the call protocol that application clients must use to invoke operations on other objects. In addition, the applications are responsible for creating dynamically their web pages.

A framework application was illustrated solving a reservoir characterization problem, critical for devising an optimal strategy for the development of oil and gas fields. The results suggest that the framework can be effectively and efficiently used for solving reservoir characterization problems and holds promise to be useful not only in other areas of petroleum engineering (e.g. hydraulic fracturing design, enhanced oil recovery processes) but also in the solution of complex system design problems found in industries such as electronics, automotive and aerospace. Currently, additional applications are being developed associated with the solution of hydraulic fracturing, steam assisted gravity drainage, and water alternating gas optimization.

ACKNOWLEDGMENTS

The authors gratefully acknowledge the financial support provided by the Consejo Nacional de Investigaciones Científicas (CONICIT – Venezuela) through the Projects G-97000824 and G-97003899.

REFERENCES

Object Management Group (OMG), 2001. *The Common Object Request Broker: Architecture and Specification (CORBA 2.4 specification).* HTTP://www.omg.org/ technology/ documents/formal/corbaiiop.htm.

Vinoski, S., 1997. 'Integrating Diverse Applications within Distributed Heterogeneous Environments', *IEEE Communications Magazine*.

Henning, M., et. al., 1999. *Advanced CORBA Programming with C++*. U.S.A: Addison Wesley.

Microsoft Corporation. 1998. *Distributed Component Object Model Protocol. DCOM/1.0.* Internet-Draft. HTTP://msdn.microsoft.com /library/ specs/ distributedcomponentobjectmodelprotocoldcom10.htm

Eddon, G., et. al., 1998. *Inside Distributed COM*. U.S.A: Microsoft Press.

Michelena, N., et. al., 1999, 'A CORBA-Based Object-Oriented Framework for Distributed System Design', *Mechanics of Structures and Machines*.

Papalambros, P., et. al., 1997, 'Distributed Cooperative Systems Designs', *Proceedings of the 11th International Conference on Engineering Design*.

Merle, P., et. al., 1996. 'CorbaWeb: A WWW and Corba Worlds Integration', *2th COOTS, Workshop on Distributed Object Computing on the Internet*.

Object Management Group (OMG), 1996. *CORBA Scripting Language. Request For Proposal*. OMG Document: orbos/96-06-13.

Bush, B. W., 2000. *Banda Java Packages. Version 8.1*. http://www.sladen.com/bwbush..

Jones, D., 1993, 'Lipschitzian Optimization without the Lipschitz Constant', *Journal of Optimization Theory and Application*.

Jones, D., 1998, 'Efficient Global Optimization of Expensive Black-Box Functions', *Journal of Global Optimization.*.

Institute for Parallel and Distributed High Performance Systems (IPVR), University of Stuttgart, 1995. *Stuttgart Neural Network Simulator Users Manual*. http://www.informatik.uni-stuttgart.de/ipvr/ bv/projekte/snns/ UserManual/UserManual.html.

Wang, L., et. al., 1995, 'Building Sugeno Type Models Using Fuzzy Discretization and Orthogonal Parameter Estimation Techniques', *IEEE Transactions on Fuzzy Systems*.

Queipo, N., et. al., 2000, 'Surrogate Modeling-Based Optimization for the Integration of Static and Dynamic Data Into a Reservoir Description', *2000 SPE Annual Technical Conference and Exhibition*.

E-BUSINESS CHANGE AND ORGANISATIONAL PERFORMANCE:

A Case Study of B2B e-Business Integration

Colin Ash

Edith Cowan University,Pearson Street, Churchlands, Perth, Australia,
Email: c.ash@ecu.edu.au

Keywords: Internet enabled ERP, B2B e-procurement, e-Business change management, Organisational performance

Abstract: Many ERP enabled organisations have undertaken significant e-business initiatives over the past two years. Initially these were concerned with cost savings but now the trend is towards revenue generation. Also, the earlier thinking on this topic indicated a significant role for information technology in these initiatives. We depart from this by emphasising the importance of managing the change of e-business projects. The paper examines a research model that proposes various antecedents to successful e-business change management in ERP environments. A case study of the first B2B e-business integration with Dell Computer Corporation and its largest corporate customer is examined in the context of this model. The study demonstrates the integration of ERP and non-ERP systems, using Web-based technologies, to provide to optimise an overall B2B value chain. The specific goal is to determine facilitators that lead to success of an e-business project. Finally the study is used to emphasise the role of change management and cultural readiness when adopting e-business solutions.

1. INTRODUCTION

Numerous papers and reports have been written about e-business and how this concept will change the way companies do business. However, little information is available on how to successfully integrate e-Business projects with ongoing ERP implementations or already productive ERP systems. As more and more established organisations realise that they need to open themselves to their customers, partners and suppliers over the Internet, integration with ERP systems becomes a critical issue.

Since 1998, both academics and practitioners have witnessed the coming together of these two dominant technologies as the next wave of systems integration (Ash, 1998). This combination of technologies offers established companies the opportunity to build interactive relationships with partners and suppliers, improve efficiency and extend its reach, all at a very low cost. According to interviews conducted by Forrester Research with 40 senior IT and e-Commerce executives, Electronic business will explode by 2002 because they expect 78% of their customers and 65% of their trading partners to have global electronic connections with them, up from 40% and 43% respectively. Online revenue growth has quadrupled each year. By 1998, it totalled $35 billion inter-company and $15 billion retail, worldwide. In 2000, out of 256 million users, 53 million buyers will average $4,090 each in e-commerce business. By 2003, online revenues will exceed $1.3 trillion (Hesterbrink, 1999:p3).

Although these technologies are fundamentally different, the fusion of their functionality offers a sound infrastructure for doing business online or electronic business. Here e-business means "making the key business processes of an organisation available over the Internet" (Boey, 1999: p.1). Although simple, this definition nevertheless incorporates some subtle but fundamental points about e-business applications with ERP systems.

The paper reports on a qualitative case study of two partner organisations, that use the Internet to integrated their non-ERP and ERP (SAP R/3) systems for electronic procurement. The case presents a recently implemented B2B e-business project by *Dell* to be used to supply computer equipment to one of its customer companies, *Customer.com*. The aim of this study is to test the suitability of the research framework for identifying the factors for success of an e-business project. The focus of the study goes beyond the economic benefits derived from implementing e-business

J. Filipe et al. (eds.), Enterprise Information Systems III, 287–294.

solutions, as it focuses on e-business change and organisational performance issues.

2. THEORETICAL FRAMEWORK

Preliminary investigations of local Western Australian and overseas SAP sites indicated the importance of environmental conditions for e-business change (e-BC) (Ash, 2000).

For example, the capability to share knowledge, the importance of the learning organisation, as well as the activities of change management teams. Although information gathered was qualitatively rich, attempts at analysis lead to the need for a comprehensive model.

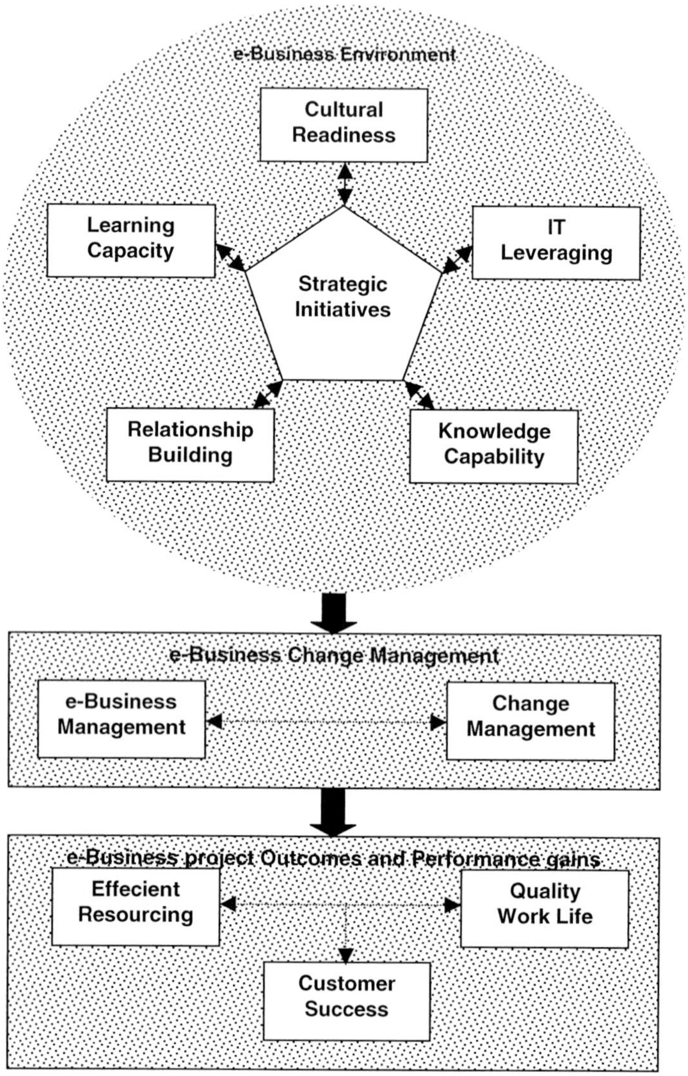

Figure 1: Theoretical Framework of e-Business Change Management

The model illustrated in Figure 1 was adapted from Guha et al, (1997). It is used to guide the researcher in identifying the facilitators and inhibitors of a successful e-BC. The relationships presented in the framework are based on relevant work in organisational change, strategic management innovation, and information systems. The general thesis of the framework is adapted from Guha's et al, (1997) work on "business process change management".

"Any significant business process change requires a strategic initiative where top managers act as leaders in defining and communicating a vision of change. The organisational environment, with ready culture, a willingness to share knowledge, balanced network relationships, and a capacity to learn, should facilitate the implementation of prescribed e-business management and change management. Both of these are requisite for customer success and ultimately in achieving measurable and sustainable competitive performance" (: 121).

The research challenge, here, is one of leveraging existing theory to circumscribe the research domain for examining diverse attributes of e-business adoption in ERP environments (e-ERP) from Ash and Rossouw, (1999).

The findings from the studies in "business process change" by Guha et al (1997), suggests that successful e-BC projects should tend to have facilitators in all dimensions of the research framework. Failure is most likely to be due to a lack of key factors such as cultural readiness, or change management. Also, the approach taken in this study adopts the view that the theoretical framework should be business focused, not industry based. It will vary in terms of the business focus of the organisation; for example customer or supplier focused, product or service focused.

Clarifying these issues requires systematic attention to learning processes, organisational culture, technology infrastructure and systems thinking. Hesterbrink (1999) stresses the impact e-business projects have on business processes, people, technology and organisation in an ERP environment. He also, emphasises the value of having ERP systems already aligned with business processes is an advantage for e-ERP adoption.

Handy, (1989) explains the important fundamental that "learning is a response to change". To puts this into context, "the creation and implementation of any e-business project is inextricably linked to the management of change" (Kalakota, et al, 1999). Further, change management of new business practices is vital for moving towards doing business via the Internet (Pereira, 1999). For the case study that follows, the business process focus is on business-to-business in the e-procurement area.

In order to avoid an original IT-centric position, e-business change (e-BC) is defined here as an organisation initiative to design an e-business project "to achieve significant (breakthrough) improvements in performance (eg quality, responsiveness, cost, flexibility, satisfaction, shareholder value, and other critical e-business measures) through changes in relationships between management, information, technology, organisational structure, and people" (Guha, et al, 1997). Therefore, in any examination of e-BC outcomes, consideration should be given to (a) the environmental conditions for change and (b) the ability of the organisation to manage change in those conditions.

3. METHODOLOGY

The current study makes use of an established theoretical framework taking from business process change (BPC) research. Figure 1 shows the adapted framework that was used as a tool for identifying the facilitators and inhibitors of successful e-business projects within ERP enabled organisations. "Embedded" multiple case-study analysis was chosen to investigate the research questions concerning the broad and new complex phenomenon of e-ERP change management. The case-studies selection criterion required a major e-business project, which has organisational implications.

"Embedded" multiple case-study analysis was chosen to investigate the research questions concerning the broad and new complex phenomenon of e-business change projects. Embedded enlists the use of multiple units of analysis; (1) the company (strategy), (2) the project team, (3) the project.

3.1 Case selection

To identify the sites, a search using secondary literature, web sites, and SAP related industry consultants were contacted to identify major e-ERP projects. Within the scope of this study the term e-ERP project is used to represent any instance of Internet-ERP technology adoption (eg SAP B2B Procurement, SAP Employee Self Service, SAP Retail Store), (SAP 1999). More than ten SAP enabled organisations known to have adopted e-business systems were selected. In each case a senior IT/SAP project manager was contacted for the purpose of conducting interviews. The e-business initiative selection criteria are given in Table 1.

Table 1: All Case Organisations Interviewed

Criterion of Project	Bank	Biotech	Charity	Dell & Cust	Employ -ment	Engin- eering	Scitech	Society
1. Major e-business project	B2E	B2B	B2C	B2B	B2E/B	B2E	B2C	B2C
2. Project completed	Locally	Yes	Sept	Yes	Yes	Locally	Yes	Yes
3. Expected breakthrough	Yes	Yes	Yes	Yes	Yes	Yes	Yes	Yes
4. Cross functional focus	Yes	Yes	Yes	Yes	Yes	Yes	Yes	Yes
5. Unambiguous outcomes	Yes	Yes	Yes	Yes	No	Yes	Yes	Yes
Size of Organisation	Large	Medium	Small	Large	Large	Large	Large	Small
Significance of Project	Medium	High	High	Very High	High	Innova- tive	High	High

3.2 Data collection

In November 1999 the researcher conducted initial interviews in person by visiting each organisation at their headquarters. Senior e-business project managers were questioned about "the benefits and barriers arising from extending their R/3 business processes onto the Internet" (Ash, 2000). A repeat visit to each site in June/July 2000, was performed to collect the primary information for this study, using the following protocol:

A qualitative structured interview questionnaire was used during the second visits to collect primary data for the study from nine (9) SAP worldwide sites. Table 1, shows only 8 cases.

- Archival documents were collected, as well as many conversations via e-mail.

In each case the focal point of contact was the senior level IT/SAP project manager.

In Table 1, one of the e-business project stands out from all the other seven mini-case studies.

4. A CASE STUDY: B2B INTEGRATION

In 2000 Dell pioneered (implemented) its first business-to-business "B2B E-Business Integration" with an established customer company. The information gathered about this case forms the basis of the discussion for rest of this paper. This case is chosen here because it illustrates a comprehensive approach to inter-enterprise computing. This is an example of an integration architecture that is made possible through a variety of backend systems and procurement systems. How does it work?

One of Dell's customers, *Customer.com*, is able to leveraging its existing SAP backend system and SAP business Connector (powered webMethods technology) to communicate directly with Dell's component-based e-business system. The integration of *Customer.com's* ERP (SAP R/3) system and (SAP B2B) procurement application to its customer Dell catalogue, automates the e-procurement of Dell's computer products via the Internet (Dell, 2000).

4.1 Technology fit

In adopting an enterprise information system, technology is only half the picture. Organisational perspective is equally important (Fan, 2000). Figure 2 illustrates the issue of business or enterprise information systems fit versus organisational performance. *Customer.com* implemented SAP as its enterprise business system. However, unlike *Customer.com,* Dell sees itself "as competing in a very dynamic environment with ever **changing** technology, customer tastes, and supplier relationships" (Fan, 2000: 29).

For this reason, Dell choose to abandon its early development in SAP and in 1996 started to use COM as a standard in developing its component-based enterprise solution. Further, Dell strongly believes that the company has to adopt a more flexible approach, in order to fit IT to its overall corporate and operation strategy.

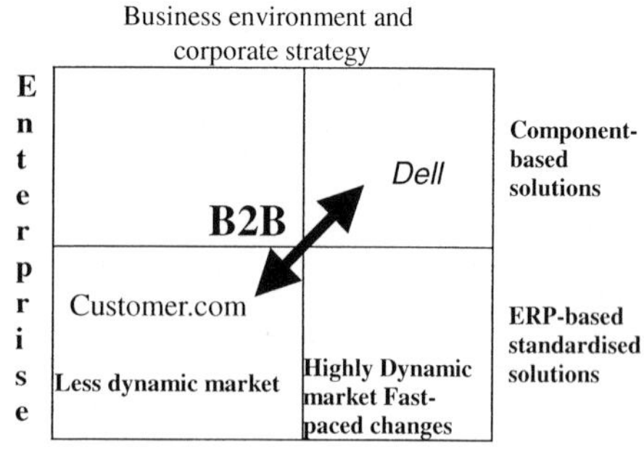

Figure 2: Decision Matrix for Dell and Partner

5. RESEARCH FINDINGS

At the case interview of the project manager answers were collected using a structured questionnaire that probed three levels of detail; from components, and their constructs with their corresponding categories. Tables 2a, 2b, and 2c represent the details of the interview questionnaire, as adapted from Guha et al, (1997) earlier research.

By analysing the data and comments captured from the interviews, a qualitative rating was first derived. The comments help to focus on the contributions of the individual components of the research or business framework. Each component of the framework was rated as having a positive or negative contribution to the e-business project.

The results given in Tables 2a, 2b, 2c indicates an overall level of success was achieved. The column of ratings draws attention to the importance of having positive contribution from all the components (synergy) for the project to be successful (Guha et al,1997). To understand these summarised findings, a more in depth discussion follows for each of the three main dimensions of e-business change - the *change environment*, the *management of change*, and the *outcomes and performance gains*.

5.1 Change environment

Strategic Initiatives This IT innovation sprang from the insights of one of Dell's IT/professional staff. This is due to the IT manager "ideas champion" (Ash and Zach, 1999) The champion had the drive and energy to make the project happen. Also, the "ideas champion" received decision making support from the central administration (board). He had the motivation to communicate and sell the vision for the project to others in the organisation so that they were willing to provide their support.

Cultural Readiness In the project, the staff showed a desire to be part of change. The change agent was the practical leadership of the management staff. "We are very please with acceptance of this integrated e-business solution." This was the view shared by both partners.

Table 2a: Findings of *Change Environment* in the Business Framework

Component *Constructs*	**Supplier Organisation "Dell"**	**Customer Organisation "Customer.com"**
Strategic Initiatives		
stimuli	pro-active	pro-active
formulation scope	**incremental**	**revolutionary**
decision making	champion emergence	champion emergence
strategy led	**onset**	**onset**
Cultural Readiness	**[+ve]**	**[+ve]**
change agents	+	+
leadership	+	+
risk aversion	welcomed	welcomed
extent open communication	+	+
IT Leveragability		
role of IT	enabling	enabling and **socio-technical**
use of Internet technology	**superior**	**adequate**
Network Relationship Balancing	**[+ve]**	**[+ve]**
inter-organisational linkages	cooperative	cooperative
cross-functional cooperation	adequate	adequate
Learning Capacity		
improve efficiency	learning by doing	learning by doing
adaptation	**learning from others**	**response to IT change**
learning type	**double-loop**	**Single loop**
external information use	**boundary spanners**	**technology gate-keeper**
declarative knowledge	focus on core competencies	focus on core competencies

Key: +ve = facilitator, -ve = inhibitor, +&- = facilitator & inhibitor

According to Mintzberg and Westley, (1992), a visionary leader is a single leader who influences change. For *Customer.com* the leadership showed inspiration for the development of a practical solutions that overcame management obstacles. However, there remains the problem of training employees. A culture of acceptance to change introduced for the benefit of the all staff, and not just the clerical employees.

Cultural Readiness In the project, the staff showed a desire to be part of change. The change agent was the practical leadership of the management staff. "We are very please with acceptance of this integrated e-business solution." This was the view shared by both partners.

According to Mintzberg and Westley, (1992), a visionary leader is a single leader who influences change. For *Customer.com* the leadership showed inspiration for the development of a practical solutions that overcame management obstacles. However, there remains the problem of training employees. A culture of acceptance to change introduced for the benefit of the all staff, and not just the clerical employees.

Network Relationships and Learning For *Customer.com* the project demonstrated positive cooperation with the interstate sub-branch of the organisation, and the beginnings of cross-functional cooperation.

In the project, learning by doing and learning from others helped improve the professional end-user IT skills. The extra time saved enabled the accountant/ IT manager to devote time to quality decision making procedures.

IT Leveragability and Knowledge Capability For *Customer.com*, the project demonstrated positive leadership, superior IT design for improved learning, and business-to-employee communication, but with some employee resistance. To overcome resistance to change, each of these components, must be aligned (along with the enabling technology) to the strategic initiatives to overcome resistance to change (Chesterbrink, 1999).

5.2 Change management

Change Management The pattern of change was reported to be a participative change tactic resulting in an evolutionary change. This was viewed as a "waterfall" progression of change, starting with an alleviation of dissatisfaction by the staff and eventually arriving at a "well managed" workflow:

alleviation of dissatisfaction,

vision for change – "doing business in a new and improved way",

evolutionary change tactics,

e-Business Management The use of computer graphics in combination with the web tools and techniques also had positive influence on the use of the by casual users.

5.3 Outcomes and performance gains

It was reported that from the outset the project showed an improvement in one of the outcome constructs - the quality of work life (QWL). However, within the area of **performance gains,** improved customer response and an expanding customer base was seen as most significant (positive). As a measure of its success and/or acceptance, this e-business solution is expected to include the B2B e-procurement of office equipment and supplies.

The performance gains for e-procurement were achieved from two sources; 25% cost savings, and reduced cycle time from 2 weeks to 2 days, and access to (real-time) customer data via ERP technology. The project enabled efficiency gains from minimising of delays in customer orders, and effectiveness gains from optimising employee/staff time. For example; fewer complaints, improved management of the customer, increase to 50% with online orders (sales), and a growth in corporate sale of 45% (DELL, 2000). Also, access to online real-time data for deciding on the optimal employee orders. The cost savings through operational efficiencies of all equipment resourcing, compare favourably to those cost savings (efficiencies) in other e-procurement case studies. In the *Biotech.com* case study (UK) the gains appear to be less; 20% cost savings, and reduced cycle time from 2 weeks to 4 days. However, improvements for staff in the QWL dimension appear the same.

Outcomes of e-business change (e-BC) can be measured at various levels within the broad complex phenomenon of an e-ERP project. In any examination of e-BC outcomes, consideration should be given to; (i) the environmental conditions for change, and (ii) the ability of the organisation to manage change in those conditions (Tables 2a, 2b).

To address these issues of change Norton (1992) and Kaplan (1996) offer the use of a balanced scorecard (BSC). The use of BSC for strategic enterprise management is a significant departure from traditional performance management programs that are to financial frameworks. The BSC provides

Table 2b: Findings of *Change Management* in the Business Framework

Component / *Constructs*	Supplier Organisation "Dell"	Customer Organisation "Customer.com"
Change Mgt Practice	**[+ve]**	**[+ve]**
mgt's readiness to change	**committed**	pro-active
nature of change	+	**revolutionary**
scope of change	**improvement**	champion emergence
managed of change	**alleviation of dissatisfaction**	onset
e-Business Mgt Practice		
e-business measurement	**use of e-bus metrics**	**audit**
use of tools and techniques	**superior**	**adequate**
use of team-based structure	+	+

Table 2c: Findings of *Outcomes and Performance Gains*in the Business Framework

Component / *Constructs*	Supplier Organisation "Dell"	Customer Organisation "Customer.com"
quality of work life	employee satisfaction	employee satisfaction
B2B resourcing	cost savings (+), choice (NA), quality (+), reliable (+)	cost savings (**25%**), choice (+), quality (+), reliable (+)
B2B networking	1st B2B customer	1st B2B supplier

that discipline that helps executive teams to articulate and better understand their strategies. In addition, the BSC enables organisations to introduce a new governance and review process that is focused on strategy and not on tactics. The governance process emphasises learning, team problems solving and coaching.

More recently, leading firms that have begun to undertake e-BC to meet strategic goals recognise that they only accomplish their objectives through people. If effectively managed, employees should ultimately be more productive in their work tasks and better able to serve customers, suppliers, and business partners. The key constructs that can be probed here are; gaps between effectiveness expectations (goals) and actual performance improvements, eg efficient company resourcing, quality of employee work life, customer satisfaction - from Venkatraman and Henderson's view of "virtual organising" (1998).

6. FUTURE STUDIES

In the future e-business with ERP technologies will play an integral part in helping established enterprises build and operate B2B e-procurement solutions, and eventually lead to the development of electronic marketplaces. Also as e-business adoption becomes common place, corporate portals for empowering employees will be considered as an economic necessity. When these corporate front-end systems begin to look and feel the same, the real competitive advantage will ultimately come from the ERP back-end systems.

The next wave of economic advantage lies in revenue generation from business opportunities in new e-business models. As business strategy shifts from just cost savings to revenue generation, this research framework is recommended as tool for future study of the broad and new complex phenomenon of e-ERP implementations.

In general future research will need to consider the theoretical conjecture; an e-business project built on the strong foundation of an ERP (or equivalent component-based system) that can provide information for all business partners, and process incoming information from customers and suppliers, is much more likely to succeed than one lacking this foundation.

7. CONCLUSIONS

The case study showed how *Customer.com* is currently using B2B integration with *Dell* and its SAP system to provide immediate process efficiencies, and should provide a model for use with all our other suppliers. This e-business solution is made possible by an integrated architecture of a variety of backend systems and procurement applications or systems. The primary beneficiaries were the corporate customers, through the automation of B2B e-procurement and customer details management.

The case presented was used primarily to test the suitability of an established research framework for gathering evidence to identify the factors for success of an e-business project. The research framework was chosen as a methodology for its ability to examine complex phenomena. It is seen as evolutionary in nature, and was content driven. It is primarily a diagnostic tool for identifying factors contributing to success of new business models. It is *not* seen as a prognostic tool. It would appear to have some use by business professionals/consultants in e-business change projects.

The adapted research framework for e-business change was used to identify the factors for success of this e-business project within an ERP environment. The results confirm the previous findings from studies in the area of "business process change". Here the e-business project was found to have facilitators in all components of the business framework, including the change environment and project management. Further, findings from the other case studies showed; the least successful e-business projects were found to have inhibitors in both dimensions, especially in the area of cultural readiness and change management. In this case, employee satisfaction was derived from an overall acceptance to change in administrative processes and IT use. This highlights the need to encourage the balancing of conflicting organisational and people needs, when contemplating the implementation of e-business solutions.

As e-business adoption becomes common place, corporate portals for empowering employees will be considered as an economic necessity, such as e-procurement for employees. The next wave of economic advantage lies in revenue generation from new business opportunities in other business-to-business models. These are complex problems that can never be solved with technology alone. They require executive commitment, leadership, with appropriate problem solving skills, for the developing a network of e-business relationships.

REFERENCES

Ash, C.G. (1998). Knowledge Management and the Electronic Consultative Enterprise: A Case for Integrating SAP R/3 with the Internet, In *Proceedings of the 8th Workshop in Information Technologies and Systems (WITS'98)* ICIS'98, Helsinki, 11-12 Dec, 1998

Ash, C.G. Rossouw, A. (1999). Internet Enterprise Resource Planning Pilot Project: A Case for Maximising the Synergy between Teaching, Research and Industry, *Proceedings of the Institutions of Higher Learning Forum* at SAPPHIRE'99, Singapore, Nov 99

Ash, C.G. Zach, A. (1999). The Friends of the Bibbulmun Track: A Case for Building e-Business Communities, In *Proceedings of BIT'99 Conference* – Manchester, UK; 3-4 Nov. 99

Ash, C.G. (2000). An e-Commerce Model for Extending ERP Systems onto the Internet: An Australian Perspective, In *Proceedings of the International Conference of Enterprise Information Systems, ICEIS'2000* -Stafford, UK 4-7 July, 2000

Boey, P. Grasso, M. Sabatino, G. Sayeed, I. (1999). Architecting eBusiness Solutions, Vol II No. 7 [http://www.cutter.com/consortium/freestuff/dcar9907.html

Dell, M. Fredman, C. (1999) *Direct from Dell: Strategies that Revolutionised an Industry*, HarperBusiness, NY, USA. Chap. 13

Fan, M. Stallaert, J. Whinston, A.B. (2000) "The adoption and design methodologies of component-based enterprise systems, "*European Journal of Information Systems,* 9; 25-35

Guha, S. Grover, V. Kettinger, W.J. Eng, J.T.C. (1997). Business Process Change and Organisational Performance: Exploring an Antecedent Model, *Journal of Management Information Systems*, Vol. 14, No1; 119-154.

Handy, C. (1989) *The Age of Unreason*, Harvard Business School Press, UK; 57-80

Hesterbrink, C. (1999). e-Business and ERP: Bringing two Paradigms together, Price Waterhouse Coopers, Sept '99. [http://www.pwc.com]

Kalakota, R. Robinson, M. (1999). *e-Business: Roadmap for Success*, Addison-Wesley Longman, MA, USA; 56-58

Kaplan, R.S. (1996) *Translating strategy into Action: The Balanced Scorecard*, Harvard Business School Press.

Mintzberg, H. Westley, F. (1992). Cycles of Organisational Change, *Strategic Management Journal*, 13; 39-59

Norris, G. Hurley, J.M. Hartley, K.M. Dunleavy, J.R. Balls, J.D. (2000) *E-Business and ERP: Transforming the Enterprise*, PricewaterhouseCoopers, John Wiley & sons, USA

Norton, R.K. (1992) "The Balanced Scorecard- Measures that Drive Performance", *Harvard Business Review* Jan-Feb '92

Pereira, R.E. (1999) "Resource View Theory Analysis of SAP as a Source of Competitive Advantage for Firms", *The DATA BASE for Advances in Information Systems*, Winter 1999, Vol. 30, No. 1; 38-46

SAP (1999). e-Business Solutions, mySAP.com, http://www.sap.com/solutions/ecommerce/

Venkatraman, N. Henderson, J.C. (1998). Real strategies for Virtual Organising, *Sloan Management Review*, Fall '98; 33-48

QOS NEGOTIATION BASED ON MANAGEMENT DELEGATES

José Luís Oliveira, Rui L. Aguiar
Dep. de Electrónica e Telecomunicações, Universidade de Aveiro, 3810-193 Aveiro, Portugal,
E-Mail: jlo@det.ua.pt , ruilaa@ua.pt

Keywords: Network Management, Service Management, Agents, QoS.

Abstract: The introduction of Quality of Service in the Internet will bring increased needs for efficient service management in the network. Current approaches to this problem rely on distributed management protocols with centralized service control points. This paper proposes the usage of software agents for this task, developed in a two-stage approach due to its implementation complexity. The usage of agents, supported by appropriate platforms, would naturally provide delegation and control mechanisms, improve management flexibility and even transparently support the existence of multiple management paradigms across network operators.

1. INTRODUCTION

With the growing complexity of network infrastructures and end-user services, Internet Service Providers (ISPs) will be faced with a major challenge: the implementation of management structures able to cope with these network improvements. Furthermore, the unpredictable nature of these evolving changes, both in terms of capabilities (the type of facilities being provided) and of dimension (the number and type of elements to be managed), will also compel these novel management paradigms to develop evolutionary capabilities. It is clear that the introduction of Quality of Service (QoS) on IP-based networks will bring a new set of management issues. Nevertheless, these new management paradigms will have to be built still upon current management structures. The convergence of both present and future management models into a common working framework is thus critical for Internet evolution, supporting the transition between current and future Internet services. This trend is followed inside the corporation by the increased trend on business process integration, with the electronic commerce proliferation and its impact on the enterprise. This situation is further complicated by telecommunication liberalisation and regulation policies, which are promoting an environment where competitors must work together behind the information society umbrella, posing new interoperation requirements to information technology management systems. Competing service providers will have to work in cooperative fashion, both between themselves and with their customers, in order to make the most of the network they have - and the introduction of QoS will place extra challenges on them.

In fact, one of the major problems of the Internet in the near future will be its (current) inability to provide efficient support to multi-service, multi-party communications, when different parties are under the administrative control of different entities, providing different services (or pursuing different goals). The interrelationships between ISPs and between ISPs and large corporations will become complex business transactions, in a multi-level service environment. This summons the issue of service management for corporation practices. Service management aspects have been outside the scope of the Internet community until now, although currently some related activities have been initiated inside this community. IP "management architecture" efforts have been concentrated over two primary issues: management information definition, and management protocols, i.e., they are focused on network device management.

In this paper we propose a framework where mobile agents can play an important role in solving some of the upcoming problems connected with service characteristics, administrative boundary definitions, and information-flow layer definitions. This framework presents large advantages in terms

J. Filipe et al. (eds.), Enterprise Information Systems III, 295–302.

of evolution and flexibility, defining interfaces between multiple management entities and levels, which can then be implemented separately by different domains. This framework will be presented for simplicity mainly from the point of view of inter-ISP management; nevertheless it can be also applied to large corporations, creating conditions for close joint service management between corporations and their ISPs. This is a foreseeable evolution following the trends inside large communication providers for the creation of specific companies for handling large customers.

2. QOS REQUIREMENTS AND SERVICES

The appearance of new transport services in the Internet has been recognized for a long time, and they are associated with the introduction of QoS in ISP-based services (Partridge, 1992). According to current transport proposals, one can cluster these new services around three main types (Aguiar, 1999), graded in terms of implementation complexity for management purposes:

A. Quantitative QoS Transport Services - these services characterize themselves by a Service Level Agreement (SLA) where a fixed minimum quantifiable QoS is assured. Example: the Virtual Leased Line (VLL) service, where the ISP provides a virtual connection line between two sites.
B. Relative QoS Transport Services - These services characterize themselves by providing the corporation with a fixed relative assurance regarding its own traffic in every situation. Example: the Olympic service, where the traffic is classified in three different classes, with different drop probabilities in case of network congestion.
C. Variable QoS Transport Services - These services present variable QoS parameters that will depend on characteristics (or requests) from the corporation traffic. The customer will be able to request/change QoS parameters for their packets, according to its own needs. Although these services may, upon instantiation, map themselves onto one of the previous service types, their on-demand characteristics increase their implementation complexity significantly, placing these services in a class by itself. Example: "Pay-per-Request", where the customer requests (and pays for) the type of QoS it requires from the network for every connection is desires to set up.

Many variants are possible, according to market demand, tariff policies, and management flexibility in the ISP network. For instance, "time-based variable tariffs" (where cost changes with a time schedule), and "time-based variable bandwidths" (where available connections change with the time of day) can be applied to most service descriptions, with more complex management functions. Time-based variable tariffs will need to register the traffic being processed, and calculate total costs according to the time of the day. Time-based variable bandwidths will allow different QoS along the time. Some simple time-based and amount-of-traffic-dependent services can already be found today, supported by proper management software (HP, 1998).

All of the above services can be used to provide some end-user guaranties across the Internet, independent of the type of traffic being carried by the network. This will advance the emergence of new services, especially in the multimedia arena. Although these services should be independent of the type of traffic being transported, quite different subjective end-user perceptions on the existing QoS may exist depending on the transport service carrying the data. Some types of data may lend itself to better end-user perception with some types of transport services than with others (e.g. real-time video distribution will generally present poor performance with relative QoS services). Thus, it is natural that in a competitive telecommunications world, different operators may specialize in the delivery of specific services.

Typical requirements for end-user applications over these transport services can be identified (Table I). These applications (ranging from video conferencing to Computer Supported Cooperative Work (CSCW), from e-commerce to voice over IP, and including video broadcasting) can be classified in terms of parameters such as the need for authentication, chargeability (who will need to support the service payment), the type of bandwidth requirements, the traffic round trip time (RTT), the importance of jitter and packet loss, the policy time horizon (PRRT), the need for multicast and for dynamic contract negotiation, and the service type, from those described above (Aguiar, 1999) (deLaat, 1999).

Mapping these end-user services over specific IP transport services is a complex decision, which will be made depending on each ISP mix of services, traffic patterns, customer requirements, and equipment characteristics. Providing corporations with these facilities across distinct ISP domains becomes a complex task, especially when several technology solutions and management strategies are used. Furthermore, corporations may implement

Table I: Typical Requirements for high-level applications in the Internet
I – Initiator, P – Peer, C – client, S – server,
MAB – minimum assured bandwidth, CBR – constant bit-rate, VBR – variable bit-rate

	Authentication	Payment	BW	RTT	Jitter allowed	Multicast	Pkt loss allowed	Max PRTT	Dynam. contract	Service type
Computer-based training	I	C	MAB			Y		min		quantit
CSCW: data	I+P	C	MAB	X		Y		days	Y	variable
CSCW control	I+P	C	MAB	X				days		quantit
E-commerce	I+P	C/S						sec		relativ
Distributed Computing	All	All						days		relativ
IP voice-telephony	I	I	CBR	X	no		Y	sec	Y	quantit
Video telephony	I	I	VBR	X	no		Y	sec	Y	quantit
Video group broadcast	I	C	VBR		no	Y				quantit
Video conferencing	I+P	All	VBR	X	no	Y	Y	min	Y	variable

their own policies in controlling their own contracted ISP-provided services (for instance, a corporation may support a "paid-connection" IP-based helpdesk). This will be the typical environment for advanced service management systems in the future.

The Internet is providing (or at least trying to…) a new set of technological solutions that support part of the issues required to control network bandwidth in order to provide network-wide QoS. A scalable mechanism for the introduction of QoS in the network has been developed by the IETF Differentiated Services (DS) group (Blake, 1998). DS define classes of service that must be provided by internetworking equipment in order to fulfill high level SLAs. Currently, with already existing products that claim to be DS conformant the degradation in flow throughput is relatively high. We have performed some tests over different network configurations (using commercial equipment in several *in-lab* topologies) and one of out main conclusions was that simply marking at an ingress router degrades transfer rates ci. 30% (Pinto, 2000). This problem can be solved through two major features: equipment enhancement and management optimization.

These technological and performance issues are disjoint from the services themselves, which are "translated" in terms of equipment characteristics by network management entities. Services, by themselves, are not defined in the DS work, and a clear separation is made between the services and the network building blocks supporting these services. SLAs are established between the corporation and the ISP; the service provider will convert this in specifications mapped in the network equipment. (Work on some aspects of SLA standardization has just begun inside the IETF).

The independence between the services and the supporting technology is an issue of paramount importance for understanding potential service management problems. On the lower transport level, some providers may resort to RSVP, MPLS or ATM for providing similar transport services – and certainly some mix of a multitude of technologies will occur in the Internet. Several management strategies may be in place at the same time across a set of distinct domains, supporting a single end-to-end service. This complexity lead to the notion of Bandwidth Broker (BB), a (logically centralized) entity able to manage and control each DS domain, handling the interaction between the device and service management.

This is quite far from basic Internet management, until recently guided by the simplicity and minimalism that originated the very successful SNMP framework. Despite its on-going evolutions (SNMPv3), it still lacks scalability due to the inherent broad range of management information and polling-based operations. The introduction of differentiated services into the network will highlight these limitations even further. Considering *system integration* as a requirement from future customers for advanced Internet services, a common platform allowing the management of network, services, systems and users is to be expected. This goal may seem to imply, for instance, that such entities as Bandwidth Brokers (Nielsen, 1999) or Police Enforcement Points (Yavatkar, 1999) should be controlled by SNMP – if it aims to remain as the reference management framework. The adequacy to SNMP to such a wide range of management operations is still an open issue.

The successive changes on network equipment imply continuously new added features that turn the management of these systems more and more complex. This is especially true as large corporations will pressure for full integration of their business processes, and thus will cooperate with ISPs for improved transport service management. Agent technology can be the metaphor that is needed to handle this complexity. With the ability to perform actions on behalf of other programs or on behalf of the user, agents can be used on areas such as information retrieval (Nekrestyanov, 1999), electronic commerce (Gleizes, 1999), personal mobility, telecommunications and user interfaces (Green, 1997)) just to name a few. Mobile agents are a special kind of agents that have also the ability to migrate from host to host, carrying data, code, and execution state. Mobile agents are increasingly being considered for managing networks and services (Lopes, 1999).

3. MOBILE AGENTS IN SERVICE MANAGEMENT

The establishment of a service with QoS across different entities will require multiple actions between multiple parties: In the example illustrated in Figure 1, if the autonomous domains (AD) A and D need to establish a QoS-enabled connection, in order to support the communication requirements of corporations 1 and 2, AD A has to establish a service agreement with B, C and D to support the QoS parameters in that connection, and agree with them to manage their network in order to maintain this contract. Service management will have to handle all the different aspects of this environment, providing support for service subscription, service invocation and negotiation, conformance validation, network configuration, etc…

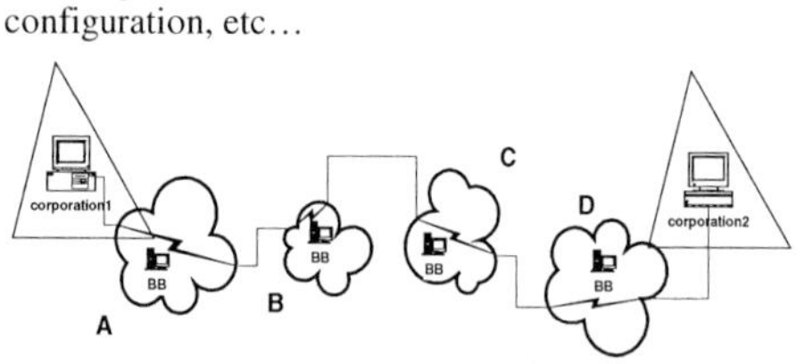

Figure 1: Two corporations establishing a connection through four autonomous domains (AD)

Even for this reasonably simple topology, on-demand VPN (a foreseeable popular service for corporations) service management, for instance, potentially encompasses quite different technologies and managements systems – some of which were referred in section II. Each AD will be under the administrative management of a (logically centralized) bandwidth broker. This entity will use its own policies and protocols to manage its domain, in a way completely unrelated with its neighbor domains. Thus inter-domain service management may be extraordinary complex. Furthermore, corporations may even be lacking information on the transport networks (B, C) connecting their service providers (A, D).

Current approaches to this problem are mainly concerned with the service subscription aspect. They rely on the definition of common sets of service specifications and usage to establish inter-BB communication. Besides handling only a small part of the service management problem, this approach presents two shortcomings: a) it impairs the global provision of special services, which may be required by corporation with needs outside the scope considered in the common set of services; and b) it places the control of a distributed service (e.g. the service being provided by ISP A to corporation1) under several administrative entities, and subject to multiple different management implementations, which may interpret service requirements in a strict (or not) sense. The ideal situation is for AD A, in close cooperation with corporation1, to control the way B implements the service requested by A; what we achieve in the inter-BB situation is AD B implementing the service A requested, by its own policies and strategies.

Previous work has shown the possibilities of integrating mobile agents (MA) technology in current SNMP-oriented environments (Lopes, 2000, 2001). Such integrated agents can ultimately provide a tool for the solution of these problems. However, due to the inherent complexity of the overall systems under discussion, we devised a two-step deployment strategy in the evolutionary path for the introduction of agents for service management. These two phases cover two different aspects on the interchange of information between bandwidth brokers (or between the corporation management system and the ISP), to be deployed in different time frames, as more knowledge and standardization on mechanisms for service management of QoS in the Internet develops. In the first phase, agents are simply treated as the entities communicating the resource reservations regarding each end-to-end service. In the second phase, these agents are treated as the actual management delegates inside BBs, with specific management capabilities being delegated on these agents.

3.1 Agents as tools for reservation information

Our initial management approach, with agents as mobile reservation tools, use MA to signal reservation between BBs in a way parallel to IntServ resource reservation via RSVP or other proposals concerning BB interoperation (Yavatkar, 1999) (T'Joens, 2000). For the establishment of an end-to-end connection, requests are sent across the autonomous domains (and not the machines, as in RSVP), and equipment configuration is performed (if required) independently by each AD. This is the simple concept discussed in Nielsen, 1999 (see Figure 2). However, in our approach this is done not by successive requests on network QoS parameters between each BB, but by sending mobile code to the required BBs, able to negotiate agreements with each AD.

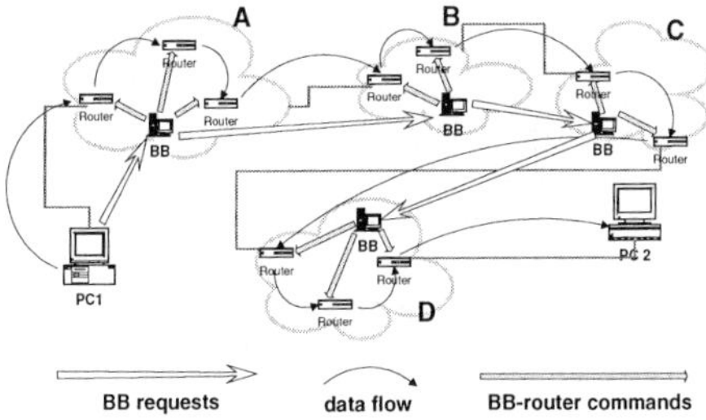

Figure 2: Two machines establishing a connection: requests and commands in the BBs

Thus we have a mobile agent that will initially run across the whole connection (in a simulated environment). This agent has clear parameters (from the point of view of the initiator) regarding the type of resources that it requires and the limits of negotiation he is able to use.

As the agent crosses the successive administrative domains, it exchanges information with each BB regarding the type of assurance it can provide in his own domain. It will collect information while transversing the network, until receiving enough information to decide upon the refusal or fulfillment of the connection. While moving from one domain to another, this agent tries to negotiate with the local BB the possibility(ies) of a connection with the specific QoS parameters that it requires. Depending on the domain, these parameters may have to be adapted and negotiated; those processing instructions are integrated in the agent (and thus completely under the control of the initiating domain) and the negotiation with the bandwidth broker in the next domain already includes results from previous domains, as the agent moves onwards. If successive constrains placed by different domains make the connection unfeasible, then the agent migrates to the initiating domain; otherwise it may reserve the resources until it releases them (either by the end of the connection or by issuing a release due "request refusal").

While the agent negotiates with each BB, it is able to collect connection parameters for each domain. In our implementation, the parameters used are: the minimum and peak bandwidths granted, and associated maximum packet drop probability; the estimated connection latency inside the domain; timing information (when the connection can be assured and for how long), cost class, and an administrative reference pointer. This pointer, currently unused, can be used for the exchange of further administrative information between domains (e.g. as an indirection to business support tools). These parameters were chosen by simplicity and flexibility to provide several of the services in Table I. The agent is issued a request with some possible values for these parameters, and uses parameters returned by the BB either to decide upon the establishment (or reservation) of the connection or to return relevant information to the initiating domain.

Each BB can return several groups of parameters to the agent (presently organized by different classes of cost). The operation of the agent can be easily exemplified. While transversing the domains, the agent is able to calculate (e.g.) the estimated connection latency that the connection will have; it is then able to interrupt the set-up of the connection if it concludes that this parameter will not be fulfilled. If the connection latency can be fulfilled, the agent may be requesting an "immediate" connection and find out that the connection can only start up after a couple of minutes – and this alternative may be acceptable for the invoking domain. It can then conclude the connection and return the information "connection to be established in five (e.g.) minutes" and request for information to proceed. It may also return two different connection setups possibilities, presenting different costs, if unable to make a final decision.

In this approach, each BB needs only to understand the requests each agent is placing to its resources, and does not have to understand what would be the reasonable negotiation rules for this particular agent. The BB-agents negotiation scenario allows for multiple possibilities of connection establishment, with different costs associated, while all the intelligence decisions will remain with the agent – issued by the BB (or by the information management system of a large corporation) that required the end-to-end service. By contrast, in a

BB-communication model (T'Joens, 2000) each node has to understand the parameters, and be able to provide composition rules for each parameter it understands (Shker, 1997). This approach is not flexible in a complex, multi-service environment, as these rules can change according to end-user applications and different network management policies. Furthermore, if corporations execute their own management on the contracted services, their own policies can change according to variable business interests, further complicating these composition rules.

The complexity of such a BB over traditional approaches is centered in the simple interface provided to the agents (typically for parameter configuration) and in the agent platform, which can be managed through SNMP (Lopes, 2000). Nevertheless the added complexity this approach allows greater scalability of service management in the network.

The advantages of using agents in this task, if one imagines a situation where many domains are transversed for a single service, and each domain has to support many connections, are centered on flexibility and timing. The "management agent" may allow for a faster connection setup (specially if large connection data is exchanged) and provides for a more flexible acceptance of service requests. This flexibility is centered in the initiator of the connections, which is the entity that has a clear knowledge of what type of compromises it is able to accept. If only two domains were involved, a simple protocol between both BBs would be sufficient. However, the concatenation of the facilities across multiple domains is a more complex issue, and the ability of the code to make the decisions in-site, without the need for the information to travel back to the originator, increases significantly its efficiency. In our view, agents do not provide "Intelligence on Demand", but they are "Pushing Management" through the network.

This paradigm presents costs in terms of network traffic. Similar results could be achieved if the invoking domain established direct negotiations with each one of the domains to be transversed in series. Instead of "pushing management" code, the invoking domain would sequentially "pull information" from the other domains (Figure 3). For each domain, multiple sets of connection parameters could have to be pulled, hence creating significant network traffic. However, when the agent is the requesting element, complex MA can present implementation sizes with significant dimension, and thus present small advantage in terms of network efficiency. Thus the biggest advantage of this methodology is the evolution path that it provides for the introduction of agents as actual management delegates inside bandwidth brokers.

3.2 Agents as management delegates

If QoS capabilities become common in the Internet, then the management of each domain will become much more complex, with technologies as Differentiated Services and MPLS, or even IntServ services, being deployed. The range of services to be provided is probably quite diverse (Aguiar, 1999), as discussed in section II, and severe management problems will appear for cross-domain service requests. No fixed management configuration will be able to provide services on-demand in this type of environment. Most of the traffic patterns across the Internet are short-lived, and long setup establishment times will not be useful in this situation. This means that each BB will need to provide response to service requests in short time, often from AD quite far (in geographic terms) from its own. This could lead to changes in the typically peering agreements between neighborhood ADs, which brings an added ISP economic complexity to this process. Complex transport agreements, with multiple entities would have to be devised, and managed.

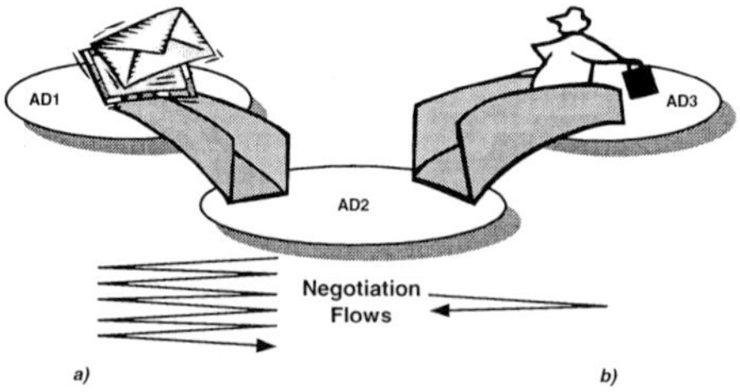

Figure 3: SLA: A message-oriented negotiation (a) versus a mobile delegate approach (b)

This last complexity is not strictly required. It is much more reasonable (and more usual in the current telecommunications world) for each AD to still establish contracts with its neighbors, and to assume that every request from its neighbor is to be charged under that contract, leaving the responsibility of passing eventual costs to other parties and their neighbors.

In this context, the contract between ISPs should still rely on bandwidth usage, improved with some associated QoS parameters. However, this basic "QoS-bandwidth" notion will need to expand from the simple interconnection interface to cover transport services across the AD. For instance, referring to our Figure 1, AD B may have a SLA with AD A stating "the neighbor AD A will have a 2 Mbps connection to me, and I will assure that 1

Mbps of its traffic will reach other domains with top priority". In this type of situation, domains are actually sub-allocating some of their resources to their neighbors. This is our reference management framework: ISPs will establish contracts where they will "rent" some of their resources to the traffic originating from their peers. As an added-bonus, this situation simplifies the setup time of each connection request, as the contracts between ISPs will naturally imply large blocks of traffic to benefit from multiplexing effects. Thus, a specific flow will not need to wait for the setup of the whole connection across the multiple domains: in principle this connection will be established (or at least all the administrative issues are already resolved).

Agents will be a natural tool for this environment. If some resources of an AD are "rented" to its peers, these may be (between certain limits) managed by these same peers. Returning to our previous example, domain A could prefer to reserve half of the top-priority 1Mbps connection (through domain B) for HTTP traffic to domain C – and could decide to change its policy at any time. This would be an independent decision by domain A. Its SLA with domain B would have to cover bounds on management capabilities, but as long as A kept these limits, it could manage these resources inside B. Thus it would configure "its" connection in domain B according to its desires. This leads to a BB architecture that is able to "delegate" internally some of its responsibilities to a "representative" of other domains – that is, a BB able to support mobile agents. An agent from domain A migrates to the BB inside B upon a first service request (or upon administrative agreement between both domains, when neighbors). This same agent will handle further service requests (with a proprietary protocol, e.g.) from domain A to domain B.

The BB is the recipient for the agents' engine - a MASIF-compliant one such as presented in Lopes, 2001, since it provides rules for MA interchange between different platforms. With the added SNMP functionality, this agent platform can be updated without changes to the BB system; the interaction between the platform and the BB is done through the SNMP MIB. The agents by themselves, their complexity and degree of autonomy, are the responsibility of the issuing domain (e.g. a corporation managing its SLA). Agents will naturally have a living period limited by peering agreements between domains, and their operation limits will be constrained by the terms of this agreement (enforced by the domain policies). In our model, two levels of policy and admission control will be performed inside the BB: each QoS-connection request from a foreign domain will have to be validated by the resident MA of this domain, and the overall resource utilization (and/or network reconfiguration) will have to be validated by the MA/BB policy manager.

This scenario is a feasible evolution for our current work of agents as tools for reservation information, and provides large management flexibility with minimal network overhead. Services become mostly independent of agreements between specific management policies of different ISPs. The introduction of a new service by an ISP will simply require the replacement of its mobile code in all ISPs where it wants to support this new service. This task is not dependent on those domains, as long as the generic conditions of the SLAs already established are fulfilled. In our envisaged scenario agents would seldom travel (this would only happen when new peering agreements are established or new services are implemented), and thus the size of the agent is not a primary issue. However, the agent could be able to provide management at such a fine degree of granularity as the issuing domain requires, and would handle all the multiple data exchange required for any supported service, and for any change in the service.

Although network traffic would still be required for service establishment, this traffic could be mostly limited to neighborhood domains. In fact, in the limit, each MA could be though as a remote instance of a primary management system, and thus, given a specific service request, could perform the required actions only with the available information in that domain. If information of other domain is still needed, the MA can integrate is own information in the request, and pass this information to this adjacent domain – where a "similar" MA would reside, equally able to answer this service request as the first MA. Naturally, a trade-off between the MA capabilities (compared with the main management system in its primary domain) and its complexity and size will exist, and this will depend on the services each domain provides and the agreements it has with its neighbors. In our scenario, complex services could eventually be provided through provider networks that are offering much simpler services.

4. CONCLUSIONS

In this paper we analyzed issues surrounding the problems of service management in the Internet, in a multi-party, multi-service framework, with large corporations performing some control of their contracted ISP-transport services. Due to the needs of increasing management complexity and simple evolution paths, agent technology seems to be a flexible tool for supporting advanced service management.

The usage of agents for bandwidth brokers has then been described, in two different situations. In a first phase we implemented agents as tools for reservation information, able to negotiate connection parameters across several autonomous domains. This approach can then be extended for agents as management delegates, creating an evolvable framework for managing services. Agents will migrate across the network as services are deployed, and will handle their own part of the network management. This framework effectively decouples service implementation from the multiple management problems specific to each domain, implementing a distributed management architecture based on mobile agents.

REFERENCES

Aguiar, R., Oliveira, J.L., 1999, "New Services on an Advanced Internet", in *Multimedia Applications, Services and Techniques*, Helmut Leopold, Narciso Garcia (Eds.), Springer-Verlang, pp.197-211.

Blake, S., et al., 1998, "An Architecture for Differentiated Services", *RFC 2475*.

deLaat, C., Gommans, L., 1999, "User scenarios for Networking Policy control".

Gleizes, M., Léger, A., Athanassiou, E. and Glize, P., 1999, "Self-Organization and Learning in MultiAgent Based Brokerage Services", *International Conference on Intelligence in Services and Networks*, IS&N'99.

Green S., Hurst L., Nangle B., Cunningham P., Somers F. and Evans R., 1997, Software Agents: A review.

HP, 1998, "Billing for Internet usage", Telecommunications News, 16, Hewlett Packard European Edition.

Lopes, R., Oliveira, J.L., 1999, "Software Agents in Network Management", *1st International Conference on Enterprise Information Systems* - ICEIS'99.

Lopes, R., Oliveira, J.L, 2000, "Managing Mobile Agents with SNMP", *Proc. of the Simposio Español de Informatica Distribuida*, SEID 2000.

Lopes, R., Oliveira, J.L, 2001, "SNMP management of MASIF platforms", *IFIP/IEEE International Symposium on Integrated Network Management*, IM 2001.

Neilsen, R., et al, 1999, "A Discussion of Bandwidth Broker Requirements for Internet2 Qbone Deployment, Version 0.7", Internet 2 Q-Bone Requirements,

Nekrestyanov, I., O'Meara, T., Patel, A., Romanova, E., 1999, "Building Topic-Specific Collections with Intelligent Agents", *International Conference on Intelligence in Services and Networks*, IS&N'99.

Partridge, Craig, 1992 "A proposed flow Specification", *RFC 1363*.

Pinto, A., Valente, R., Aguiar, R., Oliveira, J.L., 2000, "Managing QoS over IP", *Internal Report*, Universidade de Aveiro.

Shker, S., Wroclaswski, J., 1997, "General Characterization Parameters for Integrated Service Network Elements", *RFC 2215*.

T'Joens, Y., et al., 2000, "Service Level Specification and Usage Framework", IETF draft-manyfolks-sls-framework-00.txt.

Yavatkar, R., et al., 1999, "A Framework for Policy-based Admission Control", Internet Draft <draft-ietf-rap-framework-03.txt.

MAY YOUR INFORMATION SERVICE LIVE IN INTERESTING TIMES...

Engineering Dynamic Service Environments

Steven Willmott
Artificial Intelligence Laboratory, Ecolé Polytechnique Fédérale de Lausanne, Lausanne, Switzerland
Email: steven.willmott@epfl.ch

Bernard Burg
Hewlett-Packard Laboratories, 1501 Mill Page Road, MS 1u-16, Palo Alto, California
Email: bernard_burg@hpl.hp.com

Paul O'Brien
BT ExaCT, BT Adastral Park, MLB1/PP12, Martelsham Heath, Ipswich, Suffolk, United Kingdom
Email: paul.d.obrien@bt.com

Keywords: Dynamic services, Service composition and Technology convergence

Abstract: Information systems are undergoing a transformation - they are becoming faster, richer, more intelligent, personalised and mobile. Furthermore, some of the greatest advances may yet be to come with the creation of networked environments supporting complex direct interaction between heterogeneous information systems: enabling services to act autonomously, discover one another, provide services to each other and dynamically form composite information services. This paper paints a vision of such future "Dynamic Service Environments", outlines the technologies which may play a role in creating them and discusses some of the challenges that lie ahead.

1. INTRODUCTION

Information Systems as we know them are undergoing great changes – vastly increased bandwidth, access over mobile devices, an explosion of consumer users and rapidly increasing business take-up. In all this change however, arguably the largest potential paradigm shift on the horizon is the move towards enabling information services to interact directly and automatically with *one another*, to dynamically construct new and valuable compound services and pro-actively exploit business opportunities on behalf of their owners. Such advances would lead to new generations of information services able to flexibly integrate themselves into the information environment and form part of an on-line Dynamic Service Environment (DSE).

Although such an environment may seem years away, aspects of it already exist today and current technological developments provide us with many of the tools needed to make DSEs a reality.

This paper aims to:

- Paint a vision of future DSEs, including a discussion of their important requirements.
- Provide an overview of which emerging technologies are likely to contribute to the vision.
- Outline some of the challenges that lie ahead.

A discussion of this sort is clearly a major undertaking and this paper can only hope to scratch the surface. The authors hope to provide a broad overview and a useful snapshot of today's technology trends.

2. DYNAMIC SERVICE ENVIRONMENTS

The idea of environments populated by autonomous flexible information services is certainly not new. Similar ideas can be found in many places from William Gibson's fantasy vision of the matrix

J. Filipe et al. (eds.), Enterprise Information Systems III, 303–311.

(Gibson 1984) to the visions of many research projects and, increasingly, industry mission statements. Although these visions vary in scale and scope, the more concrete goals often have recurring themes:

- Independence and resourcefulness: Services should be able to achieve their goals without a great deal of supervision, acting in a resourceful manner to solve unforeseen problems.
- Flexible interaction between services: Rather than being accessible only to human users or over specially crafted interfaces, services should provide interfaces abstract enough to support useful interaction with a wide range of other services.
- Automatic integration in the environment: Services should be able to automatically search out and make use of many related services (market places, auctions, partners, suppliers, directory services etc.).
- Fast, intelligent reaction to change: Services should be able to react to changes in the environment such as failures of partner services and pro-actively seize opportunities such filling new market niches.

2.1 Definition of a DSE

Common themes such as those given above have given rise a number of definitions of systems which might fulfil their aims. A number of definitions (such as Jennings 1998) define the essential characteristics of the entities (service providing entities) involved in such a system. Other definitions focus on properties of the types of interaction or relationships between entities that might be involved (Gasser 1991 for example). Building on these definitions allows us to attempt a definition of a DSE.

Dynamic Service Environment: A dynamic service environment is a system in which all of the following properties hold[1]:

1. Autonomy: services are provided by autonomous service providing entities.
2. Interaction: service providing entities are able to communicate meaningfully with one another.
3. Heterogeneity: the system may contain services of many different types, implementations, from multiple application domains.
4. Openness: service providing entities may join and leave the environment dynamically - opening the possibility that new, previously unknown services may appear and existing known services may disappear.
5. Dynamic Composition: that service entities are able to dynamically coordinate their interactions to provide services to each other and create new compound services.

In addition different services in a DSE would likely be owned by different organisations or individuals; making the DSE a shared space supporting complex interactions between diverse systems.

This "system level" definition is useful for two reasons 1) it allows us to specify the properties of the environment without unduly restricting ourselves to a particular technology (agents, ebXML or whatever), 2) the properties can be used to identify requirements for systems which might form part of the environment. I.e. starting from the problem rather than a solution.

2.2 The challenges of building a DSE

There are already environments which have some of the properties described in Section 2.1. The World Wide Web for example is a very open (thousands of new web pages are added every day), heterogeneous (there are web sites for almost every topic imaginable) and is made up of many autonomous service entities (individual web sites administered by different people), it does not however support communication between service entities particularly well nor does it provide for easy composition of information services. A CORBA application on the other hand might link a distributed set of autonomous services, allow them to communicate and provide services to one another but is likely to be limited in heterogeneity (usually purpose built for one application) and openness (not accepting new, previously unknown services). Enterprise middleware technologies, BEA systems weblogic for example) extend the CORBA model, providing open platforms which allow message based interaction across a heterogeneous environment, but fail to provide the rich semantic interoperability which allows the dynamic interaction between and composition of services envisioned in the DSE.

Despite the existence of systems which exhibit some of the properties of a DSE, fulfilling all properties one system is non trivial since some are potentially conflicting. Each of the criteria automation, heterogeneity and openness complicate effective interaction and dynamic composition of services:

[1] Properties such as security and scalability are clearly of great practical importance but these five properties appear to be fundamental to the concept of a DSE.

- Autonomy: the more autonomous systems are, the more difficult it is to ensure coherent, consistent behaviour for any subset of systems.
- Heterogeneity: the more heterogeneous systems become, the more complex it is to ensure that they can interoperate and work together effectively.
- Openness: the greater the amount of change in the environment, the more difficult it is to ensure that the systems present can work together effectively and provide consistent services.

These potential conflicts can be directly associated with three areas of recent technological development:

1. High-level control: as systems become more complex there is an increasing need to raise the level of abstraction at which they can be managed.
2. Flexible Interaction: The power of DSEs stems from the fact that arbitrary combinations of services could work together to provide new innovative services. This composition requires highly complex interaction and coordination between services and poses difficult challenges in supporting interactions between heterogeneous systems.
3. Automated resource discovery: in an open environment, increasingly sophisticated mechanisms are required to identify those services that can be usefully aggregated with one another.

These needs have long been recognised in the Artificial Intelligence, Knowledge representation and Computer Science communities and as recent technological development (see Section 3) shows, they are also increasingly important in commercial settings.

3. TECHNOLOGY LANDSCAPE

Technology trends in both academic and commercial settings are showing strong trends towards systems which might make DSEs a reality. This section reviews the technology areas that appear most relevant to DSEs.

Figure 1 groups together several technologies into three areas. Although not the only classification possible, this grouping appears to be useful to match technologies with the primary challenges DSE's pose: Autonomy, Heterogeneity and Openness (Section 2). The following sections deal with each of these areas, highlighting trends and identifying challenges ahead.

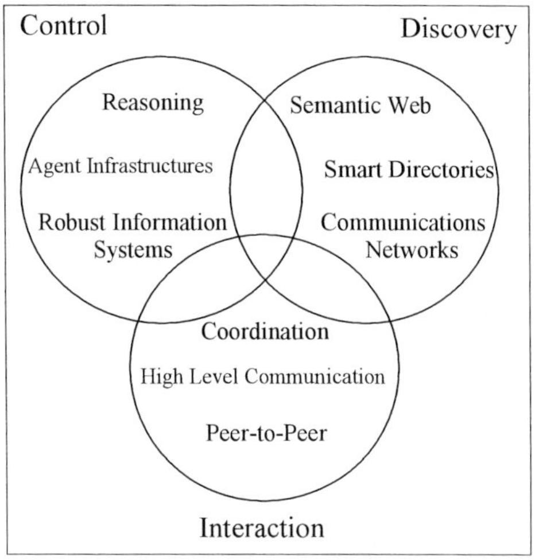

Figure 1: Technologies areas meeting the challenges of DSEs.

3.1 High Level Control

The three major technology areas are likely to contribute to making information services more autonomous and raising the level of abstraction at which they can be managed. These areas are: existing robust information system, agent infrastructure and reasoning techniques.

3.1.1 Robust Information Systems

Industrial strength information systems have been evolving rapidly, are able to handle millions of requests per day, scale effectively and provide increasingly powerful management tools.

Important trends are 1) increasingly intelligent content / systems management support tools, 2) multi-purpose/multiformat content delivery (e.g. for WAP/WML, HTML, XML, per browser optimisation) and 3) more sophisticated personalisation and customisation of information delivery, 4) A greater emphasis on interface abstraction in Business-to-business and Enterprise Application Integration tools, web service syndication, and market place management (VerticalNet others).

3.1.2 Agent Infrastructures

Agent technology's main strength is its focus on designing and managing systems of autonomous entities. Agent systems are likely to make a significant contribution to future automated services (Papazoglou 1998).

There are now a large number of toolkits available which enable developers to quickly construct multi-agent systems. Some of the most active efforts include FIPA-OS and Jade (open source implementations of the FIPA agent standard), JatLite (a popular agent platform supporting KQML), Retsina, Zeus and OAA (long running projects exploring many aspects of agent systems), Agentbuilder, JACK (commercial platforms offering a range of services), and mobile agent systems such as Grasshopper, Aglets and D'Agents.

There are strong trends towards increased standardisation (with large initiatives such as FIPA and efforts to standardise a Java Agent Services API, see JAS 2001), and a move towards supporting mobile devices (e.g. in the LEAP and Crumpet). Increasingly, toolkits are also including reasoning capabilities (see next section) and GUI management tools for deployed agents (see Section 3.2.2.)

3.1.3 Reasoning Systems

Finally, higher levels of control imply that systems will be required to perform more intelligent reasoning to match tasks assigned to them – requiring greater embedded intelligence. Artificial Intelligence research over the past 25 or more years has provided us with a large range of sophisticated reasoning techniques from symbolic methods such as: constraint satisfaction (Tsang 1994), case based reasoning (Leake 1996), expert systems (Forsyth 1984), planning (Tate 1990), automated reasoning (Wos 84) to non-symbolic AI such as genetic algorithms (Goldberg 1989), neural networks (Jordan 1996), Bayesian networks (Maritz 1989) and fuzzy logic (Zadeh 1988).

These approaches have most often been applied in stand-alone systems but increasingly more sophisticated reasoning systems are being implanted in agent-based systems. JESS (a Java based rule based reasoning system) for example has been integrated into FIPA-OS and Jade. ZEUS incorporates a planning and scheduling engine. Many agent systems (such as JAM! and dMars) are also based on particular reasoning mechanisms. Finally, AI reasoning techniques are now finding their way into commercial information systems (see Autonomy's systems for example).

3.1.4 Challenges

The three technology areas are therefore already growing together but major challenges lie ahead:

- Effectively merging agent infrastructures with robust information systems: most agent toolkits are still experimental and not robust, secure, efficient or scalable enough to be used for high traffic purposes. The task of bringing agent systems to the kind of reliability required for large-scale applications is complicated by the fact that they generally provide complex feature sets (agent language, task models, reasoning engines). Similarly, agent technology needs to become accessible to a broader software engineering community, requiring methodologies and toolkits that support the engineering of hybrid systems that combine agent technologies with traditional software technologies.
- Autonomous yet "predictable" behaviour: making services increasingly autonomous may improve their adaptability, resilience and scalability and increase their ability to exploit their environment. This deployment however opens up the possibility of less predictable behaviours requiring new approaches to management and which control but do not inhibit the beneficial effects of decentralised systems.
- Intelligence vs. Efficiency: many current implementations of reasoning systems are still research prototypes and the computations carried out are often inherently complex. Thus careful choices need to be made as to the type of reasoning systems applied in services.

3.2 Flexible Interaction

An environment supporting diverse types of services poses two types of interaction problem:

1. How to ensure that any two services can interact with one another.
2. How to ensure that groups of services interacting with one another to form a compound service coordinate their actions.

The first problem has lead to extensive work on high-level communication (agent language, ontologies); the second problem to developments in coordination technologies and new computing paradigms such as peer-to-peer.

3.2.1 High Level Communication

Agent and knowledge representation researchers in particular have long explored areas such as agent language, semantics of communication and ontologies. All of these appear to be essential if systems are to be able to communicate with each other in a sufficiently abstract manner. Agent communication languages such as FIPA-ACL and KQML are used in many contexts. Efforts in developing effective ontologies and ontology representations include work on Cyc, Ontolingua, DAML and OIL.

There are signs that what were often originally academic projects are now rapidly moving into industry (see Rapoza 2000 on DAML at W3C for example). Efforts such as ebXML, BizTalk, RosettaNet and eCo also demonstrate industry recognition of the importance of this type of semantic framework.

3.2.2 Coordination

Technologies and frameworks for coordinating large numbers of autonomous systems are an intensive area of research in the agent community. Approaches include social laws, organisations and coalition formation (studying large groups of autonomous systems) and planning, commitment, contracts, negotiation, game theory and tuple spaces (studying individual coordination problems). Research is complemented in industry by lower level coordination mechanisms such as CORBA and Enterprise Java Beans distributed transactions.

A large number of Agent toolkits include either some kind of built in coordination mechanism (TuCSoN uses tuple spaces for example), agent definition languages (MAST) or organisational design support (DeCaf, ZEUS, SIF, TuCSoN, MadKit, SWARM). Hence there is a clear effort to make coordination mechanisms available in toolkit form.

3.2.3 Peer-to-peer

Another area that has received a great deal of attention is that of peer-to-peer technologies (PtPWG 2001). Innovative services provided by companies such as Scour, Napster and Gnutella as well as projects such as SETI@Home have sparked interest by moving away from client-server based paradigms to distributing tasks and services over large numbers of independent nodes. These paradigms contribute to both new interactions models for DSEs and new ways for discovering distributed resources (see Section 3.3).

Although they are open and consist of many autonomous nodes, current examples of peer-to-peer systems are usually application driven (that is they serve a particular aim such as the sharing of music files). As heterogeneity becomes more important ("general purpose" peer-to-peer) issues such as domain and application level descriptions of services and resources are likely to become increasingly important.

3.2.4 Challenges

Current developments in these three areas are thus highly complimentary with the DSE vision, contributing understanding and models for richer, higher level interactions between individual service entities. Challenges include:

- Tools for high-level communication languages and ontologies: Agent communication language such as FIPA-ACL and KQML are logic based and have complex formal semantics. If non-logicians are to be expected to use them effectively they must either be simplified (potential resulting in loss of power) or come with comprehensive support tools.
- Verifying the validity and utility of semantic frameworks: although widely used communication languages such as FIPA-ACL are often used as "convenient syntax" and the semantics are at best loosely interpreted. There still remains a considerable way to go before these frameworks can be proven useful in large scale applications
- Integration of Agent Communication Language, Content Expressions and Ontology: It is not clear how best the work on ontology, content expressions (e.g. content languages such as KIF) and agent communication languages should be integrated. While such frameworks show promise they have yet to be applied outside highly domain dependent, small-scale demonstrators.
- Expressivity vs. Efficiency: the use of full modal logic languages (such as FIPA-ACL/SL) to express message content creates a powerful generic communication mechanism but is 1) probably beyond the needs of most applications and 2) suffers from the fact that complex reasoning engines are required to discern the meaning of messages (see Wooldridge 2000 for example).
- Complex service configurations: allowing arbitrary interactions between services opens up a Pandora's box of complex configuration and coordination issues. It is not clear that the overhead of applying automatic coordination mechanism will outweigh the gain in automation.
- Flexible composition vs. security: although increased flexibility in system-system interactions increases the potential power of information services, it also increases the risk of attack or failure. The greater the dependencies between services, the greater the risks of

catastrophic outages caused by a cascade effect resulting from attacks on or failures of key services.

3.3 Automated Resource Discovery

Once services are able to interact more directly with one another, the next major area of concern is locating the correct services to interact with and establishing the best mode of interaction. This is likely to be supported by contributions from three areas: Semantic Web developments, smart directories and advances in network technology. As recognised by many communities, this requires increasing the *semantic content* of service descriptions. Interface definitions will also need to define the kind of network services and other configuration required to support particular interactions. Such "semantic level" descriptions then need to be made available through powerful directory services.

3.3.1 Semantic web technology

Adoption of XML based solutions has been key in recent developments of information systems, with XML and RDF forming the basis for most of the current initiatives to providing more machine accessible descriptions of data (RDF usage in DAML, OIL Ontology mark-up) and interface description (serialisation to XML in SOAP). Developments such as XMI (OMG's metadata interchange framework), XSLT (enabling transformations between different XML documents) promise a second level of interoperability between heterogeneous systems.

Just as important as the technologies themselves are the extensive efforts to apply it – particularly in a business context: ebXML, BizTalk, eCo and others all use XML as a basis for defining frameworks for business interactions.

3.3.2 Smart Directories and Discovery

Recent developments have seen a number of technologies aimed at coordinating application services offered either within a single organisation or between organisations. These include E-Speak, UDDI, ebXML, BizTalk and eCo. One of the main motivations behind these systems is to create directories of registered applications with common interfaces. Applications can then be directly accessed by subscribers: creating a mechanism for dynamically discovering and accessing services.

3.3.3 Networks

Recent developments in network technology, particularly in the area of flexible Quality of Service management are essential to building effective DSEs. This need arises in IP networks with DiffServ (Bernet 1999) or MPLS (Baniramka 1999) traffic engineering as well as in connection-oriented networks. Particularly important is recent work on service level agreements that aims to make service provisioning more dynamic and flexible (Verma 1999)(Linnholt-Popien 2000). Without workable solutions for allocating network the resources needed by an information service the service cannot be delivered.

3.3.4 Challenges

The development in semantic web technologies and smart directories underlines the critical importance of flexible integration between business systems. Major challenges include:

- Effectively leveraging machine-readable content: This includes not only difficulties in merging ontologies/descriptions, but also the problem of linking acquired information to effective inference mechanisms able to make useful decisions.
- Smart Directories need to get smarter still: although efforts such as UDDI have the potential to enable automatic service composition, interfaces arguably need to be richer and more abstract still before automated systems could automatically browse UDDI directories to find partner services.
- Richness of description v's complexity: the expressiveness of service description languages must take into account the computational complexity of evaluating descriptions and combinations of descriptions.
- Interleaving services and network resource requirements: Linking service interactions (at the application layer) to resource usage at the network layer is likely to become increasingly complex as newer, more dynamic services are likely to require even closer control of network resources to function.

4. TOWARDS DSES

In addition to the challenge areas outline in Section 3, there are wider issues which cut across all three areas:

- Stability vs. Dynamism: DSEs potentially represent a major paradigm shift and it needs to be shown that such environments are potentially as secure, reliable and effective as today's information systems. Furthermore, the potential benefits must substantially outweigh costs.

- Standardisation. The success of DSE depends to a large extent on standards but as section 3 demonstrates, the technologies which may be relevant to DSEs are extremely diverse – and within the remit of different standards organisations. It is not clear how consensus will be achieved between the many different interest groups involved. Alternatively, mechanisms for interoperation across standards need to be supported.
- Verification, testing, integration of technology: with so many different component technologies, unification is a huge task. Furthermore, it will be difficult to verify the effectiveness of systems without significant deployment, usage and interoperability testing.
- Achieving Critical Mass: a DSE is only as good as the services deployed within it. This fact implies that, over time, there needs to be a convergence to core technologies or standards that attract the majority of useful services. Without this it will be unclear which DSE enabling technologies to invest in.

There is reason to be hopeful however.

Many of the technologies cited in section 3 are now freely available under open source licenses (everything from XML parsers to planners, agent toolkits, web servers, and implementations of the EJB specifications); this provides unprecedented access to emerging technologies, increasing the chance of innovative development. Secondly, standards bodies are already working together in many relevant areas: DAML at W3C being one example, the standardisation of a Java Agent Services API (JAS 2001) and FIPA's liaison with OMG are others. Finally, initiatives such as Agentcities and the DARPA CoAbs GRID are building experimental testbeds using a range of the technologies cited. Alongside efforts such as ebXML to integrate several levels of technology (ontology, business message exchanges, syntax), these testbeds should act as catalysts for different technology communities to get together and produce common solutions.

5. CONCLUSIONS

It is clear that many of the technologies available today are progressing towards:

- Greater automation: increasingly mature agent systems, improved sophistication and higher-level management for industrial information services.
- Greater semantic content of data: widespread use of XML, standardisation of domain information in ebXML, BizTalk and eCo, increased efforts towards agent communication semantics and ontology representations (DAML, OIL).
- Greater intelligence: embedding of reasoning systems such as Jess in agent toolkits, increasing use of AI approaches in (e.g.) personalisation.
- More flexible interaction: application directories and infrastructures such as UDDI and eSpeak, Agent standardisation efforts such as FIPA and innovative web services such as Napster and Gnutella.

This paper outlines a vision of the kind of systems that may result from these developments. The future may see open networks enabling diverse autonomous service providing entities to discover each other and make use of one another's services. Microcosms of this type of world already exist but it appears that current technology trends look set to quickly increase the generality and range of current solutions.

This paper intentionally takes an abstract view of developments in information systems technologies. It simplifies a number of the issues in order to focus on the broader movement towards the realisation of a dynamic service environment. In reality there is no doubt that "the devil is in the detail" and there is much work needed before information services are as flexible, intelligent and composable as the DSE vision suggests. The authors hope that the high level view of current technology trends helps set the context for dealing with the detail.

These are indeed interesting times for researchers working on information systems and perhaps it will not be all that long before information services themselves get a far "more interesting view of the world".

REFERENCES

Agentbuilder 2001. *corporate homepage:* http://www.agentbuilder.com/

Agentcities 2001. *Agentcities homepage*: http://www.agentcities.org/

Aglets 2001. *Mobile Agent Platform project homepage at IBM*: http://www.trl.ibm.co.jp/aglets/, (see also http://www.aglets.org/)

Bernet, Y. et. Al. 1999. *"A Framework for Differentiated Services"*, IETF RFC: draft-ietf-diffserv-framework-02.txt. 1999.

Bhaniramka, P., Sun, W., Jain, R. 1999. "*Quality of Service using Traffic Engineering over MPLS: An Analysis*", IETF RFC draft-bhani-mpls-te-anal-00.txt.

BizTalk 2001. *Biztalk hompage*: http://www.biztalk.org/

D'Agents 2001. *D'Agents mobile agent platform project at Dartmouth*: http://agent.cs.dartmouth.edu/

DAML 2001. "*Darpa Agent Mark-up Language*" project homepage: http://www.daml.org/

DeCaf 2001. *DeCaf Agent architecture homepage at the University of Delaware*: http://www.eecis.udel.edu/~decaf/

DMARS 1998. "*A Formal Specification of dMARS*", d'Inverno, M. Kinny, D. Luck, M. Wooldridge, M. In collection "Intelligent Agents IV: Proceedings of the Fourth International Workshop on Agent Theories, Architectures and Languages", LNAI 1365 pages 155—176, 1998.

EbXML 2001. *EbXML homepage:* http://www.ebxml.org/

ECo 2001. *eCo framework homepage*, Commerce Net, http://eco.commerce.net/

E-Speak 2001. *E-Speak homepage*: http://www.e-speak.hp.com/

FIPA 2001. *Foundation for Intelligent Physical Agents (FIPA) standards body homepage*: http://www.fipa.org/

FIPA-ACL 2000. "*FIPA ACL Message Structure Specification*", Foundation for Intelligent Physical Agents, 2000: http://www.fipa.org/specs/fipa00061/

FIPA-SL 2000. "*FIPA SL Content Language Specification*", Foundation for Intelligent Physical Agents, 2000: http://www.fipa.org/specs/fipa00008/

FIPA-OS 2001. *FIPA-OS Agent platform project homepage*: http://fipa-os.sourceforge.net

Forsyth, R. 1984. "*Expert Systems*", Chapman and Hall, England, 1984.

Gibson, W. 1984. "*Neuromancer*", (Reprint) Mass Market Paperback, 1995. Original 1984.

Goldberg, D. 1989. "Genetic Algorithms" Addison Wesley, 1989.

GRID 2001. *The DARPA GRID activity*: http://coabs.globalinfotek.com/

Grasshopper 2001. *Grasshopper2 Agent Platform product homepage at IVK++*, http://www.ikv.de/

IST-Crumpet 2001. "*Creation of User-friendly Mobile services Personalised for Tourism*", European Union IST project, project homepage: http://www.ist-crumpet.org/

IST-iCities 2001. "*Information Cities*", European Union IST project number: IST-1999-11337.

IST-LEAP 2001. "*Lightweight Extensible Agent Platform*", European Union IST project number: IST-1999-10211.

Jack 2001. *Jack product homepage at AgentSoft:* http://www.agent-software.com.au/jack.html

JADE 2001. *Jade agent platform homepage:* http://sharon.cselt.it/projects/jade/

JAS 2001. *Java Agent Services specification homepage*: http://java.sun.com/aboutJava/communityprocess/jsr/jsr_087_jas.html

JatLite 2001. *JatLite Agent platform homage at Stanford*: http://java.stanford.edu/java_agent/html/

Java 2001. *Java Programming Language homepage*: http://www.javasoft.com

Jennings et. Al. 1998. "*A Roadmap of Agent Research and Development*", Autonomous Agents and Multi-Agent Systems, 1, 275-306.

Jini 2001. *Jini technology hompage:* http://www.jini.org

Jordan M. I. Bishop, C. 1997. "*Neural Networks*". In collection "The Computer Science and Engineering Handbook", eds Allen, B. Tucker, Jr. CRC Press.

KQML 1993. "*Specification of the KQML Agent-Communication Language*", Finin et. Al. (The DARPA Knowledge Sharing Initiative External Interfaces Working Group), 1993, on-line at: http://www.cs.umbc.edu/kqml/papers/kqmlspec.ps

Leake, D. B. 1996. "Case Based Reasoning", MIT Press, USA

Linnhoff-Popien, C. and Hegering, H (eds.) 2000. "*Trends in Distributed Systems: Towards a Universal Service Market*", Lecture Notes in Computer Science No. 1890, Springer, 2000.

MadKit 2001. *MadKit project homepage*: http://www.madkit.org/

Maritz, J. S. Lwin, T. 1989 "*Empirical Bayes Methods*", Chapmann and Hall.

Napster 2000. *Napster.com homepage*: http://www.napster.com/

Gasser, L. 1991. "*Social Concepts of Knowledge and Action*", Artificial Intelligence 47, pages 107-138.

Gnutella 2001. *Gnutella project homepage*: http://gnutella.wego.com/

Rapoza, J. 2000. "*DAML could take search to a new level*", PC Week, ZDNET: http://www.zdnet.com/eweek/stories/general/0,11011,2432538,00.html

RosettaNet 2001. *RosettaNet homepage*, http://www.rosettanet.org

OAA 2001. *Open Agent Architecture Project homepage at SRI International*: http://www.ai.sri.com/~oaa/

OMG/CORBA 2001. *OMG homepage*: http://www.omg.org

Ontolingua 2001. *Ontolingua project homepage at Stanford*: http://www-ksl-svc.stanford.edu/

Oracle 2000. "*Oracle 9i Dynamic Services*", Technical White Paper, Chan C. http://www-4.ibm.com/software/developer/library/w-wsdl.html

Papazoglou, M. P. van den Heuvel, W-J. 1998. "*From Business Processes to Cooperative Information Systems: an Information Agents Perspective*", In collection Intelligent Information Agents, ed Klusch, M. Springer, 1998.

PtPWG 2001. *Peer-to-Peer Forum homepage*: http://www.peer-to-peerwg.org/

RETSINA 2001. *Retsina Agent Architecture homepage at Carnegie Mellon University*: http://www.cs.cmu.edu/~softagents/

RDF 2001. *RDF resources homepage at W3C*: http://www.w3.org/RDF/

Scour 2001. *Scour.com corporate homepage*: http://www.scour.com/

Semantic Web 2001. *Semantic Web activity homepage:* http://www.semanticweb.org

SETI@Home 2001. "*Search for Extraterrestrial Intelligence @ Home*" homepage at University of Berkley: http://setiathome.ssl.berkeley.edu/

SIF 2001. "*Social Interaction Framework*" project homepage at the DFKI: http://www.dfki.uni-sb.de/~sif/

SOAP 2001. *SOAP homepage at W3C*: http://www.w3.org/TR/SOAP/

Swarm 2001. *Swarm project homepage*: http://www.swarm.org

Tate et. Al. 1990. "*A review of AI Planning Techniques*", in collection "Readings in Planning", eds Allen, J. Hendler, J. Tate, A. Morgan Kaufmann.

Tsang, E. 1994. "*Foundations of Constraint Satisfaction*", Academic Press.

TuCSoN 1998. "*Coordination of Mobile Information Agents in Tucson*", Ominici, A. Zambonelli, F. Journal of Internet Research, 8(5).

[UDDI 2001. *UDDI homepage*: http://www.uddi.org

Verma, D. 1999. "*Supporting Service Level Agreements in IP Networks*", Macmillan.

WAP/WML 2001. "*Wireless Application Protocol/Wireless Mark-up Language*", WAP Forum homepage: http://www.wapforum.org

Wooldridge, M. 2000. "*Semantic Issues in the Verification of Agent Communication Languages*", in Autonomous Agents and Multi-Agent Systems 3(1), pages 9-31.

Wos et. Al. 1984. "Automated Reasoning- Introduction and Applications", Prentice-Hall.

WSDL 2000. "*Web Services Description Language (WSDL) 1.0*" Christensen E.,Curbera F., Meredith G., Weerawarana S., http://www-4.ibm.com/software/developer/library/w-wsdl.html

XMI 2001. *Corba, XML/XMI Resources Page at OMG*: http://www.omg.org/technology/xml/index.htm

XML 2001. *XML resources homepage at W3C*: http://www.w3.org/XML/

XSLT 2001. "*XSL Transformations (XSLT) v1.0*", W3C Recommendation 16 : http://www.w3.org/TR/xslt

Zadeh, L. 1988. "*Fuzzy Logic*", IEEE Computer 21(4).

ZEUS 2001. *ZEUS agent architecture homepage*: http://www.labs.bt.com/projects/agents.htm

AGENT-BASED PERSONALIZED SERVICES FOR MOBILE USERS OVER A VPN

Hamid Harroud, Mohamed Ahmed, Ahmed Karmouch
School of Information Technology & Engineering (SITE)
University of Ottawa
161 Louis Pasteur St. Ottawa, ON, Canada K1N 6N5
E-mail: harroud@sol.genie.uottawa.ca , mahmed@sol.genie.uottawa.ca , Karmouch@site.uottawa.ca

Keywords: software agent, authorization policies, negotiation, KQML, service presentation, media abstraction

Abstract: This paper proposes an agent-based service provisioning system for mobile users. It features a set of cooperative agents distributed over different sites that work together to provide personalized services for nomadic users within a Virtual Private Network (VPN). For instance, when a user moves outside of his office, he would like to have a similar office environment while he is at home, in a meeting at another company, on a business trip or at a temporary location such as a hotel. Agents representing the end-users and the system agents may engage into a negotiation process to help the user access personalized services at particular site. Such access is performed in accordance with the user's home policies as well as his current location policies. Adaptive Service Presentation agent is used to adapt the service presentation to the capabilities of the user's device (e.g. Workstation, Laptop, Phone, PDA). This work is part of the Mobile Agent Alliance project involving University of Ottawa, National Research Council and Mitel Corporation in Canada.

1. INTRODUCTION

Nowadays, the increasing users' mobility, have introduced the need for personalized services at different locations on the networks. Locations that a user may visit can be configured into virtual private networks. In such a network users would like to retain access to services that are provided by their home site (e.g. office), while moving across locations on the network. In the multimedia Information and Agent Research Laboratory, at the University of Ottawa, we are exploring different aspects of agent technology and mobile computing in order to provide users and organizations with a system capable of offering mobile personalized services for nomadic users.

The emerging agent technology defines agents as having capabilities to act on behalf of a user and could migrate from one location to another while performing their tasks throughout their itinerary (Magedanz 2000). This key characteristic is very useful in developing tools to manage users' mobility and to implement a flexible service provisioning system. To this end, we have designed an agent-based system that provides a (mobile) working environment, similar to the home site environment (i.e. office), that can be used by mobile users, wherever they roam and whatever devices they use.

One of the key design components of the system is the use of authorization policies and agents negotiation. Authorization policies are defined at each site to monitor the resource utilization as well as the site's overall policies. The use of policies allows the system administrator to easily change the behavior of the system without altering its components. Agent negotiation process is used to guide agents to persuade each other for making decisions on user's behalf in conformance with enabled policies. For instance, when a user moves from his home site to a visited site, agents communicate and negotiate with one another to allocate to the user a temporary profile according to her home preferences and services. The negotiated profile includes user's identity, authorized services with associated quality of service, devices that may be used, cost to be paid, etc. Furthermore, mobile users may use heterogeneous devices with different capabilities, such as a workstation, a laptop with a wireless connection, a PDA or a phone. Therefore our system should be able to identify the device used at a particular time and adapt the presentation to the device capabilities. Adaptation is a challenging issue in multimedia services such as video mail. We have

J. Filipe et al. (eds.), Enterprise Information Systems III, 312–319.

adopted a general approach that takes into consideration the characteristic of media to be presented to the user and the capabilities of the device used to access the media. This approach is based on the media abstraction techniques that are capable of summarizing and possibly converting media contents to adapt their presentation on the user's (small) device. This would help to provide alternatives for end users in the form of short summary messages of different formats.

The organization of the paper is as follows. The following section introduces the main components of our agent-based service provisioning system. The inter-agent interaction and negotiation model is then presented, with the agent communication mechanism and the policy-based negotiation protocol being presented in subsections. Then a model is used to describe a scenario for providing call forwarding and media abstraction services within a 3-sites based private network. Some aspects of the media abstraction service are then highlighted. Finally, we draw our conclusion and future work.

2. AGENT-BASED SERVICE PROVISIONING SYSTEM

The architecture of the system is depicted in figure 1. It is composed of several cooperating agents that work together to provide provisioning and delivery of personalized services across inter-working sites and heterogeneous devices. We now briefly introduce each the components.

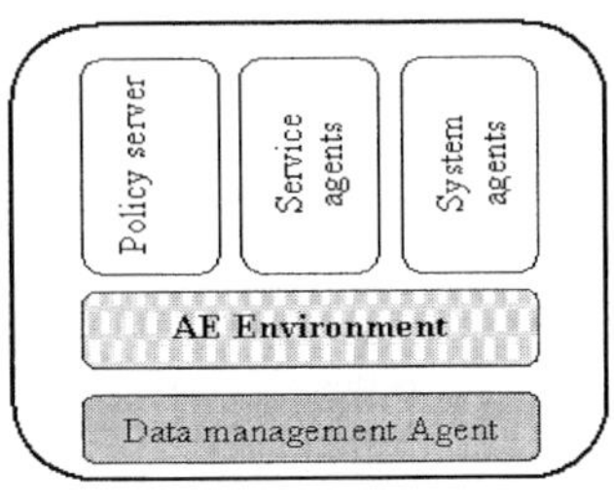

Figure 1: Basic system components

The ***data management agent (DMA)*** has the role of managing information related to the user, such as user's profile, current personalized services, preferred quality of service, and current location. The DMA maintains consistency of this information at each site.

The ***policy server (PS)*** manages rules that govern the utilization of the system and network resources at each site. For instance PS may prohibit authorizations to a user for obtaining a particular service or resources at a specific site. The policy server also maintains authorization policies that may be permitted or denied to each agent locally and when an agent interacts remotely with other agents. Policies include the monitoring of services and resource utilization as well as system configuration and quality of service.

Service agents provide access to services on a particular site. The main task of a service agent is to prepare the appropriate execution environment required by the service. Legacy services can be integrated in the system by means of agent wrappers. Two mains services are have been considered in our system, the Call Forwarding service (e.g. telephone, fax and e-mail) and media abstraction service. The Call forwarding service selects the incoming calls and forwards the authorized ones to the user at her current location. The Media abstraction service (*MediABS*) provides media summarization and conversion as required by the user's device.

System agents are those agents that manage the site processing system functionality. These agents include the Site Profile Agent (SPA), the Resource reservation Agent (RA), and the Adaptive Service Presentation agent (ASP). **SPA** is responsible for negotiating the user profile and authorized services at the visited site. **RA** is responsible for configuring each service agent execution environment (e.g. memory usage, processing time, network bandwidth) and monitoring resource consumption. For instance a negotiation between the **RA** and a service agent maybe engaged to make sure that the required resources are available at the time the service is requested by the user. **ASP** manages the user's interaction with service agents and adapts the presentation to the device capabilities and the visited site organization's policies.

Agents are executed under the control of the ***Agent execution environment***, which provides a framework for agent management and communications. Several agent platforms have been developed (Pham 1998), in our laboratory we have adopted FIPA-OS (Buckle 1999) platform. However we have used a different communication mechanism, which is based on MicMac (Mitel 1996), a Mitel Corporation product. MicMac supports hands-on experimentation with multi-agent interaction and negotiation protocols. This product has been extended to provide a secure inter-agent communication tool (Zheng 2001).

Figure 2 depicts the relationship between agents, services and the directory information base. The LDAP repository is managed by the DMA and maintains information about user preferences, resource availability, services and policies. Service agents represent the legacy services in the agent-based system. An event server (i.e. ***coordinator agent***) is deployed to synchronize and to perform agent communications using MicMac.

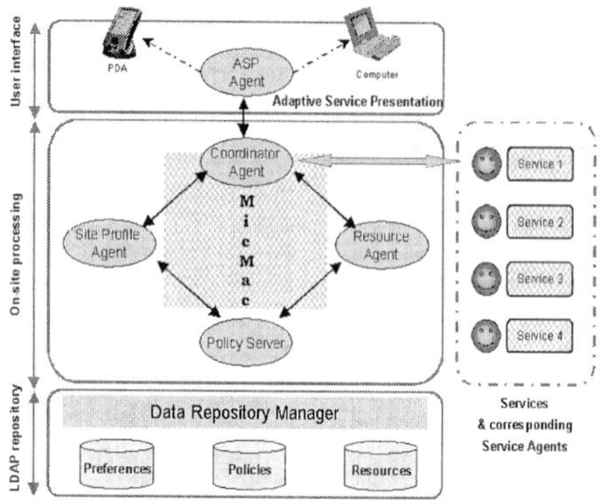

Figure 2: Agent-based architecture

The ASP agent is the access point for mobile users; its role is authenticating users and providing access to the services. The SPA identifies the user and determines his authorized profile that would be used during the working session.

3. INTER-AGENT NEGOTIATION

Each agent has the ability to initiate and to control interactions with its peers, depending on its current needs. This is performed in exchanging information messages using KQML (Knowledge Query Manipulation Language). KQML has been used, as an inter-agent communication language, in several prototypes and demonstration systems (Labrou 1994, Mayfield 1996).

3.1 Inter-agent Communication using MicMac

MicMac is a set of software tools, which provides an environment to deal with multi-agent interaction and negotiation protocols (Mitel 1996). It allows the creation and the manipulation of one or more Agoras. An Agora is an open area (shared tuple space) for posting and/or picking up information. The basic structure unit of exchanged information within an Agora is a tuple. A tuple is an unordered set of fields represented as "key-value" associations. Each KQML message is translated into or from tuple format.

Inter-site communication is performed via the Coordinator Agent. Outgoing/incoming inter-site tuples are encrypted/decrypted respectively using a session key generated by the user authentication procedure (Zheng 2001).

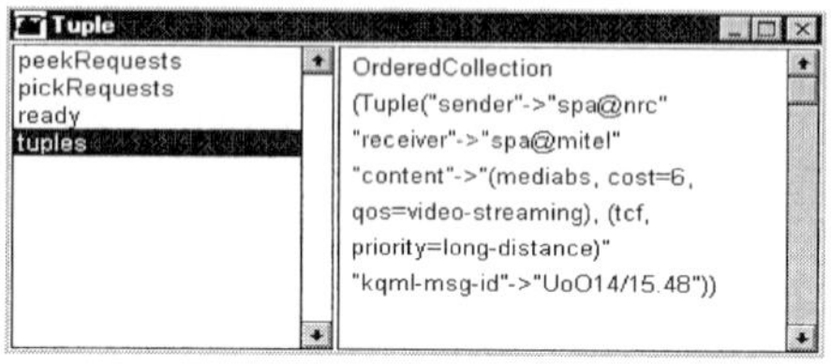

Figure 3: Sample of a request tuple on MicMac

Figure 3 shows an Agora editor, with an example of a request posted as a tuple on MicMac. In this example, "*sender*", "*receiver*" and "*content*" are the **keys** of the posted tuple, while "*spa@nrc*", "*spa@mitel*", "*(MediABS, qos=video-streaming), (CFS, priority=long-distance)*" are the corresponding **values** respectively.

Agora Editor displays and monitors a complete view of processing requests over the tuple space content. A small set of primitives is offered to trigger specific processing requests as described in table 1.

Table 1: Primitive set of Agora

Primitives	*Request Description*
Post	Add a tuple to a tuple space
Pick	Extract a tuple from a tuple space
Peek	Read a tuple from a tuple space
Cancel	Terminate a pending Pick/Peek request

The pick and peek primitives remain pending until an entry in the agora space satisfies the tuple template (anti-tuple). Duration can be specified for how long any request (tuple or anti-tuple) should remain on the agora space.

3.2 Policy-based Negotiation Protocol

Agent behavior and decision-making are monitored by a set of policies. Each site may define its own set of policies. There are two types of policies: authorization and obligation policies (Sloman 2001). An authorization policy is a set of *conditions* that prohibit or permit an agent (called the *subject*) to perform *actions* on *target* entities. Conditions may concern the subject, the target or the state of the system. An obligation policy triggers events for performing some actions when conditions are applicable. Our policies are represented using XML and visually modelled with a graphical tool (Amer 2001).

Table 2: Sample of authorization policies at avisited site

Policy ID	*Type*	*Subject*	*Action*	*Target*	*Conditions*
P-1	pAP	*SPA*	*MediABS access*	*MIRL student*	*[(cost>6, qos<v.s.) ; (cost>20)]*
P-2	*nAP*	*RA agent*	*Reservation*	Service Agent	*[(space>10);* (time>60)]

The system uses actually authorization policies only. Table 2 shows two examples of policies. P-1 is a *positive* authorization policy (permission). It indicates that a visiting student from MIRL laboratory is authorized to use the MediABS service if the local SPA agent receives a proposal with the value of the cost parameter is more than 20 units.

The cost may be less than 20 (more than 6) but the video streaming quality of service will not be provided. P-2 is a *negative* authorization policy (interdiction). It says that the resource agent is not allowed to reserve resources required by any service agent if the requested space is more than 10 Mb or time processing is more than 1 hour.

Since site policies are private and not available to other sites, conflicts may occur among inter-site agents' interactions. Therefore, negotiation takes place in an attempt to resolve these conflicts.

The negotiation protocol starts by an agent that produces a *proposal* according to the local policies and submits it to the other party, which evaluates the proposal and possibly generates a *counter-proposal* till an agreement or the deadline of negotiation, have been reached. Proposals and counter-proposals consist of a set of elements (services or resources) associated with some parameters (e.g. cost, quality of service, time, etc).

While in a proposal values of different parameters are given explicitly by the sender agent, they are not quantified within a counter-proposal (site privacy). In the counter-proposal, possible values of parameters are LOW, HIGH, and UNEQUAL or may be UNKNOWN. **LOW** specifies that the parameter should be increased for an acceptable proposal (e.g. cost). **HIGH** specifies that the parameter should be decreased (e.g. quality of service). **UNEQUAL** indicates that the value of the parameter must be modified (e.g. password). **UNKNOWN** indicates that the parameter was not specified in the proposal. The agent sender uses its own *strategy* to assign new values to the parameters received in the counter-proposal.

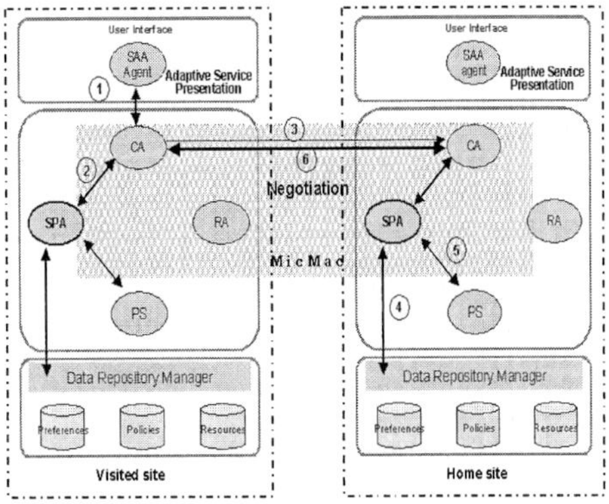

Figure 4: Negotiating the user's profile at the visited site

Figure 4 shows a generic scenario of creating a user's profile at a visited site. After the user's authentication, through the ASP (on an authorized device) has been processed (1), the Coordinator Agent establishes a connection between the visited and the home Site Profile Agents (2 & 3). The home SPA gets the user's preferences from the local database directory (4) and maps the retrieved preferences with the home Policy Server (5).

Negotiation process between home and visited SPA (to determine the final profile) is then performed (6). The visited SPA and the Home SPA negotiate according to the protocol described above. For example, we assume that the visited SPA has received a proposal specifying the MediABS service with parameters "cost=7" and "quality-of-service=video streaming". Using the policy P-1 (table 2), the visited SPA may generate a counter-proposal where it specifies parameters "*cost=LOW*" or "*quality-of-service=HIGH*". The home SPA uses its policy-based strategy that allows it to decide either to increase the cost or to decrease the quality-of-service within a new proposal.

4. AN EXAMPLE SCENARIO WITHIN A THREE PARTICIPATING SITES

We have implemented a prototype that involves three participating sites: University of Ottawa (*UoOttawa*), National Research Council of Canada (*NRC*) and Mitel Corporation in Ottawa (*Mitel*). The following scenario describes how a temporary profile of a visiting user is determined and how the user can use his personalized services. We consider the case of a user (e.g. Tom) from Mitel visiting NRC site. Figure 5 summarizes the negotiation process between Mitel and NRC sites, after authenticating Tom at NRC. The Mitel-SPA proposed two services: *MediABS* service with cost and quality of service parameters and the *CFS* service with the priority parameter (proposal *P1*). The NRC-SPA generated a counter-proposal where CFS is prohibited and the *cost* of MediABS service has to be increased or the quality-of-service decreased (counter-proposal *CP1*). The Mitel-SPA made decision to increase the cost then submitted a new proposal (proposal *P2*). The third proposal was accepted and Tom is therefore authorized to use the MediABS service with parameters *"cost=15"* and the " *quality-of-service=Color Key Frames*".

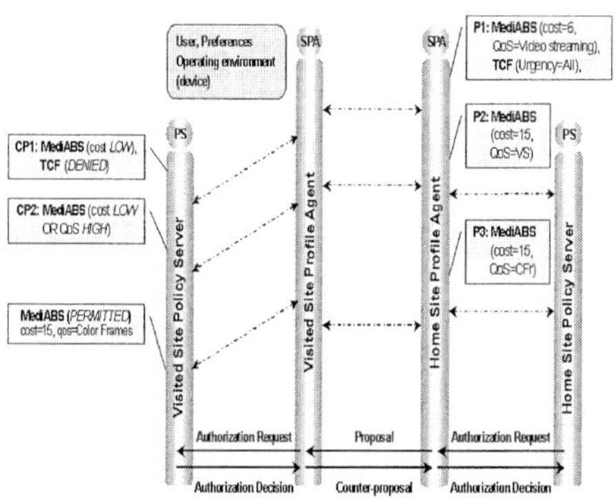

Figure 5: Negotiating Tom's profile and authorized services at NRC site

Because of resource reservation process, the negotiated quality of service may not be guaranteed at the time the user requests the service. Hence, MediABS service agent would have to negotiate local resources (e.g. *time*, *space*, *bandwidth* and *memory*) with the local RA agent. The quality of service may be reduced to the grey scale image key-frames or to a short summary message to match the available resources and the device capabilities.

Figure 6 shows an outcomes example, where the ASP displayed only some representative frames (21 KB in the total size) out of the entire video mail (about 3MB in the total size) and a short text report.

The user may disconnect before the service agent gets back with the results. The service agent stores the retrieved results in XML format (figure 7) and informs the ASP agent, so that the results could be presented next time the user logs on.

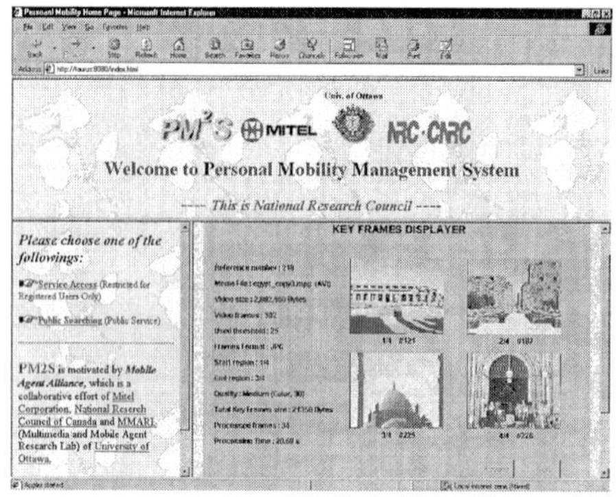

Figure 6: Outcomes example for MediABS with medium QoS


```
<user id= xyz@sol.genie.uottawa.ca,
    session=123, title=phD student>
  <vlocation>Mitel</vlocation>
  <hlocation>UoOttawa</hlocation>
  <service name=MediABS,
      location=UoOttawa>
    <parameter>
      <key>cost</key>
      <value>15</value>
    </parameter>
    <parameter>
      <key>quality-of-service</key>
      <value>colorKeyFrames</value>
    </parameter>
    <request>
      <reference>746</reference>
      <input>video122.avi</input>
      <startframe>begin</startframe>
      <endframe>end</endframe>
      <operation>key framing
      </operation>
    </request>
    <results>
      <processing>ok</processing>
      <time>9.8s</time>
      <initial_size>3Mb</initial_size>
      <frames>
        <number>5</number>
        <value>46,66,116,188,195</value>
        <total_size>21kb</total_size>
        <format>JPG</format>
        <dimension>160x120</dimension>
      </frames>
      <dlocation>
        <protocol>http</protocol>
        <host>altair.genie.uottawa.ca</host>
      <path>/mediabs/outputs/123/</path>
      </dlocation>
    </results>
  </service>
</user>
```


Figure 7: Example of results report for MediABS service in XML format

The service agent keeps a record of information related to the user (*id*, *location* and *session*), the service (*name* and *parameters*), the request (*reference*, *input* and *operation*) and the results (*processing time*, *content description* and *location*).

5. MEDIA ABSTRACTION SERVICE

The proliferation and the heterogeneity of the end devices that can be used by mobile users made it necessary to adapt service presentation accordingly at the run-time process. Therefore, we defined the media abstraction service that deals with different media summarization and conversion (e.g. Images browsing availability, Video streaming support, Text to speech converters, etc). In particular, we have developed a video segmentation algorithm based on color histograms and a Binary Penetration technique.

The algorithm addresses multiple video format analysis, and aims to provide video summaries by discovering the different cut changes within a video segment with high accuracy and better performance.

It defines various configurations for the extracted frames. They could be color or grey frames with different image qualities and different image formats to suit user's device capabilities.

For cut detection, the service implements spatial skip and temporal skip parameters to improve the performance during the analysis process, without sacrificing the accuracy of the detection. The Spatial, Temporal skips (Zhang 1993) and the use of Histogram analysis methods (Ahmed 1999) benefit from the redundant characteristic and high correlation of the video frames either in the spatial or temporal dimension. The use of color histograms has been verified to be more robust against objects and camera movements within the same shot. The adopted algorithm, called the six most significant RGB bits with the use of Blocks Intensity Difference (Ahmed 1999), makes use of the 24 bits RGB color space components of each compared pixels directly (each color component has 8 bits representation).

However, the service exploits only the two most significant RGB bits (Zhang 1993) of each color (using a masking operation). The service evaluates every corresponding two-frame histogram difference.

Then, if the overall histogram difference average exceeds some defined threshold, the two frames are said to represent an abrupt camera cut. However, in some cases, the global color distribution information may not discover the cut detection even if there is a cut detection in the compared frames. The partitioning of each frame into a number of disjoint blocks is used for resolving the missed cuts problems. This partitioning makes use of the locality information of the histogram distribution. The two examples, shown in figure 8 illustrate this problem and its solution.

Although the use of the six most significant RGB bits, with the use of blocks intensity difference algorithm provided efficient results, it lacks the performance objective required in these kind of services, especially in distributed environment. For this reason, the algorithm was updated with a new opportunistic approach using the temporal heuristic dependencies within the visual information. The objective of this extension is to relax the step of analyzing all the consecutive frames of a certain region till the algorithm suggests they may have a potential cut discontinuity between the two frames. The frames are extracted and analyzed in a binary penetration manner.

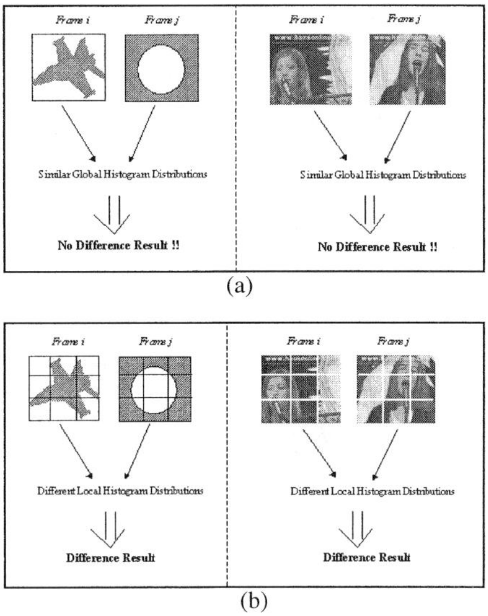

Figure 8:
(a) Wrong Frames Unchange Decision!,
(b) Cut Detection using six most significant RGB bits with the use of Blocks Intensity Difference

The algorithm initially compares frames m and k, which are separated by a number of frames that is equal to the temporal skip parameter. Then, if the difference between the two frames exceeds a histogram-difference threshold, the middle frame (m+k)/2 is extracted and compared to both ends. If one of the two differences exceeds or even if both of them exceed the threshold, the greater difference represents a potential possibility of finding a cut within its half region. The temporal skip should be a moderate value that represents a possibility of finding one camera cut operation at maximum within it.

This continues until the difference of two consecutive frames exceeds the given threshold, which represents a true camera cut operation in this region. In addition, the procedure stops when the difference in both halves, at a certain level, are lower than the threshold. That means that there is, actually, no camera cut operation in this entire region because of a large object or camera optical flow motion, which happened within this region.

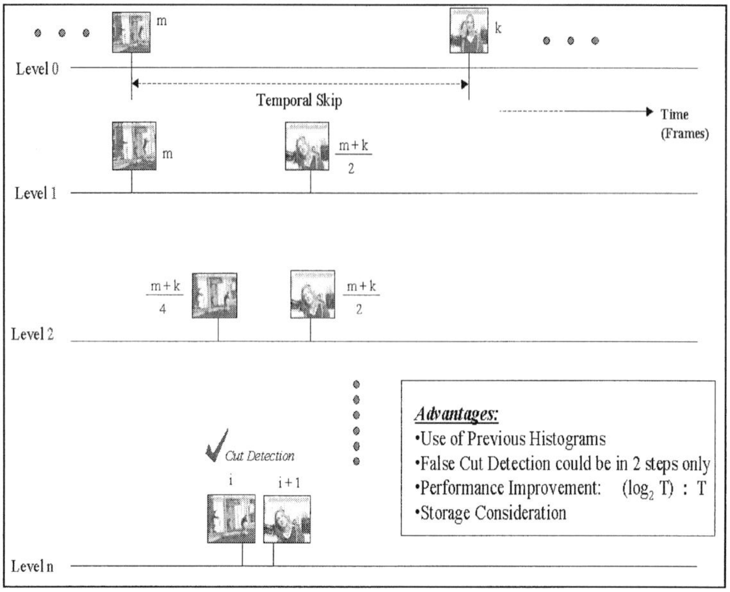

Figure 9: A successful video cut detection scenario using Binary Penetration algorithm

Figure 9 shows a visual representation of execution of the binary penetration algorithm along with its advantages.

6. RELATED WORK

The issue of service provisioning has been studied in several projects (Hooda 1998, Cameleon 1999, ITU-T 1995, Magedanz 2000). The central focus of these works has been based on the VHE (Virtual Home Environment) concept of UMTS (Universal Mobile Telecommunication System). The concept of VHE is such that users are consistently presented with the same personalized features, user interface capabilities and services in whatever network, whatever terminal and where ever the user may be located (ETSI 2000). Our work is closely related to the European ACTS project CAMELEON (Cameleon 1999), where agent technology is used for the efficient provisioning and deployment of telecommunication services for mobile users. However, while it is intended that UMTS users will have the ability to access their particular set of services from any suitable access point (ETSI 2000), we give mobile users the ability to use local services at the visited site in conformance with their pre-determined personalized preferences at their home site. In addition to this, we have introduced the concept of policies to monitor agents' behavior and their decision-making in a flexible and scalable manner. Furthermore, we have defined an appropriate inter-agents negotiation model, which deals with agent autonomy and information privacy. The policy-based negotiation model presented in this paper has been designed for fully autonomous agents and can easily be adapted to other issues such as electronic commerce, distributed scheduling, and quality of service management.

In the area of image analysis and recognition to allow the partitioning of a video source into separate segments, several contributions have been made. Pass et al. (Pass 1996) proposed a histogram refinement algorithm using color coherence vectors based on local spatial coherence and defined a notion of Joint Histograms (Pass 1999). Wolf (Wolf 1996) provided an algorithm to detect the key frames in MPEG video file format using optical flow motion analysis. Sethi et al. (Sethi 1998) used a similarity metric to measure the similarity through both the hue and saturation components of the HSI color space between two images. However, most of these works lack the optimization considerations of the processing time performance and storage requirements especially if they will be utilized throughout run-time distributed environments.

7. CONCLUSION AND FUTURE WORK

In this paper, we have presented an agent-based architecture for providing personalized services to mobile users. The system comprises several cooperative agents distributed over different sites. Agents engage into negotiation using authorization policies. Policies are defined at each site to monitor the resource utilization as well as the site's overall policies.

We believe that the agent technology provides more flexibility especially in the development of mobile computing. The use of policies is a very powerful and promising mechanism that is adopted to maintain privacy and to manage dynamic changes in a distributed environment and more importantly in the development of agent-based applications.

Future work will include integration of mobile agents to remotely use (or buy) services from a non-participating site (e.g. service provider). The use of obligation policies to efficiently monitor and control the behavior of mobile agents while performing their tasks is also part of future work.

ACKNOWLEDGEMENTS

We would like to thank Tom Gray and Sergei Mankovski from Mitel Corporation, Roger Impey, Ramiro Liscano and John Meech from National Research Council of Canada (NRC) for their helpful discussions and suggestions.

REFERENCES

Ahmed, M., and Karmouch, A., 1999, 'Improving Video Processing Performance using Temporal Reasoning', *SPIE-Applications of Digital Image Processing XXII*, Denver Co USA, Vol. 3808, pp. 645-656.

Amer, M., Karmouch, A., Gray, T., Mankovskii, S., 2001, 'An Agent Model for the Resolution of Feature Conflicts in Telephony', *Journal of network and systems management* (to appear).

Buckle, P., Hadingham, R., 1999, 'FIPA and the Internet Revolution', *Key notes speech at the 2nd International ACTS Workshop*, Singapore.

Cameleon Consortium, 1999, *the European ACTS Research Project (AC341)*, Available:http://www.dfv.rwth-aachen.de/project/cameleon/cameleon.html.

ETSI TR 122 970, 2000, 'Universal Mobile Telecommunication System (UMTS); Service aspects; Virtual Home Environment (VHE)', *Technical Report Version 3.0.1.*

Hooda, A., Karmouch, A., Abu-Hakima, S., 1998, 'Personal Mobility Management Using LDAP Distributed Directory and Static Agents', *5th Conference on Intelligence in Networks*, Bordeaux, France.

ITU-T Recommendation F.851, 1995, 'Universal Personal Telecommunication (UPT), Service Description'.

Labrou, Y., et al, 1994, 'KQML as an agent communication language', *Proceedings of the 3rd International Conference on Information and Knowledge Management (CIKM'94)*, ACM Press.

Magedanz, T., Karmouch, A., (Guest Editors), 2000, 'Mobile Software Agents for Telecommunication Applications', *Journal of Computer Communication*, Vol. 23, Issue. 8.

Mayfield, J., et al, 1996, 'Evaluation of KQML as an Agent Communication Language', *Intelligent Agents Volume II - Proceedings of the 1995 Workshop Agent Theories, Architectures and Languages, Lecture Notes in Artificial Intelligence*, Springer-Verlag.

Mitel Corporation, 1996, 'Mitel-CATA (The MicMac software Testbed)', *Technical Report, CITI/Adaptive Information Systems.*

Pass, G., Zabih, R., 1996, 'Histogram Refinement for Content-Based Image Retrieval', *IEEE Workshop on Applications of Computer Vision*, pp. 96-102.

Pass, G., Zabih, R., 1999, 'Comparing Images Using Joint Histograms', *ACM Journal of Multimedia Systems*, Vol. 7, No. 3, pp. 234-240.

Pham, V., Karmouch, A., 1998, 'Mobile Software Agents: An Overview', *IEEE Communications, Special issue on mobile agents and telecommunications*, Vol. 36, No. 7, pp. 26-36.

Sethi, I., et al., 1998, 'Color-WISE: A System for Image Similarity Retrieval Using Color', *Proc. of SPIE, Storage and Retrieval for Image and Video Databases VI*, Vol. 3312, pp. 140-149.

Sloman, M., Labo, J., Lupu, E., (Editors), 2001, 'Policies for Distributed Systems and Networks', *International Workshop*, Policy2000, Bristol, UK.

Wolf, W., 1996, 'Key Frame Selection by Motion Analysis', *Proceedings of IEEE International Conference on Acoustics, Speech, and Signal Processing*, Atlanta, Vol. 2, pp. 1228-1231.

Zhang, H., et al, 1993, 'Automatic Partitioning of Full-Motion Video', *Multimedia Systems*, Vol. 1, No. 1, pp. 10-28.

Zheng, C., Karmouch, A., Gray, T., Impey, R., 2001, 'Approaching Secure Communications in a Message-Oriented Mobile Computing Environment', *Journal of Multimedia Tools and Applications*, Kluwer Academic Publishers (to appear).

AN AGENT-BASED KNOWLEDGE SHARING MODEL FOR INFORMATION RETRIEVAL ON THE INTERNET

Bin Ling, Colin Allison
School of Computer Science, University of St. Andrews, North Haugh, St. Andrews, UK
Email:bl11@st-and.ac.uk, ca @st-and.ac.uk

Kecheng Liu
School of Computing, Staffordshire University, Beaconside, Stafford, UK
Email:K.Liu@staffs.ac.uk

Keywords: Information Retrieval, Knowledge Sharing, User Modelling, Co-operation, Middle Agent

Abstract: With the proliferation of electronically available information, and its diverse nature, a critical problem has arisen which is how to locate, retrieve and process relevant information effectively. It is impractical to build either a unified peer-to-peer system or a centralised architecture that combines all of these information resources. A more promising approach is to program specialised informative agents within an organisational structure that provide public access to information resources on the Internet. These agents can co-operate with other agents to share their knowledge when appropriate. This paper describes an integrated approach to developing this type of agent-based information retrieval system model, which employs a user-modelling strategy, co-operation methods and matchmaking middle-agents. The feasibility of the resultant knowledge-sharing environment is demonstrated by experimental results from a simulation based on requirements from the UK National Health Service.

1. INTRODUCTION

There is often a need to acquire information by employing multiple agents on a network that communicate and collaborate with each other but do not know of one another's existence in advance. Information access and retrieval capabilities provided by current agent-based applications are lacking in providing suitable mechanisms and abstractions for this type of agent co-operation and individual user modelling. One of the basic problems facing designers of open, distributed multi-agent systems for the Internet is the connection problem – finding the other agents who might have the information or other knowledge that users need. Most of those conventional agent-based applications rely on some form of direct interaction models (peer-to-peer communication), which have been argued not to be adequate for Internet applications (Omicini and Zambonelli, 1999). Direct communication between widely distributed and independent entities is inherently difficult and is not expressive enough to deal with issues such as heterogeneity, dynamicity and security, and also requires the interposition of global consistency mechanisms.

People often use the Internet to find expertise in a certain field, but such a task can be difficult and time-consuming. Asking other agents at random resembles diffusion in a gas and is extremely slow – it means each agent could be required to ask every other agent on the network, resulting in a solution that scales poorly. Also, in a large organisation, there are likely to be many initiatives that make use of the same underlying methods and techniques – project directories and job titles will be of no use in identifying them, but knowledge of people with similar backgrounds would be very useful.

The research described in this paper focuses on investigating a framework for agent-based knowledge sharing. This includes a number of informative agents who share their results with a just-in-time information presentation agent. Integrating these ensures that the presentation agent does not only suggest its own documents of relevance, but information found by the other agents as well. The framework allows agents to deposit information for later use by themselves or by other agents. In this way, knowledge sharing between

J. Filipe et al. (eds.), Enterprise Information Systems III, 320.

agents is possible, but it is also controlled in such a manner as to allow modular inclusion of agents within the framework.

2. AGENTS FOR THREE-LAYER INTERNET STRUCTURE

2.1 Three-layer Internet Structure

The framework in this paper is based on a three-layer Internet structure (Hermans, 1996). The three-layer structure makes it possible to abstract over the various techniques that are hidden under its surface. Each layer is focused on one specific part of the activity, and is supported by corresponding types of software agents: the requester agent, the provider agent and the middle agent (as shown in **Figure 1**). This combination of agent types enables the human user to perform complex tasks more efficiently.

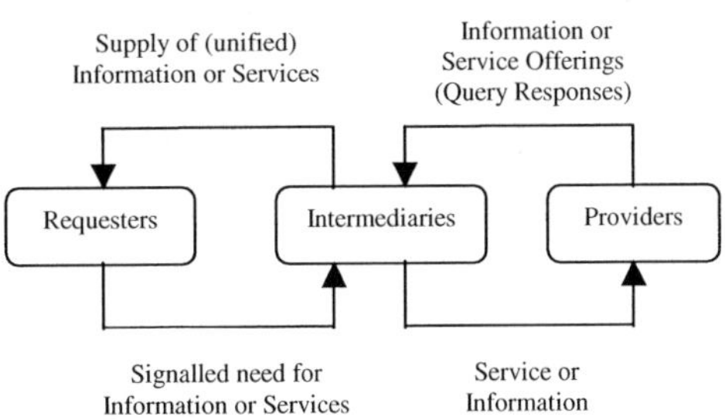

Figure 1: Overview of the Three-layer Model

2.2 Middle Layer Agents

From a privacy standpoint, preference information can flow from a requester to a provider, and capability information can flow the other way. Agents that deal with preference or capability information that are neither requesters nor providers are called middle-agents.

As we know, software agents are computer programs, which attempt to perform some tasks autonomously for their users in a trustworthy, personalised fashion. Middle layer agents are more specific than general software agents, they take more initiative, and actively inform the user when they find items that match the user's requirement. Often, such agents may not understand the knowledge domain directly, but are instead facilitators that can find other people who understand the domain better. The behaviour of middle agents has certain performance implications for efficiency, privacy, robustness and adaptive qualities (Decker *et al.*, 1996), which are related to characteristics of the external environment and of the agents themselves.

3. AN INTEGRATED MODEL FOR CO-OPERATIVE AGENT KNOWLEDGE SHARING

Software agent technology is an important advance in the management of knowledge, and has brought new potential for the improvement of efficiency and effectiveness of information retrieval systems. This paper considers an overall framework which is inspired by the ideas from *computational ecology* (Huberman, 1988), in which personal agents have only local knowledge, but self-organise into larger units. The core ideas in the approach taken here are to:

- Compare the agents' information in a peer-to-peer, decentralised fashion;
- Use middle agents to refer users to others who have similar interests and share the knowledge between users whose interests match.

This section focuses on three technical issues: the user modelling strategy, a multiple-agent architecture and the middle layer agent. These are integrated to support personal agent behaviours in the knowledge-sharing model.

3.1 User Modelling Strategy

The user-modelling strategy employed in this paper is based on the concept of a *stereotype*. Modelling users by means of stereotypes is based on the premise that given a specific application domain and known information about users, it is possible to generate stereotypes of user groups. Individual users can then be modelled by customising an instance of their profile from the general class. Each user specifies group preferences when registering with the system. For example, a doctor may specify radiology or pathology.

A profile agent is designed to locate users with common interests to facilitate knowledge networking. It informs the user about other users with similar interests within a particular user (agent) community, through the dynamic user profiles maintained by the framework. Each user's profile agent operates autonomously and contacts other registered agents periodically to compare interest profiles. During this exchange, the information disclosed to other agents is strictly controlled by their privacy settings to ensure that information is not divulged to parties that the user does not want to know. When the framework distributes user profiles across a number of servers, profile agents share their contact lists when privacy restrictions are met. It means that a profile agent does not need to contact every other agent directly to build up a picture of users sharing common interests and knowledge. The profile agent then informs the user (at intervals specified in the user preferences) about contacts made and matches found. For each interest, the list of matches found may be examined, and the user can obtain contact details or links to interest groups, for example, medical professionals with similar interests.

Two important policies are used in this knowledge-sharing model:

1. Dynamically matching user demand and provider's supply in the best possible way.
2. Maintaining current awareness - users will be able to request agents in the middle layer to notify them regularly, or maybe even instantly, when new information about certain topics becomes available or when a provider has sent an advertisement offering information or services matching certain keywords.

3.2 Co-operation of Multiple Agents

Within any multi-agent system, agreed protocols and mechanisms are required to allow an agent to operate in a distributed environment, co-operating with other agents. Our approach to co-operation is to facilitate distributed multi-agent knowledge sharing. Each agent has a knowledge-sharing model that includes other agents. Agents communicate in order to build and update their individual knowledge. Each user agent in the community has a user profile, which includes information about the multiple domains of knowledge that interest the user and the knowledge learned through knowledge acquired from other users. These agents can be called upon to assist a user who wants help in deriving knowledge. This environment also includes a middle agent, which helps a user agent search for potential agent candidates who may be able to satisfy an information request. This middle agent participates in negotiating the desired knowledge from other agents in the community. With this approach, loosely coupled agents form high-level (but possibly incomplete) knowledge and results, which they exchange which each other.

3.3 Agents Conflict Solution

This approach to knowledge sharing has the potential for agent conflicts. In some middle agent scenarios, a situation may arise when a user reviews sets of knowledge patterns acquired through an interaction and determines that an identifiable agent is unable to provide quality information, and hence should not be consulted in the future. In order to address this issue, the system uses a two-stage-filtering process to improve the performance of the middle agent. For instance, the first stage of filtering takes place when the middle agent accepts an information request. It examines the user profile encoded in the information request, and uses this information to filter out undesirable agents, or identify favourable agents from which to acquire quality information. An intelligent filter will help moderate the second stage of filtering, as the user reviews the knowledge that was acquired from the agent community, and decides whether to adopt this knowledge into his/her user dictionary. After this stage, the intelligent filter allows the user to analyse the accepted and rejected knowledge, and then determine if some agents are providing low-quality knowledge. This analysis may prompt the user to initiate a change to their profile, in order to avoid undesirable agents, or to favour helpful user agents in future requests.

3.4 Middle Agent Mechanism

Different types of middle agents have been proposed in the Internet, such as matchmakers, brokers and blackboards (Decker *et al.*, 1996). The emphasis in this model is on the *matchmaker* agent.

As shown in **Figure 2**, matchmaking has the following general form: a provider agent advertises its know-how, or capability to a middle agent that stores the advertisements. A requester agent that desires a particular service sends to the middle agent a service request that is subsequently matched with the middle agent's stored advertisements. The middle agent communicates the results to the requester. As matchmaking is usually done dynamically over large networks, and it has been observed that there is a potential trade-off between the quality and efficiency of service matchmaking on the Internet (Sycara and Klusch, 1996). Accordingly the system must be designed to perform efficiently.

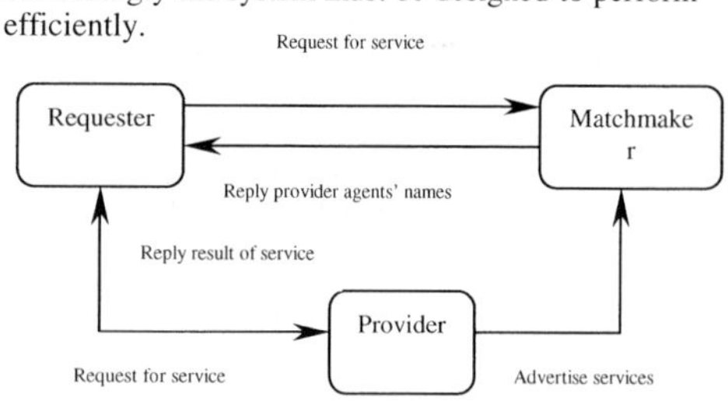

Figure 2: Service Matchmaking in Multi-agent Systems

4. CASE STUDY: NHS INFORMATION SYSTEM

In this section, the model for knowledge sharing is applied to design a framework of collaborative agents, with a particular focus on the role of the matchmaking agent.

4.1 Current Situation

To evaluate the co-operative knowledge-sharing model for agent based information retrieval, the medical domain has been chosen as a task domain. Currently, there are millions of medical related records accessible on the Intranet for the National Health Service (NHS) in the UK (NHSnet, 2000). However, in relation to the professional knowledge base, NHS professionals cannot possibly remember all current and emerging knowledge about the work they do. They are experiencing the difficulties and frustration of searching for valuable information and exchanging their knowledge with other researchers through the use of conventional Web-based information systems. Medical professionals and general practitioners (GPs) frequently request this domain specific information retrieval by simply using email to exchange information or via internal keywords search through the medical sources over the NHS Intranet. This situation is common in the medical research area. For instance, two doctors both doing research on similar cases are unaware of each other's work. The current ad hoc approach to information retrieval is neither efficient nor productive and research resources are thus wasted to some degree. This environment has some interesting features:

- There are many sources of uncertainty and dynamic change in this environment
- Resource constraints – not all data is available for all users
- There is a strong need for sharing information about research between medical professionals and GPs.

4.2 Collaborative Agents for IR

To facilitate the knowledge sharing and interoperation among agents on the organisation, a high level algorithm outlining the approach shown as following:

1. User agent **U**, who can provide extraction knowledge within this multi-agent environment, has registered its location, important information (e.g. preferences) and capabilities to a middle agent **M**. This user agent represents a requester.
2. Another kind of agent **P**, who provides user-desired information, has registered its location and its advertised capabilities with the middle agent **M**. It resides within the NHS Intranet but can also be the information resource beyond the Intranet by registering with **M**.
3. All user agents and provider agents have a common agent interface for communication and may understand the standard agent communication language such like KQML (Kuokka and Harada, 1995)
4. There is only one kind of middle agent **M** (Matchmaker) within this multiple agent environment. Of course, there will be a set of middle agents if necessary for a large agent community. **U** formulates an information request **R**, **R** contains user profile information on the domain, such as user preferences, domain ontology.
5. **U** sends the information request **R** to the middle agent **M.** Middle agent **M** decodes the message, and uses user preference information to help eliminate or favour particular agents in the community. **M** uses **R** and the advertised capabilities of the agents in the community to derive a candidate set of provider agents **A**, which are believed to be able to provide extraction knowledge to satisfy **R**.
6. After **U** has acquired extraction knowledge from the agent community **A**, it presents the user the extraction knowledge for view, using an intelligent configurable filter (Sycara *et al.*, 1998) to avoid repeating already accepted repeated knowledge, and previously rejected extraction knowledge.
7. If necessary, **U** should update its domain knowledge and updated profile then re-register its updated capabilities with the middle agent **M**.

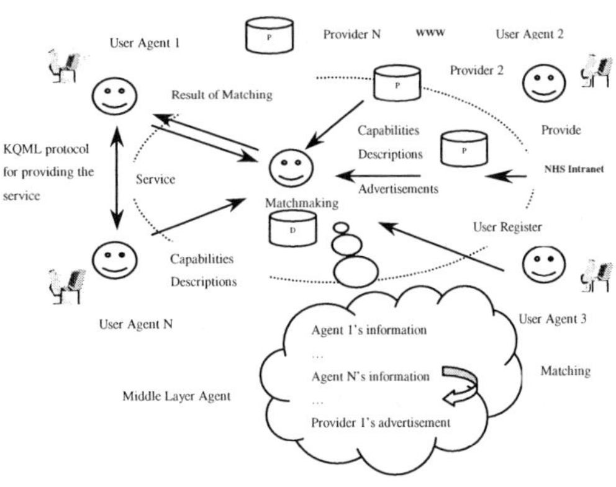

Figure 3: Co-operative Knowledge Sharing Framework

Based on this algorithm for knowledge sharing, a co-operative knowledge-sharing framework has been constructed, as illustrated in **Figure 3**.

4.3 Architecture of the Personal Agent

The personal agent architecture is designed to provide a unified environment in which several different functional agents are integrated. **Figure 4** shows the overall user task model and its components including: learning user profile information, collecting user's feedback and searching Web pages. It consists of three different agents: the profile agent, the interface agent and the search agent with their tasks being described as follows:

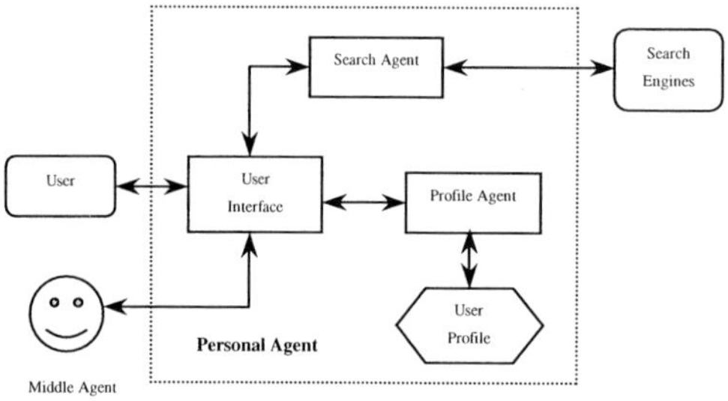

Figure 4: Architecture Design of Personal Agent

Profile Agent - the main task of the profile agent is to build and maintain a user model, which constructs the user profile and adapts to changes in a user's interests. Users trigger most of the activities of the profile agent when they provide a feedback to the system through the user interface agent.

Search Agent - searching is carried out by a meta search engine sending search commands to a search engine available on the Internet and parsing the search results. It allows the users to explore new interests. In addition, it may visit other agents in the community and fetch the user-desired information based on indications from a middle agent.

Interface Agent - the user interface agent basically serves as the general user interface (GUI) between the user and the agent community. It creates a Java/HTML interface on the fly to convey information and messages from other agents (including the middle agent) to its user and *vice versa* through an Internet browser. It also redirects messages sent through the Internet from its user to an appropriate agent in the system.

All these functional agents reside on the user (client) side and work as a whole personal agent. The personal agent is a thread that can be written in Java, but there is no central administration. Each user is associated with such an agent. They are built when a new service is created or when a user registers. The personal agent is in charge of autonomously exchanging requests or answers with others personal agents.

Constructing a user profile depends on user-supplied keywords and information provided at registration. New users register with the knowledge-sharing environment and complete a brief questionnaire about their broad areas of interest. This information is submitted to the middle agent and stored as initial advertisements for future matching. Thereafter, the user profile is automatically constructed and refined by the profile agent using information from multiple sources such as bookmarks and feedback from the user. This process analyses the pages browsed by the user and groups related documents together according to their similarity measures.

The user profile can be updated and expanded by the profile agent after new searching or new information has been found. For instance, when information has moved to another location, agents will be able to find it, and update their knowledge bases accordingly.

4.4 Information Brokering

The middle agent has the capability to accept registration from user agents, which define the user's knowledge over multiple domains of interest and capabilities to provide knowledge as well as accept advertisements from providers, which contain the user-desired information that can be retrieved by requesters. All the received information, user preferences and advertisements, will be stored as meta-data in its database. A user discovering the lack of sufficient knowledge about a particular domain can choose to ask his/her user agent to construct an information request containing detailed information about the domain of knowledge and some of the user's knowledge acquisition preferences. As long as a middle agent accepts such information requests, it will be primarily responsible for utilising previously advertised user agent capabilities to recognise which user agents (in the community) can provide the desired information by sharing the knowledge.

5. SIMULATION AND EVALUATION

In order to demonstrate the theory and the framework of collaborative agents for IR, and to evaluate the research results, a software environment has been built which simulates a part of the NHS Intranet.

5.1 The Simulation

The framework of the agent application uses a Java Voyager (Objectspace, 2000) program to support the validation (Figure 4). Within it, for example, some users and providers have a requester ***R*** requesting information while others do not. ***R***'s search agent only visits the hosts recommended by the middle agent thereby saving ***R***'s searching time and reducing the network traffic. The middle agent program contains a single instance of a middle agent. When each provider joins the system, the provider program creates a single instance of a provider and registers it with the middle agent. The middle agent also keeps a list of all advertisements supplied by each provider.

When a user starts to search for information (see **Figure 5**), the initial applet class makes a remote procedure call to the search agent class. The later class constructs and launchs an agent to find the information with its user name, a virtual reference to the applet and a virtual reference to the middle agent. It is instructed to move to the server (middle agent) to obtain the list of relevant information providers (including the users who could share their knowledge). The agent then moves to the various providers' sites to fetch the information in turn. Meanwhile, the agent uses the virtual reference to the applet and continually sends its status to the applet as long as the applet is open. After visiting each provider and relevant users, the search agent moves back to the user and dies.

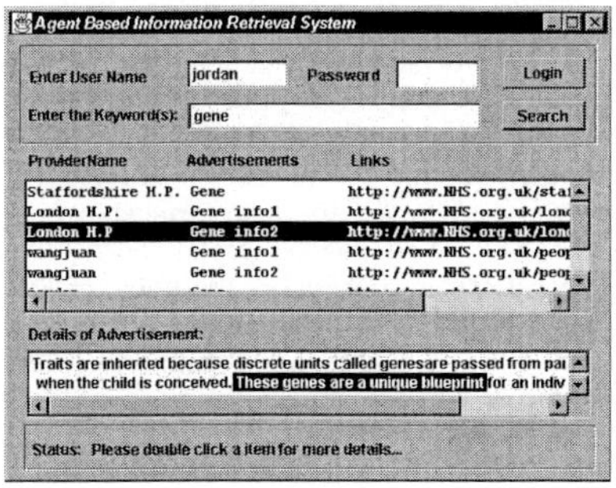

Figure 5: User IR Dialogue Interface

It is important to get the balance right to ensure the search agents find the right providers yet do not overload their hosts and capabilities of the server in the process. Thus, when the numbers of users reach the limit of a particular middle agent (primary server), the secondary server is started. If the users of the secondary server also reach its limit, the primary server directs the user to the secondary server with the fewer users. This reduces the network traffic load on the servers.

5.2 Experimental Evaluation

The framework of the agent application has been prototyped (Ling, 2000), and the results reported show the feasibility of the model design. The main performance attribute measured in this simulation is the agent response time - the total elapsed time (which is read from the main server shown in **Figure 6**) taken by a requester to satisfy a service objective. The first test runs a search agent and measures the elapsed time taken to visit all the members of the framework. The second test runs the same agent, but measures the elapsed time taken to visit a certain number of providers directed by a middle agent and judges the overall efficiency of the algorithm.

Three network groups have been tested. The test results of the first group shown in **Table 1**, validate the theoretical model with and without using a middle agent. For a fixed number of providers, who have the same interest with the requester, it is seen that the search agent's spending time is increased notably during the process along with the increase in network users. In the case of using a middle agent, it is noticed that in almost all cases, the time spent on the agent searching process is relatively constant though there is a little difference when adding a new user. It is obvious that as more users register with the middle agent, more time will be needed on matchmaking. However, the difference is still very small compared with the 'no middle agent' case.

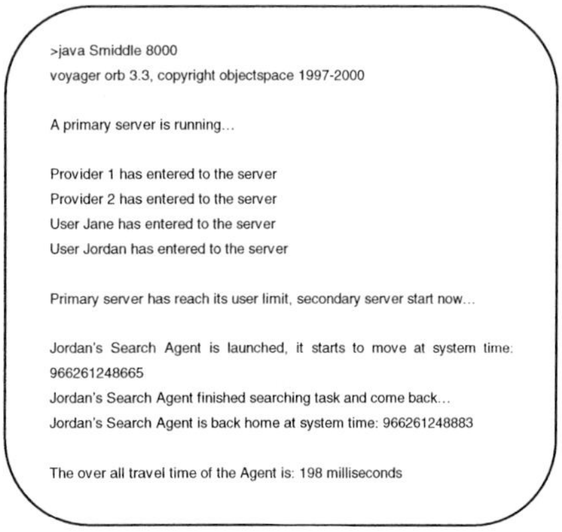

Figure 6: Voyager Simulation Window

Table 1: Simulation Results of Network Group One

Total no. of network users	No. of the providers have same interest	Without a middle agent		With a middle agent	
		Needed moving steps (unit)	Time spent (ms)	Needed moving steps (unit)	Time spent (ms)
3	2	3	153	4	168
4	2	4	198	4	177
5	2	5	237	4	185
6	2	6	274	4	197
7	2	7	310	4	206
8	2	8	355	4	215

The experimental results in **Figure 7** also provide very positive support for this. On the other hand, it can be seen from **Table 1** that the search agent takes more moving steps in the case of no middle agent if the number of network users is more than five. Consequently, from the theoretical point of view, the former case will occupy more network bandwidth and cost more network traffic, especially when the number of the network users are greatly increased. In contrast, because of employing a middle agent, the search agent in later case could save moving steps and find relevant information providers more quickly and efficiently.

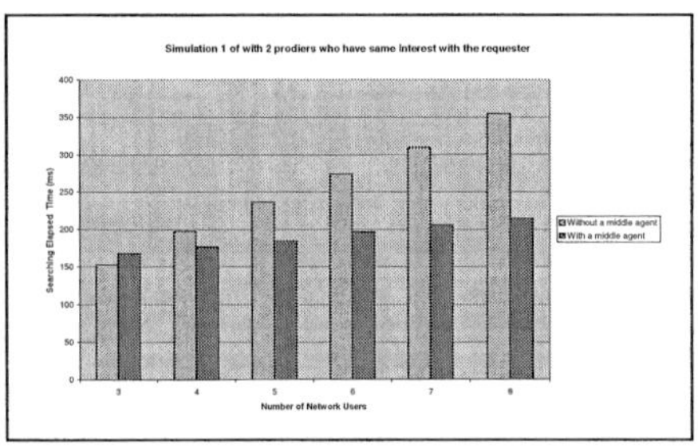

Figure 7: Simulation Chart of Network Group One

Table 2: Simulation Results of Network Group Two

Total no. of network users	No. of the providers have same interest	Without a middle agent		With a middle agent	
		Needed moving steps (unit)	Time spent (ms)	Needed moving steps (unit)	Time spent (ms)
6	5	6	308	7	299
7	5	7	360	7	310
8	5	8	415	7	321
9	5	9	463	7	332
10	5	10	511	7	344
11	5	11	564	7	353

It is obvious that for a larger number of users and providers, more time will probably be necessary, similar to the figures shown in **Table 2.** Nevertheless, the test results of another two groups also show a similar conclusion with those from group one.

The code for the system prototype is written in Java, and can be executed on many different kinds of environment such as UNIX, Windows, Macintosh, Linux etc.

6. CONCLUSIONS AND FURTHER WORK

This research goes some way to addressing the problems of IR by using personal agents and middle agents who can store meta-information about WWW pages. This is then used to retrieve relevant pages quickly and easily and makes it possible for users with common interests to share knowledge. In particular, it demonstrates how informative agents have an ability to model and learn user profiles, and communicate with other agents to improve the efficiency of IR by means of third parties in the form of middle agents.

An agent-based knowledge-sharing framework has been designed and constructed to facilitate the sharing of knowledge in a web-based NHS intranet. Co-operation behaviour and other agent functions were added to the agents to have the system perform better under a wider range of operating conditions. These behaviours made the system more robust and adaptive, distinguishing it from other distributed IR systems. The results of simulations demonstrate that referral-based matchmaking can provide acceptable results without requiring an agent to know about all the other agents, and without requiring unreasonable messaging traffic or computational load. The proposed model can also be introduced to a user who may actually be an expert, or interested in multiple domains of knowledge, thus allowing for generalised knowledge sharing in any domain.

Further value is achieved by developing user interest groups to specify their members when they register, with each interest group having its own middle agent. In this case, the jobs of IR and matchmaking are distributed and less likely to cause the type of networking bottleneck that is concomitant with a central single middle agent.

For example, students, tutors and administrators (Allison *et al.*, 1999) may use personal agents and the knowledge-sharing model, both for searching information sources and for management of virtual learning environment (VLE) activities. Personal agents can be used to locate the material that a student requires to complete some piece of work. By introducing a middle agent and interest groups, a student can find other students with similar interests to work on a group project. A specialist tutor that can then help students or a student group to achieve their goals more effectively, by monitoring activity and suggesting appropriate strategies.

On the other hand, all the middle agents of interest groups could be co-ordinated by a general middle agent. The general middle agent acts as a commander, in charge of all the co-ordination work and dispatch work as well as emergency backup. This kind of hierarchic design for an agent system may also be introduced to extend the reach of Web systems, such as the extranet or the origination of multiple Intranets connected together. It is likely that information and knowledge will be more manageable and faster to access and share using this approach.

Finally, the proposed method of approaching knowledge sharing brings up an interesting question about agent communications. Firstly, consider the middle agent approach: the matchmaker provides the opportunity for user agents to provide knowledge. This is an excellent opportunity for user agents to talk with other user agents, and to proactively acquire additional extraction knowledge that a user may seek for future IR queries. Secondly, users should be able to configure some user preferences such that their user agent negotiates (Ferber, 1999) to use the services of a particular middle agent. For example, a user may wish to use the agent community to acquire extraction knowledge that he finds useful information about some medical disease. Because of the sensitive nature of some diseases, e.g. AIDS, a user may wish that his request for information remained anonymous amongst his peers. In this situation, a user agent who requests information should choose to communicate with a Broker middle agent, since it is inherently capable of maintaining privacy (Hermans, 1996). In other situations, a user may wish to have one-on-one contact with individual user agents when deriving extraction knowledge. In this scenario, the user agent should attempt to negotiate the services of a Matchmaker middle agent. Agents need to be flexible and have the capabilities of co-ordinating communication between different middle agents in order to obtain the correct level of service as desired by the users. Although this idea is not currently represented in this model, it is thought that there is the potential for agent negotiation in the competition for contracts to provide services in the future.

REFERENCES

Allison, C., M. Bramley, R. Michaelson, and J. Serrano. (1999) "An Integrated Framework for Distributed Learning Environments" In "Advances in Concurrent Engineering", 6th ISPE International Conference on Concurrent Engineering, Bath, UK

Cabri G., Leonardi L. and Zambonelli (2000) "Mobile-agent co-ordination mobiles for Internet applications" Research Feature, IEEE

Davis J., Weeks R., Revett M. (2000) " JASPER: communication information agents for WWW", Accessed 2/2000, also see https://www.w3.org/conferences/www4/papers

Decker K., Lesser V., Prasad M.V.N., Wagner T (1996) " MACRON: An Architecture for Multi-agent Co-operative Information Gathering". UMass Computer Science Technical Report

Ferber Jacques (1999) "Multi-Agent Systems- An Introduction to Distributed Artificial Intelligence", Addison Welsley Longman Limited, ISBN 0-201-36048-9.

Hermans Björn (1996) "Intelligent Software Agents on the Internet" Thesis of Tilburg University, Tilburg, The Netherlands

Huberman B. A. (1988) " The Ecology of Computation" Elsevier Science Publishers B V.

Katia Sycara, Jianguo Lu and Wendy Klusch (1998) "Interoperability Among Heterogeneous Software Agents on the Internet". Technical Report CMU-RI-Tr-98-32, The Robotics Institution, Carnegie Mellon University.

Kuokka D. and Harada L. (1995) " On using KQML for matchmaking" In proceeding, ICMAS-95, pages 239 245. AAAAI Press

Ling Bin (2000) "Enhanced Co-operative Knowledge Sharing Model for Agent Based Information Retrieval" Research thesis, Staffordshire University

NHS Information Authority, http://www.nhsia.nhs.uk/, Access time: 5.2000

Omicini Andrea and Zambonelli Franco (1999) "Tuple Centres for Co-ordination of Internet Agents" ACM 1-58113-086-4/99/0001, SAC '99, San Antonio, Texas, USA

Sycara Katia, Klusch Matthias, Lu Jiangguo (1996) "Matchmaking among heterogeneous agents on the Internet" Technical Report of the Robotics Institute, Carnegie Mellon University, Pittsburgh, USA.

Voyager 3.3 of ObjectSpace, http://www.objectspace.com/products/voyager/ Access time: 6/2000

AUTHOR INDEX